CRITICAL SURVEY OF
Poetry
Fourth Edition

World Poets

CRITICAL SURVEY OF
Poetry
Fourth Edition

World Poets

Chinua Achebe—Daisy Zamora
Resources
Indexes

Editor, Fourth Edition
Rosemary M. Canfield Reisman
Charleston Southern University

SALEM PRESS
Pasadena, California
Hackensack, New Jersey

Editor in Chief: Dawn P. Dawson

Editorial Director: Christina J. Moose	*Research Supervisor:* Jeffry Jensen
Development Editor: Tracy Irons-Georges	*Research Assistant:* Keli Trousdale
Project Editor: Rowena Wildin	*Production Editor:* Andrea E. Miller
Manuscript Editor: Desiree Dreeuws	*Page Desion:* James Hutson
Acquisitions Editor: Mark Rehn	*Layout:* Mary Overell
Editorial Assistant: Brett S. Weisberg	*Photo Editor:* Cynthia Breslin Beres

Cover photo: Ernesto Cardenal (AFP/Getty Images)

Some of the essays in this work, which have been updated, originally appeared in the following Salem Press publications, *Critical Survey of Poetry, English Language Series* (1983), *Critical Survey of Poetry: Foreign Language Series* (1984), *Critical Survey of Poetry, Supplement* (1987), *Critical Survey of Poetry, English Language Series, Revised Edition*, (1992; preceding volumes edited by Frank N. Magill), *Critical Survey of Poetry, Second Revised Edition* (2003; edited by Philip K. Jason).

∞ The paper used in these volumes conforms to the American National Standard for Permanence of Paper for Printed Library Materials, X39.48-1992 (R1997).

Library of Congress Cataloging-in-Publication Data

Critical survey of poetry. — 4th ed. / editor, Rosemary M. Canfield Reisman.
  v. cm.
Includes bibliographical references and index.
ISBN 978-1-58765-582-1 (set : alk. paper) — ISBN 978-1-58765-761-0 (world poets : alk. paper)
1. Poetry—History and criticism—Dictionaries. 2. Poetry—Bio-bibliography. 3. Poets—Biography—Dictionaries. I. Reisman, Rosemary M. Canfield.
PN1021.C7 2011
809.1'003--dc22
                                                                        2010045095

First Printing

Publisher's Note

World Poets is part of Salem Press's greatly expanded and redesigned *Critical Survey of Poetry* Series. The *Critical Survey of Poetry, Fourth Edition*, presents profiles of major poets, with sections on other literary forms, achievements, biography, general analysis, and analysis of the poet's most important poems or collections. Although the profiled authors may have written in other genres as well, sometimes to great acclaim, the focus of this set is on their most important works of poetry.

The *Critical Survey of Poetry* was originally published in 1983 and 1984 in separate English- and foreign-language series, a supplement in 1987, a revised English-language series in 1992, and a combined revised series in 2003. The *Fourth Edition* includes all poets from the previous edition and adds 145 new ones, covering 843 writers in total. The poets covered in this set represent more than 40 countries and their poetry dates from the eighth century B.C.E. to the present. The set also offers 72 informative overviews; 20 of these essays were added for this edition, including all the literary movement essays. In addition, seven resources are provided, two of them new. More than 500 photographs and portraits of poets have been included.

For the first time, the material in the *Critical Survey of Poetry* has been organized into five subsets by geography and essay type: a 4-volume subset on *American Poets*, a 3-volume subset on *British, Irish, and Commonwealth Poets*, a 3-volume subset on *European Poets*, a 1-volume subset on *World Poets*, and a 2-volume subset of *Topical Essays*. Each poet appears in only one subset. *Topical Essays* is organized under the categories "Poetry Around the World," "Literary Movements," and "Criticism and Theory." A *Cumulative Indexes* volume covering all five subsets is free with purchase of more than one subset.

WORLD POETS

The single-volume *World Poets* contains 61 poet profiles, arranged alphabetically. For this edition, 8 new essays have been added, and 7 have been significantly updated with analysis of recently published books or poems.

The volume begins with a list of Contents and a Pronunciation Key. The poet essays follow in alphabetical order. The Resources section features three tools for interpreting and understanding poetry: "Explicating Poetry," "Language and Linguistics," and "Glossary of Poetical Terms." The "Bibliography," "Guide to Online Resources," "Time Line," "Major Awards," and "Chronological List of Poets" provide guides for further research and additional information on world poets; comprehensive versions appear in *Topical Essays* and *Cumulative Indexes*. The "Guide to Online Resources" and "Time Line" were created for this edition.

World Poets contains a Geographical Index of Poets; a Categorized Index of Poets, in which poets are grouped by culture or group identity, literary movement, historical period, and poetic forms and themes; and a Subject Index. The *Critical Survey of Poetry* Series: Master List of Contents identifies poets profiled in *World Poets* as well as poets profiled in other *Critical Survey of Poetry* subsets. The *Cumulative Indexes* also contains comprehensive versions of the categorized, geographical, and subject indexes.

UPDATING THE ESSAYS

All parts of the essays in the previous edition were scrutinized for currency and accuracy: The authors' latest works of poetry were added to front-matter listings, other significant publications were added to back-matter listings, new translations were added to listings for foreign-language authors, and deceased authors' listings were rechecked for accuracy and currency. All essays' bibliographies—lists of sources for further consultation—were revised to provide readers with the latest information.

The 7 poet essays in *World Poets* that required updating by academic experts received similar and even fuller attention: All new publications were added to listings, then each section of text was reviewed to ensure that recently received major awards are noted, that new biographical details are incorporated for still-living authors, and that analysis of works includes recently published books or poems. The updating experts' names were added to essays. Those original articles identified by the editor, Rosemary M. Canfield Reisman, as not needing substantial updating were nevertheless reedited by Salem Press editors and checked for accuracy.

ONLINE ACCESS

Salem Press provides access to its award-winning content both in traditional, printed form and online. Any school or library that purchases *World Poets* is entitled to free, complimentary access to Salem's fully supported online version of the content. Features include a simple intuitive interface, user profile areas for students and patrons, sophisticated search functionality, and complete context, including appendixes. Access is available through a code printed on the inside cover of the first volume, and that access is unlimited and immediate. Our online customer service representatives, at (800) 221-1592, are happy to help with any questions. E-books are also available.

ORGANIZATION OF POET ESSAYS

The poet essays in *World Poets* vary in length, with none shorter than 2,000 words and most significantly longer. Poet essays are arranged alphabetically, under the name by which the poet is best known. The format of the essays is standardized to allow predictable and easy access to the types of information of interest to a variety of users. Each poet essay contains ready-reference top matter, including full birth and (where applicable) death data, any alternate names used by the poet, and a list of Principal Poetry, followed by the main text, which is divided into Other Literary Forms, Achievements, Biography, and Analysis. A list of Other Major Works, a Bibliography, and bylines complete the essay.

- *Principal poetry* lists the titles of the author's major collections of poetry in chronological order, by date of original appearance. Most of the poets in *World Poets* wrote in a language other than English. The foreign-language title is given in its entirely, fol-

lowed by the first English publication and its date of publication, if a translation has been made.

- *Other literary forms* describes the author's work in other genres and notes whether the author is known primarily as a poet or has achieved equal or greater fame in another genre. If the poet's last name is unlikely to be familiar to most users, phonetic pronunciation is provided in parentheses after his or her name. A Pronunciation Key appears at the beginning of all volumes.

- *Achievements* lists honors, awards, and other tangible recognitions, as well as a summation of the writer's influence and contributions to poetry and literature, where appropriate.

- *Biography* provides a condensed biographical sketch with vital information from birth through (if applicable) death or the author's latest activities.

- *Analysis* presents an overview of the poet's themes, techniques, style, and development, leading into subsections on major poetry collections, poems, or aspects of the person's work as a poet. As an aid to students, those foreign-language titles that have not yet appeared in translation are followed by a "literal translation" in roman and lowercase letters in parentheses when these titles are mentioned in the text. If a collection of poems has been published in English, the English-language title is used in the text. Single poems that have not been translated are followed by a literal translation in parentheses. Those that have been translated are referred to by their English-language title, although the original title, if known, is also provided.

- *Other major works* contains the poet's principal works in other genres, listed by genre and by year of publication within each genre. If the work has been translated into English, the date and title under which it was first translated are given.

- *Bibliography* lists secondary print sources for further study, annotated to assist users in evaluating focus and usefulness.

- *Byline* notes the original contributor of the essay. If the essay was updated, the name of the most recent updater appears in a separate line and previous updaters appear with the name of the original contributor.

APPENDIXES

The "Resources" section provides tools for further research and points of access to the wealth of information contained in *World Poets*.

- *Explicating Poetry* identifies the basics of versification, from meter to rhyme, in an attempt to demonstrate how sound, rhythm, and image fuse to support meaning.
- *Language and Linguistics* looks at the origins of language and at linguistics as a discipline, as well as how the features of a particular language affect the type of poetry created.
- *Glossary of Poetical Terms* is a lexicon of more than 150 literary terms pertinent to the study of poetry.
- *Bibliography* identifies general reference works and other secondary sources that pertain to world poets.
- *Guide to Online Resources*, new to this edition, provides Web sites pertaining to world poetry and poets.
- *Time Line*, new to this edition, lists major milestones and events in world poetry and literature in the order in which they occurred.
- *Major Awards* lists the recipients of major poetry-specific awards in the areas covered by *World Poets* and general awards where applicable to poets or poetry, from inception of the award to the present day.
- *Chronological List of Poets* lists all 61 poets covered in *World Poets* by year of birth, in chronological order.

INDEXES

The Geographical Index of Poets lists all poets covered in *World Poets* by country or region. The Categorized Index of Poets lists the poets profiled in *World Poets* by culture or group identity (such as Jewish culture and women poets), literary movements and historical periods (such as Acmeist poets, Modernism, and Negritude), and poetic forms and themes (such as political poets, ghazals, haiku, and nature poetry). The *Critical Survey of Poetry* Series: Master List of Contents lists not only the poets profiled in *World Poets* but also those in other subsets, allowing users to find any poet covered in the complete series. The Subject Index lists all titles, authors, subgenres, and literary movements or terms that receive substantial discussion in *World Poets*. Listings for profiled poets are in bold face.

ACKNOWLEDGMENTS

Salem Press is grateful for the efforts of the original contributors of these essays and those of the outstanding academicians who took on the task of updating or writing new material for the set. Their names and affiliations are listed in the "Contributors" section that follows. Finally, we are indebted to our editor, Professor Rosemary M. Canfield Reisman of Charleston Southern University, for her development of the table of contents for the *Critical Survey of Poetry, Fourth Edition* and her advice on updating the original articles to make this comprehensive and thorough revised edition an indispensable tool for students, teachers, and general readers alike.

CONTRIBUTORS

Walton Beacham
Beacham Publishing Corp.

Harold Branam
Savannah State University

Gerhard Brand
*California State University,
Los Angeles*

J. R. Broadus
University of North Carolina

Joseph Bruchac
Greenfield Center, New York

Susan Butterworth
Salem State College

John Carpenter
University of Michigan

Carole A. Champagne
*University of Maryland-Eastern
Shore*

Julian W. Connolly
University of Virginia

Marcia B. Dinneen
Bridgewater State College

Lee Hunt Dowling
University of Houston

Desiree Dreeuws
Sunland, California

K Edgington
Towson University

Cliff Edwards
Fort Hays State University

Massud Farzan
Boston University

William L. Felker
Yellow Springs, Ohio

Margot K. Frank
Randolph-Macon Women's College

Keiko Matsui Gibson
*Kanda University of International
Studies*

Morgan Gibson
Urbana, Illinois

Ronald Gray
Grand Junction, Colorado

Robert Hauptman
St. Cloud State University

Sarah Hilbert
Pasadena, California

Donald D. Hook
Trinity College

Kenneth A. Howe
Michigan State University

Anne Howells
Occidental College

Ramona L. Hyman
Loma Linda University

Tracy Irons-Georges
Glendale, California

Maura Ives
Texas A&M University

Alfred W. Jensen
University of Idaho-Moscow

Sheila Golburgh Johnson
Santa Barbara, California

Leslie Ellen Jones
Pasadena, California

Irma M. Kashuba
Chestnut Hill College

Rebecca Kuzins
Pasadena, California

Jeanne Larsen
Hollins College

Linda Ledford-Miller
University of Scranton

Leon Lewis
Appalachian State University

R. C. Lutz
CII Group

Cherie R. Maiden
Furman University

John Marney
Oakland University

Vasa D. Mihailovich
University of North Carolina

Jane Ann Miller
*University of Massachusetts,
Dartmouth*

Monique Nagem
McNeese State University

David Nerkle
Washington, D.C.

Caryn E. Neumann
Miami University of Ohio

James O'Brien
University of Wisconsin

Mahmoud Omidsalar
*University of California,
Los Angeles*

Shannon Oxley
University of Leeds

Charles A. Perrone
University of Florida

CONTENTS

RESOURCES

INDEXES

PRONUNCIATION KEY

To help users of the *Critical Survey of Poetry* pronounce unfamiliar names of profiled poets correctly, phonetic spellings using the character symbols listed below appear in parentheses immediately after the first mention of the poet's name in the narrative text. Stressed syllables are indicated in capital letters, and syllables are separated by hyphens.

VOWEL SOUNDS

Symbol	Spelled (Pronounced)
a	answer (AN-suhr), laugh (laf), sample (SAM-puhl), that (that)
ah	father (FAH-thur), hospital (HAHS-pih-tuhl)
aw	awful (AW-fuhl), caught (kawt)
ay	blaze (blayz), fade (fayd), waiter (WAYT-ur), weigh (way)
eh	bed (behd), head (hehd), said (sehd)
ee	believe (bee-LEEV), cedar (SEE-dur), leader (LEED-ur), liter (LEE-tur)
ew	boot (bewt), lose (lewz)
i	buy (bi), height (hit), lie (li), surprise (sur-PRIZ)
ih	bitter (BIH-tur), pill (pihl)
o	cotton (KO-tuhn), hot (hot)
oh	below (bee-LOH), coat (koht), note (noht), wholesome (HOHL-suhm)
oo	good (good), look (look)
ow	couch (kowch), how (how)
oy	boy (boy), coin (koyn)
uh	about (uh-BOWT), butter (BUH-tuhr), enough (ee-NUHF), other (UH-thur)

CONSONANT SOUNDS

Symbol	Spelled (Pronounced)
ch	beach (beech), chimp (chihmp)
g	beg (behg), disguise (dihs-GIZ), get (geht)
j	digit (DIH-juht), edge (ehj), jet (jeht)
k	cat (kat), kitten (KIH-tuhn), hex (hehks)
s	cellar (SEHL-ur), save (sayv), scent (sehnt)
sh	champagne (sham-PAYN), issue (IH-shew), shop (shop)
ur	birth (burth), disturb (dihs-TURB), earth (urth), letter (LEH-tur)
y	useful (YEWS-fuhl), young (yuhng)
z	business (BIHZ-nehs), zest (zehst)
zh	vision (VIH-zhuhn)

A

CHINUA ACHEBE

Born: Ogidi, Nigeria; November 16, 1930

PRINCIPAL POETRY

Beware, Soul Brother, and Other Poems, 1971,
1972
Christmas in Biafra, and Other Poems, 1973
Collected Poems, 2004

OTHER LITERARY FORMS

Chinua Achebe (ah-CHAY-bay) is a writer who has made important contributions in every literary genre. He is known primarily for his first novel, *Things Fall Apart* (1959). His other novels include *No Longer at Ease* (1960), *Arrow of God* (1964), *A Man of the People* (1966), and *Anthills of the Savannah* (1987). Achebe's short stories are collected in *The Sacrificial Egg, and Other Stories* (1962) and *Girls at War, and Other Stories* (1972). He has also published collections of essays: *Morning Yet on Creation Day* (1975), *An Image of Africa* (1977), *The Trouble with Nigeria* (1983), *Hopes and Impediments* (1988), *Home and Exile* (2000), and *Education of a British-Protected Child* (2009). In addition to his contributions as a poet, novelist, short-story writer, and essayist, Ache has written books for children: *Chike and the River* (1966), *How the Leopard Got His Claws* (1972; with John Iroaganachi), *The Flute* (1977), and *The Drum* (1977). He has also edited numerous works, including *Don't Let Him Die: An Anthology of Memorial Poems for Christopher Okigbo, 1937-1967* (1978; with Dubem Okafor).

ACHIEVEMENTS

Chinua Achebe is known as the founder of modern African writing. His many awards include the Margaret Wrong Memorial Prize (1959) for *Things Fall Apart*, the Nigerian National Trophy for Literature (1961), the Jock Campbell-*New Statesman* Award for Literature

for *Arrow of God* (1966), the Commonwealth Poetry Prize (1972, joint winner), the Afro-Asian Writers Association's Lotus Award (1975), the Nigerian National Merit Award (1979), the Triple Eminence Award from the Association of Nigerian Authors (1990), the Langston Hughes Award (1993), the Campion Medal and Order of Kilimanjaro Award (both 1996), the German Booksellers Peace Prize (2002), and the Man Booker International Prize (2007). He was named Officer of the Order of the Federal Republic (Nigeria) in 1979, a fellow of the Royal Society of Literature in 1981, an honorary foreign fellow of the American Academy and Institute of Arts and Letters in 1982, and an honorary fellow of the American Academy of Arts and Science in 2002. In 1998, he was the McMillan-Steward Lecturer at Harvard University and the Presidential Fellow Lecturer at the World Bank.

BIOGRAPHY

Albert Chinualumogu Achebe was born the fifth of six children of educated Igbo parents, Isaiah Okafor Achebe and Janet Anaenechi Achebe. He was born in Ogidi, a town in the eastern region of Nigeria. After converting to Christianity, Achebe's father served as a catechist for the Church Missionary Society. From 1944 to 1948, Achebe attended the Government College, Umuahia, a highly competitive school, then received a scholarship to the University College, Ibadan (University of Ibadan). Initially, Achebe's collegiate goal was to study medicine; however, his goals changed because of his interest in the academic areas of religion, history, and English literature. While at the University College, Achebe and several other students founded a literary journal, *The University Herald*. In addition to publishing works in the journal, Achebe served as the editor during his third year of matriculation at the institution.

After graduation in 1953, Achebe served as a teacher at the Merchant of Light School. He began working for the Nigerian Broadcasting Corporation in 1954, and two years later, he trained at the British Broadcasting Corporation. He published the inaugural text for the Heinemann African Writers series, *Things Fall Apart*, in 1959. The publication of this novel significantly changed the trajectory of Achebe's writing

Chinua Achebe (AP/Wide World Photos)

career and his life. The novel has been published in many languages and has sold more than eight million copies. Moreover, *Things Fall Apart* ushered Achebe into the center of the critical conversation on African literature and social-political thought, giving him a central place in the canon of world literature.

In addition to a prolific writing career, Achebe has had an outstanding academic portfolio. His visiting professorships include posts at the University of Massachusetts at Amherst (1972-1975), the University of Connecticut (1975-1976), and City College of the City University of New York (1989). In 1986, Achebe was appointed pro-vice-chancellor of the State University of Anambra in Enugu. Achebe was the Charles P. Stevenson Professor of Languages and Literature at Bard College in 1990-2009. In September, 2009, he became the David and Marianna Fisher University Professor and professor of Africana studies at Brown University.

In addition to being one of Africa's most influential writers, Achebe is a family man. On September 10, 1961, he married Christie Chinwe Okoli, a professor of psychology. The couple had four children, Chinelo, Ikechukwu, Chidi, and Nwando.

ANALYSIS

The thematic concern of Chinua Achebe's life and writing is to articulate the meaning of what it is to be

African from the perspective of one who is authentically African. Critic Nahem Yousaf has said that Achebe's intent as a writer is to "challenge the insidious stories in which the colonized and dispossessed are rendered inhuman and inept in order to make heroes of the 'hunter' colonialists, and to shore up the memoirs of colonial apologists." Achebe expresses his love for and critique of Africa, specifically Nigeria, in all of his writing. Achebe's political and social critique of his country comes out of his love for the people and the place that he identifies as home.

CHRISTMAS IN BIAFRA

Christmas in Biafra is a poetic response to the Biafran War (1967-1970; also known as the Nigerian Civil War). In this collection, Achebe relates the stories of the people who suffered during the war. The images created, as in "Benin Road," are portraits of a country tortured by the reality that on a highway sometimes, "Speed is violence/ Power is violence/ Weight violence."

The book is divided into five sections: "Prologue," "Poems About War," "Poems Not About War," "Gods, Men, and Others," and "Epilogue." Although the main theme of the book is war, the book has a religious tone. Poems such as "Lazarus" suggest that this collection is a spiritual polemic grounded in the complex depictions of war and its aftermath. Achebe helps the reader realize that when a war is over, a country—and all that is associated with it—must regroup, writing that "life catches desperately at passing hints of normalcy."

COLLECTED POEMS

Collected Poems is a broad representation of Achebe's poetry, with its themes of the cultural effects of imperialism and colonialism. In its introductory "parable," Achebe details the need for this collection, which was published because the author received an "urgent call from a lady who identified herself as Curator of *Another Africa*," an exhibition that included his work. In the postmodern sense, Achebe's *Collected*

Poems was called into being because of the synergistic relationship between an author and his prospective audience.

Other major works

LONG FICTION: *Things Fall Apart*, 1959; *No Longer at Ease*, 1960; *Arrow of God*, 1964; *A Man of the People*, 1966; *Anthills of the Savannah*, 1987.

SHORT FICTION: "Dead Men's Path," 1953; *The Sacrificial Egg, and Other Stories*, 1962; *Girls at War, and Other Stories*, 1972.

NONFICTION: *Morning Yet on Creation Day*, 1975; *An Image of Africa*, 1977; *The Trouble with Nigeria*, 1983; *Hopes and Impediments*, 1988; *Conversations with Chinua Achebe*, 1997 (Bernth Lindfors, editor); *Home and Exile*, 2000; *Education of a British-Protected Child*, 2009.

CHILDREN'S LITERATURE: *Chike and the River*, 1966; *How the Leopard Got His Claws*, 1972 (with John Iroaganachi); *The Drum*, 1977; *The Flute*, 1977.

EDITED TEXTS: *Don't Let Him Die: An Anthology of Memorial Poems for Christopher Okigbo, 1937-1967*, 1978 (with Dubem Okafor); *Aka wega: Egwu aguluagu egwu edeluede*, 1982 (with Obiora Udechukwu); *African Short Stories*, 1985 (with C. L. Innes); *Beyond Hunger in Africa*, 1990 (with others); *The Heinemann Book of Contemporary African Short Stories*, 1992 (with Innes).

MISCELLANEOUS: *Another Africa*, 1998 (poems and essay; photographs by Robert Lyons).

Bibliography

Booker, M. Keith, ed. *The Chinua Achebe Encyclopedia*. Westport, Conn.: Greenwood Press, 2003. This comprehensive guide to Achebe's life and works provides substantive discussions of his fiction, nonfiction, and poetry. Contains several hundred entries, a bibliography, and a chronology.

Egejuru, Phanuel Akubueze. *Chinua Achebe: Pure and Simple—An Oral Biography*. Ikeja, Nigeria: Malthouse Press, 2002. A biography of Achebe written from the Nigerian point of view.

Emenyonu, Ernest N., and Iniobong I. Uko, eds. *Emerging Perspectives on Chinua Achebe*. Trenton, N.J.: Africa World Press, 2004. Contains two essays on Achebe as a poet, one focusing on *Beware, Soul Brother, and Other Poems*, and the other discussing Achebe as a war poet.

Lindfors, Bernth. *Early Achebe*. Trenton, N.J.: Africa World Press, 2009. Although this work deals primarily with the novels, essays, and stories published between 1951 and 1966, it helps the reader understand what formed Achebe's main themes.

Morrison, Jago. *The Fiction of Chinua Achebe*. New York: Palgrave Macmillan, 2007. Although the focus of this work is Achebe's fiction, it examines the key areas of criticism surrounding his work.

Nwodo, Christopher S. *Philosophical Perspective on Chinua Achebe*. Port Harcourt, Nigeria: University of Port Harcourt Press, 2004. Looks at the philosophical aspects of Achebe's writings, focusing on the Igbo people and questions of racism.

Opata, Damian U., ed. *The Eagle in Ascendance: More Papers from the Chinua Achebe International Symposium, 1990, with New Essays Added*. Ibadan, Nigeria: Heinemann Educational Books, 2005. This collection, which adds new critical essays to those originally from a 1990 symposium, covers most aspects of Achebe's writing.

Sallah, Tijan M., and Ngozi Okonjo-Iweala. *Chinua Achebe, Teacher of Light: A Biography*. Trenton, N.J.: Africa World Press, 2003. A biography of Achebe that looks at his life and work, discussing the intellectual life of Nigeria in the twentieth century.

Ramona L. Hyman

Anna Akhmatova
Anna Andreyevna Gorenko

Born: Bol'shoy Fontan, near Odessa, Ukraine, Russian Empire (now in Ukraine); June 23, 1889

Died: Domodedovo, near Moscow, Soviet Union (now in Russia); March 5, 1966

Principal poetry
Vecher, 1912
Chetki, 1914

Belaya staya, 1917

Podorozhnik, 1921

Anno Domini MCMXXI, 1922

Iz shesti knig, 1940

Izbrannye stikhotvoreniia, 1943

Stikhotvoreniia, 1958

Poema bez geroya, 1960 (*A Poem Without a Hero*, 1973)

Rekviem, 1963 (*Requiem*, 1964)

Beg vremeni, 1965

Sochineniya, 1965-1983 (3 volumes)

Poems of A., 1973

Requiem, and Poem Without a Hero, 1976

Selected Poems, 1976

You Will Hear Thunder, 1976

Way of All the Earth, 1979

Anna Akhmatova: Poems, 1983

The Complete Poems of Anna Akhmatova, 1990 (2 volumes)

OTHER LITERARY FORMS

In addition to poetry, Anna Akhmatova (ak-MAH-tuh-vuh) wrote an unfinished play and many essays on Russian writers. Her spirited book *O Pushkine: Stat'i i zametki* (1977), published in its complete version posthumously, is one of the most discerning tributes to the greatest Russian poet, Alexander Pushkin, by a fellow poet. Akhmatova also translated poems from the Old Egyptian, Hindu, Armenian, Chinese, French, Italian, and many other languages, most of these in collaboration with native speakers.

ACHIEVEMENTS

Anna Akhmatova enriched Russian literature immeasurably, not only with the quality of her poetry but also with the freshness and originality of her strong talent. Through Acmeism, a literary movement of which she was one of the founders and leading members, she effected a significant change of direction in Russian poetry in the second decade of the twentieth century. The Acmeists' insistence on clarity and precision of expression—much in the spirit of the Imagists, although the two movements developed independently of each other—represented a reaction against the intricate symbols and otherworldly preoccupations of the Symbolists. Akhmatova's youthful love poems brought her early fame, and her reputation was further enhanced during the long reign of terror in her country, through which she was able to preserve her dignity, both as a human being and as a poet. With Boris Pasternak, Osip Mandelstam, and Marina Tsvetayeva, Akhmatova is universally regarded as one of the four great poets of postrevolutionary Russia. Having been generously translated into English, Akhmatova's works are constantly gaining stature in world literature as well.

BIOGRAPHY

Anna Akhmatova—the pen name of Anna Andreyevna Gorenko—was born in a suburb of Odessa in 1889, into the family of a naval officer. Akhmatova began to write poetry when she was eleven, and her first poem was published in 1907. She achieved great popularity with her first books, *Vecher* and *Chetki*. After joining the literary movement called Acmeism, she played an important part in it together with Osip Mandelstam and with her husband, Nikolay Gumilyov, from whom she was later divorced. During World War I and the Russian Revolution, Akhmatova stood by her people, even though she did not agree with the ideas and methods of the revolutionaries. Never politically inclined, she saw in the war and the revolution an evil that might eventually destroy the private world in which she had been able to address herself exclusively to her own problems. When the end of that world came, she refused to accept it, believing that she would be able to continue her sequestered life. She also refused to emigrate, saying that it took greater courage to stay behind and accept what came.

The effect of the revolution on her life and creativity was not immediately evident, for she subsequently published two more collections of poetry. When her former husband and fellow Acmeist Gumilyov was shot, however, Akhmatova realized that the new way of life was inimical to her own. Compelled to silence, she ceased to exist publicly, instead remaining an inner émigré for eighteen years and occupying herself mostly with writing essays and translating. This silence may have saved her life during the purges of the 1930's, although she was not spared agony while trying to ascertain the fate of her only son, a promising scholar of Asian history, who had been sent to a labor camp three times. Only World War II brought a change to Akhmatova's dreary and dangerous life. Like many Soviet writers and intellectuals, she once again sided with her people, suppressing her reservations and complaints. She spent the first several months of the war in besieged Leningrad and then was evacuated to Tashkent, where she stayed almost to the end of the war. In Tashkent, she was brought closer to the other part of her ancestry, for her grandmother, from whom she took her pen name, was a Tartar.

When the war was over and the authorities again resorted to repression, Akhmatova was among the first to be victimized. In a vitriolic speech by Andrei Zhdanov, the cultural dictator at that time, she and the satirist Mikhail Zoshchenko were singled out as examples of anti-Soviet attitudes among intellectuals and charged with harmful influence on the young. They were expelled from the Writers' Union, and their works ceased to be published. Thus, Akhmatova vanished from public view once again in 1946, this time involuntarily, and did not reappear until ten years later. In 1958, a slender collection of her poems was published as a sign of rehabilitation. A few more of her books were subsequently published, both at home and abroad, thus reinstating the poet as an active member of society.

During the last decade of her life, she wrote some of the best poetry of her career. Shortly before her death, she received two richly deserved accolades for her work. Ironically, the recognition came from abroad: She was awarded the prestigious Italian Etna Taormina Prize in 1964 and an honorary doctorate from Oxford University in 1965. Ravaged by long illness, she died in 1966, having preserved her dignity and independence by asking for and receiving a church funeral according to the Russian Orthodox rites. After her death, Akhmatova was almost unanimously eulogized as the finest woman poet in all Russian literature.

ANALYSIS

Anna Akhmatova's poetry can conveniently be divided into three distinct periods: 1912 to

1923, 1940 to 1946, and 1956 to 1966 (with a few poems published in 1950). The interim periods were those of enforced silence. The first silence, from 1923 to 1940, came as a result of tacit admission on her part that the changed way of life in Russia was not fully acceptable to her. The second, from 1946 to 1956, was a direct result of the authorities' intervention. Needless to say, Akhmatova kept busy by further refining her poetry, by writing essays, and by translating.

VECHER AND CHETKI

Akhmatova's development as a poet can be traced from book to book. Her first books, *Vecher* and *Chetki*, impressed readers with the freshness of a young woman's concern about her feelings of love. In almost all the poems having love as a focal point, Akhmatova presents love from a woman's point of view, in a form resembling a diary. It is difficult to say whether the female voice in these poems belongs to the poet herself; probably it does, but in the last analysis it is immaterial. The beloved is almost always silent, never fully revealed or described, and at times he seems to be almost

Anna Akhmatova (The Granger Collection, New York)

secondary—only a catalyst for the woman's feelings. She is so entranced by his mere presence that, in her anguish, she draws her "left-hand glove upon [her] right." The poet expresses the whole spectrum of love—from the playfulness of a young woman trying to dismay her partner (to prove that she, too, can wield some power over him) to moments of flaming passion.

To be sure, passion is presented implicitly, in the time-honored tradition of Russian literature, yet it is also vividly indicated in unique ways. As she says, "In human intimacy there is a secret boundary,/ Neither the experience of being in love nor passion can cross it/ Though the lips be joined together in awful silence/ And the heart break asunder with love." Her fervent passion is coupled with fidelity to her partner, but as her loyalty is professed time and again, a note of frustration and a fear of incompatibility and rejection become noticeable. The prospect of unrequited love is confirmed by betrayal and parting. The ensuing feeling of loneliness leads to despair and withdrawal. The woman's reaction shows a mixture of anger, defiance, even resignation: "Be accursed . . ./ But I swear by the garden of angels/ By the holy icon I swear,/ By the passionate frenzy of our nights,/ I will never go back to you!" (These lines, incidentally, prompted Zhdanov, in his merciless attack many years later, to call Akhmatova "a nun and a harlot.") Thus, celebration, parting, and suffering receive equal play in Akhmatova's approach to love, although the ultimate outcome is a markedly unhappy one. Her love poetry is a vivid testimony both to the glories and to the miseries of her gender.

The feminine "I" of the poems seeks refuge, release, and salvation in religion, nature, and poetry. The refuge in religion is especially evident in *Chetki*. The work has a peculiar religious tone, pervaded, like Akhmatova's sentiments of love, with a mood of melancholy and inexplicable sadness. The persona seems to have found consolation for unhappiness in love when she says: "The King of Heaven has healed my/ Soul with the icy calm of love's/ Absence." Her prayers are mostly in the form of confession or intercession. It is easy to see, however, that they are used primarily to compensate for her feeling of loneliness and weariness of life. Thus, privations and misfortunes are closely tied to her religious feelings; sin and atonement are inseparable, and

her passions of the flesh are tempered by spiritual fervor. Akhmatova's poems with religious overtones have little in common with customary religious experience. They are also much more complex and psychologically laden than any of her other poetry.

BELAYA STAYA AND ANNO DOMINI MCMXXI

In Akhmatova's third collection, *Belaya staya*, a new theme joins those of love and religion: a presentiment of doom. Nourished by the horrors of war and revolution, this presentiment grows into a wake for a world on the verge of annihilation. As the revolution dragged on, Akhmatova's mood turned bleaker and more hopeless. She sought rapport with the events by writing poetry with political motifs, but to no avail.

The poems in *Anno Domini MCMXXI* clearly reveal Akhmatova's state of mind and emotions at this difficult time, as well as her awareness that an era had come to an end. "All is sold, all is lost, all is plundered,/ Death's wing has flashed black on our sight,/ All's gnawed bare with sore, want, and sick longing," she laments in one poem. She refused to emigrate, however, knowing instinctively, as did Boris Pasternak many years later when he was threatened with expulsion from the Soviet Union, that for a poet to leave his or her native land is tantamount to a death worse than physical death. She did not hesitate to criticize those who had left their country in its worst hour: "Poor exile, you are like a prisoner/ To me, or one upon the bed/ Of sickness. Dark your road, O wanderer,/ Of wormwood smacks your alien bread." These lines have been quoted often by Soviet critics for propaganda purposes, although Akhmatova wrote them sincerely, as a poet who could not tear herself away from her own land.

WAR AND LOVE OF COUNTRY

In the poems in which Akhmatova grappled with the problems of present-day reality, a gradual shift from intimate love poetry toward more worldly themes can be seen. This shift can be considered as an overture to another kind of Akhmatova's poetry. Tormented by the turbulent years of war and revolution, in which she made many personal sacrifices and witnessed many tragedies (the loss of friends, for example, including her former husband Nikolay Gumilyov), she was forced to face reality and to express her feelings and opinions about it. The silence imposed on her in 1923 only postponed further development in that direction.

When she was allowed to reappear shortly before World War II, Akhmatova wrote little in her old idiom. In many poems written during the war, she extols the beauty of her land and the magnitude of the martyrdom of her people under attack by a ruthless enemy. Leningrad, the city of her life and of her dreams, is especially the object of her affection. Tsarskoe Selo—a settlement near Leningrad, which was the residence of the czars; the town of young Alexander Pushkin; and the town of Akhmatova's favorite poetry teacher Innokenty Annensky as well as of her own youth—remained vividly and forever etched in her memory, even when she saw it almost totally destroyed in the war.

Leningrad and Tsarskoe Selo were not the only places to which Akhmatova paid homage; indeed, all Russia was her home. Her attitude toward her country is typical of many Russian intellectuals, who, despite a thick veneer of cosmopolitanism, still harbor a childlike, sentimental, and sometimes irrational love for their country. From her earliest poems to her last, Akhmatova expressed the same feeling for Russia, a strange mixture of abstract love for her country, on one hand, and down-to-earth concern for its people, on the other. In the poem "Prayer," for example, she prays to the Lord to take even her child and to destroy "the sweet power of song" that she possesses if it would help to change "the storm cloud over Russia . . . into a nimbus ablaze."

This willingness to sacrifice what is dearest to her if it would benefit her country is no mere affectation—it is expressed with utmost sincerity and conviction. In a poem written almost thirty years later, "From an Airplane," she again expresses her love for her country in no less sincere terms: "It is all mine—and nothing can divide us,/ It is my soul, it is my body, too." Perhaps the most profound and meaningful testimony to her patriotism can be found in the poem "Native Land," written in the last years of her life. For her, her country was "the mud on our gumboots, the grit in our teeth . . ./ And we mill, and we mix, and we crumble/ This innocent earth at our feet,/ But we rest in this earth at the roots of the flowers,/ Which is why we so readily say: It is ours!"

Akhmatova did not limit her gaze to European Rus-

sia, where she was reared and where she spent most of her life. Through her experiences in Tashkent, the city in which her ancestors had resided, she acquired a great admiration for, and understanding of, the Asian mind and soul. A mystical bond with Asia inspired her to write some of her most beautiful descriptive poems, such as "From the Oriental Notebook."

REQUIEM

Nevertheless, Akhmatova could not close her eyes to the Soviet reality, in which she was personally caught in a most tragic way. In a unified cycle of poems, *Requiem*, a masterpiece unpublished in the Soviet Union until 1987, she expresses her deep sorrow about not only her personal loss but also the suffering to which the Russian people were being subjected. *Requiem* was her closest approach to public castigation of the regime in her country. The tone for the entire work is set by the motto, which sadly admits that the circumstances are not those of a foreign country but, more personally, those of the poet's own country and people. In a short foreword in prose, Akhmatova tells how during the horrible years of the purges she spent seventeen months waiting in line in front of a prison to discover the fate of her son. Another woman recognized her and whispered, "Can you describe this?" "Yes, I can," Akhmatova replied.

She kept her promise by writing *Requiem*. Although much of it reflects the universal sorrow and despair of a mother on the verge of losing her son, it is the *injustice* of her suffering that most pains the poet. Using her personal sorrow to speak for all human beings who suffer unjustly, the poet created in *Requiem* a work of lasting value. Moreover, there is much encouragement to be gained from *Requiem*. The persona does not lose hope and courage. She perseveres, knowing that the victims are unjustly persecuted and that she is not alone in suffering. In the epilogue, she recalls the trying hours and the faces she has seen in those seventeen months; in her final words, she begs that her monument be erected in front of the prison where she has stood for "three hundred hours," so that the thawing snow from the face of her monument will glide like tears. Even if overt references to the political terror are overlooked, *Requiem* is still one of the twentieth century's most eloquent poetic testimonies to human tragedy.

FINAL POEMS

Akhmatova's poetry from the last decade of her life shows the greater maturity and wisdom of old age. Her approach to poetic themes is more epic and historical, with a deeper perspective. This mature poetry is also more philosophical and psychological. The best example is the autobiographical *A Poem Without a Hero*, a panoramic view of the previous century as it pertains to the present. It is a subtle and at times complex poem, difficult to fathom without a proper key.

In her last poems, Akhmatova speaks as if she has realized that her active role is over and that nothing else can hurt her. Her work at this time shows a mixture of sadness, resignation, relief, and even slight bewilderment as to what life really is after more than seven decades of coping with it: "The grim epoch diverted me/ As if I were a river./ I have been given a different life. In a new bed/ The river now flows, past the old one,/ And I cannot find my shores. . . ." She finds solace in her increasing loneliness, contemplating the past, trying to reevaluate it and to find the correct perspective on it. In one of her last poems, written slightly more than a year before her death, she speaks of the "Supreme Mystery." It has been on her mind from the beginning, changing its face from period to period. In her early poetry, it was the mystery of the man-woman relationship. Later, it became the mystery of the man-to-man relationship, with the emphasis on the cruelty of man to man. In her last years, it became the mystery of the relationship of man to eternity, indeed, the mystery of the meaning of existence. Through such organic development, Akhmatova reached the pinnacle of her poetic power, the power found in Pasternak's late poetry and in the work of other great poets of the century.

FORM AND STYLE

The stylistic aspect of Akhmatova's poetry is just as important as the thematic one, if not more so. She shows several peculiarly Akhmatovian features. Above all, there is the narrative tone that points to a definite affinity with prose. Formalist critic Viktor Zhirmunsky calls her entire oeuvre "a novel in verse." It is this affinity that enables her to switch easily from emotion to description. Connected with this skill is a dramatic quality, expressed either through inner monologue or dialogue. The second striking feature is the brief lyric form, usually consisting of three to four stanzas, rarely five to seven, and never more than seven. (Later in her career, Akhmatova wrote many poems in free verse.) Parallel to the brevity of form is a pronounced laconism: A few carefully selected details suffice to convey an entire picture. Akhmatova's economy of words, spare almost to the point of frugality, led her to the epigrammatic form and to fragmentation, understatement, and improvisation. As a result, her sentences are sometimes without a verb and even without a subject (that being quite possible in Russian). Another peculiarity is the concreteness of her images, especially with reference to space and time. She tells the reader exactly where and when, almost to the minute, the events in her poem take place. The colors are vividly and exactly given. She avoids metaphors, instead using pointed, explanatory epithets. Finally, her intonation, never scrupulously measured or regulated, is that of a syncopated rhythm, approaching the rhythm of some forms of folk poetry. Many of these stylistic features result from her adherence to the tenets of Acmeism, but many others are uniquely her own and are easily recognizable as such.

Of the poets who influenced her, Akhmatova herself admits indebtedness to Gavrila Derzhavin, Pushkin, and Annensky. The latter two can be said to have exerted the greatest influence on her, although traces of other poets' influences—Nikolai Nekrasov, Aleksandr Blok, Mikhail Kuzmin—can be found. Even Fyodor Dostoevski, who never wrote poetry, is sometimes mentioned as a possible source of influence. As for her impact on other poets, Akhmatova's influence, like that of her great contemporaries, Mandelstam, Pasternak, and Marina Tsvetayeva, is pervasive, elusive, impossible to measure. In her old age, she recognized the talent of Joseph Brodsky—then only twenty-two years old— and passed on her mantle, as Nadezhda Mandelstam has said, in a kind of poetic succession. Akhmatova, "Tragic Queen Anna," as literary historian Alexander Werth calls her, is a poet without whom modern Russian literature is unthinkable and by whom world literature has been significantly enriched.

OTHER MAJOR WORK

NONFICTION: *O Pushkine: Stat'i i zametki*, 1977.

BIBLIOGRAPHY

Driver, Sam N. *Anna Akhmatova*. New York: Twayne, 1972. This is the first English biography, written six years after Akhmatova's death. The first third of the book deals with biographical facts, and the remainder with a thematic explanation of the poetry. It is a concise yet scholarly work, still serving as the best primary introduction to Akhmatova's life.

Feinstein, Elaine. *Anna of All the Russias: The Life of Anna Akhmatova*. New York: Knopf, 2007. The extensive details of this biography bring to life Akhmatova's complex personality and grant readers insight to her poetry.

Gerstein, Emma. *Moscow Memoirs: Memories of Anna Akhmatova, Osip Mandelstam, and Literary Russia Under Stalin*. Translated and edited by John Crowfoot. Woodstock, N.Y.: Overlook Press, 2004. Literary scholar Gerstein describes her experiences with Mandelstam and Akhmatova, including the poet's reactions to her son's imprisonment.

Ketchian, Sonia. *The Poetry of Anna Akhmatova: A Conquest of Time and Space*. Munich: Otto Sagner, 1986. A brilliant scholarly study of themes and method in Akhmatova's poetry. Contains a recapitulation of Akhmatova scholarship, both Soviet and Western.

Leiter, Sharon. *Akhmatova's Petersburg*. Philadelphia: University of Pennsylvania Press, 1983. A review of Akhmatova's life in her beloved St. Petersburg and of political circumstances providing the material for, and leading to, her poetry inspired by St. Petersburg. The book also discusses Akhmatova's vision of this city.

Reeder, Roberta. *Anna Akhmatova: Poet and Prophet*. Rev. ed. Los Angeles: Figueroa Press, 2006. Reeder discusses in scholarly fashion all facets of Akhmatova's life and work. Stressing the artistic aspects of her poems, the author also examines the political circumstances in which she had to live. A forty-six-page bibliography is particularly useful.

Rosslyn, Wendy. *The Prince, the Fool, and the Nunnery: The Religious Theme in the Early Poetry of Anna Akhmatova*. Amersham, England: Avebury, 1984. An examination of the interplay of religion and love in Akhmatova's early collections, this book also contains considerable biographical detail. Poems are included in both Russian and English translation.

Wells, David N. *Anna Akhmatova: Her Poetry*. Oxford, England: Berg, 1996. Wells offers a succinct overview of Akhmatova's life and poetry from the beginnings to her later works. His is a penetrating study, with many citations from her poetry in both Russian and English, stressing her main achievements.

Vasa D. Mihailovich
Updated by Mihailovich

CLARIBEL ALEGRÍA

Born: Estelí, Nicaragua; May 12, 1924

PRINCIPAL POETRY

Anillo de silencio, 1948
Suite de amor, angustia y soledad, 1951
Vigilias, 1953
Acuario, 1955
Huésped de mi tiempo, 1961
Vía única, 1965
Aprendizaje, 1970
Pagaré a cobrar y otros poemas, 1973
Sobrevivo, 1978
Suma y sigue, 1981
Flores del volcán/Flowers from the Volcano, 1982 (Carolyn Forché, translator)
Luisa en el país de la realidad, 1987 (*Luisa in Realityland*, 1987)
La mujer del río Sumpul, 1987 (*Woman of the River*, 1989)
Y este poema-río, 1988
Fugues, 1993 (Darwin J. Flakoll, translator)
Variaciones en clave de mí, 1993
Umbrales = Thresholds, 1996 (Flakoll, translator)
Saudade = Sorrow, 1999 (Forché, translator)
Soltando Amarras = Casting Off, 2003 (Margaret Sayers Peden, translator)
Esto soy: Antología de Claribel Alegría, 2004

OTHER LITERARY FORMS

Though primarily known as a poet, the prolific Claribel Alegría (ahl-ay-GREE-ah) has published in a range of genres, sometimes in collaboration with her husband and principal translator, Darwin "Bud" J. Flakoll. Alegría and Flakoll collaborated on the novel *Cenizas de Izalco* (1966; *Ashes of Izalco*, 1989), on a translation of the poems of Robert Graves (1981), on the anthology *New Voices of Hispanic America* (1962), and on the testimonials *Nicaragua: La revolución sandinista, una crónica política, 1855-1979* (1982; Nicaragua: the Sandinista revolution, a political chronicle, 1855-1979), *Para romper el silencio: Resistencia y lucha en las cárceles salvadoreñas* (1984; to break the silence: resistance and struggle in Salvadoran prisons), and *Fuga de Canto Grande* (1992; *Tunnel to Canto Grande*, 1996). Alegría also has published novellas, three of which are collected in *Album familiar* (1982, 1986; *Family Album: Three Novellas*, 1991), as well as essays and children's literature. She has also edited poetry collections.

ACHIEVEMENTS

Claribel Alegría's *Ashes of Izalco*, a novel about the 1932 massacre known as the Matanza, was a finalist in 1964 in the Biblioteca Breve contest, sponsored by the Spanish publishing house Seix Barral. In 1978, she won Cuba's prestigious Casa de las Américas Prize for her volume of poetry *Sobrevivo* (I survive). In 2006, Alegría capped her career with the Neustadt International Prize for Literature. Perhaps most important, Alegría brought Central American literature, especially women's writing, to the attention of readers in the United States, and with it she brought a concern for the political situation in El Salvador and Nicaragua in particular. Her works have been translated into more than ten languages.

BIOGRAPHY

Clara Isabel Alegría Vides was born in Estelí, Nicaragua, to a Salvadoran mother and a Nicaraguan father, but her family soon moved to Santa Ana, El Salvador, because of the political problems her father suffered as a Sandino sympathizer. In 1932, she witnessed the Matanza, in which more than thirty thousand peasants were slaughtered by government troops after a peaceful protest against the military dictatorship.

Alegría published her first poems in 1941. In 1943, she went to the United States to attend a girls' school near New Orleans, Louisiana. She next attended George Washington University, where she met her husband, Flakoll, an American journalist from South Dakota who was studying for his master of arts degree. They married in December, 1947. In 1948, Alegría graduated with a bachelor's degree in philosophy and letters. Later that same year, her first book of poetry, *Anillo de silencio* (ring of silence), was published in Mexico. She gave birth to a daughter, Maya, in Washington, D.C., in 1949, and twin daughters, Patricia and Karen, in Alexandria, Virginia, in 1950. In 1951, the family visited El Salvador briefly before moving to Mexico, where their circle included various writers and intellectuals, some living in exile like Alegría.

In 1953, the family moved to Santiago, Chile, where they lived for almost three years, to work on an anthology (and translation) of Latin American writers and poets, *New Voices of Hispanic America*, which introduced writers such as Juan Rulfo and Julio Cortázar,

Claribel Alegría (©Miriam Berkley)

who would later be part of the "boom" in Latin American literature. Her son Erik was born in Santiago in 1954. In 1956, the family returned to the United States, where Flakoll applied to the U.S. Foreign Service. In 1958, he was appointed second secretary to the U.S. Embassy in Montevideo, Uruguay, and two years later, he was posted to Argentina. However, Flakoll became disillusioned by the world of politics and resigned from the Foreign Service. In 1962, Alegría and Flakoll moved to Paris, where they met many Latin American writers living in exile, including Carlos Fuentes, Mario Benedetti, and Mario Vargas Llosa. Alegría and Flakoll and worked on the first of many subsequent collaborations, producing her first novel, *Ashes of Izalco*, whose publication in Spain was delayed by censorship. In 1966, the family moved to Mallorca, where they lived for many years.

In 1979, after the Sandinistas overthrew the dictatorship of Anastasio Somosa in Nicaragua, Alegría and her husband went to Nicaragua to do research for a testimonial on the revolution. In 1980, a right-wing group assassinated outspoken human rights advocate and Roman Catholic archbishop Oscar Romero in El Salvador. Alegría gave a poetic eulogy for Romero at the Sorbonne in Paris. Her public criticism of Salvadoran government atrocities earned her a spot on a death list and made her a political exile from her adopted homeland. In 1983, Alegría and Flakoll moved permanently to Nicaragua. Flakoll died in 1995. Alegría remained in Nicaragua and has mentored numerous poets, including Gioconda Belli and Daisy Zamora.

ANALYSIS

Claribel Alegría has often spoken in interviews of the writer's role as the voice of the voiceless, of poetry as a weapon against repression, oppression, exploitation, and injustice. She considers herself a feminist, which she defines as wanting equality for women and men, and she both writes about women and promotes the work of women writers. Her poetry reflects her experience of exile, loss, and absence, often with a sense of nostalgia, or of longing for a happier, more innocent past. Much of her work is at least partially autobiographical, and memory serves as a powerful means of preserving the past.

FLORES DEL VOLCÁN/FLOWERS FROM THE VOLCANO

The first translation of one of Alegría's works into English was *Flores del volcán/Flowers from the Volcano*, a bilingual edition. It is through the efforts of the translator, prizewinning poet Carolyn Forché, that Alegría first came to the attention of readers in the United States. Many of the poems chosen for this collection come from the 1978 collection *Sobrevivo*. The title of the work is an indication of its contents: The volcano represents Central America as a region and El Salvador as a country, as part of the Pacific Ring of Fire, but the volcano also represents the eruption, violence, and death caused by the civil wars of the 1970's and 1980's in Nicaragua, Guatemala, and El Salvador, while flowers suggest beauty, hope, and life.

In the title poem, "Flowers from the Volcano," Alegría critiques the class structure in El Salvador, in which "the volcano's children/ flow down like lava/ with their bouquets of flowers," threatening the status quo of the well-to-do, "the owners of two-story houses/ protected from thieves by walls," who "drown their fears in whiskey." She remembers the dead in "Sorrow," with its "rosary of names," including Roque Dalton, the Salvadoran poet killed by government forces in 1975, and the Chilean folksinger Victor Jara, killed by security forces in the stadium of Santiago in 1973, along with many other Chileans.

Flowers from the Volcano contains some poems of nostalgic recollection of life in Santa Ana in simpler times, but the collection principally engages notions of class struggle and the brutal repression of liberty and life. As Forché notes in the volume's preface, five years passed between the summer that she and Alegría worked on the book and its publication, and in those five years "more than 40,000 people . . . died in El Salvador at the hands of security forces."

LUISA IN REALITYLAND

Sometimes called a novel, or a mixed-genre work, *Luisa in Realityland* combines brief autobiographical anecdotes and vignettes with poetry to tell the story of the childhood and adolescence of Luisa (who resembles Alegría) in a country much like El Salvador. (The poems from this volume also form one section of the collection *Y este poema-río*.)

For Luisa, like Alegría, the ceiba tree of her homeland (in "The Ceiba") is nearly mystical with meaning, ". . . the sentinel/ of [her] childhood." In this poem, as in most of the poems in this work, are the themes of exile and loss: "My absences/ have been lengthy/ innumerable," she says; "They won't let me return." Alegría's politics are clear in these poems. In "Personal Creed" she states:

> I believe in my people
> who have been exploited
> for five hundred years

In "From the Bridge," the adult Luisa/Alegría looks back in time at the little girl and adolescent she once was, but now through the eyes of experience:

> Do you remember the massacre
> that left Izalco without menfolk?
> You were seven years old.
> How can I explain it to you
> nothing has changed
> and they keep killing people daily.

Despite the violence and pessimism of many of the poems, however, the book ends with an invitation to a "rebellious/ contagious peace," a "return to the future."

WOMAN OF THE RIVER

Many of the poems in *Woman of the River* directly confront the political situation in Central America and condemn the United States' influence and its presence there. In "The American Way of Death," Alegría criticizes America's response to people's desire for a better life:

> if you choose the guerrilla path,
> be careful,
> they'll kill you.
>
> If you combat your chaos
> through peace,
> . . . . . .
> they'll kill you.
>
> If your skin is dark
> . . . . . .
> slowly they'll kill you.

"The American Way of Life" contrasts skyscrapers with undocumented workers, wealth with wanton destruction, and finds one dependent on the other. America, says Alegría, is a selfish "bitch" who "chews Salvadorans/ as if they were Chiclets/ chews up Nicaraguans." Perhaps here she refers to the massive U.S. funding of the war in El Salvador or the training of Salvadoran and Nicaraguan soldiers by the U.S. military.

The title poem, "Woman of the River," testifies to the results of U.S. support of the war, telling the tale of a woman who survives the 1980 Sumpul River massacre with her baby and youngest son by hiding in the river for hours after the security troops have killed everyone in their path, including her other three children.

FUGUES

With the wars over in Central America, Alegría's later work became less political. In *Fugues*, the main themes are love, death, and aging. In "Mirror Image," for example, the poet considers the aging process, speaking to an alien, skull-like image superimposed on her own as it stares at her from the mirror:

> Why do you insist
> on showing me day after day
> these sockets
> that used to be my eyes?
>
> . . . .
>
> I traverse your skin
> to embrace the little girl
> who still resides in me

Fugues also contains a fascinating series of poems relating female mythological or historical figures to contemporary psychology. In "Letter to an Exile," the legendary Penelope (from Homer's epic poem the *Odyssey*, c. 725 B.C.E.; English translation, 1614) writes to her husband Odysseus, asking him please not to return home. Each of the Greek mythical figures—Persephone, Demeter, Pandora, and Hecate—has her own poem, as does Malinche, an Aztec interpreter and lover of the Spanish conqueror Hernán Cortés and the mother of the first Mexican. Each of the poems presents an interpretation from the woman's perspective rather than the usual interpretation of a woman by a man.

SORROW

Saudade = Sorrow was written as a series of love poems to Alegría's dead husband. As her translator

Forché comments, *saudade* is "a Portuguese word for a vague and persistent desire for something that cannot be, a time other than the present time, a turning toward the past or future, a sadness and yearning beyond sorrow." *Saudade* means much more than the English title *Sorrow*. The "Nostalgia" of *Fugues*, in which she stops being herself and begins forever "being us," becomes "Nostalgia II" in *Sorrow*, in which she ceases "being us" and again becomes "this I/ with its burden of winter/ and emptiness."

However, the collection ends optimistically when the poet states that "sadness can't cope" with her. Although *Sorrow* does not have the political tone or content common to her earlier works, Alegría has not forgotten her rosary of names to remember the dead. As she says in "Every Time," the dead are resurrected when she names them. Just as she used her art as a weapon for the cause of justice and named the dead to keep them alive to memory, she now uses her art to keep her "deceased beloved" present.

CASTING OFF

Soltando Amarras = Casting Off continues Alegría's theme of bereavement. The poet, a widow approaching eighty years of age, has shifted from a focus on the political to a focus on the personal. She writes with delicacy and restraint about her life winding down. Alegría clearly is still mourning her husband as well as her other departed friends. The poems occupy a stark, grief-filled landscape that is both intimate and universal.

"Casting Off" refers to the difficulties of growing old and accepting death. Although reluctant to let go, Alegría does see death as a reunion with loved ones who have gone before her, leaving her entangled in memories and unable to sleep. "You Made the Great Leap" expresses the loneliness of being left behind as well as Alegría's readiness to meet death:

> You made the great leap
> and were reborn
> I am left on this shore
> crouched to spring

Alegría seems to rehearse her departure from this world by taking on the personae of mythological women such as Arachne, Antigone, Medea, Cassandra, and the Furies. Through them, she approaches death and accepts it, refusing to shy away from risk and expressing a willingness to accept change. As she writes in "Limbo," she feels good because she is "all alone/ with my dead," and soon she will join them. Alegría is content to conclude a well-lived life.

OTHER MAJOR WORKS

LONG FICTION: *Cenizas de Izalco*, 1966 (with Darwin J. Flakoll; *Ashes of Izalco*, 1989); *El detén*, 1977; *Pueblo de Dios y de mandinga*, 1985; *Despierta mi bein, despierta*, 1986.

SHORT FICTION: *Album familiar*, 1982, 1986 (*Family Album: Three Novellas*, 1991).

NONFICTION: *Nicaragua: La revolución sandinista, una crónica política, 1855-1979*, 1982 (with Flakoll); *No me agarran viva: La mujer salvadoreña en lucha*, 1983 (with Flakoll; *They Won't Take Me Alive: Salvadoran Women in Struggle for National Liberation*, 1987); *Para romper el silencio: Resistencia y lucha en las cárceles salvadoreñas*, 1984 (with Flakoll); *Fuga de Canto Grande*, 1992 (with Flakoll; *Tunnel to Canto Grande*, 1996); *Somoza: Expediente cerrado, la historia de un ajusticiamiento*, 1993 (with Flakoll; *Death of Somoza: The First Person Story of the Guerrillas Who Assassinated the Nicaraguan Dictator*, 1996).

TRANSLATION: *Cien poemas de Robert Graves*, 1981 (with Flakoll).

CHILDREN'S LITERATURE: *Tres cuentos*, 1958.

EDITED TEXTS: *New Voices of Hispanic America*, 1962 (with Flakoll); *Homenaje a El Salvador*, 1981; *On the Front Line: Guerrilla Poetry of El Salvador*, 1988 (translated with Flakoll).

BIBLIOGRAPHY

Aparicio, Yvette. "Reading Social Consciousness in Claribel Alegría's Early Poetry." *Cincinnati Romance Review* 18 (1999): 1-6. Contends that Alegría's earlier, more metaphorical and less overtly "resistant" poetry contains implicit social criticism and deals with issues of injustice and power relations in a more allegorical manner than her later overtly politicized poetry.

Beverly, John, and Marc Zimmerman. *Literature and Politics in the Central American Revolutions*. Austin: University of Texas Press, 1990. Traces the development of popular revolutionary poetry and testimonial narrative as reactions to historical events in Nicaragua and El Salvador, and stresses the importance of revolutionary Salvadoran women poets such as Alegría.

Boschetto-Sandoval, Sandra M., and Marcia Phillips McGowan. *Claribel Alegría and Central American Literature: Critical Essays*. Athens: Ohio University Center for European Studies, 1994. An excellent collection of essays on Alegría's major works and themes. One essay specifically treats her poetry. Includes an interview with the poet and a chronology of her life and works, along with a bibliography of publications by and about her.

Craft, Linda J. *Novels of Testimony and Resistance from Central America*. Gainesville: University Press of Florida, 1997. The chapter on Alegría examines two works written in collaboration with her husband, Flakoll, *Ashes of Izalco* and *They Won't Take Me Alive*, and the multigenre *Luisa in Realityland*.

Harrison, Brady. "'The Gringos Perfected It in Vietnam': Torture and the American Adviser in Claribel Alegría's *Family Album* and Carlos Martinez Moreno's *El Infierno*." *Atenea* 26, no. 2 (2006): 9-19. Examines the theme of the psychological trauma of torture while showing how Alegría's work exemplifies how torture can discipline dissidents and regime alike.

McGowan, Marcia P. "Mapping a New Territory: *Luisa in Realityland*." *Letras Femeninas* 19, nos. 1/2 (Spring/Fall, 1993): 84-99. Considers *Luisa in Realityland* a "new form of autobiographical discourse" that incorporates poetry, testimony, and elements of fiction.

Sternbach, Nancy Saporta. "Remembering the Dead: Latin American Women's 'Testimonial' Discourse." *Latin American Perspectives* 18, no. 3 (Summer, 1991): 91-102. Examines the testimonial voice of prose and poetry in *They Won't Take Me Alive* and *Flores del Volcán/Flowers from the Volcano*.

Treacy, Mary Jane. "A Politics of the Word: Claribel Alegría's *Album familiar* and *Despierta mi bien, despierta*." *Intertexts* 1, no. 1 (Spring, 1997): 62-77.

Discusses the "elite" or "bourgeois" woman as a marginalized "woman of porcelain," aware of her privileged status but not its political and economic underpinnings. In contrast to the passive bourgeois woman depicted in many of the female characters in novels by Isabel Allende, Rosario Ferré, and Teresa de la Parra, the two works by Alegría examined here portray "the struggles of the bourgeois woman to extricate herself from domesticity and to forge an independence through a 'progressive' political identity."

Van Delden, Maarten. "Claribel Alegría, the Neustadt Prize, and the World Republic of Letters." *World Literature Today* (May/June, 2007): 45-48. Discusses the significance of the Neustadt Prize and Alegría's critical reception in the world of letters.

Van Delden, Maarten, and Yvon Grenier. *Gunshots at the Fiesta: Literature and Politics in Latin America*. Nashville, Tenn.: Vanderbilt University Press, 2009. Discusses the political thought of Latin American writers. The chapter on Alegría focuses on *Ashes of Izalco* to argue that a writer does not have to abandon cultural nationalism to achieve literary excellence.

Linda Ledford-Miller
Updated by Caryn E. Neumann

YEHUDA AMICHAI

Born: Würzburg, Germany; May 3, 1924
Died: Jerusalem, Israel; September 22, 2000

PRINCIPAL POETRY
Akshav u-ve-yamim aherim, 1955
Ba-ginah ha-tsiburit, 1958
Be-merhak shete tikvot, 1958
Shirim, 1948-1962, 1962
Akshav ba-ra'ash, 1968
Selected Poems, 1971
Ve-lo 'al menat lizkor, 1971
Songs of Jerusalem and Myself, 1973
Me-ahore kol zel mistater osher gadol, 1974

Travels of a Latter-Day Benjamin of Tudela, 1976
Amen, 1977
Ha-zeman, 1978 (*Time*, 1979)
Shalyah gedolah, she-elot uteshuvot, 1980 (*Great Tranquility: Questions and Answers*, 1983)
Love Poems, 1981 (bilingual edition)
She'at ha-hessed, 1983
Me'adam ve-el adam tashav, 1985
The Selected Poetry of Yehuda Amichai, 1986, 1996
Travels, 1986 (bilingual edition)
The Early Books of Yehuda Amichai, 1988
Poems of Jerusalem: A Bilingual Edition, 1988
Even a Fist Was Once an Open Palm with Fingers, 1991
Nof galui 'enayim/Open Eyed Land, 1992
Poems of Jerusalem and Love Poems: A Bilingual Edition, 1992
Yehuda Amichai: A Life of Poetry, 1948-1994, 1994
Akhziv, Kesaryah ve-ahavah ahat, 1996
Patuah sagur patuah, 1998 (*Open Closed Open*, 2000)

OTHER LITERARY FORMS

Yehuda Amichai (ahm-ih-KI) has written three volumes of fiction and a book for children. *Lo me-'akshav, lo mi-kan*, a novel, was published in Hebrew in Tel Aviv in 1963 and translated into English as *Not of This Time, Not of This Place* in 1968. A collection of short stories, *Be-ruah ha-nora'ah ha-zot*, was published in Tel Aviv in 1961; a translation of about half the stories appeared in English in 1984 under the title *The World Is a Room, and Other Stories*. Amichai also wrote a play for the radio, titled *Pa 'amonim ve-rakavot* (1968; pr. as *Bells and Trains*, 1966). Two of his plays, *No Man's Land* and *Masa' le-Ninveh* (journey to Nineveh) were performed in 1962 and 1964, respectively.

ACHIEVEMENTS

With Amir Gilboa, Abba Kovner, and Dan Pagis, Yehuda Amichai was a leading member of the first generation of Israeli poets. They were born in Europe and Hebrew was not their mother tongue, yet they came to Palestine and were soon writing in the resurrected tongue of Hebrew.

A continuous tradition of secular Hebrew poetry has existed since 1000 B.C.E., flourishing first in Spain, Portugal, Provence, Italy, and the Netherlands, migrating in the nineteenth century to Central and Eastern Europe. However, the language that the poets used was literary rather than colloquial, and no one spoke it; the poet's Hebrew was largely derived from sacred texts. Amichai and his contemporaries were the first literary generation to use Hebrew as a vernacular. The new generation felt the need to break with the preceding poetic traditions, yet the new spoken language alone did not suffice as a literary instrument. It was this first generation that provided different models and showed how an everyday language—though still replete with biblical and talmudic echoes—might be transformed into contemporary poetry.

Amichai was one of the leaders of this generation, and the various forms, tonalities, and influences that he introduced into Hebrew literature have had a lasting effect. As the critic Gabriel Josipovici has written, Amichai and his colleagues were European Jews first and Israelis second; the dreadful history of Europe and the Middle East in their lifetime forced them to contemplate their relationship to both Judaism and the State of Israel. Amichai's generation was unique in Hebrew literature, and of this group, it is perhaps Amichai who explored the broadest range of poetic forms.

His poetry and prose were awarded the Shlonsky Prize, two Acum prizes, and the especially coveted Israel Prize. His radio play *Bells and Trains* won the first prize in Kol, the country's competition for original radio plays. Although his country bestowed on him its top honors, the Nobel Prize, which many felt he rightly deserved, eluded him. His own belief was that he had been passed over because the choice had become increasingly politicized.

BIOGRAPHY

Yehuda Amichai grew up in an Orthodox Jewish home; his father was a shopkeeper, his grandfather a farmer. His mother tongue was German. Although he entered the government-sponsored Israelitische Volkschule at the age of six and learned to read and to write Hebrew, he did not begin to speak Hebrew until 1935, when he moved to Palestine with his parents and settled in Jerusalem. His outlook was influenced by the Social-

Yehuda Amichai (The Granger Collection, New York)

ist youth movement, to which most Jewish adolescents belonged in the Palestine of the 1930's and early 1940's. He fought with the British army in World War II, then with the Palmakh in the Israeli War of Independence of 1948. He also fought with the Israeli army in 1956 and 1973.

For most of his life, Amichai made his living as a schoolteacher and was a familiar figure on Jerusalem streets. His poetry was popular in Israel, and after the publication of his first book in 1955, his writing was an important source of supplemental income. Although there are fewer than three million readers of Hebrew in Israel, the collection of his early work, *Shirim, 1948-1962* (poems, 1948-1962), several times reprinted, has sold fifty thousand copies. Translations brought thousands of new readers and additional income for Amichai. He was a visiting poet at the University of California, Berkeley, in 1971 and frequently traveled abroad to give poetry readings.

Though he always served his country militarily when called, he came to view warfare ever more cyni-

cally and sadly. When he died, his passing was particularly lamented by the peace movement in Israel and Jewish America, which had come to view him as a spokesperson. He was survived by a much-loved second wife frequently celebrated in his poetry, two sons, and a daughter.

ANALYSIS

Yehuda Amichai was not a poet of a single major theme, and a variety of approaches to his work are open to the reader and critic. He was—perhaps above all—an autobiographical poet, yet it is also possible to consider him as a national poet whose personal concerns overlap those of his country. Amichai was one of the few poets of the late twentieth century who could be called genuinely popular, and it is important to consider the nature of his relationship to his audience. Other important features of Amichai's poetry are the apparent effortlessness of his poems, with their agile, attractive speaking voice and complex tone; his use of conceits (his early poetry especially has been called Metaphysical) and his consistent success in finding striking, original metaphors; the rich variety of forms he tried, from quasi-Shakespearean sonnets to mock-heroic couplets and free verse; his emphasis on the concrete, palpable events of everyday life, as opposed to the abstract phraseology of ideologies and philosophers; and finally, his love poetry, the major theme of his work from the 1950's and 1960's. Today Amichai is recognized as the author of a body of work that is extremely varied, rich, and inventive in form. One of Amichai's most remarkable traits is that his poems have the ability to surprise.

AUTOBIOGRAPHICAL NATURE OF WORK

The autobiographical nature of Amichai's poetry was the cause of some attacks on his work. Spontaneous reference to his own experiences characterized his entire oeuvre. The other, equally important, impulses are also present: the desire to describe what is real, immediate, and concrete and the need to reach out to his surroundings. In his second collection of poems, he wrote about his thirty-second birthday: "Thirty-two times I have put on the world/ and still it doesn't fit me./ It weighs me down,/ unlike the coat that now takes the shape of my body."

His references to himself were usually self-demeaning and rueful. He did not choose to present the "beautiful soul" held up for admiration by many contemporary American poets. The persona of his poems was always complex and viewed with levels of irony. Clearly there is no barrier between the speaker and his surroundings. Amichai's self—his autobiography—proves to be remarkably synoptic and inclusive. Always he saw himself not as an individual, but as a human being against a rich, ambiguous backdrop of Hebrew history, European birth, and Israeli environment. Amichai described himself at home in Jerusalem in his poem "Travels of the Last Benjamin of Tudela":

> I've been patched together
> from many things, I've been gathered in different times,
> I've been assembled from spare parts, from disintegrating
> materials, from decomposing words. And already now,
> in the middle of my life, I'm beginning to return them
> gradually.

The speaker of such a passage is intimate, his mind agile and far-reaching, never confined. The critic Robert Alter has stressed that archaeology was always one of Amichai's primary metaphors for his perception of the human condition; he saw both the individual self and history as an elaborate depositing of layers in which nothing is entirely buried from sight. There was also an uncanny overlapping between his own life and that of the country of Israel. He wrote in the poem titled "When I Was Young, the Whole Country Was Young":

> When I first fell in love, they proclaimed
> her independence, and when my hair
> fluttered in the breeze, so did her flags.
> When I fought in the war, she fought, when I got up
> she got up too, and when I sank
> she began to sink with me.

The combination of the two themes seems spontaneous and unstudied, always accompanied by humor, irony, and the special effortlessness that by the mid-1970's had become one of the most distinctive features of Amichai's poetry.

MATURE STYLE OF THE 1980'S

After 1980, Amichai fused the two themes to the point of self-parody. In "You Mustn't Show Weakness" he wrote, "This is the way things stand now:/ if I pull out the stopper/ after pampering myself in the bath,/ I'm afraid that all of Jerusalem, and with it the whole world,/ will drain out into the huge darkness." Although such a thought might have actually occurred to him while taking a bath, it is doubtful whether the passage could be called autobiographical; Amichai built a different, much more synoptic persona than the "I" of the earlier poems. This development is confirmed by a passage such as this: "If I'm a hedgehog, I'm a hedgehog in reverse,/ the spikes grow inward and stab./ And if I'm the prophet Ezekiel, I see/ in the Vision of the Chariot/ only the dung-spattered feet of oxen and the muddy wheels."

After the 1980's, it is no longer possible to speak of Amichai's poetry as predominantly autobiographical. He had achieved an inclusive view of the world in which the speaker's observations and his use of a first-person pronoun are strictly vehicles at the service of other concepts: of society and time, of reality, and of the world.

THE REALITY OF CONCRETE EXPERIENCE

Looking back from the vantage point of Amichai's mature style of the 1980's, it is clear that he always appreciated the reality of concrete, individual experience, and of the personalities of other people. For example, some poems were excellent portraits of women, especially "You Are So Small and Slight in the Rain," "The Sweet Breakdowns of Abigail," and the devastating and sensual "A Bride Without a Dowry," which ends:

> And she's got a will of iron inside
> that soft, self-indulgent flesh.
> What a terrible bloodbath
> she's preparing for herself.
> What a Roman arena streaming with blood.

In another poem he wrote that as a child, when he banged his head on the door, he did not scream "Mama" or "God," but simply, "my head, my head," and "door, door." The meaning is clear: He always preferred solid, palpable reality to subjective notions.

LIMITS OF TRANSLATION

Gabriel Josipovici has written that, "like much postwar East European poetry, Amichai's is poetry which can travel"; that is, it is easily translated. His fluctuating tone, the humor, irony, and playfulness with words were extremely subtle; however, much is lost, both in style and content, in translation. Amichai's poetry remains powerful in the hands of such talented translators as Chana Bloch and Stephen Mitchell. But even they cannot fully render into English the complex historical stratifications of the Hebrew tongue. Words and images have acquired multiple resonances through the millennia, in biblical, talmudic, and kabbalistic writings.

An example of the limits of translation is the ending of "When a Man's Far Away from His Country," a wry, bitter poem whose subject is the quality of language. The tone and spoken rhythms are all-important, not only in style but also in theme. One translation, by Bloch, whose work has been justly praised, ends:

> In my words
> is the soul's garbage, the trash of lust,
> and dust and sweat. In this dry land even the water I drink
> between screams and mumblings of desire
> is urine,
> recycled back to me by a twisted route.

An English translation by Amichai himself reads:

> In my words there is garbage of soul
> and refuse of lust and dust and sweat.
> Even the water I drink in this dry land,
> between screams and memories of love,
> is urine recycled back to me
> through complicated circuits.

Amichai's version has one line less (like the original) and a different system of emphases, stresses, and tonalities. In the first translation, it would be difficult for the reader to divine that the "twisted route" could refer to the theme of memory, while the humorous "complicated circuits" clearly recalls the theme—and process—of memory. The stress on excretion in the first translation shifts the meaning.

Much is lost in even the best translations. As Robert Alter writes, "His Hebrew is often rich in sound play, wordplay, allusion, and other traits of virtuosity that are not readily evident in translation, and his language is a shifting mixture of colloquial and literary." Colloquial, spoken tone is important: Puns, employed seriously

even by Hebrew prophets in the Bible, are either lost or misunderstood. Amichai was influenced by W. H. Auden: When he was a soldier in the British army, he found a Faber and Faber anthology of contemporary British and American poetry. Perhaps the best way for an English-speaking reader to have a sense of Amichai's verbal textures is to read the selections in *The Modern Hebrew Poem Itself* (1965), edited by Stanley Burnshaw, and the *Penguin Book of Hebrew Verse* (1981), edited by T. Carmi. These provide literal translations and full commentaries that give the English speaker an idea of the density of Amichai's style in the original Hebrew.

USE OF METAPHOR

One feature of Amichai's style much easier to translate is the use of metaphor. From the very beginning, Amichai was a virtuoso of metaphor. He seemed to produce metaphors effortlessly—perhaps too effortlessly, as some early poems became metaphorical tours de force. He could write about Jerusalem as "the Venice of God," or in another context, as "An operation that was left open." A fig tree is "that brothel where ripe figs/ couple with wasps and are split to death." The metaphors were sometimes witty, as in "Jerusalem's a place where everyone remembers/ he's forgotten something/ but doesn't remember what it is" or "tears/ remain longer than whatever caused them." However, the wit often is turned into profound meaning, as in this stanza:

> There are candles that remember for a full twenty-four
>   hours,
> that's what the label says. And candles that remember
> for eight hours, and eternal candles
> that guarantee a man will be remembered by his children.

One of the vices of Amichai's poetry was that often he was willing to settle for easy metaphors. This might have been partly a result of his respect for solidity, for reality; as a young poet his posture was of assent, of necessary yet ironic acceptance. His concept of life was basically linear: "Our lives were stamped *To the last stop: one way*." He made a similar statement in another volume of poems: "I am always Cain:/ a fugitive and a vagabond before the deed that I won't do,/ or after the deed that/ can't be undone." This had its pious side; although he could be irreverent about God (Amichai ceased to believe in a deity at the age of fifteen), there was another, greater loyalty to his community: "When I was a child I sang in the synagogue choir,/ . . . and I'll go on singing/ till my heart breaks, first heart and second heart./ A Psalm." It required some time, perhaps two decades, for him to pass through the stage in which he thought of himself primarily as a vehicle—a head "like the heads of those senseless weeds" through which fate passes like wind from one place to another—to his later and far more dynamic, nonlinear version of history and life.

LOVE POEMS

It is in Amichai's earlier volumes that he was primarily a love poet. When he was in his twenties and thirties, it seemed as if the love of women, and especially one woman, was to be his overriding theme. Some of these poems express wonder at a woman's beauty and a concentrated dedication to sensual heterosexual love. He wrote: "I tried to go out into my times, and to know,/ but I didn't get further/ than the woman's body beside me."

Many of Amichai's love poems are very moving, and they are frequently anthologized. A bilingual collection was selected from his different volumes by Amichai himself and published as *Love Poems* in 1981. The poems are sensual, savage, nothing seems to be held back, and they range through a broad spectrum of emotions. "Six Songs for Tamar" and "Songs for a Woman" are especially beautiful. The note of wonder Amichai expresses could be very moving: "If you open your coat/ my love must widen." In many poems, however, there is a note not only of deep sadness but also of self-pity, as in the much-admired poem "A Pity. We Were Such a Good Invention," which ends:

> A pity. We were such a good
> and loving invention.
> An airplane made from a man and a wife.
> Wings and everything.
> We hovered a little above the earth.
>
> We even flew a little.

The note of mingled psychological realism and irony that became more pronounced as Amichai matured also crept into his verses contemplating love:

> The singer of the Song of Songs sought his beloved so
>   long
> and hard
> that he lost his mind and went looking for her with a
>   simile
> And fell in love with the images he himself had imagined.

Although the clipped, elegiac mood is obviously ironic, it spread from poem to poem and became obsessive, threatening to swamp Amichai's other concerns. Despite this trend, he grew and added new themes.

OPEN CLOSED OPEN

As a younger man, rejecting the jingoistic military phrases of a nation frequently embattled, Amichai had affirmed in verse his desire to die peacefully in his own bed rather than gloriously on the battlefield. In his last book, *Open Closed Open*, he reiterated this message, at the same time rejecting the burial practices of his Orthodox upbringing:

> When I die I want only women to tend to me at the burial
> society,
> To do to my body what seems right in their pretty eyes and
> clean out my ears from the
> last words
> I heard and wipe from my lips the last words I uttered
> And rub my flesh with perfumed oil so as to anoint me the
> King of Death for a single
> day.

His last book also continued his lifelong argument with the God whose existence he doubted, a deity so negligent of his chosen people. The image of Jewish scholars reading the Torah aloud to God all year long, a portion each week, and then starting all over again the next year, called to his mind Scheherazade frantically talking to save her life. Jews, he suggested, hastened to put themselves in the hand of God merely to avoid that same punishing hand. In other lines, he spoke of the Christian God as a suffering Jew and the Muslim God as an Arab Jew, still hoarse from the desert. Only the Jewish God seemed not really Jewish at all.

In addition, he was ready to face head-on the Holocaust that his family had escaped by their early migration from Germany. How, he asked, could there be any desire to know God after Auschwitz? He observed that white smoke rises from Vatican chimneys when popes are chosen, while black smoke rose from Auschwitz crematoria to signify that "God has not yet chosen the Chosen People!"

Finally, Amichai was left to question one of the last verities of his life, the value and mission of the State of Israel. His chosen metaphor was the Huleh swamp, whose drainage had been an early article of Zionist pride. Later it was discovered that what had seemed a valiant land reclamation had been in fact an ecological disaster. The results of all human efforts seemed now equally uncertain.

While Amichai's last published poems conveyed a compassionate skepticism of all endeavor and despite war and world weariness, the poet did not totally abandon hope. Might it still be possible, he wondered, for Palestine and Israel to lay down their arms and, like their proverbial ancestors Ishmael and Isaac, come together after many grievances and bury their father Abraham in the Cave of Machpelah?

OTHER MAJOR WORKS

LONG FICTION: *Lo me-'akshav, lo mi-kan*, 1963 (*Not of This Time, Not of This Place*, 1968); *Mi yitneni malon*, 1972.

SHORT FICTION: *Be-ruah ha-nora'ah ha-zot*, 1961; *The World Is a Room, and Other Stories*, 1984.

PLAYS: *Masa' le-Ninveh*, pb. 1962; *No Man's Land*, pr. 1962.

RADIO PLAY: *Pa 'amonim ve-rakavot*, 1968 (pr. as *Bells and Trains*, 1966).

BIBLIOGRAPHY

Abramson, Glenda. *The Writing of Yehuda Amichai: A Thematic Approach*. Albany: State University of New York Press, 1989. First full-length English-language study devoted to the author. Examines Amichai's thematic preoccupations across a variety of genres.

Alter, Robert. "The Untranslatable Amichai." *Modern Hebrew Literature* 13 (Fall/Winter, 1994). A clear, succinct discussion of the problems of linguistic and cross-cultural translation, with attention to Hebrew writing in general and Amichai's verse in particular. Alter, who has discussed biblical translation in earlier writings, is well equipped to elucidate the multilayered cultural heritage of Israeli poetry.

Amichai, Yehuda. "Yehuda Amichai." Interview by Joseph Cohen. In *Voices of Israel: Essays and Interviews with Yehuda Amichai, A. B. Yehoshua, T. Carmi, Aharon Appelfeld, and Amos Oz*, edited by Joseph Cohen. Albany: State University of New York Press, 1990. An examination of five "new wave" Israeli writers regarded as literary spokespersons for their nation. Both the introductory essays on the individual writers and the questions asked in their interviews highlight the special opportunities offered creative artists by the environment of Israel, a nation resurrected from antiquity and precariously situated at a crossroads of global cultures.

Gold, Nili Scharf. *Yehuda Amichai: The Making of Israel's National Poet*. Waltham, Mass.: Brandeis University Press, 2008. A biographical criticism that traces Amichai's life and relates it to his works, including his love poetry.

Green, David B. "The Most Accessible Poet: Yehuda Amichai, 1924-2000." *Jerusalem Report*, October 23, 2000. An obituary and overview of the achievements of Amichai, from a respected news magazine that surveys worldwide Jewry. Replete with facts and provocative observations, Green's article celebrates a beloved cultural hero of his nation.

Mazor, Yair. "Farewell to Arms and Sentimentality: Reflections of Israel's Wars in Yehuda Amichai's Poetry." *World Literature Today* 60 (Winter, 1986). Considers Amichai's poems a moral measure of Israel's wars through the Lebanon campaign.

Ramras-Rauch, Gila. "Remembering Yehuda Amichai, 1924-2000." *World Literature Today* 75, no. 1 (Winter, 2001): 86. A biographical sketch as well as thematic analysis of Amichai's poetry and its influence on other Israeli writers, by a professor of Hebrew literature.

Roth, John K., ed. *Holocaust Literature*. Pasadena, Calif.: Salem Press, 2008. Contains an essay on *Open Closed Open* that examines both Amichai and the volume of poetry.

Williams, C. K. "We Cannot Be Fooled, We Can Be Fooled." *The New Republic*, July 3, 2000. Ostensibly a review of Amichai's last book published in English but actually an identification of the central themes of the poet's career through a close reading of passages from some of his most important poems. Williams finds a clear "ethical focus" in the poet's work and places him within the grand tradition of Western humanistic letters, even while acknowledging the Hebraic sources.

John Carpenter
Updated by Allene Phy-Olsen

INNOKENTY ANNENSKY

Born: Omsk, Siberia, Russia; September 1, 1855
Died: St. Petersburg, Russia; December 13, 1909

PRINCIPAL POETRY

Tikhie pesni, 1904
Kiparisovy larets, 1910 (*The Cypress Chest*, 1982)

OTHER LITERARY FORMS

In addition to his two collections of poetry, for which he is best remembered today, Innokenty Annensky (uhn-YEHN-skee) wrote four tragedies and was a critic and pedagogue of note. His tragedies include *Melanippa-Filosof* (pb. 1901), *Tsar Iksion* (pb. 1902), *Laodamiia* (pb. 1906), and *Famira Kifared* (pb. 1913). Annensky's major critical effort consists of the essays constituting the two collections entitled *Kniga otrazhenii* (1906) and *Vtoraia kniga otrazhenii* (1909). They were reissued in a single volume in 1969. The remainder of Annensky's critical and pedagogical essays have never been collected in book form; they remain scattered throughout the Russian journals in which they first appeared.

ACHIEVEMENTS

Innokenty Annensky has always been considered a "poet's poet" because of the subtlety of his poetic imagery and the intricacy of his thought. In contrast to such contemporary poets as Aleksandr Blok and Konstantin Balmont, who were enormously popular in their own time, Annensky's main impact was rather on the aesthetic theory of Acmeism, one of the great Russian poetic schools of the twentieth century. Two gifted and famous Acmeists, Anna Akhmatova and Osip Mandelstam, were especially drawn to Annensky both as a poet and as a formulator of poetic doctrine.

Although he has often been regarded as a member of the older, "first generation" of Russian Symbolists (in contrast to the younger or "second generation"), Annensky does not truly fit into a particular category. His style can be designated as Symbolist insofar as his use of literary allusions is concerned, yet his worldview and aesthetic ideals, as well as his treatment of non-Symbolist stylistic elements, set him apart from this movement. Annensky differs from his contemporaries in his aesthetic independence. He is considered unique among twentieth century Russian poets in that he combined aspects of Symbolism with experimental stylistic devices to produce verse that cannot easily be labeled. He is regarded today as one of the more interesting and significant modern Russian poets, and he has a reputation far exceeding that which he enjoyed during his own lifetime.

BIOGRAPHY

Innokenty Fyodorovich Annensky was born in Omsk, Siberia, on August 20, 1856, but the family returned to St. Petersburg in 1858. Both parents having died when Annensky was quite young, he was reared by his brother, Nikolay Fyodorovich Annensky, publisher of the important journal *Russkoe bogatstvo*. Nikolay and his wife, Alexandra Nikitichna Annenskaya, held liberal political and social views typical of the positivistic thinkers of their generation.

Educated at home, possibly because his health was poor, Annensky mastered several foreign languages, including Latin and Greek. He completed a degree in philology at the University of St. Petersburg in 1879; in the same year, he married a widow named Dina Khmara-Barshchevskaya. The marriage was apparently a happy one; he was close to his two stepsons, and his own son Valentin was born in 1880.

Annensky embarked on his pedagogical career following graduation. After teaching Greek and Russian in several private institutions in St. Petersburg, he went to Kiev between 1890 and 1893, where he became director of the Pavel Galagan College. He returned to St. Petersburg in 1893, assuming the directorship of a high school there, and in 1896, he was appointed head of the famous lyceum at Tsarskoe Selo. It was during his tenure at Tsarskoe Selo that he issued his first volume of original verse and translations, *Tikhie pesni*; the book was virtually unnoticed by the critics.

Annensky's last post was as inspector of the St. Petersburg School District; he also lectured on classical literature at a private university for women. During this period, his friendship with the Acmeist poet and theoretician Nikolay Gumilyov gave him entrée into the literary world of St. Petersburg and brought him belated fame. Annensky died of a heart attack on November 30, 1909, the very day his retirement had been granted.

ANALYSIS

Innokenty Annensky's lyrics reflect an intimate knowledge of French poetry, particularly the verse of the Parnassians and the French Symbolists. Like many of these French poets, Annensky heeded Stéphane Mallarmé's dictum that to name was to destroy, while to suggest was to create. Like the French, Annensky concentrated a lyrical theme in one symbolically treated subject or in a complex of interconnected subjects. Although he made use of symbol and suggestion, the fact that the lyrical theme was related to a single subject or a complex of related subjects lent greater impact to his poems.

Annensky's link with the French Symbolists was paralleled by his close ties with the Parnassians. The latter, particularly their principal poet, Théophile Gautier, advocated art for art's sake and the composition of a carefully constructed poetry equally removed from subjective emotions and contemporary events. The Parnassians also expressed a renewed interest in the classical world; indeed, the Parnassians had a greater impact on Annensky than did the Symbolists, for he shared with the former a cult of poetic form and a love of the word as such, as well as subscribing to their notion that there was no affinity between aesthetics and ethics.

Annensky's relationship with the Russian Symbolists is somewhat ambiguous for there was an ab-sence of any kind of organizational tie or even any close relationship between him and representatives of the "new poetry." Unlike his contemporaries, he considered Symbolism to be an aesthetic system rather than a literary school. He neither rebelled against civic poetry, for example, as the Symbolists generally did, nor rejected his poetic heritage. Unlike the later Symbolists, he did not regard art as a means of mystical escape, maintaining that Symbolism was intended to be literature rather than a new form of universal religion.

The approximately five hundred lyrics that Annensky wrote are the center of his creative work and can be divided into six major themes: death, life, dream, nature, artistic creation, and time. The themes of death, life, dream, and nature are actually subordinate to that of time, which binds all of them together. In this very emphasis on temporality, Annensky transcended Symbolism and anticipated later poetic movements. His exemption of artistic creation from the strictures of time illustrates the enormous emphasis he placed on aesthetics.

Death played an important role in Annensky's verse, for he considered it as an ever-intruding end to a life without hope. He devoted a number of lyrics to this theme, one of the most important of which was "Siren' na kamne" ("Lilac on the Gravestone"). Here Annensky touches on the transitory nature of human life, on the contrast between life and death, and on the awareness that the seemingly infinite possibilities of the intellect are thwarted by the intrusion of an awareness of physical death. Annensky's realization that death is a physical, inescapable end demonstrates his acceptance of the limitations of the material world and stresses thereby one of the most significant differences between him and the Symbolists.

"DEPRESSION" AND "THE DOUBLE"

One of Annensky's major themes is life. This category is dominated by lyrics about *toska* (depression, melancholy, or yearning personified), as exemplified by the poem "Toska" ("Depression"). The persona in "Depression" is an invalid, suspended, as it were, between life and death. The setting for the poem is a sickroom decorated with flowered wallpaper, around which flies hover. The unnaturalness of the surroundings, coupled with Annensky's frequent use of participles rather than finite verbs, separates both persona and reader from the normal, lively world of action and imprisons them in a static, banal realm. Like his poems on death, Annensky's lyrics about life are characterized by pessimism derived from his constant awareness of the limitations and frustrations of life.

In *The Influence of French Symbolism on Russian Poetry*, Georgette Donchin suggests that because the dream symbolizes an escape from reality, it was a common poetic theme for Russian Symbolists. The dream also occupies a special place in Annensky's poetry. Simon Karlinsky, in his 1966 essay "The Materiality of Annensky," argues that the dream represents a world divorced from the strictures of time, an alternative existence for the poet. Annensky's dream verses can be subdivided into three categories according to theme: disorientation, oblivion, and nightmare. In "Dvoinik" ("The Double"), the persona experiences a loss of orientation, with the primary differentiation of identity, that between the I and the non-I, blurred. Annensky's deliberate grammatical confusion of the first, second, and third persons destroys the normal distinctions between conversation and narration, even of existence. When the distinct separateness of the individual consciousness is eradicated, nothing is certain. Annensky has, in fact, placed the rest of the poem outside reality by erasing the conceptions of definite time and space, with all existence transformed into a dream.

EPHEMERALITY AND DEATH

In "Kogda b ne smert', a zabyt'e" ("If There Were Not Death, but Oblivion"), oblivion represents the cessation of time. It is a state divorced from temporality, which is seen in the poem as the creator and destroyer of beauty. The poet's awareness of the ephemerality of artistic as well as natural beauty is a source of torment for him; he is trapped by time and is doomed to solitude.

Unlike disorientation and oblivion, the nightmare threatens the sufferer with annihilation. In "Utro" ("Morning"), Annesky has erased the distinction between dream and reality, making the nightmare vividly real. When day comes at the end of the poem, it is not merely a unit of time but a symbol of the force of light against the power of darkness, good against evil, life against death.

NATURE

Nature is the backdrop against which thoughts and emotions can be projected, the external mirror of human existence. As such, it constitutes a significant theme in Annensky's verse. The winter poem "Sneg" ("Snow") is characterized by a sharpness of line and by the specificity resulting from the repeated use of the definite demonstrative adjective *eto* ("this"). In addition to crispness of outline and color contrast, Annensky's employment of oxymoron makes his images clearer still. The clarity of nature has become a foil for the clarity of the thought of the persona.

"TO A POET"

In contrast to the later Symbolists, Annensky considered the poet a creator of clear, linear art. His divergence from the Symbolists is especially marked in the lyric "Poetu" ("To a Poet"), a lesson in how to write poetry. Annensky focuses on the importance of clarity and concreteness, opposing them to abstraction and indefiniteness. He asserts that poetry is a "science" governed by certain laws and is, within limits, exact, as the measuring triad of dimensions in the poem suggests. The figure with the triad is the Muse, who in turn symbolizes the art of classical Greece with its emphasis on clarity and beauty of form. The link with Greece is reinforced by the reference to Orpheus and the significance of form. The Muse is juxtaposed to veiled Isis, emblematic of the mystery and distortion of the later Symbolists. She perhaps stands for the figure of Eternal Wisdom that informed much of the philosophy of the Symbolist philosopher-poet Vladimir Soloviev. The poet is not an intermediary between Earth and a higher realm; he is not a seer or transmitter, but a writer.

"POETRY"

Like "To a Poet," "Poeziia" ("Poetry") is a metapoem, in which art transcends the everyday world and allows the poet limited access to a realm of absolute beauty. The poem is set in the Sinai Desert, a region of intense light and heat; the word "flaming" in the first line not only describes the concentrated heat of the desert but also carries the religious connotation of the fire that can purge sin and memory (as in Alexander Pushkin's famous poem "Prorok," "The Prophet"). Annensky personifies poetry in the last stanza, where he speaks of the "traces of Her sandals." The narrator never sees Poetry directly; he entreats Her, although not "knowing Her."

The desert can be seen here as a haven from society and from the decay of the established religion (in this case, Symbolism) from which the poet seeks to escape. Poetry is contrasted to the vision of Sophia (Eternal Wisdom) that Soloviev saw in Egypt, and the poem as a whole may well represent Annensky's escape from a burdensome, "official" school of poetry in his quest for pure art.

"THE STEEL CICADA"

Time is centrally important in Annensky's verse, for it is the regulator of the days and seasons, the ruler of life. Time connects and dominates all of Annensky's other themes, providing a focal point for understanding his conception of the material world and his emphasis on art. "Stalnaia cikada" ("The Steel Cicada") portrays time as an invention of the mind. In this lyric, Annensky has equated the timepiece with a cicada and has thus transformed it into something alive, thereby implying process and change. When the lid of the watch has been slammed shut in the last stanza, time has stopped. The intrusion of *toska*, having cut the poet off from external events (by shutting the watch lid), has stopped time.

Time, the medium of change, causes the alteration of moods and conditions that is the antithesis of depression. Annensky speeds up time through his poetic lexicon, employing short phrases without enjambment to achieve a staccato effect. Near the end of the poem, the persona has become reconciled to the return of depression; his companionship with the cicada is called a "miracle" that will last only for a minute. With the removal of the cicada comes the realization that the passing moment is beyond recall. The poet's attempt to escape from constancy into a realm of change that he has invented himself (symbolized throughout the poem by the watch, a mechanical object) has failed. In the end, he is the victim of his own immutability.

SYMBOLISM OF TIME

For Annensky, time symbolizes process and the final disintegration that characterizes life, nature, and death, while life represents the temporary immersion in process. It is the poet's realization of the relentless flow of time that produces the psychological state of depression, an awareness that the extreme limitations of exis-

tence are nevertheless the highest human achievement. Annensky's cognizance of depression amounts to a rejection of mysticism, separating him irrevocably from the later Symbolists. Time represents reality and is inescapable except through the momentary conquest by the mind and spirit of the artist.

USE OF PERSONIFICATION

Although he did not experiment in metrics and rhyme, Annensky was more adventurous stylistically in his employment of personification. He frequently capitalizes the first letter of a word denoting an object or abstract term to identify it with a human being, utilizing the simile and metaphor for the same purpose. Annensky's reliance on personification causes the reader to view nature, at least within the scope of these poems, as an extension of the conscious mind. His poetic universe centers on the mind, extends to artifacts, includes surrounding nature (especially the garden), and is limited only by the clouds. Beyond the clouds lies infinity, which cannot be understood and hence cannot be encompassed within the realm dominated by the mind. Because his universe can be considered as having a rational basis, Annensky should be regarded as a precursor of the rationalism of the Acmeists.

ROLE IN THE SYMBOLIST MOVEMENT

Although classified as a Symbolist by a number of critics, Annensky should rather be regarded as a transitional figure between Symbolism and later poetic developments in Russia. Annensky differs from the Symbolists in his use of conversational elements and in his preference for concrete, distinct objects as poetic images. Like his thematic emphasis on time, his predilection for the concrete and real as opposed to the abstract and mystical denotes an acceptance of the actual world. His literary orientation was toward new poets rather than toward those who were already established. His later poetry contains stylistic elements more compatible with Acmeism, even with Futurism, than with Symbolism.

Annensky's ambiguous position in relation to the Symbolists is underscored by his avoidance of the polemics characterizing the Symbolist school. This may have been partially a result of the fact that he was not a professional poet but instead was an educator who lacked sufficient time or opportunity to develop exten-

sive personal contacts with the Symbolists. His abstention from the literary quarrels that were to climax in
1910, the year after his death, indicates an unwillingness to involve himself in the intricacies of literary battles. In addition, Annensky's avoidance of Symbolist
polemics parallels his emphasis on poetry as an artistic
phenomenon rather than a literary school. He believed
that the intrinsic aesthetic value of poetry precluded its
use as a vehicle. His abstention from mysticism and literary polemics resulted from a desire to preserve the integrity of the art and thus to prevent its prostitution to
other ends.

INFLUENCE ON ACMEISTS

Annensky stood out from the poets of his time in de-
vising a poetic world that was concrete rather than abstract, worldly rather than mystical. He employed personification and focused on images and objects that
made his language concrete. Although he was interested in the musical elements of poetry, he emphasized
its pictorial and visual aspects. He thus created a definitive background for the philosophical or aesthetic argument of a particular lyric. These factors, coupled with a
respect for the intrinsic worth of art, relate him more
closely to writers following him, particularly to such
poets as the Acmeists, than to his contemporaries. In
tracing the development of Russian poetry and, indeed,
of Russian literature as a whole in the twentieth century, the pivotal position of Annensky and the great
scope of his contribution must be taken into account.

OTHER MAJOR WORKS

PLAYS: *Melanippa-Filosof*, pb. 1901; *Tsar Iksion*, pb.
1902; *Laodamiia*, pb. 1906; *Famira Kifared*, pb. 1913.

NONFICTION: *Kniga otrazhenii*, 1906; *Vtoraia
kniga otrazhenii*, 1909.

BIBLIOGRAPHY

Fedorov, Andrei V. *Innokentij Annenskij: Lichnost' i
tvorchestvo*. Leningrad: Khudozhestvennaia Literatura, 1984. A succinct biography by a leading Russian scholar on Annensky. It details the poet's life
and discusses the essential aspects of his lyrics,
prose, and plays, with the emphasis on poetry. In
Russian.

Ljunggren, Anna. *At the Crossroads of Russian Modernism: Studies in Innokentij Annenskij's Poetics*.
Stockholm: Almqvist & Wiksell International,
1997. A thorough discussion of Annensky's poetry,
addressing both the Russian and international links
of his work, with the emphasis on how the French
Symbolists were received and transformed by Annensky within the Russian Symbolist poetry. His
poetics are discussed at length. His similarities with
Boris Pasternak, Ivan Bunin, Vladislav Khodasevich, and Vladimir Nabokov are also discussed.

Setchkarev, Vsevolod. *Studies in the Life and Work of
Innokenty Annensky*. The Hague, the Netherlands:
Mouton, 1963. This seminal work includes a biography and a discussion of Annensky's works and is
one of the best on the subject. Setchkarev discusses
in detail Annensky's rise to prominence and his
contribution to the Russian literature of the first decade of the twentieth century. The author analyzes
Annensky's significance in the second wave of
Russian Symbolists. A must for students of Annensky by a Russian scholar transplanted in the West.

Tucker, Janet G. *Innokentij Annenskij and the Acmeist
Doctrine*. Columbus, Ohio: Slavica, 1986. In this
studious examination of Annensky's poetry, the
author analyzes the poet's contribution to Symbolist poetry, the themes and devices of his poetry, his
role as a literary critic, and, above all, his views of,
and relationship to, the doctrine of Acmeism and his
links with that movement. A valuable contribution
to the critical evaluation of Annensky by a Western
scholar.

Janet G. Tucker
Updated by Vasa D. Mihailovich

KOFI AWOONOR

Born: Weta, Ghana; March 13, 1935

PRINCIPAL POETRY

Rediscovery, and Other Poems, 1964
Night of My Blood, 1971
Ride Me, Memory, 1973

The House by the Sea, 1978
Until the Morning After: Selected Poems, 1963-1985, 1987
Latin American and Caribbean Notebook, 1992

OTHER LITERARY FORMS

Kofi Awoonor (AH-wew-nohr) is an accomplished writer in a range of genres. He has shown a lifelong interest in the oral poetry of his Ewe-speaking Anlo people and acted as translator of this culture's oral history and literature. His best-known work in this vein is his translation of three modern Ewe poets in *Guardians of the Sacred Word: Ewe Poetry* (1974). He is well known as a political essayist, a role reflected in his larger nonfiction titles, which include *The Breast of the Earth: A Survey of the History, Culture, and Literature of Africa South of the Sahara* (1975), *The Ghana Revolution: Background Account from a Personal Perspective* (1984), and *Africa, the Marginalized Continent* (1994). He is also a capable fiction writer, with works that include *This Earth, My Brother* (1971) and *Comes the Voyager at Last: A Tale of Return to Africa* (1992).

ACHIEVEMENTS

Kofi Awoonor has been honored with several awards and fellowships. He held Rockefeller, Longmans, and Fairfield Fellowships and won the University of Ghana's Gurrey Prize for creative writing in 1959 and for poetry in 1979, the National Book Council award for poetry in 1979, the 1988 Commonwealth Poetry Prize for the African region, and numerous other honors, including the Columbia University Translation Award, Brazil's Cruzeiro do Sol, and the Ghana Association of Writers Distinguished Author Award.

BIOGRAPHY

The childhood of Kofi Awoonor, born George Awoonor-Williams, was spent in the Volta region of Ghana near the seacoast town of Weta. Long a meeting place for the East and the West, both through agricultural commerce and the slave trade, the Weta area is also known for the strength of its traditional customs and the eloquence of its oral poets who speak the Ewe language. Such poems of Awoonor as "Night of My

Blood" and "My Uncle, the Diviner Chieftain" show how deeply and personally the history and culture of his Anlo people influenced his formative years, despite the European surname Williams once appended to his African name (indeed, his first poems were published under the name George Awoonor-Williams). Though highly educated, Awoonor has never turned his back on the culture and beliefs that shaped his early years. In a 1975 interview, he said,

> As society progresses, this whole technological society in which we are living today, we tend to forget about those other mysterious areas of human experience. But hocus-pocus is part of our waking world. I believe strongly, very, very strongly, that I am never alone.

In a way, then, Awoonor's biography is that of a tribal man and cannot be separated from the history of his people. An understanding of his life should include an awareness of the traditions, for example, of the Ewe migration from the town of Notsie in present-day Togo, where the Ewe were held captive by an African tyrant, as well as some knowledge of how deeply the drumbeat penetrates every aspect of his life. While recognizing the holistic virtues of the "African way," Awoonor grew up knowing that all the evils of African life could not be attributed to colonialism.

Awoonor received his secondary education at the famous Achimota Secondary School near the capital city of Accra. At the University of Ghana at Legon, he won his first major literary recognition, the university's Gurrey Prize for the best original creative writing. After graduation, he lectured in English at the university from 1960 to 1963 before taking an appointment as a research fellow and lecturer in African literature at the university's pioneering Institute of African Studies. During the years that followed, he was constantly active, traveling to China, Russia, and Indonesia, editing the literary review *Okyeame*, acting as the managing director of the Ghana Film Corporation, and founding the Ghana Playhouse, where he worked as both producer and actor.

The overthrow of Ghanaian president Kwame Nkrumah in 1966 coincided with Awoonor's decision to study abroad. In 1967, with the aid of a Longmans Fellowship, he went to the University of London, where he obtained a master's degree in modern English, focusing on the linguistic features of English in West Africa. A Fairfield Fellowship brought him in 1968 to the University of California, Los Angeles. In 1969, he accepted a position at the State University of New York at Stony Brook, where he eventually obtained his doctorate and became chair of the comparative literature program. Aside from brief trips to Europe and Africa, Awoonor did not leave the United States until 1975, when he ended his eight years of exile at the invitation of the Ghanaian head of state, Colonel Ignatius Kutu Acheampong, to become the chair of the English Department at the University of Ghana at Cape Coast. Awoonor's years in the United States were most productive: He published two volumes of poetry, a novel, a critical study of African literature, and an anthology of Ghanaian poets, which is also a seminal work on traditional oral poets.

Awoonor returned to Ghana with a number of ambitious projects in mind, including the launching of a publishing company, but political turmoil in Ghana interfered with his plans. The Ewe have a long history of nationalistic aspirations (because of arbitrary colonial boundaries, they are divided almost evenly between the present-day nations of Ghana and Togo), and Awoonor was linked to an Ewe military officer's alleged plot to overthrow the government of Ghana. On December 31, 1975, Awoonor was arrested for "harboring a fugitive" and placed in detention in Ussher Fort. His imprisonment lasted more than a year. His poems written during that period (later published in *The House by the Sea*) were smuggled out of prison and sent in letters to the United States, to one of his publishers, signed with such pseudonyms as I. H. A. Birdcry. Following an international outcry and efforts by Amnesty International, Awoonor was released and, in 1977, was sent as Ghana's representative to the International Festival of African Arts and Culture (FESTAC) in Nigeria. In 1978, however, his home was surrounded by troops, and he escaped in the night, slipping over the border to Togo.

From 1978 to 1982, political turmoil continued in Ghana, with elections, coups, and the execution for political corruption of no fewer than three of Ghana's former heads of state, including Acheampong. During this period, Awoonor returned to Cape Coast as dean of the faculty of arts. In 1981, he was awarded a Rockefeller Foundation Fellowship to further a study of "the moral perspective in the folktale and the modern novel in Africa."

A paucity of Awoonor's imaginative writings in the 1980's and 1990's attested to his growing involvement in government and foreign diplomacy. In 1989, he was appointed Ghana's Ambassador to Brazil, was reassigned to Cuba in 1988, and from 1990 to 1994 served as his country's permanent representative and ambassador to the United Nations.

ANALYSIS

Generally acknowledged as one of Africa's most exciting poets, Kofi Awoonor has been a significant presence since the publication in 1963 of his first poems, in Gerald Moore and Ulli Beier's *Modern Poetry from Africa*. His work is included in every anthology of contemporary African literature and has been translated into many languages, including Russian, French, Chinese, and German. His presence at various international forums on African literature and the awards he has won to encourage his continued study of oral traditions and contemporary African literature attest his stature, and he has been invited to read his poetry and discuss his work at colleges and universities throughout the United States and Europe.

Although he is one of the most widely traveled contemporary African writers, Awoonor has maintained and continued to explore those links to his Ewe-speaking culture and language that make his poetry effective and unique. He has captured the feel and rhythms of traditional oral poetry in an English which, unlike that of such African poets as Christopher Okigbo and Wole Soyinka, is seldom obscure. In the words of one of Africa's foremost literary critics, Ezekiel Mphahlele (in his introduction to Awoonor's *Night of My Blood*), Awoonor's verse is "the truest poetry of Africa." As Mphahlele says, "Although Awoonor's poetry is packed with ideas, his gentle diction carries us there with its emotional drive, its traditional speech patterns. For all that, the poetry stays on the ground, avoiding any intellectual horseplay."

The most critically acclaimed African poet of Awoonor's generation, Christopher Okigbo (born in Nigeria in 1932 and killed in action with the Biafran army in 1967), said that he wrote for other poets. Awoonor, however, has sought a much broader audience, emulating, within the context of African and world literature, the role of the Ewe oral poets among their own people.

Awoonor has led a life exemplary of the committed writer, saying once that he "thrives on opposition and conflict" and stating early in his career that his pet aversions are "poseurs and hypocrites and righteous men." Always political but never doctrinaire or propagandistic, he speaks with passion about the inequities of the world in a voice that avoids stridency. Indeed, his voice is often as gentle as a lover's, but his vision is unclouded by romanticism. His stance is closest, perhaps, to that of another well-traveled poet who addressed his verse to the common people—Pablo Neruda.

Awoonor's greatest accomplishment may lie in his synthesis of African ideas and Western experience. He reveres the philosophy of Africa yet moves in the technological world of the late twentieth century with ease, drawing from both cultures to forge a literary voice at once genuinely African and distinctly modern. Awoonor's language effects a similar synthesis, carrying the strong music of his native Ewe into English. (He continues to write in his native language, often doing first drafts in Ewe and producing both Ewe and English final versions.) Ewe is a highly tonal language, sung as much as spoken, with tonality determining the meaning of innumerable words. That Awoonor has made the transition from Ewe to English without sounding strained, stilted, or incomprehensible is almost an act of magic.

Awoonor's synthesis of language and ideas strengthens his expression of that "conflict between the old (traditional) and the new (foreign)" that the Nigerian critic Romanus Egudu rightly sees as characteristic of Awoonor's poetry. Indeed, there is a central theme that unifies all of Awoonor's works: the search for a new tomorrow in a recently independent Africa still confused by its bitter colonial past, a search for a synthesis of Western values and technology with the basically humanistic African culture that holds Awoonor's first allegiance. Awoonor, however, unlike many of his contemporaries, does not stop at that point of conflict. Instead, he works toward a resolution, building a bridge to a new land that may not yet exist but that his work foresees, shaped from both past and present and based on the soil where ancestors are buried but never truly dead.

Awoonor's eloquent exhortation at the end of *The Breast of the Earth* serves as a concise statement of his poetic stance:

> Those who call for a total Europeanization of Africa are calling for cultural suicide. Those who are asking for a pure and pristine journey into the past are dreamers who must wake up. For in the center, somewhere between those two positions, lies the only possibility.

It is in that center, a center that does hold, that the poetry of Awoonor lives.

EARLY PERIOD

A useful key to understanding Awoonor's poems may be found in his own description in 1971 (in *Palaver: Interviews with Five African Writers in Texas*, 1972) of his poetic development to date, which he divides into three phases "punctuated by my relationship to technique and my relationship to theme." The first phase, which Awoonor calls his apprenticeship, saw the creation of work that drew heavily on the tradition of the Ewe song, especially the dirge form. These laments—which have, as Awoonor puts it, a "lyrical structure with the repetitions of sections, segments, lines, along with an enormous, a stark and at times almost naive quality"—shaped his often anthologized "Songs of Sorrow" and "Song of War."

In the traditional Ewe dirge, the poet usually sings from the point of view of a man overwhelmed by the weight of life and by the enormity and inevitability of death. One should be careful, however, not to mistake this tone for one of total despair or hopelessness. An awareness of death is linked in African philosophy with an understanding that the departed ancestor's spirit still cares for the living left behind, and the bridge between life and death, or—to use a metaphor that both the Romans and the Ewe understand well—the ferry that crosses the river from the land of the living is a much more visible presence to the Ewe than to a contemporary Westerner. Awoonor's early poems fall squarely within that tradition and have images and even whole lines that are direct translations from the dirge poets of Anlo. Thus, it is with a distinctly Ewe voice that Awoonor speaks in "Songs of Sorrow" when he writes,

> My people, I have been somewhere
> If I turn here, the rain beats me
> If I turn there, the sun burns me
> The firewood of this world
> Is only for those who can take heart
> That is why not all can gather it.

The poem's proverbial message is that suffering must be expected in any human life. It is only those who are able to "take heart," who continue to strive in the face of adversity, who can collect the firewood of the world, not merely surviving within the often hostile environment but husbanding it for their good and the good of others. The catalog of woes that follows—the loss of children, the extinction of great households, the fall of leaders ("the tree on which I lean is fallen")—is thus intended as a realistic appraisal of the worst events that might befall one. Knowing that these things can happen, the person of resolve should be inspired to strive that much harder.

"THE SEA EATS THE LAND AT HOME"

"The Sea Eats the Land at Home" also draws on the tradition of the lament, but it is a more original poem, one that points toward Awoonor's mature style. Blending wide personal experience with ancestral rhythms, the poem describes with photographic accuracy the erosion that has so often threatened the existence of the town of Weta. It captures the living presence of the sea, a capricious deity that men may propitiate but can never control. Awoonor has witnessed its capriciousness more than once (there are destroyed remnants of half a dozen breached seawalls in front of Fort Prinzenstein in Weta), and he has made it visible even to those who have never been to the coast. There is nothing vague or unclear in the poem. It moves with a slow, inexorable dignity that echoes the movement of the sea, ending with lines that resound like the ebb and flow of the waves: "In the sea that eats the land at home,/ Eats the whole land at home." It was a remarkable achievement for a young poet.

"THE WEAVER BIRD"

Awoonor's poems never operate on a single level. As in the traditional Anlo poems, where a leopard is never merely a leopard but may also be a number of other things, including death, an enemy, or the Ewe cult, Awoonor's references to nature are symbolic. Nowhere is this more clear than in "The Weaver Bird." These birds are found throughout Africa. In Ghana, they are brightly colored and raucous birds that make large colonies of finely constructed hanging nests. Beautiful yet obstreperous, creative yet crowding out the other birds in the environment—what better symbol for the colonizing European? At first, in Awoonor's poem, the weaver seems little more than a bird, even though it "built in our house/ And laid its eggs on our only tree." When the bird begins "Preaching salvation to us that owned the house," however, it is obvious that it represents the Christian missionary presence in Africa, a source of confusion for the true owners of the house. Awoonor's poem offers a powerful image of that clash of cultures in which the African is forced to conform to a European value system: "Its sermon is the divination of ourselves/ And our new horizons limit at its nest." Nevertheless, though their traditional ways have been sullied by the invaders, the poet and his people have not been defeated; indeed, the last lines of the poem might serve as an anthem for postcolonial Africa:

> We look for new homes every day,
> For new altars we strive to rebuild
> The old shrines defiled by the weaver's excrement.

SECOND PHASE

The second phase of Awoonor's poetry is hinted at by "The Weaver Bird." Influenced by his study of Western literature, and particularly by the poetry of T. S. Eliot, Gerard Manley Hopkins, and William Butler Yeats, Awoonor began to write poems that embody in their linguistic texture as well as in their themes the collision of Western and African values.

In his second phase of poetry, Awoonor has said, he dealt "continuously with the theme of the conflict of cultures." The poetry is meant to be a commentary on the way the poet was torn in two by his allegiance to that side and his allegiance to this side, without this conflict ever being resolved. "The Years Behind" and "We Have Found a New Land" are two excellent examples. The former begins with lines that have the tone and diction of an English lyric, flowing with an almost artificial ease: "Age they say cannot wither the summer smiles/ nor will the trappings of our working clothes/ change into the glamour of high office./ Twenty-eight seasons have passed/ and the fleshy flushes of youth are receding/ before the residuary worm's dominion/ in the house of the fire-god." At that point, though, one third of the way into the poem, something begins to happen; the imagery leaves England far behind: "On the sacred stone with the neglected embers/ the cock-offering has fluttered and gone./ The palm-oil on the stone gods has turned green/ and the gods look on concerned and forgotten." The focus of the poem, then, is not on the poet's own approaching age but on the condition of his people and their gods, their culture. Though still alive, that culture is in neglect, while the speaker himself is in exile "among alien peoples whose songs are mingled with mine." What, then, can be done? The answer comes in the last four of the poem's twenty-three lines, with the beat and the wording of a traditional Anlo song. Neither working clothes nor the robes of high office are the proper garb for the poet. He must have a garment that is at once traditional and newly made, much as the famed Ewe weavers make kente cloth from the fine imported threads of England, embroidering it with old symbols that have proverbial connotations:

> Sew the old days for me, my fathers,
> Sew them that I may wear them
> for the feast that is coming,
> the feast of the new season that is coming.

"WE HAVE FOUND A NEW LAND"

A similar movement can be traced in "We Have Found a New Land," with its ironic image of "smart professionals in three piece" who find this Western costume inappropriate for their tropical homelands and begin "sweating away their humanity in driblets." They think they have "found a new land/ This side of eternity/ Where our blackness does not matter/ And our songs are dying on our lips." In their view, it is the poet—who wears traditional dress and speaks of the old ways, despite his Western education—who has "let

the side down," their language reflecting their British overlay. The poet weeps for them—and for that part of himself which has not yet been reborn, for those who "have abjured the magic of being themselves." The conclusion of the poem again holds out a hope for a renewed future by looking to the past: "Reaching for the Stars we stop at the house/ of the Moon/ And pause to relearn the wisdom of our fathers."

THIRD PHASE

In Awoonor's third phase of poetry, his political vision obtains a sense of urgency. Almost absent are poems in which he chooses only to reflect with a sense of detachment on politics, history, and culture. Most indicative of this change are the poems in *The House by the Sea*, which stem from his incarceration at Ussher Fort Prison (the "house" in the title referring to the prison). His words seem inspired by a larger vision, an experience of political repression and cultural genocide, and he urges action in word and deed.

In this phase, his stylistic preference turns to the long poem. In the more than four hundred lines of "The Wayfarer Comes Home," the imprisoned poet looks far beyond the borders of his native Ghana to witness a worldwide struggle for human dignity. Like Awoonor's other long poems, "Night of My Blood" (which retells the story of the Ewe migration), "I Heard a Bird Cry," and "Hymn to My Dumb Earth," "The Wayfarer Comes Home" makes great use of Ewe rhythms, at times even breaking into the native language itself. Like "Hymn to My Dumb Earth," the poem modulates between a prose rhythm tone and a stress rhythm, but this is not a departure from Awoonor's traditional roots. Interestingly enough, this seemingly modern structure, with something like reportage flowing into song (reminiscent of the works of Robert Duncan and Allen Ginsberg), characterizes the Ewe technique in poetry, whereby the cantor makes his address to the audience and then swings into the story.

The unifying image of "The Wayfarer Comes Home" is the "evil animal," the creature that has been created by colonialism, by the misuse of power, by human greed. The poet sees his mission as destroying that beast and prophesies its demise. At the end of the poem, when the poet-hunter—whose vision has ranged throughout the world seeking that empowering feminine presence that is his one true love and his native land—predicts his eventual triumph, it is a triumph for all humanity, one which all human beings should strive for and celebrate.

UNTIL THE MORNING AFTER

Until the Morning After collects a range of Awoonor's poetry from his earliest published work, *Rediscovery, and Other Poems*, through *The House by the Sea* and contains nine previously unpublished poems, some of which are translations of works originally composed in Ewe. These new poems mirror Awoonor's lifelong preoccupation with "life's tears" or "life's winds and fate." In typical Awoonor and Ewe dirge tradition, there is hope beyond death. Life itself is seen as the ultimate "act of faith." The collection also includes a brief autobiographical appendix explaining his relationship with language and writing. *Until the Morning After* helps trace Awoonor's development as a poet, from his early lyrics about nature and heritage, through his politically oriented period formed by his experiences in prison. The title of the volume is based on Awoonor's belief in the basic human need for freedom, and two of his later poems explain that freedom is so important that death will be postponed "until the morning after" it is finally achieved.

LATIN AMERICAN AND CARIBBEAN NOTEBOOK

Awoonor's role as a foreign diplomat and his travels in Brazil, Cuba, and Nicaragua inspired his collection titled *Latin American and Caribbean Notebook*. He takes a defensive and self-accusatory tone here, calling himself "the braggart loudmouth boastful/ uncertain diplomat" ("Rio de Janeiro: Fearful and Lovely City") who serves other countries while his own is being wrecked by corrupt politics and criminals. His feelings of displacement among victims of the black diaspora in other lands—for example, Brazilian squatters or African gardeners in England—is palpable. He notes an ironic solidarity with those who have fallen from the regal ancestral glories of their African heritage "down the vast saharas of my history." Coupled with his self-scrutinizing pieces are those that adulate revolutionary heroes of Nicaragua and Cuba and a number of poems that are nostalgic love lyrics ("Time Revisited," "Distant Home Country," "Lover's Song," "Readings and Musings"). In the love poems, he reflects on time and

aging and melds childhood memories with the everyday business of a diplomat, condemned to lonely beds in distant cities.

OTHER MAJOR WORKS

LONG FICTION: *This Earth, My Brother*, 1971; *Comes the Voyager at Last: A Tale of Return to Africa*, 1992.

NONFICTION: *The Breast of the Earth: A Survey of the History, Culture, and Literature of Africa South of the Sahara*, 1975; *Fire in the Valley: Ewe Folktales*, 1983; *The Ghana Revolution: Background Account from a Personal Perspective*, 1984; *Africa, the Marginalized Continent*, 1994; *The African Predicament: Collected Essays*, 2006.

TRANSLATIONS: *Guardians of the Sacred Word: Ewe Poetry*, 1974; *When Sorrow-Song Descends on You*, 1981 (of Vinoko Akpalu).

EDITED TEXT: *Message: Poems from Ghana*, 1970 (with G. Adali-Mortty).

BIBLIOGRAPHY

Awoonor, Kofi. "African Literature: The Common Tongue—A Conversation with Kofi Awoonor." Interview by John Goldblatt. *Transition* 75/76 (1997): 358. Awoonor explores the roots and commonalities in African literature.

_____. "Kofi Awoonor." Interview. In *Palaver: Interviews with Five African Writers in Texas*, edited by Bernth Lindfors. Austin: African and Afro-American Research Institute, University of Texas, 1972. Awoonor discusses the phases of his poetic development, as well as other topics.

_____. "Kofi Awoonor: In Person." Interview. In *In Person: Achebe, Awoonor, and Soyinka at the University of Washington*, edited by Karen L. Morrell. Seattle: African Studies Program, Institute for Comparative and Foreign Area Studies, University of Washington, 1975. Awoonor discusses his work, his life, and African poetry.

Egudu, Romanus. *Four Modern West African Poets*. New York: NOK, 1977. Examines the etiology of conflict in the poetry of Kofi Awoonor and cultural oppression in the poetry of Christopher Okigbo, John Pepper Clark, and Lenrie Peters.

Ojaide, Tanure. "New Trends in Modern African Poetry." *Research in African Literatures* 26, no. 1 (Spring, 1995): 4. Examines the ways in which younger African poets have rejected many of the poetic practices associated with the early Awoonor, Christopher Okigbo, Wole Soyinka, and others. Among the characteristics of the new poetry are the national experience, indigenous and oral modes, and a loosening and diversification of language.

Roscoe, Adrian A. *Mother Is Gold: A Study in West African Literature.* New York: Cambridge University Press, 1971. Examines the roots and historical criticism of a range of West African authors, including Awoonor. Includes bibliography.

Wilkinson, Jane. *Talking with African Writers: Interviews with African Poets, Playwrights, and Novelists.* Studies in African Literature. London: J. Currey, 1992. Provides a discussion of the history and criticism of African literature as well as a series of interviews with African writers, including Awoonor. Bibliographical references and index.

Joseph Bruchac
Updated by Sarah Hilbert

B

ALEKSANDR BLOK

Born: St. Petersburg, Russian Empire (now in Russia); November 28, 1880

Died: Petrograd, Russian Soviet Federation of Socialist Republics (now St. Petersburg, Russia); August 7, 1921

Stikhi o prekrasnoy dame, 1904
Nechayannaya radost, 1907
Snezhnaya maska, 1907
Zemlya v snegu, 1908
Nochyne chasy, 1911
Skazki, 1912
Krugly god, 1913
Stikhi o Rossii, 1915
Sobraniye stikhotvoreniy i teatr v 4 kigakh, 1916
    (4 volumes; includes the poetic cycles *Puzyri zemli, Gorod, Faina*, etc.)
Dvenadtsat, 1918 (*The Twelve*, 1920)
Skify, 1918 (*The Scythians*, 1982)
Solovinyy sad, 1918
Iamby: Sovremennye stikhi, 1907-1914, 1919
Sedoe utro, 1920
Za granyu proshlykh dnei, 1920
Vozmezdie, 1922 (wr. 1910-1921)
Poems of A. B., 1968
Selected Poems, 1972

OTHER LITERARY FORMS

Aleksandr Blok wrote three lyrical plays, the first of which, *Balaganchik* (pr., pb. 1906; *The Puppet Show*, 1963), was staged immediately and widely. The second, *Korol' na ploshchadi* (pb. 1907; *The King in the Square*, 1934) was never staged, although its material was absorbed into other works. *Roza i krest* (pb. 1913; *The Rose and the Cross*, 1936) was popular in print and had more than two hundred rehearsals at the Moscow Art Theater, but was never publicly staged. Several additional dramatic monologues failed before presentation. Blok also wrote critical essays on poetry and drama as well as a series of articles dealing with the role of the intelligentsia in Russian cultural development, translated several plays from French and German for stage production, and edited his mother's translation of the letters of Gustave Flaubert. Much of his work was reissued in various collections during his lifetime, and posthumous editions, including diaries, letters, and notebooks, have appeared regularly. A scholarly collected works in nine volumes has been completed in the Soviet Union.

ACHIEVEMENTS

Aleksandr Blok was the leading Russian Symbolist and is universally regarded as one of the most important Russian poets of the twentieth century. The Symbolists were interested in poetic reform to reshape the partly sentimental, partly social-oriented poetic idiom of the second half of the nineteenth century. They favored a return to mysticism, albeit with modern overtones, free from the rational tenor of the scientific age. The movement's early exponents, notably Konstantin Balmont and Valery Bryusov, incorporated French Symbolist ideas into their work, but when Blok began to write at the turn of the century, Symbolism was no longer a single unit. It had disintegrated into literary factions that reflected the movement's precepts in their own way. Though Blok paid homage to the search for spiritual values, his mysticism owes as much to the writings of his uncle, the religious philosopher Vladimir Solovyov, as to Stéphane Mallarmé, with whom he shared the striving to give shape to the "music of the spheres," the elusive entities beyond reality.

In contrast to his eccentric fellow Symbolists and the equally whimsical linguistic experimenters of other movements, Blok stood out as a contemplative, sincere individual whose philosophical concerns were as important as the language used to express them. He attached an almost metaphysical significance to the creative power of the poet, and this belief in the transcendental quality of art led him to reach beyond the partisan interests of his contemporaries to create a solid, coherent poetical system reminiscent of the "golden age" of

Alexander Pushkin, Mikhail Lermontov, and Fyodor Tyutchev almost a century earlier. Blok's considerable talent and natural sense of rhythm facilitated the realization of these aspirations, resulting in an amazing output during twenty years of literary activity. Thematically, Blok brought the cult of the Eternal Feminine to Russia, using the concept as focal point in his search for spiritual unity. The immense range of this vision, incorporating, among others, the Virgin Mary, Holy Sophia, Mother Russia, Blok's wife, and St. Petersburg prostitutes, permitted the poet to extend early mystical longings to the concrete realities of his own life and to revolutionary changes. His verse cycles dedicated to his native land, his perceptive essays on the role of the intelligentsia, and his refusal to emigrate during the famines of the civil war brought him deference from all segments of the Russian public. Stylistically, he honored the conventions of the past by building on existing rhyme schemes in much of his work, even as he changed from the traditional counting of syllables in a metric foot to modern tonic verse patterns.

Blok's poetry appealed to fellow poets, critics, and the public at large alike. He managed to avoid censorial confrontations with both prerevolutionary and postrevolutionary regimes to emerge as the most esteemed writer of the Silver Age, at once a preserver of tradition and a precursor of modern poetry. His work is widely translated and discussed abroad, and he remains a respected literary figure in Russia.

Biography

The artistically, academically, and socially illustrious family into which Aleksandr Aleksandrovich Blok was born on November 28, 1880, contributed significantly to his poetic development and success. His maternal grandfather was Andrey Beketov, the prominent botanist and rector of St. Petersburg University, and his grandmother was an editor and translator—from English, French, and German—of artistic and scientific works. Blok's mother, one of the prime influences on his life, wrote poetry herself and established a reputation as a translator of French literature. Several other female members of the family were also engaged in literary activity, especially the interpretation of French writers to the Russian public, thus exposing Blok early

to the ideas of European literature. The Blok side of the family consisted of outstanding professional people, though tainted with a strain of insanity that affected Blok's father, a law professor at Warsaw University. Blok believed that his father's mental instability contributed to his own frequent despondency. Blok's parents, highly individualistic and incompatible in personality, did not remain together for long. The poet was born in his mother's ancestral home and reared by a household of solicitous women, who nourished both his physical and artistic development until age eleven, when he was finally enrolled in a boys' school. By that time, he had already written poems, coedited an informal family journal, and taken part in domestic theatricals. Blok's lifelong attachment to the feminine principle in his poetry and his first book of verse specifically devoted to that concept may well reflect the influence of the women in the Beketov household.

In 1898, Blok entered the law school of St. Petersburg, but changed three years later to the philology department, from which he graduated in 1906. In 1903, he published his first verses and married the daughter of the scientist Dmitry Mendelyev, a family friend. He had also become interested in mystic philosophy, contributing essays to the Religious-Philosophical Society, of which he was a member. By the time his first verses were printed, he had amassed more than six hundred poems, most of which found ready acceptance after his debut. From this point on, a steady stream of poems, dramas, and essays issued from Blok's pen with seeming effortlessness. In 1904, the collection *Stikhi o prekrasnoy dame* (verses about the Beautiful Lady) appeared, to be followed in 1907 by his second book, *Nechayannaya radost* (unexpected joy), and several plays. Under the influence of his mystical beliefs, Blok had transferred the cult of a divine feminine vision to his wife, Lyubov, an aspiring actress, to whom many of the Beautiful Lady poems were dedicated. Blok's close friend and fellow mystic, the poet Andrey Bely, carried this adoration to extremes, causing family disharmony. Blok's wife rejected all mysticism, lived a life of her own, and bore a short-lived son conceived in an extramarital liaison. Nevertheless, the couple remained together as trusted friends. Blok to the end admired, needed, and relied on Lyubov's strong, earthy personality, as he had earlier relied on his mother and grandmother.

The shattered idealism of Blok's marriage and the miscarried 1905 uprising drew the poet away from the otherworldly themes of his early work. As he developed a more skeptical, practical outlook, he immersed himself in the street life of St. Petersburg, giving himself up to several passions. His infatuation with Natalia Volokhova, an actress in his play *The Puppet Show*, inspired the verse cycles *Snezhnaya maska* (the snow mask) and "Faina," which are among his finest works. A happier love affair with the opera singer Lyubov Delmas in 1914 engendered the cycle "Karmen."

Blok made five journeys abroad. As a young man, he accompanied his mother twice to Germany. Later, in 1909, he traveled with his wife to Italy and transformed his impressions of that country into the group of "Italyanskie stikhi." In 1911, the Bloks toured Europe, which provided inspiration for the verse tale *Solovinyy sad* and the play *The Rose and the Cross*, reflecting experiences on the Basque coast and in Brittany respectively. A nagging feeling of guilt about having neglected his father is reflected in the unfinished epic "Vozmezdie" (retribution).

Blok's political involvements were minor, though controversial. His ideas on the state of the country were published in *Rossia i intelligentsia* (1918), a series of essays spanning a decade. Blok accuses his own upper class of having created a cultural schism by looking to Europe while slighting its own people and heritage. This negative attitude toward the existing ruling circles encouraged him not to condemn the revolution, though he did not welcome it enthusiastically. A stint at the front contributed to his unhappiness, as he saw the philosophical unity sought in his work disappear in the ravages of war and revolution. He served briefly on a provisional government commission investigating suspect czarist officials, then composed his best-known and most controversial poem, *The Twelve*, which depicts a murderous Red Army detachment as disciples to an ineffectual, effeminate Christ. The equally provocative *The Scythians* followed a few days later. Between 1918 and his death on August 7, 1921, Blok wrote little, though he continued work on "Vozmezdie." The Bolshevik government, grateful for his conciliatory stance,

Aleksandr Blok (Library of Congress)

printed and reissued many of his works and appointed him to several literature boards and artistic commissions. Through these activities, his material circumstances became less desperate than those of his fellow citizens, but his health declined quickly just the same. Depression and doubts about the future of his country hastened his end. Russia's artistic, literary, and governing elite and more than a thousand people followed his coffin in recognition of his cultural contributions.

ANALYSIS

Aleksandr Blok sought to give a metaphysical dimension to his poetry by creating a persona that pays homage to a supernatural ideal, in his own words "an essence possessed of an independent existence." This ideal is usually represented by the concept of the Eternal Feminine, which takes on a range of embodiments in the various stages of Blok's development. Initially, he depicted an ephemeral, distant spirit, the Beautiful Lady, whose presence the poet perceives in almost every poem, but who is never made manifest. As Blok matured, his mental discipline, inquiring mind, and sensuous disposition prompted him to alter the image, until it became more of a literary device and less of a religious inspiration. While the vision retained some of its ethereal, purifying characteristics in later works, it also assumed demoniac, physically alluring aspects. In many other poems, desperate city women, whose misfortunes Blok ascertained from newspapers, represent the feminine ideal, as do the poet's female friends and relatives. The persona's attitude to the changing image is ambiguous. He is inexplicably and fatally drawn to some embodiments, observing others wistfully and indifferently. Eventually, social pressures, war, and revolution drew Blok further from the transcendental sphere, causing him to blend his vision with the concept of Mother Russia. Blok then saw the Beautiful Lady in the lined faces of praying peasant women and urban prostitutes, and even in the Russian landscape. A final attempt to revive the religious dimension of the image occurs in the revolutionary poem *The Twelve*, in which an effeminate, Christ-like ghost silently and gently accompanies marauding Bolshevik revolutionaries.

Blok was the forerunner of modern Russian poetry. He replaced the realistic, low-quality verse of the second half of the nineteenth century with a new lyricism, to which he gave a mystical dimension. Technically, he freed Russian verse from rigid meter and led the way to modern tonic patterns. The social upheavals of his era are reflected in his work but are always subordinate to artistic requirements. Blok appealed to all segments of the public and continues to be popular at home and abroad.

"GOROD" AND "ARFY I SKRIPKI"

Although the Eternal Feminine is a constant in Blok's work, it does not exhaust his poetic themes. After witnessing the bloodbath of the unsuccessful 1905 uprising in St. Petersburg, he devoted an entire cycle, "Gorod," to his hometown. Only a few of these poems express political observations; most of them deal with the darker aspects of street life. Feelings of impending catastrophe, both personal and societal, pervade the poetic atmosphere. The later cycle "Strashny mir" (a terrible world) extends this theme of urban degradation and misery. In one of the sections of the cycle, "Plyaski

smerti" (dances of death), which echoes Charles Baudelaire's "Danse Macabre," Blok evokes the disintegration of his society, which the persona views in the shape of a corpse, no longer believing in transcendence, while soulless St. Petersburg citizens dance their own deaths through empty lives. In the seventy-two-poem cycle "Arfy i skripki" (harps and violins), Blok endeavors to link poetry to music, and several of his verses were later set to music. He manages to reproduce the rhythm of ballads, romances, and factory and folk songs in these and many other poems. Finally, the unfinished epic "Vozmezdie" is a lyrical chronicle of his family's and nation's destiny. Blok's general poetic mood ranges from mystical belief and idealistic expectation to false rapture, skeptical, even cynical visions of life, and eventually sadness, despair, and critical aloofness.

POETIC STYLE

Stylistically, Blok stands between the traditional syllabic meter and modern tonic patterns. In his earlier work, metric regularity and exact rhyme dominate, to be followed by syllabotonic verse and experiments with *vers libre*. His rhymes become approximate, until he evolves a very modern, conversational style. Typically, his line has three stresses, interrupted by one or two unstressed syllables, but his rather extensive output shows great stress and syllable diversity within the line. He favors lexical repetition and occasionally repeats the first stanza as the last, with slight lexical change, to achieve a musical effect. Not the least of his skills is to transform vague, mystical notions into concise, elegant verse. Blok's poetry is more accessible than the linguistic experiments of the Futurists and other innovators, and theme or thought are not as completely subordinated to technique. This accessibility, achieved with no loss of artistic quality, and the generally held belief that he re-created the great poetic traditions of the nineteenth century, give him a fame and exposure not matched by other modern Russian poets.

CELEBRATION OF THE ETERNAL FEMININE

Blok's celebration of a feminine ideal is a twentieth century version of earlier cults, encompassing the Gnostic image of Holy Sophia, the adoration of the Virgin Mary in its various guises, Dante's devotion to Beatrice, and Johann Wolfgang von Goethe's evocation of the Eternal Feminine in *Faust: Eine Tragödie* (pb. 1808, 1833; *The Tragedy of Faust*, 1823, 1838). Blok was not directly influenced by Western manifestations of the concept, though he employed all of them. His interest in the symbol came from the writings of the mystic philosopher Vladimir Solovyov, who incorporated Holy Sophia into his ideological system. Blok called his ideal more generally the Beautiful Lady, devoting not only his first collection, *Stikhi o prekrasnoy dame*, to her, but also extending the vision in diverse guises in all major subsequent work. His choice of an ancient symbol was influenced by the belief that familiar, even proverbial, concepts call forth deeper emotions than newly created metaphors. The more than three hundred poems of his first collection portray the Beautiful Lady as a godlike essence which can never assume concrete, earthly shape, but is accessible in spirit to the perceptive poetic persona. The image thus appears in fleeting poses, in the flickering of a candle, the rustle of a curtain, a breeze, or simply as a felt presence. Particularly prominent is Blok's evocation of a distant shadow: "I waited for You. But Your shadow hovered/ In the distance, in the fields . . ." or "You are leaving into crimson sunset/ Into endless circles."

In this semblance, the Beautiful Lady is sometimes an elemental, an almost pagan spirit, enveloped in mists and twilight, floating by in a snowflake or glistening in a star. She appears as a figure in a song and is herself a song, perceived in snatches of distant melodies. In line with traditional symbolism, she is frequently represented by a radiant light: "I wait. Unexpectedly a door will open,/ And vanishing light will fall on me." The association with light extends naturally to religious settings, in which the Beautiful Lady is an incarnation of the Virgin. She is anticipated by the persona at the temple entrance: "The church steps are illuminated/ Their stones alive—and waiting for Your steps," and immediately perceived within: "Holy Lady, how caressing the candles,/ How comforting Your features." The poems tend to follow a rigid scheme: a physical setting empty of other people, the persona's anticipation, his ritualistic incantations, and the resultant perception of the vision.

Blok often used dark/light contrasts to separate image from persona and the rest of the world. In a well-known poem of this type, "I Go into Darkened Temples," the worshiper waits in the dim edifice, contemplating the flickering candle before the icon of the Virgin. The intense longing produces a state of excitement, in which real or imaginary creaks, rustles, and movements translate into a perception of her presence. The icon seems to come alive as the worshiper falls into a trance, engulfed by dreams and fairy-tale images. The final impression is an instant of joy and relief. These verses are not so much a lyrical diary, though Blok designated them as such, as they are a glimpse of his spiritual search. The intensity of his emotions carries a hint of immaturity, even sentimentality, which is redeemed, however, by the careful transmutation of the ecstasy into a restrained poetic idiom, and by the gossamer quality of the dreamlike reflections.

Several factors led the poet to change the image and thus extend the range of his spiritual odyssey. The idea of constant longing and expectation, interrupted only by vague, insubstantial moments of revelation, failed to satisfy the poet on a permanent basis. Doubt in the validity of his adoration, even in the existence of the Beautiful Lady and impatience with her remoteness already appear in the first collection. Blok sees himself as her "Obscure slave, filled with inspiration/ Praising You. But You don't know him." He also reproaches her: "You are different, mute, faceless,/ Hidden away. You bewitch in silence." In the end, he challenges the symbol more directly: "You are holy, but I don't believe You." In one of Blok's most quoted poems, "I Have a Premonition of You," he fearfully anticipates other embodiments: "The entire heaven is on fire, and Your appearance near,/ But I am terrified that You will change your visage." The changes were inevitable in the light of the poet's determination to transfer some of the mystique to his fiancé Lyubov, who became his wife in 1904. This attempt at earthly incarnation miscarried, for while he implored Lyubov to serve as his inspiration, addressing her with the same capitalized "You" often lavished on the Beautiful Lady, she refused all mysticism and insisted on an ordinary flesh-and-blood relationship.

NECHAYANNAYA RADOST

Blok's second book, *Nechayannaya radost*, features an altered image of the Beautiful Lady. The thirteen-poem lead cycle "Puzyry zemli" identifies the symbol with the Macbethian witches, described by William Shakespeare: "The earth has bubbles, as the water hath/ And these are of them." Religious adoration is here replaced by riotous cavorting amid the demons of the St. Petersburg marshes. The second cycle of the book, "Nochnaya fialka," a fantastic tale composed in 1905-1906, expands this underground involvement. A new version of the Eternal Feminine appears in the form of a graceful but lethally poisonous flower princess. The dreamer-poet leaves his city and friends to venture far into a swampy netherworld, where he encounters a faceless, ageless vegetable female. This sweet-smelling woman flower eternally spins, casting her devastating marsh breath over others, while she herself blooms in the poisonous atmosphere. The sleepy hero perceives distant echoes of a happier land, now forever lost to him. The style of "Nochnaya fialka" demonstrates Blok's increasing technical mastery. Though he preserves traditional regular rhythm, he uses free verse and uneven rhyme and syllable schemes. This poem is considered one of Blok's best.

In Blok's subsequent collections, the Eternal Feminine assumes whatever aspect suits the poetic theme. When casting his unrequited love for Natalia Volokhova into verse in the cycle *Snezhnaya maska*, the vision becomes a glacial force, indifferently condemning the persona to a frozen wasteland. In "Faina," she is a cruelly teasing gypsy. Blok's most famous poems feature other embodiments of the ideal. In "The Stranger," she is a prostitute, uncannily reflecting the purity and mystery of the Beautiful Lady, and in "A Girl Sang in a Church Choir," she is a young singer transformed into a ray of light, promising salvation, while the piercing cries of a child reveal her deception. When the poet does make contact with his vision, the encounter is usually unsatisfactory or violent, as in "Humiliation," where the persona wrestles with a prostitute and shouts in despair: "I am neither your husband, nor bridegroom, nor friend!/ So go ahead, my erstwhile angel and plunge/ Your sharp French heel into my heart."

THE TWELVE

Blok's most controversial manifestation of a divine vision occurs in the final stanza of his revolutionary poem *The Twelve*. Technically, *The Twelve* is a master-piece. It pits the icy, howling snowstorm of the revolution against the vulnerable population, seen as unsure of its footing and slipping on the ice. All segments of society confront and attempt to hurdle the Bolshevik snowdrift. A fur-clad upper-class lady fails and lies prostrate; a fat-bellied priest attempts to squeeze by furtively; a bourgeois stands undecided at the crossroad; an intellectual shouts his dissent; and a peasant woman, not understanding the political event, succeeds in clambering across the snowdrift. Prostitutes using incongruous political jargon establish union fees for their services. These scenes are background for the main drama dealing with twelve Red Army men who think they safeguard the revolution, but really loot and kill. One of them murders his lover in a jealous rage, only to be overcome by religious scruples and feelings of guilt. At poem's end, the revolutionaries continue on their violent path, boldly asserting their freedom from religion, but—unknown to them—they are led by the shadowy, gentle, garlanded figure of an effeminate Christ, whose unexpected appearance transmutes the marauders into the twelve disciples. Blok was vilified by both the Left and the Right for this inexplicable ending, but insisted that his poetic instinct dictated it. The controversy over this image for a long time obscured appreciation of the poem's exquisite artistic craftsmanship. Blok wrote very little after *The Twelve*.

OTHER MAJOR WORKS

PLAYS: *Balaganchik*, pr., pb. 1906 (*The Puppet Show*, 1963); *Korol' na ploshchadi*, pb. 1907 (wr. 1906; *The King in the Square*, 1934); *Neznakomka*, pb. 1907 (*The Unknown Woman*, 1927); *Pesnya sudby*, pb. 1909, 1919 (*The Song of Fate*, 1938); *Roza i krest*, pb. 1913 (*The Rose and the Cross*, 1936); *Ramzes*, pb. 1921; *Aleksandr Blok's Trilogy of Lyric Dramas*, 2003 (Timothy C. Westphan, translator and editor).

NONFICTION: *Rossia i intelligentsia*, 1918; *Katilina*, 1919; *O simvolizme*, 1921 (*On Symbolism*, 1975); *Pis'ma Aleksandra Bloka*, 1925; *Pis'ma Aleksandra Bloka k rodnym*, 1927; *Dnevnik Al. Bloka, 1911-1913*, 1928; *Dnevnik Al. Bloka, 1917-1921*, 1928; *Zapisnye knizhki Al. Bloka*, 1930; *Pis'ma Al. Bloka k E. P. Ivanovu*, 1936; *Aleksandr Blok i Andrey Bely: Perepiska*, 1940.

BIBLIOGRAPHY

Berberova, Nina. *Aleksandr Blok: A Life*. Translated by Robyn Marsack. New York: George Braziller, 1996. A biography originally published in 1996 by Carcanet Press Limited, Britain, and by Alyscamps Press, France.

Briggs, A. D. P. *A Comparative Study of Pushkin's "The Bronze Horseman," Nekrasov's "Red-Nosed Frost," and Blok's "The Twelve": The Wild World*. Lewiston N.Y.: Edwin Mellen Press, 1990. Blok's "The Twelve" is compared to works by Nikolai Nekrasov and Alexander Pushkin.

Chukovsky, Kornei. *Alexander Blok as Man and Poet*. Translated and edited by Diana Burgin and Katherine O'Connor. Ann Arbor, Mich.: Ardis, 1982. A very good Soviet monograph, equally divided between biography and critical analysis of Blok's work. Best known as a scholar of children's literature, Chukovsky was a friend of Blok, and his account is enriched by personal reminiscence.

Hellman, Ben. *Poets of Hope and Despair: The Russian Symbolists in War and Revolution, 1914-1918*. Helsinki: Institute for Russian and East European Studies, 1995. Surveys and compares the work of half a dozen Russian Symbolists of the World War I period, including Blok. Includes bibliographical references.

Pyman, Avril. *The Life of Aleksandr Blok*. 2 vols. New York: Oxford University Press, 1979-1980. One of the most exhaustive treatments of Blok as a man and a writer by a leading scholar of Russian literature. The emphasis is on biography, but there are also discussions of Blok's poems. Excellent illustrations.

Rylkova, Galina. *The Archaeology of Anxiety: The Russian Silver Age and its Legacy*. Pittsburgh, Pa.: University of Pittsburgh Press, 2007. This discussion of the Silver Age (c. 1890-1917) in Russia contains a chapter on Blok and his work.

Sloane, David A. *Aleksandr Blok and the Dynamics of the Lyric Cycles*. Columbus, Ohio: Slavica, 1987. A penetrating study of Blok's lyrics, especially his tendency to write in cycles throughout his career.

Soboleva, Olga Yu. *The Silver Mask: Harlequinade in the Symbolist Poetry of Blok and Belyi*. Oxford, England: Peter Lang, 2007. The author compares and contrasts how Blok and Andrey Bely use the harlequin in their Symbolist poetry.

Vickery, Walter, ed. *Aleksandr Blok Centennial Conference*. Columbus, Ohio: Slavica, 1984. A collection of twenty-one essays on various aspects of Blok's life and work, prepared for a seminar in Chapel Hill, North Carolina, in 1981, the centennial of Blok's birth. The topics tend to concentrate on the stylistic elements of his poetry and other aspects of Blok's portrait.

Vogel, Lucy, ed. *Blok: An Anthology of Essays and Memoirs*. Ann Arbor, Mich.: Ardis, 1982. A collection of informative memoirs by people who knew Blok, including Lyubov Mendeleeva (his wife), Maxim Gorky, Osip Mandelstam, and Boris Pasternak. Includes a twenty-six-page bibliography.

Margot K. Frank

JORGE LUIS BORGES

Born: Buenos Aires, Argentina; August 24, 1899
Died: Geneva, Switzerland; June 14, 1986
Also known as: F. Bustos; H. Bustos Domecq; B. Suárez Lynch

PRINCIPAL POETRY

Fervor de Buenos Aires, 1923, 1969
Luna de enfrente, 1925
Cuaderno San Martín, 1929
Poemas, 1923-1943, 1943
Poemas, 1923-1953, 1954
Obra poética, 1923-1958, 1958
El hacedor, 1960 (*Dreamtigers*, 1964)
Obra poética, 1923-1964, 1964
Seis poemas escandinavos, 1966
Siete poemas, 1967
Elogio de la sombra, 1969 (*In Praise of Darkness*, 1974)
El otro, el mismo, 1969
Para las seis cuerdas: milongas, 1970 (illustrated by Héctor Basaldua)

El oro de los tigres, 1972 (translated in *The Gold of Tigers: Selected Later Poems*, 1977)

La rosa profunda, 1975 (translated in *The Gold of Tigers*)

La moneda de hierro, 1976

Historia de la noche, 1977

Sonetos a Buenos Aires, 1979

Antología poética, 1923-1977, 1981

La cifra, 1981

Los conjurados, 1985

Obra poética, 1923-1985, 1989

Selected Poems, 1999

OTHER LITERARY FORMS

Jorge Luis Borges (BAWR-hays) is best known for his short stories, especially those written during the period when he made each the exploration of a metaphysical paradox, often with the pretense that he was summarizing some larger work. These metaphysical themes pervade most of his poems, which give them even more condensed treatment.

ACHIEVEMENTS

The best measure of the achievement of Jorge Luis Borges is his enormous influence on world literature and literary criticism, especially on Latin American Magical Realism and North American fantasy. Borges, along with Samuel Beckett, received the International Publishers' Prize (Prix Formentor) in 1961. Other recognitions include the Ingram Merrill Foundation's Annual Literary Award (1966), various honorary degrees (beginning in 1971 with Columbia University), Israel's Jerusalem Prize (1971), Mexico's Alfonso Reyes Prize (1973), the Nebula Award for Best Short Story (1975), a Special Edgar Allan Poe Award from the Mystery Writers of America (1976), the World Fantasy Award (1979), Spain's Miguel de Cervantes Prize (1979), shared with Gerardo Diego), the International Balzan Prize (1980), France's Cino Del Duca World Prize (1980), the Ingersoll Foundation's T. S. Eliot Award for Creative Writing (1983), and the National Book Critics Circle Award in criticism (1999). Argentina honored him with the directorship of its National Library from 1955 to 1973. He became a member of the French Legion of Honor in 1983.

BIOGRAPHY

Jorge Luis Borges was born in Buenos Aires, Argentina, in 1899. Borges grew up bilingual in Spanish and English, largely because he had a British grandmother, and later learned some French, German, and Latin during the family's four years in Switzerland (1914-1919). The major conflict during his early years was between forcefulness and literary refinement. Before leaving for Switzerland (to seek treatment for his father's growing blindness), his family lived in a suburb plagued with knife-fighting gauchos and other criminals, a fascination with which often surfaced in Borges's writings. In partial contrast, his father was a lawyer, psychology teacher, and amateur novelist. Once, however, when Borges was being bullied by Argentine classmates, his father handed him a knife. Another incentive toward assertiveness may have come from his mother (a dominant figure until she died at the age of ninety-nine), who prided herself on being descended from famous warriors. Edwin Wilson's biography of Borges argues that he was made to feel that a literary life was less valid than a military one.

After a period in Spain, where he fell under the influence of Ultraists (who reduced poems to a series of metaphors), Borges and his family returned to Argentina in 1921. He cofounded the Ultraist journal *Prisma*, and in 1923, he published his first collection of poetry, *Fervor de Buenos Aires* (fervor of Buenos Aires), paid for by his father and with a cover by his sister. After the family returned to Europe later that year for his father's eye treatments, he received a positive review of the book in the Spanish journal *Revista de Occidente*; thus his literary reputation was founded.

Borges was seen as a Europeanized intellectual, whom critics contrasted with the populists. In protest at being classified as a member of the elite, he spent years exploring and writing about the Argentine lower class (for example, the kind of criminal nightclubs where the tango was then danced). From this time forward, he suffered from various unrequited loves, particularly of Norah Lange, whose house figures nostalgically in many of his poems.

By 1937, his father could no longer provide for the family, so Borges took a menial position in a library, where he would finish his duties quickly each day and spend the rest of the time reading, translating, and composing articles, including antifascist essays. In 1946, this political activity had caused him to be forced out of his job by the profascist government of the populist president Juan Perón, who had been elected that year. Borges's resistance to the Perónists continued throughout his life, sometimes placing him on the liberal (antifascist side) and sometimes on the conservative (antipopulist) side. His reputation had grown to the extent that he could earn a living by writing and giving lectures, which he continued to do, even after his hereditary eye disease brought eight operations for cataracts and then blindness. He served as professor of English and American literature at the University of Buenos Aires from 1956 to 1968. He married Elsa Astete Millán in 1967, but she was rejected by his intellectual friends, and the marriage ended in divorce in 1970. He left Argentina, disappointed by its 1982 invasion of the Falkland Islands, for Geneva. There, in 1986, the last year of his life, he was married to the photographer María Kodama. He died of liver cancer in Geneva.

ANALYSIS

Even more obviously than his other writings, the poetry of Jorge Luis Borges focuses on psychological orientation, reconciling the cultural contradictions associated with the poet's place in the world. In the early poetry, this issue of place tends to be quite literal, especially in his first volume, *Fervor de Buenos Aires*, about various locations in that city. Inspired partly by the French Symbolist poets he had read during his high school years in Switzerland, he made urban landscapes into representations of modern angst—consonant with the cynicism he was gleaning at that period from his literary mentor Macedonio Fernándéz but juxtaposed with his mother's patriotism.

In his preface to a 1969 reprint of *Luna de enfrente* (moon across the way), he contrasts the introverted way he mapped the city in *Fervor de Buenos Aires* with the ostentation of the later volume. It ushers in a splattering of the lines with local slang, typical of those periods when he acted as if he had to prove his virility that way. This, however, never led him to abandon the allusive or metaphysical, since the goal was always to make the physical locations metaphors for states of

mind. That situation becomes more explicit in his third volume, *Cuaderno San Martín* (San Martin copybook), with "Fundación mítica de Buenos Aires" ("The Mythical Founding of Buenos Aires"), in which, after speculating about the actual origins of Buenos Aires, he recognizes the place is for him an eternal mental state.

This marks a transition from his poetic apprenticeship toward his long second period of mastery. Beginning with his 1960 collection *Dreamtigers*, he tended to set poems in the mind itself (often in some version of a dream). After his mother's death in 1975, he gradually shifted into a third period, old age. Particularly in the 1980's during his relationship with Kodama, he achieved greater independence from his mother's influence (for example, a growing pacifism and a lessening of embarrassment over not being a warrior). During this time, his poems incorporated more short sentences as if sometimes gasping for breath and were prone to complain of ill health, but they also celebrated his new love. It was a time of dreams coming true (albeit awk-

Jorge Luis Borges (©Washington Post; reprinted by permission of the D.C. Public Library)

wardly and belatedly), as with the prose poem "Mi última tigre" ("My Last Tiger"), about the time when, blind and frightened, he nonetheless managed the courage to pet a real tiger.

FERVOR DE BUENOS AIRES

Although less directly than during his middle period, self-division characterizes *Fervor de Buenos Aires*. In "Las calles" ("The Streets"), for example, the speaker of the poem situates his soul as being on those streets—yet not on the avaricious, crowded ones (the core of the city) but on nearly empty, suburban ones, diminishing into eternal expanses. Despite this antiurban sentiment, the poem ends with an injunction to literal flag waving in praise of his country. Since the center of Buenos Aires was expensive property and its suburbs much less so, his rejecting the former for the latter has perhaps a liberal slant but not a populist one, because of his denouncing crowds. The poet longs for the timeless peripheries, where the streets (and presumably the speaker's soul) end. Throughout Borges's entire poetic opus, this is a common metaphor—a longing to move outside time, even at the cost of extinction, but in interviews, he said repeatedly that he kept remarking this precisely because he feared loss of himself. Indeed, in "The Streets," the poet counters this drift toward the timeless void with the image of separate souls recognized as such by God and also by the poem's patriotic affirmation of his country at the end. The streets themselves thus become a metaphor for a place where the poet's soul connects difficult-to-join opposites. This poem establishes the ambivalent attitude of the volume.

Even as patriotic a poem as "Inscripción sepulchral" ("Sepulchral Inscription") ends with Isidoro Suárez turned not merely into glory but also into dust. Because he provides the fact that Suárez is his great-grandfather, Borges advertises himself as being the speaker. Conversely "Calle desconocida" ("Unknown Street") is about a longing for oblivion, imaged as night and a downward path, derived from the pessimism of his favorite philosopher Arthur Schopenhauer. The poem portrays life as a locus of pain, where every step one takes is on some site of agony, compared to the Golgotha of Christ's crucifixion. Despite all this, the poem's speaker feels tenderness toward the earthly locals. In

"Unknown Street," his imaginative power is so intense that poetry seems real to him to the point that the most he can say of the silver evening's vividness is that it resembles that of verse. In contrast, "El sur" ("The South") merely lists pleasant but plain images, such as stars whose names he does not know, and it concludes lamely that the place, not his words, constitutes the true poem. The volume is thus even ambivalent about the poet's qualification as poet—a theme persistent enough in Borges's subsequent poetry to be presumably his own.

DREAMTIGERS

Even more than *Antología personal* (1961; *A Personal Anthology*, 1967), *Dreamtigers*, a collection of verse and prose poems, was one he considered a very personal selection of his works. The intense self-division of the volume is established with his most famous prose poem, "Borges y yo" ("Borges and I"). It describes the tension between his physical self and his literary one, who keeps robbing the former of its experiences, even though the two manage to live together in Buenos Aires fairly peacefully. Also impressive is his prose poem "Dreamtigers," its title in English, which for Borges was a literary language dissociated from his Argentine existence. The whole point of the poem is to contrast literary tigers he loves with real ones and lament the difficulty of fixing either in the dreaming imagination—a part of himself not entirely under his control.

THE GOLD OF TIGERS

The Gold of Tigers is a bilingual edition that contains Alastair Reid's translation of *El oro de los tigres* and *La rosa profunda*. It helped to establish Borges's American reputation as a poet and marked the close of his middle period. Like all the poetry of that middle period, it is pervaded by the theme of life as a dream; nonetheless, it foreshadows his final period. It already laments that time is running out; thus some desires (such as to master the German language) will never be fulfilled. Two of its major themes are that his blindness stripped his sight of all colors but gold and that certain objects (such as the rose and coins) have resonances of events once connected to them. They may thus perhaps unite one to the whole universe.

OTHER MAJOR WORKS

LONG FICTION: *Un modelo para la muerte*, 1946 (with Adolfo Bioy Casares, under joint pseudonym B. Suárez Lynch).

SHORT FICTION: *Historia universal de la infamia*, 1935 (*A Universal History of Infamy*, 1972); *El jardín de senderos que se bifurcan*, 1941; *Seis problemas para don Isidro Parodi*, 1942 (with Bioy Casares, under joint pseudonym H. Bustos Domecq; *Six Problems for Don Isidro Parodi*, 1981); *Ficciones, 1935-1944*, 1944 (English translation, 1962); "Tres versiones de Judas," 1944 ("Three Versions of Judas," 1962); *Dos fantasías memorables*, 1946 (with Bioy Casares, under joint pseudonym Domecq); *El Aleph*, 1949, 1952 (translated in *The Aleph, and Other Stories, 1933-1969*, 1970); *La muerte y la brújula*, 1951; *La hermana de Eloísa*, 1955 (with Luisa Mercedes Levinson); *Cuentos*, 1958; *Crónicas de Bustos Domecq*, 1967 (with Bioy Casares; *Chronicles of Bustos Domecq*, 1976); *El informe de Brodie*, 1970 (*Doctor Brodie's Report*, 1972); *El matrero*, 1970; *El congreso*, 1971 (*The Congress*, 1974); *El libro de arena*, 1975 (*The Book of Sand*, 1977); *Narraciones*, 1980.

SCREENPLAYS: *"Los orilleros" y "El paraíso de los creyentes,"* 1955 (with Bioy Casares); *Les Autres*, 1974 (with Bioy Casares and Hugo Santiago).

NONFICTION: *Inquisiciones*, 1925; *El tamaño de mi esperanza*, 1926; *El idioma de los argentinos*, 1928; *Evaristo Carriego*, 1930 (English translation, 1984); *Figari*, 1930; *Discusión*, 1932; *Las Kennigar*, 1933; *Historia de la eternidad*, 1936; *Nueva refutación del tiempo*, 1947; *Aspectos de la literatura gauchesca*, 1950; *Antiguas literaturas germánicas*, 1951 (with Delia Ingenieros; revised as *Literaturas germánicas medievales*, 1966, with Maria Esther Vásquez); *Otras Inquisiciones*, 1952 (*Other Inquisitions*, 1964); *El "Martin Fierro,"* 1953 (with Margarita Guerrero); *Leopoldo Lugones*, 1955 (with Betina Edelberg); *Manual de zoología fantástica*, 1957 (with Guerrero; *The Imaginary Zoo*, 1969; revised as *El libro de los seres imaginarios*, 1967, *The Book of Imaginary Beings*, 1969); *La poesía gauchesca*, 1960; *Introducción a la literatura norteamericana*, 1967 (with Esther Zemborain de Torres; *An Introduction to American Literature*, 1971); *Prólogos*, 1975; *Cosmogonías*, 1976; *Libro de sueños*, 1976; *¿Qué es el budismo?*, 1976 (with Alicia Jurado); *Siete noches*, 1980 (*Seven Nights*, 1984); *Nueve ensayos dantescos*, 1982; *This Craft of Verse*, 2000; *The Total Library: Non-fiction, 1922-1986*, 2001 (Eliot Weinberger, editor).

TRANSLATIONS: *Orlando*, 1937 (of Virginia Woolf's novel); *La metamórfosis*, 1938 (of Franz Kafka's novel *Die Verwandlung*); *Un bárbaro en Asia*, 1941 (of Henri Michaux's travel notes); *Bartleby, el escribiente*, 1943 (of Herman Melville's novella *Bartleby the Scrivener*); *Los mejores cuentos policiales*, 1943 (with Bioy Casares; of detective stories by various authors); *Los mejores cuentos policiales, segunda serie*, 1951 (with Bioy Casares; of detective stories by various authors); *Cuentos breves y extraordinarios*, 1955, 1973 (with Bioy Casares; of short stories by various authors; *Extraordinary Tales*, 1973); *Las palmeras salvajes*, 1956 (of William Faulkner's novel *The Wild Palms*); *Hojas de hierba*, 1969 (of Walt Whitman's *Leaves of Grass*).

EDITED TEXTS: *Antología clásica de la literatura argentina*, 1937; *Antología de la literatura fantástica*, 1940 (with Bioy Casares and Silvia Ocampo); *Antología poética argentina*, 1941 (with Bioy Casares and Ocampo); *El compadrito: Su destino, sus barrios, su musica*, 1945, 1968 (with Silvina Bullrich); *Poesía gauchesca*, 1955 (with Bioy Casares; 2 volumes); *Libro del cielo y del infierno*, 1960, 1975 (with Bioy Casares); *Versos*, 1972 (by Evaristo Carriego); *Antología poética*, 1982 (by Leopoldo Lugones); *Antología poética*, 1982 (by Franciso de Quevedo); *El amigo de la muerte*, 1984 (by Pedro Antonio de Alarcón).

MISCELLANEOUS: *Obras completas*, 1953-1967 (10 volumes); *Antología personal*, 1961 (*A Personal Anthology*, 1967); *Labyrinths: Selected Stories, and Other Writings*, 1962, 1964; *Nueva antología personal*, 1968; *Selected Poems, 1923-1967*, 1972 (also includes prose); *Adrogue*, 1977; *Obras completas en colaboración*, 1979 (with others); *Borges: A Reader*, 1981; *Atlas*, 1984 (with María Kodama; English translation, 1985).

BIBLIOGRAPHY

Boldy, Steven. *A Companion to Jorge Luis Borges*. Rochester, N.Y.: Tamesis, 2010. Provides biographical information and a general appreciation of Borges's themes.

Cortinez, Carlos. *Borges the Poet*. Fayetteville: University of Arkansas Press, 1986. Three interviews with Borges about poetry, followed by articles on his poetry, including an essay by María Kodama about his haiku.

Egginton, William, and David E. Johnson, eds. *Thinking with Borges*. Aurora, Colo.: Davies Group, 2009. Contains essays on Borges, including one on his poetry.

Jenckes, Kate. *Reading Borges After Benjamin: Allegory, Afterlife, and the Writing of History*. SUNY Series in Latin American and Iberian Thought and Cure. New York: State University of New York, 2007. Interprets his works, particularly his early poetry, as metaphors for a nonlinear approach to the history of Buenos Aires.

McNeese, Tim. *Jorge Luis Borges*. New York: Chelsea House, 2008. This biography, part of the Great Hispanic Heritage series, examines Borges's life and works. Contains a chapter on his poetry.

Milne, Ira Mark, ed. *Poetry for Students*. Vol. 27. Detroit: Thomson/Gale Group, 2008. Contains an analysis of Borges's "Borges and I."

Waisman, Sergio. *Borges and Translation: The Irreverence of the Periphery*. Lewisburg, Pa.: Bucknell University Press, 2005. Because Borges's writings have multilingual sources related to translations he made and because he sometimes took a very active part in the translation of his works into English, this is an important source.

Williamson, Edwin. *Borges: A Life*. New York: Viking, 2004. A generally convincing interpretation of his literary themes as disguised autobiography.

Wilson, Jason. *Jorge Luis Borges*. London: Reaktion, 2006. Part of the Critical Lives series, this biography looks at the life and works of Borges.

Woodall, James. *Borges: A Life*. New York: BasicBooks, 1996. Provides a wealth of photographs and anecdotal material derived from Borges's friends.

James Whitlark

JOSEPH BRODSKY

Born: Leningrad, Soviet Union (now St. Petersburg, Russia); May 24, 1940
Died: Brooklyn, New York; January 28, 1996

PRINCIPAL POETRY

Stikhotvoreniya i poemy, 1965
Elegy to John Donne, and Other Poems, 1967
Ostanovka v pustyne: Stikhotvoreniya i poemy, 1970
Debut, 1973
Selected Poems, 1973
Chast' rechi: Stikhotvoreniya, 1972-1976, 1977
Konets prekrasnoi epokhi: Stikhotvoreniya, 1964-1971, 1977
V Anglii, 1977
A Part of Speech, 1980
Verses on the Winter Campaign 1980, 1980
Rimskie elegii, 1982
Novye stansy k Avguste: Stichi k M.B., 1962-1982, 1983
Uraniia: Novaya kniga stikhov, 1987
To Urania: Selected Poems, 1965-1985, 1988
Chast' rechi: Izbrannye stikhi, 1962-1989, 1990
Bog sokhraniaet vse, 1991
Forma vremeni, 1992 (2 volumes; volume 2 includes essays and plays)
Rozhdestvenskie stikhi, 1992 (*Nativity Poems*, 2001)
Izbrannye stikhotvoreniya, 1957-1992, 1994
So Forth, 1996
Collected Poems in English, 2000
Nativity Poems, 2001

OTHER LITERARY FORMS

The essays and reviews of Joseph Brodsky (BRODskee), some of which have been collected in *Less than One: Selected Essays* (1986), are valuable in their own right; brilliant, arrogant, and idiosyncratic, they establish Brodsky as one of the finest poet-essayists of the twentieth century. Among Brodsky's subjects are Osip and Nadezhda Mandelstam, Marina Tsvetayeva (unlike most of his prose, his two essays on Tsvetayeva, one brief and one extended, were written in Russian, the language Brodsky normally reserves for his poetry), W. H. Auden, Constantine P. Cavafy, and Eugenio Montale. The essay "Less than One" is an extraordinary meditation on the city of Leningrad, part memoir and part cultural history.

ACHIEVEMENTS

Joseph Brodsky is generally recognized as one of the most gifted poets writing in Russian in the twentieth century; for many, there is little question of his having any rivals. Perhaps Brodsky's most remarkable achievement was his ability to continue writing poems in Russian despite the hardships of political persecution within the Soviet Union and, later, the alienation from the everyday rhythms of the Russian language imposed by his exile to the United States. Brodsky matured as a poet in a Leningrad devoid of poetic movements; indeed, the sense of being alone as a poet pervades his work to an unusual degree. It is difficult to assess Brodsky's generation of poets. The work of contemporaries whom he has praised, poets such as Evgeni Rein and Anatol' Naiman, is available only sporadically in the West, and then in the limited distribution of the émigré presses.

Brodsky's poems have been translated into many languages, including French, German, Italian, Swedish, Czech, and Hebrew, but it is the English translations that won him high regard and a rather wide audience in the West. Brodsky's participation in the translation process, given his own fine skills as a translator, ensured high-quality versions that sound like anything but adaptations from another language. Brodsky was accorded many honors, including Guggenheim and MacArthur Fellowships, an honorary doctorate from Yale University, membership in the American Academy of Arts and Letters, and the Nobel Prize in Literature in 1987. He served as the United States poet laureate consultant in poetry in 1991-1992.

BIOGRAPHY

Joseph Aleksandrovich Brodsky was born in Leningrad on May 24, 1940. Brodsky's mother worked as a translator, an occupation her son was to take up as well; his father worked as a news photographer. During the German blockade of the city, Brodsky spent some time with his grandparents. He has recalled a somewhat later time of fear during the government-orchestrated anti-Semitic hysteria of 1953, when it seemed that his family might be "resettled" far from Leningrad. During these last years of Stalinism, Brodsky was an unenthusiastic student; he left school in 1955 to pursue independent studies in various languages and literatures. In 1956, he began learning Polish, a language that gave him access to Western literature not available in Russian; he recalled that he first read the works of Franz Kafka and William Faulkner in Polish translation, and he encountered the poetry of Czesław Miłosz, whom he called "one of the greatest poets of our time, perhaps the greatest."

The year 1956, when Brodsky was only sixteen, was crucial in establishing his sense of himself and of Russia. When Brodsky referred to himself as a member

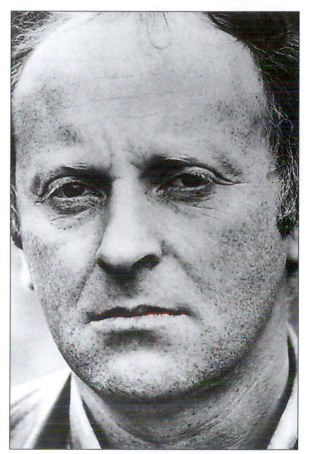

Joseph Brodsky (©The Nobel Foundation)

of the "generation of 1956," he had in mind the shock of recognition forced by the invasion of Hungary, a recognition of his status as a poet in a totalitarian state. If Brodsky saw Stalinism less as a political era than as a "state of mind," then the events of 1956, three years after the death of Stalin, proved the ugly endurance of a repressive regime that soon began to harass Brodsky personally.

Brodsky made several trips away from Leningrad on geological expeditions, traveling throughout the Soviet Union to the Amur River near China, Central Asia, the Caspian Sea region in the south, and the White Sea area in the north, where he was to spend nearly two years in exile a few years later. These travels exposed Brodsky to a variety of landscapes and may in part account for the powerful, if unattractive, natural descriptions in his mature verse. His travels permitted him a great deal of freedom, but his vaguely unorthodox movements and affiliations eventually drew the attention of KGB officials. Brodsky was first arrested in 1959 and twice confined to mental hospitals. These visits provided the setting for his most ambitious long poem, a dialogue between "Gorbunov i Gorchakov" ("Gorbunov and Gorchakov"). Brodsky had begun writing poems as early as 1958, though he later dated his first serious work from about 1963 (the year of his elegy to John Donne).

Arrested again and tried in 1964, Brodsky was sentenced in March to five years exile and hard labor; the charge was "parasitism." In effect, Brodsky was put on trial for identifying himself as a poet without "proof" in the form of a university degree or membership in the Writers' Union. The notes from his trial, smuggled out of Leningrad and excerpted often in articles about Brodsky, make for perverse evidence for his belief that the spiritual activity of writing poetry cannot be tolerated by a state that defines writing as a political act. Many Soviet cultural figures of international renown, including Dmitri Shostakovich and Kornei Chukovskii, testified on Brodsky's behalf and agitated for his early release, often at great professional and personal risk. As a result, Brodsky served only twenty months of his term, doing agricultural work in a small "village"—actually just a few huts in the wilderness—near Arkhangel'sk. He continued reading and writing; his first acquain-

tance with the works of Auden came in 1965, in translation. (He had known Robert Frost's poems as early as 1962 and was astonished by Frost's "hidden, controlled terror.")

Auden's influence is apparent in Brodsky's poem written on the occasion of T. S. Eliot's death in 1965; the lament looks ahead to the mature verse that Brodsky was writing on his return to Leningrad that year. It was at this time that his friends succeeded in shortening the length of his prison term. Anna Akhmatova, whom Brodsky had first met in 1960, was chief among this group of friends. Though he did not recall initially feeling an affinity with Akhmatova, Brodsky and she became close friends. His work owes more to the style and preoccupations of Mandelstam than to Akhmatova, but Brodsky found in Akhmatova a living link to Russia's great poetic tradition, a poet who had known Mandelstam well, a poet who incarnated Russia's great upheavals in her life and in her verse.

Brodsky matured a great deal as a poet between 1965 and 1972. He gave readings to small groups of students and even managed to have four of his poems published in 1966 and 1967 in official publications of Soviet cultural organs. A first volume of his poems had appeared without his authorization in the United States in 1965; a revised version, which included new poems, came out in 1970. Brodsky supported himself in Leningrad as a translator during these years, producing Russian versions of writers ranging from Andrew Marvell and Donne to Tom Stoppard. Brodsky did nothing, however, to become more acceptable to the Soviet regime during these seven years in Leningrad. In 1972, he was exiled from the Soviet Union; he was not even told where the airplane he was boarding would take him—to Siberian exile, or to freedom in the West. The plane landed in Vienna, where Brodsky was met by an American Slavicist, Carl Proffer, with an invitation to teach in Ann Arbor, Michigan. In Vienna, Brodsky sought out Auden, who arranged for him to participate in the Poetry International in London and generally smoothed his way for his introduction to the West.

Settling in the United States, Brodsky slowly began a life of teaching, writing, giving readings, and meeting fellow poets. He taught at the University of Michigan, Queens College, the Five Colleges (Amherst, Hampshire, Mount Holyoke, Smith, and the University of Massachusetts), New York University, and Columbia University. In 1981, he became the Five College Distinguished Professor of Literature, with tenure at Mount Holyoke College; he also spent time teaching at Columbia. Brodsky became a U.S. citizen in 1977. He won the Nobel Prize in Literature in 1987. He died in Brooklyn, New York, on January 28, 1996.

ANALYSIS

In describing his poetry, Joseph Brodsky had said that his "main interest is the nature of time," a theme that also recurs with obsessive frequency in his essays. Beginning even before his exile to Arkhangel'sk in 1964 and persisting in his later works, there is a preoccupation with endings, with concluding moments that illuminate with sudden new depth the meaning of all that has come before. Brodsky, whose stance as a poet is that of a watcher and listener rather than that of a participant and speaker, records his sense of a period of time in a manner that is more transcendental than teleological. In a 1962 poem, "Ogon', ty slyshish' . . ." ("The Fire Is Dying Down"), Brodsky observes how the room and objects around him absorb the shifts in time marked by the changing fire. A sense of lateness advances on the poet "from the corners"; he finds himself "suddenly at the center." Time has paused so palpably that the "clock hands have completely disappeared." The fire dies by the end of this twenty-line poem, but its brightness does not abandon the attentive watcher, who remains behind in the room's darkness. Just as it is important that the clock hands are not only invisible but also silent, silence being the analogue of time's halt, so it is crucial in the last line that the fire glows not in the poet's eyes but in the room itself. The encroaching darkness of the dying fire becomes an external event that marks the inner fact of the poet's eyes growing cold, "motionless."

"SONNET"

In another short lyric of 1962, a poem of fourteen lines with only a few near-rhymes and simply titled "Sonet" ("Sonnet"), Brodsky explores a moment defined by a different kind of ending. Speaking to a loved woman, the poet envisions a new eruption of Vesuvius that will someday cover their dusty city with ash. He

hopes that when the eruption begins, he will be able to set off for her house, so that future excavators will find them still embraced. The poem stops time in that final embrace, preserved by a layer of ash. The embrace and the ash are equally sustaining for the poet, who notes the passing clouds, a frequent emblem for the passing of time in Brodsky's poems. It is typical of Brodsky's poems that the very moment that destroys a city and all life in it also contains the possibility of preservation against decay.

The poem mirrors this contrast between the threat of change and the saving power of volcanic ash in its formal arrangement. As in many early Brodsky poems, the unit of division in the poem is the line. Without enjambments and virtually without rhyme (there is some sound interlocking in the first four lines), the poem's ordering principle is the sequence of its thoughts, expressed at the even pace of one clause per line. The exception is line 12, "then I would like for them to find me," a single thought in two clauses (in Russian), the crucial turning point of the poem. The meter of the poem is iambic, mostly feminine pentameter, five-footed iambs being the commonest line length in Brodsky's repertoire in the 1960's, and the most successful. The sonnet feels experimental, though, because there are two lines of two and four metric feet, respectively, and virtually no rhyme, as if it were testing the boundaries of its own timing. Like Brodsky's many unrhymed sonnets, the poem shows how time can be controlled, slowed or hurried, within the conventions of meter and rhyme; the final picture of an unending embrace literally suspends time, so that the poem challenges, visually as well as verbally, the unspoken condition of all Brodsky's work, the effect of time on humans.

The tender lyrics of early, as well as later, Brodsky, are balanced by verses of ironic distance and glittering wit. In some poems, such as the famous "Pamiatnik" ("Monument"), the serious if slightly mocking tones of the first lines ("Let's build a monument/ at the end of a long city street") turns toward a sarcastic finale—in this case prepared for by the poem's accumulation of petty details from Leningrad life: "Let's build a monument to lies." That final sentence indicts monument building as yet another hypocritical activity in a society whose public life proves inevitably false. In a longer poem,

"Dva chasa v rezervuare" ("Two Hours in a Reservoir"), Brodsky mixes German and Yiddish phrases into a running monologue. The speaker pronounces his thoughts as they furiously charge past him in whatever language comes to his lips: "Enter and *exeunt* devils, thoughts./ Enter and *exeunt* guests, years." Narrative fragments about Faust and Johann Wolfgang von Goethe, Dr. Faustus and Thomas Mann, interrupt speculations about God and poetry and the fact that humans are hurtling toward their deaths. The poem extends Brodsky's preoccupation with time, quoting Faust's famous desire to seize and hold one beautiful moment, a line Brodsky might be expected to appreciate—indeed, one he uses more than once. The poem's pace, though, is breakneck, the puns (particularly between languages) rampant, and the humor of the piece as pungent as it is inventive. Brodsky's search for ways to understand the passing of time, often defined by its endpoints, emerges in poems as varied as the witty "Odnoi poetesse" ("To a Certain Poetess"), where a relationship has outlived love, or the delicate "Aeneas i Dido" ("Aeneas and Dido"), in which the moment of parting is captured poignantly by details—passing clouds, the hem of a tunic, a fish chasing after a ship at sail.

"AENEAS AND DIDO"

"Aeneas and Dido" deals with the end of a myth, and the poem concludes with a memorable picture. Dido watches Aeneas looking through a window, both of them realizing that the new gusts of wind will make it possible for Aeneas to set sail and leave Dido behind. Windows appear frequently in Brodsky's poems, often framing a landscape seen from within a room. Indeed, space becomes almost the conceptual framework through which time is explored in Brodsky's poems: His remark that literature shows what time does to a person was made in a talk titled "Language as Otherland," and the titles of his poems often locate lyrics spatially as well as temporally. Examples of this can be found in each stage of his career, including "Zimnim vecherom v Ialte" ("A Winter Evening in Yalta"), "Dekabr' vo Florentsii" ("December in Florence"), and "Osen' v Norenskoi" ("Autumn in Norenskaia").

SETTINGS

Brodsky's settings are occasionally interiors; small rooms become intimate settings for discovering the world

outside and, always, oneself. In "Sumev otgorodit'sia . . ." ("Now that I've walled myself off from the world"), glimpses of puddles and fir trees merge with the domestic drama of a poet studying his face in a mirror. Brodsky has moments of self-description, framed by mirrors and windows, reminiscent of the later works of Akhmatova, though Brodsky always seems in search of some truth deeper than the self-image a piece of glass presents him. Self and other, interiors and landscapes interpenetrate one another in Brodsky's poems; as furiously as he seeks boundaries, walling himself off spatially, or describing endpoints in time, spaces and periods of time run into one another, and the confusions press the poet all the more in his attempt at self-definition.

Brodsky's landscapes are inseparable from the homesickness that pervades his verse. There is no place called "home" that is exempt. While he was in internal exile in Arkhangl'sk, Brodsky compared himself to Ovid; in the West, he has described scenes as diverse as Cape Cod and Cuernavaca, hills and lagoons and sluggish rivers, stopovers in St. Mark's Piazza or along Roman roads. Brodsky loves Venice, a city that glows through his poems like Leningrad, but there is not any landscape, any visual image of indoor or outdoor space with which the poet is not somehow at odds.

New places provide fresh scenes for seeing, new ways to show what one must see. If the goal of his poetry is, as Brodsky said in 1972, "to show man the true scale of what is happening," then landscape and cityscape finally offer a figurative vocabulary for philosophical apperceptions. The "scale" for Brodsky is never political but always personal, a fact that made him politically suspect in the Soviet Union.

PHILOSOPHY

Brodsky's philosophical preoccupations (the nature of "reality," and what it means for time to pass) and figures of expression (mythological plots, interior and exterior landscapes) are constants in his poetry, of which he continued to find new variations. There is, however, a more distinct sense of development in the prosodic features of Brodsky's poems, and these changes provide the clearest indications of his battle with Russian poetic tradition. Certain Brodskian themes resemble those of poets whom he is known to admire: the parting and exile of Mandelstam, the meditations on death of Evgeni Baratynskii, the monuments of Alexander Pushkin if not of Gavrila Derzhavin, the epistolary acts of self-definition of Dmitry Kantemir. In the case of Brodsky's verse forms, however, there are only a few poems with rather self-conscious and specific models, the most notable being his poem on the death of Eliot, written in the form and spirit of Auden's "In Memory of W. B. Yeats."

POETIC FORMS

Brodsky's early poems strive to carve their own prosodic molds, using simple, assertive sentences, and a structuring free-verse line the firm closure of which allows few enjambments. The rhymes are experimental, often only hints at sound repetitions. In the early 1960's, Brodsky experimented with the placement of the line in such poems as "Ryby zimoi" ("Fish in Winter") and "Stikhi pod èpigrafom" ("Verses with an Epigraph"). Poems such as these make the most startling break with Russian prosodic tradition, spread over a page in complex patterns of indentation like those of E. E. Cummings (whom Brodsky admired in his youth). More deeply radical, though, and more difficult to sustain, are poems with very long verse lines, such as "Proplyvaiut oblaka" ("Clouds Swim By"). Here Brodsky repeats and interweaves similar phrases to break up long lines, while subtly binding them more tightly one to another. In later poems, Brodsky has used refrains to the same effect: The word "stifling" recurs as a one-word sentence in "Kolybel'naia Treskovogo Mysa" ("Lullaby of Cape Cod"). The long line led Brodsky to explore ternary meters (several poems use anapest pentameter); in some cases, various kinds of ternary meters appear fleetingly with rhymes or near-rhymes structuring the poem. The impression in "Clouds Swim By" is one of fluidity that is being formidably if flexibly shaped, perhaps the most appropriate form for a poem that describes the changing shapes of clouds overhead.

Longer verse lines came into Brodsky's work with complex sentences, as well as enjambments more abrupt than those previously found in Russian poetry. Regular meters are usually used, though they are the less common meters of iambic pentameter (not the common meter in Russian as it is in English; Russian depends far more on iambic tetrameter) and anapest pentameter. There are striking ventures in stanzaic form, the most remarkable in "Gorbunov and Gorchakov." In this long poem, Brodsky limits himself to an *ababab.abab* sequence in each ten-line stanza; the poem contains fourteen sections of ten such stanzas and is actually a conversation, sustaining the rhythms and dictions of colloquial speech within its very demanding form.

With these additional formal complexities, Brodsky entered a grammatical universe adequate to the expression of his metaphysical questions. As has been noted by Richard Sylvester, Brodsky's complex sentences convey an ever-changing nexus of logical relationships, where words such as "because," "despite," "when," "where," and "if" become the all-important links in sentences dependent on several semantic fields. In such later poems as the cycle "Chast' rechi" ("A Part of Speech"), subject matter, diction, even stylistic level may change in such quick succession as to seem arbitrary: One poem in the cycle begins "A list of some observations." However, Brodsky's poetry is anything but inscrutable; his complex forms provide myriad vehicles perfectly suited for exploring themes of fragmentation, decay, solitary observation, and intense recollection.

A PART OF SPEECH

In Brodsky's well-received *A Part of Speech*, images and underlying questions extend the issues raised in his earlier poems. The desire to focus on particular points in time finds him often retreating into memory. This orientation toward the past was felt keenly in poems from the 1960's; one of Brodsky's best-known poems is "Ostanovka v pustyne" ("A Halt in the Wilderness"), where the razing of an Orthodox church is witnessed as a gesture of senseless modernization. Time as a category has tragic dimensions for Brodsky, as he himself has said. Near the end of "A Halt in the Wilderness," he speaks acerbically of "the relay race of human history." That poem looks ahead to ask what sacrifices the new era might demand, but there is no redeeming belief in progress for Brodsky. In his essays, Brodsky dwelt on the evils of the twentieth century; he offers his readers little consolation and certainly no respite from personal responsibility in the dogmas of ideology or religion. In "Lullaby of Cape Cod," Brodsky defines his sense of human knowledge and its limitations in lines that resonate beyond his experience of emigration: "Having sampled two/ oceans as well as continents, I feel that I know/ what the globe itself must feel: there's nowhere to go."

Akhmatova found that in Brodsky's first poems the speaking voice was extremely solitary. The sense of bearing a unique vision is undiminished in Brodsky's later poems, ranging from the varieties of quantification in "Lullaby of Cape Cod" to the equation that acts as a fluctuating refrain in "Èkloga IV-ia (Zimniaia)" ("Winter Eclogue: IV"): "Time equals cold." The more nearly oxymoronic Brodsky's declarations, the more finely he has sharpened his sense of the metaphysical conceit into an instrument for measuring a vision that is always just evading the poet's means of expression.

There is no expectation of finding the "right" metaphor, as frequent images of echoless space imply. "A glance," wrote Brodsky in "A Part of Speech," "is accustomed to no glance back." Brodsky's poems are less a relief from solitude than a journey forth, a journey deeper and farther into the "otherland" of language. To say that the journey is "merely long" is to say nothing, and to say everything. Brodsky writes in "Lullaby of Cape Cod":

> Far longer is the sea.
> At times, like a wrinkled forehead, it displays
> a rolling wave. And longer still than these
> is the strand of matching beads of countless days;
> and nights.

To observe that the break between "days" and "nights" is radical in terms of syntax and prosody is to describe Brodsky's poetics; to add that the break is unbearably long, that it expresses a discontinuity central to his metaphysical premises, is to initiate an examination of Brodsky's underlying themes at the level on which he deserves to be understood.

TO URANIA

Two collections of Brodsky's poetry contain translations of his Russian poems, by him and by others, as well as poems written in English. For this reason, there is a noticeable incongruence of themes and styles. *To Urania* contains poems from his earlier collections *A Part of Speech* and *Uraniia*. They express the poet's nostalgia for his homeland and are elegies for parents

and friends, mixed with his musings about historical events and European cities, in which intellectually he felt at home as much as in his homeland. Moreover, fourteen cantos in his peculiar bardic style are actually a dialogue between two patients in a Soviet psychiatric ward. Brodsky indulges in his familiar attempts to fathom the mysteries of memory of the things past and to reconcile the limits of time and space, as he did throughout his poetic career. References to political matters, especially their seamy side, are also vintage Brodsky. Elements of a realistic and a spiritual, almost metaphysical approach to poetry are masterfully proportioned, as in many of his collections. Subdued sorrow of an exile unable or unwilling to forget the old and fully accept the new breaks through the veneer of bombastic intonations. Finally, his difficulties in mastering fully the idiom of a foreign language are manifested in sporadic rough renditions of English idioms.

SO FORTH

So Forth offers poems written during the last decade of Brodsky's life. As in *To Urania*, they are both translations and poems written originally in English. Considered by some critics as a collection of perhaps his best poetry (while others point out his awkwardness in juggling the two languages), *So Forth* displays Brodsky's ability to conform his remarkable erudition and never fully satisfied curiosity to his unique style. Even though, as in *To Urania*, he tries his best to be a poet-citizen of the world, the deep sorrow that he was forced out of his homeland is beautifully expressed in the poem "In Memory of My Father: Australia," in which the poet sees in a dream his father sailing as a ghost to Australia, that is, being free to travel. Not all poems are somber and heavy. Some are surprisingly light, as is the poem "A Song"—dancing, as it were, like a child in play. However, most of Brodsky's later poems are elegiac, somber, ironic, always reminding his readers of sorrow and death.

OTHER MAJOR WORKS

PLAY: *Mramor*, pb. 1984 (*Marbles*, 1985).

NONFICTION: *Less than One: Selected Essays*, 1986; *Vspominaia Akhmatova*, 1992; *Watermark*, 1992; *On Grief and Reason: Essays*, 1995; *Homage to Robert Frost*, 1996 (with Seamus Heaney and Derek Walcott).

BIBLIOGRAPHY

Bethea, David M. *Joseph Brodsky and the Creation of Exile*. Princeton, N.J.: Princeton University Press, 1994. A critical analysis that compares and contrasts Brodsky to the poet's favorite models—John Donne, W. H. Auden, Osip Mandelstam, and Marina Tsvetayeva—and analyzes his fundamental differences with Vladimir Nabokov. Various critical paradigms are used throughout the study as foils to Brodsky's thinking. Includes a bibliography and index.

Brodsky, Joseph. Interviews. *Joseph Brodsky: Conversations*. Edited by Cynthia L. Haven. Jackson: University Press of Mississippi, 2002. Contains numerous interviews with Brodsky in which he talks about life in exile and his poetry.

Grudzinska-Gross, Irena. *Czesław Miłosz and Joseph Brodsky: Fellowship of Poets*. New Haven, Conn.: Yale University Press, 2010. Examines the relationship between the two poets and how their work was influenced.

Jason, Philip K., ed. *Masterplots II: Poetry Series*. Rev. ed. Pasadena, Calif.: Salem Press, 2002. Contains analysis of two of Brodsky's poems, "A Part of Speech" and "Elegy for John Donne."

Loseff, Lev, and Valentina Polukhina, eds. *Joseph Brodsky: The Art of a Poem*. New York: St. Martin's Press, 1999. These essays concentrate on individual poems and on purely aesthetic aspects of Brodsky's poetry. The essays, written in both Russian and English, analyze the most significant of Brodsky's poems, using citations in Russian and English.

MacFadyen, David. *Joseph Brodsky and the Baroque*. Montreal: McGill-Queen's University Press, 1998. A thorough analysis of the baroque elements in Brodsky's poetry and of the affinities with, and influence of, philosophers Søren Kirkegaard and Lev Shestov and the poet John Donne. The comparison of Brodsky's poetry before and after exile is especially poignant.

_____. *Joseph Brodsky and the Soviet Muse*. Montreal: McGill-Queen's University Press, 2000. An assessment of Brodsky's significance as a shaper and remaker of Soviet poetry in his early years. The contact with, and influence of, the writings of James Joyce, John Dos Passos, Ernest Hemingway, Robert Frost, Boris Pasternak, and Marina Tsvetayeva are chronicled, with suitable citations, in Russian and English, from Brodsky's poetry. Very useful for the understanding of Brodsky's development as a poet.

Polukhina, Valentina. *Brodsky Through the Eyes of His Contemporaries*. Rev. ed. 2 vols. Boston: Academic Studies Press, 2008. A leading Russian expert examines the poet as his fellow poets saw him.

Rigsbee, David. *Styles of Ruin: Joseph Brodsky and the Postmodernist Elegy*. Westport, Conn.: Greenwood Press, 1999. Rigsbee examines Brodsky's contribution to postmodernist poetry, particularly through his pronounced trend toward elegy. A poet himself and a translator of Brodsky, the author adds to his analyses a personal touch as well as that of an expert of the craft.

Turoma, Sanna. *Brodsky Abroad: Empire, Tourism, Nostalgia*. Madison: University of Wisconsin Press, 2010. This biography of Brodsky focuses on his life as an exile.

Stephanie Sandler
Updated by Vasa D. Mihailovich

C

ERNESTO CARDENAL

Born: Granada, Nicaragua; January 20, 1925

PRINCIPAL POETRY

Gethsemani, Ky., 1960

La hora cero, 1960

Epigramas: Poemas, 1961 (*Epigramas*, 1978)

Oración por Marilyn Monroe, y otros poemas, 1965
    (*Marilyn Monroe, and Other Poems*, 1975)

El estrecho dudoso, 1966 (*The Doubtful Strait*, 1995)

Antología de Ernesto Cardenal, 1967

Salmos, 1967 (*The Psalms of Struggle and
    Liberation*, 1971)

Mayapán, 1968

Homenaje a los indios americanos, 1969 (*Homage
    to the American Indians*, 1973)

Poemas reunidos, 1949-1969, 1969

Antología, 1971

La hora cero, y otros poemas, 1971 (*Zero Hour,
    and Other Documentary Poems*, 1980)

Poemas, 1971

Canto nacional, 1973

Oráculo sobre Managua, 1973

El Evangelio en Solentiname, 1975 (*The Gospel in
    Solentiname*, 1976)

Poesía escogida, 1975

Apocalypse: And Other Poems, 1977

Antología, 1978

Canto a un país que nace, 1978

Nueva antología poética, 1979

Poesía, 1979

Poesía de uso: Antología, 1949-1978, 1979

Tocar el cielo, 1981

Antología: Ernesto Cardenal, 1983

Poesía de la nueva Nicaragua, 1983

Wasala: Poems, 1983

Vuelos de Victoria, 1984 (*Flights of Victory*, 1985)

Quetzalcóatl, 1985

*With Walker in Nicaragua, and Other Early Poems,
    1949-1954*, 1985

From Nicaragua with Love: Poems, 1976-1986,
    1986

Cántico cósmico, 1989 (*The Music of the Spheres*,
    1990; also known as *Cosmic Canticle*, 1993)

Los ornis de oro, 1991

Golden UFOs: The Indian Poems, 1992

*El Río San Juan: Estrecho dudoso en el centro de
    América*, 1993

Telescopio en la noche oscura, 1993

Antología nueva, 1996

Versos del pluriverso, 2005

Pluriverse: New and Selected Poems, 2009
    (Jonathan Cohen, editor)

OTHER LITERARY FORMS

Part 1 of the autobiography of Ernesto Cardenal (kahr-day-NAHL), *Vida perdida* (lost life), was published in 1999 by Seix Barral in Barcelona. It is an excellent biographical resource and starting place for exploring the poet's fascinating life and thought. The chapters devoted to his years as a Trappist monk in Gethsemani, Kentucky, and his correspondence with the Catholic mystic, theologian, and writer Thomas Merton enlighten the reader attempting to comprehend the corpus of Cardenal's poetry.

Cardenal wrote essays and other prose works as he served as minister of culture in Nicaragua and as a director of Casa de los Tres Mundos, a literary and cultural organization in Granada, Nicaragua. *Vida en el amor* (1970; *To Live Is to Love*, 1972; *Abide in Love*, 1995) is a collection of meditations written after his novitiate years at Gethsemani.

ACHIEVEMENTS

Ernesto Cardenal was instrumental in the rebirth of Nicaragua's identity as "a nation of poets," as it became known after Rubén Darío immortalized the poet-nation at the beginning of the twentieth century. Cardenal's life is as fascinating as his poetry. Controversy over the literary and political value of his work resulted from his attempts to reconcile the many roles he had played, from monk to priest to governmental official to promoter of literacy and the arts. His political ideology seemed inconsistent as he switched public roles. From a bourgeois family background, he espoused Marxism and militancy, then Christianity and nonviolent resistance. This dichotomy is evident in his work, but these ideological conflicts enhance rather than detract from his poetic corpus.

Consistent in his belief that art is linked to politics, his poetry actively supported the revolution that in 1979 overthrew the regime begun by dictator Anastasio Somoza García. After a functional social democracy was established in Cardenal's homeland, he served as an unofficial yet visible cultural ambassador. He was instrumental in the organization of community-based literacy and poetry workshops that have earned national as well as international success.

The poet has also been praised as an artist. His sculpture won recognition in the United States as well as in Central America and Mexico. A stone sculpture of Christ dominates the courtyard of the Trappist monastery in Gethsemani, Kentucky, where he served as a novitiate from 1957 to 1959.

Cardenal has been honored with several awards for his literary achievements as well as for his public service. In 1972, he received the Christopher Book Award for *The Psalms of Struggle and Liberation*. In 1980, he received the Premio de La Paz grant, sponsored by Libreros de la República Federal de Alemania. He has received state-sponsored honors and honorary doctorates from several European nations. Cardenal was nominated for the 2005 Nobel Prize in Literature and received the Pablo Neruda Ibero-American Poetry Prize in 2009.

BIOGRAPHY

Ernesto Cardenal Martínez was born in 1925 in Granada, Nicaragua. He studied at the Universidad Nacional Autónoma de México. After graduating in 1947, he moved to the United States to study North American literature at Columbia University in New York from 1948 to 1949.

After traveling for a year throughout Europe, Cardenal returned to Nicaragua. He translated and published North American poetry and anonymously wrote political poems against the dictatorship of Somoza. The Chilean poet Pablo Neruda published works by the then-unknown Cardenal in *La Gaceta de Chile*. While

Ernesto Cardenal (Thomas Lohnes/AFP/Getty Images)

in Nicaragua, Cardenal managed a bookstore that promoted national writers and published *El hilo azul*, a poetry journal.

In 1954, Cardenal participated in an armed assault against the Somoza regime known as the April Rebellion and continued to write anonymous political poems. Three years later, he drastically changed directions by entering the monastery of Our Lady of Gethsemani in Kentucky, where he met Thomas Merton, his spiritual mentor and lifelong friend. Poor health forced Cardenal to transfer to the Benedictine monastery in Cuernavaca, Mexico. There, he wrote his poetry collection *Gethsemani, Ky.* and the meditations *Abide in Love*. He continued his theological studies at the seminary of La Ceja in Colombia. While at the seminary, he wrote poems later collected and translated as *Homage to the American Indians*. He was ordained a Roman Catholic priest in 1965.

With the guidance of Merton, Cardenal planned to establish the spiritual community of Solentiname on Lake Nicaragua. He created a school for the native folk arts, poetry workshops, and the political movement of liberation theology. He visited Cuba to study its revolutionary process. In 1976, he represented Solentiname in the Russell tribunal for human rights violations in Latin America. In 1977, after Sandinista leaders had ordered Cardenal on a diplomatic mission, Somoza's army destroyed Solentiname. Cardenal was exiled from Nicaragua until the government of reconstruction appointed him minister of culture in 1979. He served internationally in the cause of peace and disarmament. After earning the Rubén Darío Prize, the highest Nicaraguan honor, he was honored by the governments of France and Germany, among those of other nations. Several international universities bestowed honorary doctorates upon Cardenal.

Cardenal's autobiography, *Vida perdida*, is an excellent source for biographical information, though not necessarily more accurate than objective sources. References to literary influences and Cardenal's creative contemporaries permeate the text. His complex values and belief system shine through his personal history as he reminisces about his literary production as spiritual experiences, with an unaffected style laced with self-effacing humor.

In *Vida perdida*, Cardenal defines himself as a Christian Marxist whose first calling is to serve God. His service is politically committed, focusing on the Central American peasants. His poems not only spoke for the voiceless; they enabled Cardenal to promote and publish poetry collections by "ordinary people," allowing them a personal as well as collective poetic voice.

ANALYSIS

Revolutionary political ideology is blended with Roman Catholic theology in Ernesto Cardenal's poetry. Like Pablo Neruda, he hopes to motivate readers to change social injustices. His overt messages do not overshadow their poetic forms, and technical mastery is not compromised by theme. Cardenal's poetry is not just his second calling. Rather, it serves as an integral part of his first calling, operating as a tool of his spiritual mission to convert and enlighten. His poems reveal hard and ugly truths about Nicaragua and contemporary societies as they evangelize.

He developed the concept of *exteriorismo* with his poet friend José Coronel Utrecho. Through this technique, words present the world directly through its object rather than by abstraction. Cardenal referred to impure poetry as that seeming closer to prose for its prosaic references. *Interiorista* poetry is composed of abstract or symbolic words that have traditionally poetic connotations. Utrecho and Cardenal believed that the only poetry that could express the Latin American reality and reach the people in a revolutionary way was *exteriorista*. Cardenal's presentation of prosaic elements is innovative, and he connects images through techniques of montage, interpolation, and intertextuality.

"ZERO HOUR"

Among the most militant political poems that serve as a call to action, "La hora cero" ("Zero Hour") epitomizes Cardenal's *exteriorista* mission of words: "I did it," dijo después Somoza./ "I did it for the good of Nicaragua./ . . . de armas;/ todos marcados U.S.A., MADE IN U.S.A. . . ." The vivid reality of the United States supplying arms to the Nicaraguan dictatorship is juxtaposed with William Walker's invasion and scenes of exploitation, oppression, and glimpses of truth filtered through sound bites, news clips, and elements from the mass media.

"MARILYN MONROE"

"Oración por Marilyn Monroe" ("Marilyn Monroe") exemplifies *exteriorismo* as it is applied to themes beyond the Nicaraguan experience. This prayer reveals how a woman was destroyed by Hollywood. Cardenal relates the cultural icon to the degradation and exploitation of women. This poem connects Monroe to the Virgin Mary and demonstrates how both images of the ideal woman have been desecrated and violated by a godless, hedonistic society. He begins his prayer:

Father
Receive this girl known throughout the world as
    Marilyn Monroe
though that was not her real name
(but You know her real name, that of the orphan raped
    at nine
and the shopgirl who had tried to kill herself at just 16.)
and who now appears before You without makeup
without her Press Agent
without photographs or signing autographs
lonely as an astronaut facing the darkness of outer
    space . . .

THE MUSIC OF THE SPHERES

Cardenal developed the genre of the canto in the way that Ezra Pound and Neruda created their own cantos. Cardenal credited Pound as a major influence on his poetic style. Disparate images are juxtaposed, lyrical and prosaic lines are mingled, and spiritual elements are combined with images of materialism and consumerism, in which commercialization replaces emotional and spiritual spontaneity. Technical skill is balanced by immediate and relevant messages.

The Music of the Spheres encapsulates the canto form. More than forty cantos create a vision of cosmic development that refers to astronomy, biology, physics, history, mythology, philosophy, politics, and theology. Science blends with spirituality to form a harmonic whole.

The organization of interconnected canticles resembles Pound's subdivisions of a long poem into thematic units. As a whole, the canticles' lyric quality predominates. They sing their praises to creation as they reach out to the cosmos to grasp its elemental clues to origins. These cantos chronicle political and economic realities, harmoniously combined with spiritual transcendence.

Cardenal's original masterwork follows the tradition of epic poems from Homer to Dante to Pound.

OTHER MAJOR WORKS

NONFICTION: *Vida en el amor*, 1970 (*To Live Is to Love*, 1972; also known as *Abide in Love*, 1995); *En Cuba*, 1972 (*In Cuba*, 1974); *Cardenal en Valencia*, 1974; *La santidad de la revolución*, 1976; *La paz mundial y la revolución de Nicaragua*, 1981; *Vida perdida*, 1999; *Los años de Granada*, 2001; *Las ínsulas extrañas*, 2002; *Memorias*, 2003; *La revolución perdida*, 2004; *Thomas Merton—Ernesto Cardenal: Correspondencia (1959-1968)*, 2004.

TRANSLATIONS: *Catulo-Marcial en versión de Ernesto Cardenal*, 1978 (of Gaius Valerius Catullus); *Tu paz es mi paz*, 1982 (of Ursula Schulz's *Dein Friede sei mein Friede*).

EDITED TEXTS: *Antología de la poesía norteamericana*, 1963 (with Coronel Urtecho); *Literatura indígena americana: Antología*, 1966 (with Jorge Montoya Toro); *Poesía nicaragüense*, 1973; *Poesía nueva de Nicaragua*, 1974; *Poesía cubana de la revolucíon*, 1976; *Antología de poesía primitiva*, 1979; *Poemas de un joven*, 1983 (by Joaquín Pasos); *Antología: Azarias H. Pallais*, 1986.

BIBLIOGRAPHY

Cardenal, Ernesto. *Abide in Love*. Translated by Thomas Merton and Mev Puleo. Maryknoll, N.Y.: Orbis Books, 1995. Merton provides a detailed introduction and Puleo's meticulous translations enhance this new edition of the collection *Vida en el amor*.

_____. *Apocalypse and Other Poems*. Edited by Robert Pring-Mill and Donald D. Walsh. New York: New Directions, 1977. Both editors, Cardenal experts, provide insightful introductions to the collection. The translators include the editors, along with Thomas Merton, Kenneth Rexroth, and Mireya Jaimes-Freyre.

_____. *The Doubtful Strait = El estrecho dudoso*. Translated by John Lyons. Bloomington: University of Indiana Press, 1995. Tamara Williams provides a substantial introduction to this collection. It is a detailed critical study of its genesis, technical, thematic, and stylistic elements, and historical and literary influences. Demonstrates how an epic quality is developed through the continuous thread of the quest throughout this collection.

_____. "Ernesto Cardenal Describes Sandinista Split." Interview by Leslie Wirpsa. *National Catholic Reporter* 31, no. 30 (May 26, 1995): 9. Cardenal describes Nicaraguan politics and reflects on the efforts made during the years immediately following the establishment of the Sandinista government.

_____. *Flights of Victory*. Translated by Marc Zimmerman. Maryknoll, N.Y.: Orbis Books, 1985. Presents the collection with a critical study of the historical context as well as technical and thematic elements that distinguish it from other works. Zimmerman examines the elements of *exteriorismo*, which was influenced by the Central American vanguards of revolutionary poets. This study demonstrates how Cardenal utilized *exteriorismo*.

Dawes, Greg. *Aesthetics and Revolution: Nicaraguan Poetry, 1979-1990*. Minneapolis: University of Minnesota Press, 1993. The chapter "Poetry and Spiritual Materialism: Ernesto Cardenal" discusses how Cardenal's Marxism, seen through a Christian lens, affected his poetry. Dawes believes that Cardenal's work reinterprets theology itself. Through liberation theology, religious states such as faith and salvation are returned to the social sphere. Examines Cardenal's impact on Nicaraguan politics and literature.

Elias, Edward. "Prophecy of Liberation: The Poetry of Ernesto Cardenal." In *Poetic Prophecy in Western Literature*, edited by Jan Wojcik and Raymond-Jean Frontain. Cranbury, N.J.: Associated University Presses, 1984. The author considers Cardenal's poetry within the Old Testament context of prophecy. He notes the poet's continuous efforts to move others to action and makes comparisons to the Hebrew prophets of old.

Gibbons, Reginald. "Political Poetry and the Example of Ernesto Cardenal." *Critical Inquiry* 13, no. 3 (Spring, 1987): 648-671. The poet speaks against injustice and oppression and in favor of compassion and revolution. It is impossible to separate the political from the poetic in Cardenal's work, Gibbons suggests.

Lee, Jongsoo. "The Colonial Legacy in Ernesto Cardenal's Poetry: Images of Quetzalcoatl, Nezahualcoyotl, and the Aztecs." *Hispania* 87, no. 1 (March, 2004): 22-31. Argues that Cardenal, in his poetry, "presents the Aztecs as a symbol of evil due to their militarism and practice of human sacrifice, while the two pre-Hispanic Mexican heroes, Quetzalcoatl and Nezahualcoyotl, symbolize righteousness because of their peaceful religious and civilized practices." Offers further critical analyses of Cardenal's representations.

Rowe, William. *Poets of Contemporary Latin America: History and the Inner Life*. New York: Oxford University Press, 2000. In the chapter "Ernesto Cardenal: Eros and Belief Under Epic Necessity," Rowe explores the poems as differing proposals of attention for each collection. He avoids making critical artistic decisions from political, religious, or erotic perspectives. Rowe believes that these preconceptions make the poems' words a vehicle for a higher cause, rather than enable them to be appreciated for their intrinsic artistic value.

Sarabia, Rosa. *Poetas de la palabra hablada*. London: Tamesis, 1997. This study, in Spanish, examines the oral nature of several Latin American writers. The chapter "La historia como musa en la poesía de Ernesto Cardenal" focuses on historical influences, including Native American mythology. The contemporary reality also influences the politically conscious poet as spokesman for the voiceless who are suffering injustices. This study demonstrates how past and contemporary realities, along with an oral tradition, find their voices in Cardenal's poetry.

Carole A. Champagne

AIMÉ CÉSAIRE

Born: Basse-Pointe, Martinique; June 26, 1913
Died: Fort-de-France, Martinique; April 17, 2008

PRINCIPAL POETRY

Cahier d'un retour au pays natal, 1939, 1947, 1956 (*Memorandum on My Martinique*, 1947; better known as *Return to My Native Land*, 1968)
Les Armes miraculeuses, 1946 (*Miraculous Weapons*, 1983)
Soleil cou coupé, 1948 (*Beheaded Sun*, 1983)
Corps perdu, 1950 (*Disembodied*, 1983)
Ferrements, 1960 (*Shackles*, 1983)
Cadastre, 1961 (revised editions of *Soleil cou coupé* and *Corps perdu*; *Cadastre: Poems*, 1973)
State of the Union, 1966 (includes abridged translation of *Miraculous Weapons* and *Shackles*)
Moi, Laminaire, 1982
Aimé Césaire: The Collected Poetry, 1983
Lyric and Dramatic Poetry, 1946-82, 1990
La poésie, 1994

OTHER LITERARY FORMS

Poet, dramatist, and essayist Aimé Césaire (say-ZEHR) is recognized not only for his poetry but also for his political and dramatic works. The first major poem he wrote, *Return to My Native Land*, set the tone and thematic precedence for his subsequent writings. *Tropiques*, a cultural magazine of which the poet was one of the principal founders, featured Césaire's own poems, which were reprinted in the Gallimard edition of *Miraculous Weapons* in 1946. As well as a vehicle for literary content, the magazine was used to arouse the cultural and political consciousness that would continue to mark Césaire's personality throughout his life.

Césaire's poetry attests his exceptional talent as an artist, and his polemical and historical works, *Discours sur le colonialisme* (1950; *Discourse on Colonialism*, 1972), born of the poet's disillusionment with the inferior role Martinique continued to play in its relations with France, and *Toussaint Louverture: La Révolution française et le problème coloniale* (1960), named after the black hero Toussaint-Louverture, who led the 1802-1803 revolution in Haiti, demonstrate the poet's effort to assail racism, colonialism, and the cultural alienation of blacks from all sides. He continued to explore the problems of the existence of blacks in the world and African culture, especially the issue of decolonization, in his drama—which is more accessible than his poetry.

His plays include *La Tragédie du Roi Christophe* (pr. 1963; *The Tragedy of King Christophe*, 1969), *Une Saison au Congo* (pb. 1966; *A Season in the Congo*, 1968), and a reworking of William Shakespeare's play *The Tempest* (pr. 1611) entitled *Une Tempête, d'après "La Tempête" de Shakespeare: Adaptation pour un théâtre nègre* (pr., pb. 1969; *A Tempest*, 1974).

Aimé Césaire (©Sophie Bassouls/Sygma/CORBIS)

ACHIEVEMENTS

Aimé Césaire's contribution to literature goes beyond his exceptional use of Surrealist techniques, his extraordinary mastery of the French language, and his attempt to articulate the inhumane effects of racism and colonialism. In 1982, he received the French Grand Prix National de la Poésie. By his example, Césaire helped to give impetus to the first great outpouring of written literature in Africa and the West Indies.

BIOGRAPHY

One of several children, Aimé Fernand David Césaire was born on June 26, 1913, in Basse-Pointe, Martinique; his father, Ferdnand, was a comptroller with the revenue service. Most of his childhood was spent in the midst of poverty, and as Césaire grew older, he became acutely aware of the oppressive conditions of the majority of the Martinicans. At the Lycée Schoelcher in Fort-de-France, he excelled in his studies, winning a scholarship to the Lycée Louis-le-Grand in Paris. Ironically, this sojourn in Paris paved the way for Césaire's political maturation.

His friendship with Léopold Senghor, whom he met at Louis-le-Grand, was instrumental in changing Césaire's view of Africa, which would serve time and again as a source of inspiration for him. Once he completed his studies, he returned to Martinique with his wife, Suzanne, whom he had married while he was a student at the École Normale Supérieure. They would have six children.

Césaire's return to Martinique, a journey he had envisioned in his first poem, was as significant as his departure. He (as well as his wife) enjoyed a brief teaching career (1940-1945) at his former *lycée* in Fort-de-France. As usual, Césaire left his mark, inspiring his students with his love of poetry and instilling in them an enthusiasm for learning. Like many of his black contemporaries, Césaire took on the dual role of artist and political leader. Elected mayor of Fort-de-France (1945) and deputy to the National Assembly in France (1946), Césaire worked diligently to improve the plight of the Martinicans. During his fourteen years in office in the National Assembly, he was a member of the French Communist Party. He left the party when he perceived its indifference to the particular interests of Martinique.

In 1957, Césaire founded the Martinican Progressive Party (Parti Progressiste Martiniquais), and despite his disillusionment, he never ceased to play an active role in shaping the political life of his homeland. He assumed the presidency of the local "regional council," but he retired from electoral politics entirely in 1993. Although he did not publish any new poetry after 1982, the collection of his work published in Paris in 1994 by the prestigious Seuil firm was a major event. Césaire died in Fort-de-France, Martinique, on April 17, 2008. Césaire remains the best-known writer of the West Indies.

ANALYSIS

Aimé Césaire arrived in France in 1931, at a time when Surrealism had already begun to dominate the literary scene. Instead of an ideology, this movement provided Césaire with the poetic vision and creative license to set his own creative Muse into action. Fleeing the oppressive poverty of his native Martinique, Césaire was ripe for the ideals put forth by the Surrealists. He was attracted, in particular, to the notion of *écriture automatique* (automatic writing) and the Freudian concept of the self, hidden in the recesses of the subconscious, waiting only for a propitious moment to reveal itself. Armed with these two concepts, Césaire destroyed the poems he had written previously and began writing his epic poem *Return to My Native Land*, which would eventually gain for him great fame. More significant, he adopted the methods of the Surrealists in the service of a truly revolutionary cause.

Thus, Césaire's sojourn in France, originally envisioned as an escape from the hopeless conditions in Martinique, resulted instead in his own cultural and political awakening. While pursuing his studies in Paris at the Lycée Louis-le-Grand, he met Senghor (who later became the first president of Senegal and one of Africa's greatest francophone writers). Thanks to their friendship, Césaire acquired a greater knowledge and appreciation of Africa. Together, they joined forces with Léon Damas, another young poet, to establish the journal *L'Étudiant noir*, which replaced a previous journal, *Légitime défense*, that had been silenced after its first publication. Thus, Césaire's cultural and political consciousness gradually began to take on a more concrete form. Before, racism and colonial exploitation were, in his perception, limited mainly to the geographical confines of the West Indies and, especially, to Martinique. Once in Paris, however, he began to realize that the suffering of blacks extended well beyond the boundaries of his homeland. For Césaire, Senghor, and Damas, the creation of *L'Étudiant noir* was an acknowledgment that blacks in the West Indies, Africa, and elsewhere underwent a common experience.

Although Césaire worked zealously to produce a poem that would express the range, depth, and complexity of his poetic vision, his efforts were not initially received with enthusiasm. The first publisher to whom he submitted *Return to My Native Land* refused to publish the poem. Césaire succeeded in having only excerpts from the poem published in the magazine *Volonté* in 1939. Consequently, both the poet and his work went unnoticed for the most part, but this did little to dampen his creative spirit. When Césaire finally returned to Martinique, where he founded the journal *Tropiques* with the aid of his wife, Suzanne Césaire; René Menil; and Aristide Maugée, he continued to bring to life his poetic inspirations. It was not, however, until Césaire met André Breton (who became aware of Césaire's poetic genius after having read, in *Tropiques*, the poems that make up *Miraculous Weapons*) that Césaire was reintroduced to France's reading public. Subsequent admiration of Césaire's work was not limited to writers or political figures. The 1950 deluxe edition of *Disembodied* contained thirty-two engravings by Pablo Picasso that richly illustrated the ten poems in the collection. The poetic genius that caught the attention of Breton continues to be recognized by Césaire's critics.

RETURN TO MY NATIVE LAND

In his preface to the first complete edition of Césaire's *Return to My Native Land*, Breton remarked that this poem represented the "greatest lyrical monument of the times." Indeed, Césaire's first major poem has left an indelible mark upon literature. Of all his works, *Return to My Native Land* is, by far, the most criticized, analyzed, and quoted.

If poetry allows the human spirit to liberate itself from the bonds of reason, as the Surrealists suggest, then it becomes quite clear why Césaire's first major work has such a strong autobiographical tone. The ever-present "I" calls attention to the poet's desire to become rooted once again in his history and culture. Thus, *Return to My Native Land*, a poem of revolt, self-awakening, and "engagement," represents, first and foremost, the poet's personal testimony. From the start, it recalls the town where Césaire grew up, an image that seems both to attract and to repel him. He vividly evokes the stagnant existence of black peasants in Martinique, trapped in poverty and despair, resigned and silent. The emphasis placed on the geographical isolation of the island reinforces, as well, the idea of cultural alienation from the African sources of the black people.

Césaire presents a distressing picture of the poverty in which he and his six brothers and sisters lived. His father's health was being destroyed by an unknown illness, and his mother spent her days and nights operating a Singer sewing machine to help provide the family's daily sustenance. However, poverty and illness were not the most tragic effects of colonialism and racism, for Césaire saw an entire race reduced to a state of intellectual and emotional apathy, convinced of their inability to build, to create, to take control of their own destiny. It was in response to this sense of apathy and self-contempt that Césaire developed the concept of negritude, emphasizing a very proud self-awareness of "blackness" and the distinctive qualities of black culture.

Césaire's recognition and acceptance of Martinique's history, which also represents his own as well, makes it possible for him to purge himself of his feelings of cultural inferiority and to begin his ascent toward a new sense of racial consciousness. From the abyss of despair there arises a magnificent cry of pro-test. In *Return to My Native Land*, Césaire undertakes what he envisions as a messianic mission: He becomes the voice of the downtrodden, the victims, the exploited, the oppressed—those who are unable to verbalize and articulate their own cry of protest. Critics often compare the poet to Christ, citing as examples the lines in which Césaire takes on himself the prejudices held against blacks. At one point, his account of the inhumanities suffered by blacks is reminiscent of the scourging of Christ. Césaire's acceptance of his Christ-like role strongly underscores the message of "engagement," the poet's role as a socially and politically committed artist.

SHACKLES

The themes and motifs found in Césaire's first major poem recur throughout his oeuvre. *Shackles*, published in 1960, explores the vicissitudes of the black experience in Martinique and the evolution of African culture. The title, which denotes the forging of iron, suggests the era of slavery. Césaire recaptures this brutal moment in black history in the title poem, which is replete with nautical expressions used to evoke the voyage of the slave ship. He uses this image to draw a comparison between the agony suffered by the slaves and the misery which plagues the lives of the Martinicans, "arrimés de cœurs lourds" (stowing heavy hearts). It is with this new generation of slaves, who are not necessarily physically bound by chains, that Césaire is primarily concerned.

The poet recognizes the need to reconcile the present with the past, heretofore rejected and denied, before there can be any real and permanent cultural revolution. Therein lies the salvation of Martinique, cut off physically and emotionally from its African roots. The past represents, in Césaire's words, an old "wound" which has never healed, an "unforgettable insult." Thus, Césaire, with other negritude writers, has finally been able to set the record straight, to place colonialism and slavery in their proper perspective. Like all the other sons and daughters of humanity, black people were not destined to be slaves for all time.

African independence has signaled the beginning of a new phase in the history of blacks. Suddenly, it became apparent that the masters of colonialism were not entirely invincible. This is a positive sign for Césaire, who sees in these events a confirmation of the latent force among blacks—a force needed to overcome years of inferiority and submission. His poem "Pour saluer le Tiers Monde" ("Salute to the Third World") is above all one of praise and exaltation. The poet feels an immense sense of pride in the advent of a new Africa. Césaire punctuates the text, several times, with the emphatic words "I see," calling attention to the fact that he is a witness to these changing times. The image Césaire presents of Africa, unexpectedly standing upright, contrasts, significantly, with his image of Martinique, made powerless by its somnolence. Césaire laments the lack of racial and cultural consciousness among the Martinicans and celebrates Africa, the maternal source of his people. Indeed, to some degree, Césaire places the burden of leadership for the West Indies on Africa. The poet depicts a symbolic ritual in which he covers his body with the soil of Africa in such a way as to infuse himself with its strength. It is important to note that Césaire's treatment of Africa in *Shackles* recalls his original theme of the "return to his native land," which signifies not only a physical journey but also a return to his African heritage.

While he grapples with the larger problems of Martinique's fate, Césaire continues to confront his personal dilemma as a committed artist. His situation is not a unique one; it is one he shares with the educated elite of all Third World nations. With this privileged status comes the awesome responsibility to represent the voice of the masses. In his public life, Césaire does this through his active involvement in the political affairs of Martinique. In the same way, his poetry reaffirms continually his message of racial consciousness and commitment. There is no art for art's sake in Césaire's work; style and content are so closely intertwined that it is virtually impossible to talk about one without the other.

In *Return to My Native Land*, Césaire refers to the creative power of words, a power that enables the individual to alter reality. Poetry has allowed the poet the freedom to manipulate and violate the French language in ways that would not have been possible in prose. Thus, the very texture of his language is political; his style is a declaration of independence, shattering conventions associated with the oppressors of his people.

Despite the thematic consistency that characterizes Césaire's oeuvre, a certain movement can be traced from *Return to My Native Land* to *Shackles*. The former deals with the necessity to affirm and reclaim the dignity of blacks. It was the product of a period of intense soul-searching for the poet, who had to overcome his own sense of cultural and racial inferiority. In *Shackles*, on the other hand, Césaire seeks to reconcile the ideals of negritude with the existing realities in the West Indies. The masses do not appear to be ready to take their destiny into their own hands, and Césaire has come to realize that the effects of years of silent resignation will be reversed only gradually. In all his works, however, Césaire has remained committed to his people, serving them as visionary, storyteller, historian, and poet.

OTHER MAJOR WORKS

PLAYS: *Et les chiens se taisaient*, pb. 1956; *La Tragédie du Roi Christophe*, pb. 1963 (*The Tragedy of King Christophe*, 1969); *Une Saison au Congo*, pb. 1966 (*A Season in the Congo*, 1968); *Une Tempête, d'après "La Tempête" de Shakespeare: Adaptation pour un théâtre nègre*, pr., pb. 1969 (*A Tempest*, 1974).

NONFICTION: *Discours sur le colonialisme*, 1950 (*Discourse on Colonialism*, 1972); *Toussaint Louverture: La Révolution française et le problème coloniale*, 1960.

MISCELLANEOUS: *Œuvres complètes*, 1976.

BIBLIOGRAPHY

Arnold, A. James. Introduction to *Césaire's Lyric and Dramatic Poetry, 1946-82*, by Aimé Césaire. Translated by Clayton Eshleman and Annette Smith. Charlottesville: University Press of Virginia, 1990. Provides a succinct introduction to Aimé Césaire's life and work. Offers critical observations that supplement and extend many of the readings in Arnold's important *Modernism and Negritude*.

_____. *Modernism and Negritude: The Poetry and Poetics of Aimé Césaire*. Cambridge, Mass.: Harvard University Press, 1981. This work is certainly the definitive study of Césaire's poetry and its relationship to both negritude and modernism. Highly readable and elegantly written.

Davis, Gregson. *Aimé Césaire*. New York: Cambridge

University Press, 1997. A generally chronological examination of the evolution of Césaire's poetic and intellectual development and its connection to his aesthetics and politics.

Eshelman, Clayton, and Annette Smith. Introduction to *Aimé Césaire: The Collected Poetry*. Berkeley: University of California Press, 1983. In this illustrated collection of more than four hundred pages, Eshelman and Smith offer commentary on Césaire to accompany their translations of a selection of his poems for the English-language audience and students. Bibliographical references.

Figueroa, Victor. *Not at Home in One's Home: Caribbean Self-Fashioning in the Poetry of Luis Palés Matos, Aimé Césaire, and Derek Walcott*. Madison, N.J.: Fairleigh Dickinson University Press, 2009. Contains a chapter on Césaire's *Return to My Native Land* and describes Caribbean poetry.

Martin, Gerald, ed. *Men of Maize*. Pittsburgh, Pa.: University of Pittsburgh Press, 1993. A collection of essays by various authors relevant to Césaire, poetry as a genre, and Caribbean culture.

Munro, Martin. *Shaping and Reshaping the Caribbean: The Work of Aimé Césaire and René Depestre*. Leeds, England: Maney, 2000. Munro examines Caribbean literature through the works of Césaire and Depestre. Bibliography and index.

Pallister, Janis L. *Aimé Césaire*. New York: Twayne, 1991. Short biography and a critical analysis of Aimé Césaire's work and career. Includes bibliography and index.

Scharfman, Ronnie Leah. *Engagement and the Language of the Subject in the Poetry of Aimé Césaire*. Gainesville: University Press of Florida, 1987. This monograph addresses issues of race awareness and politics as well as literature. Bibliography, index.

Suk, Jeannie. *Postcolonial Paradoxes in French Caribbean Writing: Césaire, Glissant, Condé*. Oxford, England: Clarendon Press, 2001. This study of Caribbean writing includes analysis and discussion of the works of Césaire.

Cherie R. Maiden
Updated by Gordon Walters

MICHELLE CLIFF

Born: Kingston, Jamaica; November 2, 1946

PRINCIPAL POETRY

Claiming an Identity They Taught Me to Despise, 1980 (prose and poetry)
The Land of Look Behind: Prose and Poetry, 1985

OTHER LITERARY FORMS

Michelle Cliff writes in a wide variety of genres including essays, novels, short stories, and literary criticism as well as poetry. She began writing after having read an article about Jamaica that she felt did not portray Jamaica as she had known it. In all of her writings, she depicts the real Jamaica as she believes it to be and elucidates what it means to be Jamaican. Throughout her works, she addresses the problems of oppression, colonialism, postcolonialism; prejudice in regard to color, race, gender, and sexual orientation; and the loss of oral history. In her novels, in particular, she treats the need for revising mainstream history to include the lost oral history of the oppressed and ostracized. Cliff is also recognized as an important literary critic.

ACHIEVEMENTS

Michelle Cliff is considered one of the most important writers addressing the issues of race, color, feminism, sexual orientation, and heritage and identity, particularly as faced by mixed-race individuals in a postcolonial society. Through her fictional works and prose poetry, she has made an important contribution to the "rewriting" of history by revealing the "other" history that has been omitted from official history. She is also esteemed for her literary criticism. Cliff received a MacDowell Fellowship (1982), National Endowment for the Arts grants (1982, 1989), a Massachusetts Artists Foundation Fellowship (1984), an Eli Kantor Fellowship from Yaddo (1984), and a Fulbright Fellowship (1988).

BIOGRAPHY

Michelle Cliff, a light-skinned Creole, was born in Kingston, Jamaica, on November 2, 1946. Her father was American and her mother was Jamaican. She grew up in a mulatto family that placed extreme importance on skin color and highly valued light skin. Consequently, her family continually insisted that she pass for white. As she matured, Cliff gradually realized that this rejection of her black heritage was unacceptable to her. Cliff spent her childhood both in the United States and Jamaica. When she was three years old, her family moved to the United States. She remained in Jamaica for a short period of time but soon joined her family in New York City. They lived in a Caribbean neighborhood. Cliff and her family made many visits to Jamaica during the late 1940's and early 1950's. In 1956, Cliff returned to live in Jamaica and attend boarding school.

Upon graduation from secondary school, she returned to the United States to attend Wagner College. During this time, she became involved in politics and in the feminist movement. In addition, she actively opposed the war in Vietnam. In 1969, she received an A.B. degree. She worked in the publishing field as a reporter, a researcher, and an editor. In 1974, she completed a master of philosophy and subsequently earned a Ph.D. from the Warburg Institute at the University of London. While a student at the girls' boarding school in Jamaica, Cliff had been attracted to a classmate, but it was during her stay in England that she truly became aware of her lesbian orientation. In 1976, she began her relationship with the poet Adrienne Rich, and she also began to write poetry. In 1980, she published her first book of poetry *Claiming an Identity They Taught Me to Despise*. From 1981 to 1983, with Rich, she coedited a multicultural lesbian journal *Sinister Wisdom*. She published her second collection of poetry, *The Land of Look Behind*, in 1985.

In 1984, Cliff published her first novel, *Abeng*, which portrays the multiracial, multicultural world in which she grew up. She published a sequel, *No Telephone to Heaven*, in 1987. She followed this with the novels *Free Enterprise* (1993) and *Into the Interior* (2010). She also published the short-story collections *Bodies of Water* (1990), *The Store of a Million Items* (1998), and *Everything Is Now: New and Collected Stories* (2009). In addition to writing, Cliff has held several university teaching positions.

ANALYSIS

At the start of her career as a writer, Michelle Cliff published two collections of prose poetry, *Claiming an Identity They Taught Me to Despise* and *The Land of Look Behind*. In her poetry, she begins to address the issues that she later explores in her fictional works. Although both her fiction and her poetry are based on her life, experiences, and reactions to her environment, her poetry is more intimate and personal than her fiction. Cliff's poetry addresses two major themes: passing and denying her black heritage and revealing what she calls the "real" Jamaica. She seeks to correct the "false" history of Jamaica to reveal the hidden or ignored history—the black history of Jamaica. Her poetry deals with what it means to be Jamaican, to be racially mixed, to be other. From her two major themes, she branches out to discuss issues of sexual difference, oppression, and postcolonialism. Separation is also an important theme of her poetry. By including quotations from other writers in her poetry collections, Cliff connects her poetry, which focuses on Jamaica and Jamaicans, to the universal problems of racism, intolerance, oppression, and separation.

Cliff has stated that she does not consider herself a poet but rather a writer of prose. She has also expressed a concern that language, in its beauty of expression and its sounds, will obscure the thoughts expressed. Her poetry is an expression of her ideas and beliefs written in a language filled with images, wordplay, and an intense portrayal of her view of the world. It has a richness of color and texture, and the images she creates, some beautiful, others disturbing, remain with the reader. The purple-skinned fruit with the star-shaped center, the dark Polynesian woman rowing between the white ice cliffs, a chipped crystal doorknob, the translucent skin of green tomatoes, the sow suspended for slaughter, the breast milk of the black charwoman mixing with her mop water—these images all become part of the reader's remembering.

CLAIMING AN IDENTITY THEY TAUGHT ME TO DESPISE

Claiming an Identity They Taught Me to Despise contains five selections that Cliff had previously published in journals and five new writings. The poetry examines Cliff's life, particularly her childhood, in terms of being imprisoned in a false life, controlled by others, and forced to assume an identity created by others. Through random thoughts and disjointed memories, her poetry expresses what will become the organized themes of her fiction In the first section, "Passing," Cliff begins with a quotation from Oscar Wilde that expresses the idea that it is not what people do not see but what they do see that is the world's mystery. This quotation sets the tone of the section and also elicits a multitude of questions regarding passing for what one is not. Cliff leads the reader to see the mystery of societal attitudes toward color, sexual orientation, and oppression of particular groups. It can only be mystery because of its lack of logic, reasonableness, and justice. Cliff then delves into how passing affects an individual's life. She emphasizes the importance of camouflaging oneself, of hiding, as she says, like the lizards in the schoolyard. She expresses her fear of camouflage but also recognizes its importance for self-protection; by becoming invisible like the lizards who blend with the leaves, one becomes safe. However, this safety requires one to lead a ghost life, to make one's real self invisible, and to reject connections to the unacceptable. For Cliff personally, as for any light-skinned Creole, this means rejecting her black heritage, ignoring her black family traditions and history. She poignantly expresses the pain of such an existence as she describes incidents from the time she spent with her grandmother among those of color in the rural "real" Jamaica.

In the sections "Filaments," "Obsolete Geography," and "Accurate Record," Cliff continues to recount incidents from the time spent with her grandmother and also from her life in Kingston and in the United States. She addresses the issue of separation or splitting. She describes how the importance placed on color by her family, particularly her father's family, resulted in a splitting of the family based on color of skin. Even within her own immediate family, the splitting occurred because Cliff was light skinned, called "fair" by her family, while her younger sister was dark skinned like her mother. She became her father's daughter, and her sister, her mother's daughter. Thus Cliff was removed from the mother-daughter bond. In all three sections, Cliff emphasizes the constant manipulating of

what is revealed and how the unacceptable and the unpleasant are kept hidden.

"Against Granite," "The History of Costume," and "Women's Work" explore the lives of women who are marginalized, exploited, rejected, persecuted, and ignored. "Against Granite" portrays the efforts of black women to preserve the history of incarceration, to revise history by writing it from the viewpoint of the slave, the servant, and those who are not free. These black women maintain a normal lifestyle, yet they write. "Women's Work" is a series of vignettes of women used up by excruciating work, burned for offenses, and threatened by gang rape. Starting with a quote from Virginia Woolf dealing with the mutilation and destroying of birds of paradise for their feathers, "The History of Costume" addresses how costume deforms women's bodies and becomes a sort of bondage. It concludes with an image of a nineteenth century mother and daughter in mourning attire. The small child is dressed exactly like the mother; the daughter is bonded to her mother but in a deformed way.

"Claiming an Identity They Taught Me to Despise," "The Garden," and "Separation" return to a more personal focus. Cliff claims her black heritage as she recalls the history of the slaves in colonial Jamaica and declares herself sister to them. She is Jamaican, she is Creole, and she is black, not white. In "The Garden," she expresses her need to garden and gardening's connection to her grandmother, who found comfort in watching things grow. "Separation" deals with the final separation of Cliff from her family as she and her sister help her mother divide the family possessions, keeping some and disposing of others. Her sister and her mother have decided to live together. They are sending her sister's daughter to live with her father. As a child, the light-skinned Cliff was left in New York with her father; her dark-skinned mother and sister returned to Jamaica.

THE LAND OF LOOK BEHIND

The Land of Look Behind includes seven of the sections of poetry already published in *Claiming an Identity They Taught Me to Despise* and four new writings, plus a preface, in which Cliff explains how she came to write poetry. The title, *Land of Look Behind*, is another name for Jamaica, but here it means not only Jamaica but also Cliff's act of looking back at her life in colonized, anglicized Jamaica and her looking behind the anglicized Jamaica to the black Jamaica and even further behind to African history and tradition. In "Travel Notes," she writes about a visit to the home of Emily and Charlotte Brontë, suffragists, the murder of children, and a female Ku Klux Klan member, emphasizing oppression and death. However, she concludes with a vignette about women in Texas capturing and moving rattlesnakes to a safe place.

"If I Could Write This in Fire I Would Write This in Fire" retells events from Cliff's life in Jamaica and London. It is permeated with her anger over the value placed on skin color and the oppression of Jamaicans by British colonizers and the subsequent oppressions of dark-skinned Jamaicans by light-skinned middle-class Jamaicans. She writes about her grandmother and her dark-skinned friend Zoe. Cliff emphasizes the impact of skin color on their lives. The light-skinned Cliff went to college in London; Zoe remained in Jamaica in poverty and was beaten by her husband. The collection concludes with "Love in the Third World" and "A Pilgrimage, A History Lesson, Two Satires and A Vision," in which Cliff treats the issues of color, oppression, and hatred of difference on a worldwide scale.

OTHER MAJOR WORKS

LONG FICTION: *Abeng*, 1984; *No Telephone to Heaven*, 1987; *Free Enterprise*, 1993; *Into the Interior*, 2010.

SHORT FICTION: *Bodies of Water*, 1990; *The Store of a Million Items*, 1998; *Everything Is Now: New and Collected Stories*, 2009.

EDITED TEXTS: *The Winner Names the Age: A Collection of Writings*, 1978 (with Lillian Smith).

MISCELLANEOUS: *If I Could Write This in Fire I Would Write This in Fire*, 1982; *History as Fiction, Fiction as History*, 1994.

BIBLIOGRAPHY

Cliff, Michelle. *Abeng*. New York: Penguin, 1995. Cliff's novel, based on her own life, makes her poetry more meaningful and understandable.

_____. "Journey into Speech: A Writer Between Two Worlds—An Interview with Michelle Cliff." Interview by Opal Palmer Adisa. *African American Review* 28, no. 2 (1994): 273-275. Cliff speaks on the color issue, oppression in Jamaica, resistance as community, and the importance of women in the history of resistance.

Elia, Nada. *Trances, Dances, and Vociferations: Agency and Resistance in Africana Women's Narratives*. New York: Garland, 2001. Among other topics, Elia discusses Cliff's use of alternative and oral history, sexual disguise, and racial passing.

Page, Yolanda Williams, ed. *Encyclopedia of African American Women Writers*. Westport, Conn.: Greenwood Press, 2007. Contains a brief biography of Cliff that examines her life and works.

Paravisini-Gebert, Lizabeth. *Literature of the Caribbean*. Westport, Conn.: Greenwood Press, 2008. Provides historical background for understanding Cliff's writings and placing her in the context of Caribbean writers.

Shawncey Webb

SOR JUANA INÉS DE LA CRUZ

Born: San Miguel Nepantla, New Spain (now in Mexico); November, 1648 (baptized December 2, 1648)
Died: Mexico City, New Spain (now in Mexico); April 17, 1695
Also known as: Sor Juana

PRINCIPAL POETRY

Inundación castálida, 1689
Segundo volumen de las obras, 1692 (the long poem *Primero sueño* is translated as *First Dream*, 1983)
Fama y obras póstumas, 1700
The Sonnets of Sor Juana Ines de la Cruz in English Verse, 2001

OTHER LITERARY FORMS

The most readable prose work of Sor Juana Inés de la Cruz (WAH-nah ee-NAYS day lah krews), *Respuesta de la poetisa a la muy ilustre Sor Filotea de la Cruz* (1700; *The Answer*, 1994), is an appealing autobiographical defense of her precocious interest in learning, an emotional plea for acceptance as a woman and a scholar, and an obsessive declaration of faith. Sor Juana tries to convince her superiors that, despite her lifelong curiosity about the material world, theological concerns are still the most important to her.

El divino Narciso, pr. c. 1680 (*The Divine Narcissus*, 1945), a religious one-act play, is a tasteful and imaginative treatment of divine love in which Narcissus, as a figure of Christ, falls in love with human nature as a reflection of himself. With this short play, the fantasy of desire that takes so many forms throughout Sor Juana's work finds its ultimate synthesis of eros and agape.

ACHIEVEMENTS

Sor Juana Inés de la Cruz was a Mexican literary virtuoso who was called the tenth muse during her lifetime and who is generally considered the most important writer of colonial Spanish America. Although she wrote more than four hundred poems, twenty-three short plays, two full-length comedias, and various prose works, Sor Juana's reputation rests on a handful of poems (about two dozen in all), *The Divine Narcissus*, and *The Answer*. Although a reassessment of her works begun in the 1950's promises a more extensive list of her most important writings, it is likely that, with the exception of her extremely complex *First Dream*, the few pieces that earned her the admiration of Marcelino Menendez y Pelayo one hundred years ago will continue to be the ones that will ensure her a place of prominence in Spanish letters.

At her best, Sor Juana was able to manipulate the often unwieldy and intricate language of the Spanish Baroque, with its rich heritage from the Golden Age, into expressions of delicate, feminine vision and sensibility. Her aesthetic documentation of the search for knowledge, love, and God is the most complete personal and artistic record of any figure from the colonial period. Sor Juana's love poetry appears to reflect frustrating and painful experiences before her entry into the convent at about the age of seventeen. Few of the poems are concerned with fulfillment or the intimate communication of personal feelings; most are, instead,

variations on the themes of ambivalence and disillusionment in love. Sor Juana's philosophical poems are linked to her amatory verse by a sense of disenchantment. An exception to her general pessimism is *First Dream*, in which the poet takes delight in depicting the joys and dangers of her intellectual explorations. More of Sor Juana's writings bear witness to her theological concerns. Although some of her religious lyrics express the same kind of anguish about God's love that she expressed about human love, she clearly attempted in her *villancicos* to use her poetic talent in the service of the Roman Catholic Church.

BIOGRAPHY

Juana Inés de Asbaje y Ramírez de Santillana was born in November, 1648, in San Miguel Nepantla, some sixty kilometers southeast of Mexico City. She was the illegitimate child of a Spanish captain and a Creole mother. In the charming *The Answer*, she tells how she learned to read at the age of three and tagged along with one of her sisters to La Amiga, an elementary school, where she took her first formal lessons. She says that, at the age of eight, she begged her mother to let her cut her hair and dress like a boy so she could attend the university. That being denied her, she continued her self-education by reading the classics she found in her grandmother's house. Around 1659, she was allowed to go to Mexico City and live with the family of one of her aunts. Although not enrolled in the university, Juana privately continued her studies, which included twenty lessons in Latin. Twenty was apparently sufficient, for subsequently she was able to write Latin poetry as well as anyone in the viceroyalty.

By 1664, Sor Juana was a member of the viceregal court and was the darling of the vicereine. She so impressed the viceroy, the marques de Mancera, with her knowledge, that he arranged for forty professors from the university to give her tests. Sor Juana passed them all, amazing the local elite. Her several years of court life must have been intense, emotional years. She was a beautiful woman and was doubtless wooed by gentlemen of some wealth and position. Nevertheless, by 1669, she had entered the convent and had taken religious vows, as much from aversion to marriage as from attraction to the celibate life. It was her desire to be free

Sor Juana Inés de la Cruz (Library of Congress)

to learn, she states in *The Answer*, that was the primary motivation for her vocation.

For the next twenty-three years, Sor Juana was the major literary figure in colonial Spanish America, composing everything from love sonnets to a treatise on music, almost all her writing being done on request from high-ranking officials of the Roman Catholic Church or the state. She wrote elaborate pieces for performance at liturgical functions, occasional verse for political events, and scenarios and scripts for afternoons of royal entertainment. Not long after the brilliant defense of her studies in *The Answer*, and at the height of her career, when her collected works were beginning to be published and acclaimed in Spain, pressures by her religious superiors induced her to give away her library of more than four thousand volumes and all her scientific and musical instruments and to abandon writing altogether. Several years later, on April 17, 1695, she died in an epidemic that swept Mexico City.

ANALYSIS

Although most of the compositions have merit, the lyric poems, in the order of their treatment here, are usually considered to be the best, and they may be used as a point of departure for delineating a canon of Sor Juana Inés de la Cruz's most significant writings.

Sor Juana was a deeply passionate and intelligent woman who dedicated her life to knowledge and spiritual perfection. On one hand, she seems to have renounced love for intellectual freedom, and from her amatory and philosophical writings, it appears that her renunciation of the world, along with her commitment to learning, paradoxically caused an obsession with intimacy and a profound disillusionment with any reality except that of spiritual intimacy. On the other hand, judging from her other prose and verse, Sor Juana was also a writer engaged with her society, closely involved with its institutions and its native culture. An anthology of Sor Juana's most popular compositions may slight this more social side of her personality, but it is important to remember as one reviews her major poems of love and disillusionment that the poetess wrote more concerning religion than about any real or imaginary love and that she was as adept at elaborate versification about current events and visitors to the viceroyalty as at revealing her most private feelings. It is not difficult to dwell on the more romantic side of the "tenth muse," to use certain of her poems to enhance the image of a jilted, precocious, disenchanted teenage intellectual sequestering herself in a convent and spending her life in extremely elaborate sublimation. Her most famous pieces contribute to such an image, but as the reader is exposed to a wider spectrum of her talents, a more balanced picture emerges; a trajectory of maturation becomes visible in which Catholicism and the Baroque are means to the self-fulfillment and self-expression originally thwarted in her youth by her lack of social position and her fascination with scholarship.

PROGRESSION OF LOVE

If one reads Sor Juana's writings to observe a progression from human to divine love, it is appropriate to begin with the sonnet "Esta tarde, mi bien" (this afternoon, my love). The poem is one of the few in which she relates a moving encounter with another person, and it contrasts the impotency of words with the efficacy of tears in the communication of love. Here, there is none of the love-hate dialectic that colors most of her amatory poems; instead, one finds the description of a delicately feminine, sensitive, and formidably talented personality in a moment of unguarded abandon. It is only a slight exaggeration to say that after "Esta tarde, mi bien," one sees in Sor Juana's verse the psychological effects of an unhappy affair rather than the experience of love itself. Even the tender *lira* "Amado dueño mio" (my beloved master), while documenting in a poetic sense the dimensions of intimacy, is a conventional lament of the lover separated from the beloved. The lover, like a Renaissance shepherdess, tells her misfortunes to the wind, which carries her complaints, her passion, and her sadness to the distant partner. Alfonso Méndez Plancarte states that the poem contains some of Sor Juana's finest lines and that it may surpass the eclogues of Garcilaso de la Vega. The comparison with Garcilaso is appropriate, and poetry in his likeness is fitting to express the absence of consummation rather than its presence; significantly, the *lira* keynotes a thematic transformation from completion to emptiness.

The sonnet "Detente, sombra de mi bien esquivo" (stay, shadow of my scornful love) can be considered an introduction to a series of poems that admit both the positive and negative effects of passion as well as the inconclusive status of unconsummated love. In "Detente, sombra de mi bien esquivo," the beloved himself eludes the poet, but his image cannot escape the prison of her fantasy. Important in this and the poems under discussion below is the counterpoint of conceits and emotions about the love "por quien alegre muero" (for whom I would happily die) but also "por quien penosa vivo" (for whom I live in agony), which develops to an extreme in the sonnet "Al que Ingrato me deja, busco amante" (I seek the one who spurns me) and "Que no me quiera Fabio, al verse amado" (that Fabio does not love me as I love him), and the *redondilla* "Este amoroso tormento" (this torment of love). In the latter piece, as in the other poems of this group, the poet never finds fulfillment, "porque, entre alivio y dolar, hallo culpa en el amor y disculpa en el olvido" (because between relief and pain, I find blame in love and exoneration in forgetfulness).

Beyond frustration and the love-hate duality that the poet attributes to romantic feeling lie disillusionment and bitterness. The sonnets "Silvio, yo te aborezco" (I hate you, Silvio), "Amor empieza por desasosiego" (love begins uneasily), and "Con el dolor de la mortal herida" (with the pain of a mortal wound) are among Sor Juana's strongest denunciations of the men she once might have loved, as well as of herself for having given in to loving them: "no solo a tí, corrida, te aborrezco,/ pero a mí por el tiempo que te quise" (not only do I abhor you/ but myself for the time that I loved you). Here the bittersweet of "Este amoroso tormento" turns to anger. The image of the lover purposely retained in "Detente, sombra de mi bien esquivo" is repeatedly banished, and it is a logical movement from such rejection to the *sátira filosófica*, "Hombres necios" ("Foolish Men"), one of Sor Juana's more popular denunciations of men as the source of all women's problems. In these feminist *redondillas*, the poet exposes the ways in which men "acusan lo que causan" (blame us for the things they cause). Why, she asks, do men want women to be good if they tempt them to be bad? Who, she questions, is the greater sinner, "la que peca por la paga o el que paga por pecar" (she who sins for pay or he who pays for sin)?

Because Sor Juana's poems are not usually dated, there is no way of knowing whether the progression from the delicate, loving "Esta tarde, mi bien" to the sarcastic "Hombres necios" reflects the sequential effects of an increasingly unhappy situation. In any case, these poems of erotic experience do fit a pattern that begins with brief reciprocal affection and degenerates into ambivalence, then finally into contempt. There are, at the same time, a great number of poems written to women which do not fit this generalization. Sor Juana apparently had very meaningful relationships with the wives of two of the Mexican viceroys, and her many verses to Lysi show a far more consistent emotional response than that depicted in poems of male-female interaction. Certainly the Lysi poems, perhaps especially the ornate "Lámina sirva el cielo al retrato" (the sky is lamina of your portrait), are a moving contrast to her more widely read poems' heterosexual canon.

PHILOSOPHIC POEMS

Sor Juana's philosophic poems complement her negative attitude toward worldly love. "Verde embeleso de la vida humana" (green charm of human life) rejects illusions and hope as deceptive: "solamente lo que toco veo" ("I only see what I can touch"). It represents the repression of vain dreams, the acceptance of life without romance or even platonic fantasy. "Diuturna enfermedad de la Esperanza" (lasting infirmity of hope) reiterates this concept, and "Este que ves, engaño colorido" (this painted lie you see), a sonnet on her portrait, is an intense affirmation of the Roman Catholic view that the flesh is "polvo, es sombra, es nada" ("is dust, is a shadow, is nothing"). Her "Rosa divina" (divine rose) is a variation on the universal theme of the brevity of beauty and life. Perhaps her most powerful renunciation is "Finjamos que soy feliz" (pretend that I am happy), in which she denies the validity of knowledge and maintains that because humans can know nothing for certain, ignorance is preferable to imperfect knowing: "aprendamos a ignorar" ("let us learn to not know"). "Finjamos que soy feliz" is a moment of despair within the context of Sor Juana's self-confessed lifelong passion, the pursuit of knowledge. Her monumental *First Dream*, the only work that she admitted to writing for her own pleasure and not to please someone else, is far more balanced in presenting her attitude toward learning.

FIRST DREAM

First Dream, which is among the best philosophic poems in Spanish, is the height of Sor Juana's exploration of the Baroque. The poem begins with a description of nightfall, in which the entire physical world eventually succumbs to sleep. The human spirit, freed from the constraint of the body, soars upward to find a perspective from which it can comprehend the immensity of the universe. Once it glimpses the overpowering dimensions of creation, the soul retreats to the shadows. Finding a mental shore on the sea of knowledge, it decides to approach the challenge of learning by dividing things into categories and mastering each division separately. In spite of doubts that the mind can really know anything, echoes of the dark vision of "Finjamos que soy feliz," the soul continues its search for truth. Dawn arrives, however, and the dream ends inconclusively. Universal knowledge has eluded the soul, but the dreamer has not despaired.

Once considered to be on the fringe of literature because of its purposeful Gongorism, *First Dream* is enjoying the positive reconsideration accorded the entire Spanish Baroque, in the course of which Luis de Góngora y Argote himself has been reinstated into the canon of major Spanish poets. Accepting the style of this poem as not only valid but also essential to its meaning, one can better appreciate Sor Juana's most mature and complex statement about the human condition. It is the culmination of a lifetime of study and reflection.

SACRED BALLADS

Sor Juana's religious writings include several "sacred ballads," among which "Amante dulce del alma" (sweet love of my soul), "Mientras la Gracia me exita" (while Grace moves me), and "Traigo conmigo un cuidado" (I have a deep concern) are generally held in high regard. All three attempt to express the effects of divine love. "Amante dulce del alma" asks why Christ might have willed to visit the poet in Holy Communion: Has he decided to be present from love or from jealousy? She decides for the former, reflecting that since God knows all things, he can see into her heart and has no reason to be jealous. "Mientras la Gracia me exita" tries to clarify some of the feelings involved in the inner struggle between "la virtud y la costumbre" (virtue and habit). Like "Amante dulce del alma," this is a poem of scruples rather than a meditation of universal religious significance. "Traigo conmigo un cuidado" carries the analysis of spiritual love further and contrasts it with the poet's experience of human love. "La misma muerte que vivo, es la vida con que muero" ("the same death that I live is the life in which I die"), she writes at the end of the poem, attempting to sum up her contradictory mental state. Even though it is divine love that causes her to feel the way she does, there are parallels between the *contrarias penas* ("contradictory anxieties") of "Este amoroso tormento" and those expressed in "Traigo conmigo un cuidado."

It is more fruitful to look for a developed sense of religious experience in Sor Juana's *villancicos* and her play *The Divine Narcissus* than in her personal religious lyrics. Although these works have generally been neglected, scholar Méndez Plancarte and others have made convincing defenses of their genres as well as of the verse itself. *The Divine Narcissus* contains some of Sor Juana's best writing, and, with the *loa* (or one-act play) that precedes it, shows how she introduced local themes into her work. The most significant element of the play, however, is the successful depiction of divine love, sufficiently anthropomorphized to give it comprehensible human beauty. Here is also the full evolution of a spiritual maturity that finally quiets the older, worldly concerns.

OTHER MAJOR WORKS

PLAYS: *El divino Narciso*, pr. c. 1680 (*The Divine Narcissus*, 1945); *Los empeños de una casa*, pr. c. 1680 (adaptation of Lope de Vega Carpio's play *La discreta enamorada*; *A Household Plagued by Love*, 1942); *Amor es más laberinto*, pr. 1689 (wr. 1668; with Juan de Guevara); *El cetro de José*, pb. 1692; *El mártir del Sacramento, San Hermenegildo*, pr. c. 1692; *The Three Secular Plays of Sor Juana Inés de la Cruz*, 2000.

NONFICTION: *Neptuno alegórico*, 1680; *Carta atenagórica*, 1690; *Respuesta de la poetisa a la muy ilustre Sor Filotea de la Cruz*, 1700 (*The Answer*, 1994).

MISCELLANEOUS: *Obras completas de Sor Juana Inés de la Cruz*, 1951-1957 (4 volumes: I, *Lírica personal*, poetry; II, *Villancicos y letras sacras*, poetry; III, *Autos y loas*, drama; IV, *Comedias sainetes y prosa*, drama and prose; Alfonso Méndez Plancarte, editor); *A Sor Juana Anthology*, 1988.

BIBLIOGRAPHY

Bergmann, Emile L., and Stacey Shlau, eds. *Approaches to Teaching the Works of Sor Juana Inés de la Cruz*. New York: Modern Language Association of America, 2007. Contains several essays about Sor Juana's poetry as well as a wealth of material on her life and other works.

Cruz, Sor Juana Inés de la. *A Woman of Genius: The Intellectual Autobiography of Sor Juana Inés de la Cruz*. Translated with an introduction by Margaret Sayers Pedén. Salisbury, Conn.: Lime Rock Press, 1982. Contains a translation of Sor Juana's defense of her life, *The Answer*. Also contains a list of basic sources at the end.

Flynn, Gerard. *Sor Juana Inés de la Cruz*. Boston: Twayne, 1971. Introduces the reader to Sor Juana and her work. The first chapter gives biographical information, and the others review her poetry and drama. A discussion of the criticism of several au-thors is included, as are a number of quotations from Sor Juana's work with English translations provided by Flynn.

Gonzalez, Michelle A. *Sor Juana: Beauty and Justice in the Americas*. Maryknoll, N.Y.: Orbis Books, 2003. A biography of Sor Juana that examines all aspects of her life, including her poetry.

Kirk, Pamela. *Sor Juana Inés de la Cruz: Religion, Art, and Feminism*. New York: Continuum, 1998. An examination of Sor Juana's role in the Roman Catholic Church as well as her literary efforts. Bibliography and index.

Lucianai, Frederick. *Literary Self-fashioning in Sor Juana Inés de la Cruz*. Lewisburg, Pa.: Bucknell University Presses, 2004. Four essays in a roughly chronological order that track how Sor Juana created a literary self in her writings.

Merrim, Stephanie. *Early Modern Women's Writing and Sor Juana Inés de la Cruz*. Nashville, Tenn.: Vanderbilt University Press, 1999. Situates the work of Sor Juana within the field of seventeenth century women's writing in Spanish, English, and French. The protofeminist writings of Sor Juana are used as a benchmark for the examination of the literary production of her female contemporaries. Includes bibliographical references and index.

_____, ed. *Feminist Perspectives on Sor Juana Inés de la Cruz*. Detroit: Wayne State University Press, 1991. A collection of essays by important literary critics and translators of Sor Juana. Discusses her life, time, and work in the context of feminist criticism.

Montross, Constance M. *Virtue or Vice? Sor Juana's Use of Thomistic Thought*. Washington, D.C.: University Press of America, 1981. Examines Sor Juana's use of Scholastic doctrine and methodology, specifically the ideas of Saint Thomas Aquinas. The author analyzes the combination of belief and questioning in the *Carta atenagórica*, *The Answer*, and *First Dream*. Extensive bibliography and the Spanish text of *First Dream* is included.

Paz, Octavio. *Sor Juana: Or, The Traps of Faith*. Translated by Margaret Sayers Peden. Cambridge, Mass.: Harvard University Press, 1988. A biography of Sor Juana by a leading Mexican poet, essayist, and cultural critic. Paz emphasizes Sor Juana's uniqueness as a poet and focuses on her struggle for her intellectual and creative life. Historical settings and traditions are detailed. Included are illustrations, among them portraits of Sor Juana, and a helpful listing of Spanish literary terms.

_____, ed. *Mexican Poetry: An Anthology*. Translated by Samuel Beckett. Reprint. New York: Grove Press, 1985. Contains a discussion of the place of Sor Juana in Mexican poetry as part of Paz's introduction to the history of Mexican poetry. Within the anthology itself are translations of twelve of Sor Juana's poems.

William L. Felker

D

Rubén Darío
Félix Rubén García Sarmiento

Born: Metapa (now Ciudad Darío), Nicaragua;
January 18, 1867
Died: León, Nicaragua; February 6, 1916

Principal poetry

Abrojos, 1887

Rimas, 1887

Azul, 1888

Prosas profanas, 1896 (*Prosas Profanas, and Other Poems*, 1922)

Cantos de vida y esperanza, los cisnes, y otros poemas, 1905

Canto a la Argentina, oda a mitre, y otros poemas, 1914 (English translation, 1920)

Selected Poems of Rubén Darío, 1965 (Lysander Kemp, translator)

Other literary forms

The fame of Rubén Darío (dah-REE-oh) rests primarily on his poetry, but he wrote serious prose as well. *Azul* (azure), his first major publication, contained poems and short stories alike. Both the poetry and the prose portions were widely acclaimed, but Darío's mature work includes almost no fiction. He published several volumes of essays based on his experience as a foreign correspondent, a traveler, and a diplomat, and two such collections have gained international attention: *La caravana pasa* (1903; the caravan passes) was among the earliest chronicles of the experience of American artists in Paris, while *Tierras solares* (1904; the sunny lands) is a collection of affectionate and melancholy essays celebrating the countryside of southern Spain, which Darío considered the common ground of Spanish and Latin American history. Darío also published literary criticism, political commentary, an autobiography, and exegeses of his own works.

The most famous of Darío's critical works is *Historias de mis libros* (1914; stories of my books), a compilation of three explanatory pieces he wrote about his greatest works of poetry, *Azul*, *Prosas Profanas, and Other Poems*, and *Cantos de vida y esperanza, los cisnes, y otros poemas*. In *Historias de mis libros*, he responded to the most frequent criticism of his work, that he had abandoned the traditional themes of Latin America in pursuit of a European art. He branded the criticism "myopic" and answered that the literature of the New World needed no more stylized odes to nature or patriotic battle hymns.

Achievements

Rubén Darío was a giant of Spanish-language literature and a pioneer of the literature of the American continents. One of the founders of the indigenous Latin American literary movement known as *Modernismo*, Darío introduced European influences—particularly from France—to the poetry of Latin America, but perhaps more important, he introduced the *Modernismo* of Latin America to Europe. His dramatic innovations in theme, language, meter, and rhyme influenced the poetry of both the New World and the Old.

The publication of *Azul* in 1888 was acclaimed by European as well as South American critics, and the book's title was adopted by the *Azure Review*, a Mexican journal that became a principal forum for South America's experimental *Modernista* poetry. When Darío was only twenty-one years old, the influential Madrid critic Juan Valera praised the Nicaraguan's "singular artistic and poetic talent" and the "pure Spanish form" of his writing. With the publication of later works, Darío's renown grew, and he was widely acknowledged as a spokesperson for Latin American culture.

Darío was a colorful public figure, equally at home in Paris, Madrid, and Latin America. He traveled constantly and was acquainted with literary figures throughout Europe and Latin America. He exerted a profound cultural influence through his poetry, his literary criticism, and his journalism. At the height of his fame, he was Nicaragua's minister to Spain; an internationally celebrated lecturer, poet, and journalist; and an éminence grise among artists of Europe and the Americas. In a 1934 tribute, Chile's Pablo Neruda and Spain's Federico García Lorca pronounced Darío "the poet of America and Spain."

BIOGRAPHY

Rubén Darío's life was adventurous and bohemian. He traveled constantly in Europe and the Americas, renowned for his literary achievements but dogged by debt, sickness, and alcoholism throughout his life.

Darío was born Félix Rubén García Sarmiento in 1867 to a poor, part-Indian family in rural Nicaragua. He published his first poem at the age of thirteen, and his early promise as a poet won for him scholarships that enabled him to gain an education.

In 1886, Darío left Nicaragua for Santiago, Chile. There, he suffered a life of severe poverty and wrote in obscurity until the publication of *Azul*. Through Darío's friend Pedro Balmaceda, the son of Chile's president, *Azul* came to the attention of Juan Valera, a Spanish critic attentive to South American literature.

Rubén Darío (Hulton Archive/Getty Images)

Valera published an encouraging review in Spain and Latin America in 1889, but although this brought Darío literary recognition, it did little to ease his poverty. In the same year, the poet returned to Central America, where his writing in literary journals and other periodicals won regional fame for him.

In 1892, Darío traveled to Europe as an assistant to a relative who was an official of the Nicaraguan government. He made his first visits to Madrid and to Paris, developing a lifelong love for the artistic communities of Europe. On his return to Central America, Darío called on Rafael Nuñez, a former president of Colombia, who was, like Darío, a writer. Nuñez arranged for a consular appointment for Darío in Buenos Aires, Argentina. Darío remained in Buenos Aires from 1893 to 1898, writing for many Latin American newspapers and other periodicals, including *La nación*, Argentina's most influential newspaper. In the course of his Argentine stay, Darío's literary reputation continued to grow. *Prosas Profanas, and Other Poems*, his second major volume, was published in 1896 and attracted critical attention in Spain and South America alike. Both the work's literary maturity and treatment of erotic themes ensured Darío's notoriety in the Spanish-speaking literary world.

In 1898, Darío returned to Europe as a foreign correspondent for *La nación*. In the course of the following ten years, he became a fixture of the literary life in Spain and France. He collaborated in establishing a number of fledgling literary journals, contributed to periodicals in Europe and Latin America, and produced important works of nonfiction as well as collections of poetry. Despite his commission from *La nación* and appointments to consular positions for Nicaragua in both Paris and Madrid, however, Darío's financial difficulties continued.

In 1907, Darío returned to Nicaragua to an enthusiastic public reception but stayed in his native country only briefly; he remained restless until his death, spending the last ten years of his life traveling throughout Central America and Europe, holding a variety of diplomatic and ceremonial posts, lecturing, and publishing poetry and essays in periodicals of both continents. In 1914, he published his last major work, *Canto a la Argentina, oda a mitre, y otros poemas*, commissioned by

La nación on the occasion of Argentina's centenary of independence.

In 1915, Darío took his last trip home from Europe. His health was poor, and he died the following year in León, Nicaragua, at the age of forty-nine.

ANALYSIS

Rubén Darío is remembered as one of the first poetic voices of postcolonial Latin America, enormously influential as a founder of *Modernismo*. His work, however, underwent constant change, and no single school can claim him. He was acclaimed a Prometheus who brought modern trends of European art to newly independent Latin America; at the same time, he was an innovator in poetic form who exercised a major influence on the poetry of twentieth century Spain. In his later years, Darío retreated from the exotic imagery of *Modernismo* and returned to more traditional Latin American themes, including patriotism and religion.

The birth of *Modernismo* in Latin America coincided with South America's transition from colonialism to independence. The declining influence of Spanish culture made way for new literary sources. Latin American intellectuals had long recognized French culture as the navigational star for their society, which was throwing off the control of monarchies. Thus, in the late nineteenth century, with much of Latin America freed from the cultural sway of Spain, the influence of France was everywhere ascendant, particularly in the universities and in the world of the arts. Darío's work in particular and *Modernismo* in general derived primarily from the interplay between French and Spanish culture, with a rich diversity of other foreign influences.

At its heart, *Modernismo* was an assertion of artistic freedom—the manifesto of those whom Darío described as a "new generation of American writers [with] an immense thirst for progress and a lively enthusiasm." The *Modernistas* idealized art, seeking to range freely for symbolic images in the worlds of the fantastic, the mysterious, and the spiritual. Emphasizing the eclectic internationalism that characterized the movement, Darío spoke of a "close material and spiritual commerce with the different nations of the world."

Darío's work spanned thirty-five years. It consists of thousands of poems, most of them short and many of them in sonnet form. Darío's best-known works also include longer pieces, and his shorter works are sometimes grouped as suites of poems with common themes.

The most common subjects of Darío's poetry are the members of his international family of friends, his romantic loves, and the world of nature. In the tradition of French Parnassianism, he portrayed his subjects through dramatic ideals, using lavish symbolic imagery. Whatever the subject, Darío's portraits are rich in exotic imagery and symbolism. The world of his images is European as much as it is American. In places real and imagined, the reader finds unusual animals and woodland flora, and characters plucked from myth and history. Darío's poetry abounds in allusion, and he often arrays his poetic portraits of the most commonplace themes with the exotic trim of myth and history.

"A VÍCTOR HUGO"

Early evidence of Darío's debt to French art and literature appears in the 1884 poem "A Víctor Hugo" (to Victor Hugo), a paean directed not only to the French master but also to an enumerated multitude of figures who inspired the seventeen-year-old Darío: authors, scientists, and philosophers from Europe and the United States as well as figures from mythology and the Bible. The poem describes the explosion that Hugo touched off in the heart of the self-proclaimed "sad troubadour from the New World." Throughout the work, Darío blends his pious attention to the noise and movement of nature with the voices of myth and history. The influential Spanish critic Juan Valera acknowledged the obvious: The poetry of the young Darío was marked by an immersion in the images and ideas of centuries of Western civilization. Throughout his literary life, Darío wore his new religion proudly.

"A Víctor Hugo" explodes with pithy tributes to Darío's Olympus of heroes. Venus smiles. Apollo discourses with Erato, the Muse of love poetry, and with her sister Muses. Christ preaches and dies. Galileo utters his apocryphal words of defiance ("And still, I say, it moves"). Benjamin Franklin, Robert Fulton, and Ferdinand de Lesseps move Earth with their inspired plans.

International recognition did not immediately follow the publication of "A Víctor Hugo," but the work heralded Darío's fame. In it, he affirmed his proud association with the artist. His profusion of references to the geniuses of Western civilization, too, reflected his captivation by European art and writing. Finally, his portrait of the world was of an extraordinary setting, a site of spectacular animation, anticipating explicitly *Modernista* works. Although emotional and sincere, his descriptions were not so much true to life as true to an ideal.

At the close of "A Víctor Hugo," the New World's sad but well-read troubadour echoes a famous theme of Spain's first poet of the modern era, Gustavo Adolfo Bécquer: the yearning to give voice to the transcendent and the frustration at the limits of language. Darío unconvincingly gasps: "Oh, but I am left breathless at my lyre/ And unable to continue my song." The breathless recollection of Hugo, France's "immortal genius" and "prophet," however, provides a reviving breeze: "Thoughts of your just fame/ Echo in my mind/ And ardor inflames my heart. . . ."

AZUL

The publication of *Azul* in 1888 marked the beginning of Darío's international recognition. An unusual combination of short stories and poetry, the collection revealed not only Darío's ebullience but also his sympathy with Parnassianism, with its exotic symbolism, lavish portrayal of ideals through striking imagery, and departure from metric formalities.

The centerpiece of *Azul* is the suite of four poems that constitute "El año lírico" (the lyrical year), corresponding to the seasons and beginning with spring. The poems describe settings rich in exotic scenery and stirring with activity. "Primaveral" (spring) is by far the most dramatic. It portrays a vast forest alive with the awakening activity of nature. Darío's treatment of the arrival of spring, with suggestions of pagan and mythic ritual, reveals his fascination with a favorite theme of nineteenth and twentieth century European art and literature: the vision of untamed nature as the face of the savage world. The theme received its most celebrated treatment in Igor Stravinsky's ballet *Le Sacre du printemps* (*The Rite of Spring*), which premiered in Paris in 1913. Darío's "Primaveral" begins with an invitation to the same celebration. The poem is composed of six stanzas of nearly uniform length, five of which end with the antiphonal cry: "Oh, my beloved, It is the sweet springtime!" The grand forest hosts the bathing nymphs, a stalking Pan, and the stirring Muses. Throughout the poem, colors flicker in the light. The locusts chirp to the sun, and all of nature highlights the beauty of a woman's face. "Primaveral" is not simply a seasonal celebration of love; the forest is the beautiful face of the world.

Azul also introduced influential formal innovations. The traditional Spanish sonnet of the nineteenth century consisted of rhymed lines with an even distribution of metric feet within the lines. Darío's sonnets generally abide by those conventions, but he experimented with longer lines and innovative patterns of rhyme. His sonnet "Caupolicán" (added to editions of *Azul* after 1890) is an early example. Each of its lines far exceeds the conventional eleven metric feet; in addition, Darío's rhyme scheme is unorthodox, and instead of the usual rhyming device of assonance, he employs sharp, syllabic rhymes. The first quatrain of the sonnet is representative:

> Es algo formidable que vio la vieja raza;
> robusto tronco de árbol al hombro de un campeón
> salvaje y aguerrido, cuya fornida maza
> blandiera el brazo de Hércules, o el brazo de Sansón.

> They saw Something formidable, the now-gone ancient race:
> A robust tree trunk on the shoulder of the champion
> Savage and war-wise with the mighty mace
> Fit for the arm of Hercules or the arm of a Samson.

Azul, if not the first *Modernista* work in Latin America, is a literary landmark and supremely representative of the movement. Its departure from formality and its thematic audacity reveal the literary freedom of what was then a new, and largely young, generation of artists in Latin America, apace of Europe's artistic evolution.

PROSAS PROFANAS, AND OTHER POEMS

With his next major collection, Darío established his reputation as a mature poet and aroused controversy as well. Published in 1896, while Darío was living in Argentina, the work received considerable attention in Spain. Although it developed themes familiar to readers of *Azul*, it also included many poems exalting erotic love. The Spanish poet Pedro Salinas, a Darío partisan, describes the work as the "daydream of a cultured and erotic man."

In exploring sexual themes, Darío was both playful and frank, enhancing his reputation as a libertine and a rascal, and he provoked predictable outrage from some conservative critics. Others saw uncommon beauty and innovation in the work, and *Prosas Profanas, and Other Poems* won acclaim, particularly among young readers in Europe.

One of the best-known poems in the collection *Prosas Profanas, and Other Poems*, "Blasón" ("Blazon") is a panegyric to the swan (*Modernista* doctrine and French Parnassians). The work contributed to one of literary history's most colorful exchanges, a contest between Darío and his contemporary, the Mexican poet Enrique González Martínez, fought by symbolic proxies.

In "Blazon," Darío proudly adopts the swan as his blazon—his emblem. He sings of the swan's haunting unreality and decorative beauty in numerous poems, extolling its mythic and regal qualities—"Olympic is the swan, . . . Wings, short and pure . . . as the sun they seek." In time, the swan became closely associated both with Darío and with *Modernismo*, symbolizing the depiction of the exquisite, for which the *Modernistas* strived.

Some Latin American artists believed that Darío was guilty of excessive fidelity to the symbols, themes, and forms of European art. The growing "New World" movement did not entirely reject *Modernismo* but rather scolded what it perceived as its symbolic excesses and favored development of truly Latin American themes. In his later works, Darío himself showed just such an inclination, but at the height of his swan worship, he was a target of the New World movement.

González Martínez chose to attack the symbol of the swan in his famous repudiation of the elegant excesses of *Modernismo*, "Tuércele el cuello al cisne" ("Wring the Swan's Neck"), something of a New World credo. The 1911 work began, "Wring the neck of the deceitfully-plumed swan/ Who sings his white note to the blue of the fountain." Ironically, by the time "Wring the Swan's Neck" was published, Darío had turned to themes more conspicuously South American, in-cluding traditional Christian subjects and songs to the awakening continent.

CANTOS DE VIDA Y ESPERANZA, LOS CISNES, Y OTROS POEMAS

This growing South Americanism is obvious in the last of Darío's three great collections, *Cantos de vida y esperanza, los cisnes, y otros poemas*. Published when Darío was thirty-eight and in the depths of ill health and despondency, the work was widely acclaimed in Europe and South America and recognized as a new departure for the poet. Although it carries on themes associated with Darío's early works, it also includes a number of poems featuring traditional Christian imagery as well as several political poems—both uncommon in his previous collections.

"A Roosevelt" ("To Roosevelt"), the best known of the *Cantos de vida y esperanza, los cisnes, y otros poemas*, is sharply political. It voices a stern warning to the United States to forswear colonial designs on Latin America. The poem is a confident address to President Theodore Roosevelt, a celebrated big-game hunter, whose personification of the United States is clear.

"To Roosevelt" followed close on the heels of Spanish defeat in the Spanish-American War. Voicing as it did a solemn warning to the United States and a disarming affinity with Spain, the poem did much to enhance the reputation of Darío, then living in Europe, as a spokesperson of Latin America. The poem boasts of the proud Spanish spirit and the strong literary traditions of Latin America—both ironic choices for Darío—as the sources of South America's potential resistance to the United States.

Darío enjoys a lasting place in Hispanic literature. His art reunited Spain and its former empire after the wars of independence. He infused Latin American literature with the cosmopolitanism of the European avant-garde, while his own achievement drew European critical attention to the literary activity of Latin America. He was, to many, the quintessential American artist: an earnest student of tradition and an eager captive of the future.

OTHER MAJOR WORKS

SHORT FICTION: *Cuentos completos de Rubén Darío*, 1950 (Ernesto Mejía Sánchez, editor).

NONFICTION: *La caravana pasa*, 1903; *Tierras solares*, 1904; *Historias de mis libros*, 1914.

MISCELLANEOUS: *Obras desconocidas de Rubén Darío*, 1934 (Raúl Silva Castro, editor); *Escritos inéditos de Rubén Darío*, 1938 (Erwin K. Mapes, editor); *Rubén Darío, Obras completas*, 1950-1953 (5 volumes).

BIBLIOGRAPHY

Acereda, Alberto, and Rigoberto Guevara. *Modernism, Rubén Darío, and the Poetics of Despair*. Lanham, Md.: University Press of America, 2004. An examination of *Moderismo* and how it was expressed in the works of Darío.

LoDato, Rosemary C. *Beyond the Glitter: The Language of Gems in Modernista Writers Rubén Darío, Ramón del Valle-Inclán, and José Asunción Silva*. Lewisburg, Pa.: Bucknell University Press, 1999. A critical study of Latin American and Spanish modernist writers. Includes bibliographical references and index.

Morrow, John A. *Amerindian Elements in the Poetry of Rubén Darío: The Alter Ego as the Indigenous Other*. Lewiston, N.Y.: Edwin Mellen Press, 2008. An analysis of Darío's works that looks at the Indian influence on his work.

Mujica, Barbara. "Uncovering a Literary Treasury." *Americas* 44, no. 2 (1992): 53. A profile of the early modernist magazine *Revista de América* and its publishers, including Rubén Darío.

Solares-Larrave, Francisco. "A Harmony of Whims: Towards a Discourse of Identity in Darío's 'Palabras Liminasies.'" *Hispanic Review* 66, no. 4 (Autumn, 1998): 447-465. An examination of Rubén Darío's ability to manipulate words to evoke a "soul" and to create beauty.

Torres-Rioseco, Arturo. *The Epic of Latin American Literature*. Berkeley: University of California Press, 1964. History and criticism of Latin American literature. Includes commentary on Rubén Darío's poetry and an index.

Watland, Charles. *Poet Errant*. New York: Philosophical Library, 1965. A biography of Darío with bibliographic references.

David Nerkle

CARLOS DRUMMOND DE ANDRADE

Born: Itabira, Brazil; October 31, 1902
Died: Rio de Janeiro, Brazil; August 17, 1987

PRINCIPAL POETRY

Alguma poesia, 1930
Brejo das almas, 1934
Sentimento do mundo, 1940
Poesias, 1942
A rosa do povo, 1945
Poesia até agora, 1947
Claro enigma, 1951
Viola de bolso, 1952
Fazendeiro do ar, 1953
Cincoenta poemas escolhidos pelo autor, 1958
Poemas, 1959
Antologia poética, 1962
Lição de coisas, 1962
In the Middle of the Road, 1965
José e outros: Poesia, 1967
Boitempo, 1968
A falta que ama, 1968
Reunião: 10 livros de poesia, 1969
Seleta em prosa e verso, 1971
As impurezas do branco, 1973
Menino antigo, 1973
Esquecer para lembrar, 1979
The Minus Sign: Selected Poems, 1980
A paixão medida, 1980
Carmina Drummondiana, 1982 (with Silva Belkior)
Nova reunião: 19 livros de poesia, 1983
Corpo, 1984
Sessenta anos de poesia, 1985
Travelling in the Family, 1986
Amar se aprende amanda: Poesia de convívio e de humor, 1987
Poesia errante: Derrames líricos (e outros nem tanto, ou nada), 1988
O amor natural, 1992
José: Novos Poemas, 1993
A paixão medida: Poesia, 1993
Carlos Drummond de Andrade: Poesia, 1994
Poesia completa: Conforme as disposições do autor, 2002

OTHER LITERARY FORMS

In addition to many books of poetry, Carlos Drummond de Andrade (druh-muhnd juhn-DRAH-juh) published three volumes of stories, nine collections of *crônicas* (journalistic "chronicles," or short prose pieces which may take the form of anecdotal narratives or commentary on current events or behavior), and numerous Portuguese translations of works of French literature. The language of many of his prose-narrative poems is closely related to that of his *crônicas*.

ACHIEVEMENTS

In a distinguished career spanning six decades, Carlos Drummond de Andrade produced a formidable body of poetry and prose. Appealing to connoisseurs of literature and the broader public alike, he became one of Brazil's most beloved modern writers. With a vast poetic repertory of considerable thematic and stylistic variety, Drummond is widely regarded as the leading Brazilian poet of the twentieth century; many consider him to be the most important lyrical voice in that nation's entire literary history. He rightly stands alongside the great Portuguese-language poets, the classic Luís de Camões and the modern Fernando Pessoa, as well as the major contemporary Latin American poets Pablo Neruda, César Vallejo, and Octavio Paz.

Brazilian *Modernismo* of the 1920's and 1930's sought to free poetry from the lingering constraints of Parnassian and Symbolist verse. Iconoclast writers combated conservative tradition, infusing poetry with New World awareness and revitalizing lyric through application of avant-garde techniques. Perhaps more than any other poet of *Modernismo*, Drummond was capable of crystallizing the aims of the movement to institute newness and give value to the national variety of the Portuguese language, while forging an intensely personal style with universal scope.

Drummond received numerous literary prizes in Brazil for individual works and overall contribution, including those of the PEN Club of Brazil and the Union of Brazilian Writers. He was twice nominated (in 1972 and 1978) for the Neustadt International Prize for Literature awarded by *World Literature Today*. In his modest way, Drummond refused many other prizes and declined to seek a chair in the Brazilian Academy of Letters. His work has had a tremendous and continuing impact on successive generations of Brazilian artists, influencing emerging lyric poets since the 1930's. On another front, more than seventy musical settings of his poems have been made. Composers inspired by Drummond include the renowned Heitor Villa-Lobos (who set Drummond's poems to music as early as 1926) and the popular vocalist Milton Nascimento. Academic studies of Drummond's work abound; hundreds of articles and dozens of book-length analyses of his poetry have appeared in Brazil.

BIOGRAPHY

Carlos Drummond de Andrade was born in a small town in the interior of Brazil, the ninth son of a rancher with strict traditional values. His rural origins and family life were to be constant sources of inspiration for his poetry. As a rebellious youth, he studied in Belo Horizonte, the capital city of the state, where the family moved in 1920. The young Drummond had already published several items when, in 1922, he became aware of the Modern Art Week in São Paulo, an event that officially launched *Modernismo* as a program of artistic renovation and nationalist spirit.

In 1924, two leaders of the movement from São Paulo, Oswald de Andrade and Mário de Andrade (no relation), took Swiss-French poet Blaise Cendrars on a tour of Brazil; Drummond met them in Belo Horizonte. The young poet from Minas corresponded with Mário de Andrade, one of Brazil's most influential men of culture, until the death of the latter. Still in his home state, Drummond was a cofounder, in 1925, of *A revista* (the review), a modernist organ which lasted through three issues. In the same year, Drummond received a degree in pharmacy, a profession which he never practiced. Instead, he began to earn his living in journalism. In 1928, Oswald de Andrade's radical literary journal *Revista de antropofagia* (review of anthropophagy) published a neoteric poem by Drummond which generated much controversy and some early notoriety for the author. His first two books of verse were published in 1930 and in 1934, the year Drummond moved to Rio de Janeiro, the political and cultural capital of the nation.

In Rio, the writer from Minas served as chief of staff for the minister of health and education and collaborated on magazines and literary reviews. By 1942, he had been contracted by a major publishing house that would regularly publish cumulative editions of the poet's work, affording renewed exposure to poetry that had originally appeared in limited first editions of narrow circulation. Drummond lost his position in the ministry when the government fell in 1945. For a brief period, he was part of the editorial board of the tribune of the Communist Party. Later in that same year, he found work with the directorship of the National Artistic and Historical Patrimony, a bureaucratic position he held until his retirement in 1962.

During his years of public service, Drummond kept up a prolific pace as a journalist, narrator, and poet of diverse talents. In 1954, he obtained a permanent column in a major Rio daily to publish his *crônicas*; he maintained this activity until the early 1980's. Throughout these four decades, the author periodically joined the best of his journalistic prose pieces with other original writings for publication in volumes. A significant part of his wide-ranging recognition and popularity can be attributed to these endeavors. During this time, Drummond's reputation as a poet steadily grew. His work has been translated into Spanish, German, French, Swedish, Bulgarian, Czech, Russian, and English.

ANALYSIS

In 1962, Carlos Drummond de Andrade edited an anthology of his own poetry. Rather than follow a standard chronological sequence or order selections according to the book in which they originally appeared, the author chose poems from each of his collections and organized them into nine representative thematic divisions. This self-characterization reflects, in very general terms, the main preoccupations of Drummond's poetry before and after the publication of the anthology. Each of what the poet calls his "points of departure" or "materials" corresponds to a titled subdivision: the individual ("Um eu todo retorcido," a totally twisted self), the homeland ("Uma província: Esta," a province: this one), the family ("A família que medei," the family I gave myself), friends ("Cantar de amigos," singing of friends), social impact ("Amar-amaro," better-bitter love), knowledge of love ("Uma, duas argolinhas," one, two jousts), lyric itself ("Poesia contemplada," contemplated poetry), playful exercises ("Na praça de conuites," in the square of invitations), and a vision, or attempt, of existence ("Tentativa de exploração e de interpretação do estar-no-mundo," efforts at exploration and interpretation of being-in-the-world).

These are, as the author himself noted, imprecise and overlapping sections. Indeed, any effort at classificatory or chronological categorization of Drummond's poetry, like that of any complex and prolific verse maker, is subject to inconsistencies and inaccuracies. In addition to the wide thematic concerns enumerated above, several stylistic constants run through the whole of Drummond's work. Certain traits of form and content fade and reappear; other aspects merit consideration from a cumulative point of view. There is much transitional overlap between the broadly defined phases of his production. With these caveats in mind, the general lines of Drummond's poetic trajectory can be traced.

His earliest production, in the 1930's, following the antinormative paths of *Modernismo*, is direct, colloquial, and circumstantial. Sarcastic tones abound within a somewhat individualistic focus. Broader perspective is evident in the next stage, in the 1940's, as the poet explores the physical and human world around him. Existential questions are raised within the context of community; social and historical events move the poet, whose own anguish is a reflection of a generalized crisis of consciousness. A third phase, in the 1950's, incorporates personal and social concerns into an all-encompassing consideration of humanity and the environment from a philosophical standpoint. A certain formal rigidity accompanies this more contemplative and speculative poetry.

The development of Drummond's verse from the 1930's to the 1950's reveals, in broad strokes, a process of opening and expansion. This unfolding can be described with a tripartite metaphor of sight and attitude. The dominant voice of the early poetry is ironic yet timid; the poet observes but the lyric vision is uninvolved, hardly surpassing the limits of self. As the poet begins to confront the surrounding world, he looks more intently at the faces of reality. Existential meditations lead to a project of encounter; the struggles of others are seen and internalized. In his most mature stage, the poet not only observes and looks but also contemplates objects and subjects in an effort to see essences or the roots of contradictions. Having developed this broader vision, Drummond returns, in a cycle of books beginning in 1968, to examine his provincial origins. These latest works—in a reflection of the predominance of paradigms over temporal progression in Drummond's work—are permeated with the vigorous irony that characterized his earliest verse.

A thoroughly modern poet, Drummond can be inspired by and effectively use almost any source for his poetry. Much of his raw material is quotidian; the molding of everyday reality into poetic frameworks may be anecdotal or manifest utopian aspirations. One of his notable strengths is the ability to strike a balance between the light, vulgar, direct, or colloquial and the heavy, elevated, evocative, or contemplative. He is at home with the concrete and the abstract, finding the structures of language most adequate for a particular situation. His is a poetry of discovery, whether of a provincial past in its psychic and mythical dimensions or of the relationships and values that form modern society. Drummond's literary discoveries are not presented as truths or absolutes. His poetry is informed by a fundamental skepticism; however, bouts with relativism and anguish do not result in nihilism or cynicism. His lyric universe is fundamentally secular, and his speculative and metaphysical considerations of essences and human experience rarely involve concepts of gods or divinity.

Throughout, there operates a dialectic of inner examination and outward projection, of introspection and denunciation of social problems. Expressions of anguish and impotence unveil emblematic poetic selves threatened by technology and a hostile world. The poet seeks to apprehend the profound sense of unresolved differences and change for the individual, the family and affective relationships, society at large, his nation, and the community of humankind. When he bares himself and his personal psychic states, well-tuned devices filter or block the potential for self-indulgence or confession. The revelation of oppressive senses of reality is related to a view of the human condition, to the crises of modern humanity and civilization. T. S. Eliot said that great poets writing about themselves are writing about

their times. A clear sign of Drummond's greatness is his linkage of substances of private, public, and transcendent planes.

WORDS AND MEANING

A particularly important aspect of Drummond's poetry is the explicit preoccupation with words and expressive means. At the outset, the poet expressed his disquiet through attacks on worn values and stale traditions. As his impulsive impressionism evolved, he undertook an ever-expanding search for nuances, keywords, the secrets of language and its virtualities. Words themselves and the making of poetry are the themes of some of Drummond's most important poems. In such works, the necessity of expression may be played against incommunicability or the imperfections of language. There is no tendency or approach in his poetry without a corresponding questioning of linguistic instruments or the sense of poetry. The modernist period in Western culture has been characterized as the age of criticism. Drummond's poetry is marked by self-consciousness; he is a constant critic of his own art. After *Modernismo* had effectively dissolved as a movement in Brazil, only its most complete poet would be able to write: "And how boring it's become to be modern/ Now I will be eternal."

Drummond's prime linguistic concern is with meaning. In his poetry, conceptual dimensions are generally more important than visuality or sonorousness. Occurrence, idea, and conceit dominate over imagery or symbolism. He seeks to use words in unusual and provocative combinations. Drummond's verse, moreover, is not very musical, in the sense of melodious and harmonious formation of words. There is notable formal variety in the poet's repertory, which incorporates everything from minimalist epigrams to long prose poems, both lyrical and narrative. Much of the poetry seems direct or simple. In the fashion of an Ernest Hemingway character who can "know that it's complicated and write it simple," Drummond, in the realm of poetry, has an uncanny ability to sculpt seemingly spontaneous airs. The simplicity of the poet is deceptive or even duplicitous. While Drummond's customary approach is free verse, he has written in consecrated forms such as the sonnet. He has cultivated the ode, the ballad, and the elegy as well.

MODERNISMO

Drummond's earliest work is written under the sign of *Modernismo* and demonstrates a combative frame of mind with respect to conservative notions of belles lettres associated with Parnassian and Symbolist traditions, long surpassed in Europe but slow to die in South America. Following the Brazilian modernists who preceded him in the 1920's, Drummond sought, once and for all, to pierce the "sacred air" of poetry by abandoning the idea of "noble" thematics and insisting on a more colloquial approach. In 1930, *Modernismo* had already conquered some ground. Thus, Drummond's poetry could not constitute rebellion alone. He was presented with the challenges that liberation presents and had to forge an iconoclasm of the second degree. Drummond succeeded in delivering the coup de grace on propriety, academic language, and mandatory stylization of diction. Humor and irony, never perverse, permeate the early poems, several of which can be called, in the Brazilian fashion, "joke-poems."

"IN THE MIDDLE OF THE ROAD"

Two memorable selections from Drummond's first book, modestly titled *Alguma poesia*, illustrate the poet's characteristically daring and provocative attitudes. In the ten lines of the poem "No meio do caminho" ("In the Middle of the Road"), the speaker simply announces, in a starkly unadorned and repetitive fashion, that he, with "fatigued retinas," will never forget that "there was a stone in the middle of the road." Readers wondered whether the poem was sheer mockery or designed to baffle. Conservative critics laughed at the author, some even suggesting that the poem demonstrated a state of schizophrenia or psychosis. The extent of the controversy enabled Drummond, many years later, to edit a book consisting solely of commentaries and critiques of the neoteric set of verses. On the positive side, the poem can be read as a drama of obsession with ideas or as an expression of a monotonous human condition. It can also represent confrontation with impediments of any kind, be they personal, related to self-fulfillment, or literary (that is, ingrained norms). "In the Middle of the Road" can further be considered as a premonition of the hermetic mode in which Drummond would operate in subsequent poetry.

"POEM OF SEVEN FACES"

Another symptomatic modernist work is the seemingly disjunct "Poema de sete faces" ("Poem of Seven Faces"). The opening lines—"When I was born, a crooked angel/ one of those who live in shadows/ said: Go on, Carlos! be *gauche* in life."—embody senses of repudiation, marginality, and awkwardness that inform the poet's early work and never completely disappear. This is the first presentation of the "twisted self" that inhabits Drummond's poetic world. The penultimate group of verses of the heptagonal poem alludes to a neoclassical poem, well known by Brazilian readers, to present aspects of a new poetics: "World world oh vast world/ If I were called Earl'd/ it would be a rhyme, it wouldn't be a solution." Here Drummond attacks the canons of rhyme and meter as external formalities that restrict expressive plenitude. This aggressive insistence on artistic freedom is again formulated with reference to rhyme in "Considera ção do poema" (consideration of the poem), in which the poet writes that he will not rhyme *sono* (slumber) with "the uncorresponding word" *outono* (autumn) but rather with "the word flesh/ or any other for all are good for me." Such statements should not be misconstrued, for Drummond has utilized delicately all manners of rhyme (verse-initial, verse-final, horizontal, vertical, diagonal, and internal), especially in his middle years. The question is not rhyme per se but the adaptation of form to the exigencies of particular poetic situations. In the early years of modernist enthusiasm, free verse indeed dominates Drummond's output.

NATIONALISM

As for the nationalistic concerns of *Modernismo*, the young Drummond did present a series of poetic snapshots of Brazil, focused on his home state of Minas Gerais, but these poems were not strictly regionalist. Even the validation of national reality did not escape the ironic provocations of the young poet. In a poem titled "Também já fui brasileiro" (I have been Brazilian too), he writes: ". . . I learned that nationalism is a virtue/ But there comes a time when bars close/ and all virtues are denied." Unwillingness to be restricted by the imposition of new values can also be read between lines such as "A garden, hardly Brazilian . . . but so lovely." Drummond's all-encompassing irony is crystalline in a poem called "Hino naçional" (national anthem), which begins, in typical Brazilian modernist fashion "We must discover Brazil!" only to declare, toward the conclusion of this exercise in skepticism, "We must, we must forget Brazil!" This distancing effect is a good measure of the poet's independence and unyielding search for revelations beyond given and constituted frames of reference, above and below evident surfaces.

SOCIAL-HISTORICAL PHASE

The social phase of Drummond's poetry is identifiable not so much by formal development but rather by attitudinal and ideological shifts. The titles of two of his early collections, *Sentimento do mundo* (feeling of the world) and *A rosa do povo* (the people's rose), clearly indicate in what directions the poet moved. Personal and family preoccupations are linked to the surrounding world, as the poet explores the consequences of pragmatism, mechanization, and the reification of humanity. The disquiet of the ironic self gives way to concerns with the other and with more far-reaching societal problems. Within this orientation, one of Drummond's masterpieces is "Canto ao homem do povo Charlie Chaplin" ("Song to the Man of the People C. C."). Harry Levin has written that Chaplin was one of the greatest modernists for his brilliant renderings of the frustrations and incongruities of modern urban life. Drummond, master of Brazilian *Modernismo*, pays homage to that cinematographic genius and incorporates reverberations of his work into a long (226-line) Whitmanesque piece that speaks for the "abandoned, pariahs, failures, downtrodden." In general, Drummond's poetry of this period gives rise to an existential raison d'être that is determined via interaction and giving. Individuality is encompassed by new perspectives: ethics, solidarity with the oppressed and the international community. The symptomatic poem "Os ombros suportam o mundo" ("Shoulders Bear the World") establishes a vital perspective—"Just life without mystifications"—alongside "Mãos dadas" ("Hand in Hand"), which presents the poetic voice of commitment: "I am shackled to life and I see my companions/ They may be taciturn but they nourish great hopes/ It is among them that I consider the enormity of reality." The 1940's were marked by the ravages of world war, and events touched Drummond the poet. The effects of the war in Europe are reflected, for example, in his "Congresso internacional do medo" (international congress of fear). Antifascist positions and socialist sympathies are evident in such representative poems as "Carta a Stalingrado" (letter to Stalingrad) and "Con o russo em Berlin" (with the Russians in Berlin).

"RESIDUE" AND "SEARCH FOR POETRY"

In the midst of this social and historical commotion, Drummond wrote two of his most enduring poems, "Resíduo" ("Residue"), an instigating inventory of emotive and objective presences, and "Procura da poesia" ("Search for Poetry"), which voices an ideal poetics. Here the persona speaks against making poetry of events, feelings, memories, or thoughts. Instead, he advises one to "penetrate quietly the kingdom of words" and contemplate the "thousands of secret faces under the neutral face" of each word. This advice might seem to point out inner contradictions, for much of Drummond's poetry itself derives from the sources he seems to reject. Without discounting a touch of ironic self-commentary, a less literal reading would not hold occurrences, sentiment, recollection, and ideas to be, in themselves, ill-advised for poets. Indeed, unmediated experience will not yield poetry; the true search is for a linguistic craft capable of reformulating experience into viable art.

NEOCLASSICAL PHASE

Formal and thematic properties alike permit establishing a third phase in Drummond's poetic career, beginning in the 1950's and continuing into the next decade. The free-verse and colloquial emphases of his eminently modernist and *engagé* poetry give way to somewhat neoclassical methods. The poet rediscovers the sonnet (and other measured forms) and withdraws from events into a philosophical mode. Reflection on the self, the world, and words takes place at the level of abstract expression. Drummond's confrontation with issues of metaphysics and transcendence signifies an interpretative poetry, which becomes somewhat hermetic. The book titles *Claro enigma* (clear enigma) and *Fazendeiro do ar* (farmer of the air) are suggestive of the evolution of the poet's endeavors, as are the names of specific poems such as "Ser" ("Being"), "Entre o ser e as coisas" ("Between Being and Things"), "Aspiração" ("Aspiration"), "Dissolução" ("Dissolution"), and "Contemplação no banco" ("Contemplation on a Bench"). In this more "pure" poetry, love (carnal and psychic) may constitute a means of sublimation. Consideration of family and of the past may evoke wonder about immortality or heredity as a cognitive category. What Drummond calls the most representative poem of this period, "A máquina do mundo" ("The Machine of the World"), is not to be understood in terms of personal accommodation or social structure but as phenomenological totality with mythical and archetypal dimensions. The poet reports an awakening:

> the machine of the world half-opened
> for whom its breaking was avoiding
> and at the very thought of it moaning . . .
> the whole of a reality that transcends
> the outline of its own image drawn
> in the face of mystery, in abysms . . .

Such poetry of paradox and enigma is also present in *Poemas*, but narrative procedures and concrete referents are reminiscent at times of the more "realistic" poetry of earlier years. The title of the poem "Especulações emtornoda palavra homem" ("Speculations Around the Word Man") suggests its philosophical stance, but rather than affirmations, the poem is made up entirely of questions. In this way, one is reminded of the celebrated poem "José," which portrayed disillusionment and the potential for resignation through a series of questions. "A um hotel em demolição" ("To a Hotel Under Demolition") is a long, digressive work which was inspired by an actual event and has prosaic moments. The wandering poem is anchored at the end of the metaphor of the hotel, as the speaker, who has "lived and unlived" in the "Great Hotel of the World without management," finds himself to be "a secret guest of himself." Here Drummond balances narrative and lyrical impulses, private and social dimensions, as well as observation and contemplation.

LIÇÃO DE COISAS

The two most important selections of *Lição de coisas* (lesson of things), which represents fully the author's mixed style, operate within strict binomial structures. Philosophical speculation is tempered in (by) "A bomba" (the bomb), an extended series of reactions to and statements about atomic explosive devices, the most humbling and frightening invention of modern technology. Each line begins with "the bomb," except the last, in which "man" appears with the hope that he "will destroy the bomb." The realism of this lyric contrasts, but ultimately links, with the experimental "Isso é aquilo" ("this is that). This second work is measured and balanced, consisting of ten numbered sets of ten, two-item lines. The pairs of words or neologisms in each line are determined by free lexical, morphological, or semantic associations, for example, "The facile the fossil/ the missile the fissile. . . . the atom the atone . . . the chastity the castigate . . ." The final two lines have but one item—"the bombix/ the pytx"—and connect the playful linguistic exercise to the thematic of destruction. These two poems reflect how philosophical, humanitarian, and poetically inventive concerns can interpenetrate and synthesize in Drummond's poetry.

BOITEMPO

The publication of *Boitempo* (oxtime) begins a homonymous trilogy that incorporates hundreds of poems. This production constitutes a detailed return to historical roots and rural origins. The poet sets out to explore memories, incidents, and personages of his childhood and adolescence in Minas Gerais, much as he did in the 1930's. Inherent in this project is the potential for self-indulgence, cathartic sentimentalism, or autobiographical nostalgia. However, Drummond undertakes this effort with all the perspective of his varied poetic activities—modernist struggles, committed verse, metaphysical divagations, and metapoetics—and makes poetic distance of the chronological distance that separates him from his material. His moods are serene, and a generalized irony tempers the tenderness of memory. The poet is sufficiently detached to employ light, humorous tones in his review of a parochial (and paternalistic) past. There are certainly literarily self-conscious moments in the flow of Drummond's *Boitempo*. Passages that might appear to be dialogues with what was lived long ago are actually evocations of a literary oeuvre. There are returns to the birth of the "totally twisted self" as well as dramatizations of the genesis of nonconformity and rebelliousness. The poetry's comic character signifies a turning away from problematic relations as the center of poetic concern. Only about a tenth of the first set of the

Boitempo poems are suggestive of Drummond's philosophical muses. The continuation of that mode is to be found in *A falta que ama* (loving lack) and in parts of the brief *A paixão medida* (measured passion).

LEGACY

The contributions of Drummond to the modern art of poetry can be measured in regional, national, continental, and international terms. His regional role in *Modernismo* developed into Brazil's most powerful body of poetry. His reformulation of academic verse as idiomatic lyricism was unique in the diversity of tones, depth of psychological probing, and complexity of thought. With its linguistic flexibility, Drummond's poetry has the eminent capacity to represent metamorphoses, the mobility of sentiment, and the multiplicity of being. In his craft, he achieves a balance of emotion, intelligence, ethical senses, and irony. While Drummond's poetry has been a vehicle for expressions of social awareness, self-discovery, and transcendent inquiry, none of these is more fundamental than the poet's disquiet with the instrument of language itself. Drummond's truest vocation is not the profession of a literary creed or promulgation of any set of ideas but the very uncovering and shaping of words and verbal structures to reflect and explore multiple moods and attitudes.

OTHER MAJOR WORKS

SHORT FICTION: *Contos de aprendiz*, 1951; *70 historinhas*, 1978; *Contos plausíveis*, 1981; *O sorvete e outras histórias*, 1993; *Histórias para o rei: Conto*, 1997; *As palavras que ninguém diz: Crônica*, 1997.

NONFICTION: *Confissões de Minas*, 1944; *Passeios na ilha: Divagaçoes sôbre a vida literária e outras matérias*, 1952; *Fala, amendoeira*, 1957; *Cadeira de balanco*, 1966; *Versiprosa: Crônica da vida cotidiana e de algumas miragens*, 1967; *Caminhos de João Brandão*, 1970; *A bôlsa e a vida*, 1971; *O poder ultra jovem*, 1972; *Os dias lindos*, 1977; *Discurso de primavera e algumas sombras*, 1977; *Setenta historinhas: Antologia*, 1978; *Boca de luar*, 1984; *O observador no escritório*, 1985; *Tempo, vida, poesia: Confissões no rádio*, 1986; *Moça deitada na grama*, 1987; *Conversa de livraria 1941 e 1948*, 2000; *Carlos e Mário: Correspondência completa entre Carlos Drummond de Andrade (inédita) e Mário de Andrade*, 2002 (Lélia Coelho Frota, editor); *Quando é dia de futebol*, 2002.

TRANSLATION: *Fome*, 1963 (of Knut Hamsun).

CHILDREN'S LITERATURE: *Historia de dois amores*, 1985.

EDITED TEXTS: *Rio de Janeiro em prosa e verso*, 1965 (with Manuel Bandeira); *Minas Gerais*, 1967; *Uma pedra no meio do caminho: Biographia de um poema*, 1967.

BIBLIOGRAPHY

Armstrong, Piers. *Third World Literary Fortunes: Brazilian Culture and Its International Reception*. Lewisburg, Pa.: Bucknell University Press, 1999. Contrasts Brazilian writers with their Spanish American counterparts and compares Drummond's poetic persona to such "paradigmatic antiheroes" as T. S. Eliot and Franz Kafka.

Di Antonio, Robert Edward. "The Confessional Mode as a Liberating Force in the Poetics of Carlos Drummond de Andrade." *Quaderni Ibero-Americani* 8, nos. 61/62 (December/January, 1986/1987): 201-207. Considers Drummond an existentialist with a personal, often humorous vision of the absurdity of existence.

Lima, Luiz Costa. "Carlos Drummond de Andrade." In *Latin American Writers*. Vol. 2. New York: Charles Scribner's Sons, 1989. This lengthy essay discusses Drummond's early work in the context of conflicting aspects of Brazilian *Modernismo*, his later work as evidence of "the corrosion principle," and his even later work as the "postcorrosion phase," in which memory is privileged over history.

Roncador, Sonia. "Precocious Boys: Race and Sexual Desire in the Autobiographical Poems of Carlos Drummond de Andrade." *Afro-Hispanic Review* 27, no. 2 (Fall, 2008): 91-115. Roncador discusses the relationships between boys in privileged households and the black maids and other servants, using numerous poems by Drummond.

Sternberg, Ricardo da Silveira Lobo. *The Unquiet Self: Self and Society in the Poetry of Carlos Drummond de Andrade*. Valencia, Spain: Albatros/Hispanófila, 1986. Analyzes Drummond's work as representing the inherent conflict in the relationship between self and others, and the tendency toward both withdrawal from and engagement with the world.

_____. "The World Within: Carlos Drummond de Andrade's *Alguma poesia*." *Luso-Brazilian Review* 21, no. 2 (Winter, 1984): 57-69. Focusing on Drummond's "first phase," from 1930 to 1945, Sternberg examines *o choque social*, or social shock inherent in the conflicts between individual and society, self and others, in Drummond's poetry.

Vargas, Claret M. "A Poetics of Bafflement: Ethics and the Representation of the Other in Carlos Drummond de Andrade's Poetry." *Neophilologus* 92, no. 8 (July, 2008): 457-470. Explores the self and the Other in three poems by Drummond: "Menino Chorando na Noite," "O Operário no Mar," and "Jose."

Charles A. Perrone

———

Du Fu

Born: Gongxian, China; 712
Died: Tanzhou (now Changsha), Hunan Province, China; 770
Also known as: Tu Fu

Principal poetry

Quan Tang shi, 1706
Tang shi san bai shou, 1763 (*The Jade Mountain: A Chinese Anthology*, 1929)
Tu Fu: Selected Poems, 1962 (Zhi Feng, editor; Rewi Alley, translator)
The Selected Poems of Du Fu, 2002 (Burton Watson, translator)
Du Fu: A Life in Poetry, 2008
Spring in the Ruined City: Selected Poems, 2008

Other literary forms

Du Fu (dew few) is known primarily for his poetry. The 1,450 poems he wrote have been collected through the years in frequently revised and reprinted anthologies and collections such as *Quan Tang shi* and *The Jade Mountain*.

Achievements

Born during the Tang Dynasty (618-907), the classical period in Chinese literary history, Du Fu was one of four poets whose greatness marked the era. Some fifty thousand poems from that period have survived, the large number resulting primarily from the talents of Du Fu; Wang Wei, basically a nature poet; Bo Juyi, a government official whose poetry often reflected official concerns; and Li Bo, probably the best known of all Chinese poets, a poet of the otherworldly or the sublime.

Du Fu sums up the work of all these poets with the wide range of topics and concerns that appear in his poems. Known variously as "poet-historian," "poet-sage," and "the Master," Du Fu may be China's greatest poet. His "Yue ye" ("Moonlit Night") is perhaps the most famous poem in Chinese literature. His more than fourteen hundred extant poems testify to his productivity; the range of topics in his poetry and the variety of verse that he employed constitute Du Fu's main contribution to Chinese literature.

One of Du Fu's major contributions to Chinese literature was his extensive occasional verse—poems inspired by a journey or by a mundane experience such as building a house. Many of Du Fu's occasional poems were addressed to friends or relatives at some special time in their lives. Distant relatives who held official positions and achieved distinction would receive a laudatory poem. These poems could also be addressed to special friends. Du Fu traveled much in his life, both by choice and involuntarily, relying on friends to shelter and support him, because, for the majority of his life, he was without an official governmental position and salary. His poems would therefore be addressed to these persons as expressions of gratitude and friendship on the occasion of his visit.

Poems about nature abounded during the Tang period, and Du Fu contributed extensively to this genre as well. In contrast to Li Bo, who followed the Daoist philosophy of withdrawal from the world, Du Fu was very much a poet of everyday life, both in his response to nature and the physical world and in his active engagement in the social and political life of his times. Indeed, it has been said that Du Fu's poetry provides a running history of the Chinese state during his era.

Finally, Du Fu was a master of poetic form; his verse forms were as varied as his content. During the Tang period, the *gutishi* (old forms) in Chinese poetry coexisted with the *lushi* (new forms). The old, or "un-regulated," forms placed no restrictions on the word tones used in the verse, did not limit the number of lines in a poem, and did not require verbal parallelism. The new forms, or "regulated verse," however, were much more demanding. They mandated certain tonal patterns, especially in rhyme words, a requirement which markedly affected word choice. They also usually restricted the total number of lines in a poem and utilized verbal parallelism. Each of these two major categories of Chinese poetry was also divided into subcategories depending on the meter, which in Chinese poetry depends on the number of words in each line rather than on stressed and unstressed syllables, as in Western poetry. Du Fu adeptly used both old and new forms in his verse, justifying in this respect as in every other his reputation as "the Master."

BIOGRAPHY

Du Fu's life could best be described as one of frustration. Although his mother's family was related to the imperial clan, and both his father and grandfather held official positions in the government, much of Du Fu's life was spent in poverty. Unable to pass the examination for entrance into official service, Du Fu remained, more often than not, a "plain-robed" man, a man without official position and salary. His poems from the mid-730's allude to "the hovel" in which he lived on the outskirts of the capital while the court members resided in the splendor of the palace. One of Du Fu's sons died from starvation in 755 because of the family's poverty, and the poet's sadness and anguish caused by his son's death is reflected in several of Du Fu's poems.

Du Fu was born in Gongxian, Henan Province, in 712. His natural mother died at an early age, and Du Fu's father remarried, eventually adding three brothers and a sister to the family. Du Fu was apparently a very precocious child. In his autobiography, he states unabashedly that

at the age of seven he pondered "only high matters" and wrote verses about beautiful birds, while other children his age were dealing with puerile subjects such as dogs and cats. At an early age, Du Fu also mastered a great number of the characters which make up written Chinese. He was writing so extensively by the age of nine, he claims, that his output could easily have filled several large bags. Not much else is known about Du Fu's early years. As would be expected, he was schooled in literary matters in preparation for entrance into official service. A firsthand knowledge of the many facets of Chinese life and the geography of the country also became a part of Du Fu's education: He traveled for about three years before taking the official examination for public service. His poetry of this period reflects the experiences and sights he encountered while traversing the countryside.

In 735, at the age of twenty-three, Du Fu finally took the test to enter government service and failed. Appar-

Du Fu (The Granger Collection, New York)

ently there was something in Du Fu's writing style, in the way he handled the Chinese characters, which did not suit the examiners. This setback in Du Fu's plans ushered in the first of several important phases in his life. Since the poet had failed the examination and was without a position, he resumed his travels. During these travel years, several significant changes occurred in his life. His father died in 740, which prompted a series of poems on the theme of life's impermanence. This event was followed by Du Fu's marriage to a woman from the Cui clan, a marriage which ultimately produced two sons and four daughters for the poet. Finally, and probably most important in terms of his literary work, Du Fu met Li Bo in 744.

Following the Daoist tradition, Li Bo, who was ten years Du Fu's senior, had become a "withdrawn" poet after his banishment from the court. As such, he represented a viewpoint opposite to that of Du Fu concerning a literate man's obligations to Chinese society at that time. Du Fu's poetry exhibits his grappling with these contending views. He was sometimes attracted to the simple lifestyle of Li Bo, but the Confucian ethic under which Du Fu had been reared persevered, and he returned to the capital in 746, eleven years after his first attempt, to repeat the test for an official position. He failed again; this time, according to the historians, one of the emperor's officials was afraid that new appointees to the bureaucracy would weaken the latter's power in the court, so he saw to it that everyone who took the examination failed. The frustration and humiliation resulting from this second failure to pass the examination, perhaps heightened by the fact that his younger brother had passed the examination earlier, did not seem to deter Du Fu from his goal of securing an official post. Although he was forced to move outside the capital with his family and to rely on support from friends and relatives to survive, Du Fu seemingly resolved to gain an official position through another route, this time by ingratiating himself with important people who could aid his quest.

Wei Ji was one such person. As an adviser to the emperor, he was in a position to help Du Fu when the occasion arose. Du Fu was also well acquainted with Prince Li Jin, a pleasure-loving, undisciplined figure who was an embarrassment to the court. The prince had a great appreciation for literature, however, and after Du Fu wrote several poems dealing with "The Eight Immortals of the Wine Cup," as the prince and his coterie were called, the prince took a special liking to the poet. Because of these friendships, Du Fu's name was heard around the court, and when he wrote the "Three Great Ceremonies" poems, their excellence and their laudatory treatment of the emperor engendered imperial recognition and favor. A third examination for an official position ensued as a result. Whether Du Fu passed or failed this one was of little consequence; finally, at the age of forty-four, he was given an official position by imperial decree. (Li Bo's position with the court had also been established by imperial decree because he had refused to take the civil-service exam as a matter of principle.) Ironically, Du Fu refused the position. It apparently involved moving to a distant western district, and because the position required him to be a part of the police administration, it would also have involved beating people for infractions of the law, something Du Fu was not inclined to do. The poet's refusal found some sympathy in the court, and he was appointed instead to the heir apparent's household. Thus, the years 755 and 756 stand as pivotal ones in Du Fu's life: He received his first official position in the government after many years of struggle, and strangely enough, he gave up that position because he rapidly grew to dislike the servile aspects of the job. Amid all this, the An Lushan Rebellion began.

For the remainder of his life, Du Fu was one of the many who endured the misfortunes of this war. When the rebellion began in 756, the emperor was forced to flee the capital, as did Du Fu. The latter's poems from that period depict the many defeats of the imperial army. Once he had established his family in the relative safety of Fuzhou in the north, Du Fu set out to join the Traveling Palace of the displaced emperor, but he was captured by rebel forces and taken back to the capital, which they occupied. Held by the rebels for several months, he finally escaped and joined the Traveling Palace as a censor, an official responsible for reminding the emperor of matters which required his attention. During this period, Du Fu did not hear from his family for more than a year, and he wrote possibly the most famous poem in Chinese literature, a love poem to his wife and children entitled "Moonlit Night."

The capital was retaken the next year, 757, and Du Fu was reunited with his family. His "Journey North" describes the effects of the war on the Chinese people and countryside, as well as his homecoming to his family. With the government reestablished in the capital, Du Fu returned there with his family for official service. This period of service was also short-lived; he once again grew tired of the bureaucratic life and its constraints. Floods and the war had devastated the countryside around the capital, so Du Fu took his family west to flee the war and to find food. The war, however, also spread to the west, and as a result, Du Fu once again shifted his family, this time southward to Zhengdu, five hundred miles from the fighting.

The time he spent in the south has been labeled Du Fu's "thatched hut" period. This was something of a pastoral period in his life, during which he seemed to emulate Li Bo and the Daoist ethic to some degree. The war, however, persisted both in the countryside and in Du Fu's poems. The rebellion finally spread even to the south, and Du Fu was forced to leave his thatched hut in 765. He spent the remaining five years of his life in restless travel, cataloging in poetry his journeys and the events he witnessed. Du Fu, "the Master," died in 770, at the age of fifty-eight, as he traveled the Xiang River looking for a haven from the ill health and ill times which had beset him.

ANALYSIS

Du Fu's poetry deals with a multitude of concerns and events. His verses express the moments of self-doubt and frustration which plagued the poet, such as when he failed the civil-service examinations or when he became increasingly afflicted by physical ailments later in life, referring to himself in one verse as an "emaciated horse." Du Fu's poems also deal with painting and the other arts, and they often employ allusions to outstanding figures in China's literary and political past to comment on contemporary conditions. It is, however, in his poems addressed to family and friends and in his nature poems that the substance and depth of his verse can be most clearly seen.

Among Du Fu's finest poems are those which ex-press his love for friends and family. Poems addressed to friends constituted both a literary and a social convention in China during the Tang period. In literate society, men sought one another for friendship and intellectual companionship, and poems of the "address and answer" variety were often composed by the poet. Several examples occur in the poems which Du Fu wrote either to or about Li Bo, his fellow poet. After the two met in 744, they traveled together extensively, and a firm bond, both personal and scholarly, was established between them. In one poem commemorating the two poets' excursion to visit a fellow writer, Du Fu explained his feeling toward Li Bo: "I love my Lord as young brother loves elder brother/ . . . Hand in hand we daily walk together." In "A Winter Day," Du Fu writes that "Since early dawn I have thought only of you [Li Bo]," thoughts which may have been both pleasant and painful for Du Fu as he grappled with the question of whether he wanted to continue his quest for a governmental position or follow Li Bo's example and become a "withdrawn" poet. Du Fu also highly praised Li Bo's verses. In a later poem, "the Master" laments the fact that Li Bo has become unstable, but he also rejoices in the gift of Li Bo's talent: "My thoughts are only of love for his talent./ Brilliant are his thousand poems."

The concern and admiration which Du Fu felt and expressed poetically were not directed solely to other poets. Many of his poems of this type were addressed to longtime friends. "Zeng Wei ba chu shi" ("For Wei Ba, in Retirement") is one example which not only expresses Du Fu's friendship for Wei Ba but also describes the life stages the two have passed through together. The poet comments on how briefly their youth lasted, observing that "Though in those days you were not married/ Suddenly sons and daughters troop in." The two friends have not seen each other for twenty years, "both our heads have become grizzled," and Du Fu knows that the next day will separate them again. He is elated, however, by the "sense of acquaintance" his friend revives in him, and the poet captures that sense in his verse.

"MOONLIT NIGHT"

Du Fu was separated from his family several times, sometimes by the war, sometimes by economic conditions. His most famous poem, "Moonlit Night," expresses his deep concern for his wife as "In her chamber she alone looks out/ . . . In the sweet night her cloud-like tresses are damp/ In the clear moonlight her jade-like arms are cold." The poet wonders how long it will be before ". . . we two nestle against those unfilled curtains/ With the moon displaying the dried tear-stains of us both?" Essentially a love poem for the poet's wife, "Moonlit Night" was an unconventional work in its time. Wives in ancient China were seen primarily as pieces of reproductive machinery, with no intellectual capabilities. A poet might lavish great sentiment in verse on a male companion, but tender thoughts concerning a wife were rarely expressed in poetry.

"The River by Our Village"

In true classical fashion, Du Fu was also a nature poet. He could portray nature in an idyllic vein, as in "The River by Our Village," in which the poet describes how "Clear waters wind around our village/ With long summer days full of loveliness/ Fluttering in and out from the house beams the swallows play/ Waterfowl disport together as everlasting lovers." These lines reflect the contentment of Du Fu's pastoral or "thatched hut" period; he ends the poem by asking: "What more could I wish for?"

"The Winding River"

While many of Du Fu's nature poems are distinguished by their vivid evocation of landscapes and wildlife for their own sake, he also treats nature symbolically. In "The Winding River," falling blossoms signify the changing of the seasons and cause the poet to ". . . grieve to see petals flying/ Away in the wind. . . ." This evidence of mutability engenders further reflection; as the poet watches "Butterflies going deeper and deeper/ In amongst the flowers, dragonflies/ Skimming and flicking over the water," he is reminded that "Wind, light, and time ever revolve," that the only constant factor in life is change. In turn, the poet is led to reflect on the inconsequential and often futile nature of his and other men's ambitions: ". . . why should I be lured/ By transient rank and honours?" Nature instructs him ". . . to live/ Along with her" in a rich and full harmony rather than existing in the pale semblance of living which men have created for themselves.

Because of the range of his sympathy, Du Fu has been compared to William Shakespeare: Both were able to encompass in their works the whole teeming life of their times. Although Du Fu's declaration "In poetry I have exhausted human topics" may seem an overstatement, his many poems and their varied concerns seem almost to justify such a claim.

Bibliography

Chou, Eva Shan. *Reconsidering Tu Fu*. 1995. Reprint. New York: Cambridge University Press, 2006. Chou examines the styles and techniques of Du Fu's poetry as well as his literary legacy. Contains some translations of poems. Bibliography and index.

Davis, A. R. *Tu Fu*. New York: Twayne, 1971. General and concise, addressing simply the often complicated problems of form and theme.

Du Fu. *The Selected Poems of Du Fu*. Translated by Burton Watson. New York: Columbia University Press, 2002. A collection of Du Fu's poems, translated into English by a noted specialist on China. The introduction provides a great deal of biological and background information.

_____. *The Selected Poems of Tu Fu*. Translated by David Hinton. New York: New Directions, 1989. A collection of Du Fu's poetic works, translated into English.

Hawkes, David. *A Little Primer of Tu Fu*. Oxford, England: Clarendon Press, 1967. Written for readers who know little Chinese. The volume contains the texts of thirty-five of Du Fu's poems in Chinese characters and Pinyin romanization, with descriptions in English of titles, subjects, and poetic forms followed by exegeses and translations. Can be employed as a very useful textbook.

Hung, William. *Tu Fu: China's Greatest Poet*. New York: Russell and Russell, 1969. The most valuable study in English. Clear and highly readable, it includes a volume of notes and incorporates translations of 374 poems.

McCraw, David R. *Du Fu's Laments from the South*. Honolulu: University of Hawaii Press, 1992. An examination of Du Fu's travels in Sichuan and his poetic output. Bibliography and indexes.

Pine, Red, trans. *Poems of the Masters: China's Clas-*

sic Anthology of T'ang and Sung Dynasty Verse. Port Townsend, Wash.: Copper Canyon Press, 2003. A collection of poetry from the Tang and Song Dynasties that includes the work of Du Fu. Indexes.

Seaton, J. P., and James Cryer, trans. *Bright Moon, Perching Bird: Poems by Li Po and Tu Fu.* Scranton, Pa.: Harper & Row, 1987. This work, part of the Wesleyan Poetry in Translation series, features the works of Li Bo and Du Fu, two Tang poets. Provides some information on Tang Dynasty poetry.

Seth, Vikram, trans. *Three Chinese Poets: Translations of Poems by Wang Wei, Li Bai, and Du Fu.* Boston: Faber and Faber, 1992. A collection of poems by Du Fu, Li Bo, and Wang Wei. Commentary provides useful information.

Kenneth A. Howe

E

SERGEI ESENIN

Born: Konstantinovo (now Esenino), Ryazan
province, Russia; October 3, 1895
Died: Leningrad, Soviet Union (now St. Petersburg,
Russia); December 28, 1925

PRINCIPAL POETRY

Radunitsa, 1915 (*All Soul's Day*, 1991)
Goluben', 1918 (*Azure*, 1991; includes
     "Preobrazhenie," "Transfiguration";
     "Prishestvie," "The Coming"; and
     "Inonia")
Ispoved' khuligana, 1921 (*Confessions of a
     Hooligan*, 1973)
Pugachov, 1922
Stikhi skandalista, 1923
Moskva kabatskaia, 1924
Anna Snegina, 1925
"Cherni chelovek," 1925
Persidskie motivi, 1925
Rus' sovetskaia, 1925
Strana sovetskaia, 1925
Sobranie sochinenii, 1961-1962 (5 volumes)
Selected Poetry, 1982
Complete Poetical Works in English, 2008

OTHER LITERARY FORMS

Sergei Esenin (yihs-YAYN-yihn) wrote little besides poetry. Some autobiographical introductions and
a few revealing letters are helpful in analyzing his poetry. The short story "Bobyl i druzhok" and the tale
"Yar" are rarely mentioned in critical discussion of
Esenin's work, but his theoretical treatise "Kliuchi
Marii" (1918; the keys of Mary) helps to explain his
early revolutionary lyrics. This economically written,
perceptive study traces the religious origins of various
aspects of ancient Russian culture and art.

ACHIEVEMENTS

Perhaps the most controversial of all Soviet poets,
Sergei Esenin is certainly also one of the most popular,
among both Russian émigrés and citizens. The popularity of his poetry never diminished in Russia, despite
a period of twenty-five years during which his work
was suppressed and his character defamed. Officially,
Esenin was labeled the Father of Hooliganism, and his
works were removed from public libraries and reading
rooms. In the early 1950's, however, his reputation was
fully rehabilitated, and his poems have become widely
available in Russia. In the twenty-first century, Esenin
rivals Aleksandr Blok, Vladimir Mayakovsky, and even
Alexander Pushkin as the most popular of all Russian
poets.

Although Esenin welcomed and supported the 1917
October Revolution, he soon began to have second
thoughts. He did not like the transformation that was
taking place in the rural areas, and he longed for the traditional simple peasant life and the old "wooden Russia." His flamboyant lifestyle, his alcoholism, and his
dramatic suicide eventually brought him the scorn of
the Soviet authorities.

The most important representative of the Imaginist
movement in Russian poetry, Esenin at his best achieved
a distinctive blend of deep lyricism, sincerity, melancholy, and nostalgia. Calling himself "the last poet of
the village," Esenin used folk and religious motifs, images of nature, and colorful scenes from everyday village life, which he painted with a natural freshness and
beauty. His disappointment with his own life, his unhappy marriages, and his apprehensions concerning the
changes he saw at every hand—all are reflected in the
mood of unfulfilled hope and sadness that pervades his
poetry.

BIOGRAPHY

Sergei Aleksandrovich Esenin was born in the small
village of Konstantinovo, since renamed Esenino in the
poet's honor, in the fertile Ryazan province. His parents were poor farmers, and because his mother had
married against the will of her parents, the Titovs, the
couple received no support from their families. Esenin's father had to go to Moscow, where he worked in a
butcher shop, in order to send home some money.

When he stopped sending the money, his wife had no other choice but to find work as a live-in servant. Her parents at last decided to help and took the young boy to live with them.

Esenin's grandfather, Feodor Andreevich Titov, belonged to a religious sect known as the Old Believers; he frequently recited religious poems and folk songs, and he approached life with an optimistic vigor. Esenin's grandmother sang folk songs and told her grandson many folktales. Both grandparents adored the young Esenin, who lived a happy and relatively carefree life. They made a great impression on the young boy.

From 1904 to 1909, Esenin attended the village school, where, with little effort, he graduated with excellent marks. His grandfather Titov decided that Esenin should become a teacher and sent him to the church-run Spas-Klepiki pedagogical school from 1909 to 1912. At first, Esenin was extremely unhappy in the new surroundings; he even ran away once and walked forty miles back to his grandparents' home. Eventually, however, he became reconciled to his fate, and he was noticed by his teachers and peers for the unusual ease with which he wrote poetry. The boy with the blond, curly hair became self-confident and even boastful, which made him unpopular with some of his fellow students.

At the age of sixteen, after his graduation in 1912, Esenin decided not to continue his studies at a teacher's institute in Moscow. Instead, he returned to his grandparents' home and devoted his life to poetry. He was happy to be free to roam aimlessly through the fields and the forests, and his early poems reflect his love for animals and for the rural landscape. Although he also used religious themes in his early poems, Esenin was probably not very religious, certainly not as devoted as his grandfather. He was, however, very familiar with the religious traditions of the Old Believers and with the patriarchal way of life.

Esenin realized that to become known as a poet, he had to move to a big city. In 1912, he moved to Moscow, taking a job in the butcher's shop where his father worked. He disliked the job but soon found work as a bookstore clerk, where he was happier. Esenin also joined the Surikov circle, a large group of proletarian and peasant writers.

Esenin lost his job in the bookstore, but in May of 1913, he became a proofreader in a printing shop. The work strengthened his interest in the labor movement, and though he never completely accepted the ideology of the Social Revolutionary Party, he distributed illegal literature and supported other revolutionary activities. To learn more about history and world literature, Esenin took evening courses at the Shaniavski People's University in Moscow. With his goal of becoming a great poet, he recognized the need to broaden his education.

The foremost Russian writers of the time, however, lived in St. Petersburg rather than in Moscow, and in March of 1915, Esenin moved to Petrograd (as St. Petersburg was known between 1914, when Russia went to war against Germany, and 1924, when it became Leningrad). Upon his arrival, Esenin went to see Blok, who helped the young "peasant" and introduced him to well-known poets such as Zinaida Gippius, Feodor Sologub, and Vyacheslav Ivanov and to novelists such as Ivan Bunin, Aleksandr Kuprin, and Dmitry Merezhkovsky. The young poet Anatoly Mariengof became Esenin's intimate friend. Esenin was appointed as an editor of the political and literary journal *Severnie Zapiski*, an appointment that brought him in contact with other writers and intellectuals. Through the help of a fellow peasant poet, Nikolai Klyuyev, Esenin met the publisher M. V. Averyanov, who published Esenin's first volume of poems, *All Soul's Day*, in 1915.

In the autumn of 1915, Esenin was drafted into the army, which for him was a tragedy. He agonized in the dirty barracks and under the commands of the drill sergeant. Eventually, he succeeded in being transferred to the Commission of Trophies, a special unit for artists, but he neglected his duties so flagrantly that he was ordered to a medical unit stationed near the czar's residence in Tsarskoe Selo. The czarina discovered that the young poet was stationed nearby and invited him to the court to read his poetry. Esenin was flattered, but he also carried in his heart a deep hatred for the monarchy. Under some still unclear circumstances, Esenin left Tsarskoe Selo before February of 1917, and in 1918 he published his second volume of poetry, *Azure*.

In August of 1917, Esenin married Zinaida Raikh, who was then working as a typist for a newspaper published by the Socialist Revolutionary Party. The marriage ended in divorce in October, 1921, following the birth of two children. Raikh, who subsequently became a famous actress, married the great theatrical director Vsevolod Meyerhold. Esenin maintained ties with Raikh until the end of his life, and the dissolution of his first marriage established the pattern that was to mark his last years.

In 1918, however, Esenin was hopeful and ambitious, on the verge of fame. In March of 1918, he again moved to Moscow and continued to write optimistic, mythical poetry about the future of Russia. He tried to understand the revolution, although he abhorred the suffering it brought. In late 1918, during a visit to his native Konstantinovo, Esenin observed the passivity of the peasants. With the poem "Inonia," he tried to incite them to positive action.

During this period, Esenin, with several minor poets such as Mariengof, formed a literary movement known as Imaginism. The Imaginists (*imazhinisty*) had been inspired by an article about the Imagist movement in English and American poetry, founded by Ezra Pound. Except for the name, however, and—more important—the doctrine that the image is the crucial component of poetry, there was little connection between Pound's Imagism and the Russian Imaginism. For Esenin, the movement encouraged liberation from the peasant themes and mythical religiosity of his early verse. In addition, as is evident in the Imaginist manifesto of 1919, the movement was useful in attracting publicity, of which Esenin was very conscious.

In the fall of 1921, at a studio party, Esenin met the well-known American dancer Isadora Duncan, who was giving a series of dance recitals in Russia. Although Esenin spoke no English and Duncan knew only a few phrases in Russian, they found enough attraction in each other for Esenin to move immediately into Duncan's apartment. The turbulence of the relationship became notorious. In 1922, Duncan needed to raise money for her new dancing school in Moscow. She wanted to give a series of dance recitals in Western Europe and in the United States, but she also realized the difficulties she and Esenin would face in the United States if they were not legally married. On May 2, 1922, they were married, and Esenin became the first (and the only legal) husband of Duncan.

The United States disappointed Esenin. He could not communicate, and even Prohibition did not slow down his acute alcoholism. In the United States, he was seen merely as the husband of Duncan, not as a famous Russian poet. The skyscrapers could not replace the gray sky over the Russian landscape. After a nervous breakdown, Esenin returned alone to Russia, and when Duncan returned some time later, he refused to live with her again.

After his return to the Soviet Union, Esenin became increasingly critical of the new order. He was never able to accept the atmosphere of cruelty and destruction during the civil war, and the ruthless law of vengeance carried out by many fanatics, even after the war, was criminal in his eyes. It was difficult for Esenin both as an individual and as a poet to conform to Lenin's new economic policy period. To some extent, he regarded this difficulty as a personal failure and reacted to it with spells of depression alternating with outbursts of wild revelry. He styled himself a "hooligan," and he excused his heavy drinking, drug taking, barroom brawls, blasphemous verse, and all-night orgies as fundamentally revolutionary acts.

At the same time, Esenin saw himself as a prodigal son. He yearned for motherly love, the healing touch of nature, and the peaceful countryside. In 1924, he returned to his native village, but he could not find the "wooden Russia" that he had once glorified in his poems. *Rus' sovetskaia* (Soviet Russia), his famous poem of 1925, expresses his isolation in his own country. The revolution had not fulfilled Esenin's dreams of a rural utopia, and he, "the last poet of the village," was among its victims.

From September, 1924, until February, 1925, Esenin visited Baku and the Crimea, a trip that resulted in the publication of the collection *Persidskie motivi* (Persian motifs). In 1925, he married Sofya Tolstaya, one of Leo Tolstoy's granddaughters. The marriage was predictably unhappy; Esenin's deteriorating health caused him to be admitted repeatedly to hospitals. He managed to write the somewhat autobiographical long poem *Anna Snegina*, which describes the fate of the prerevolutionary people in the new Soviet society. The poor reception of the poem and the harsh criticism it provoked devastated Esenin.

The poet began to mention suicide more frequently. Even though his physical health improved, Esenin remained very depressed. In December of 1925, he left his wife in Moscow and went to Leningrad, where he stayed at the Hotel Angleterre. He was there for several days and was frequently visited by friends. On December 27, Esenin cut his arm and in his own blood wrote his last poem, "Do svidan'ia, drug moi, do svidan'ia . . ." ("Good-bye, My Friend, Good-bye"); later that day, Esenin gave the poem to friends (who neglected to read it) and showed the cut to them, complaining that there was no ink in his room. In the early hours of December 28, the poet hanged himself on a radiator pipe.

Esenin's widow arrived the next day and took her husband's body in a decorated railroad car to Moscow. In Moscow, thousands of people waited for the arrival of the train. Fellow writers and artists carried the coffin from the train station to its temporary resting place in a public building, where thousands more paid their last respects. Esenin was buried on the last day of 1925.

ANALYSIS

Sergei Esenin's poetry can be divided into two parts: first the poetry of the countryside, the village, and the animals and, second, the primarily postrevolutionary poetry of *Moskva kabatskaia* (Moscow the tavern city) and of *Rus' sovetskaia*. Generally, the village poetry is natural and simple, while many of the later poems are more pretentious and affected. The mood of country landscapes, the joys of village life, and the love for animals is created with powerful melodiousness. The poet's sincere nostalgia for "wooden Russia" is portrayed so strongly that it becomes infectious. Esenin creates idylls of the simple Russian village and of country life with the freshness of a skilled painter, yet the musicality of his verse is the most characteristic quality of his poetry. His simple, sweet, and touching early lyrics are easy to understand and are still loved by millions of readers in Russia.

As a "peasant poet," Esenin differed from some other Russian peasant poets of the time, such as Nikolai Klyuyev and Pyotr Oreshin. Esenin stressed primarily the inner life of the peasant, while the others paid more attention to the peasants' environment. His peasants are free of material things, even though they are part of

their environment, while in the work of other peasant poets, things are preeminent.

Esenin's early poems chiefly employ the vocabulary of the village; they reveal the influence of the *chastushki*, the popular folk songs widely heard in any Russian village. When he arrived in Petrograd, Esenin presented himself as "the poet of the people"; dressed in a peasant blouse adorned with a brightly colored silk cord, he chanted his poems about harvests, rivers, and meadows.

When Esenin moved to Petrograd, he began to learn the sophisticated techniques of the Symbolists, particularly from the poet Blok. Esenin was able to create a complete picture of a landscape or a village with a single image. He continued, however, to maintain the melancholy mood and the sadness that would always be typical of his poetry.

At the time of his suicide, Esenin was still quite popular, both in the Soviet Union and among Russian émigrés. Beginning in 1926, the State Publishing House published Esenin's collected works in four volumes, but many poems were missing from this edition. By that time, the "morally weak Eseninism" had been officially denounced. In 1948, a one-volume selection of Esenin's poetry was published, and it sold out immediately. By the early 1950's, Esenin was fully rehabilitated, and in 1961, a five-volume edition appeared, which has since been reprinted several times. According to Russian critics, Esenin's tremendous popularity can be explained by the fact that his poetry was consonant with the feelings of the Russian people during the most difficult days in their history.

ALL SOUL'S DAY

Esenin's first collection, *All Soul's Day*, radiates happiness, although it is not free of the melancholy typical of his works. These early poems express the joy of village life, the poet's love for his homeland, and the pleasures of youth; even the colors are light and gay: blue, white, green, red. Esenin employs religious themes and Christian terminology, but the poems are more pantheistic, even pagan, than Christian. *All Soul's Day* was well received by the critical Petrograd audience, and this response immeasurably boosted Esenin's confidence. The poet was only twenty years old when he proved his mastery of the Russian language.

AZURE

Esenin's second collection, *Azure*, appeared after the revolution, in 1918, but the majority of the poems were written during World War I. These poems reflect Esenin's uncertainty concerning the future, although he did accept and praise the October Revolution. He visualized the revolution as a glorious cosmic upheaval leading to a resurrection of Russia and its rural roots. The style, mood, and vocabulary of *Azure* reveal the influence of Blok and Klyuyev.

Although Esenin undoubtedly was initially on the side of the Bolsheviks, his vision of the revolution was a highly individual one. He saw a return to peasant communities and to a primitive democratic simplicity. The threatening industrialization and the technological development of the mysterious electricity, the hidden source of power, which he witnessed later, horrified him. Three long poems with religiously symbolic titles, which were part of the *Azure* cycle, reflect this attitude: "Preobrazhenie" ("Transfiguration") "Prishestvie" ("The Coming"), and "Inonia."

The well-known poem "Inonia" reflects with particular clarity Esenin's wish for a peasant utopia, an anti-capitalist, agricultural republic that could resist the industrial giants. Esenin saw himself as the prophet of a new religion that had to overcome the peasants' traditional Christianity to bring about a happy, rural, socialist paradise. By 1920, however, Esenin realized that the results of the revolution were slowly destroying his "rural Russia," and he saw himself as "the last poet of the village."

PUGACHOV

During this period of growing disillusionment, Esenin began to forsake the simplicity and the rural spirit of his early verse, although folk elements never disappeared from his work. Among the most significant of his more experimental Imaginist poems was the long dramatic poem *Pugachov*, published in 1922. This unfinished verse drama exhibits the unusual metaphors and verbal eccentricities that were characteristic of the Imaginists. The hero of Esenin's poem, the Cossack leader of a peasant rebellion in the 1770's, is highly idealized and bears little resemblance to the historical Pugachev. In contrast to Pushkin, who treated the same subject in his novella *Kapitanskaya dochka* (1836; *The*

Captain's Daughter, 1846), Esenin passionately sympathized with Pugachev and his peasants. He also drew parallels between Pugachev's revolt and the October Revolution: In his view, both had failed because of human egotism and people's unwillingness to sacrifice for the common good.

"STRANA NEGODIAEV"

In 1922 and 1923, partially during his trip to the United States and Western Europe and partially after his return, Esenin wrote another dramatic poem. "Strana negodiaev" (the country of scoundrels), influenced by Western cinema, marked a departure from the Imaginist style of *Pugachov*. In it, Esenin abandoned striking imagery in favor of a rather crude realistic style. He never completed the poem, however, realizing that it was a failure. In the poem, Esenin refers to America as a greedy trap in which deceit is the key to survival; at the same time, he acknowledges the industrial achievement of the West. In sympathizing with the anti-Soviet hero of this dramatic poem, Esenin confirmed that he had lost much of his enthusiasm for the revolution.

MOSKVA KABATSKAIA

Indeed, by 1923, Esenin saw himself as lost in his own country. He did not reject the revolution itself but the results of the revolution. He was already notorious for his alcoholism, his orgiastic lifestyle, and his escapades around Moscow. His most decadent poems were included in the collection *Moskva kabatskaia*. In these poems, he confessed that he would have become a thief if he had not been a poet, and he exposed all his vices. These poems reflect Esenin's disappointment with himself, with love, and with religion. The critics accused him of wallowing in filth.

The poet of the village and the countryside became overshadowed in the 1920's by the alcoholic of *Moskva kabatskaia*. Esenin's manner became harsher, reflecting the worsening crisis of his life. Gentle laments for the passing of the idealized countryside were replaced by nostalgia for lost youth and the search for a home. Esenin largely abandoned the devices cultivated by the Imaginists, returning to the materials of his early verse yet handling them in a new manner—stark, assured, despairing.

With the poems of *Moskva kabatskaia*, Esenin sought to reconcile himself with the new Russia. In the celebrated poem "Rus' sovetskaia," he admits that he is too old to change, and he fears that he will be left behind by younger generations. In a mixture of resignation and defiance, he accepts the new order and resolves to continue writing poetry not by society's standards but by his own.

PERSIDSKIE MOTIVI

Although Esenin never visited Persia, during his visit to Baku and the Caucasus in 1925, he wrote a cycle of short poems entitled *Persidskie motivi*. Technically, the poems are well written, but Esenin's love lyrics addressed to different girls, in which genuine nostalgia mingles with superficiality and a lack of conviction, suggest that the poet was nearing a dead end.

ANNA SNEGINA

In 1925, Esenin also published the long autobiographical poem *Anna Snegina*, written during his stay in Batum. The poem describes a love affair set in a Russian village during the civil war. Soviet critics, however, were not interested in decadent love affairs; they expected poetry promoting the revolutionary spirit. Esenin was not able to produce this; he remained the anachronistic dreamer of a rural utopia. In his eyes, Soviet society had no need of him nor of his poetry.

OTHER MAJOR WORK

NONFICTION: "Kliuchi Marii," 1918.

BIBLIOGRAPHY

Brengauz, Gregory. *Yesenin: Lyrics and Life—Introduction to Russian Poetry*. 2d ed. Tallahassee: Floridian Publisher, 2006. This biography, in Russian and English, looks at Esenin's life and works.

Davis, J. *Esenin: A Biography in Memoirs, Letters, and Documents*. Ann Arbor, Mich.: Ardis, 1982. Davis culls the autobiographical material from the poet's work and complements it with biographical commentaries, shedding light on various aspects of Esenin's life. These materials, in turn, shed light on his poetry.

De Graaff, Frances. *Sergei Esenin: A Biographical Sketch*. The Hague, the Netherlands: Mouton, 1966. In his valuable study of Esenin's life and poetry, De Graaff combines biography with the poet's works, bolstering his observations with citations from many poems, in Russian and English. Includes an extensive bibliography.

Esenin, Sergei. *Complete Poetical Works in English*. Translated by Victoria Bul. Tallahassee: Floridian Publisher, 2008. Contains an introduction and biography by the translator, poems by poets who influenced or were influenced by Esenin, and a section of Isadora Duncan's autobiography.

McVay, Gordon. *Esenin: A Life*. Ann Arbor, Mich.: Ardis, 1976. In this definitive biography of Esenin in English, the author encompasses the poet's entire life, including his tragic death by suicide. The book offers brief analyses of Esenin's works along with copious illustrations.

Mariengof, Anatoli. *A Novel Without Lies*. Translated by Jose Alaniz. Chicago: Ivan R. Dee, 2000. A detailed memoir of Mariengof's association with Esenin and the literary avant-garde of the 1920's.

Prokushev, Yuri. *Sergei Esenin: The Man, the Verse, the Age*. Moscow: Progress, 1979. In this biography of Esenin by a Russian scholar, Prokushev offers the Russian point of view of the poet and his poetry. The emphasis is on the biographical details. It is somewhat tinted ideologically, stressing Esenin's often failed efforts to adapt to the Soviet reality, his love for Russia, and the realistic aspects of his poetry. Despite its politically motivated slant, the book is full of interesting observations.

Thurley, Geoffrey. Introduction to *Confessions of a Hooligan*, by Sergei Esenin. Cheadle, England: Hulme, 1973. A book of translations of Esenin's poems about his struggle against alcoholism. In the introduction, Thurley examines circumstances that led to the writing of these poems.

Visson, Lynn. *Sergei Esenin: Poet of the Crossroads*. Würzburg, Germany: Jal, 1980. Visson undertakes a thorough, expert analysis of the stylistic features of Esenin's poetry, with extensive quotations from the poems, in Russian and in English, offering penetrating insights into the artistic merits of Esenin's poetry and gauging the scope of his contribution to Russian poetry.

Rado Pribic

F

FIRDUSI
Abū ol-Qāsen Manṣūr

Born: Ṭūs, Khorāsān Province (now in Iran);
  Between 932 and 941
Died: Tabaran, near Ṭūs (now in Iran); between 1020
  and 1025
Also known as: Ferdowsī; Firdawsī; Firdouṣi

PRINCIPAL POETRY
  Shahnamah, c. 1010 (*Sah-name*, 1906)

OTHER LITERARY FORMS

Although the only surviving work by Firdusi (fur-DEW-see) is the *Sah-name*, another long poem titled *Yusuf u Zulaikha* (Joseph and Zulaikha), detailing the story of the biblical character Joseph and Potiphar's wife, has been attributed to Firdusi. This poem, however, is not Firdusi's and belongs to a much later period. Other verses scattered in various anthologies of the classical period have been ascribed to the poet, but none of these fragments can be assigned to him with certainty. These fragments have been collected and studied by H. Ethé in his *Firdûsî als Lyriker* (1872-1873).

ACHIEVEMENTS

The names of Firdusi and his *Sah-name* (the book of kings) became synonymous with the national epic of Iran. With the birth of the discipline of Orientalism, this book was brought to the West through translations and influenced Western authors such as Matthew Arnold, who based his "Sohrab and Rustum" on it. Thus, Firdusi's poem was established as an important work in world literature.

BIOGRAPHY

Little factual information is available concerning Firdusi's life. The character of the poet is overgrown by a thicket of tales that sprang up around him shortly after his death. He was born Abū ol-Qāsen Manṣūr in or around the city of Ṭūs, Khorāsān Province, in northeastern Iran. His date of birth is given as any year between 932 and 941. His father was a country gentleman of the *dihqān* class, the rural landowners. Firdusi's youth was spent in circumstances of financial ease. When still young, he versified individual heroic tales, but it was not until the age of thirty-five or forty that he systematically attempted the versification of one of the existing prose *shahnamahs* of his time, spending between twenty and thirty-five years of his life on this project. During this time, he completed at least two redactions of his work, one in 994-995 and the other in 1009-1010.

Apparently Firdusi was hoping to offer his great epic to a king whom he considered worthy of it. Thus, when he finished the first redaction, he kept it for nearly twenty years before finally offering it to King Mahmūd of Ghazna in the hope of receiving some reward. During this time, the poet had grown old and destitute. It would be incorrect to assume that Firdusi began his project with the intention of offering the finished product to King Mahmūd or even for the sake of financial gain: From references to the project scattered throughout the epic, it is clear that he began the work at least twenty years before Mahmūd ascended the throne. That the poet was relatively young and financially secure when he began his versification of individual stories is evident from the introduction to the story of Bīzhan and Manīzha, in which he paints a picture of himself as a young and affluent country gentleman. In the middle of his great project, however, his life had already changed for the worse. He was old, tired, and poor. When he submitted his poem, completed around 1010, the court disregarded his great effort.

It is known from references within his poem that Firdusi lost a son, who was about thirty-seven years old at the time of his death and probably not very loving toward his father. The classical Persian sources refer to a daughter of the poet as well, but Firdusi himself mentions nothing about her. Firdusi lived some ten or fifteen years after his disappointment with the court of Mahmūd, busying himself with making corrections to and insertions in the text of his poem, and finally dying between 1020 and 1025.

Whereas dependable historical data about Firdusi's life are difficult to unearth, a wealth of folklore concerning him exists in the classical accounts of his life. This folk biography of the poet exists not only in the living oral tradition but also within the classical Persian texts. The contents of the classical Persian sources recounting the biography of the poet demonstrate standard folk motifs. They further disregard historical facts by telling of Firdusi's meeting with famous persons long dead when the poet was born. These texts seem to be largely retellings, in courtly prose, of the stories circulating about the poet in the oral tradition of the period of their composition.

According to these sources, the poet began the versification of the *shahnamah* so that he could supply his daughter with an adequate dowry out of the reward he expected to obtain for it. When he finished the work, he had it transcribed in seven volumes and took it to the court of King Mahmūd. There, with the help of a great minister, he presented it, and it was accepted by the king, who promised the poet sixty thousand gold coins, or one coin per verse. However, the monarch paid Firdusi only twenty thousand silver coins in the end. The reason for this change of heart on the part of the king was that Firdusi was accused of heresy by those who wished him ill. Firdusi, bitterly disappointed, went to the bath, and on coming out, bought a drink of sherbet and divided the money between the bath man and the sherbet seller. Knowing, however, that he had thus insulted the king, he fled the capital, taking his poem with him. Firdusi sought refuge with a noble Iranian prince, and in his palace, he composed a satire of one hundred or more couplets on King Mahmūd, which he inserted as a preface to the *Sah-name*. When he recited this satire to his host, the prince, a prudent man, told him: "Mahmūd is my liege-lord, sell me these one hundred satirical verses for one thousand coins each." The poet agreed, and the prince took possession of the verses and destroyed them. Of the one hundred verses, it is said, only six remain. This account, however, is inconsistent with the fact that the entire text, showing every sign of authenticity, remains.

After this episode, Firdusi retired to his native city of Tūs, where he lived his last years in the company of his daughter. Meanwhile, the king had a change of heart and decided to send the poet his just reward. As the camels bearing the royal reward were entering the city through one gate, however, the corpse of Firdusi was being borne forth through another. Such is the account of the classical Persian texts.

ANALYSIS

The national saga of Iran, which constitutes an ethnic history of the Iranians, existed in written form long before the time of Firdusi. Sagas of this type formed a genre of classical Persian literature, both in verse and in prose, which were known by the generic name *shahnamah*. Firdusi chose an existing prose *shahnamah* to versify during his long poetic career. He included in his narrative other relevant tales from the oral tradi-

The earliest known depiction of the game of polo, from an illustration in Firdusi's Shahnamah *(c. 1010). (Getty Images)*

tion, creating a coherent narrative detailing the national saga of Iran in verse. His masterful verse gradually replaced the original prose work, and in time the term *shahnamah* came to be applied exclusively to his poem.

SAH-NAME

The *Sah-name* is a long epic poem that in the great majority of manuscripts comprises between forty-eight thousand and fifty-two thousand distichs. In some later manuscripts, the number of distichs reaches fifty-five thousand or more. The *Sah-name* is composed in the meter of *mutaqarib*, which is made of a line of eight feet in two hemistichs. Whereas the hemistichs of each line have end rhyme, successive lines do not rhyme with one another. As in the case of all other classical Persian poetry, a regular caesura exists between hemistichs. The *mutaqarib* meter, although used in the work of pre-Firdusian poets in different kinds of narrative poetry, came to be almost exclusively reserved for epic poems after Firdusi. The *Sah-name* has been repeatedly published in Iran, Europe, and India, and has been translated either in whole or abridged form into many languages.

The narrative of the *Sah-name* can be divided into three parts. The first, a mythological section, begins with the reign of the first king, Kayūmars, and deals with a dynasty of primordial rulers, or demigods, who function as creative kings or culture heroes. They either invent some useful item or teach men a new craft. This group of kings, possibly based on an ancient class of old Iranian gods, are called the Pīshdādīs (the ancient creators).

The second part of the epic deals with a series of kings called the Kayāniyān. The rule of this group constitutes the purely legendary section of the *Sah-name*. As all creative activities have already been dealt with by the Pīshdādīs, the Kayāniyān dynasts mark the beginning of the legendary and the heroic section. Their reign is filled with great wars and lofty deeds of heroes and kings. In this section, men become the main figures of the tales. Although the men encountered in these stories are heroic, or idealized, they are nevertheless completely human, lacking the creative powers of the demigods of the previous section. While they may be sorcerers, makers of illusions, they are not divine.

The third part of the *Sah-name* is the semihistorical section, which narrates an idealized version of the reign of historical monarchs who ruled Iran from roughly the sixth century B.C.E. to the Arab conquest in the seventh century C.E. Incorporating a version of the medieval Alexander romances, of which Alexander of Macedonia is the central figure, this semihistorical section is comparatively lacking in action and includes much didactic verse. Recounting the tales that sprang up around the characters of certain historical monarchs of this period, it ends with an account of the fall of the Sāsānian Empire (224-651 C.E.) and the Muslim conquest of Iran.

One gets the impression that in composing the narrative of the first two parts, the mythical and the heroic/legendary section, the poet exercised his imagination to a greater extent than when working with the semihistorial section. Scholars such as W. L. Hanaway have suggested that this feature of the *Sah-name* results from a greater availability of detailed material relating to the historical monarchs of Iran at the time of its composition. The availability of this detailed material limited the extent to which the poet could exercise his imagination. Firdusi repeatedly states that he tried to remain faithful to the sources from which he was working. As a result of his faithfulness to these sources, Hanaway observes, he became more of a historian than an epic poet. In one instance, at the end of a long episode in the reign of King Anūshīravān and his grand vizier Būzarjumihr, just before he began to compose the legend of the invention of the game of chess, Firdusi writes:

Thanks be to the lord of the sun and of the moon
That I was finally rescued from Būzarjumihr and
    the king.
Now that this boring task has come to an end
Let us begin to relate the tale of Chess.

Thus, the poet seems to have been restricted by a text, one that bored him, but to which he remained faithful.

Amin Banani has observed that Firdusi is in a sense the historian of his race. Firdusi often specifies the source from which he obtained his information, a habit that enables scholars to distinguish between the tales that have an oral origin and those that are based on written sources. The *Sah-name* narrates, in chronological order, the progression and the evolution of the concept of kingship in the context of the Iranian legendary history. Individual kings may fall, but the line of kings continues uninterrupted. In the course of the steady progression of the institution, kings evolve from divine priest-kings/culture heroes (such as Jamshīd) to monarchs who rule by divine grace through their royal glory (called *farr* in the epic).

A motif that runs through the poem is that of the royal person who is recognized and restored to his rightful place. Sometimes it is a hero who helps establish the new king. The central hero of the epic, Rustam, is one such protector of king and crown. At other times, the king is restored through the efforts of more obscure persons, such as shepherds or blacksmiths. However, as G. M. Wickens observes, "at no point in the vast cavalcade are we in any serious doubt that the true line of kingship, as distinct from individual kings, will survive." Exploits of individual heroes, such as Rustam's mortal battle with his son Suhrāb, his battles with demons, and the tale of his seven trials, are couched in the overriding motif of the protection of the crown.

Similarly, there is a recurring dramatic tension between good and evil, legitimacy and illegitimacy, and Iranian and non-Iranian. It is in this context that the tale of the perpetuation of the institution of kingship is told. This dramatic tension in the epic is heightened by a skillful use of characterization. There are, as Banani has pointed out, no archetypes in the *Sah-name*. Every character is so minutely developed that he ceases to be a hero in the abstract and develops instead into an individual with a well-defined pattern of behavior. Through this characterization, "the goodness of the best is possible and the evil of the most wretched is not incredible." Thus, there is no fairy-tale world of black and white, or absolute good and absolute evil, in Firdusi's poem.

Because of its size, the *Sah-name* is not easily manageable as an object of literary criticism. It should be remembered that the two great classical epics of the Western world, Homer's *Iliad* (c. 750 B.C.E.; English translation, 1611) and *Odyssey* (c. 725 B.C.E.; English translation, 1614), together comprise no more than approximately twenty-seven thousand lines. The *Sah-name*'s great length, as well as its relative linguistic in-

accessibility, have made it a poor candidate for literary criticism. Thus, Firdusi's poem still remains virtually virgin territory for critical analysis.

B<small>IBLIOGRAPHY</small>
Clinton, Jerome W. *In the Dragon's Claws: The Story of Rostam and Esfandivar*. Washington, D.C.: Mage, 1999. Clinton's translation of the tale of the epic hero king Rostam (Rustam) includes genealogical tables of the royal heroes of *Sah-name*.

Davis, Dick. *Epic and Sedition: The Case of Ferdowsi's Shāhnāmeh*. Fayetteville: University of Arkansas Press, 1992. Examines Firdusi's epic work and the politics surrounding it.

_____. "The Problem of Ferdowsi's Sources." *Journal of the American Oriental Society* 116, no. 1 (January-March, 1996). Argues that Firdusi used mainly versified oral sources rather than written sources for his epic, and any written sources used most likely were in verse form that came from an oral tradition. Bibliographic footnotes.

De Blois, François, ed. *Persian Literature: A Biobibliographical Survey*. 2d ed. Vol. 5. London: RoutledgeCurzon, 2004. A vast bibliography from the Royal Asiatic Society that has information on Firdusi's writings.

De Brujin, J. T. P., ed. *General Introduction to Persian Literature*. London: I. B. Taurus, 2008. Part of the A History of Persian Literature series, this volume places Firdusi in context.

Firdusi. *The Epic of the Kings: "Shahnama," the National Epic of Persia*. Translated by Reuben Levy. 2d ed. Costa Mesa, Calif.: Mazda, 1996. An abridged translation of the epic, with a foreword by Ehsan Yarsater, a preface by Amin Banani, and an introduction by Dick Davis.

Meisami, Julie Scott. *Persian Historiography to the End of the Twelfth Century*. Edinburgh: Edinburgh University Press, 1999. Explores the writing of Persian-Iranian history during the time of the Sāsānid, Ghaznavid, and Seljuk dynasties, and discusses Firdusi's *Sah-name* as historical prose. Maps, bibliography, index.

Nizāmī Arūzī Samarqandi. *The Chahár Maqála (The Four Discourses) of Nizāmī Arūzī Samarqandi*.

Translated by Edward G. Browne. 1921. Reprint. London: Luzac, 1978. These anecdotal accounts of poets, astrologers, and others by a twelfth century belletrist include the earliest surviving biographical information about Firdusi. Bibliography, index.

Robinson, B. W. *The Persian Book of Kings: An Epitome of the Shahnama of Firdawsi.* London: RoutledgeCurzon, 2002. Illustrations, bibliography, index. A concise introduction to and summary of Firdusi's epic work. Illustrations include early Persian paintings depicting events and actions. Includes a table listing kings in the book, a bibliography, and an index.

Yarshater, Ehsan, ed. *Persian Literature.* Albany: State University of New York Press, 1988. Essays of particular interest in this volume cover such topics as early Persian court poetry, the development of epic Persian verse, and Firdusi and the tragic epic. Bibliography, index.

Mahmoud Omidsalar

G

ENRIQUE GONZÁLEZ MARTÍNEZ

Born: Guadalajara, Jalisco, Mexico; April 13, 1871
Died: Mexico City, Mexico; February 19, 1952

PRINCIPAL POETRY

Preludios, 1903
Lirismos, 1907
Silénter, 1909
Los senderos ocultos, 1911
La muerte del cisne, 1915
El libro de la fuerza, de la bondad y del ensueño, 1917
Parábolas, y otras poemas, 1918
Jardins de Francia, 1919 (translation)
La palabra del viento, 1921
El romero alucinado, 1923
Las señales furtivas, 1925
Poemas truncas, 1935
Ausencia y canto, 1937
El diluvio del fuego, 1938
Tres rosas en el ánfora, 1939
Poesía, 1898-1938, 1939-1940
Bajo el signo mortal, 1942
Segundo despertar, y otras poemas, 1945
Vilano al viento, 1948
Babel, poema al margen del tiempo, 1949
El nuevo narciso, y otras poemas, 1952

OTHER LITERARY FORMS

The reputation of Enrique González Martínez (gohn-SOL-ays mor-TEE-nays) rests entirely on his poetry. He was active as a journalist, and his only published fiction—three short stories—appeared in a provincial newspaper and in a magazine that he coedited early in his career. These stories show a marked influence from the naturalist movement. The first one, "Una hembra" (a female), which appeared in *El heraldo de Mexico* in 1895, narrates the transformation experi-

enced by a girl of the humblest class when the illicit love affair into which she is forced by the terrible circumstances of her life results in the birth of a child. The second story, "La chiquilla" (the girl), which was published in *Arte* in 1907, relates the sensual awakening of a young girl being reared in the house of a priest. In the third of the stories, "A vuelo" (ringing bells)—also published in *Arte*, in 1908—a sick boy dies when he is unable to suppress his desire to ring his favorite bell in the church on the day of the town fiesta.

González Martínez's acceptance speech on his admission to the Mexican Academy of Language, "Algunos aspectos de la lírica mexicana" (1932; some aspects of Mexican lyricism), examines the history of Mexican lyric poetry and draws the picture of its evolution, analyzing the best Mexican poets, pointing out weaknesses and virtues, and determining influences and trends. It has been considered one of his most refined prose pieces.

González Martínez wrote two autobiographical volumes *El hombre del búho* (1944; the man of the owl) and *La apacible locura* (1951; the peaceful madness). In these two books, written during the author's advanced years, he recalls the most important moments and events of his life in a plain and clear style, without literary pretentiousness. Sincerity and humility are perhaps the most impressive features of these two works, in which the poet talks about his contemporaries, describes his friends, and tells of his successes and his disappointments.

ACHIEVEMENTS

Enrique González Martínez achieved his first literary success at an early age. When he was fourteen years old, he won first prize in a contest organized by the English-Spanish newspaper of Guadalajara, *The Sun*, for his translation of an English poem about John Milton. Later in his life, he was an effective member of the prestigious Mexican Academy of Language, president of the Athenaeum of the Youth of Mexico, member of the Seminary of Mexican Culture, founding member of the renowned National College of Mexico, president of the organizing committee of the American Continental Congress of Peace, and a professor of language and literature at various institutions of higher education. He received the Manuel Ávila Camacho Literary Award in 1944 and was a candidate for the Nobel Prize in Literature in 1949.

BIOGRAPHY

Enrique González Martínez was born in Guadalajara, the capital of the state of Jalisco, Mexico, on April 13, 1871. He was the son of a schoolteacher, José María González, and his wife, Feliciana Martínez. González Martínez attended the grade school directed by his father, and in 1881, he entered the preparatory school run by the Roman Catholic Church in the Conciliar Seminary of his native city. Five years later, when he was only fifteen, he entered the School of Medicine of Guadalajara.

González Martínez's fondness for poetry began at a very early age. As a child, he often amazed his parents and other adults with his achievements as a student as well as with his ability to write verse. Although he devoted himself with enthusiasm to the study of medicine during his student years, his interest in poetry grew. When he graduated as a medical doctor in 1893, he had already published a number of poems in newspapers and magazines, earning for himself a reputation as a provincial poet.

Despite his appointment upon graduation as an adjunct professor of physiology in the School of Medicine in Guadalajara, González Martínez did not have much success practicing medicine in his native city. At this time, González Martínez's father was offered the post of headmaster in a school that was going to be opened in Culiacán, the capital of the state of Sinaloa. It was an excellent opportunity to improve the family's economic situation, and since González Martínez had yet to establish himself as a physician, he decided to move to Culiacán with his parents and his younger sister, Josefina. They arrived there at the end of 1895, and for the next six months, González Martínez tried without success to establish his professional practice. After this time, he decided to move to the small town of Sinaloa, where he finally established himself and resided for the next fifteen years. In 1898, González Martínez married Luisa Rojo y Fonseca, a girl who had strongly impressed him when he had first seen her on his initial visit to Sinaloa. Their marriage produced four children—Enrique, María Luisa, Héctor, and Jorge—the youngest child, however, lived only sixteen months.

The fifteen years that González Martínez lived in Sinaloa were a period of intense professional activity as a doctor as well as of incessant literary production. For some time, the poet seemed to be content with publishing his poems in newspapers and magazines of the provinces as well as the capital, where he was beginning to be known. Nevertheless, in 1900, an event took place that prompted González Martínez to publish his first book of poetry. For reasons not yet fully understood, a newspaper in Guadalajara published a false report of his death. Several publications in different cities expressed their sorrow for the early death of such a promising poet and reprinted poems of his that had previously appeared in their pages. One of González Martínez's friends published a long article lamenting the death of the poet, recalling his life, listing his successes, and praising his virtues as a physician, a man of letters, and a citizen. When all this came to the attention of González Martínez in the small town where he lived, the poet rushed to deny the false information, and in a letter written in a joking tone he thanked his friend from Guadalajara for the informative and sorrowful article. After the uproar occasioned by this event had passed, the poet concluded that his poems must be good enough to be published in book form, and thus his first collection, titled *Preludios* (preludes), appeared in 1903.

Although González Martínez continued practicing medicine, his other activities seemed to multiply after the publication of his first book. In 1907, he published *Lirismos* (lyricisms), his second book of poetry, and between 1907 and 1909, he edited, along with his friend Sixto Osuna, the magazine *Arte*, which was published in Mocorito. Between 1907 and 1911, he occupied the position of political prefect in the districts of Mocorito, El Fuerte, and Mazatlán in the state of Sinaloa, and at the beginning of the Revolution of 1910, he was the secretary general of the government in Culiacán, the capital of the state of Sinaloa. In 1909, he published another book of poetry, *Silénter* (silently), and was appointed correspondent member of the Mexican Academy of Language.

In 1911, González Martínez published *Los senderos*

ocultos (the concealed paths). That same year, he decided to abandon his medical career completely to devote the rest of his life to poetry, changing his residence and that of his family to Mexico City. There, he began to work as an editorial writer for the newspaper *El imparcial*. Finally, he was designated effective member of the Mexican Academy of Language and affiliated himself with the Athenaeum of the Youth of Mexico, becoming its president a year later. In 1912, he founded the magazine *Argos*, which appeared for only one year, and in 1913, he was appointed under secretary of public instruction and fine arts. After occupying this position for a year, he spent a year as secretary general of the government in Puebla. In 1915, he returned to Mexico City to devote himself to teaching and was appointed a professor of Spanish language and literature and of general literature in the National Preparatory School, as well as in the Normal School for Women. He was also appointed a professor of French literature in the School of Higher Studies, later called the Faculty of Philosophy and Letters. He soon lost his professorial positions, however, for political reasons.

After 1915, the poetic production of González Martínez increased, and his books of poetry followed one another with a frequency uncommon even among the most prolific poets. Nevertheless, despite his constant dedication to poetry, in 1917, he went back to work for a newspaper, this time as an editorial writer for *El heraldo de México*, while at the same time acting as coeditor of the magazine *Pegaso*.

In 1920, González Martínez began his diplomatic career with an appointment as minister plenipotentiary to Chile; he was transferred to a similar position in Argentina two years later. After another two years, he was appointed minister plenipotentiary for Mexico in Spain and Portugal, and he held this position for six years, until 1931.

The relatively peaceful life of González Martínez suffered two serious disruptions. The first was the death of his wife, Luisa, in 1935, and the second was the death of his son Enrique in 1939. The poet expressed in his poems the sorrow and the solitude that these two deaths caused him.

In 1942, González Martínez was admitted into the

Seminary of Mexican Culture. A year later, he was appointed founding member of the important cultural organization the National College of Mexico, and in 1944, he received the Manuel Ávila Camacho Literary Award. In 1949, he presided over the organizing committee of the American Continental Congress of Peace and was nominated for the Nobel Prize in Literature. He died as he was approaching his eighty-first birthday, on February 19, 1952.

ANALYSIS

Placing Enrique González Martínez in the global picture of the movements and tendencies of Hispanic literature is not an easy task. Among the factors contributing to this difficulty is the fact that the poet was active for more than a half century, during which time many styles and techniques succeeded one another. Nevertheless, although González Martínez was influenced by many poets, both from his own epoch and from other eras, he never permitted another poet's idiom to smother his own voice.

González Martínez began to write when the poetic environment in the Hispanic world was dominated by *Modernismo*. The great Nicaraguan poet Rubén Darío had succeeded in imposing his peculiar modality on this movement not only in Latin America but also in Spain. *Modernista* poetry was greatly influenced by the Parnassian and Symbolist schools of French origin, often featuring landscapes of ancient Greece or of eighteenth century France and including all kinds of exotic plants and flowers. The preferred fauna were animals known for their beauty, such as the peacock and the swan—especially the latter, which became a symbol of the movement. Metals and precious stones were used constantly as poetic motifs. The language of the *Modernistas* was musical and richly textured; adjectives were used profusely, and the imagery evoked strange impressions and sensations, synesthesia appearing with extraordinary frequency.

It was only natural that a movement so generalized and powerful as *Modernismo* had an influence on a young poet such as González Martínez, who had an expansive concept of poetry and who was well equipped for artistic creation to the most refined degree. In his poetry can be found Parnassian and Symbolist notes, satyrs and beautiful animals, musically elegant adjectives and synesthesia—everything with the clear desire to produce a refined artistic creation. For these reasons, many would consider González Martínez a member of the *Modernismo* movement.

Nevertheless, González Martínez was never a *Modernista* in the style of Darío. His satyrs and nymphs suffer from a lack of realism, and his fowls and stones—they are not always precious—do not function as mere ornaments in his poetry but contribute to the development of its ideas as well as communicate emotion. Closer connections could be found between González Martínez and *Modernistas* with the tendencies of the Cuban José Martí and the Colombian José Asunción Silva or with Darío in his later years, when his poetry was richer in insight and profundity. In González Martínez, interior concentration, simplicity of expression, and directness of communication are dominant characteristics.

"WRING THE SWAN'S NECK"

For these reasons, González Martínez fits better as a postmodernist. It is true that he was only four years younger than Darío and that he was several years older than the *Modernistas* Leopoldo Lugones, from Argentina, and Julio Herrera y Reissig, from Uruguay. Nevertheless, it must be considered that González Martínez published his first book of poetry in 1903, when he was already thirty-two years old, and that he reached his peak when *Modernismo* was fading and postmodernism was at its apex. In this connection, the sonnet "Tuércele el cuello al cisne" should be mentioned.

This is the famous poem in which González Martínez recommended the death of the swan, the symbol of *Modernismo*, and its replacement by the owl as less ornamental but more wise and thoughtful. The poet himself said that his sonnet was not intended as an attack on Darío and the other first-class *Modernistas*; rather, it was directed against Darío's epigones. Nevertheless, González Martínez's poem was widely regarded as the death blow to *Modernismo* and the beginning of postmodernism. In any case, González Martínez's aesthetic was fundamentally different from that of the *Modernistas*: He was inclined toward meditation and the patient study of the mysteries of life rather than toward verbal brilliance for its own sake.

PRELUDIOS

When González Martínez published his first book of poems, he was already an experienced poet, with perfect technical control. In each poem of his first book, *Preludios*, the formal perfection of a master craftsperson can be observed, although the poet still had not found his direction. In *Preludios*, many different influences can be noted. The strongest is that of the *Modernistas*, which came to the poet through his compatriots Manuel Guitérrez Nájera and Salvador Días Mirón. Other influences were those of Latin poets, such as Horace, and of Mexican traditional poets, such as Manuel José Othon. Some of González Martínez's phrases have all the brilliance and elegance characteristic of *Modernismo*, as in "Ríe" (laugh)—"over the warm ermine of your shoulders,/ your laugh, fair blond, come forth/ as rainy gold"—or in "Baño" (bath), in which he says that the sculptural nude body of a girl is a "volcano of snow in an eruption of roses." His descriptions of nature, and of the love scenes that take place in it, have all the charm and delicacy of the classical or the national poets, as can be seen in the series of sonnets grouped under the title of "Rústica" (rustic).

The presence of these diverse influences and orientations clearly indicates that in *Preludios* the poet was still trying to find his voice and a more profound source of inspiration. The distinctive voice that would later be characteristic of the best of González Martínez's production is heard in only a few poems in *Preludios*, as when in "A una poeta" (to a poet) he exhorts a fictitious colleague to go to nature in search of "an ideal for your longings," telling him: "See the country, look at the sea, contemplate the sky:/ there is beauty there, inspiration and everything!" Likewise, when he talks of the healthy effects of night and silence, he says: "when the angel of the night spreads/ his sweet peace . . . under the blue silence the poet stretches/ his wings towards the world of dreams."

LIRISMOS

Lirismos, the poet's second collection, was a continuation of the search for himself that began in *Preludios*, and an intensification of his desire for formal perfection. The book is composed mostly of sonnets, and the influences of the *Modernistas* and the ancient classics continue, although somewhat mitigated by characteristics of the French Parnassian and Symbolist movements. Upon the appearance of this book, many praised the artistic perfection of its poems and, based on this perfection, considered the book superior to the first one. The poet, however, was not deceived by these opinions and noticed that the Parnassian coldness had frozen his own voice.

SILÉNTER

As a result, in his next book, *Silénter*, with the sonnet of the same title, he seems to advise himself to look for inspiration in self-intimacy, saying, "give forms to your desires, crystallize your idea/ and wait proudly for a distant dawn." In the first tercet of this sonnet, he calls on himself to achieve interior silence, advising himself that "a sacred silence sets you apart from the uproar." In one of the central poems of *Silénter*, which is also one of the poet's best known, "Irás sobre la vida de las cosas . . ." (you will go over the life of things . . .), he persists with his idea of returning to nature and investigating silence. He extols nature—"the soliloquy of the fountain, as well as/ the weak blinking of the star"—and advises "that you refine your soul until you are able to listen to the silence and see the shadow."

In another of his best-known poems, "A veces una hoja desprendida . . ." (sometimes a fallen leaf . . .), González Martínez goes deeper in his understanding of nature, expressing a greater intimacy with it: "that star and I know each other,/ that tree and that flower are my friends." In this poem, his identification with nature becomes complete; the poet exclaims "Divine communion! . . . I finally know what you murmur, clear fountain;/ I finally know what you tell me, errant breeze." In "Soñé con un verso . . ." (I dreamed of a verse . . .), the poet tells of having dreamed of a vibrant, clear, and strong verse; when, after waking, he attempts to relate his dream, he gives a fairly accurate description of his calm and peaceful way of writing poetry: "with mournful crepe my lyre veiled its cords/ and my verse was made of a soft melancholy/ like the steps that glide over the rug." In another poem, "En voz baja" (in a soft voice), the poet tells about his struggle to discover the secret of Nature. He begins by saying, "in all that exists/ I have heard many times your voice, nature"; then, describing his efforts to Nature, a woman, he tells

her: "I pursue you and you escape; I adore you and everything is in vain./ Hermetically you hide the clue to the arcanum"; finally he asks when the moment will come in which "devoted lover . . ./ you will tell me in a soft voice the divine secret?"

LOS SENDEROS OCULTOS

In *Los senderos ocultos*, González Martínez continues the process initiated in his preceding books—that is, of trying to understand and identify with nature. Here this process reaches its greatest intensity and achieves the most satisfactory results. Perhaps for this reason, *Los senderos ocultos* has been considered by many to be the poet's best work. In "Busca en todas las cosas . . ." (seek in all things . . .), the author adds "the soul of things" as a new objective of the poet's search. That is why he advises: "seek in all things a soul and a hidden/ meaning," adding later that "you will know little by little how to decipher their language . . ./ Oh divine colloquy of the things and the soul!" In "Renovación" (renovation), the poet continues his search for identification, which now is not with the soul or the life of things, but with life itself, in its more universal and comprehensive sense. That same desire for identification includes the poet's beloved in the poem "A la que va conmigo" (to the one who goes with me), in which he tells her that "we will go through life identified with it" and that the "soul of things will be our own soul."

The pantheistic overtones of "Renovación" are even more evident in "Doux pays" (French for "sweet country"), in which the poet dreams of "a divine marriage between human life/ and the life of the world." Later, these thoughts will be embellished with a kind of Christian sweetness, as, for example, in "Cuando sepas hallar una sonrisa . . ." (when you learn how to find a smile . . .): "when you learn how to find a smile in the drop of water, in the mist,/ in the sun, in the bird, and in the breeze," then "like the Saint of Assisi, you will call brothers/ the tree, the cloud, and the beast"; then "you will reverently take off your sandals/ not to wound the stones in the road." In "Tiendo a la vida el ruego . . ." (I have a request for life . . .), the poet expresses his desire for total possession of and identification with life when he says that he does not ask for "the incomplete gift, but for the totality of life"; in the previously mentioned

"Wring the Swan's Neck," he elevates life to the category of a goddess: "adore life intensely/ and let life understand your homage."

In the beautiful and well-known "Como hermana y hermano" (like sister and brother), the poet describes the peaceful way in which he and his beloved are traversing the road of life, and he admits that life has secrets and mysteries that humans cannot discover. When, in the silence of the night, the poet and his beloved hear their hearts beating, he says, "do not fear, there are songs heard/ but we will never know who signs them. . . ." When she, upon feeling a strange sensation, asks if he has kissed her, his answer is, "you will never/ know who gives those kisses." Finally, when she feels a tear sliding down her forehead, she asks him if he is crying, but the poet says, "we will never know who sheds those nocturnal tears."

LA MUERTE DEL CISNE

Although González Martínez maintained his preoccupation with the themes of his early collections, in *La muerte del cisne* (the death of the swan), he began to show a desire for innovation leading to new themes and more varied formal techniques. The result is greater diversity, but also a loss of cohesiveness and the appearance of contradictions. In "Ánima trémula" (trembling soul), the poet aspires to totality and wants to be, at the same time, "the viewer and the spectacle,/ and be the dreamer and the dream." In "A una alma ingenua" (to a simple soul), he shows a preference for what is simple and humble, asking "the soul without ideas," to whom he is talking, to "give me your eyes to see life." In "Iba por un camino" (I was going on a road), the poet shows a powerful desire for life: "Let's live, let's live, because life is escaping!" In "Hortus conclusus" (Latin for "the enclosed garden"), on the other hand, he chooses to detach himself from life; when life calls, his soul "quietly and taciturnly . . . has closed the door . . . and does not answer." A kind of pessimism now appears with some frequency. In "Los días inútiles" (the useless days), the poet, reconstructing his past, feels the awakening of "an immense desire/ to sob by myself and ask for pardon"; in "Mañana los poetas" ("Tomorrow the Poets Will Sing"), he says that the poets of the future, despite all their successes, "will pick up the abandoned lyre from the floor/ and will sing with it our same song."

LATER POETRY

In his subsequent books, González Martínez continued to write his own very personal poetry, meditating in silence on his ideas, in intimate communion with nature, and expressing himself in his direct, simple, and polished language. He was for a long time the most admired poet of Mexico, and several generations of younger poets considered him their guide and inspiration. In his later years, when he was no longer in vogue, his poetry suffered a radical devaluation, and he has never regained his former eminence. Nevertheless, he dominated an entire epoch in his country, and he wrote poems that will not disappear with the passing of time.

OTHER MAJOR WORKS

SHORT FICTION: "Una hembra," 1895; "La chiquilla," 1907; "A vuelo," 1908.

NONFICTION: "Algunos aspectos de la lírica mexicana," 1932; *El hombre del búho*, 1944; *La apacible locura*, 1951.

BIBLIOGRAPHY

Brushwood, John S. *Enrique González Martínez*. New York: Twayne, 1969. An introductory biographical study and critical analysis of selected works by González Martínez. Includes bibliographic references.

Geist, Anthony L., and José B. Monleón, eds. *Modernism and Its Margins: Reinscribing Cultural Modernity from Spain and Latin America*. New York: Garland, 1999. A rereading of modernism and the modernist canon from a double distance: geographical and temporal. It is a revision not only from the periphery (Spain and Latin America), but also from this new fin de siècle, a revisiting of modernity and its cultural artifacts from that same postmodernity.

González, Aníbal. *A Companion to Spanish American Modernismo*. Rochester, N.Y.: Tamesis, 2007. This work covers *Modernismo* in various genres, including poetry. Provides context for understanding González Martínez.

Sharman, Adam. *Tradition and Modernity in Spanish American Literature: From Darío to Carpentier*. New York: Palgrave Macmillan, 2006. This survey examines modernism in Spanish American literature and places González Martínez in context.

Tapscott, Stephen, ed. *Twentieth-Century Latin American Poetry: A Bilingual Anthology*. Austin: University of Texas Press, 1996. Provides a brief analysis of the poetry of González Martínez and translations of some of his better-known poems, including "Wring the Swan's Neck" and "Como hermana y hermano."

Washbourne, Kelly, and Sergio Gabriel Waisman, eds. *An Anthology of Spanish American Modernismo: In English Translation, with Spanish Text*. New York: Modern Language Association of America, 2007. Contains translations from the works of González Martínez and provides context for their understanding.

Rogelio A. de la Torre
(including original translations)

H

HAFIZ
Shams al-Din Muhammad

Born: Shīrāz, Persia (now in Iran); c. 1320
Died: Shīrāz, Persia (now in Iran); c. 1389 or 1390
Also known as: Ḥāfez; Shams al-Dīn Muḥammed;
  Shams al Dīn Muḥammed of Shīrāz

PRINCIPAL POETRY
  Dīvān, c. 1368 (*The Divan*, 1891)

OTHER LITERARY FORMS

Apart from manuscripts he is known to have copied, the only existing works that Hafiz (HAH-feez) is known to have written are poetry. Other Persian writers have referred to prose works by the author, but no such writings are extant.

ACHIEVEMENTS

In the hands of Hafiz, the lyric poem, or *ghazal*, reached its highest level of development as the author combined technical virtuosity with sublime poetic inspiration. With subtle, meticulous craftsmanship, this literary form, which otherwise could be reproached as stilted and artificial, reached under Hafiz the zenith of its expressive qualities. The author's spiritual and romantic quests are evoked in delicate tones that are admirably suited to the Persian metric forms. The exquisite aspects hidden in everyday experience merge with elements of the author's larger vision, which is tinged with mystical yearnings in places as well. It is a measure also of Hafiz's unexpected depth that simple odes, with their seemingly transparent imagery, upon closer examination reveal multiple patterns of meaning that reflect the timeless qualities of daily joys and sorrows. At its finest, the poetical raiment of Hafiz's work displays meticulous, seemingly effortless construction as the diverse, multicolored threads of thought and feeling are interwoven in bright and perennially appealing designs.

In addition to the odes, or lyric poetry, Hafiz wrote elegies (*qasa'id*), of which two are included in his collected verse; he also wrote a certain number of shorter works (*qita*) and at least forty-two quatrains (*rubai'yat*). These forms, with their own harmonic and metrical requirements, demonstrate the author's attainments with other kinds of poetry. Although outwardly the entire corpus of Hafiz's known work does not exemplify a single unitary or holistic theme, the various elements of his poetical canon combine patterns and topics that are in keeping with the standards of versification upheld by classical Persian prosody.

During his lifetime, Hafiz earned the title *khwajah*, or learned man. It would appear that he was honored, as well as tolerated, by some of the rulers of his day. The claims of some writers that, possibly with the support of the shah, he was at one time a professor of Qur'ānic exegesis at an institution of religious learning have not been confirmed. Hafiz never obtained an appointment as a court poet; while he gained some renown during his lifetime, the honor with which his name is held was conferred largely by subsequent generations of poets and literary men.

BIOGRAPHY

Little is known with exactitude about the life of the great poet Hafiz, born Shams al-Din Muhammad. Even the outlines of his biography are uncertain, and rather few details may safely be accepted from the historical works and literary studies that deal with his age. Hafiz's own work has been examined for hints and allusions that would reveal more about his personal circumstances or his station in society. Some poems contain dedications, which would indicate some of the political figures to whom they were addressed; some works conclude with chronograms, by which numerical values assigned to characters yield certain dates. Nevertheless, such evidence may be gleaned only from some writings, mainly from the middle period of the author's life. The entire problem has been exacerbated by the incompleteness of existing manuscript texts, the earliest of which were transcribed possibly twenty years after the poet's death; other texts date from thirty to sixty years or more after Hafiz's own time. In its turn, the lack of a single accepted body of work limits the usefulness of biographical research based on Hafiz's own writings. Tantalizing suggestions, which can be neither proved nor disproved, add an aura of the legendary to the rather sparse data that have been established beyond doubt.

It would seem that the poet's father was a merchant who moved from Isfahan to Shīrāz under conditions suggesting family circumstances of relative poverty. The author was probably born about 1320, the date most often mentioned by the pertinent authorities, though some works cite 1317 and others suggest 1325 or 1326. When he was quite young, Hafiz's father died; nevertheless, he evidently received a thoroughgoing education. To his given name, Shams al-Din Muhammad, was added the epithet Hafiz, which is bestowed on those who have learned the Qurʾān by heart. In his poetry, there are enough learned references to Arabic theology and Persian literature to suggest that he gained familiarity with classical subjects relatively early in life.

During his youth, Hafiz is reputed to have served as a dough maker in a baker's shop and as a manuscript copyist. Some of Hafiz's poems were dedicated to Qiwam al-Din Hasan (died 1353), who served at times as vizier to a local ruler who had arisen during the waning years of the Mongol period of Persia's history. While Hafiz thus wrote some of his most important works by about the age of thirty, political upheaval, and the struggle between rival dynasties for the control of Shīrāz, probably complicated the poet's life. During the reign of Mubariz al-Din Muhammad (died 1358), religious differences arose between the Sunni ruler and the Shiite citizenry; Hafiz still may have enjoyed protection from one of the shah's ministers.

The most important creative period for the author evidently occurred early in the reign of Jalal al-Din Shah Shujaʿ (died 1384); it would seem that Hafiz's renown spread across Persia, into the Arab lands, and as far as India. There is some evidence that he was invited to serve other rulers, though he declined, as he was notoriously reluctant to leave his native city. He may well have been married; one poem from 1362 or 1363 seems to have been meant as a eulogy for a deceased son.

It is thought that Hafiz lost favor at the shah's court and remained in some disgrace from 1366 to 1376.

Though the grounds remain obscure, it has been alleged that the author's exuberant celebration of the joys of wine and love disquieted those in political power. He may have spent a year or two in other Persian cities, such as Isfahan or Yazd. One account, which is generally deemed apocryphal, has the poet undertaking a journey to India, only to turn back at Hormuz, on the Persian Gulf, from fear of the open sea. Much of the rest of Hafiz's life, so far as is known, was spent in Shīrāz. He may have regained some favor with patrons in the government; whether he held any academic position is unclear. There are no records, in any event, of his appointment to any educational institutions in Shīrāz. Moreover, it is quite possible that the recurrent complaints about personal poverty, which appear at intervals throughout *The Divan*, actually did reflect the poet's own situation to some extent.

The last years of the author's life occurred during the unsettled period that followed Timur's invasion of Persia. While Hafiz may have been assisted sporadically by members of the earlier government who remained in Shīrāz, by some accounts, which historical research has actually tended to confirm, he met with the great conqueror in 1387 and half-seriously set forth his justification for placing love's attractions above the control of provinces and nations. Hafiz died in 1389 or 1390, and subsequently his tomb became one of the most celebrated monuments in Shīrāz, at which later generations of literary aficionados would gather.

ANALYSIS

While Hafiz's lyrics have widely been considered the most nearly perfect examples of this genre, his poetry has an ineffable quality that seemingly eludes exact analysis. For that matter, specialists have contested whether cohesiveness may be found in specific poems and whether shifting levels of meaning may account for abrupt transitions in topical content. In a technical sense, however, the felicitous union of diction, metric length, emphasis, and rhyme is everywhere in evidence. Hafiz's appeal is veritably universal: Romantic, often lighthearted, and alive to the joys of this world, his poems reveal sublime attributes in the experiences and perceptions felt on this earth. It is from this point of departure that metaphysical or theological speculation may begin, but while concerns of this sort are taken up in the author's writings, they are far from obtrusive. Indeed, in some connections they may appear inscrutable. The poet's philosophical interests, though immanent, do not impede the measured, melodious currents that guide his thoughts across specific series of lines.

In some quarters, Hafiz was reproached as a hedonist and a libertine; he has been charged as well with the use of blasphemous motifs, both in his attitude toward the clergy and for poetic symbolism suggesting affinities with mystical schools of thought. The cast of mind revealed in his verse is effulgent and slightly irreverent; in calling for the wine bowl or in depicting woman's beauty, however, he shows little that is immoderate or overly indulgent. He may seem bedazzled, but he is not really helpless in the face of love's charms or the lure of the tavern; at least the precision with which his verses are delivered would suggest controlled self-awareness. There are some rhetorical flights of fancy that most readers probably will tolerate. The features of women conjured forth in Hafiz's poems point to an idealized romantic conception, the embodiments of which would appear now and again before the writer.

The poet seems wistfully conscious that this life is fleeting; but unburdened by fatalism, he has resolved to accept the world's pleasures where they may be found. Literary and theological references crop up here and there; they suggest the author's familiarity with learned works even as his own views on life's deeper issues are recorded. When they make their appearances, reflections on death and ultimate designs to this existence reveal a thoughtful, broadly tolerant outlook that, for all its mystical, seemingly heterodox inspiration, complements and affirms the positive values the author has proclaimed elsewhere in his verse.

COMMAND OF IMAGERY

The enduring qualities of Hafiz's poetry are maintained in the first instance through his consummate use of imagery; indeed, memorable lines and passages are recalled specifically from these associations. Although classical Persian poetry to an extent depended on specific, fixed points of reference—the roses and nightingales that make their appearances in Hafiz's works originated in prototypes handed down by generations of versifiers—his poetic vision placed these stock im-

ages in fresh and distinctively personal literary settings. The allegorical and the actual merge gracefully in the gardens where many of his poetic encounters take place; directly and through allusions, visions of orchards, meadows, and rose gardens are summoned forth. These settings, almost certainly taken from those in and around the author's own city, are typically flanked by box trees, cypresses, pines, and willows. The wind, likened sometimes to the breeze of paradise, wafts scents of ambergris, musk, and other perfumed fragrances; at times there is jasmine in the air.

Roses also figure prominently in many of Hafiz's lines, often as buds, blossoms, and petals; at other times hyacinths, lilies, violets, and tulips appear. The narcissus seems to have its own self-answering connotation. The nightingale, which at places alights on the roses, provides musical accompaniment to the poet's fonder thoughts; at some junctures swallows or birds of paradise enter the poet's landscape. Celestial bodies often mark transitions to metaphorical passages: The Pleiades sparkle but sometimes provoke tears; at times Venus or Saturn is in the ascendant. The moon mirrors and hurls back images of the beloved's features.

Archetypal visions of women enter many of the lyrics, though generally by hints and partial references. Seemingly bemused by the eyebrows, the pupils of the eyes, the hair, the neck, or the moonlike visage of the loved one, the author must have readily conceived a host of similes. Tresses resemble a tree's leafy growth; lips recall roses in the fullness of their blossom. Perfumed winds mingle with the lover's soft voice. Hafiz seems to have been particularly entranced by the mole, or beauty spot (*khal*), to be found on the cheeks of some women. This fascination, and his willingness to place love above riches and power, led him to compose some of the most celebrated lines in all poetry: "If that beauteous Turk of Shiraz would take my heart in hand,/ I would barter for her dark mole Bukhara and Samarqand."

In other moods, the author wrote from the standpoint of a *rind*, or vagabond; in this frame of mind, the cares of this world are gently shunted aside for the tavern and the bowl of wine. Many such lyrics at the outset are addressed to the *saqi*, or cupbearer; sad tidings and glad are greeted with the thought that the rosy glow of drink will set matters in perspective. The intrinsic pleasures of fellowship around the bowl are evoked; at times there are melancholy images as well, as when the poet's heart-blood, or the ruby lips of an absent lover, are contrasted with the tawny drink before him. Poverty and the vicissitudes of romantic encounters could seemingly be offset by the mellowing reflections good wine could bring. There are occasions as well when the bowl suggests another quest, when the pursuit of enigmatic romance might be superseded by concern with the ultimate questions. Another image is introduced here and there, that of the cup of Jamshid from old Persian lore, which was supposed to provide magical visions of the universe. Another very famous ode begins with the lines

> Long years my heart had made request
> Of me, a stranger, hopefully
> (Not knowing that itself possessed
> The treasure that it sought of me),
> That Jamshid's chalice I should win
> And it would see the world therein.

This poem ends with speculation on the views of divinity propounded by thinkers and groups from various persuasions that were out of favor in the Persia of Hafiz's day.

RELIGIOUS THEMES

The religious themes developed in Hafiz's verse betray heterodox influences coupled with a broadly tolerant point of view. Some references merely bear the outward stamp of mystic ways of life: the dervish's cloak (*khirqah*) and the dusty, stony path of the spiritually inclined mendicant are featured in some notable lyrics; there are odd juxtapositions of the religious search and the meditations of the wine bibber. Although in some passages the author suggests that his innate liberality and profligacy precluded any commitments to the religious life, he seems nevertheless to have been struck by the free and open spiritual journeys of the peripatetic dervish, or *qalandar*. The impious, slightly scandalous regard with which Hafiz was held in some quarters was given added weight by his references to religious views that went beyond those officially upheld by the authorities.

Mystical currents in Islamic thought had been dis-

seminated under the general rubric of Sufism; such habits of mind eluded the strict doctrinal categories of more orthodox thinkers. Sufi interpretations of philosophical and religious questions still had found adherents among important men of letters in Persia; the evidence from Hafiz's works suggests a more than casual acquaintanceship with mystical teachings. Indeed, though without conferring his entire approval, the poet refers to the distinctive spiritual orientation of the Sufis in many places. More controversial were his quotations from al-Husayn ibn Mansur al-Hallaj, who was executed in Iraq in 922 for his alleged personal identification with God. Hafiz apparently found some inspiration in the celebrated martyr's beliefs in love and manifestations of the divine all around in the world. Moreover, in keeping with the multiple sources of Sufism, where elements of several religious doctrines could be acknowledged in the continuing quest for spiritual guidance, Hafiz's lyrics also point to vital truths in Christianity and in Magian (Zoroastrian) traditions. Elsewhere the author quotes from the Qurʾān, generally where matters of love and tolerance embracing diverse ways of life are involved.

Conflicting interpretations have been advanced on another level, however; it has been contended that hidden meanings lie within the outwardly simple and straightforward compositions of Hafiz. It has been averred, for example, that the vocabulary of mystical sects appears with enough regularity that two, or several, connotations were intended in many of the author's verses. This approach, which can be applied to certain Persian expressions, as well as to loan words from Arabic, assumes great depth in lyrics whose nominal subject matter already is handled through direct and metaphorical means. In this light, mentions of roses may be taken, specifically and obliquely, as references to love, but also (in Sufi usage) may denote initiates in a religious order. The common term *sihr* (magic), originally from Arabic, acquires numerous connotations where contexts involving both romantic and mystical-theological concerns arise. No single pattern of such underlying meanings, beyond those to be found in a literary language that is rich in poetic and theological usage, has been uncovered that may be used uniformly throughout Hafiz's works. On the other hand, it may well have been the case that the poet at certain junctures freely adopted semantic forms that would reflect the several concerns that at various times bemused him.

POLITICAL WORKS

Political concerns across the range of Hafiz's works may be considered briefly under two headings. In the first place, there are a certain number of frankly panegyric poems, which openly were meant to gain or retain the benevolent attention of rulers during his age. Such works are useful largely in that they cast some light on the poet's position in society and may readily be assigned dates; most are from the 1350's and 1360's. Flattery here is couched in terms that to some extent recall the images from other verse. Other poems, however, disclaim interest in political controversies, and indeed regard power as one of the less desirable ends in this life. In some notable lines, the reader is advised to practice kindness with friends and courtesy toward enemies; beyond this point, the author evidently had little interest in the polemical issues of political philosophy.

POETIC CRAFTSMANSHIP

By inference and from direct references, it may be learned that two of the most important literary predecessors of Hafiz were Nizami Ganjavi (c. 1140-c. 1202) and Saʿdi (c. 1200-c. 1291). By his own time, the *ghazal* had long been established as a major vehicle of poetic expression. It had become a standard form by which a certain number of distichs, or *bayt*, could be set to a single rhyme; the hemistichs also are made to rhyme. The final distich often contains the author's identifying name; in these lines Hafiz often addressed himself in self-congratulatory tones or in wry and self-effacing expressions. A set number of line feet are used in the verses of a single poem; emphasis follows a pattern that is strictly consistent throughout. To be sure, some variations may be observed among separate compositions. The number of lines may vary, generally between five and twelve; syllables may be emphasized in different patterns from one poem to the next. A notable feature in many of Hafiz's lyrics is the conclusion of each line with the same word; this practice, as a further demonstration of his virtuosity, lends added impact to many poems. Specific standards of emphasis and metric construction may also be found in other poetic forms, such as the elegies and quatrains Hafiz wrote; these works, while expressing some of the same concerns as the lyrics, are of interest largely as illustrating other facets of the author's poetic craftsmanship.

The troubled question of unity was raised by early critics, possibly including some readers from the poet's own lifetime. In discussing the works of the Persian author, Hafiz's first English translator, Sir William Jones, described his verse as "like orient pearls at random strung." One of the British scholar's contemporaries contended that Hafiz's works were utterly incoherent, although he nevertheless managed to produce Latin translations of some poems. Later writers have reached decidedly mixed conclusions on this vexed issue, which has also preoccupied leading Iranists of the twentieth century. Even when allowance is made for the diversity of themes and subjects in works composed possibly over a number of years, there are outward and rather conspicuous signs of inconsistency in individual compositions. Separate lyrics often enough will deal abruptly with two or more topics; sometimes transitions are not clearly made. This trait has given added credibility to theories of multiple mystical meanings in Hafiz's works, but even in this sense internal discrepancies arise. Although metaphorical usage may be considered to conjoin elements in the frankly romantic lyrics, in some poems, the setting is transferred from the garden to the tavern with no specific mode of passage. Other lyrics, after the contemplation of worldly cares and joys, shift rather sharply to essentially philosophical or religious concerns. Apart from the poetic conventions of metric length, emphasis, and rhythm that unite the lines within specific compositions, some passages would not be incongruous if affixed or transposed to other works. At the same time, it should be noted that allegations of disunity have been made against only a certain number of poems; it may be argued that in the author's works as a whole, continuity of themes and outlook may readily be discerned. Moreover, where combined meanings are concerned, suggesting both a symbolic and an actual realization of the author's design, it may be contended that conceptual integrity is preseved where imagery and allusion are interwoven about issues of major concern to the poet.

INFLUENTIAL LEGACY

The influence of Hafiz has been very great. In Persia, though the example he set probably precluded yet further summits in the development of the classical *ghazal*, many later writers derived inspiration from his works; the most notable from the great early age of Persian poetry probably was Jami (1414-1492). A number of commentaries and transcribed manuscripts, as well as poetry composed along similar lines, attest the reception of Hafiz in the lands of the Ottoman Empire. Although it was several centuries before Hafiz's works were printed, translations eventually did much to acquaint important creative thinkers with the poems of the Persian author. Among writers in the English language, there are notable references to Hafiz in the works of Alfred, Lord Tennyson, and Ralph Waldo Emerson; even given the vagaries of translation and comparative availability, it has been maintained that among classical Persian authors only Omar Khayyám made a more definite impression in England and the United States. In continental Europe, Hafiz's renown was spread particularly with the publication of a German translation of *The Divan* in 1812-1813, by the Austrian Orientalist Joseph von Hammer-Purgstall. Johann Wolfgang von Goethe utilized this work in according Hafiz pride of place in his *Westöstlicher Divan* (1819; *West-Eastern Divan*, 1877). Later translations of Hafiz, eventually into a number of languages, assisted both in the scholarly assessment and the public availability of his works. In Russia, a number of poets were notably influenced by Hafiz's lyrics, beginning probably with Afanasii Afanas'evich Fet (Shenshin) in the middle of the nineteenth century. The modern Islamic world, in particular, Sir Muhammad Iqbal of Pakistan, has also drawn inspiration from the Persian poet's works. In Iran itself, a spate of articles, studies, and scholarly editions of Hafiz's poetry have maintained his high reputation into modern times.

BIBLIOGRAPHY

Hafiz. *The Divan of Hafez: A Bilingual Text, Persian-English*. Translated by Reza Saberi. Lanham, Md.: University Press of America, 2002. Presents a translation of Hafiz's *The Divan*, with facing Persian-English pages. Hafiz's life and work are discussed in the introduction. Includes a glossary.

_____. *The Gift: Poems by Hafiz the Great Sufi Master*. Translated by David Ladinsky. New York: Penguin Putman, 1999. Ladinsky is a well-known translator of Hafiz, and his translations are playful, contemporary, and rich in surprising metaphors. His introduction surveys the life and work of Hafiz.

Hillmann, Michael C. "Classicism, Ornament, Ambivalence, and the Persian Muse." In *Iranian Culture: A Persianist View*. Lanham, Md.: University Press of America, 1988. An attempt to discern enduring Iranian cultural attitudes in an examination of aesthetic aspects and criteria discernible in Hafiz's *ghazals*, among them appreciation of tradition, formality, and ceremony, a penchant for embellishment and the ornamental, and a capacity for ambivalence in attitudes, ideas, beliefs, and standards. Bibliography.

_____. *Unity in the Ghazals of Hafez*. Minneapolis, Minn.: Bibliotheca Islamica, 1976. A formalist analysis of sixteen Hafizian *ghazals* in a response to longstanding charges by Iranian scholars and scholars of Asia that Hafiz' poems lack unity. Includes an extensive list in notes and bibliography of writings on Hafiz in European languages. Bibliography, index.

LeMaster, J. R., and Sabahat Jahan. *Walt Whitman and the Persian Poets: A Study in Literature and Religion*. Bethesda, Md.: Ibex, 2009. Hafiz and Walt Whitman are examined for the religious content of their poetry.

Loloi, Parvin. *Hafiz, Master of Persian Poetry: A Critical Bibliography—English Translations Since the Eighteenth Century*. New York: I. B. Tauris, 2004. A bibliography of Hafiz's works that helps the researcher sort out the many translations.

Pourafzal, Haleh, and Roger Montgomery. *The Spiritual Wisdom of Haféz: Teachings of the Philosopher of Love*. Rochester, Vt.: Inner Traditions, 2004. A good introduction to Hafiz's poetry. Explores how his work speaks to scholarship in philosophy, psychology, social theory, and education. Bibliographical references, index.

J. R. Broadus

JOSÉ HERNÁNDEZ

Born: Chaera de Pueyrredón, Buenos Aires,
    Argentina; November 10, 1834
Died: Belgrano, Argentina; October 21, 1886

PRINCIPAL POETRY

El gaucho Martín Fierro, 1872 (*The Gaucho
    Martin Fierro*, 1935)
La vuelta de Martín Fierro, 1879 (*The Return of
    Martin Fierro*, 1935; included in *The Gaucho
    Martin Fierro*, 1935)

OTHER LITERARY FORMS

José Hernández (ehr-NON-days) dedicated his life to poetic and prosaic elucidation, illumination, and explanation of all aspects of the lifestyle, politics, and moral values of the Argentine gaucho (a type of cowboy and occasional laborer located in rural Argentina). He wrote many lengthy articles and essays about the political situation of the gauchos in relation to the power struggle between Argentine forces in favor of federalism and those in favor of regional autonomy. Hernández composed many of these works for a sophisticated readership that principally included the well-educated population of Buenos Aires and the provincial capitals of Argentina. While a journalist, he produced various works that depicted the gaucho lifestyle in biographical and instructional prose forms.

ACHIEVEMENTS

Known almost exclusively for his epic poem, *The Gaucho Martin Fierro*, José Hernández received no formal literary awards during his lifetime. However, he is remembered and honored through the Martín Fierro Award, given each year to the most outstanding television and radio productions in Argentina. The small statues that are awarded are in the shape of a gaucho.

BIOGRAPHY

José Rafael Hernández y Pueyrredón was born on the family ranch near San Martín in the province of Buenos Aires, Argentina, on November 10, 1834. By the age of four, he was enrolled in school and was said to have been able to read and write. When he was nine years old, his father (the foreman on the ranches of General Juan Manuel de Rosas) moved the family to the south of the province, where he came into close contact with the rural gaucho lifestyle and customs. It was here that he witnessed at first hand the armed suppression of the Indian population that still occupied much of this part of the province. Hernández received little formal education, but he developed an aptitude for reading, writing, and speaking that impressed his contemporaries. In 1857, he moved to the city of Paraná, where he met his wife, Carolina. They were married in 1863 and had seven children.

He moved to Buenos Aires in 1863 and began his career as a journalist for the newspaper *El Argentino*. He began to write poetic and prose works and penned articles for the paper *El Eco de Corrientes*. Between 1853 and 1871, he became involved in the Argentine Civil War. He actively participated in the armed rebellion of the gauchos against President Domingo Faustino Sarmiento. The failure of this movement necessitated his self-exile to Brazil in 1871. On his return to Buenos Aires, he began composing his long epic poem, *The Gaucho Martin Fierro*, with the aim of presenting the gaucho lifestyle and mythology to the population of Argentina, at that time still a young country. The first part of the epic poem was published in the newspaper *La Repúblicá*. Shortly thereafter, it was published in book format. Because of his intimate knowledge of the language, culture, and morals of the gaucho people, he was able to create an authentic presentation that became extremely popular with the gauchos as well as various factions of the Argentine population. In 1879, the second part of the work was published.

In 1873, Hernández founded the newspaper *Río de la Plata*, in which he advocated regional autonomy, freedom from conscription of gauchos for the Indian wars, and a country based on agriculture and education. However, the newspaper was soon shut down by political foe and fellow author Sarmiento, who was also the president of Argentina. In his lengthy editorial essays, Hernández expressed disdain for the Europeanized and elitist factions that backed Sarmiento and who considered the gauchos to be unfit as a model for Argentina's future.

Under a new federal administration, Hernández was elected as a congressman in 1879 and a senator from the province of Buenos Aires in 1881. He was still serving in this capacity when he died of cardiac problems on October 21, 1886.

ANALYSIS

José Hernández represents one of the first markedly Latin American voices in literature. That is, his Argentine perspective was based on firsthand knowledge, and he wrote in a style that was not copied or transplanted from a European approach. Hernández lived in a tumultuous time during the nation-forming period of Argentina. The nation was undergoing a struggle between those who wanted to use the gaucho as a national hero and model and those who wished to eliminate the gaucho influence entirely. Hernández favored the incorporation of gaucho values into mainstream Argentine politics and realities. Therefore, he wrote his epic poems to enlighten the educated masses in Buenos Aires, the capital of Argentina.

Hernández's original audience was the educated and urban reader. The author himself had experienced prejudicial treatment during his lifetime in rural, marginalized sections of Argentina, and he believed the gaucho existence was threatened. His goal went beyond education of the urban elites, and he clearly hoped his epic poems would help bring about reconciliation between the urban and rural groups in Argentina. Later, his focus shifted to the gauchos themselves. Hernández was successful in his efforts to accurately describe the gauchos, as can be seen in the fact that his works were immediate best sellers and have continued to be considered essential reading for any serious study of historical and contemporary Argentine values and culture. The author's goal was not limited to describing the lifestyles of the gauchos; he also sought to present their thoughts and values.

The poems address the day-to-day life of the gauchos, relating their social manners and colloquial language. Much like the American Wild West hero, the gaucho is presented as a hardworking, hard-fighting individualist who takes on the corrupt elements of an expanding frontier. Most of the challenges to this individualism result in a physical confrontation, generally a

José Hernández

fight between two or more men. Literally all the fights are provoked by women. Unlike the North American counterpart, the gaucho does not win the respect of a woman in the end.

In *The Gaucho Martín Fierro*, the reader finds a determined defense of a marginalized group. The gauchos are presented as unfairly oppressed by a society that cannot or will not treat them fairly. Literally every governmental, military, and legal entity encountered in the poems is presented as corrupt. In this manner, Hernández extorts the reader to empathize with the neglected gaucho. Clearly, one of the goals of the author was to change his society through literature. The concept of the gaucho as a noble example of the new Argentine citizenship was revolutionary at the time of the publication of *The Gaucho Martin Fierro*. Hernández's nemesis, Argentine president Sarmiento, had published *Facundo: Civilización y barbarie—Vida de Juan Facundo Quiroga i aspecto físico, costumbres i habitos de la Republica Argentina* (1845; *Life in the Argentine Republic in the Day of the Tyrants: Or, Civilization and Barbarism*, 1868), a work that portrayed the gauchos as backward and uneducated.

THE GAUCHO MARTIN FIERRO

Hernández used prologues in both parts of *The Gaucho Martin Fierro*. In the part published in 1872, his stated mission was to lament the gauchos' situation, with the goal of demonstrating to an urban audience in Buenos Aires that the preservation of the gaucho lifestyle was a necessary component in the building of an Argentine national identity. Hernández starts by informing the reader that the happy and meaningful life of the gaucho had degenerated into suffering at the hands of indifferent urban intruders. He uses the colloquial speech of the gauchos to emphasize their different culture. They are portrayed as competent speakers, but without much formal education.

Hernández relates how Fierro and his gaucho friend Cruz decide that the only way to escape the injustices heaped on them by an ignorant and corrupt authority system in the evolving frontier lands of Argentina is to flee the society entirely and align themselves with the indigenous culture. This symbolic break with mainstream Argentina was meant to awaken the urban dweller to the injustices that were being wrought with their acquiescence. The problems that Cruz and Fierro endured were not just unfortunate fate, but rather systematic abuse of an entire culture. The two gauchos are presented as universal "others" who are not being noticed by the powers in the distant capital of the nation. Hernández attempts to reconcile the long-standing differences between rural and urban values by exposing the members of the urban segment to his somewhat romanticized but generally accurate descriptions of their rural counterparts.

THE RETURN OF MARTIN FIERRO

The seven years that had passed between the publication of the first and second parts of Hernández's epic poem had produced a markedly different political and social reality in Argentina. By 1879, Hernández had come to back the new Argentine president, who had called for the assimilation of the gauchos into the geopolitical structure of the country. This time, in the prologue to *The Return of Martin Fierro*, the Hernández's intentions are more complex: He intends to give advice to the gaucho himself. Hernández does mention how he educated the urban elites about gaucho culture in the first part of the poem, but his focus in the second part is on instructing gauchos themselves. He encourages good work habits and more education, so that gauchos could become more productive and respected citizens.

Hernández updates the tale of Martín Fierro and Cruz by describing how their sons had integrated themselves into the Argentine national culture by means of productive work and education, as opposed to marginal work efforts and the physical brawling that was portrayed in the first part of the poem. By analogy, the gauchos are advised as to what they must to become more in line with the future needs of the new country. The work reads like a guidebook, instructing the gauchos on how to leave the misery and instability of the past behind.

Numerous examples of education by analogy can be found in the work. One is the speech that Fierro delivers to his sons, in which he relates that the future will not be as easy as the past. It will require productive work, education, and adherence to the concepts of God and country. Another example is found at the end of the poem. A conflict arises that in the 1872 version would have led to a physical fight between the two antagonistic men. Instead, the quarrel is resolved without violence when the men compete to see who is the better singer.

BIBLIOGRAPHY

Foster, David William, and Daniel Altamiranda, eds. *From Romanticism to Modernismo in Latin America*. New York: Garland, 1997. A collection of essays on literary genres in Latin America, including poetry. The introduction is helpful and the work includes a segment on Hernández's *The Gaucho Martin Fierro*. The epic poem is examined from the viewpoint of Romanticism in Latin American poetry. Includes a bibliography.

Hanway, Nancy. *Embodying Argentina: Body, Space, and Nation in Nineteenth Century Narrative*. Jefferson, N.C.: McFarland, 2003. This bilingual anthology is useful for the student who requires information on the history of Argentine nation building in order to understand the importance of Hernández's epic poem. It specifically presents an excerpt from *The Gaucho Martin Fierro*, which deals with the tragedy of the slave ship. The introduction provides a historical summary of Latin American poetry. Includes bibliography and index.

Hernández, José. *The Gaucho Martín Fierro*. Edited by Kate Kavanagh. Albany: State University of New York Press, 1967. Bilingual edition of José Hernández's epic poem with a very useful introduction. Includes bibliography.

Quiroga Lavié, Humberto. *Biografia de José Hernández*. Buenos Aires: Librería História, 2004. Although written in Spanish, this work is the definitive account of the life, writings and events that gave birth to them in the nineteenth century Argentina of Hernández. It explains the intricate relationship between Hernández and his adversary, Argentine president Sarmiento, himself a recognized author and poet.

Scroggins, Daniel C. *A Concordance of José Hernández's "Martín Fierro."* Columbia: University of Missouri Press, 1971. Easy-to-read edition of the epic poem of Hernández. Includes an introduction to nineteenth century Argentine poetry.

Slatta, Richard W. *Gauchos and the Vanishing Frontier*. Lincoln: University of Nebraska Press, 1992. This excellent history presents the gauchos of nineteenth century Argentina in a cultural perspective that pits them against the evolving modern nation of Argentina. It is valuable for anyone who wants a better understanding of Hernández's portrayal of the gauchos. As with the epic poem, it presents the gaucho as a romanticized character but nonetheless an essential component in the struggle for Argentine nationhood.

Vicuña, Cecilia, and Ernesto Livon-Grosman, eds. *The Oxford Book of Latin American Poetry: A Bilingual Anthology*. New York: Oxford University Press, 2009. This bilingual anthology, considered the best introduction to Latin American poetry, includes an excerpt from Hernández's epic poem. It provides a brief biography and critique of Hernández, biography, and index.

Paul Siegrist

NAZIM HIKMET

Born: Salonika, Ottoman Empire (now Thessaloniki, Greece); January 20, 1902
Died: Moscow, Soviet Union (now in Russia); June 3, 1963

PRINCIPAL POETRY

Güneşi içenlerin türküsü, 1928
835 satir, 1929
Jokond ile Si-Ya-U, 1929
1 + 1 = bir, 1930
Varan 3, 1930
Sesini kaybeden şehir, 1931
Benerci kendini niçin öldürdü?, 1932
Gece gelen telgraf, 1932
Portreler, 1935
Taranta Babu'ya mektuplar, 1935
Simavne Kadisi oğlu Şeyh Bedreddin destanı, 1936 (*The Epic of Sheik Bedreddin*, 1977)
Moskova senfonisi, 1952 (*The Moscow Symphony*, 1970)
Poems by Nazim Hikmet, 1954
Kurtulus Savaşı destanı, 1965 (expanded as *Kuvayi Milliye*, 1968)
Piraye için yazilmis saat 21-22 şiirleri, 1965
Şu 1941 yılında, 1965
Dört hapisaneden, 1966
Rubailer, 1966 (*Rubaiyat*, 1985)
Yeni şiirler, 1966
Memleketimden insan manzaralari, 1966-1967 (5 volumes; *Human Landscapes*, 1982)
Selected Poems, 1967
The Moscow Symphony, and Other Poems, 1970
Son şiirler, 1970
The Day Before Tomorrow, 1972

*Things I Didn't Know I Loved: Selected Poems of
Nazim Hikmet*, 1975
Kerem gibi, 1976
The Epic of Sheik Bedreddin, and Other Poems,
1977
Selected Poetry, 1986
A Sad State of Freedom, 1990
Beyond the Walls: Selected Poems, 2002

OTHER LITERARY FORMS

Although he is remembered primarily for his poetry, Nazim Hikmet (HIHK-meht) also became known early in his career for his plays; among the most notable of these are *Kafatası* (pb. 1931; the skull) and *Unutulan adam* (pb. 1935; the forgotten man), which deal with the practice of psychology and the conflict between worldly recognition and inner dissatisfaction. Other works in this genre, however, have been criticized for a facile identification of personages with political and social standpoints that they were meant to represent. Hikmet subsequently moved in other directions in his dramatic writing, first with works such as *Bir aşk masalı* (pb. 1945; a love story), which attempted a modern interpretation of traditional Middle Eastern characters. Other plays involved experiments with old and new technical forms, as a part of the author's effort to adapt classical literary themes to contemporary concerns. Among later plays, by far the most widely known was *İvan İvanoviç var mıydı yok muydu?* (was there or was there not an Ivan Ivanovich?), which was written in exile and was first published in a Russian translation in 1956. In this contribution to the literary "thaw" in the Soviet Union, the author took issue with the personality cult and rigid, unswerving norms of criticism that had dominated creative writing under dictator Joseph Stalin.

Hikmet's narrative fiction is rather uneven; there is some moving and effective writing in *Sevdalı bulut* (1968; the cloud in love), which brings together short pieces, including children's stories, written over many years. His novels tend to display his ideological concerns. Of these perhaps the most interesting is *Yeşil elmalar* (1965; green apples), which deals with crime, corruption, and penal detention. Also of interest as a semiautobiographical effort is *Yaşamak güzel şey bekardeşim* (1967; *The Romantics*, 1987). Works of

political commentary furnish direct statements of the author's views on leading issues of his time; his treatises on Soviet democracy and on German fascism, both originally published in 1936, are particularly revealing in this regard. Other insights into the writer's thought may be gathered from his collected newspaper columns and compilations of his personal letters.

ACHIEVEMENTS

Throughout his creative lifetime, Nazim Hikmet was regarded as a politically controversial figure whose poetry expressed ideological concerns that situated him well to the left among Turkish writers of his generation. Although officially he was almost invariably out of favor in his own country—indeed, much of his adult life in Turkey was spent in prison, and work from his later years was composed under the shadow of Soviet cultural standard-bearers—his experiments with versification produced poetic forms that, more than any other works, announced the introduction of modern techniques into Turkish writing in this genre. During the last years of the Ottoman Empire, major innovations had been attempted by leading literary figures; language reform movements proceeded alongside the development of literary vehicles suitable for wider circles of readers among the masses. Enlarging on the earlier efforts of Mehmet Tevfik Fikret and other important writers, Nazim Hikmet devised new and strikingly resonant verse patterns that in their turn pointed to the possibilities that could be achieved with the use of free verse. Moreover, while admittedly experimental, his verse was distinctive in the unusual confluence of models chosen: Hikmet's poems show the influence of Soviet post-Symbolists while, in some notable works, recalling classical Islamic traditions in modern, reworked guises. Hikmet's poetry is alternately strident in its political declamations and intensely personal in its evocations of the writer's sufferings and innermost wants. Many of his prose works, while never really descending to the level of Socialist Realism, are somewhat more narrowly symptomatic of the ideological persuasions that guided him.

Apart from his literary fame, Hikmet became well known from the political charges for which he served an aggregate of seventeen years in Turkish prisons. In

1949, an international committee was formed in Paris to press for his release; among others, Jean-Paul Sartre, Pablo Picasso, Louis Aragon, and Paul Robeson petitioned for the reopening of the Turkish government's case against him. In 1950, the Soviet Union conferred its World Peace Prize on Nazim Hikmet, an award he shared with Pablo Neruda. During the last years of Hikmet's life, he made a number of public appearances in Moscow, Warsaw, and capitals of other Soviet bloc countries. After his death, his work became the subject of lively discussion, much of it favorable, in his native Turkey, and important writings once more were published. Students of and specialists in Turkish literature have widely acknowledged his leading position among modern poets.

BIOGRAPHY

On January 20, 1902, Nazim Hikmet was born in Salonika, the port city in Thrace that was then part of the Ottoman Empire. His father was a physician who had held government appointments; his mother was a painter, and his grandfather, Nazim Paşa, was a poet and critic of some note. As a boy, Hikmet was introduced to local literary circles. His first poems were written when he was about seventeen. He was educated in Istanbul, at the French-language Galatasaray Lycée and at the Turkish Naval Academy. Although poor health precluded a military career, he went oxn to Moscow during the early period of Soviet-Turkish friendship; between 1922 and 1924, he studied at the University of the Workers of the East. He derived inspiration from the events of the Russian Revolution and probably was influenced as well by the bold new literary ventures of Soviet poets such as Sergei Esenin and Vladimir Mayakovsky. Upon his return to his native country, Hikmet joined the Turkish Communist Party, which by then had been forced into a clandestine existence; in Izmir, he worked for a left-wing publication and was sentenced to fifteen years in prison. He fled to the Soviet Union and returned only after a general amnesty was proclaimed in 1928. By that time, his first book-length collection of poems had been published in Soviet Azerbaijan. In Turkey, the Communist Party had been formally outlawed, and Hikmet was arrested forthwith. Nevertheless, Turkish publishers brought out verse collections such as *835 sat r* (835 lines) and others; his works were deemed inflammatory by the authorities, who claimed that they incited workers against the government. He was imprisoned twice and later was able to find work mainly as a proofreader, translator, and scriptwriter. Indeed, some of his early poems refer to the tedious routine of his daily work, to which he was effectively restricted because of his political convictions. Although his plays won critical recognition and some acclaim for their introduction of new, unconventional dramatic forms—here Hikmet may in some ways have followed the technical innovations of Bertolt Brecht—political writings and newspaper columns had to be published under a pseudonym. He turned to historical topics, which nevertheless allowed range for his leftist populist outlook: The last work published in Turkey during his lifetime was *The Epic of Sheik Bedreddin, and Other Poems*, which includes a long poem narrating events surrounding the life and death of the leader of a fifteenth century peasant revolt.

Nazim Hikmet (AP/Wide World Photos)

In January, 1938, new charges were brought against Hikmet; because copies of his poems were found in the possession of military cadets, he was arraigned for inciting unrest in the armed forces. A military court found him guilty, though the original sentence of thirty-five years was reduced to twenty-eight. During his imprisonment in Bursa, Hikmet embarked on his poetic magnum opus, *Human Landscapes*, which was to be published only after his death, in a five-volume edition of 1966-1967. This monumental, and sometimes disjointed, work was circulated in parts among the poet's friends, family, and confidants; some portions of it were confiscated by the Turkish police or otherwise disappeared. Much of the writing Hikmet produced in prison has a musing, poignant, indeed bittersweet quality that was not so pronounced in his earlier works. On the other hand, some poems alight on world events of which he had heard in passing: Germany's invasion of the Soviet Union, in 1941, and the United States' use of an atom bomb against Hiroshima at the end of World War II, are discussed in his verse from this period. In 1949, in spite of having suffered a heart attack, Hikmet undertook a hunger strike that lasted seventeen days. In response to international pressure, the Turkish government released him from prison in 1950, but shortly thereafter, to curb the expression of his political views, he was made liable for conscripted military service. The following year, Hikmet fled the country alone in a small fishing boat; he was taken on board a Romanian ship in the Black Sea and eventually made his way to Moscow.

During his years in exile, the last period of his life, Hikmet lived for some time in the Soviet capital and in Warsaw; he took out a Polish passport under the name Borzęcki, after a family to which he had traced some of his ancestors. Sometimes he also used the added surname Ran. He traveled widely and attended literary congresses in other Soviet bloc countries; he also spent much time in Paris. He visited China, Cuba, and Tanganyika. Once he was refused a visa to enter the United States. Although he was not a literary conformist, he continued to uphold Soviet positions on international security. Some of his works from this period did him little credit, though they dealt with issues similar to those of his earlier activist poems. He suffered from angina pectoris, which had developed during his longest prison term, and other chronic health complaints arose later. While he lived in Turkey, he had married three times; his imprisonment had made settled family life impossible. In Moscow, he took up residence with a fetching young "straw blonde" Vera Tuliakova. Some of his later poems wistfully call back images of the women in his life or point to the hopes he still cherished in spite of his advancing age and his problematical physical state. After a final heart attack, Hikmet died in Moscow on June 3, 1963. Homage was rendered him from leading literary figures in many countries. Since his death, his reputation among Turkish writers has grown apace.

ANALYSIS

According to some estimates, the poetry of Nazim Hikmet has been translated into at least fifty languages. Perhaps more than that of any other Turkish writer, his work transcended the bounds of stylized Ottoman versification. At their best, his poems call to mind settings the author knew well, while extending a universal appeal on behalf of his social beliefs. Lyrical and rhetorical passages occur alternately in some of his major works; his epics exhibit narrative powers that in some segments are used to depict events from the distant past or to evoke those from the author's lifetime.

Moreover, though early in his career he came to be known as much for his outspoken ideological positions as for his literary achievements, Hikmet's poetry conveys the sudden dramatic impact of historical occurrences; social issues are depicted in ways that can be felt beyond the strict limits of party politics. On a more personal level, romantic yearnings, whimsical observations of street scenes and travel, and indeed nature and the weather are discussed in simple yet deeply felt lines that complement Hikmet's more directly expressed political concerns. Some of his poems communicate the loneliness and anxiety he felt as a political prisoner, without indulging particularly in self-pity. On the whole, he cannot be classified purely as a rationalist or a romantic; rather, his works combine elements of both inclinations.

LANGUAGE

From the outset, Hikmet's poetry was brash, vibrant, and politically engaged; defiantly casting aside traditional poetic styles, the author's work exuberantly mixed ideology and amorous inclinations in lines that at first glance resemble dismembered declarative sentences punctuated by crisp, staccato repetitions of phrases and nouns. Statements begun on one line are carried forward, with indentations, to the next, and sometimes further indentations are inserted before the thought is concluded. Question marks and exclamation points enliven stirring passages in which the author seems to be carrying on a dialogue with himself, if not with nature or society.

The vowel harmony characteristic of the Turkish language is used to impart added force and velocity to some passages; moreover, the author's writing drew from folk songs, time-honored national sagas, and other sources in eclectic and distinctive combinations. Colloquial expressions, lower-class idioms, and outright vulgarisms appear from time to time. This approach, which seems ever fresh and lively in the hands of a talented practitioner, is notably well suited to Hikmet's subject matter. One early poem, evidently composed in a devil-may-care mood, contrasts the author's straitened and difficult circumstances—his many monotonous hours as a lowly proofreader were rewarded with a pittance—and the effervescent sensations of springtime, with Cupid urging him after a comely girl.

JOKOND ILE SI-YA-U

Considerable powers of creative imagination were called on in early poetry of a political character. In the long poem *Jokond ile Si-Ya-U* (the Gioconda and Si-Ya-U), various narrative transitions are conjoined with abrupt changes of setting, from Paris to the open sea to Shanghai under the white terror; eventually the author's summary is presented from his vantage point in Europe. Some of Hikmet's experiences during his travel—he had met Chinese revolutionaries during a visit to France—appear in an ultimately fictional and somewhat fantastic form. The author, who is bored and chafing at what he regards as hidebound aesthetic classicism in the Louvre, comes upon a modern Gioconda in a most unusual guise. Her modern incarnation is exotic and remote, but deeply concerned about mass upheaval that aims at the transformation of traditional Asian society. Still inscrutable, she is made to stand

by as the soldiers of nationalist leader Chiang Kai-shek execute a Chinese Communist spokesperson. Ultimately the Gioconda is tried and found guilty by a French military court; hers is a fate quite different from spending centuries on canvas as a creation of Leonardo da Vinci. Other works express Hikmet's proletarian views of art: Beethoven's sonatas, he maintains, should be played out on wood and metal in the workplace. The raw power of the industrial age is reflected in his taut descriptive lines about iron suspension bridges and concrete skyscrapers. However, the workers in his native Turkey were invariably badly off: They were bound to an unthinking routine and could afford only the lowest quality of goods.

TARANTA BABU'YA MEKTUPLAR

One early composition took up the cause of striking transportation workers in Istanbul in 1929. At times Hikmet considered events that were not too far removed from his own experience; his sojourns in Russia during the early years of the Soviet government probably furnished impressions recaptured in verses about the revolutionary events of 1917. Poems collected in *Taranta Babu'ya mektuplar* (letters to Tarantu Babu) raised another problem in world politics; they are letters in verse purportedly written by a young Italian to a native woman caught up in the Ethiopian war launched under Benito Mussolini. The author's commentary on the brutal excesses of fascism reveals a measure of political prescience as well as an expanded sense of solidarity with like-minded people in many nations.

THE EPIC OF SHEIK BEDREDDIN

Historical dimensions of class struggle are explored in *The Epic of Sheik Bedreddin*. Government pressure by this time had restricted Hikmet's choice of subject matter, making it almost impossible for him to publish work on contemporary issues, so the author turned to more remote ages with the avowed intent of rescuing major events from the antiquarian dust that had gathered around them. This epic, based on a book he had read during one of his early prison terms, was given added intensity by the author's experience of seeing a man hanged outside the window of his cell. While set in the early fifteenth century, Hikmet's work underscores the solidarity that brought together Turkish peasants, Greek fishermen, and Jewish merchants. In places, he suggests that though historical works had depicted this era as the prelude to an age of imperial greatness, it in fact was rife with social unrest and discontent provoked by inequality and injustice. Ten thousand common people took up arms to oppose the sultan before the rebellion was finally put down. The eventual execution of his protagonist, one of the insurgents' leaders, was a grim, bloody business that Hikmet recounts in unsparing detail but with impassioned sensitivity. This long poem, one of the most celebrated in Turkish literature of the twentieth century, is also notable for the author's broadening concern with different verse techniques, which reached fruition with his works combining modern usage with classical Persian meters.

Prison poems

During Hikmet's longest period of imprisonment, between 1938 and 1950, works displaying other facets of his poetic consciousness were composed. His outlook seemed to become more deeply personal, though perhaps not so brash and self-assertive as in some of his first poems. His meditations on the springtime reveal a sense of yearning and melancholy that was previously absent. For a time, he was held in solitary confinement. He wrote of singing to himself and watching shadows on the wall; simple things began to matter more to him. There are a number of touching passages in prison poems that he addressed to Piraye, his second wife; brief, bittersweet phrases recall their shared joys together, aspects of her appearance, and simple pleasures that mattered most to him.

The long period of his incarceration led to some brooding reflections on the transitory and changeless issues of this life. In some poems, there is speculation on the seasons that have come and gone, children who have been conceived and grown since he entered prison; mountains in the distance, however, remain fixed points separated by specific spatial intervals. There are also some ironic musings on the fates of common criminals from among his fellow prisoners: One of them was held for murder but was paroled after seven and one-half years; after a second, much shorter, sentence for smuggling, he was released for good and eventually married. The couple's child would be born while much of Hikmet's term, as a political prisoner, still remained to be served.

Angina pectoris, followed by a heart attack, aroused uncertainty about the author's physical condition. He wrote poems reaffirming the necessity to go on living, particularly with half his heart devoted to social concerns in Turkey or to political struggles in Greece and China. Some works that begin by marking the passage of time in prison contain brief but intense reactions to events of World War II, including bombing raids, the liberation of concentration camps at Dachau, and the dawn of the nuclear age.

Rubaiyat

One collection of poems, *Rubaiyat*, written in 1945 but published posthumously in 1966, reveals the author's search for further literary forms that would express the ideological and philosophical content of his thought. Beginning with the example of the thirteenth century Sufi poet and religious thinker Jalāl al-Dīn Rūmī, Hikmet took up the position in effect that mysticism is merely a veiled means of approaching material and social reality. Hikmet purposely adopted the quatrain, on a pattern similar to that used by Omar Khayyám, specifically to take issue with the Persian poet's supposed hedonism. In some lines, counsel to take wine and be joyful is contrasted with the harsh, inescapable routines of working-class life. Elsewhere the philosophical idealism of classical writers is challenged by Hikmet's own commitment to dialectical materialism; in poems dedicated to Piraye, the poet asks whether the images he retains of her correspond to the material reality he remembers. On a technical level, this work is notable as well for the author's provocative insertion of colloquial language in passages that otherwise conform to time-honored standards of versification.

Human Landscapes

Contemporary history on a panoramic scale is taken up in *Human Landscapes*, which was written during the author's prison years but was published several years after his death. Beginning with an epic study of Turkish history during the twentieth century, at intervals the poet's narrative also turns to major events in adjoining regions, notably naval action of World War II in the Mediterranean and the work of Soviet forces against Nazi invaders. His commentary on the Turkish War of Independence (1919-1922) stands in stark contrast to the heroic national themes repeatedly invoked by other writers of that period. In Hikmet's view, it would seem that the people as a whole contributed to final victory but only through an inchoate mass rising that did not also lead to a social revolution. Indeed, many passages suggest that class differences remained acute but were altered by Turkey's changed status in the world economy. There are a number of brief sketches of individual lives, both from the wealthy and from the lower orders, often to state unpleasant truths about the people's living situation. Some characters, it is recorded, died of disease at early ages; farmers retained their land but lost all means of production. Many of the personages are war veterans from one conflict or another. There is much attention to dates, but not in the sense of commemorating events with patriotic connotations; important occurrences in individual lives are accorded the same emphasis as major developments in the nation's history. There is also a fair amount of random, seemingly senseless violence: Family quarrels lead to murder; after a man kills his wife, children use the head as a ball in a macabre game. A wrenching, gripping scene records the lynching of a Turk who had collaborated with the British occupation forces. There are some sardonic religious references that call to mind folk superstitions; in some later passages, Turks of a pro-German inclination speculate about whether Adolf Hiler could be a Muslim. Leading Turkish statesmen and thinkers figure as portraits on the walls of business offices; the memories associated with them are quirky bits of characterization that are far from flattering.

The work as a whole darts about and circumambulates historical epochs as they affected different, indeed opposing, social classes. After nearly fifteen years of national independence, homeless and desperately hungry men are to be found outside a newspaper office; if wealthy businessmen cannot turn a profit in some branches of the export trade because of government restrictions, they move readily to other sectors where their fortunes can be augmented. Some of them end up dealing with both the Allied and the Axis powers during World War II. The incidence of suicide on either side of the class divide is fairly high; among the poor, childbirth is difficult, painful, and sometimes ends in tragedy. Although this exercise in historical realism,

based on the author's own observations of Turkish life, does not seem to hold out any immediate hopes for a better future, the poet's descriptions of nature and simple joys serve to leaven an otherwise grim and unsentimental saga.

Some later segments of this work are essentially similar to portions of *The Moscow Symphony, and Other Poems*, an imaginative lyrical reconstruction of German-Soviet fighting that in the first instance was probably based on news stories that Hikmet received in prison. After allowance for the different languages, it may be argued that some passages would do credit to a Soviet wartime poet: the anxiety of the war's first year, the vast human drama of armies locked in combat, and the camaraderie of soldiers brought together in common struggle are evoked in brisk, telling lines. Hikmet's own allegiances are discussed in another section, which depicts the execution of an eighteen-year-old Russian girl for partisan action against the Nazis. He wrote, "Tanya,/ I have your picture here in front of me in Bursa Prison," and, before returning to the Turkish settings where his epic had commenced, he added:

> Tanya,
> I love my country
>   as much as you loved yours.

LAST POEMS

Hikmet's last poems in some ways chronicled the tribulations of exile; many works had to do with his travels about the Communist world, as well as into Switzerland and to Paris. The impression arises that he considered many of his destinations as way stations; hotel balconies, train depots, arrivals and departures are recorded repeatedly and almost mechanically. His political works from this period, albeit written in countries that were openly receptive to his views, were lacking perhaps in the combative spirit that had distinguished the poems written in Turkey. Among such productions, there may be found some caustic observations in verse on the Korean War—he deplored Turkey's participation in that conflict—as well as more positive and uplifting efforts composed for May Day celebrations or in response to the Cuban revolution. One poem was meant to commemorate the fortieth anniversary of the foundation of the Turkish Communist

Party. His personal concerns, perhaps, were handled more effectively in his later works. One poem describes his meeting with a young blonde woman in an express train; as the sights pass by outside afterimages of her hair and eyelashes and of her long black coat repeatedly appear before his eyes. Some poems expressed his desire to be reunited with his lover, Tuliakova, after journeys about various East European countries. In other works, there are somewhat sour comments on his physical condition, which continued to deteriorate during his years in exile. Although he continued to cherish the values of this existence, some passages became dour and premonitory. Toward the end of his life he speculated:

> Will my funeral start out from our courtyard?
> How will you take me down from the third floor?
> The coffin won't fit in the elevator,
> and the stairs are awfully narrow.

LEGACY

For many years, Hikmet was regarded as Turkey's best-known Communist; his conspicuously partisan poetry on behalf of the working classes created more controversy than the pronouncements of many political figures. His importance as a poet, however, may be measured by the extent to which his works have been read even as interest in his ideological agitation, the long-standing scandal of his imprisonment, and his life in exile have become past concerns. While it is possible to distinguish major phases in his career as a poet—and arguably within those periods he was subject to variable moods—there are also elements of continuity that in their turn point to the enduring features of his work. Although some of his efforts may have aged more gracefully than others, his concerns with social justice and with the struggle against fascism in Europe certainly would find sympathy with many subsequent readers. He maintained that Marxism interested him largely for its literary possibilities and that his work was involved largely in the basic human issues of his time. His poems are quite possibly the most readily recognized of those from any Turkish writer of the twentieth century. Aside from his political fame, or notoriety, it may be contended not only that he had discovered forms by which modern free verse might be composed

in Turkish but also that he had come upon themes and techniques that have been found to be intrinsically appealing on a much wider level.

OTHER MAJOR WORKS

LONG FICTION: *Kan konuşmaz*, 1965; *Yeşil elmalar*, 1965; *Yaşamak güzel şey bekardeşim*, 1967 (*The Romantics*, 1987).

SHORT FICTION: *Sevdalı bulut*, 1968.

PLAYS: *Ocak başında*, pb. 1920; *Kafatası*, pb. 1931; *Bir ölü evi yahut merhumun hanesi*, pb. 1932; *Unutulan adam*, pb. 1935; *Bir aşk masalı*, pb. 1945; *İvan İvanoviç var mıydı yok muydu?*, pb. 1956, in Russian (pb. 1971 in Turkish); *Enayi*, pb. 1958; *İnek*, pb. 1958; *İstasyon*, pb. 1958; *Yusuf ve Zeliha*, pb. 1963; *Sabahat*, pb. 1966; *Yolcu*, pb. 1966; *Damokles'in kı lı cı*, pb. 1971; *Fatma, Ali ve başkalari*, pb. 1971; *Her şeye rağmen*, pb. 1971.

NONFICTION: *Alman faşizmi ve ırkçı lığı*, 1935; *Sovyet demokrasisi*, 1936; *İt ürür kervan yürür*, 1965; *Cezaevinden Mehmet Fuat'a mektuplar*, 1968; *Kemal Tahir'e mahpusaneden mektuplar*, 1968; *Oğlum, canim evladim, Memedim*, 1968; *Bursa cezaevinden Va-Nu'lara mektuplar*, 1970; *Nazim ile Piraye*, 1975.

MISCELLANEOUS: *Bütün eserleri*, 1967-1972 (8 volumes; collected works).

BIBLIOGRAPHY

Başak, Ergil. *The Image of Nâzim Hikmet and His Poetry: In Anglo-American Literary Systems*. Istanbul: Nâzim Hikmet Culture and Art Foundation, 2008. The work, from the Turkish perspective, looks at how Hikmet is portrayed in Europe and America.

Göksu, Saime, and Edward Timms. *Romantic Communist: The Life and Work of Nazim Hikmet*. 1999. Reprint. New York: Gardners Books, 2006. The authors propose in this biography of Hikmet that his life and career form a microcosm of twentieth century politics. Göksu and Timms explore Hikmet's life chronologically through ten well-researched chapters. The clear structure helps the narrative to flow from one chapter to the next and allows the reader to grasp both the detail and the broad picture. Includes bibliographical references and index.

Halman, Talât Sait. *Rapture and Revolution: Essays on*

Turkish Literature. Edited by Jayne L. Warner. Syracuse, N.Y.: Syracuse University Press/Crescent Hill, 2007. This study on Turkish literature contains a chapter that notes Hikmet's importance in Turkey and sees him as the voice of iconoclasm.

Kinzer, Stephen. "Turkish Poet Is Lauded, but Stays Exiled in Death." *The New York Times*, February 27, 1997, p. A4. As Turkey settles into what is likely to be an extended confrontation between secular and pro-Islamic forces, symbols take on exaggerated political importance for both sides. Perhaps no individual crystallizes the conflict better than Hikmet, atheist and Communist and also one of the greatest literary figures ever to emerge from this country.

J. R. Broadus

I

ISSA
Kobayashi Yatarō

Born: Kashiwabara, Japan; June 15, 1763
Died: Kashiwabara, Japan; January 5, 1827

PRINCIPAL POETRY
Kansei kuchō, 1794
Kansei kikō, 1795
Kyōwa kuchō, 1803
Bunka kuchō, 1804-1808
Shichiban nikki, 1810-1818
Hachiban nikki, 1819-1821
Kuban nikki, 1822-1824
The Autumn Wind, 1957
A Few Flies and I, 1969
The Spring of My Life, and Selected Haiku, 1997

OTHER LITERARY FORMS

Although Issa (ee-sah) is known primarily as one of the three great haiku poets, he also wrote prose—in *Chichi no shūen nikki* (1801; *Diary of My Father's Death*, 1992), a response to his father's death—and mixed prose and verse, or *haibun*, in *Oragu haru* (1819; *The Year of My Life*, 1960), an autobiographical account of his most memorable year.

ACHIEVEMENTS

Ezra Pound's recognition of the power of a single image that concentrates poetic attention with enormous force and his examination of the complexity of the Japanese written character led to an increasing awareness of the possibilities of haiku poetry for Western readers in the early part of the twentieth century. Combined with a growing interest in Asian studies and philosophy, haiku offered an entrance into Japanese concepts of existence concerning the relationship of humans and the natural world. Because the brevity of haiku is in such contrast to conventional ideas of a complete poem in the Western tradition, however, only the most accomplished haiku poets have been able to reach beyond the boundaries of their culture.

The most prominent among these are Matsuo Bashō (1644-1694), Yosa Buson (1715-1783), and Issa. As William Cohen describes him, "in humor and sympathy for all that lives, Issa is unsurpassed in the history of Japanese literature and perhaps even in world literature." A perpetual underdog who employed humor as an instrument of endurance, who was exceptionally sensitive to the infinite subtlety of the natural world, and who was incapable of acting with anything but extraordinary decency, Issa wrote poetry that moves across the barriers of language and time to capture the "wordless moment" when revelation is imminent. More accessible than the magisterial Buson, less confident than the brilliant Bashō, Issa expresses in his work the genius that is often hidden in the commonplace. The definition of haiku as "simply what is happening in this place at this moment" is an apt emblem for a poet who saw humans forever poised between the timely and the timeless.

BIOGRAPHY

The poet known as Issa was born Kobayashi Yatarō in 1763 in the village of Kashiwabara, a settlement of approximately one hundred houses in the highlands of the province of Shinano. The rugged beauty of the region, especially the gemlike Lake Nojiri two miles east of the town, led to the development of a tourist community in the twentieth century, but the harsh winter climate, with snowdrifts of more than ten feet not uncommon, restricted growth in Issa's time. The area was still moderately prosperous, however, because there was a central post office on the main highway from the northwestern provinces to the capital city of Edo (now Tokyo). The lord of the powerful Kaga clan maintained an official residence that he used on his semiannual visits to the shogun in Edo, and a cultural center developed around a theater that featured dramatic performances, wrestling exhibitions, and poetry readings.

Issa was the son of a fairly prosperous farmer who supplemented his income by providing packhorse transportation for passengers and freight. His composition of a "death-verse" suggests a high degree of literary awareness. In the first of a series of domestic tragedies, Issa's mother died when he was three, but his grandmother reared him with deep affection until Issa's father remarried. Although his stepmother treated him well for two years, on the birth of her first child, she relegated Issa to a role as a subordinate. When she suggested that a farmer's son did not need formal schooling, Issa was forced to discontinue his study of reading and writing under a local master. When her baby cried, she accused Issa of causing its pain and beat him so that he was frequently marked with bruises.

According to legend, these unhappy circumstances inspired Issa's first poem. At the age of nine or so, Issa was unable to join the local children at a village festival because he did not have the new clothes the occasion required. Playing by himself, he noticed a fledgling sparrow fallen from its nest. Observing it with what would become a characteristic sympathy for nature's outcasts, he declared:

> Come and play,
> little orphan sparrow—
> play with me!

The poem was probably written years later in reflection on the incident, but Issa displayed enough literary ability in his youth to attract the attention of the proprietor of the lord's residence, a man skilled in calligraphy and haiku poetry, who believed that Issa would be a good companion for his own son. He invited Issa to attend a school he operated in partnership with a scholar in Chinese studies who was also a haiku poet. Issa could attend the school only at night and on holidays— sometimes carrying his stepbrother on his back—when he was not compelled to assist with farm chores, but this did not prevent him from cultivating his literary inclinations. On one of the occasions when he was assisting his father by leading a passenger on a packhorse, the traveler ruminated on the name of a mountain that they were passing. "Black Princess! O Black Princess!" he repeated, looking at the snow-topped peak of Mount Kurohime. When Issa asked the man what he was doing, he replied that he was trying to compose an appropriate haiku for the setting. To the astonishment of the traveler, Issa proclaimed: "Black Princess is a bride—/ see her veiled in white."

Issa's studies were completely terminated when his grandmother died in 1776. At his stepmother's urging, Issa was sent to Edo, thrown into a kind of exile in which he was expected to survive on his own. His life in the capital in his teenage years is a mystery, but in 1790, he was elected to a position at an academy of poetics, the Katsushika school. The school had been founded by a friend and admirer of Bashō who named it for Bashō's home, and although Issa undoubtedly had the ability to fulfill the expectations of his appointment, his innovative instincts clashed with the more traditional curriculum already in place at the school. In 1792, Issa voluntarily withdrew from the school, proclaiming himself Haikaiji Issa in a declaration of poetic independence. His literary signature literally translates as "Haikai Temple One-Tea." The title "Haikai Temple" signifies that he was a priest of haiku poetry (anticipating Allen Ginsberg's assertion "Poet is Priest!"), and as he wrote, "In as much as life is empty as a bubble which vanishes instantly, I will henceforth call myself *Issa*, or One Tea." In this way, he was likening his existence to the bubbles rising in a cup of tea—an appropriate image, considering the importance of the tea ceremony in Japanese cultural life.

During the next ten years, Issa traveled extensively, making pilgrimages to famous religious sites and prominent artistic seminars, staying with friends who shared his interest in poetry. His primary residence was in Fukagawa, where he earned a modest living by giving lessons in haikai, possibly assisted by enlightened patrons who appreciated his abilities. By the turn of the century, he had begun to establish a wider reputation and his prospects for artistic recognition were improving, but his father's final illness drew him home to offer comfort and support. His father died in 1801 and divided his estate equally between Issa and his half brother. When his stepmother contested the will, Issa was obliged to leave once again, and he spent the next thirteen years living in Edo while he attempted to convince the local authorities to carry out the provisions of his father's legacy. His frustrations are reflected in a poem he wrote during this time: "My old village calls—/ each time I come near,/ thorns in the blossom."

Finally, in 1813, Issa was able to take possession of

his half of the property, and in April, 1814, he married a twenty-eight-year-old woman named Kiku, the daughter of a farmer in a neighboring village. Completely white-haired and nearly toothless, he still proclaimed that he "became a new man" in his fifties, and during the next few years, his wife gave birth to five children. Unfortunately, all of them died while still quite young. Using a familiar line of scripture that compares the evanescence of life to the morning dew as a point of origin, Issa expressed his sense of loss in one of his most famous and least translatable poems:

> This dewdrop world—
> yet for dew drops
> still, a dewdrop world

In May, 1823, Issa's wife died, but he remarried almost immediately. This marriage was not harmonious, and when the woman returned to her parent's home, Issa sent her a humorous verse as a declaration of divorce and as a statement of forgiveness. Perhaps for purposes of continuing his family, Issa married one more time in 1825, his bride this time a forty-six-year-old farmer's daughter. His wife was pregnant when Issa died in the autumn of 1828, and his only surviving child, Yata, was born after his death. Her survival enabled Issa's descendants to retain the property in his home village for which he had struggled during many of the years of his life.

In his last years, while he was settled in his old home, he achieved national fame as a haikai poet. His thoughts as a master were valued, and he held readings and seminars with pupils and colleagues. After recovering from a fairly serious illness in 1820, he adopted the additional title Soseibo, or "Revived Priest," indicating not only his position of respect as an artist and seer but also his resiliency and somewhat sardonic optimism. As a kind of summary of his career, he wrote a poem that legend attributes to his deathbed but that was probably given to a student to be published after his death. It describes the journey of a man from the washing bowl in which a new baby is cleansed to the ritual bath in which the body is prepared for burial: "Slippery words/ from bathtub to bathtub—/ just slippery words." The last poem Issa actually wrote was found under the

pillow on the bed where he died. After his house had burned down in 1827, he and his wife lived in an adjoining storehouse with no windows and a leaky roof: "Gratitude for the snow/ on the bed quilt—/ it too is from Heaven." Issa used the word *jōdo* (Pure Land) for Heaven, a term that describes the Heaven of the Buddha Amida. Issa was a member of the largest Pure Land sect, Jōdo Shinshū, and he shared the sect's faith in the boundless love of Amida to redeem a world in which suffering and pain are frequent. His final poem is an assertion of that faith in typically bleak circumstances, and a final declaration of his capacity for finding beauty in the most unlikely situations.

Analysis

The haiku is a part of Japanese cultural life, aesthetic experience, and philosophical expression. As Lafcadio Hearn noted, "Poetry in Japan is universal as air. It is felt by everybody." The haiku poem traditionally consists of three lines, arranged so that there are five, seven, and five syllables in the triplet. Although the "rules" governing its construction are not absolute, it has many conventions that contribute to its effectiveness. Generally, it has a central image, often from the natural world, frequently expressed as a part of a seasonal reference, and a "cutting word," or exclamation that states or implies the poet's reaction to what he sees. It is the ultimate compression of poetic energy and often draws its strength from the unusual juxtaposition of image and idea.

It is very difficult to translate haiku into English without losing or distorting some of the qualities that make it so uniquely interesting. English syllables are longer than Japanese *jion* (symbol sounds); some Japanese characters have no English equivalent, particularly since each separate "syllable" of a Japanese "word" may have additional levels of meaning; a literal rendering may miss the point while a more creative one may remake the poem so that the translator is a traitor to the original. As an example of the problems involved, one might consider the haiku Issa wrote about the temptations and disappointments of his visits to his hometown. The Japanese characters can be literally transcribed as follows:

*Furosato ya
yoru mo sawaru mo
bara-no-hana*

Old village:
come-near also touch also
thorn's-flowers

The poem has been translated in at least four versions:

At my home everything
I touch is a bramble. (*Asataro Miyamori*)

Everything I touch
with tenderness alas
pricks like a bramble. (*Peter Beilenson*)

The place where I was born:
all I come to—all I touch—
blossoms of the thorn. (*Harold Henderson*)

My old village calls—
each time I come near,
thorns in the blossom. (*Leon Lewis*)

Bashō's almost prophetic power and Buson's exceptional craftsmanship and control may be captured fairly effectively in English, but it is Issa's attitude toward his own life and the world that makes him perhaps the most completely understandable of the great Japanese poets. His rueful, gentle irony, turning on his own experiences, is his vehicle for conveying a warmly human outlook that is no less profound for its inclusive humor. Like his fellow masters of the haiku form, Issa was very closely attuned to the natural world, but for him, it had an immediacy and familiarity that balanced the cosmic dimensions of the universal phenomena that he observed. Recognizing human fragility, he developed a strong sense of identification with the smaller, weaker creatures of the world. His sympathetic response is combined with a sharp eye for their individual attributes and for subtle demonstrations of virtue and strength amid trying circumstances. Although Issa was interested in most of the standard measures of social success (family, property, recognition), his inability to accept dogma (religious or philosophical) or to overlook economic inequity led him to a position as a semipermanent outsider no matter how successful he might be.

OBSERVER OF NATURAL PHENOMENA

Typically, Issa depicts himself as an observer in the midst of an extraordinary field of natural phenomena. Like the Western Romantic poets of the nineteenth century, he uses his own reactions as a measuring device and records the instinctive responses of his poetic sensibility. There is a fusion of stance and subject, and the world of business and commerce occurs only as an intrusion, spoiling the landscape. What matters is an eternal realm of continuing artistic revelation, the permanent focus of humankind's contemplation: "From my tiny roof/ smooth . . . soft . . ./ still-white snow/ melts in melody." The poet is involved in the natural world through the action of a poetic intelligence that recreates the world in words and images and, more concretely, through the direct action of his participation in its substance and shape: "Sun-melted snow . . ./ with my stick I guide/ this great dangerous river." Here, the perspective ranges from the local and the minimal to the massively consequential, but in his usual fashion, Issa's wry overestimation of his actions serves to illustrate his realization of their limits. Similarly, he notes the magnified ambition of another tiny figure: "An April shower . . ./ see that thirsty mouse/ lapping river Sumida." Amid the vast universe, humans are much like a slight animal. This perception is no cause for despair, though. An acceptance of limitations with characteristic humor enables him to enjoy his minuscule place among the infinities: "Now take this flea:/ He simply cannot jump . . ./ and I love him for it."

Because he is aware of how insignificant and vulnerable all living creatures are, Issa is able to invest their apparently comic antics with dignity: "The night was hot . . ./ stripped to the waist/ the snail enjoyed the moonlight." The strength of Issa's identification of the correspondence between the actions of human beings and animals enables him to use familiar images of animal behavior to comment on the pomposity and vanity of much human behavior. In this fashion, his poems have some of the satirical edge of eighteenth century wit, but Issa is much more amused than angry: "Elegant singer/ would you further favor us/ with a dance, O Frog?" Or if anger is suggested, it is a sham to feign control over something, because the underlying idea is essentially one of delighted acceptance of common concerns: "Listen, all you fleas . . ./ you can come on pilgrimage, o.k. . . ./ but then, off you git!" Beyond mock anger and low comedy, Issa's poems about his participation in the way of the world often express a spirit of contemplation leading to a feeling of awe. Even if the workings of the natural world remain elusive, defying all real comprehension, there is still a fascination in considering its mysterious complexity: "Rainy afternoon . . ./ little daughter you will/ never teach that cat to dance."

FORBIDDING NATURE

At other times, however, the landscape is more forbidding, devoid of the comfort provided by other creatures. Issa knew so many moments of disappointment that he could not restrain a projection of his sadness into the world: "Poor thin crescent/ shivering and twisted high/ in the bitter dark." For a man so closely attuned to nature's nuances, it is not surprising that nature would appear to echo his own concerns. When Issa felt the harsh facts of existence bearing heavily on him, he might have found some solace in seeing a reflection of his pain in the sky: "A three-day-old moon/ already warped and twisted/ by the bitter cold." Images of winter are frequent in Issa's poetry, an outgrowth of the geographical reality of his homeland but also an indication of his continuing consciousness of loss and discouragement. Without the abundant growth of the summer to provide pleasant if temporary distraction, the poet cannot escape from his condition: "In winter moonlight/ a clear look/ at my old hut . . . dilapidated." The view may be depressing but the "clear look" afforded by the light is valuable and, in some ways, reassuringly familiar, reminding the poet of his real legacy: "My old father too/looked long on these white mountains/ through lonely winters."

HOME AND FAMILY

Issa spent much time trying to establish a true home in the land in which he was born because he had a strong sense of the importance of family continuity. He regarded the family as a source of strength in a contentious and competitive environment and wrote many poems about the misfortune of his own family situation. Some of his poems on this subject tend to be extremely sentimental, lacking his characteristic comic stance. The depth of his emotional involvement is emphasized

by the stark pronouncement of his query: "Wild geese O wild geese/ were you little fellows too . . ./ when you flew from home?" These poems, however, are balanced by Issa's capacity for finding some unexpected reassurance that the struggle to be "home" is worthwhile: "Home again! What's this?/ My hesitant cherry tree/ deciding to bloom?" Although nothing spectacular happens, on his home ground, even the apparently mundane is dressed in glory: "In my native place/ there's this plant:/ As plain as grass but blooms like heaven." In an understated plea for placing something where it belongs, recalling his ten-year struggle to win a share of his father's property, he declares how he would dispense justice: "Hereby I assign in perpetuity to wit:/ To this wren/ this fence." For Issa, the natural order of things is superior to that of society.

The uncertainty of his position with respect to his family (and his ancestors) made the concept of home ground especially important for Issa as a fixed coordinate in a chaotic universe. His early rejection by his stepmother was an important event in the development of an outlook that counted uncertainty as a given, but his sense of the transitory nature of existence is a part of a very basic strain of Japanese philosophy. The tangible intermixed with the intangible is the subject of many of his poems: "The first firefly . . ./ but he got away and I—/ air in my fingers." A small airborne creature, a figure for both light and flight, is glimpsed but not caught and held. What is seen, discernible, is rarely seen for long and never permanently fixed. The person who reaches for the elusive particle of energy is like the artist who reaches for the stuff of inspiration, like any person trying to grasp the animating fire of the cosmos. The discrepancy between the immutable facts of existence and the momentary, incredible beauty of life at its most moving is a familiar feature of Issa's work: "Autumn breezes shake/ the scarlet flowers my poor child/ could not wait to pick." Issa's famous "Dewdrop" haiku was also the result of the loss of one of his children, but in this poem too, it is the moment of special feeling that is as celebrated—a mixture of sadness and extraordinary perception.

SPIRITUALISM AND FAITH

The consolation of poetry could not be entirely sufficient to compensate for the terrible sense of loss in

Issa's life, but he could not accept standard religious precepts easily either. He was drawn to the fundamental philosophical positions of Buddhist thought, but his natural skepticism and clear eye for sham prevented him from entering into any dogma without reservation. Typically, he tried to undermine the pomposity of religious institutions while combining the simplicity of understated spiritualism with his usual humor to express reverence for what he found genuinely sacred: "Chanting at the altar/ of the inner sanctuary . . ./ a cricket priest." Insisting on a personal relationship with everything, Issa venerated what he saw as the true manifestation of the great spirits of the universe: "Ah sacred swallow . . ./ twittering out from your nest in/ Great Buddha's nostril." The humanity of his position, paradoxically, is much more like real religious consciousness than the chanting of orthodox believers who mouth mindless slogans although unable to understand anything of Amida Buddha's message to humankind: "For each single fly/ that's swatted, 'Namu Amida/ Butsu' is the cry." Above all, Issa was able to keep his priorities clear. One is reminded of the famous Zen description of the universe, "No holiness, vast emptiness," by Issa's determination to keep Buddha from freezing into an icon: "Polishing the Buddha . . ./ and why not my pipe as well/ for the holidays?" As translator Henderson points out, "the boundless love attributed to Amida Buddha coalesced with his own tenderness toward all weak things—children and animals and insects." Even in those poems of a religious nature that do not have a humorous slant there is a feeling of humility that is piety's best side: "Before the sacred/ mountain shrine of Kamiji . . ./ my head bent itself." In this poem, too, there is an instinctive response that does not depend on a considered position or careful analysis, thus paralleling Issa's reacion to the phenomena of the natural world, the true focus of his worship.

While most of Issa's haiku are like the *satori* of Zen awareness, a moment of sudden enlightenment expressed in a "charged image," Issa's "voice" also has a reflective quality that develops from a rueful realization of the profound sadness of existence. What makes Issa's voice so appealing in his more thoughtful poems is his expression of a kind of faith in the value of enduring. He can begin the new year by saying: "Felicitations!/ Still . . . I guess this year too/ will prove only so-so." Or he can draw satisfaction from triumphs of a very small scale: "Congratulations Issa!/ You have survived to feed/ this year's mosquitos." The loss of five children and his wife's early death somehow did not lead to paralysis by depression: "If my grumbling wife/ were still alive I just/ might enjoy tonight's moon." When his life seemed to be reduced almost to a kind of existential nothingness, he could see its apparent futility and still find a way to feel some amusement: "One man and one fly/ buzzing together in one/ big bare empty room." Or he could calculate the rewards of trying to act charitably, his humor mocking his efforts but not obscuring the fact that the real reward he obtained was in his singular way of seeing: "Yes . . . the young sparrows/ if you treat them tenderly—/ thank you with droppings."

SOMBER POEMS

There were moments when the sadness became more than his humor could bear. How close to tragic pessimism is this poem, for example: "The people we know . . ./ but these days even scarecrows/ do not stand upright." How close to despair is this heartfelt lament: "Mother lost, long gone . . ./ at the deep dark sea I stare—/ at the deep dark sea." Issa is one of those artists whose work must be viewed as a connected body of creation with reciprocal elements. Poems such as these somber ones must be seen as dark seasoning, for the defining credo at the crux of his work is that his effort has been worthwhile. In another attempt at a death song, Issa declared: "Full-moon and flowers/ solacing my forty-nine/ foolish years of song." Since death was regarded as another transitory stage in a larger vision of existence, Issa could dream of a less troubled life in which his true nature emerged: "Gay . . . affectionate . . ./ when I'm reborn I pray to be/ a white-wing butterfly." He knew, however, that this was wishful thinking. In his poetry, he was already a "white-wing butterfly," and the tension between the man and the poem, between the tenuousness of life and the eternity of art, energized his soul. As he put it himself, summarizing his life and art: "Floating butterfly/ when you dance before my eyes . . ./ Issa, man of mud."

OTHER MAJOR WORKS

NONFICTION: *Chichi no shūen nikki*, 1803 (*Diary of My Father's Death*, 1992).

MISCELLANEOUS: *Oragu haru*, 1819 (*The Year of My Life*, 1960); *Issa zenshū*, 1929; *Issa zenshū*, 1979 (9 volumes).

BIBLIOGRAPHY

Blyth, R. H. *Eastern Culture*. Vol. 1 in *Haiku*. 4th ed. Tokyo: Hokuseido Press, 1990. Discusses Issa in the context of the spiritual origins of haiku in Zen Buddhism and other Eastern spiritual traditions. Sees Issa as the poet of destiny, who saw his own tragic experiences as part of the larger motions of fate. Also interprets him both as a poet within Japanese culture and as a poet of universal appeal.

_____. *From the Beginnings Up to Issa*. Vol. 1 in *A History of Haiku*. 1963. Reprint. Tokyo: Hokuseido Press, 1973. Devotes four chapters to Issa, presenting Issa's work in chronological order, ending in the haiku of Issa's old age. Includes interpretations of Issa's work plus examples of his portrayals of plants and the small creatures of the earth and of meaningful personal incidents, such as the deaths of his wife and children. Compares and contrasts him with the great haiku poet Bashō.

Issa. *Autumn Wind Haiku: Selected Poems by Kobayashi Issa*. Translated by Lewis Mackenzie. New York: Kodansha International, 1999. This volume was originally published as *Autumn Wind* in 1957. The translator provides an informative introduction to a selection of Issa's haiku. Mackenzie assesses Issa's contributions to the haiku form, includes a detailed narrative of Issa's often troubled life, and comments on individual haiku. Includes both English translations of the poems and phonetic Japanese versions.

Kato, Shūichi. *A History of Japanese Literature: The Modern Years*. Vol. 3. Translated by Don Sanderson. New York: Kodansha International, 1990. Includes a short chapter on Issa as a realistic, down-to-earth poet of everyday life and in the context of the Japanese society of the time.

Ueda, Makoto. *Dew on the Grass: The Life and Poetry of Kobayashi Issa*. Boston: Brill, 2004. A biography of Issa that incorporates his poetry and modern Japanese scholarship. In the preface, Ueda notes that Issa has had a marked influence on Japanese poets and novelists but is viewed as less skilled than Buson and Bashō by Japanese scholars.

Yasuda, Kenneth. *Japanese Haiku: Its Essential Nature, History, and Possibilities in English, with Selected Examples*. Rutland, Vt.: Charles E. Tuttle, 1994. References to Issa and samples of his work in the context of a thorough analysis of the theory and practice of haiku.

Leon Lewis

K

VLADISLAV KHODASEVICH

Born: Moscow, Russia; May 28, 1886
Died: Paris, France; June 14, 1939

PRINCIPAL POETRY
Molodost', 1908
Shchastlivy domik, 1914
Putem zerna, 1920
Tyazhelaya lira, 1922
Evropeiskaya noch', 1927

OTHER LITERARY FORMS

In addition to his poetry, Vladislav Khodasevich (kuh-DAY-zah-vihch) published many critical essays and memoirs. The most important of these are collected in *Nekropol'* (1939), *Literaturnye stat'i i vospominaniia* (1954), and *Belyi koridor: Isbrannaia proza v dvukh tomakh* (1982). His biography of the eighteenth century poet Gavrila Derzhavin (*Derzhavin*, 1931) is also notable. As is the case with Khodasevich's poetry, very little of his prose is available in English translation.

ACHIEVEMENTS

Vladislav Khodasevich was one of the most highly regarded Russian poets of his time and is one of the least known poets in modern times. Twelve years of poetic silence before his death contributed to that obscurity, and a virtual ban on publishing his work in the then Soviet Union as well as difficult relations within the Russian émigré community in Western Europe negatively affected his reputation for years. Interest in him revived in the 1980's, when a growing interest in him emerged in both the Soviet Union and the West.

BIOGRAPHY

Vladislav Felitsianovich Khodasevich was born in Moscow on May 28 (May 16, Old Style), 1886. Neither his father nor his mother was a native Russian (Felitsian

Khodasevich was Polish, Sophie Brafman a Jewish convert to Catholicism and a fervent Polish nationalist), but perhaps as much because of his background as despite it, young Khodasevich considered himself thoroughly Russian in both allegiance and sensibility. The youngest of six children, he was educated at Moscow's Third Classical Gimnazium. Even before he left school, his ambitions turned to writing, and it was through a schoolmate that he made his first shy forays into the febrile world of fin de siècle Moscow literary life—the world of Valery Bryusov, Andrey Bely, and Aleksandr Blok. After graduation, Khodasevich began writing and publishing, and except for an almost comic bureaucratic interlude immediately after the revolution, he practiced no other profession.

Chronic ill health aggravated by hardship and privation kept Khodasevich out of military service during World War I and the Russian Revolution. In April of 1921, Khodasevich moved with his second wife, Anna Chulkova, and her son Garik to St. Petersburg, the abandoned capital, to work and live in the subsidized House of the Arts. It was there that Khodasevich, in a concentrated burst of energy, wrote many of his finest poems. Roughly one year later, however, spurred by private difficulties and by doubts about the future for writers in the new Soviet state, he and young poet Nina Berberova left for Western Europe. Khodasevich, like many other artists and intellectuals who left at the same time, did not expect his sojourn there to be a permanent one, and he maintained literary and personal ties with his homeland. However, Khodasevich soon found himself on the list of those who were to be barred from returning, and his skepticism about the Soviet Union began to harden into conviction.

Khodasevich was not of like mind with much of the émigré community, and although he settled permanently in Paris in 1927, he—like Marina Tsvetayeva—found that their aesthetic isolation in Russian letters and their lack of a convenient niche was to become an oppressive physical and spiritual isolation as well. Khodasevich, unlike Tsvetayeva, was never ostracized by fellow émigrés and was able to earn a meager living writing criticism for Russian periodicals, but there were few kindred spirits to be found among his own countrymen, let alone among the left-leaning French

Vladislav Khodasevich (Russian Literature Triquarterly)

intellectual community of 1930's Paris. Khodasevich believed that he was witnessing the final eclipse of Russian letters and, ironically, continued to insist on the primacy of tradition even as his own poetics were discarding their much-vaunted classical proportions.

Khodasevich's last years were difficult ones: He wrote practically no poetry after 1927, and a final break with Berberova in 1932, financial straits, and failing health all contributed to depression. He did remarry and continue to write remarkable prose, and he was at work on an Alexander Pushkin study when he was fatally stricken with cancer in 1939. He died in the spring of that year.

ANALYSIS

A pupil of the Symbolists who soon freed himself from their poetics if not their perceptions, a contemporary of Boris Pasternak, Anna Akhmatova, Tsvetayeva, and Osip Mandelstam but resembling none of them, Vladislav Khodasevich is a poet not easily classified. He is often described as a classicist because of his loy-alty to Pushkin and Russian verse tradition, yet his always ironic and sometimes bleak vision of the world is no less a product of the twentieth century. His poetic output was small and his demands on himself severe, but his mature verse, with its paradoxical combination of domesticity and exile, banality and beauty, harmony and grotesquerie, places him among the finest Russian poets of the twentieth century.

Khodasevich made his poetic debut in the heyday of Russian Symbolism. For the Symbolists, passion was the quickest way to reach the limits of experience necessary for artistic creation, and so all the motifs that accompany the Symbolist/Decadent notion of love—pain, intoxication, hopelessness—are explored by Khodasevich, diligent student of Decadence, in his first collection.

MOLODOST'

In *Molodost'* (youth), Khodasevich treats the transcendent themes of death, love, art, and eternity (so dear to the Symbolist canon) to both facile versifying and facile dramatization. His lyric voice is that of the seer, the magus, the seeker—a pale youth with burning eyes, a self-conscious poet risking all for revelation and encounters with mystic dread. *Molodost'* is the work of a talented beginner, but no more.

The poems are infused with vague mystery and vague premonitions, full of hints of midnight trysts at crypts, of confounding of realities, of fashionable madness and jaded melancholy. Khodasevich's problem is the problem of Symbolism in general: Its claim to universality of experience was undercut by the lack of any universal, or even coherent, symbolic system. In seeking to create a language of those "Chosen by Art," they plumbed for the emblematic, "creative" meaning of words, but the choosing and the chosen—hence the meaning—might vary from salon to salon. No word or deed was safe from symbolic interpretation, but the poet's own self-absorbed consciousness was the sole arbiter of meaning. Indeed, at times it seemed that literature itself was secondary to the attempt to divine hidden meaning in everyday events, thereby creating a life that itself was art enough.

Khodasevich's poetics would begin to change with the advent of his next book, but his apprenticeship among the Symbolists would affect him for the rest of his life. From them, he learned to perceive human existence as the tragic incompatibility of two separate realities, and all his poetic life would be an attempt to reconcile them.

SHCHASTLIVY DOMIK

His second volume of verse, *Shchastlivy domik* (the happy little house), shows Khodasevich replacing his early mentors—Bely, Blok, Bryusov, Innokenty Annensky—with eighteenth and nineteenth century classics such as Pushkin, Evgeny Baratynsky, and Derzhavin. His new persona is both more accessible and more distant than the pale pre-Raphaelite youth of the first book: He is more personal and biographical, surrounded by more concrete visual imagery and fewer abstractions, although the stylization, the deliberate archaisms, and the traditional meter in which those details are given serve to keep the poet's mask a generalized one—one poet among many, the latest heir to an elegiac tradition. *Shchastlivy domik* is still a diary of the emotions, kept by a self-absorbed "I," but here the spheres of emotion and art begin to separate. This poet belongs to a guild of craftsmen, not a hieratic brotherhood intent on perceiving life as a work in progress. A sense of history and linear time replaces the boundless "I" of the Symbolist/Decadent, defining both past and present and imposing different sorts of limits on the power of language to conjure, transform, or even affect reality. In this context, death becomes an even rather than a sensuous state of mind, and art becomes a means of overcoming death by very virtue of its formality and conventionality. These characteristics, not sibylline utterances, will carry the work beyond its creator's physical end.

Gone, then, are sadness and frustration at the utter futility of words, replaced by a less literal quietism—elegiac contemplation, meditation, and pride not in one's own oracular powers but in a tradition. Dignified humility replaces bombast, domesticity replaces exotica, and Pushkin is the chief guide. Although Khodasevich never lost his sense of the split between the world of appearance and the higher reality, in this collection he discovered inspiration in everydayness, in ordinary, prosaic, humble moments. In his next collection, his first book of truly mature work, he worked out the poetics appropriate to that discovery.

PUTEM ZERNA

Most of the major poems in *Putem zerna* (the way of grain) were finished by 1918, but the book itself did not see print until 1920. In lexicon, choice of themes, and lyric voice, it is a testament to a sober but still joyful everyday life; the poet is an ordinary human, subject to the laws of time and space, vulnerable to cold, hunger, illness, and death, no more and no less significant than any other man on the street. Like his fellow Muscovites in times of war and revolution, he observes history, participates in it "like a salamander in flame," but possesses no Symbolist second sight and no power to guess, let alone prophesy, the future. Although the poet, unlike his fellows, does have occasion to transcend his human limits, his small epiphanies, too, depend on the physical world. Their source is earthly. They derive from moments in which the poet experiences an acute awareness of things heard, felt, seen, smelled, and tasted.

Straightforward syntax, simplicity of lexicon, an intimate, slightly ironic, conversational tone, and the unrhymed iambic pentameter of the longer poems all make *Putem zerna* a deliberately prosaic book of poetry. Its persona is both public and private—public in his identification with the lives and deaths of his fellow creatures, private in facing his own mortality. The two are linked by the central metaphors of the book; the biblical seed that dies to be born again and the life-giving bread baked from buried grain—the eternal cycle of being.

Many of the book's poems have an identifiable setting in both space and time, coordinates usually lacking in Khodasevich's earlier works. The homely images of Moscow neighborhoods lead to meditations on the passing of time, nations, generations, and the poet himself as he feels the onset of physical weakness, illness, and old age. The poems chronicle what Khodasevich called "holy banality": common, collective experiences such as hauling wood, selling herring rations to buy lamp oil, and watching the local coffin maker finish his latest order. Moments of transcendence come unrequested and unexpected, with the thump of a seamstress's treadle or the sight of an all-too-ordinary suicide in a local park. The thump of the poet's own rocking chair, for example, marking time, sparks this moment in "Epizod" ("Episode"). In this poem, the observer of others leaves his own body and instead observes himself—thin, pale, dying, cigarette in hand. He also observes all the objects surrounding him—a bookcase; the ubiquitous yellow wallpaper of modest; older apartments; Pushkin's death mask; the children and their sleds. As the soul returns to its body, it journeys over water—a crossing of Lethe described in painstakingly physical terms.

The balance achieved in *Putem zerna* is both an acrobatic and a poetic feat, as Khodasevich points out in one of his short poems. It requires both muscle and brain. In his incarnation as ordinary man, Khodasevich has to balance life against death; in his role as poet, he has to balance creativity and the everyday world. For the moment, poetry makes that reconciliation possible by imposing order on the chaos and disarray of everyday life. However, just as the poet cannot exist without the man, the poetry cannot exist without the chaos.

TYAZHELAYA LIRA

If earthly and divine principles complement each other in *Putem zerna*, they come into conflict in Khodasevich's 1922 collection, *Tyazhelaya lira* (the heavy lyre). Here the divine side of the poet's nature turns dominant and becomes a condition for the existence of all else. Poetic order is no longer simply one possible means of reconciliation but the only order possible if the "I" is to survive in any way. Equilibrium shifted, the prosy external world lends itself less and less to ordering. Unlike the poet in the previous collection (an ordinary man save for his flashes of kinship with "child, flower, beast"), the poet of *Tyazhelaya lira* is unmistakably a creature different from his fellows, one for whom the creative moment has expanded to fill his entire consciousness. His state is one of constant awareness of human limitations and his own duality, of constant service to his craft. This awareness reveals not affinities but differences, not community but isolation.

Exalted, yes, but smug—never. Khodasevich's version of the conventional antagonism between the two worlds of the poet is not at all simple and clear-cut. The two realities are mutually exclusive yet do, paradoxically, overlap. Each seeks to free itself of the other, but only in their uncomfortable union does the lyric "I" of this collection exist. This voice may be much more

ironic and self-deprecating than that of the high priests of Symbolism, but the poet's gifts—vision and "secret hearing"—allow him to see and hear, not over, but through physical existence. They allow him to escape, however briefly, from his captivity in an aging, unattractive, bodily prison. Indeed, the collection is dominated by a set of images that provide that escape to the soul's true homeland: Eyes, windows, mirrors, and reflections all open onto another reality, an escape route for the spirit. Wings, wounds (sometimes mortal, death being the ultimate flight), verbs with transitional prefixes, and negative definitions also belong to a poetics whereby the word, the soul, and the spirit break out of the enclosed cell of body or world. Angels, Psyche, Lucifer, an automobile winged by headlights, and acid consuming a photographic negative move across and through the tissue of existence.

One of the most striking poems of the collection, "Ballada" ("Ballad"), describes another journey out of the body. Here, as in "Episode," the poet is transformed into a creature with knowledge of the realms of both life and death. In both cases, the journey to the underworld begins with the speaker of the poem alone in his room, surrounded by familiar objects; the room has a window, and time passes strangely. While "Episode" ends with a return to the mortal body and an understanding of life and death as kindred states, "Ballad" ends with the man transfigured, changed into Orpheus, and that transformation takes place because of poetry. Cut by the sharp blade of music, the man grows up and out of himself, setting dead matter into motion with him, recreating both himself and the world around him. His instrument, his blade, is the heavy lyre handed him through the wind.

EVROPEISKAYA NOCH'

Khodasevich's last book, *Evropeiskaya noch'* (European night), did not appear separately but came out as part of his *Sobranie stikhov* (collected verse) of 1927. Like his two earlier books, *Evropeiskaya noch'* treats of both spiritual and material worlds. The epiphanies of *Putem zerna*, however, are long gone, as are the neat oxymorons and epigrammatic resolutions of *Tyazhelaya lira*. There are no escape routes here. Instead, there is the Gnostic's anti-Paradise, a grotesque Gogolian world of inferior time and space, demoniac in its unrelenting banality and tawdry stupidity. The poet is doubly exiled, for even language seems to have lost its ability to transform either the self or what surrounds it. Now the physical world shapes both the language and the voice, distorting them and depriving them of their fragile unity and identity. The possibility—or rather impossibility—of creativity involves three things: the victory of matter over spirit and the distortion of both; the confusion of masks, or the poet's inability to recognize even himself; and the dismemberment of the once coherent lyric "I," as in a poem that ends with the poet exploding, flying apart "Like mud, sprayed out by a tire/ To alien spheres of being."

Savagely funny, *Evropeiskaya noch'* covers a world densely populated by humans, animals, and objects as well as the trappings, gadgetry, and attitudes of the modern century. Animate and inanimate objects obey the same laws, are objects of the same verbs, undergo the same processes. The natural world is at best askew, at worst hostile. The luminous, sanctified domesticity of *Putem zerna* has turned paltry and pitiful, the entire universe reduced to a collection of "poor utensils." The lyric hero, a petty Cain, is exiled from his age and from himself: "Like a fly on sticky paper/ He trembles in our time." Too inarticulate to give voice, he merely groans in mute despair.

The breakup of coherent vision and the loss of sense of self and genuine creativity take poetic form in the breakup of a once smooth line, disjointed stanzaic structure, abrupt changes of rhythm, and incongruous rhyme. Imagery, too, disintegrates: The poet looks in mirrors and cannot recognize his past selves in the aging face confronting him, gazes at a shiny tabletop and sees his own severed head reflected in the window of a passing streetcar, looks at the "asphalt mirror" of a Berlin street at night and sees himself and his friends as monsters, mutants, and human bodies topped by dogs' heads. The creation of art, so closely tied to the re-creation of self, seems impossible in a world of dusty galleries and cheap cinemas. Appropriately enough, *Evropeiskaya noch'* ends with a counterfeit act of creation, a parody of Jehovah's Fourth Day and of the poet's ability to bring dead matter to life. In this last poem, called "Zvezdi" ("Stars"), the cosmos emerges at the wave of a seedy conductor's baton. The show be-

gins, and light comes forth from darkness in the form of prostitutes: the chorus line as the Big Dipper and the soloists as the North Star and "l'Étoile d'Amour." In Khodasevich's earlier works, the poet had been able to create or re-create an earlier, truer existence, a cosmos of his own. He came to doubt his ability to perform such a task. In Khodasevich's later poems, it appears that corrupt and perverted forms—vaudeville comedians and down-and-out dancing girls—may be the only artistic order left to the modern world.

OTHER MAJOR WORKS

NONFICTION: *Derzhavin*, 1931; *Nekropol'*, 1939; *Literaturnye stat'i i vospominaniia*, 1954; *Belyi koridor: Isbrannaia proza v dvukh tomakh*, 1982.

MISCELLANEOUS: *Sobranie stikhov*, 1927.

BIBLIOGRAPHY

Bethea, David M. *Khodasevich: His Life and Art*. 1983. Reprint. Princeton, N.J.: Princeton University Press, 1986. A thorough study by a leading Western expert on Khodasevich. The monograph examines Khodasevich's life and works, underscoring his main achievements in poetic artistry and his contribution to the Russian literature at home and in exile.

Brintlinger, Angela. *Writing a Usable Past: Russian Literary Culture, 1917-1937*. Evanston, Ill.: Northwestern University Press, 2000. Contains two chapters on Khodasevich, one concerning *Derzhavin* and the other on the writer's view of Alexander Pushkin. Notes Khodasevich's devotion to the past.

Hughes, Robert P. "Khodasevich: Irony and Dislocation—A Poet in Exile." In *The Bitter Air of Exile: Russian Writers in the West, 1922-1972*, edited by Simon Karlinsky and Alfred Appel, Jr. Berkeley: University of California Press, 1977. Main stations in Khodasevich's life are marked, followed by brief but pertinent comments on his poetry and his place in Russian literature.

Khodasevich, Valentina, and Olga Margolina-Khodasevich. *Unpublished Letters to Nina Berberova*. Edited by R. D. Sylvester. Berkeley, Calif.: Berkeley Slavic Specialties, 1979. Previously unpublished letters casting light on Khodasevich. Bibliographical references, illustrated.

Kirilcuk, A. "The Estranging Mirror: The Poetics of Reflection in the Late Poetry of Vladislav Khodasevich." *Russian Review* 61, no. 3 (2002): 377-390. Provides an analysis of the later poetry, which treats of spiritual and material worlds.

Miller, Jane A. "Kodasevi's Gnostic Exile." *South and East European Journal* 28, no. 2 (1984): 223-233. Miller concentrates on Khodasevich's exile poetry, notably on *Tyazhelaya lira* and *Evropeiskaya noch'*. She points out the success of the former and the relative failures of the latter. She also broaches the question of creativity and the artist, especially his mirror of himself and his relation to the material world around him.

Nabokov, Vladimir. "On Khodasevich." In *The Bitter Air of Exile: Russian Writers in the West, 1922-1972*, edited by Simon Karlinsky and Alfred Appel, Jr. Berkeley: University of California Press, 1977. A terse but significant article on Khodasevich, written in 1939 in Russian on his death. The article has added weight because it was written by another famous writer in exile.

Rubins, Maria. *Twentieth-Century Russian Émigré Writers*. Vol. 317 in *Dictionary of Literary Biography*. Detroit: Gale, 2005. Brief essay on Khodasevich discusses his life and works.

Jane Ann Miller

KO UN

Born: Kunsan, Korea (now Gunsan, South Korea); January 8, 1933

PRINCIPAL POETRY

Pian kamsŏng, 1960
Sentence to Death, 1963
Haebyŏn ŭi unmunjip, 1966
Sin, ŏnŏ ch'oehu ŭi maŭl, 1967
Senoya Senoya, 1970
Saebyŏk kil, 1978
Choguk ŭi pyŏl, 1984
Si yŏ nara kara, 1986

Maninbo, 1986-2007 (26 volumes; *Ten Thousand Lives*, 2005)
Na ŭi p'ado sori, 1987 (*The Sound of My Waves: Selected Poems*, 1993; also known as *Traveler Maps*, 2004, and *The Three Way Tavern: Selected Poems*, 2006)
Paektusan, 1987-1991 (7 volumes)
Ne nuntongja, 1988
Nirvana, 1988
Ach'im isŭl, 1990 (*Morning Dew*, 1996)
Mwŏnya Simma, 1991 (*Beyond Self: 108 Korean Zen Poems*, 1997; revised as *What? 108 Zen Poems*, 2008)
Ajik kaji anŭn kil, 1993
Tokto, 1995
Nam kwa puk, 2000 (*Abiding Places: Korea South and North*, 2006)
Sun'gan ŭi kkot, 2001 (*Flowers of the Moment*, 2006)
Songs for Tomorrow, 1992
Tugo on si, 2002
Nŭjŭn norae, 2002
Pukkŭrŏum kadŭk, 2006
The Three Way Tavern: Selected Poems, 2006
Hŏgong, 2008

OTHER LITERARY FORMS

Although Ko Un (koh ewn) is primarily known as a poet, he is also an extremely prolific writer in a wide variety of genres and has published more than 135 books. Ko has written short stories and Buddhist novels, the most famous of which is *Hwaŏmgyŏng* (1991; *The Garland Sutra—Little Pilgrim*, 2005). He has also published travel books, books for children, biographies, autobiographies, and books of literary criticism, and he has translated several collections of traditional Chinese poetry.

ACHIEVEMENTS

Ko Un is widely considered Korea's foremost contemporary poet. He has been nominated four times for the Nobel Prize in Literature, and is a winner of the prestigious Lifetime Recognition Award from the Griffin Trust for Excellence in Poetry (2008) and the Cikada Prize (2006), a Swedish literary prize for East Asian poets. Ko has also won the Korean Literature

(1974, 1987), Daesan (1994), and the Manhae (1989) literary prizes. His poetry has been acclaimed by such noted American poets as Allen Ginsberg, Gary Snyder, and Robert Hass. His works have been translated into English, Chinese, Japanese, Russian, Arabic, Swedish, Spanish, Czech, Italian, Norwegian, German, and French, and he has given poetry readings in the United States, Japan, and Europe.

Biography

Ko Un was born into a farming family in a small village near what is now Gunsan, South Korea, in 1933. At that time, Korea had not been divided into two, but it was a colony of Japan. The Japanese colonial administration outlawed the teaching of Korean, so Ko studied Chinese classics at school (and was secretly taught Korean by a neighbor's servant). He started to write poems at the age of twelve. In 1945 (the year Korea was liberated from Japan), he discovered a book of poems by the famous leper-poet Han Ha-un (1920-1975) lying on the wayside, and he decided to become a poet. The Korean War (1950-1953) had a major impact on his life. When the war broke out, he was forced to repair runways at a South Korean air force base. Ko saw a great deal of violence during the war, and as a result, he attempted suicide several times and suffered a nervous breakdown. He entered a Sŏn (Zen) Buddhist monastery when he was nineteen and became a student of the noted monk Hyobong. In 1958, his first poem "Pyekgyeolhaek" ("Tuberculosis") was published in the review *Modern Poetry*, and in 1960, his first collection of poems, *Pian kamsŏng* (other world sensibility), was published.

Two years later, Ko left the monastery. He lived in Seoul for a time, and from 1963 to 1966, he taught Korean and art at a charity high school on the southern island of Cheju. During this period, Ko drank heavily. His second collection of poetry, *Haebyŏn ŭi unmunjip* (seaside poems), was published in 1966. He returned to Seoul, where he continued to drink and sporadically write and publish poetry with strong nihilist themes. In the winter of 1970, his life suddenly changed after he picked up a newspaper from a barroom floor and read about a poor laborer who had committed suicide by self-immolation. Ko decided to take up the causes of civil rights and democracy, and he became a political activist and nationalist poet, helping to organize the Council of Writers for Practice of Freedom and becoming a leader in the *minjung munhak* (people's literature) movement. Ko was arrested many times for protesting against the governments of presidents Park Chung-hee and Chun Doo-hwan. He was imprisoned four times (1974, 1979, 1980, 1989). The second time he was imprisoned, one of his eardrums was damaged as a result of torture. He was still able to publish several biographies, novels, and collections of poem during this time. In 1980, he was sentenced to life in prison, where he conceived of writing his most famous work of poetry, *Ten Thousand Lives*, which fills twenty-six volumes. Ko was released from prison in 1982 because of a general pardon, but in 1989, he was again briefly imprisoned.

In 1983, at the age of forty-nine, he married Lee Sang-wha, a young professor of English literature, and moved to Ansong, Gyeonggi-do, two hours south of Seoul. In 1985, his daughter Cha-ryong was born. After his move to Ansong, Ko has been very prolific. Since 1984, he has published more than one hundred works, as well as a seven-volume epic poem, *Paektusan* (Paektu mountain), about the Korean struggle for independence from Japan. From 1994 to 1998, he was resident professor in the graduate school of Kyonggi University in Seoul. Ko made numerous visits to North Korea in 2002, 2005, 2006, and 2007. In 2008, he became resident poet and professor at Dongook University in Seoul.

Analysis

Ko Un has frequently stated that he does not know why he writes poetry but that words are his religion and he is fascinated with discovering the spiritual traces of past poets. He has strongly rejected the idea that modern Korean poetry is essentially a clone of Western literature. In 1986, he declared that he is completely free of foreign literary influences. His poetry, which ranges in form from the short lyric to the pastoral and epic, reflects his tumultuous personal life, and is frequently concerned with discerning the simple truths of everyday existence. His poetic style is colloquial, arrestingly vivid, frequently earthy, and democratic in both spirit and tone. Although he has been, and continues to be, politically very active, his poetry is rarely political. He has many loyal supporters, but some commentators have criticized his lack of literary refinement.

Ko's poetry can be divided chronologically into three periods. In his early period, Ko's work is antirealist, highly emotional, and centered on romantic nihilism and emptiness. During this stage, Ko was strongly influenced by the French Symbolists, particularly Charles Baudelaire, and by Imagism. In his middle period, the 1970's, which Ko refers to as "post nihilism," he was a politically and socially engaged poet, rejected modernism, and opposed the official government literary theory of "pure literature." In his late period, which started in the 1980's, he has concentrated on realistically depicting the lives and language of ordinary people.

TEN THOUSAND LIVES

Ten Thousand Lives is Ko's most famous work of poetry. When he was imprisoned, he decided to write a very long series of short poems describing all the people he knew, including the historical and literary figures he was acquainted with through reading, as well as individuals from Korean legends and myths. This ongoing epic begins with character vignettes about the people of the village in which he grew up. The Korean original spans twenty-six volumes, but the English version is a collection of poems translated by Brother Anthony of Taizé (An Sonjae of Sogang University), Young-moo Kim, and Gary Gach.

The title of the work is self-explanatory. Ko's portraits are short (usually no longer than one page), direct, and humanistic; often speak in an exclamatory and informal voice; and have been compared to miniature Korean folk tales. His dignified and deeply human subjects stand in strong contrast to the horrors of twentieth century Korean history that they have endured. The poems in *Ten Thousand Lives* are written in Korean spoken idiom and display Korean literature's traditional stress on nature poetry, animism, and shamanism.

"The Women from Sŏnjei-ri" is a good example of his style. This poem is a group portrait of women from Sŏnjei-ri who are returning home at night after an exhausting day of selling garlic bulbs at the local market. Ko simply but precisely captures their long, lonely trek home: "Several miles gone/ several miles left to go in deepest night!/ The empty baskets may be light enough/ yet I wonder: just how light are they/ with empty stomachs, nothing to eat." However, the women's difficulties are offset by the warmth of their characters and relationships: "Still, they share this pain/ these plain, simple people/ these plain, simple women./ What a good homely life!"

"Hyegong: A Monk in the Days of Old," tells the story of the Silla dynasty monk, Heyegong, who was born of a slave. Ko concisely describes the earthy yet spiritual charms of this eccentric monk:

> Although he was a monk, he never once put on silken
>   robes
> and when he was famished
> in the course of his roaming, he'd catch a fish in some
> shallow streamlet,
> chew it up raw and still flapping:
> "*Ah*! I'm full.
> *Ah*! Buddha's full."
> Then he'd piss and his piss
> would bring the fish he'd eaten back to life
> and it would go swimming down the streamlet again,
> or so people said.

WHAT?

The purpose of *What?*, a widely acclaimed collection of Zen mini-poems, is to train the reader's mind to focus on the intense immediacy of everyday experience. They display the traditional Zen distrust of words and reason and its strong emphasis on viewing the world like a child, directly, with an open mind, constantly seeing things as fresh and new. "The Winter Sky" captures this approach well, using repetition to drive home the unobstructed and spontaneous nature of daily existence: "What aching blue!/ Though it shouts,/ nothing can be heard./ What aching blue!/ Birds fly away for days."

In "Daylight," Ko challenges the perception that life is too short by offering another perspective on viewing time: "Three hundred-millionths of a second./ If that's how long one particle lasts/ think how endless one day is./ You say a day's too short?/ You greedy thing."

SONGS FOR TOMORROW

Songs for Tomorrow, a collection of Ko's poems translated into English, covers all periods of his writing. The poems are one to two pages long and show his varied poetic styles. In the first stanza of "The Thirteenth Night of the Month," Ko lyrically describes the maternal yearnings of the village's young women: "The scent of hay from last autumn's rich harvest is truly potent./ Out behind the deadly silent village/ naked young women gather armfuls of moonlight./ Now for the very first time it seems they long to be mothers."

Ko's images in this poem, as in many of the poems in this collection, are sharp and sensuous.

OTHER MAJOR WORKS

LONG FICTION: *Hwaŏmgyŏng*, 1991 (*The Garland Sutra—Little Pilgrim*, 2005); *Sosŏl: Sŏn*, 1995; *Sumi san*, 1999.

SHORT FICTION: *San nŏmŏ san nŏmŏ pŏkch'an ap'nigŏra*, 1980.

NONFICTION: *Si wa hyŏnsil*, 1986; *Yŏksa nŭn hŭrŭnda*, 1990; *Sanha yŏ, na ŭi sanha yŏ*, 1999.

TRANSLATIONS: *Tangsi sŏn*, 1976; *Sigyŏng*, 1976.

CHILDREN'S LITERATURE: *Ch'aryŏngi norae*, 1997; *Nanun chonsaga aniya*, 1997.

BIBLIOGRAPHY

Hass, Robert. "Poet of Wonders." *The New York Review of Books* 52, no. 17 (November 3, 2005). In this profile of Ko, Hass describes his meeting with the poet and situates his poetry in the context of modern Korean poetry.

Ko Un. "Human Nature Itself Is Poetic: An Interview." Interview by Patricia Donegan. *Manoa* 18, no. 1 (2006): 1-8. Ko discusses his life and poetic inspirations.

_____. "Ko Un Poet." http://www.koun.co.kr. Ko's official Web site, in both English and Korean, contains information about his life, a list of his writings, and links to articles about him.

_____. *Songs for Tomorrow*. Translated by Brother Anthony of Taizé, Young-moo Kim, and Gary Gach. 1992. Reprint. Los Angeles: Green Integer, 2008. Contains a revealing introduction by the poet and poems representing a broad range of Ko's work.

Lee, Peter. *A History of Korean Literature*. New York: Cambridge University Press, 2003. Provides a short but informative discussion of Ko's poetry and places him within the literary history of that country.

McCann, David R., ed. *The Columbia Anthology of Modern Korean Poetry*. New York: Columbia Press, 2004. Provides a comprehensive discussion of modern poetry in Korea, a short biography of Ko, and ten of his poems.

Paik, Nak-chung. "Zen Poetry and Realism: Reflections on Ko Un's Verse." *Positions* 8, no. 2 (2000): 559-578. Presents a good overview of Ko's Zen poetry.

Ronald Gray

L

MIKHAIL LERMONTOV

Born: Moscow, Russia; October 15, 1814
Died: Pyatigorsk, Russia; July 27, 1841

PRINCIPAL POETRY

Pesnya pro tsarya Ivana Vasilyevicha, molodogo oprichnika i udalogo kuptsa Kalashnikova, 1837 (*A Song About Tsar Ivan Vasilyevitch, His Young Body-Guard, and the Valiant Merchant Kalashnikov*, 1911)

Stikhotvoreniya M. Lermontova, 1840

Demon, 1855 (*The Demon*, 1875)

The Demon, and Other Poems, 1965

Mikhail Lermontov: Major Poetical Works, 1983

OTHER LITERARY FORMS

In addition to his position as one of the foremost Russian poets of the nineteenth century, Mikhail Lermontov (LYAYR-muhn-tuhf) holds the distinction of producing what many consider to be the first major novel in Russia, *Geroy nashego vremeni* (1840; *A Hero of Our Time*, 1854). The state of Russian prose during the 1820's and 1830's was far from satisfactory. Although several writers had tried their hands at historical novels in the 1820's, writers in the 1830's were still wrestling with such basic matters as narrative structure and a suitable literary language for the larger forms of prose fiction. Lermontov himself had begun two novels in the 1830's—a historical novel, *Vadim* (1935-1937; English translation, 1984), and a novel of St. Petersburg life, *Knyaginya Ligovskaya* (1935-1937; *Princess Ligovskaya*, 1965)—but he never completed them. In *A Hero of Our Time*, he solved the problems of structure and point of view by turning to the current fashion for combining a series of discrete short stories in a single cycle and taking it a step further. *A Hero of Our Time* consists of five tales linked by the figure of the central protagonist, Grigory Pechorin. Lermontov uses the device of multiple narrators and points of view to bring his readers ever closer to this hero, first providing secondhand accounts of the man and then concluding with an intimate psychological portrait arising from Pechorin's own diary records, all the while maintaining his own authorial objectivity. The figure of Pechorin himself, a willful yet jaded egoist, made a strong impact on the reading public, and the Pechorin type had many successors in Russian literature.

Lermontov also wrote several plays, beginning with *Ispantsy* (pb. 1935; the Spaniards) and *Menschen und Leidenschaften* (pb. 1935; people and passions), which were inspired by the Storm and Stress period of Friedrich Schiller's career, and concluding with *Maskarad* (pb. 1842; *Masquerade*, 1973), a drama exposing the vanity of St. Petersburg society. Lermontov is most remembered, however, for his prose and poetry.

ACHIEVEMENTS

In poetry, Mikhail Lermontov stands out as a Romantic writer *par excellence*. Influenced in his youth by such writers as Schiller and Lord Byron, he transformed Russian verse into a medium of frank lyric confession. The reserved and often abstract figure of the poet found in earlier Russian poetry gave way to a pronounced and assertive lyric ego in Lermontov's work, and Lermontov's readers were struck by the emotional intensity of his verse. Striving to express his personal feelings as forcefully as possible, Lermontov developed a charged verse style unmistakably his own. Although he seldom invented startling new poetic images, he often combined familiar images in sequences that dazzled his readers, and he used repetition, antithesis, and parallelism to create pithy and impressive verse formulations. Lermontov's poetic vision and his unabashed approach to the expression of his emotions had a considerable effect on subsequent Russian writers, from Nikolay Nekrasov in the next generation to Aleksandr Blok and Boris Pasternak in the twentieth century.

Iconoclastic in his approach to genre as well, Lermontov completed a trend already apparent in Russian poetry of the 1820's—the dismantling of the strict system of genre distinctions created during the era of classicism in Russian literature. Lermontov drew on disparate elements from various genres—the elegy, ode, ballad, and romance—and forged from them new verse forms suitable for his own expressive needs. The poet also showed a willingness to experiment with diverse meters and rhythms, and he employed ternary meters, primarily dactyls and amphibrachs, to an extent not seen previously in Russian poetry. Lermontov's exploration of such meters would later be continued by writers such as Nekrasov.

Although Lermontov's career was exceptionally brief, his accomplishments were extensive. He is justly considered to be, along with Alexander Pushkin, one of the two most important Russian poets of the nineteenth century. He left a rich legacy for future generations of Russian poets. Having moved past the poetic practices of Pushkin and his contemporaries, Lermontov forged a new style for the expression of the poet's emotions, a style both rugged and pliant, charged and evocative. His bold assertiveness as a poet and his skilled handling of rhythm and meter found an echo in the work of several generations of later writers. These achievements have earned Lermontov the right to one of the foremost places in the pantheon of Russian poets.

B<small>IOGRAPHY</small>

Mikhail Yurievich Lermontov was born in Moscow on October 15, 1814. According to family tradition, the Lermontovs were descended from a Scottish mercenary named George Learmont, who entered the service of the Muscovite state in the seventeenth century. Mikhail's mother, Mariya Arsenieva, belonged to an old and aristocratic family, the Stolypins, and her relatives did not approve of her match with Lermontov's father. Mariya died in 1817, and the child was reared by his maternal grandmother, Elizaveta Arsenieva, on her estate, Tarkhany. Because Lermontov's father Yury did not get along with Elizaveta Arsenieva, he left his son at Tarkhany and seldom met with him again before dying in 1831.

Lermontov had a comfortable upbringing. His grandmother provided him with a series of private tutors, and he occupied himself with painting and music as well as his studies. He moved with his grandmother to Moscow in 1827, and in the following year, he en-

tered a private preparatory school connected with the University of Moscow. There, he became interested in poetry and began to write voluminous amounts of verse, inspired by such authors as Schiller, Byron, Pushkin, Vasily Zhukovsky, and others. The influence of Byron and Pushkin is evident in Lermontov's first attempts at narrative poetry, "Cherkesy" ("The Circassians") and "Kavkazsky plennik" ("A Prisoner of the Caucasus"). It was also during this period that Lermontov began work on his most famous narrative poem, *The Demon*.

In the fall of 1830, Lermontov entered the University of Moscow, where he remained immersed in his own personal world, reading and writing poetry and drama, including *Stranny chelovek* (pb. 1935; *A Strange One*, 1965). At the same time, he began to make a name for himself in social circles and experienced his first serious infatuations. His romance with one woman, Varvara Lopukhina, left a lasting imprint on the young man. Lermontov's romantic experiences and his encounter with society as a whole were filtered through

Mikhail Lermontov (Library of Congress)

his absorption with the figure of Byron. Constantly comparing his life with Byron's, he would become excited by any perceived similarities.

In 1832, Lermontov withdrew from the University of Moscow and sought admission to the University of St. Petersburg. Because the university would not give him credit for work done in Moscow, Lermontov instead entered the School of Guard Ensigns and Cavalry Cadets. There, he took up the lifestyle of an average cadet and wrote little in the way of serious poetry. Most of his creative energies went into the composition of salacious verse for his comrades' amusement, although he did begin work on his first novel, *Vadim*, a historical piece depicting the activities of a demoniac hero during the time of the Pugachev rebellion in the 1700's. After receiving his commission in the Life Guard Hussar Regiment stationed outside St. Petersburg in Tsarskoe Selo, Lermontov continued to sustain an active social life and rather calculatingly tried to generate a reputation as a Don Juan. Lermontov's cynicism about the values and mores of St. Petersburg society found expression in his verse play *Masquerade*, which, because of censorship problems, was approved for publication only after his death. In addition to this dramatic piece, Lermontov began work on the novel *Princess Ligovskaya*, which depicts an encounter between a young aristocrat and a St. Petersburg clerk, but the book was never finished.

Lermontov's literary reputation received a dramatic assist in 1837, when he wrote a bold poem about Pushkin's untimely death as a result of a duel in January of that year. The duel—the culmination of Pushkin's long frustration with life in St. Petersburg and with the attentions paid to his wife by Baron Georges d'Anthès, a French exile and the adopted son of a Dutch diplomat—had taken place on January 27. Pushkin was mortally wounded and died on January 29. Lermontov immediately penned a sharp poem expressing his dismay at Pushkin's death and the sufferings he had endured that led him to the duel. When some of d'Anthès's supporters began to cast aspersions on Pushkin, Lermontov added sixteen more lines that gave vent to his indignation with the court aristocracy itself. The poem received wide circulation in manuscript form and created a sensation in St. Petersburg. When it came to the

czar's attention, Lermontov was arrested and sent to serve in the Caucasus.

This exile did not last long, however, and after several months in the south, Lermontov was transferred to Novgorod and then back to St. Petersburg. There, the poet circulated in society as a figure of note, and he reacted to the situation with ironic amusement. He also entered into close relationships with other important literary figures of the day—Zhukovsky, Pyotr Vyazemsky, and Andrey Kraevsky, the editor of the new journal *Otechestvennye zapiski*, in which several of Lermontov's poems appeared. Although his production of lyric poetry declined at this time, he completed several noteworthy works, including the narrative poems "Tambovskaya kaznacheysha" ("The Tambov Treasurer's Wife") and "Mtsyri" ("The Novice"), which contains the confessions of a young monk who had briefly fled the monastery to find out "if the earth is beautiful" and "if we are born into this world/ For freedom or for prison." The first portions of his great novel *A Hero of Our Time* also began to appear in 1839.

Early in 1840, however, Lermontov again found himself in trouble with the authorities. Within the span of a few weeks, he succeeded in insulting the czar's daughters at a masquerade ball and took part in a duel with Ernaste de Barante, the son of the French ambassador. Again Lermontov was arrested, and again he was sent to the Caucasus for military service. Once there, Lermontov managed to obtain an assignment with a regiment actively engaged in fierce battles with rebel Caucasian tribes, and he soon distinguished himself in hand-to-hand combat with the rebels. Suitably impressed, Lermontov's commanders recommended that he be given a gold saber in recognition of his valor, but he never received this commendation, perhaps because he continued to incur the disfavor of the authorities back in St. Petersburg.

Having been given permission to take a two-month leave in the capital early in 1841, Lermontov overstayed his leave and was ordered to depart for the Caucasus within forty-eight hours. He was in no hurry to rejoin his regiment, however, and his return journey became a leisurely affair, during which he wrote several of his finest lyrics. Reaching the town of Pyatigorsk in May, he spent several weeks taking the waters and indulging in pleasant diversions with a company of friends and other young people. Unfortunately, Lermontov chose to mock a certain Nikolay Martynov, an officer and former schoolmate at the Guards' School who had adopted the habit of wearing native dress in an attempt to impress the women in town. Martynov took umbrage at Lermontov's repeated needling, and he finally challenged him to a duel. The duel took place on July 27, 1841. Deadly serious, Martynov advanced to the barrier with determination and shot Lermontov, killing him instantly. Lermontov was subsequently buried at Tarkhany.

ANALYSIS

The hallmark of Mikhail Lermontov's mature verse—a fine balance between the intensity of the poet's emotion and the controlled language he uses to express it—took several years to achieve. In his early work, Lermontov did not check his desire to convey his feelings directly, and his verse seems raw and effusive, often hyberbolic and unformed. He wrote hundreds of poems as an adolescent, and he later recognized their immaturity, for he refused to publish them with his subsequent work. They would appear only after his death.

EARLY POETRY

A study of the early poetry reveals Lermontov's aggressive absorption of the work of other writers. Imagery, phrases, and individual lines are taken whole from the poetry of such authors as Zhukovsky, Pushkin, Alexander Polezhaev, and Ivan Kozlov among the Russians, and of Byron, Thomas Moore, Alphonse de Lamartine, and Victor Hugo among foreign writers. Lermontov's tendency to lift excerpts from one work and to insert them into another was a lifelong characteristic of his artistic method. He not only appropriated elements from other writers' works but also cannibalized his own poetry. The narrative poem "The Novice," for example, contains elements drawn from an earlier work, "Boyarin Orsha" (the Boyar Orsha), which in turn contains elements from an even earlier work, "Ispoved" (a confession). As the Russian Formalist critic Boris Eikhenbaum put it in his noted study of 1924, *Lermontov* (English translation, 1981): "His attitude was not directed toward the creation of new mate-

rial, but to the fusion of ready-made elements." In his greatest works, however, Lermontov's art of fusion resulted in some very distinguished pieces.

LORD BYRON'S INFLUENCE

Perhaps the most influential figure in Lermontov's formative years as a poet was Byron. Lermontov's early lyrics repeatedly feature heroes who possess a special sensitivity or gifted nature but who have been crushed by fate. Such characters may carry a dark secret or wound in their souls, but they bear their suffering proudly and without complaint. Typical are these lines from a poem of 1831, "Iz Andreya Shenie" ("From André Chénier"): "My terrible lot is worthy of your tears,/ I have done much evil, but I have borne more." Lermontov himself recognized his affinity with Byron, while seeking at the same time to assert his individuality; a poem of 1832 begins, "No, I am not Byron, I am another/ As yet unknown chosen one." This sense of his own uniqueness is characteristic of the young Lermontov, and his fascination with the traits of the Byronic hero is further evident as he compares himself to Byron: "Like him, I am a wanderer persecuted by the world/ But with a Russian soul." Other Romantic features in the poem include a comparison between the unfathomable depths of his soul and the depths of the ocean (recalling Byron's celebrated verses on the same theme), a statement about the separation of the poet from "the crowd," and a complaint about the difficulty of expressing one's inner feelings. Lermontov airs this last concept in a demonstrative final line. Asking "Who will tell the crowd my thoughts?" the poet exclaims: "I—or God—or no one!" Many of Lermontov's poems conclude with such dramatic flair. Also characteristic here is Lermontov's penchant for concise lines structured by parallelism and antithesis. Comparing himself with Byron, he writes: "I began earlier, I will end earlier." This line seemed particularly prophetic to the Russian reading public when the poem first appeared in 1845, after Lermontov's early death. Curiously, Lermontov's apprehension of an early death remained with him throughout his career.

"THE SAIL"

One of Lermontov's early lyrics, the short poem "Parus" ("The Sail"), became well known after his death. Written in three stanzas of iambic tetrameter, the most popular meter in Russian poetry at the time, the poem is wholly constructed on a strict scheme of parallels and repetitions. The first two lines of each stanza provide a description of a sea setting, while the second two depict the psychological condition of a person, perhaps a sailor, metonymically evoked by the image of the sail moving across the open sea (the word for "sail" in Russian is masculine, and the Russian pronoun *on* can be translated as either "he" or "it"). Within this framework of parallels, Lermontov uses a series of antitheses or oppositions that perhaps reflect the contradictory flux of emotions in the subject's soul. The poet asks in the first stanza: "What is it seeking in a distant land?/ What has it abandoned in its native region?" In the second stanza, however, he provides only negative answers: "Alas,—it is not seeking happiness/ And it does not flee from happiness!" Nor do the final lines provide a concrete resolution: "Rebellious one, it seeks the storm,/ As if in storms there is peace!" Lermontov's evocation of a rebellious spirit seeking peace through turmoil was given a political interpretation by some contemporary Russian readers, but the poem's generalized nature makes other interpretations possible, too. It is likely that Lermontov simply wanted to suggest the fundamental contradictions and confusion inherent in restlessness itself.

THE DEMON

Images of rebellion and negation occupied a prominent place among Lermontov's lyrics in the 1830's, and at the end of the decade he completed his most impressive portrait of a Romantic "spirit of negation"—the title character of the long narrative poem *The Demon*. Like many of Lermontov's other narrative poems, *The Demon* is less a tale involving several characters in a concrete setting than a forum for the lyric expression of the protagonist's emotional impulses. In its earlier versions, the poem was set in Spain, and the female protagonist was a nun, but Lermontov later shifted the setting to the Caucasus, and the austere mountain ranges of this region proved to be an excellent backdrop for his portrayal of human frailty and superhuman passion. The central character of the poem is the Demon, a dark spirit who becomes captivated by the beauty of a Georgian maiden, Tamara. After her fiancé has been killed, the Demon tries to persuade her to give her love to him,

telling her that her love can restore him to goodness and reconcile him with Heaven. Having delivered his impassioned speech, he destroys her with a fatal kiss. As her soul is carried to Heaven by an angel, the Demon seeks to claim his victim, but the angel spurns him, and the furious Demon is left alone with his frustrated dreams.

The Demon is an enigmatic character. Lermontov does not provide the reader with a clear psychological portrait of his hero. He is not the stern, philosophizing rebel of Byron's verse drama *Cain* (1821) and of similar Western European treatments of the metaphysical Romantic hero. Rather, he resembles the protagonists of a number of Lermontov's other works in that he is a willful spirit motivated more by boredom than by Promethean ambitions. The Demon recalls happier times "When he believed and loved/ . . . And knew neither malice nor doubt," but his turn to evil is essentially unmotivated, and his speeches to Tamara are not logically structured arguments but rather dazzling torrents of charged phrases and images. When he identifies himself to her, he states: "I am the scourge of my earthly slaves,/ I am the tsar of knowledge and freedom,/ . . . And you see,—I am at your feet!"

When the Demon claims that he is ready to renounce evil and reconcile himself with the good, the reader is not sure how to gauge the Demon's sincerity. His attitudes are susceptible to instantaneous change. When he hears Tamara sing, he begins to enter her room "ready to love/ With a soul open to the good . . . ," yet when an angel blocks his way, he flares up: "And again in his soul awoke/ The poison of ancient hatred." He tells Tamara that as soon as he saw her, he suddenly hated his immortality and power, but as he tries to convince her to love him, he offers her both of these gifts. Perhaps the best way to understand the Demon is to view him as a figure who has truly become bored with doing evil ("He sowed evil without enjoyment/ . . . And evil grew boring to him"), and therefore he allows himself to become caught up in his own rhetoric about renunciation of evil and reconciliation with the good. At the moment of his declarations, he may feel sincere, but at the core of his soul, he is cold and unfeeling. Tamara, on the other hand, is given little to say; she seems to serve merely as a pretext for Lermontov's hero to pour out his soul.

The interaction between the Demon and Tamara is played out against the forbidding landscape of the Caucasus. Lermontov's descriptions of the icy mountains that stand guard over small patches of inhabited land serve as an apt emblem of the cosmos itself. The universe of *The Demon* and of many other Lermontov works is an impersonal realm in which human activity plays but a small and insignificant role. Lermontov's readers, however, have been less moved by his descriptions of nature than by the glittering oratory of the Demon, and the work has left significant traces on the creative consciousness of later Russian artists. The painter Mikhail Vrubel painted a series of studies inspired by *The Demon*, and the composer Anton Rubinstein wrote an opera based on the work.

"THE DEATH OF A POET"

Lermontov's development beyond the narrow thematics of his early Romantic period is most apparent in his shorter lyric works, beginning with his famous poem on Pushkin's death, "Smert poeta" ("The Death of a Poet"). The poem can be divided into three parts. The first two parts were written immediately after Pushkin's death, while the third was composed several days later. Throughout the poem, Lermontov's talent for declamatory verse comes to the fore. The first section, written in lines of iambic tetrameter, is marked by frequent exclamations, rhetorical questions, and strong intonational breaks, as in the lines: "He rose up against the opinion of society/ Alone, as before . . . and was killed!/ Killed!" In an interesting form of homage to Pushkin, Lermontov draws on Pushkin's own poetry to depict the poet's death, echoing the images used by the earlier poet in his brilliant novel in verse, *Evgeny Onegin* (1825-1832, 1833; *Eugene Onegin*, 1881).

During the second part of the poem, which is written in iambic lines of varying lengths, Lermontov adopts an elegiac tone as he questions why Pushkin left the peaceful diversions of close friendships to enter into "this society, envious and suffocating/ To a free heart and fiery passions." In the final section, also written in iambic lines of varying lengths, Lermontov's elegiac tone gives way to a torrent of bitter invective. His charged epithets and complex syntax seem to boil over with the heat of his indignation. He begins with a harsh characterization of those who spoke ill of the dead

poet—"You, arrogant offspring/ Of fathers renowned for notorious baseness"—and he continues with an attack on the court itself: "You, standing in a greedy crowd around the throne,/ The executioners of Freedom, Genius, and Glory." After reminding these villains of the inevitability of divine punishment, which cannot be bought off with gold, Lermontov concludes: "And you will not wash away with all your black blood/ The righteous blood of the poet!" "The Death of a Poet" heralded Lermontov's growing maturity as a poet. Although revealing his continued reliance on certain Romantic formulas, it indicated that he was beginning to find a workable poetic style for himself.

"MEDITATION"

Lermontov employed the declamatory style of "The Death of a Poet" with great success in his late period. A forceful poem of 1838, "Duma" ("Meditation"), for example, presents a concentrated indictment of the coldness and emptiness of Lermontov's entire generation. The poem begins, "I gaze on our generation with sadness!" and it contains such well-known lines as "We are disgracefully faint-hearted before danger/ And contemptible slaves before power." As Lidiya Ginzburg points out in her important study, *Tvorchesky put Lermontova* (1940), the lyric ego of Lermontov's early works had become a more generalized "we"; this shift perhaps reflected a greater objectivity on Lermontov's part as he soberly measured himself and the society in which he had come to maturity. Certainly the poet knew how to pinpoint the falsity and vanity of his peers. In a poem of 1840 that begins "How often, surrounded by a motley crowd . . . ," Lermontov contrasts his feelings of boredom at a masquerade ball with his warm recollections of childhood and spontaneous dreaming. Noting that he hears "the wild whisper of speeches learned by rote" and is touched "with carefree audacity" by urban beauties' hands, "which long ago had ceased to tremble," the poet concludes by confessing an urge "to confuse their frivolity/ And to throw boldly into their faces an iron verse/ Steeped in bitterness and spite!"

MATURE WORKS

Lermontov's declamatory "iron verse," however, was only one style he used in his mature work. It is futile to look for sharp genre distinctions in his late verse, for he did not pay close attention to such distinctions, and one can find in individual poems a blending of features from various genres. Eikhenbaum identifies three categories of poetry in Lermontov's mature period: poems of an oratorical, meditational character; poems of melancholy reflection; and poems resembling lyric ballads with a weakened plot. Indeed, several of Lermontov's late poems resemble small verse novellas: "Uznik" ("The Prisoner"), "Sosed" ("The Neighbor"), "Kinzhal" ("The Dagger"), "Son" ("A Dream"), and "Svidanie" ("The Meeting"). In part, Lermontov's predilection for such brief verse "novellas" may have signified a dissatisfaction with the unrestrained confessional tenor of his early work and a desire to create works that displayed greater objectivity and universality. For the same reason, perhaps, Lermontov also favored short allegorical poems in which natural settings and objects convey human situations and feelings. One example of this type is "Utyos" ("The Cliff"), the first stanza of which depicts a cloud nestling for the night against the breast of a great cliff. In the morning, the cloud moves on, "gaily playing in the azure," but it has left behind a moist trace in a crack in the cliff. The poem concludes with a picture of the cliff: "Solitarily/ It stands, plunged deep in thought,/ And quietly it weeps in the wilderness." Again, one can contrast the restrained evocation of abandonment and isolation here with the unchecked egotism of Lermontov's early work. The "plot" of this poem is further enhanced by the fact that in Russian, the word for "cloud" is feminine while the word for "cliff" is masculine. Also noteworthy is the trochaic meter of the verse; Lermontov moved beyond the poetic models of his predecessors to develop new rhythmic patterns.

"IT'S BORING AND SAD . . ."

At times, Lermontov's new rhythms produced an impression of ruggedness that aroused commentary from his readers. One such work is the poem "I skuchno i grustno . . ." ("It's Boring and Sad . . ."). Written in alternating lines of five-foot and three-foot amphibrachs, the poem stands out for its colloquial, almost prosaic diction, as at the beginning of the second stanza, where the poet writes: "To love . . . but whom? . . . for a short time—it's not worth the effort,/ But to love forever is impossible." After examining his situation and judging it dull, the poet concludes: "And life, if you look around

with cold attentiveness,/ Is such an empty and foolish joke. . . ." The mood of pessimism and disillusionment is familiar from Lermontov's early work, but the detachment and impassivity of the verse are new. The poet is no longer swept away with the importance of his emotions. He surveys his own flaws and the flaws of his generation with an analytical eye that retains no illusions about the glamorous posturings of the Romantic hero. This detachment is precisely what makes Lermontov's portrait of Pechorin, the protagonist of *A Hero of Our Time*, so gripping and accurate.

"I WALK OUT ALONE ONTO THE ROAD . . ."

Lermontov's innovative approach to rhythmic patterns was perhaps most influential in his reflective poem of 1841, "Vykhozhu odin ya na dorogu . . ." ("I Walk Out Alone onto the Road . . ."). This work, one of the last that Lermontov wrote, depicts the poet alone in the midst of nature on a quiet, starlit night. Within his soul, however, he is troubled. He wonders why he feels so pained, and he confesses that he no longer expects anything from life; he merely wants to fall into a deep sleep. Yet it is not the sleep of the grave that he seeks; rather, he would like to fall asleep in the world of nature, eternally caressed by a sweet song of love.

Of special interest in this poem is Lermontov's use of trochaic pentameter with a caesura after the third syllable of the line. This meter creates a special rhythmic effect in which the line seems to fall into two segments. The first segment is often anapestic, because the first syllable is frequently unstressed or weakly stressed, while the second part of the line seems to consist of three iambic feet. This structure creates an impression of an initial upsweep of movement, emphasizing the semantic charge of the poem's first word—"vŭkhŏzhú" ("I walk out")—followed by a more calm or stable interval over the rest of the line. Such a contrast or imbalance is itself emblematic of the poem's message, for despite the initial suggestion of movement conveyed by the poet's statement about walking out onto the road, he does not in fact go anywhere, and the poem concludes with images of passivity or stasis. This remarkable harmony between the rhythmic pattern of the poem and its message has had a lasting impact on the artists who followed Lermontov. Not only was the poem set to music and introduced to the general public as a song, but it also initiated an entire cycle of poems in which a contrast between the dynamic theme of the road or travel and the static theme of life or meditation is rendered in lines of trochaic pentameter. Among Lermontov's successors who wrote poems of this type were Fyodor Tyutchev, Ivan Bunin, Aleksandr Blok, Andrey Bely, Sergei Esenin, Boris Poplavsky, and Boris Pasternak.

OTHER MAJOR WORKS

LONG FICTION: *Geroy nashego vremeni*, 1839, serial (1840, book; *A Hero of Our Time*, 1854); *Knyaginya Ligovskaya*, 1935-1937 (wr. 1836-1837; in *Polnoe sobranie sochinenii v piati tomakh*; *Princess Ligovskaya*, 1965); *Vadim*, 1935-1937 (wr. 1832-1834; in *Polnoe sobranie sochinenii v piati tomakh*; English translation, 1984).

PLAYS: *Maskarad*, pb. 1842 (wr. 1834-1835; *Masquerade*, 1973); *Dva brata*, pb. 1880 (wr. 1836; *Two Brothers*, 1933); *Ispantsy*, pb. 1935 (wr. 1830; verse play); *Menschen und Leidenschaften*, pb. 1935 (wr. 1830); *Stranny chelovek*, pb. 1935 (wr. 1831, verse play; *A Strange One*, 1965); *Tsigany*, pb. 1935 (wr. 1830).

MISCELLANEOUS: *Sochtsnentsya M. Ya. Lermontova*, 1889-1891 (6 volumes); *Polnoe sobranie sochinenii v piati tomakh*, 1935-1937 (5 volumes; includes all his prose and poetry); *Polnoe sobranie sochinenii v shesti tomakh*, 1954-1957 (6 volumes; includes all his prose and poetry); *A Lermontov Reader*, 1965 (includes *Princess Ligovskaya*, *A Strange One*, and poetry); *Michael Lermontov: Biography and Translation*, 1967; *Selected Works*, 1976 (includes prose and poetry).

BIBLIOGRAPHY

Allen, Elizabeth Cheresh. *A Fallen Idol Is Still a God: Lermontov and the Quandaries of Cultural Transition*. Stanford, Calif.: Stanford University Press, 2007. In this volume, Allen takes a critical look at Lermontov's writing, applying literary theories, and placing it in the context of his time and culture. He is portrayed as a writer who defies categorization, straddling the line between Romanticism and Realism.

Briggs, A. D. P., ed. *Mikhail Lermontov: Commemorative Essays*. Birmingham, England: University of Birmingham, 1992. A collection of papers from a conference at the University of Birmingham in July, 1991, on Lermontov and his works. Bibliography and index.

Eikhenbaum, Boris. *Lermontov*. Translated by Ray Parrot and Harry Weber. Ann Arbor, Mich.: Ardis, 1981. A translation of the Russian monograph by a leading Russian critic of the 1920's, this thorough study of Lermontov's poetry and prose remains the seminal work on him. Many poems are offered in both Russian and English.

Garrard, John. *Mikhail Lermontov*. Boston: G. K. Hall, 1982. Presents Lermontov and his works meticulously in a concise, easy-to-understand fashion. Lays the foundation for more ambitious studies of Lermontov in any language.

Golstein, Vladimir. *Lermontov's Narratives of Heroism*. Evanston, Ill.: Northwestern University Press, 1998. Tackles the topic of heroism, prevalent in Lermontov's works, and how he presents and solves it. The emphasis is on "The Demon," "The Song," and Pechorin of *A Hero of Our Time*. Citations of works are in Russian and English translation.

Kelly, Laurence. *Lermontov: Tragedy in the Caucasus*. 1977. Reprint. New York: Tauris Park, 2003. Colorfully illustrated biography of Lermontov covers his childhood in the "wild" East, his education, the rise and fall in the society, and his attitudes toward war as reflected in his works.

Lermontov, Mikhail. *Major Poetical Works*. Translated with a biographical sketch, commentary, and an introduction by Anatoly Liberman. Minneapolis: University of Minnesota Press, 1983. A thorough detailing of Lermontov's life that takes good advantage of the previous works together with translations of more than one hundred of Lermontov's poems, not all of which have appeared in English previously. The translations have won much professional praise for their surprising poeticality that does not compromise accuracy. Includes more than fifty illustrations and is annotated and indexed.

Reid, Robert. *Lermontov's "A Hero of Our Time."* London: Bristol Classical Press, 1997. This analysis of the novel casts light on Lermontov's work as a whole. Includes bibliographical references.

Turner, C. J. G. *Pechorin: An Essay on Lermontov's "A Hero of Our Time."* Birmingham, England: University of Birmingham Press, 1978. A pithy discussion of various aspects of Lermontov's main character, of the relationship of the narrator and the reader, the narrator and the hero, the hero and himself, the hero and the author, and the hero and the reader.

Vickery, Walter N. *M. Iu. Lermontov: His Life and Work.* Munich, Germany: O. Sagner, 2001. A biography of Lermontov that examines his life and work. Includes a bibliography.

Julian W. Connolly

Li Bo

Born: Xinjiang Uygur, China (now in Chinese Turkistan); 701
Died: Dangtu, Anhwei Province, China; December, 762
Also known as: Li Bai; Li Pai; Li Po; Li Taibo; Li T'ai-pai; Li T'ai-po

Principal poetry

"Ballad of Chang-an," n.d. (as "The River Merchant's Wife: A Letter"; Ezra Pound, translator, 1915)
The Poetry and Career of Li Po, 1950 (Arthur Waley, editor)
Li Po and Tu Fu, 1973 (Arthur Cooper, editor)

Other literary forms

Some of the letters and other prose writings of Li Bo (lee boh) survive, but his reputation rests entirely on his poetry.

Achievements

Li Bo and his younger contemporary Du Fu (Tu Fu) rank as the two greatest poets in the three thousand years of Chinese literary history. Each has the reputation, and the merit, of William Shakespeare in the English tradition.

By the age of forty, Li Bo was a popular poet, well known for the audacity of his poetry and his personality, but he was not widely considered an outstanding poet in his own lifetime. Contemporaries who liked his work despite its unconventional extravagance were highly enthusiastic about it. His friend Zui Zongzhi praised it as "incomparable," and for several years Li Bo held a special position as a favored writer in the court of the emperor. In the last few years of his life, however, Li Bo's influence waned.

Interest in Li Bo's work began to revive several decades after his death, and the acclaim he received from the leading poets and critics early in the next century established him in the position of high regard that he has held ever since. His works were read, and memorized, by educated people throughout East Asia. Many later poets reveal debts to his compelling language, his gift for visualizing imagined scenes, and his intensely personal way of viewing the world. Li Bo's ability to produce a unique twist in image, language, or perspective set his poems apart, even those on traditional topics.

In many ways, Li Bo's playfulness, his individualism, and his visionary flamboyance make him the most accessible of all traditional Chinese poets for the modern Western reader. One measure of Li Bo's effect on modern-day readers of English is the number of translations available. Some of the strongest of Ezra Pound's poems after Chinese originals in *Cathay: Translations by Ezra Pound for the Most Part from the Chinese of Rihaku, from the Notes of the Late Ernest Fenollosa and the Decipherings of the Professors Mori and Ariga* (1915) are those attributed to "Rihaku," which is the Japanese pronunciation of the Chinese "Li Bo." Shigeyoshi Obata's free renditions will appeal to some readers, though others will find the English old-fashioned and too ornate. Arthur Waley's brief book on Li Bo's life and poetry at times reflects Waley's lack of affinity with his subject. The layers of meaning in the poems are sometimes overlooked and the slippery facts of Li Bo's life get muddled, but Waley's skill in Chinese and in English gives the book value. Extensive notes to individual poems are only one of the strengths of Arthur Cooper's translations.

Among the many excellent translations are the lucid, striking renditions by the poet David Young, and the more scholarly—but highly readable—work of

Eiling Eide and Stephen Owen. In addition, most anthologies of translated Chinese poetry include works by Li Bo. *Sunflower Splendor* (1975) makes an excellent starting place; it contains a bibliography of anthologies for further reading. Li Bo's daring and robust spirit, his vivid sense of the sublime and the supernatural, and his profound understanding of the creative power of the poetic mind have as much to say to the modern Westerner as they have said to Asian readers for more than a millennium.

BIOGRAPHY

Li Bo lived at the height of one of China's richest eras of cultural and political greatness. The Tang Empire stretched in some places beyond the borders of China today, and trade flourished, ranging to India, Japan, the Middle East, and even Greece. The poets of Li Bo's generation rode the crests of twin waves of innovation and the consolidation of earlier achievements. Despite the political instability that marred the final period of Li Bo's life, he lived for forty-four of his sixty-odd years under an emperor whose reign is rightly called a golden age.

It is difficult to pin down the facts of Li Bo's life. So colorful a figure naturally has inspired a number of legends. The poet evidently encouraged such legend making in his own lifetime, the more extravagant the better, such as the story that he was fathered by the spirit of the planet known in the West as Venus.

While the great majority of the people under the Tang Empire, especially the people in power, were Han Chinese, Li Bo himself was probably at least partly of Turkish or Iranian descent. Li Bo claimed that an ancestor of his had been exiled from China and that his family had lived for about a century in various settlements along trade routes in and around what is now Afghanistan. A good bit of evidence suggests the family's non-Chinese cultural orientation: Li Bo's ability to write poetry in "a foreign language," several family members' names (including those of Li Bo's two sons), the affinity for Central Asian culture shown in the content and form of many of his poems, and such stereotypically "foreign" personality traits as Li Bo's love of drinking. None of this evidence is conclusive, but it is the first of several indications that Li Bo's life was

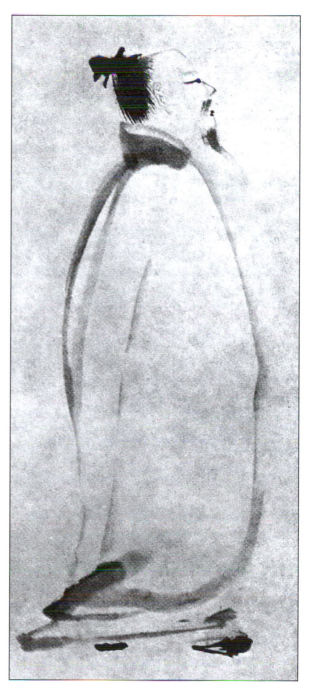

Li Bo (The Granger Collection, New York)

shaped by his position as an outsider in the empire. The Tang taste for the exotic and the Turkish connections of the imperial family meant that the work of a "foreigner" would have had a special appeal (many poets of the era were influenced by Central Asian themes and music), but Han Chinese ethnocentricity meant that the "foreigner" himself would always have been regarded as exactly that.

Li Bo's family moved to Sichuan Province, in southwest China, when he was about five years old. They were probably traders. Family wealth would explain how Li Bo managed to live without a job in the government, which was the occupation of most male poets and scholars in traditional China, but the low status of merchants would have made his family background another strike against Li Bo in the eyes of the establishment. Even to have grown up in Sichuan would have given him a markedly regional air. Owen points out the impact the particular traditions of the area may have had on Li Bo in defining himself as a nonconformist, a bold and impulsive person, and a writer not of mainstream aristocratic verse, but of a poetry that returns to the greatness of the past.

Stories of Li Bo's youth suggest the intelligence and the interest in occult learning revealed in his poems. The biographies of most poets of Li Bo's era routinely claim that their subjects were brilliant students in childhood and that they could compose verse at an early age; the reports on Li Bo are the same, but there is no reason not to believe them, if taken with a grain of salt. Poems written when he was about fifteen show Li Bo's great talent and his already distinctive violation of contemporary ideas of "proper" restraint in poetry. Li Bo apparently also lived and studied as a mountain recluse for some time before leaving Sichuan.

In his early twenties, Li Bo began a period of wandering in the great valley of the Yangzi River in central China. The role he adopted, that of a daring and noble-hearted knight errant who righted wrongs with his sword, again shows his energy and his taste for an unconventional lifestyle.

At the time of Li Bo's first marriage, in the early 730's, he was living in what is now Hubei Province, in the north-central Yangzi Basin. He made exaggerated claims for the ancestry of his wife, whose family name was Xu, as he did for his own. It was to her that his daughter Pingyang and his elder son Boquin were born. His younger son's name was Poli. The poet probably had one other formal wife and two concubines, but the facts are unclear.

Li Bo then moved north and east to Shandong Province, where he continued writing and enjoying the company of friends, and from where he traveled to the scenic regions of southeast China. He enjoyed poem exchanges, banquets in the entertainment district, and poeticizing excursions to sites famous for their natural beauty. The constant succession of occasions calling for a poem had good results; like that of so many Chinese poets, Li Bo's work developed greatly in his middle years.

It was during this period that Li Bo met the Daoist religious teacher who finally arranged for his long-awaited introduction to the imperial court in 742. In that year or the next, the poet was granted a position in the Hanlin Academy, a prestigious group of scholars, holy men, and poets who enjoyed imperial favor.

The outsider had penetrated the inner sanctum of Emperor Xuanzong himself. Perhaps Li Bo never took the civil service exams that were the more usual route of upward mobility because he disdained orthodox learning and officialdom, as he claimed, or perhaps he never took them because he lacked the well-rounded education and influential connections that were necessary to obtain a post. Not all the famous male writers of the Tang era managed to pass the test, but, except for Li Bo, they all tried. Nevertheless, for nearly three years, Li Bo was an eccentric and admired figure in a brilliant court, carousing, composing poems and song lyrics for the emperor and the women of the imperial household, and dashing off imperial decrees on command.

Things changed. The boastful, impetuous Li Bo was no courtier. In 744, evidently as the result of an intrigue, he lost the emperor's favor and was given "permission" to "return to the hills." This banishment began another period of wandering and visiting whomever might take interest in the company of this colorful and brilliant poet. Li Bo and Du Fu met when Li Bo was in his early forties and Du Fu in his early thirties; Du Fu's many admiring poems addressed to Li Bo suggest the force of the older poet's personality.

A decade later, a rebellion forced the emperor to abdicate. Li Bo, who was then in the southeast, joined the court of a secretly disloyal prince. It is not clear whether Li Bo was naïve, coerced, or a willing participant in the treason, but when the prince was defeated in

757, Li Bo was imprisoned and condemned to death. The poet's reputation saved him: His sentence was reduced to banishment to the far southwest frontier lands. Li Bo dawdled on the long journey, was finally granted amnesty in 759, and returned to his life of travel and visiting. Late in 762, the official and calligrapher with whom he was staying published the first collection of Li Bo's works. The preface records that the poet was at the time seriously ill; this illness was evidently his last. There are, however, legends of his death by drowning, in a drunken attempt to embrace the moon's reflection on a river, and of the spirits who came on dolphin-back to summon him to heaven.

Analysis

Li Bo acquired—and liked—the nickname Exiled Immortal. Its implication of a rule breaker who transcends conventional limitations describes his poetry as well as his life. He could use the standard devices and postures of his rich literary heritage, but he usually did so in his own original manner. He wrote many kinds of poems, in many moods and wearing many masks, but behind them all is the unique quality of the poet himself.

Among the poems by Li Bo that have the greatest immediate appeal for the modern Western reader are those that suggest that the poetic mind operates on the level of the universe itself. This theme often appears in Li Bo's poems about famous mountains, those nodes—in the traditional Chinese worldview—of cosmic spiritual energy. For example, in the poem "Climbing Mount Emei," the speaker of the poem ascends the best known of Sichuan's "faerie mountains," entering a realm of weird beauty that calls into question normal evaluations of both perception and ambition. At the summit, he proclaims, his aesthetic and his supernatural abilities are released, as he finally grasps esoteric Daoist teachings and the secrets of making poetry and music. Li Bo closes the poem with a characteristically grand movement up and out: He is loosed from earthly ties ("All at once I lose the world's dust"), meets a youthful sprite, and hand in hand they move across the sky to the sun. This is not the only place where the poet sets himself in moments of inspiration on a par with the great forces of nature.

"Climbing the Peak of Mount Taibo"

Still, Li Bo acknowledges, the human mind cannot always achieve this sublime state. Sometimes the power dwelling within the mountains is elusive, or the response to it is uncertain. In "Climbing the Peak of Mount Taibo," the mountain is again a jumping-off point for heavenly realms, but here the poet adopts a persona that imagines a transcendent journey of the spirit—straddling the wind and raising a hand that could almost touch the moon—only to hesitate at the end and ask, "Once I've left Wugong county/ When could I come back again?" This undercutting of the traditional spirit-journey motif is prepared for by a typical bit of linguistic playfulness. There is a multiple pun in the poem's third line: "Then Taibo speaks to me." "Taibo" is, first, the mountain itself, a peak in modern Shensi Province that was thought to be especially magical because one of the fantastic Daoist "cave-heavens" was said to be located within its summit. "Taibo" is also both the evening star (the ascent is made at sunset) and the very planetary spirit said to have been Li Bo's true father. Finally, "Taibo" is Li Bo's pen name; for an instant, at least, the reader is invited to wonder if the poet is talking only to himself.

"Wandering About Mount Tai"

One of the best examples of the multiplicity of stances and personas Li Bo could adopt when considering the relationship of the individual to the suprahuman is a poem cycle titled "Wandering About Mount Tai: Six Poems." In this description of travel around the easternmost of China's cosmos-ordering "Five Sacred Peaks," the poet achieves a mythic fusion of various traditional paradises: the ancient utopias located far away, across the sea or sky; the cave-heavens that riddle sacred ground; and the spiritually charged natural world itself. He also manages an emotional fusion of the various responses of a single persona to manifestations of the divine, ranging from frustration and embarrassment, through ecstasy and awe, to a final confident accommodation with the world and its spiritual force.

In the first poem of the group, despite the speaker's appreciation of the mountain's beauty, the stone gate of a cave-heaven is closed to him and the gold and silver pavilions of the Faerie Isles can be imagined but remain distant. Moreover, the beautiful "Jade Women" who come in response to the poet's magic, spirit-summoning whistle tease him, laughing and giving him nothing more than a cup of "Liquid Sunrise," the immortals' wine. He can only bow to them, ashamed of his mundane nature. Here as elsewhere, though he sorrows, he never lapses into self-pity. The second and third poems underline the theme of human limitations: The speaker meets a strange man who has achieved immortality through Daoist training, but the figure vanishes and the antique writing of the text he leaves behind cannot be deciphered; then, the wanderer has a moment of vision, only to chance on a youthful divinity who laughs at him for trying to achieve immortality so late, "when I've lost my grip, rosy cheeks faded." The exuberant fourth poem records a moment of hard-won spiritual achievement gained through Daoist study, fasting, and chanting. This otherworldly goal is replaced in the following poem by an awareness of the power in the natural landscape itself.

The resolution appears in the last poem of the sequence, as the poet's persona travels through sublime scenery alive with spirits. Although he is cut off from that sacred force of the Dao in which nature and spirits participate so freely, the poet presents himself as capable of actively making contact with the transcendent: He imagines a wedding dance of spirits; he reaches up to grope among the constellations. It is precisely the force of his own capacity for vision that wins that vision. Even though he acknowledges the evanescence of this magical night, he closes by stating that he will still be able to see the variegated clouds of dawn, clouds that are traditionally vehicles for immortals and that remind the reader of the Liquid Sunrise wine that was his gift from the divinities in the first poem of the group. The ability for imaginative action on the world's phenomena remains even when the moment of inspiration passes—as do the poems that have been created with it.

"In the Mountains"

The theme of the "spirit journey" noted above, and other symbols found in China's ancient shamanistic tradition, appear in many of Li Bo's works. Not all of his "mystical" poems, however, are so grandiose. In the famous "In the Mountains: Question and Answer," he quietly (and slightly smugly) strikes the pose of the reclusive sage who lives in the mountains for reasons that

only a fool would ask to have put into words; behind this persona is the perhaps even more smug poet who has just done exactly that:

> You ask me for the reason
> I roost among emerald hills.
> I smile and yet do not reply,
> heart at its natural ease.
> Peach-blossom petals on Paradise Creek
> flow on their mysterious way.
> There is another heaven and earth
> that's not the human world.

"Gazing at Yellow Crane Mountain"

Parallel to Li Bo's interest in the strange chemistry of poetic creation was his interest in alchemy. In China, this arcane science developed as part of the Daoist search for elixirs that could give long life or even immortality. Li Bo used terms found in a textual tradition running back to the ancient holy book, the *Yijing* (eighth to third century B.C.E.; English translation, 1876; also known as *Book of Changes*, 1986). Such language was popular in the poetry of the era; whether Li Bo actually conducted experiments, alchemy served him well as a source of metaphors.

For example, in the poem "Gazing at Yellow Crane Mountain," alchemical imagery describes the catalytic moment in which mutability and human limitations are accepted. The mountain's cosmic power is forcefully described in the opening lines. The peak is "bold and virile, thrusting up in mid-air"; it "gives birth to clouds"; as an *axis mundi*, it links earth and sky. It is famous, moreover, for the hermit living there who—unlike the poet—achieved transformation into an immortal long ago and left his stone cell for the Faerie Isles. At this point, the poem pivots. An alchemical reaction is described: "The Golden Crucible gives birth to a haze of dust." The concluding passage focuses on images of sustenance amid aging and physical frailty. Finally, the poet presents himself as making peace with the gap between mortal flesh and transcendental power: "I'll knot my heart's pledge, to lodge under blue pines,/ Awakened forever, my wanderlust done with!"

"Drinking Alone in the Moonlight"

Natural wonders, such as mountains, and mysteries, such as alchemy, are only two of the sources of recurring metaphors by means of which Li Bo examines the multifaceted relationship of the self with the great forces outside it. The most famous of his metaphors are those concerning wine. In reading Li Bo's many deservedly famous poems on wine, it is important to remember the traditional Chinese view of intoxication as exhilaration and release. Li Bo the gregarious man enjoyed drinking; Li Bo the lover of life's pleasures found in that enjoyment a solace for their brevity; Li Bo the eccentric and spontaneous poet could hardly not have had a reputation for enjoying it—that was a hallmark of the type; finally, Li Bo the seeker after actualization of his original unrestricted nature used the drug—as others had before him—as an instrument of that search. Poems such as the four on "Drinking Alone in the Moonlight" are the first to come to mind when this poet's name is mentioned. In this witty sequence, nature, personalized through the imaginative inspiration of wine, recognizes Li Bo's particularity. The loneliness of individuality is eased by communion with the universal order, made possible through alcohol. In "Drinking Alone in the Moonlight" (titled "Drinking Alone by Moonlight" in Owen's translation), Li Bo, drinking alone, raises his glass to the moon and his shadow, so that they drink together: "When still sober we share friendship and pleasure,/ then, utterly drunk, each goes his own way—/ Let us join to roam beyond human cares/ and plan to meet far in the river of stars."

"THE ROAD TO SHU IS HARD"

In stressing Li Bo's individualism, it is important not to overlook his adept use of Chinese tradition. Well-known poems such as "The Road to Shu Is Hard" show the unique qualities of his work: the bold language of the opening line ("Ee-hoo-hee! Steep, whoo! High, phew!"); the irregular and musical outpouring of the wildly varied lines and stanzas; the powerful evocation of the natural scene and of the visions it inspires in the imagination; and the insistence on his own panting, persistent voice ("With dangers, yes! like these,/ ahh, man from afar,/ why oh why come, eh?"). At the same time, the poem's title is that of an old folk song that for centuries had been used by educated poets as a point of departure, stressing the difficulties of the rugged mountain road just as Li Bo does. Moreover, Li Bo weaves into the poem evocative legends of the early

history of the region; allusions to historical events and to classical literature are characteristic of his work. It is his revitalizing variations, in form and content, on familiar themes that make this and other such poems so rich.

Li Bo, like many Chinese poets, sought to restore to the verse of his own era the greatness of the past, or his idealized version of the past. Throughout his oeuvre, there are reflections of his intimate knowledge of earlier poets, though the effect is never that of a mere imitation. One of his many "Ancient Airs," translated by Joseph J. Lee in *Sunflower Splendor*, proclaims, "I desire to select and transmit the old,/ So that its splendor will last a thousand ages."

Poems in this mode frequently combine the spare language and unadorned technique of earlier times with a strong moral statement. Another ancient air (translated by Pound as "Lament of the Frontier Guard") takes the traditional stance against the waste of human life and the cost to society when men serve as soldiers in the frontier lands. Such poems, with their serious messages and generally simple presentation, stood in conscious opposition to the decorative poetry associated with courtly writers of the preceding era.

FEMALE PERSONAS

Another group of poems in which Li Bo approaches a traditional subject in his own way includes those written with female personas. (Many men in traditional China wrote poems in which the speaker was a winsome chartreuse or a lonely wife.) In works such as "Poem Written on Behalf of My Wife" and "Song of Changgan" (in Pound's translation, "The River Merchant's Wife: A Letter"), the poet expresses longings common to all people through the figure of a woman addressing her husband. The vivid pictorial presentation of scenes from such women's lives reminds the reader of the skill of the man behind the mask.

TECHNIQUE AND FORM

It may be that the very force of Li Bo's images contributed to the traditional slighting of his technical skill as a poet. His was an era when many poets were directing their talents to the relatively recent "regulated verse," in which certain patterns of word pitch were to be created, somewhat like the stressed and unstressed syllables in English meter. Li Bo, however, usually preferred the freer form of old-style verse, though like a good writer of free verse in English, he still used the sounds of his language. He played with alliteration, assonance, and off rhyme. He varied line length to suit content or rhythmic need. He created striking patterns of word pitch, for example, in his powerful description of the thunderstorm in "In a Dream, I Wander Tianmu Mountain: A Chant of Farewell."

One trait of inferior Chinese poetry is a tendency to break down into a string of neat two-line units; as Owen points out, Li Bo's exuberant outpourings avoid this trap, though his effects are sometimes too easy or too loose. Eide's discussion of Li Bo's use of allusion and "revived" clichés to enrich his poems and to tighten the links between lines suggests how well crafted the poet's apparently spontaneous verse could be at its best.

In looking to the past for form, as he looked there for his poetic lineage, Li Bo found a fertile base for his own distinctive way of writing. He wrote in a variety of genres, from the old rhapsodic "rhyme-prose," or *fu*, to pseudofolk songs, *yuefu*. A high proportion of his poems have words such as "song," "ode," or "melody" in their titles, and many were actually written to be accompanied by music. Li Bo could write skillful, regulated verse when he chose or when the occasion (a formal farewell, for example) called for it. In addition, it may be that he was one of the first of the educated elite to write poems, called *ci* (lyrics), that were written to tunes of irregular line length; if he really wrote certain of these poems attributed to him, Li Bo made an important contribution to the development of a verse form that was to dominate the subsequent poetic era. In form, then, as in mood and theme, Li Bo's verse is marked by the skilled diversity often associated with greatness.

In all this wealth of poems, there is much for those who read Li Bo more than twelve hundred years after the poet's death. Even in translation, the power of his images and of his poetic personality comes through. Without knowledge of Li Bo's literary, political, or philosophical background, one can still experience his intense, expansive way of knowing the world. Indeed, Li Bo's skill is such that the reader is moved to put on the masks that the poet fashioned and walk into the landscapes he painted. For the duration of such mo-

ments, one shivers in the Gobi wind, eyes a tipsy, lisping exotic dancer, or rakes one's fingers through the Milky Way.

BIBLIOGRAPHY

Kroll, Paul. *Studies in Medieval Taoism and the Poetry of Li Po*. Burlington, Vt.: Ashgate, 2009. Focuses on Li Bo's poetry as it expresses Daoist concepts.

Li Bo. *Li Po and Tu Fu: Poems Selected and Translated with an Introduction and Notes*. Translated by Arthur Cooper. Harmondsworth, England: Penguin Books, 1973. The translations are generally excellent, and the extensive background material on the history of Chinese poetry and literature is helpful. Li Bo's connection with Du Fu is usefully discussed.

_____. *The Selected Poems of Li Po*. Translated by David Hinton. New York: New Directions, 1996. Includes commentary and background information as well as translations.

Owen, Stephen. *An Anthology of Chinese Literature: Beginnings to 1911*. New York: W. W. Norton, 1996. Contains background information and commentary on Li Bo as well as a selection of his poetry.

_____. *The Great Age of Chinese Poetry: The High T'ang*. New Haven, Conn.: Yale University Press, 1981. Provides information on Li Bo in the political and cultural milieu of the Tang Dynasty.

Pine, Red, trans. *Poems of the Masters: China's Classic Anthology of T'ang and Sung Dynasty Verse*. Port Townsend, Wash.: Copper Canyon Press, 2003. A collection of poetry from the Tang and Song Dynasties that includes the work of Li Bo. Indexes.

Varsano, Paula M. *Tracking the Banished Immortal: The Poetry of Li Bo and its Critical Reception*. Honolulu: University of Hawaii Press, 2003. Examines the critical reception of Li Bo's poetry, from early Chinese scholars to later Western ones. Besides being noted as worthy of praise, his poetry has been termed "all fruits and flowers" and morally decadent. Also provides analysis of the poetry.

Waley, Arthur. *The Poetry and Career of Li Po*. 1950. Reprint. London: G. Allen & Unwin, 1979. A still-useful introduction, although Waley's obsession with what he considers the immoral aspects of Li

Bo's character sometimes prejudices his judgment of the poetry. Includes many translations.

Weinberger, Eliot, ed. *The New Directions Anthology of Classical Chinese Poetry*. New York: New Directions, 2003. Contains an informative commentary on the evolution of translations of classical Chinese poetry. Information on Chinese poetry and translators is provided as well as translations of the poetry of many Chinese poems. Includes translations of Li Bo's poetry by Ezra Pound, William Carlos Williams, and David Hinton.

Jeanne Larsen

Li Qingzhao

Born: Jinan, Shandong Province, China; 1084
Died: Hangzhou, Zhejiang Province(?), China; c. 1155
Also known as: Li Ch'ing-chao

Principal poetry

Li Ch'ing-chao chi, 1962 (collected works)
The Complete Ci-Poems of Li Qingzhao, 1989

Other literary forms

Li Qingzhao (lee chihng-JOW) was a serious scholar of antiquities and objets d'art and compiled book annotations and catalogs of antiques with her husband Zhao Mingcheng. An essay appended to one of the catalogs, *Jinshilu houxi* (c. 1135; epilogue to a catalog of inscriptions on bronze and stone), is a major source of biographical information. She also wrote a brief critical essay on *ci* poetry. A number of other prose pieces were collected posthumously, but nearly all of them are now lost.

Achievements

Li Qingzhao's gender has certainly affected critical response to her work and has given her the mixed blessing of being regarded as "China's greatest poetess," but the high quality of her work is beyond question. It is impossible to know to what extent the preservation and transmission of those of her texts that have survived were influenced by traditional ideas of what kinds of poems were appropriate for women to write. Clearly, she understood and used the voices and the literary gestures of China's rich heritage of female persona poetry. Equally clearly, she could and did write on themes—politics and mysticism among them—outside the range found in the extant work of most Chinese literary women before the modern era.

One strength of Li Qingzhao's work, then, is its emotional variety. There are love poems ranging from the melancholy to the erotic. There are poems of despair at old age or at the defeat of the Northern Song Dynasty. Some poems exhort those in power to moral rectitude; others suggest with transcendental imagery the glories of spiritual transport to a world beyond this one.

Equally important are Li Qingzhao's contributions to the *ci* verse form. Her critical comments on the work of other *ci* poets suggest the seriousness with which she approached her art, as well as her capacity for innovation. At a time when the *shi* form—which had dominated Chinese poetry for nearly a millennium—was in danger of stagnation, she helped develop the newer kind of poetry, broadening its scope in theme and language.

The word *ci* is often translated as "lyrics"; indeed, the form had its origins in the lyrics to popular songs. Consequently, although *ci* were often beautiful to hear, they tended to focus on such lightweight topics as the pleasures of drinking and the appreciation of female beauty. Li Qingzhao, like her father's famous friend Su Shih (Su Dongbo) before her, wrote on more complex subjects and moods; her work retains the emotional delicacy associated with the *ci* while giving it more serious applications. Moreover, the wide range of levels of diction in her poems—from the elegant to the conversational—opened up new potential for self-expression and broadened options for later poets. One contemporary critic commented on her use of colloquialisms: "The fantastically vulgar expressions of the back alleys and streets, whatever suited her mood, she would write down in her poetry" (translation by Gaiyou Xu). Even after the old melodies were lost, *ci* were composed to set patterns of line length, word pitch, and rhyme; Li Qingzhao's variations on these patterns were so euphonious that they sometimes became the preferred versions. Finally, her skillful use of alliteration and assonance in this extremely difficult form has served as a benchmark of musicality that has seldom been equaled.

Ultimately, though, it is the effect of the individual poems that has earned for Li Qingzhao widespread critical regard. Her poetry retains a strongly personal vision without lapsing into self-absorption or self-pity; her sensuous descriptions of scenes come alive for the reader as they subtly express complicated moods through actions and objects in the external world. The poet used allusion to the literary tradition, as well as the repetitive phrases (for example, "chill, chill, clear, clear") that are a traditional ornament of Chinese verse. Both qualities show that her innovations were grounded in a sensitive understanding of the work of those before her.

BIOGRAPHY

Li Qingzhao's early life was one of privilege and happiness, but that happiness did not last. Political infighting resulted in her father's temporary exile and her father-in-law's disgrace. Her beloved husband's official duties caused repeated separations, and he died in his late forties. The conquest of North China by the Tartars meant the loss of her extensive art collection and difficult years as a widowed refugee. Despite the nostalgic and sorrowful tone of many of her poems, however, her work suggests the personal strength that enabled her to survive in such difficult times.

Li Qingzhao was born to a family that placed a high value on literature and education. Her father, Li Kefei, was an important figure in the national government and was well known for such prose writings as his essay on the famous gardens of the city of Luoyang. Her mother, whose family name was Wang, was a poet who had been educated at home by her grandfather, an outstanding scholar and former prime minister. Family friends of talent, influence, and learning filled the household. The lively, intelligent girl's abilities were encouraged by this literary atmosphere and by the approval of the adults around her, despite the strictures concerning education for women that were prevalent in her time. Her

reputation for poems in the respected *shi* form was established while she was still in her teens, and she developed her talents for painting and calligraphy as well.

By most accounts, Li Qingzhao was eighteen when she married Zhao Mingcheng, a young student from another important family. The two were well-matched. In two years, her husband entered the civil service, and the couple developed their collection of books, antique bronzes, and other art objects. In 1134, she wrote a charming retrospective description of how the couple had enjoyed each other's company as they compiled information on their acquisitions. The marriage has attracted much interest. There is the story of her husband's prophetic childhood dream, signifying that he would marry a poet, and another in which he attempts unsuccessfully to outdo his wife's poem "Zui huayin" ("Tune: Tipsy in the Flower's Shade"). A portrait of Li Qingzhao at age thirty-one depicts a woman of beauty and refined sensibilities.

The factional politics that caused her father's exile early in this period of Li Qingzhao's life also sent her father-in-law into disfavor. He died shortly after, in 1107. The two men belonged to opposing political groups, which must have made her position as a daughter-in-law difficult. Perhaps it also gave her a clearer perspective on governmental folly; her political poems suggest that this was so.

Li Qingzhao's husband's career was affected by his father's fall, but the following years, while her husband was out of office, were perhaps the zenith of their happiness. In the early 1120's, he returned to government service; poems written while he was traveling on official business or in search of items for their art collection suggest her unhappiness during his absence, for upper-class women were not allowed to travel as men did.

Li Qingzhao was in her early forties when North China fell to the Tartars in 1127. She fled Shandong for the South, where her husband was serving as a magistrate. Much of their valuable collection of books, paintings, and antiques was left behind and burned. After a brief time of reunion, her husband was posted to another city, fell ill with malaria, and died.

Civil disorder increased as the Tartars pressed southward and the Chinese emperor retreated before them. Most of Li Qingzhao's remaining artworks were lost as she, too, repeatedly made her way to safety. Two unsubstantiated stories suggest further pressures on the poet. She was accused of attempting a treasonous bribery, and she is said by some sources to have had a brief and unhappy marriage. The cruelty of Zhang Ruzhou, the minor government official she reportedly married and divorced, was no more shocking to biographers of later centuries than the poet's defiance of social expectations by remarrying.

Li Qingzhao's last years were evidently spent in the household of her younger brother, Li Hang, in Zhejiang Province in southeastern China, but little else is known, except that she did continue writing. Most estimates of the year of her death put it around 1155.

ANALYSIS

Li Qingzhao's work combines affective force with the aesthetic appeal of refined, well-crafted expression. The emotions behind her poems were powerful, but they are never simply self-indulgent. The exquisite sound effects of the originals are lost in English versions, yet the images, and the textures of joy or contemplation or loss that they generate, convey the poet's emotions to Western readers.

"TUNE: TIPSY IN THE FLOWER'S SHADE"

One of the best-known and most frequently translated of Li Qingzhao's poems, "Tune: Tipsy in the Flower's Shade," shows her ability to develop such a texture, revealing feeling through ambiguous language and the accretion of sensations of vision, smell, and touch. The first line of the poem offers several possible readings. The "Thin mists—thick clouds" at the line's beginning are appropriate to the autumn festival day on which the poem is set, for the festival is associated with the uprising of the cloudy *yin* principle that, according to traditional Chinese cosmology, controls the autumn and winter months. It is the second half of the line that offers multiple levels of meaning. Are the mists and clouds themselves "sad all day long," or, as is often the case in Chinese poetry, is the subject of "sadness" an unstated "I," or is the line best understood as "Thin mists and thick clouds: sorrow makes the day endless"?

The poem's subsequent images build a tone of suppressed sexuality and murky melancholy: The reader catches the dull metallic gleam of an ornamental burner

through streamers of incense smoke and feels the chill that works its way past the translucent gauze of the bed curtains. The poem is said to have been sent to her husband, and the subtle eroticism of the boudoir setting is underlined by "midnight" and "jade pillow." The bedroom trappings conjure up the traditional figure of the attractive woman alone and longing for her absent beloved. "Jade" is a common ornamental epithet, and the pillow was probably not literally made of jade. To the poet's audience, however, the word would have suggested the cool whiteness of the speaker's skin. This suits the tone established at the poem's start, inasmuch as the *yin* principle is further associated with women and with sexuality.

In the second stanza, the poet intensifies the mood of painfully stifled passion with mention of "dusk," "furtive fragrances," and the force of a wind that pushes the blinds aside. Moreover, she uses the standard imagery linked to the festival in her own way, increasing the complexity of the mood established in stanza 1. The fourth century poet Tao Qian, whom Li Qingzhao admired greatly, invariably came to mind on the day of the mid-autumn festival. Her allusion to the "eastern hedge" mentioned in one of his most famous poems immediately recalls other images associated with Tao Qian's work: Wine, a sad nobility in the face of the season's change, and the yellow chrysanthemums that endure when all the other flowers have yielded to the cold. The chrysanthemums of the last line also had been linked poetically with feminine beauty long before Tao Qian's time; Li Qingzhao uses all this in her much-praised closing assertion that she is "more fragile than the yellow chrysanthemum."

"TO THE TUNE: SOUND UPON SOUND, ADAGIO"

A similar nexus of coldness, wine, dark, and the wasted beauty of the late-blooming flowers appears in the famous poem "To the Tune: Sound upon Sound, Adagio." *Ci* were not required to fit their content to the old melodies' titles, but they sometimes did. Just as Li Qingzhao made use of the intoxication, the flowers, and the shadiness (literally, *yin*) indicated by the previous poem's title, here she creates a musical tour de force through repeated words and sounds and careful attention to the effect of word pitch. This dazzling focus on language—syllables falling one by one, like the fine rain she pictures drizzling drop after drop on the autumnal trees—prepares the reader for the poem's final twist. The poet denies the adequacy of words to relieve, or even to express, her grief. "How," she asks, "can the one word 'sorrow' finish off all this?"

MELANCHOLY THEMES

Some of Li Qingzhao's other poems, especially those written in the final period of her life, explore this theme of melancholy. In "Qingping yue" ("Tune: Pure Serene Music"), images of whiteness and purity—snow, plum blossoms, clear tears—set the scene for her description of graying hair that, to overtranslate the Chinese idiom, "engenders flowery patterns." The reference to intoxication, despite the ambiguous intimation that it is as if the plum blossoms themselves were exhilarating, is a reminder of the remarkable number of references to wine in Li Qingzhao's work. A great many Chinese writers in the nonconformist mode—including Tao Qian and the eighth century poet Li Bo—expressed their liberation from conventionality through praise of the effects of alcohol; it may be that the particularly bold stance necessarily taken, in traditional China, by the woman who claimed the role of artist made such references to the untrammeled state of inebriation especially apt. Just as characteristic is the closure, a depiction of nature that describes by implication the speaker's condition: The cutting evening wind suggests the force of aging as it scatters the pale flowers of spring.

AMATORY POEMS

Li Qingzhao's husband's death naturally figures in many of her poems of depression. The title of one well-known example is "Wuling chun" ("Tune: Spring at Wu-ling"). In an atmosphere that blends emotional stasis with a sense of time's inevitable passing ("The wind subsides—a fragrance/ of petals freshly fallen;/ it's late in the day . . ."), the speaker—like bereft women in poems written for centuries—neglects her grooming and broods on her man's absence. The poem's famous final image refers ironically to a place in the region where the poet lived out her widowhood: "I hear at Twin Creek spring it's still lovely." She, no longer part of a happy couple, says she would like to go pleasure-boating there, but she fears that "at Twin Creek my frail boat/ could not carry this load of grief."

Earlier poems on temporary separations from her husband range from loneliness to a teasing reminder of the pleasures of reunion. "Xiaochongshan" ("Tune: Manifold Little Hills"), for example, exploits the conventional association of spring with burgeoning sexuality. The grass is green, the swollen plum-blossom buds are ready to open, and "Azure clouds gather, grind out jade into dust" as the trees burst into jade-white bloom. The speaker's sensuous enjoyment of the springtime ends in a plea to her absent beloved to return so that they might more fully enjoy the season.

The attribution to Li Qingzhao of some other openly amatory poems is questionable. Some editors were doubtless quick to assign any free-floating, female-persona poem to the woman poet who stood foremost in their minds; others must have been shocked at the thought that a married woman of good family might have written on such a topic. However, there are poems that are certainly hers and are certainly sexual. The analysis by William H. Nienhauser, Jr., in an article published in *T'oung Pao* in 1978, of Li Qingzhao's poem "Ru mengling" ("Tune: As in a Dream a Song") shows how she used the technique of accreted implications to develop a fabric of delicately suggestive language, rhythm, images, and action. The poem has enjoyed long-lasting popularity; as Nienhauser observes, it is not pornography but a work of aesthetically pleasing subtlety, requiring considerable poetic skill.

POLITICAL POEMS

If Li Qingzhao's poems of joy and nostalgia reflect the events of her private life, there are others that show her concern for the disordered state of her nation. Some of these poems remain in the personal mode. This is true of her poem "Caisang ci" ("Tune: Song of Picking Mulberry") (another poem written to the same tune is among the frankly erotic poems attributed to her). Here, the huge exotic leaves of banana trees exemplify the strange new landscape of South China, to which the poet and others from the fallen heartland of the empire have fled before the Tartar onslaught. In her mind, the leaves, opening and furling, evoke human hearts pulsing with emotion. Here, too, the closely woven repetitions of sounds and words suggests the brooding, monotonous dripping of "rain at the midnight watch." The sentiments of grief and restless obsession voiced by this northerner are those of a generation in exile.

More strongly in a public voice are the admonitory poems that Li Qingzhao, like most of China's greatest poets, wrote on political themes. They display, in their form and their language, her understanding of the literary decorum so important in her culture. These poems are not *ci* but the older, loftier *shi*. (Some are written according to the rules of versification called "tonal regulation"; others are in the freer "old style.") Most of the poet's contemporaries would have considered *ci* no more appropriate to her public subject matter than a limerick would be. Moreover, the poems' diction suits the exalted positions of those to whom many of them were sent.

The message of these verses is that of the Confucian moralist, calling for righteousness on the part of the ruler and abstention from greed on the part of government officials. The poet reminds her readers of the value of learning and the consolations of study. She warns the emperor of the defeated dynasty against the reckless enjoyment of immediate pleasures and criticizes the nation-weakening dangers of political infighting. Through references, often satirical ones, to a variety of historical figures, the poet reveals her own knowledge of the classics. She also uses these allusions to cast her admonitions into a safer form. Indirectly, she censures the failure of the dynasty to stand up to the invaders and the subsequent appeasement of the Tartars.

TRANSCENDENTAL POEMS

Li Qingzhao was not the first woman to write on transcendental themes. In the eighth and ninth centuries, for example, Xue Tao, Li Ye, and Yu Xuangji all drew in their own ways on the rich stream of Daoist visionary imagery. Still, it was not usual for women to write such poems. Unconventional or not, Li Qingzhao is successful in her evocation of spiritual longing. She describes the lure of the contemplative life and reminds her readers of the value of the ascetic's pursuit of ritual purity and immortality. In "Tune: A Fisherman's Honor," the speaker sails through the sky to the paradise of the distant Faerie Isles in a spirit journey that has its origins in the shamanistic cults of centuries before. A *shi* poem, "Dream at Daybreak," relates a journey through dawn clouds to the marvelous realm of the im-

mortals. The speaker awakens, however, asking ruefully, "Since human life can be like this,/ Why must I return to my old home?" Finally, she sits in meditation, covering her ears against the clamor of this world, thinking deeply on what she will not meet with again, and sighing. The poem expresses such yearnings with ethereal grace.

What remains of Li Qingzhao's work both tantalizes and satisfies. The various *ci* and *shi* poems just discussed, the few remaining essays, and at least one long rhyme-prose (*fu*) believed to be her work, provide a frustrating glimpse of the much larger corpus of her poetry and prose that was once in circulation. Nevertheless, what has survived is enough to stand on its own merits. The evocative, sometimes surprising imagery, lively and musical language, sensitive depiction of emotional nuance, and range of mood and tone ensure that her poetry will continue to be read a thousand years after her death.

BIBLIOGRAPHY

Chang, Kang-i Sun, and Haun Saussy, eds. *Women Writers of Traditional China: An Anthology of Poetry and Criticism.* Stanford, Calif.: Stanford University Press, 1999. Part 1 of this anthology contains the poets' works, divided by dynasty, and part 2 contains criticism. Biographies of the poets, including Li Qingzhao, are included. Bibliography and index.

Djao, Wei. *A Blossom like No Other: Li Qingzhao.* Toronto, Ont.: Ginger Post, 2010. A biography of the Chinese poet, with analysis of her works.

Hansen, Valerie. "Li Qingzhao." *Calliope* 13, no. 4 (December, 2002): 24. A brief profile of the poet and her works.

Hu, P'ing-ch'ing. *Li Ch'ing-chao.* New York: Twayne, 1966. This critical study on Li Qingzhao treats both her life and her works in great detail and provides one with a clear sense of her achievements. Most of her famous poems are translated in a lucid, though sometimes prosaic, style.

Idema, W. L., and Beata Grant. *The Red Brush: Writing Women of Imperial China.* Cambridge, Mass.: Harvard University Asia Center, Harvard University Press, 2004. This work on women writers in China includes a chapter on Li Qingzhao and her writing. Other chapters shed light on the culture in which she wrote.

Li Qingzhao. *The Complete Ci-Poems of Li Qingzhao.* Translated by Jizosheng Wang. Philadelphia: Department of Oriental Studies, University of Pennsylvania, 1989. A translation that strives to be accurate to the Chinese texts. Bilingual text.

_____. *Li Ch'ing-chao: Complete Poems.* Translated and edited by Kenneth Rexroth and Ling Chung. New York: New Directions, 1979. A collection of Li Qingzhao's poetry, with critical notes and a biography.

Rexroth, Kenneth, and Ling Chung, eds. *Women Poets of China.* Rev. ed. New York: New Directions, 1990. This collection of works by women poets of China, which first was published in 1972, contains works by Li Qingzhao and other notable poets.

Yang, Vincent. "Vision of Reconciliation: A Textual Reading of Some Lines of Li Qing-zhao." *Journal of the Chinese Language Teachers Association* 19 (1984): 10-32. This essay is a close reading of four representative poems by Li Qingzhao. Focusing on the imagery and structure of the poems, the author attempts to show the poet's art of lyricism. At the end, the particular nature of her imagination is illustrated through her use of poetic techniques. The analysis is an application of Western literary criticism to Chinese poetry.

Jeanne Larsen

M

OSIP MANDELSTAM

Born: Warsaw, Poland, Russian Empire (now in Poland); January 15, 1891

Died: Vtoraya Rechka, near Vladivostok, Soviet Union (now in Russia); probably December 27, 1938

PRINCIPAL POETRY

Kamen, 1913 (enlarged 1916, 1923; *Stone*, 1981)

Tristia, 1922 (English translation, 1973)

Stikhotvoreniya, 1928 (*Poems*, 1973)

Complete Poetry of Osip Emilievich Mandelstam, 1973

Voronezhskiye tetradi, 1980

The Voronezh Notebooks: Poems, 1935-1937, 1996

OTHER LITERARY FORMS

Osip Mandelstam (muhn-dyihl-SHTAHM) was writing essays on Russian and European literature as early as 1913. Many of the theoretical essays were collected, some in considerably revised or censored form, in *O poezii* (1928; *About Poetry*, 1977). These, as well as his otherwise uncollected essays and reviews, are available in their original and most complete versions in *Sobranie sochinenii* (1955, 1964-1971, 1981; *Collected Works*, 1967-1969). Mandelstam's prose was not republished in the Soviet Union, with the exception of his single most important essay, "Razgovor o Dante" ("Conversation About Dante"), written in 1933 but not published until 1967, when an edition of twenty-five thousand copies sold out immediately and was not reprinted. Mandelstam's prose has been seen both as a key to deciphering his poetry and as a complex body of nonpoetic discourse of great independent value. All his prose has been translated into English.

ACHIEVEMENTS

Osip Mandelstam's poetry won immediate praise from fellow members of Russian literary circles, and he now holds an indisputable position as one of Russia's greatest poets. Like many of his contemporaries, however, Mandelstam experienced anything but a "successful" literary career. His work appeared often in pre-Revolutionary journals, but Mandelstam was not among the writers whom the Bolsheviks promoted after 1917. By 1923, the official ostracism of independent poets such as Mandelstam was apparent, though many continued writing and publishing whenever possible. Mandelstam did not write poetry between 1925 and 1930, turning instead to prose forms that were as inventive and as idiosyncratic as his verse. Attempts to discredit him intensified after 1928. He was arrested twice in the 1930's and is believed to have died while in transit to a Siberian labor camp.

Even during the "thaw" under Premier Nikita Khrushchev, Mandelstam's works were kept out of print, and it was not until 1973 that his "rehabilitation" was made credible by the publication of his poetry in the prestigious *Biblioteka poeta* (poet's library) series. That slim volume was reissued. During the Soviet era in Russia, scholarly writing about Mandelstam, although limited, appeared; his name was mentioned in many but by no means all studies of literature. Official publications, such as textbooks or encyclopedias, relegated him to minor status and often commented disparagingly on his "isolation" from his age. The deep respect commanded by his poetry in the Soviet Union was nevertheless measured by the evolution of scholarly interest in his work.

Mandelstam's reputation outside Russia was initially slow in developing because of the extreme difficulty in obtaining reliable texts of his works and because of the scarcity of information about the poet. As texts and translations became available, Mandelstam's reputation grew steadily. The single most important factor in making his work known in the West was the publication of two volumes of memoirs by his wife, Nadezhda Mandelstam. *Vospominania* (1970; *Hope Against Hope: A Memoir*, 1970) and *Vtoraya kniga* (1972; *Hope Abandoned*, 1974), issued in Russian by émigré publishers and translated into many Western languages, are the prime source of information concerning Mandelstam's life. Works of art in their own right, they also provide invaluable insights into his poetry.

BIOGRAPHY

Osip Emilievich Mandelstam was born in Warsaw, Poland, on January 15, 1891. His family moved almost immediately to St. Petersburg, where Mandelstam later received his education at the Tenischev School (as did Vladimir Nabokov only a few years later). Mandelstam's mother was a pianist; his father worked in a leather-tanning factory. Little is known about Mandelstam's childhood or young adulthood; he recorded cultural rather than personal impressions in his autobiographical sketch, *Shum vremeni* (1925; *The Noise of Time*, 1965).

Mandelstam took several trips abroad, including one to Heidelberg, where he studied Old French and the philosophy of Immanuel Kant at the University of Heidelberg from 1909 to 1910. He returned to St. Petersburg University's faculty of history and philology but seems never to have passed his examinations. Mandelstam had a highly intuitive approach to learning that foreshadowed the associative leaps that make his poetry so difficult to read. His schoolmate Viktor Zhirmunsky, later a prominent Formalist critic, said of Mandelstam that he had only to touch and smell the cover of a book to know its contents with a startling degree of accuracy.

Mandelstam had been writing in earnest at least as early as 1908, and he began publishing poems and essays in St. Petersburg on his return from Heidelberg. By 1913, his literary stance was defined by his alliance with the Acmeists, a group dedicated to replacing the murky longing of Russian Symbolism with a classical sense of clarity and with a dedication to the things of this world rather than to the concepts they might symbolize. Among the acquaintances made in the Acmeist Guild of Poets, Mandelstam formed a lifelong friendship with the poet Anna Akhmatova.

The ideological positions taken by poets were soon overwhelmed by the political upheavals of the decade. Mandelstam did not serve in World War I. He greeted the Revolution with an enthusiasm typical of most intellectuals; he grew increasingly disappointed as the nature of Bolshevik power became apparent. Mandelstam worked in several cultural departments of the young Soviet government, moving between Moscow and St. Petersburg (renamed Leningrad) in connection with these and other jobs. In May, 1919, he met and later married Nadezhda Yakovlevna Khazina. The civil war parted the Mandelstams at times, but they were virtually inseparable until Mandelstam's second arrest in 1938. Nadezhda Mandelstam became far more than her husband's companion and source of strength. She recorded his poems after he had composed them mentally; she memorized the poems when it became clear that written texts were in jeopardy; and she ensured her husband's poetic legacy many years after his death with her two volumes of memoirs and her lifelong campaign to have his poems published.

An early indication of Mandelstam's difficulties came in 1925, when the journal *Rossiya* rejected *The Noise of Time*. Living in or near Leningrad after 1925, Mandelstam busied himself with popular journalistic articles, children's literature, translations, and, by the end of the decade, hack editorial work. Although he published volumes of poetry, prose, and literary criticism in 1928, an attempt to entrap him in a plagiarism scandal the same year demonstrated the general precariousness of his status under the new regime. Nikolai Bukharin, who saved Mandelstam more than once, arranged a trip to Armenia and Georgia that proved crucial in ending his five years of poetic silence. Mandelstam wrote a purgative account of the plagiarism trial, *Chetvertaia proza* (1966; *Fourth Prose*, 1970), as well as poetry and prose inspired by the Armenian land and people.

After the journey, Mandelstam and his wife lived in near poverty in Moscow. Though he gave several readings, Mandelstam saw his prose work *Puteshestviye v Armeniyu* (1933; *Journey to Armenia*, 1973) denounced soon after its publication in the periodical *Zvezda*. On May 13, 1934, Mandelstam was arrested, ostensibly for a poem about Stalin's cruelty; the act of reciting such a poem even to a few friends was characteristic of his defiance of the authorities and of the Soviet literary establishment, which he openly despised. Bukharin again intervened, and the terms of exile were softened considerably. First sent to Cherdyn, the Mandelstams were allowed to select Voronezh, a southern provincial city, as the place where they would spend the next three years.

Mandelstam attempted suicide in Cherdyn and suffered intense periods of anxiety whenever Nadezhda Mandelstam was away, even briefly. He could find little work in Voronezh. Despite periods of near insanity, Mandelstam wrote (and actively sought to publish) three notebooks of poems in Voronezh. In May, 1937, the couple returned to Moscow, where Mandelstam suffered at least one heart attack. Heart ailments had plagued him for years, and throughout his poetry, shortness of breath was always to be a metaphor for the difficulty of writing.

In the fall of 1937, a final respite from the hardships of Moscow was arranged. In the sanatorium in Samatikha, Mandelstam was again arrested in the early morning of May 2, 1938. In August, he was sentenced to five years' hard labor for counterrevolutionary activities. In September, he was sent to a transit camp near Vladivostock, from which he wrote to his wife for the last time. The actual circumstances of Mandelstam's death will probably never be known. The conditions of the camp almost certainly drove him, and not a few others, to the point of insanity. In 1940, his brother Aleksandr received an official statement that Mandelstam had died December 27, 1938, of heart failure.

Nadezhda Mandelstam lived another forty-two years, sustained by her friendship with Anna Akhmatova and by her commitment to preserving her husband's poems for a generation that could read them. As Mandelstam's works began appearing in print, Nadezhda Mandelstam published her two invaluable volumes of memoirs, *Hope Against Hope* and *Hope Abandoned*. On December 31, 1980, she achieved her great wish, an achievement rare enough for Russians of her generation: She died in her own bed.

Analysis

In Osip Mandelstam's first published essay, "O sobesednike" (1913; "On the Addressee"), he describes the ideal reader as one who opens a bottle found among sand dunes and reads a message mysteriously addressed to the reader. Mandelstam's poetry, like the message in the bottle, has had to wait to find its reader; it also demands that a reader be aggressive and resourceful. His poems are intensely dependent on one another and are frequently comprehensible only in terms of ciphered citations from the works of other poets. The reader who wishes to go beyond some critics' belief that Mandelstam's lexicon is arbitrary or irrational must read each poem in the context of the entire oeuvre and with an eye to subtexts from Russian and European literature.

Acmeism

Mandelstam's attempt to incorporate the poetry of the past into his works suited both the spirit and stated tenets of Acmeism, a movement he later defined as a "homesickness for world culture." Mandelstam always saw the Acmeist poets as the preservers of an increasingly endangered literary memory. "True" poetry could arise only from a celebration of its dependence on the old. Poetry plows up the fields of time, he wrote; his own poems bring forth rich layers of subsoil by their poetics of quotation. Apparently opaque lyric situations, when deciphered, yield transparent levels of meaning. Mandelstam especially loved the myths of Greece and Rome, though his quotations are most often from nineteenth and twentieth century Russian poets.

Using another metaphor, perhaps the most typical metaphor for the Acmeists, Mandelstam wrote in the early 1920's that Russian poetry has no Acropolis. "Our culture has been lost until now and cannot find its walls." Russia's words would build its cultural edifices, he predicted, and it is in the use of the word that one must seek the distinctive feature of Mandelstam's poetry.

"Happily Neighing, the Herds Graze"

An example of Mandelstam's use of quotations will indicate how far interpretation of his poetry must stray from the apparent lyric situation. Referring to Mandelstam's first collection of poems, *Stone*, Kiril Taranovsky has noted that a line in the poem "S veselym rzhaniem pasutsia tabuny" ("Happily Neighing, the Herds Graze") quotes Alexander Pushkin's famous statement, "My sadness is luminous." Mandelstam's line is "In old age my sadness is luminous." Nineteen years later, Mandelstam wrote, in a poem memorializing Andrei Bely, "My sadness is lush." The epithet here comes from the *Slovo o polku Igoreve* (c. 1187; *The Tale of the*

Armament of Igor, 1915), but the syntax still recalls Pushkin. Interpreting the stylized line "My sadness is lush" thus requires knowing Pushkin and *The Tale of the Armament of Igor*, to say nothing of Mandelstam's first quotation of Pushkin in "Happily Neighing, the Herds Graze" or the often ornate works of Andrei Bely.

In "Happily Neighing, the Herds Graze," Pushkin's presence is also felt in the poem's seasonal setting, his beloved autumn. The month mentioned, August, suggests Augustus Caesar, and the ancient Roman context is as significant as the Pushkinian overtones. The poem thus has more to do with the ages of human culture than with grazing herds; the poem contrasts the "classical spring" of Pushkin's golden age of Russian literature with the decline of Rome. The dominant color in the poem is gold, specifically the dry gold of harvest. Russia in 1915 resembled Rome during its decline, as the Romanov dynasty faced its end, so that three historical periods come to bear on an interpretation of this apparently pastoral poem. The rise and decline of civilizations do not upset this poet, for whom the cyclical nature of the seasons suggests that historical change is itself cyclical. As Mandelstam wrote in 1918, "Everything has been before, everything will repeat anew. What is sweet to us is the moment of recognition." To achieve such moments, the reader must allow Mandelstam's metaphors to acquire meaning in more than one context. The contexts will border on one another in surprising ways, but it is his peculiar gift to his readers that when they read his poems, they see past poets and past ages of man from new vantage points.

STONE

Mandelstam's first volume of poetry, *Stone*, was published in 1913, with successive enlargements in 1916 and 1923. *Stone* contains short lyrics, many of only three or four quatrains. The title evokes the volume's dominant architectural motifs. Aside from the well-known triptych of cathedral poems in *Stone*, there are also poems of intimate interiors, designs in household utensils, and seashells. The patterns of crafted objects or complex facades allow Mandelstam to write in *Stone* about the structures of language, about how poems may best be written. At times, his metapoetic statements emerge completely undisguised. A landscape is described by the technical language of poetics in "Est'

ivolgi v lesakh" ("There Are Orioles in the Woods"), in which the birds' singing is measured by the length of vowel sounds, their lines ringing forth in tonic rhythms. The day "yawns like a caesura."

Mandelstam pursues the probable relationship between the oriole and the poet in "Ia ne slyxal rasskazov Ossiana" ("I Have Not Heard the Tales of Ossian"). Here, a raven echoing a harp replaces the oriole; the poem's persona intones, "And again the bard will compose another's song/ And, as his own, he will pronounce it." Mandelstam contrasts his own heritage with that of another land, as distinct as the singing of birds and men. Despite the differences between the battles of Russian soldiers and the feigned tales of Ossian, the poet's entire received heritage is "blessed," "the erring dreams of other singers" ("other" connotes "foreign" as well as "not oneself" in Russian). It is in making the dreams his own that the poet finds victory.

In "Est' tselomudrennye chary" ("There Are Chaste Charms"), Mandelstam concludes with an equally victorious quatrain. The poem has evoked household gods in terms derived from classical Rome and from eighteenth century poetry. After three quatrains of listening to ancient gods and their lyres, the poet declares that the gods "are your equals." With a careful hand, he adds, "one may rearrange them."

Among the poems that both assert and demonstrate Mandelstam's strength as an independent poet is "Notre Dame," the shortest and most clearly Acmeist of his three 1912 cathedral poems. The Acmeists consistently praised the Gothic optimism of medieval architecture and art, and they shared that period's devotion to art as high craft. In "Notre Dame," Mandelstam praises the church's "massive walls," its "elemental labyrinth." The cathedral becomes both that which the poet studies and that from which he is inspired to create something of his own. The outstretched body of Adam furnishes a metaphor for the opening description of the cathedral's vaulted ceiling. Adam's name, and his having been "joyful and first," had once provided an alternative name for Acmeism, Adamism, which never took hold. The name "Adam," nevertheless, invokes in "Notre Dame" the poetic principles of the movement, its clarity, its balance, its sense of the poem as something visibly constructed. "Notre Dame" is as close to a programmatic statement in verse as Mandelstam ever came; the poem does what a Gothic cathedral should do, "revealing its secret plan from the outside."

TRISTIA

Mandelstam's second volume, *Tristia*, appeared in 1922. Compared to the architectural poems of *Stone*, many drawing on the Roman tradition in classical culture, *Tristia* depends more on the myths of ancient Greece. It evokes the landscape of the Mediterranean or Crimean seas to frame tender, interiorized poems. The title is the same as that of a work by Ovid, written during his exile, and the connotations of *tristia*, both emotional and literary, resonate throughout the volume, though the title was not initially of Mandelstam's choosing. The title poem, "Tristia," addresses the difficulties of separation, the science of which the speaker says he has studied to the point of knowing it well. There are several kinds of separation involved, from women seeing men off to battle in stanza 1 to men and women facing their particular deaths in stanza 4. The poet feels the difficulty of moving from one kind of separation to another in stanza 3, where he complains, "How poor is the language of joy." Ovid's exile has been a continuous event since he wrote his *Tristia* (after 8 C.E.). There is joy in recognizing the repetition of historical and personal events; Mandelstam here performs his usual chronological sleight of hand in juxtaposing several ages in history, rising toward divinations of the future in the final stanza.

The moment of recognition or remembrance is sought after in vain in "Ia slovo pozabyl, chto ia khotel skazat'" ("I Have Forgotten the Word I Wanted to Say"). Like its companion poem "Kogda Psikheia-zhizn' spuskaetsia k teniam" ("When Psyche-Life Descends to the Shades"), the poem evokes the failure to remember poetic words as a descent into Hades. The close correspondence between these two psyche poems is characteristic of Mandelstam: The presentation of variants demonstrates his belief that the drafts of a poem are never lost. These poems also demonstrate the general Acmeist principle that there is no final or closed version of any work of literature.

PSYCHE POEMS

In the psyche poems, mythological figures are mentioned, such as Persephone or Antigone for their de-

scent into the Underworld or for their devotion to the funeral ritual, respectively. The river mentioned in both poems is not Lethe, the river of forgetfulness, but Styx, the boundary of Hades. Forgetfulness plagues both poems, however; "I Have Forgotten the Word I Wanted to Say," a formula repeated in one poem, equates the fear of death's oblivion with the loss of poetry. The images of the dry riverbed, of birds that cannot be heard, of a blind swallow with clipped wings—all suggest an artist's sterility. It is the dead who revive an ability to remember (hence their avoidance of the river Lethe), to recognize meanings as significant as those of the divining women at the end of "Tristia." With the slowness so crucial to the entire volume, something develops in "I Have Forgotten the Word I Wanted to Say." In "When Psyche-Life Descends to the Shades," the soul is slow to hand over her payment for crossing the river. The "unincarnated thought" returns to the Underworld, but the black ice of its remembered sound burns on the poet's lips. For Mandelstam, lips (like breathing), suggest the act of composing poetry, so that these twin poems conclude with a kind of optimism, however fearful.

Several poems in *Tristia* treat the social causes of Mandelstam's fear of poetic failure, among them two of his most famous: "Sumerki svobody" ("The Twilight of Freedom") and "V Peterburge my soidomsia snova" ("In Petersburg We Shall Meet Again"). Both poems respond to the Revolution of 1917 ambiguously if not pessimistically. The sun both rises and sets in "The Twilight of Freedom," where the "twilight" of the title could mean "sunset" as well as "dawn." "In Petersburg We Shall Meet Again" also chooses an ambiguous source of light; the sun is buried and the "night sun" illuminates the final stanza.

Images from the psyche poems reappear with more pronounced political overtones. In "The Twilight of Freedom," there are immobilized swallows, bound into "fighting legions." The people appear as both powerful and restrained, expressing perfectly Mandelstam's perception of the Revolution as potentially empowering but finally overpowering. In "In Petersburg We Shall Meet Again," the "blessed, meaningless word" that the poet feared forgetting in the Psyche poems seems miraculously renewed. The poem displays terrifying sights and sounds, from ominous patrols to whizzing sirens, yet the speaker clings to his "word" as if oblivious of everything else. The poem closes with a crowd leaving a theater, where the end of the performance suggests the end of an entire culture. Yet, as in the exhortation to be brave in "The Twilight of Freedom," the poetic voice affirms its power to live beyond the threats of "Lethe's cold" or the "Soviet night." What endures in *Tristia*, though with difficulty, is what seemed immutable in *Stone*: faith in the word as the center of Russian culture.

Poems

In 1928, Mandelstam published a volume of poems comprising revised versions of *Stone* and *Tristia*, as well as some twenty new poems. Several had appeared in the second edition of *Tristia*. These poems are even less optimistic than the ambiguous poems of *Tristia*; they are permeated by a fear of disorder that so threatened Mandelstam's voice that he ceased writing poems altogether from 1925 to 1930. The city arches its back threateningly in "In Petersburg We Shall Meet Again"; the back is broken in "Vek" ("The Age"). The age is dying in "Net, nikogda nichei ia ne byl sovremennik" ("No, I Was Never Anyone's Contemporary"), a poem whose first line discloses as well as any of his works Mandelstam's alienated state of mind. The source of light in these poems is not the sun, not even the occluded or nighttime sun, but stars that look down menacingly from the evening firmament. The air is steamy, foamy, dark, and watery, as impossible to breathe as the sky is to behold. Not being able to breathe, like not being able to speak, conveys Mandelstam's extraordinary difficulty in writing during this period.

"Slate Ode" and "The Horseshoe Finder"

Two of Mandelstam's most startling and most difficult poems date from the early 1920's: "Nashedshii podkovu" ("The Horseshoe Finder") and "Grifel' naia oda" ("Slate Ode"). The poems test and affirm poetry's ability to endure despite the shifting values of the age. "The Horseshoe Finder" binds together long, irregular verse lines without rhyme (a new form for Mandelstam) by repeating and interweaving clusters of consonants. Rejecting the slow realizations of *Tristia*, the poem moves quickly from one metaphorical cluster to another. Finding the horseshoe, also a talismanic

emblem for poetry in "Slate Ode," is like finding the bottled message in Mandelstam's essay "On the Addressee." The past can still be transmitted in "The Horseshoe Finder": "Human lips . . . preserve the form of the last spoken word," but these lips "have nothing more to say."

"Leningrad"

Mandelstam resumed writing poetry in 1930, and, had the official literary establishment not been forcing him out of print, there could easily have emerged a third volume of verse from the poems written in Moscow and Voronezh. A clear task unites many of these poems, a task of self-definition. The fate of the poet has become a metaphor for the fate of the culture, so that intensely personal poems avoid all solipsism. The triangular relationship "world-self-text" emerges as a conflict to be resolved anew in each poem. Mandelstam returned to Leningrad, "familiar to the point of tears." In his poem "Leningrad," Mandelstam proclaims against all odds, echoing the famous Pushkin line, that he does not want to die. Death moves inevitably through the poem, though, as his address book leads only to "dead voices"; the poet lives on back stairs, awaiting guests who rattle a ball and chain.

Mandelstam was arrested for the often-quoted epigram about Stalin; describing "cockroach whiskers" and "fat fingers, like worms," the poem was perhaps his angriest of the period. The secret police could have arrested Mandelstam, however, for any number of works from the early 1930's. Hatred of the "songs" with which the Soviets had supplied the new age, disgust at the ethos of the Socialist Utopia, and fear that Russia's genuine cultural heritage would perish are frequent themes. Mandelstam wanted no part of the changes around him; he names himself as the "unrecognized brother, an outcast in the family of man" in a poem dedicated to Anna Akhmatova, his dear friend and fellow poet who also suffered ostracism.

In the South and in Moscow, Mandelstam was befriended by several biologists. They inspired him to read Jean-Baptiste Lamarck, Charles Darwin, and other authors who in turn provided Mandelstam with a new metaphor for expressing his dislike of the age's paeans to "progress." In "Lamarck," Mandelstam chooses to occupy the lowest step on the evolutionary ladder rather than join in the false advances urged by the government. These steps bring humankind down in the evolutionary chain, observes the poet, toward species that cannot hear, speak, or breathe—toward those that do not produce poetry. The age, in copious images of the silence of deafness, has grown dumb; self-definition nears self-denigration as the surrounding cultural edifices crumble and threaten to bring the new Soviet literature down with them.

Destruction, pain, death, terror—these are the themes that dominate the post-1930 poems to a degree that would separate them from the poems written before 1925 even if there were no other distinctions. As Mandelstam wrote poems inspired by the chaos around him, so also the poems formally demonstrated the pervasiveness of chaos. Disintegration became both subject matter and structuring principle: The late poems demonstrate an openness, fragmentation, and avoidance of conventional poetic diction, meter, and rhyme that would have been inconceivable in the beautifully formed poems of *Stone* or *Tristia*. The early predilection for exact rhyme is reshaped by an admixture of near rhymes of all sorts. The poems grow rich in internal paronomasia, where interweavings of sounds create controlling structures in lines that seem otherwise arbitrarily ordered. The rhythms grow freer during the 1930's as well. Mandelstam had used free verse in the 1920's, as in "The Horseshoe Finder," and returned to it for longer, more complex works such as "Polnoch' v Moskve" ("Midnight in Moscow"). Conventionally metered poems include aberrant lines of fewer or more metrical feet or with entirely different schemes; conversely, the free verse of "Midnight in Moscow" permits interpolated lines of perfect or near-perfect meter.

The spontaneity that the late poems explore represents the final version of Mandelstam's longstanding commitment to the openness of the poetic text. Including fragments of conversation and unconventional constructions in these poems, Mandelstam was converting the destructive chaos around him to his own ends. Hence the fluidity of "cross-references" in his poetry, particularly in the late verse, where there are not only "twin" or "triplet" poems, as Nadezhda Mandelstam called them, but also entire cycles of variants, among

them the poems on the death of Bely in 1934. Moving beyond the concrete referentiality of the early poems, the late Mandelstam dramatizes rather than describes the act of self-definition. The communicative act between poet and reader overrides the encoding act between poet and world, as the reader is drawn deeply into the process of decoding the poet's relationships with his world and his poems.

Mandelstam's confidence that a reader would someday seek to understand even his most labyrinthine poems shines through unexpectedly during the late period. There are love poems to his wife and others—among the most remarkable is "Masteritsa vinovatykh vzorov" ("Mistress of Guilty Glances")—as well as poems wherein renunciation yields extraordinary strength. Mandelstam's enduring gift, long after he had himself fallen victim to the society at odds with him, was to find strength in the deepest threats to his identity. Hence, the halfhearted desire to write an ode to Stalin, which might save his wife after his own death, gave rise instead to a host of deeply honest poems that were as hopeful as they were embattled. Though the simple longings of the late poems may be futile, the act of recording his desires into completely threatened poems represents Mandelstam's typical achievement in the late works.

OTHER MAJOR WORKS

SHORT FICTION: *Yegipetskaya marka*, 1928 (*The Egyptian Stamp*, 1965).

NONFICTION: *O prirode slova*, 1922 (*About the Nature of the Word*, 1977); *Feodosiya*, 1925 (autobiography; *Theodosia*, 1965); *Shum vremeni*, 1925 (autobiography; *The Noise of Time*, 1965); *O poezii*, 1928 (*About Poetry*, 1977); *Puteshestviye v Armeniyu*, 1933 (travel sketch; *Journey to Armenia*, 1973); *Chetvertaia proza*, 1966 (wr. 1930 or 1931; *Fourth Prose*, 1970); *Razgovor o Dante*, 1967 (*Conversation About Dante*, 1965); *Selected Essays*, 1977; *Slovo i kul'tura: Stat'i*, 1987.

CHILDREN'S LITERATURE: *Dva tramvaya*, 1925; *Primus*, 1925; *Kukhnya*, 1926; *Shary*, 1926.

MISCELLANEOUS: *Sobranie sochinenii*, 1955, 1964-1971, 1981 (*Collected Works*, 1967-1969); *The Complete Critical Prose and Letters*, 1979.

B<small>IBLIOGRAPHY</small>

Baines, Jennifer. *Mandelstam: The Later Poetry*. New York: Cambridge University Press, 1976. Scholarly treatment of Mandelstam's poems written in Moscow and Voronezh in the 1930's. The study of these poems has been somewhat neglected because of their enigmatic nature.

Brown, Clarence. *Mandelstam*. New York: Cambridge University Press, 1973. The best authority on Mandelstam in the English-speaking world presents his seminal work, covering all aspects of Mandelstam's life and work. Brown's analyses of Mandelstam's poems are particularly valuable.

Broyde, Steven. *Osip Mandelstam and His Age: A Commentary on the Themes of War and Revolution in the Poetry, 1913-1923*. Cambridge, Mass.: Harvard University Press, 1975. A detailed analysis of Mandelstam's poems inspired by, and centered on, war and revolution. There are many citations of poems, in Russian and in English.

Cavanagh, Clare. *Osip Mandelstam and the Modernist Creation of Tradition*. Princeton, N.J.: Princeton University Press, 1995. Places Mandelstam within the modernist tradition of T. S. Eliot and Ezra Pound of reflecting a "world culture" divorced from strict national or ethnic identity.

Glazov-Corrigan, Elena. *Mandel'shtam's Poetics: A Challenge to Postmodernism*. Toronto, Ont.: University of Toronto Press, 2000. Analyses Mandelstam's thoughts on poetry and art in the context of the major postmodern literary debates and traces their development throughout his writings. Describes Mandelstam's intellectual world and its effect on his evolution as a thinker, specifically, on differences in his attitude toward language.

Mandelstam, Nadezhda. *Hope Against Hope: A Memoir*. New York: Atheneum, 1970. The first volume of memoirs written by Mandelstam's wife, dealing with biographical details but also with the genesis of many of Mandelstam's poetms.

_____. *Hope Abandoned*. New York: Atheneum, 1974. The second volume of the memoirs.

Pollack, Nancy. *Mandelstam the Reader*. Baltimore: The Johns Hopkins University Press, 1995. A study of Mandelstam's late verse and prose. The two genres receive approximately equal treatment, but the analyses of poems tend to be deeper.

Prsybylski, Ryszard. *An Essay on the Poetry of Osip Mandelstam: God's Grateful Guest*. Translated by Madeline G. Levine. Ann Arbor, Mich.: Ardis, 1987. A noted Polish scholar treats Mandelstam's attraction to, and reflection of, Greek and Roman classicism, the musical quality of his poetry, his affinity to architecture and archaeology, and other features of the poetry. The author places Mandelstam in the framework of world literature.

Zeeman, Peter. *The Later Poetry of Osip Mandelstam: Text and Context*. Amsterdam: Rodopi, 1988. Detailed interpretations and analyses of Mandelstam's poems written in the 1930's. Zeeman uses primarily contextualization and historical reconstruction in his discussion of the poems, some of which are among the most difficult of all Mandelstam's poems.

Stephanie Sandler

M<small>ATSUO</small> B<small>ASHŌ</small>

Born: Ueno, Iga Province, Japan; 1644
Died: Ōsaka, Japan; October 12, 1694
Also known as: Matsuo Kinsaku

P<small>RINCIPAL POETRY</small>

Sarumino, 1691 (*Monkey's Raincoat*, 1973)
Bashō's Haiku: Selected Poems by Matsuo Bashō, 2004
Haikai shichibu-shū, n.d.

O<small>THER LITERARY FORMS</small>

The literary works of Matsuo Bashō (mah-tsew-oh bah-shoh) are difficult to classify, even for those acquainted with Japanese literary history. Bashō is popularly known as the greatest of all haiku poets, although the literary form was not defined and named until two hundred years after his death. Modern collections labeled "Bashō's *haiku*" are generally bits and pieces taken from his travel journals and *renku* (linked poems). In a sense, all Bashō's literary works are broader and more complex than the seventeen-syllable haiku for which he is remembered. The seven major anthologies of his school, listed above, contain *hokku* (opening verses) and *renku* composed by Bashō and his disciples, as well as an occasional prose piece. Besides *hokku* and *renku*, Bashō is known for his *haibun*, a combination of terse prose and seventeen-syllable *hokku* generally describing his pilgrimages to famous sites in Japan. His best-known travel journals include *Nozarashi kikō* (1687; *The Records of a Weather-Exposed Skeleton*, 1966), *Oku no hosomichi* (1694; *The Narrow Road to the Deep North*, 1933), *Oi no kobumi* (1709; *The Records of a Travel-Worn Satchel*, 1966), and *Sarashina kikō* (1704; *A Visit to Sarashina Village*, 1957). Bashō's conversations on poetry were preserved by disciples, and his surviving letters, numbering more than a hundred, are treasured today.

ACHIEVEMENTS

Matsuo Bashō is the favorite poet of Japan and one of the only poets of Asia whose verses are known popularly in the West. It is paradoxical that this complex poet whose profundity continues to tease the minds of Japan's greatest literary critics is read and recited by schoolchildren in many lands. Although technically he never wrote a haiku, Bashō serves as a model for many children, East and West, writing their first verses as haiku. The wedding of simplicity and profundity that characterizes Bashō's work provides a true measure of his stature as a poet.

The continuing popularity of Bashō in his homeland, a country where laymen pride themselves on being aesthetic critics, is itself an extraordinary tribute to his work. Japanese still make pilgrimages to the stone monuments marking the stopping places on his journeys. Many recite his verses when they hear a frog splash, smell plum blossoms on a mountain trail, or hear a cicada's shrill voice. Thanks in no small part to his work, many average citizens of Japan still write poetry, hang scrolls containing verse, and read the poetry column in Japan's daily newspapers.

In an age when aristocrats were the arbiters of taste, setting the complex rules for the writing of *waka* and *renga*, the chief poetic forms of Japan, Bashō devoted himself to *haikai*, an informal style of poetry celebrating the seasons of nature and the round of ordinary life among peasants and merchants. Without Bashō, *haikai* was in danger of sliding into slavish imitation of aristocratic canons or of degenerating into a display of vulgarity, coarse humor, and puns. Bashō democratized literature in Japan, and through literature, he helped democratize Japanese aesthetics. Bringing to bear his own sensitivity to the nature mysticism of Chinese Daoism and the radical sacramentalization of the ordinary in Zen Buddhism, he created a poetry of breadth and depth for the Japanese populace. As he observes in one of his *hokku*: "The beginning of art:/ Songs sung by those planting rice/ In the back country."

More specifically, Bashō's achievements in literature led to the maturing of three forms: the *hokku*, the *haikai no renga* (informal linked verse), and the *haibun*. Devoting a lifetime of effort to *hokku*, those seventeen-syllable verses intended as openings for linked poems, Bashō prepared the form for its modern independence as haiku. Working tirelessly with disciples in Japan's cities and countryside, Bashō infused a sense of the shared spirit of poetry that led to Japan's greatest *renku*, perhaps the high point of *za no geijutsu* (group art) in the history of world literature. Finally, his mastery of the combination of prose and poetry in travel journals set a new standard for the form the Japanese call *haibun*.

Describing himself in one of his *haibun*, *The Records of a Travel-Worn Satchel*, Bashō suggested a further unity, the unity of all arts when sounded to their depths, and the unity of art with nature, a philosophy that has given Japan its unique character:

> Finally, this poet, incapable as he is, has bound himself to the thin line of poetry. One and the same thread runs through the *waka* of Saigyō, *renga* of Sōgi, paintings of Sesshū, and tea ceremony of Riky. What the arts hold in common is a devotion to nature and companionship with the four seasons.

BIOGRAPHY

Centuries of warfare among the lords and samurai of Japan's chief clans came to an end when Tokugawa Ieyasu established a military dictatorship, the Shogunate, about 1600. With a Tokugawa shogun established in the thriving merchant city of Edo (modern-day Tokyo) and a ceremonial imperial court in ancient Kyoto, Japan officially closed its doors to the outside world in 1638. Such was the setting in which Matsuo Bashō was born as Matsuo Munefusa in 1644 at Ueno in Iga province, only thirty miles from the imperial palace in Kyoto and two hundred miles from the powerful shogun in Edo.

Bashō was one of several children born to Matsuo Yozaemon, a minor samurai nominally in the service of the Tōdō family that ruled the Ueno area. Bashō's father had limited means and probably provided for his family by farming and giving lessons in calligraphy. At about age twelve, perhaps the year his father died, Bashō entered the service of the Tōdō family as a study companion to one of the Tōdō heirs, Yoshitada, a youth two years his senior with a bent toward poetry. A genuine

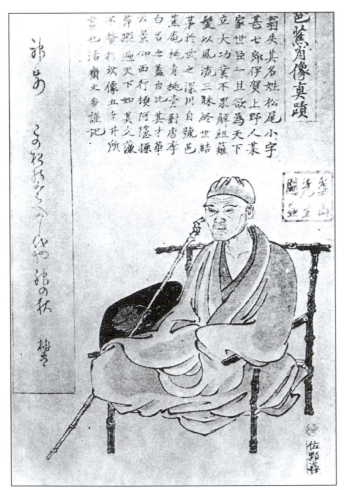

Matsuo Bashō (The Granger Collection, New York)

friendship with Yoshitada encouraged young Bashō in the study of poetry and gave him access to one of the leading teachers of the day, Kitamura Kigin (1624-1705). When Yoshitada died suddenly in 1666, Bashō, only twenty-two years of age, lost both a friend and a patron. He apparently remained in the area of Ueno and Kyoto, devoting himself to poetry in the *haikai* style of the Teitoku school favored by his teacher Kigin. Pursuing a career as a poet, by 1672, he had published at his own expense *Kai-ōi* (seashell game), a collection of humorous verses by local poets that he matched and commented upon as poet-teacher. Some scholars believe that during this period, Bashō entered a relationship with a woman later known by her religious name, Jutei, and perhaps fathered children by her, but other scholars have dismissed this as pure speculation.

In 1672, at age twenty-eight, Bashō established himself in the bustling city of Edo, where his reputation as *haikai* poet and teacher increased. In 1680, he published *Tōsei montei dokugin nijū kasen* (twenty *kasen* by Tōsei's pupils), a collection of thirty-six-link *renku*. That year, he settled in a hut on the outskirts of Edo, next to which one of his disciples planted a *bashō*. In time, the poet's residence became known as the *Bashō-an* (banana-plant hut), and his students began to address him as "Master Bashō." Thus was born the nickname by which he was known for the rest of his life.

Bashō's early poetry was influenced by the Teitoku or Teimon style of *haikai*, using clever literary allusions and wordplay. In Edo, he came under the influence of the Danrin school, which explored greater freedom in theme and diction and demonstrated genuine interest in the life of the merchants and laborers of Edo. By about 1681, his own style, called *shōfū*, had begun to emerge, as evidenced in his *hokku* describing a crow on a withered branch in autumn twilight. Bashō also began practicing meditation under the direction of a Zen priest, Butchō (1642-1715).

In the fall of 1684, Bashō put on the robes of a Buddhist priest and began a series of pilgrimages over the roads and rugged mountain trails of Japan to perfect the new ideal of his art, *sabi* (solitariness). The final twelve years of his life were given largely to strenuous travel, the perfecting of the *haibun*-style travel journal, and sessions with disciples along the way who responded to his teaching and joined him in the art of *haikai no renga*, the linking of verses to produce *renku*. By 1686, he had written his most famous verse, describing the contrast of an old pond and a frog's splash, and by 1689, he had taken the difficult inland journey that led to the height of *haibun* art, *The Narrow Road to the Deep North*. Near the end of his life, to the chagrin of some of his disciples, Bashō had begun to advocate a new principle for the writing of *haikai*: *karumi* (lightness), a focus on the ordinary and unadorned.

During a final trip to Ueno and Ōsaka to preach *karumi* and to patch up a quarrel among his disciples, Bashō's strength failed and an old illness flared up; he dictated a final verse from his deathbed: "Ill on the journey/ My dreams going round and round/ Over withered fields."

ANALYSIS

At a time when many *haikai* poets wrote hundreds of verses during a single night's linked-poetry session, Matsuo Bashō's lifetime accumulation of barely a thousand seventeen-syllable *hokku* is indicative of the seriousness with which he took his art. Constantly struggling with each of these verses, Bashō established a standard of craftsmanship and profundity that would later lead to *hokku*'s independent status as haiku.

The *hokku* often singled out as Bashō's first masterpiece is his crow verse of 1681: "On a withered branch/ A crow settles itself down—/ Autumn evening." The stark tableau of a black branch against the darkened sky is broken by the sudden movement of a crow alighting. Here, timelessness and the momentary meet, and as they merge, the wider and deeper cycle of nature's seasonal pattern is revealed. The darkness of branch, crow, and autumn nightfall interpenetrate, suggesting the Japanese aesthetic qualities called *wabi* (poverty) and *sabi* (solitude).

THEMES

What the poet has not said is as significant as his choice of theme. The traditional aristocratic themes of

Japanese court poetry, the scented love notes, koto music, and tear-drenched sleeves of *waka* are absent. Bashō reaches back to the themes and cadences of the great Tang Dynasty poets of China, Du Fu and Li Bo, to lend universality to his verse. The monochromes of the great Chan masters are suggested by the black branch and crow, and perhaps the *hokku* itself suggests the Chinese poetic topic, "shivering crow in leafless tree." The merging of all in the mystery of darkness suggests Bashō's reading preferences: Daoism's Zhuangzi (Chuang-tzu) and Japan's poet-priests Saigyō and Sōgi. The rhythm and repetition of sounds, lost in English translation, witness Bashō's careful craftsmanship in the crow verse: *kare* (withered), *karasu* (crow), *aki no kure* (autumn evening).

FROG VERSES

One of Bashō's Edo disciples, Senka, compiled a *haikai* matching of verses on the subject "frog" in 1686, *Kawazu awase* (frog contest). Bashō provided the opening verse, or *hokku*, the most famous of all his works: "An age-old pond—/ A frog leaps into it/ Splash goes the water." The presence of *kawazu* (frog), a *kigo* (season word), tells the reader that it is spring. The poet sees the still surface of a murky pond, probably an ancient pond edged by rocks and reeds designed centuries earlier by some Zen priest as a setting for a temple. A sudden splash shatters the stillness of the pond, and in that disruption a new awareness of the eternal is sealed on the consciousness. Asian philosophy's yin-yang complementarity is revealed in the relation of stillness to sound, and the Daoist theme of a void from which momentary forms of life emerge and to which they return is celebrated. The consummate demonstration of just how much can be suggested in a few words constitutes Bashō's principal contribution to the *hokku* and suggests the Asian "one-corner philosophy": Sensitivity to the smallest creature or the briefest moment within the cycle of nature provides a gateway to the motion and meaning of the entire universe. In the words of Zen Buddhism, "The mountains, trees, and grasses are the Buddha."

ZEN AND DAOISM

Bashō's training in Zen Buddhist meditation and his donning the robes of a Buddhist priest for his travels might suggest that the key concept of Buddhism, *sunyata* (emptiness), would find expression in his verses. It is significant that many of Bashō's *hokku* focus not on a presence but rather on an "absence," a creative emptiness that suggests "pure potentiality." He writes of a skylark "clinging to nothing at all," of Mount Fuji "disappearing in mist," of flowers "without names," and of "a road empty of travelers." The Daoist void and Buddhist emptiness are expressed in the aesthetic quality Japanese call *yūgen* (mysterious vagueness), a quality of the *hokku* akin to the vacant spaces in a Zen scroll painting.

KARUMI

In 1693, just a year before his death, Bashō "shut his gate" for a time, refusing all visitors. When he opened the gate again to his disciples, he began teaching a further development of *haikai* poetry, the principle of *karumi* (lightness). Even close disciples had misgivings and uncertainties about this principle to which the poet devoted his final year. Moving beyond *wabi, sabi,* and *yūgen,* Bashō sought a return to some primal simplicity in the ordinariness of life, simplicity beyond both technical excellence and poetic response to the past. He wrote of a "sick wild duck/ falling in the cold of night," of "salted fish" in a street market, of a "white-haired/ graveyard visit," a "motionless cloud," and "autumn chill." The experience of eternity was no longer simply intensified by the momentary; for Bashō, it had become incarnate in the unadorned ordinariness of life.

THE ART OF HAIKAI

Modern interest in Bashō's art has generally focused on the *hokku.* Bashō himself, however, believed the art of *haikai* was to be found less in isolated verses than in cooperative effort of a like-minded school of poets involved in "sequence composition," and apparently he felt his greatest achievements occurred in this area: "Among my disciples many are as gifted as I am in writing *hokku.* But this old man knows the true spirit of *haikai.*" The art of *haikai,* or *haikai no renga,* is so foreign to Western experience that appreciation of its merits and of Bashō's contribution is especially difficult.

The *waka* was the chief poetic form of the Japanese from prehistory through the thirteenth century. The special possession of the aristocracy at court, short *waka* called *tanka* were sometimes created by two persons, one composing the upper seventeen syllables and

another responding with the lower fourteen. When *tanka* rules became too confining, some poets began to compose *renga* (linked verses) of a *haikai* (informal) or *mushin* (frivolous) sort. *Renga* soon became adopted by the court and developed its own *ushin* (serious) rules, and so by the sixteenth century a *haikai no renga* movement sought to democratize the form again.

Bashō, an artist of *haikai no renga,* sought to keep the form open to creative contact with everyday life, yet sought also to transcend common wordplay and vulgarities. His cooperative poetic efforts with four Nagoya merchants in *Fuyu no hi* (a winter's day) and with sixteen disciples in a hundred-verse sequence called *Hatsu kaishi* (*First Manuscript Page*), culminating in a series of thirty-six-link *renku* collected in *Monkey's Raincoat.* Using the rules regarding season sequences and moon and flower verses with freedom yet sensitivity, he advocated linking alternate seventeen-syllable and fourteen-syllable verses through the principle of *nioi* (fragrance), a vague but effective sense of atmosphere and mood conveyed by one poet and verse to another.

"IN THE CITY"

A *renku* in thirty-six verses titled "Ichinaka wa" ("In the City") appears in *Monkey's Raincoat.* Its opening verse (*hokku*) is by the poet Bonchō, who introduces the "heavy odor of things" in the city and uses the seasonal words "summer moon." Bashō responds with the answering verse (*waki*), describing voices in the night at "gate after gate." They repeat, "It is hot, so hot." From there, a third poet shifts the scene to a rice paddy, Bonchō continues with a verse describing a farmer's "smoked sardine" meal, and Bashō adds a link that pictures himself as a visitor to this poor farm neighborhood, where "they don't even recognize money." Within the next half dozen verses, a young girl's religious experience is described, the season shifts to winter, and Bashō introduces an aged peasant who "can only suck the bones of fish." Sounds and word associations linking one verse to another are so subtle that even experienced *haikai* poets disagree in their analysis, though not in their high evaluation of the *renku.*

Perhaps the greatest facet of Bashō's art, linked poetry written cooperatively through a shared "fragrance," is largely closed to the Western reader, though a good *renku* translation and commentary may be of some aid. Those familiar with Western chamber music may detect similarities, as themes pass from one player to another, exciting changes in tempo and mood are introduced, and one instrument modulates to support the contribution of another.

THE NARROW ROAD TO THE DEEP NORTH

Finally, it should be noted that some critics view neither the *hokku* nor the *haikai no renga* as the height of Bashō's art. They would view his travel journals, culminating in *The Narrow Road to the Deep North*, as the epitome of his creative efforts.

In *The Narrow Road to the Deep North*, widely regarded as one of the finest works in all Japanese literature, the pilgrim-poet seeks to mature his art by hiking to those sites of beauty and history that inspired Saigyō and other poet-priests of the past. Taking arduous trails both to the inner country of Japan and the inner reaches of his own art, Bashō weaves prose and poetry into a record of a pilgrimage of the Japanese spirit as it responds to the history and beauty of the homeland. The famous opening declares that "moon and sun are eternal travelers," and bids the reader to join in the journey. Bashō describes famous sites and views at Matsushima, Hiraizumi, and Kisagata, pausing to muse over ruined castles and ancient battlefields:

> The summer grasses—
> For courageous warriors
> The aftermath of dreams.

In a land ruled by powerful military shoguns who had closed Japan to all outside contacts, such musings in the spirit of the great T'ang poets of China made this travel journal an act of courage and a proclamation that art cannot be confined by political borders. Allusions to Chinese poetry and philosophy, Japanese history and aesthetics, are woven together in such a complex tapestry that, once again, the Western reader is in need of a superior translation and a helpful commentary, but the treasures to be discovered are worth the effort.

Bashō, the poet whose verses are loved by children yet challenge the best efforts of mature scholars, spent his life in pilgrimage for his art and died on the road. In *The Narrow Road to the Deep North*, he sums up the relevance of his wanderings in a few simple words,

identifying his readers as pilgrims, too: "For each day is a journey, and the journey itself is home."

OTHER MAJOR WORKS

NONFICTION: *Nozarashi kikō*, 1687 (travel; *The Records of a Weather-Exposed Skeleton*, 1966); *Oku no hosomichi*, 1694 (travel; *The Narrow Road to the Deep North*, 1933); *Sarashina kikō*, 1704 (travel; *A Visit to Sarashina Village*, 1966); *Oi no kobumi*, 1709 (travel; *The Records of a Travel-Worn Satchel*, 1966).

MISCELLANEOUS: *The Essential Bashō*, 1999.

BIBLIOGRAPHY

Aitken, Robert. *A Zen Wave: Bashō's Haiku and Zen.* New York: Weatherhill, 1978. One of the few studies of Bashō by a Western roshi, or master teacher of Zen. This overview evaluates the poet's work in the context of Zen philosophy, offering the claim that Bashō's haiku transcend mere nature poetry and instead serve as a way of presenting fundamental religious truths about mind, nature, and cosmos.

Caws, Mary Ann, ed. *Textual Analysis: Some Readers Reading.* New York: Modern Language Association of America, 1986. Earl Miner's chapter on Bashō has as its main thesis that Bashō has not been known in the West as he would have wished to be known. The focus of his discussion is the fact that the Western concept of mimesis, what is real and what is fiction, differs from its Eastern counterpart, opening the way to misunderstanding.

Hamill, Sam, trans. *The Essential Bashō.* Boston: Shambhala, 1999. The introduction to this work represents Bashō as a consummate writer. In this work, religious issues are significantly downplayed. Instead Hamill presents his subject as a poetic and philosophical wanderer: someone engaged in a lifelong process of literary experimentation and discovery. Particularly fascinating is the overview of Bashō's transformation from a highly derivative stylist to a powerfully original poet.

Qiu, Peipei. *Basho and the Dao: The Zhuangzi and the Transformation of Haikai.* Honolulu: University of Hawaii Press, 2005. Examines the relationship between Daoism and Bashō's poetry. Contains considerable discussion of themes and influences.

Shirane, Haruo. *Traces of Dreams: Landscape, Cultural Memory, and the Poetry of Bashō*. Stanford, Calif.: Stanford University Press, 1998. This work puts the poet in the position of cultural conservationist, arguing that Bashō's poems drew on deeply held concepts of nature.

Ueda, Makoto. *Matsuo Bashō*. New York: Twayne, 1970. This study offers a brief biography as well as general perspectives on the author's major works. In addition to the expected focus on haiku, it treats Bashō's *renku* (long, collaboratively written poems) and prose works.

_____, ed. *Bashō and His Interpreters: Selected Hokku with Commentary*. Stanford, Calif.: Stanford University Press, 1992. This work is a chronologically organized anthology of Bashō's poems, each accompanied by the original Japanese text (transliterated into Western characters) and literal translations. Although this anthology offers little new insight into Bashō's life or interpretations of his work, this volume does demonstrate the tremendous influence of translation on the written word.

Cliff Edwards

VLADIMIR MAYAKOVSKY

Born: Bagdadi, Georgia, Russian Empire (now Mayakovsky, Georgia); July 19, 1893

Died: Moscow, Soviet Union (now in Russia); April 14, 1930

PRINCIPAL POETRY

Ya, 1913

Oblako v shtanakh, 1915 (*A Cloud in Pants*, 1945)

Chelovek, 1916

Fleita-pozvonochnik, 1916 (*The Backbone Flute*, 1960)

150,000,000, 1920 (English translation, 1949)

Pro eto, 1923 (*About That*, 1965)

Vladimir Ilich Lenin, 1924 (English translation, 1939)

Khorosho!, 1927 (*Fine!*, 1939)

Vo ves' golos, 1930 (*At the Top of My Voice*, 1940)

Polnoe sobranie sochinenii, 1955-1961 (13 volumes)

Mayakovsky: Poems, 1965

Poems, 1972

OTHER LITERARY FORMS

Vladimir Mayakovsky (muh-yih-KAWF-skee) was primarily a poet, but he also wrote several plays, some prose works, and numerous propaganda pieces. His first play, *Vladimir Mayakovsky: Tragediya* (pr. 1913; *Vladimir Mayakovsky: A Tragedy*, 1968), displayed the characteristics that would become associated with him throughout his career: audacity, bombastic exuberance, a predilection for hyperbole, an undercurrent of pessimism, and, above all, an uncontrollable egotism (underscored by the title). In *Misteriya-buff* (pr., pb. 1918, 1921; *Mystery-bouffe*, 1933), subtitled "A Heroic, Epic and Satiric Presentation of Our Epoch," which Helen Muchnic has termed "a cartoon version of Marxist history," Mayakovsky presents the events of World War I as a class struggle between the Clean (the bourgeoisie) and the Unclean (the proletariat). His best two plays, written in the last years of his life, contain sharp satirical attacks on Soviet society. *Klop* (pr., pb. 1929; *The Bedbug*, 1931) depicts a proletarian in the 1920's who forsakes his class by showing bourgeois tendencies. He perishes in the fire during his tumultuous wedding. Resurrected after fifty years, he finds himself forsaken in turn by the future Soviet society. Mayakovsky's warnings about the possibly pernicious direction of the development of Soviet society fell on deaf ears, as did his attacks on Soviet bureaucracy in his last major work, *Banya* (pr., pb. 1930; *The Bathhouse*, 1963). Both plays were complete failures when they were performed in the last year of the author's life. Among the best plays in Soviet literature, they met with greater approval three decades later.

ACHIEVEMENTS

Perhaps Vladimir Mayakovsky's greatest achievement as a poet was his incarnation of the revolutionary spirit in Russian literature. He was indeed the primary poet of the Russian Revolution: Right or wrong, he was able to instill the revolutionary spirit into his poetry and to pass it over to his readers. His hold on their fancy and admiration is still alive today. As a member of the Futurist movement, which he helped to organize in Russia, he brought new life into poetry by providing a viable alternative to Symbolism, which had been the dominant force in Russian poetry in the preceding two decades. Mayakovsky effected many innovations by following trends in other national literatures, thus bringing Russian poetry closer to the mainstream of world literature. He could not speak or read any foreign language, but he was always keenly interested in other literatures. His inimitable free verse set a standard for decades. He made the language of the street acceptable to the newly developing taste of both readers and critics, thus appealing to a wide audience despite his excesses. He has had many followers among poets, but none of them has been able to approximate his greatness.

BIOGRAPHY

Vladimir Vladimirovich Mayakovsky was born on July 19, 1893, in Bagdadi (a small town that was later renamed after him), where his father was a forester. From his early childhood, he showed himself to be independent and strong-willed. Although he was not a very good student, he possessed a remarkable memory for facts and long passages from poetry and other books. His childhood and early youth passed amid social unrest and rebellions. Because his entire family leaned toward the revolutionaries, Mayakovsky, too, participated in workers' demonstrations, giving his father's guns to the rebels, reading Socialist literature, and preparing himself for a lifelong revolutionary activism.

In 1906, after the death of Mayakovsky's father, the family moved to Moscow, where Mayakovsky entered high school and continued his association with the revolutionaries. He was accepted by the Communist Party when he was only fourteen and was arrested three times for his underground work. The last time, he was kept in jail eleven months, during which he read voraciously, becoming familiar with the classics of Russian literature for the first time. After his release, he decided to go back to school rather than devote all his time to political activity. Because of his activism, however, he was al-

lowed to enroll only in an art school, where he fostered his natural talent for drawing and painting. There, he met David Burlyuk, an artist and poet who encouraged him not only in his artistic endeavors but also as a poet, after Mayakovsky's timid beginnings. Together they formed the backbone of the Russian Futurists, a group that had some affinities with Filippo Tommaso Marinetti's Futurism, although Russian Futurism originated independently from the Italian movement. In 1912, the Russian Futurists issued a manifesto, appropriately titled "Poshchechina obshchestvennomu vkusu" ("A Slap in the Face of the Public Taste"), which included a poem by Mayakovsky. He spent the years before the Russian Revolution writing and publishing poetry, making scandal-provoking public appearances, continuing his revolutionary activity, and impressing everyone with his powerful voice and imposing phy-

Vladimir Mayakovsky (©Bettman/CORBIS)

sique, especially the police. He was not called into the czarist army because of his political unreliability, but during the Revolution, as well as in its aftermath, he helped the cause by drawing posters and writing captions for them and composing slogans, marching songs, and propaganda leaflets.

After the Revolution, however, Mayakovsky began to voice his dissatisfaction with Soviet policies and to fight the burgeoning bureaucracy, which remained his greatest enemy for the rest of his life. He especially disliked the seeming betrayal of revolutionary ideals on the part of the new Soviet establishment. He fell in love with Lili Brik, the wife of his close friend, the critic Osip Brik. He traveled abroad often, including a four-month-long trip to the United States, to which he reacted both favorably and critically. During his visit to Paris, he fell in love with a young Russian émigré woman. His efforts to persuade her to return with him to the Soviet Union were fruitless. This failure, along with other disappointments, led to periods of depression. He had become one of the leading poets in Soviet literature and the poet of the Russian Revolution, yet he and the circle centered on the journal *LEF* (founded by Mayakovsky in 1923) fought protracted and bitter battles with the literary establishment.

LEF, an acronym standing for *Levy front iskusstva* ("left front of art"), was an independent movement of avant-garde artists and writers organized under Mayakovsky's leadership. As Soviet cultural policy, initially supportive of the avant-garde, turned more conservative, LEF was suppressed, and its eponymous journal was forced to cease publication. In January of 1930, an exhibition that Mayakovsky organized to celebrate his twenty years of writing and graphic work was boycotted by Soviet cultural officials and fellow writers. His increasing dissatisfaction with the regime, his repeated failures in love, a prolonged throat illness, the failure of his plays, and a deep-seated disposition toward self-destruction, which he had often expressed in the past, caused him to commit suicide in his Moscow apartment on April 14, 1930. His death stunned the nation but also provoked harsh criticism of his act. A few years later, however, he received his due as a poet and as a revolutionary, a recognition that is increasing with time.

ANALYSIS

Vladimir Mayakovsky's poetry can be divided into three general categories. In the first group are the poems with political themes, often written on ephemeral occasions as everyday political exigencies demanded. These poems represent the weakest and indeed some of the silliest verses in his opus and are, for the most part, forgotten. The second group contains his serious revolutionary poems, in which he expressed his loyalty to the Revolution as a way of life and as "the holy washerwoman [who] will wash away all filth from the face of the earth with her soap." There are some excellent poems in this group, for they reflect Mayakovsky's undying faith in, and need for, an absolute that would give him strength to live and create, an absolute that he found in communism. Undoubtedly the best poems from the aesthetic point of view, however, are those from the third group, in which Mayakovsky writes about himself and his innermost feelings. These poems, which are more revealing of his true personality than all the loudly proclaimed utterances that made him famous, are the most likely to endure.

Mayakovsky's development as a poet parallels closely his life experiences. As he was growing into a fiery young revolutionary, his early poetry reflected his ebullience and combative spirit. His first poems, contained in Futurist publications, revealed his intoxication with the enormous power of words, a spirit that informs his entire oeuvre. The Futurist movement offered Mayakovsky a suitable platform from which to shout his messages. Indeed, it is difficult to say whether he joined Futurism for its tenets or Futurism embraced his volcanic energy, both as a poet and an activist, for its own purposes. The Futurists conceived of art as a social force and of the artist as a spokesperson for his age. To this end, new avenues of expression had to be found in the form of a "trans-sense" language in which words are based not so much on their meaning as on sounds and form.

YA AND A CLOUD IN PANTS

Much of Futurist dogma found in Mayakovsky an eager practitioner and an articulate spokesperson. His first serious work, a collection of four poems under the title *Ya*, already shows his intentions of "thrusting the dagger of desperate words/ into the swollen pulp of the sky." His most important prerevolutionary work, the long poem *A Cloud in Pants*, begins as a lamentation about an unanswered love but later turns into a treatise on social ills, punctuated forcefully with slogans such as "Down with your love!" "Down with your art!" "Down with your social order!" "Down with your religion!" Such pugnacity corresponds closely to the irreverent rejection of the status quo in the Futurist manifesto "A Slap in the Face of the Public Taste":

> The past is stifling. The Academy and Pushkin are incomprehensible hieroglyphs. We must throw Pushkin, Dostoevsky, Tolstoy, etc. from the boat of modernity.

The title of the poem reveals Mayakovsky's predilection for a striking metaphor: The cloud symbolizes the poet flying high above everything, while the trousers bring him down to Earth.

150,000,000

The poems Mayakovsky wrote during the Revolution bear more or less the same trademarks. The most characteristic of them, *150,000,000*, was inspired by the American intervention in the Russian Civil War on the side of anti-Bolsheviks. It was published anonymously (the ruse did not work, though), as if 150 million Soviet citizens had written it. The central theme, the struggle between the East and the West, is depicted in a typically Mayakovskian fashion. The East is personified by Ivan (the most common Russian name), who has 150 million heads and whose arms are as long as the Neva River. The West is represented by President Woodrow Wilson, who wears a hat in the form of the Eiffel Tower. Undoubtedly the poet believed that the more grotesque the expression, the more effective the message. He sets the tone at the very beginning:

> 150,000,000 are the makers of this poem.
> Its rhythm is a bullet.
> Its rhyme is fire sweeping from building to building.
> 150,000,000 speak with my lips.
> This edition is printed
> with human steps
> on the paper of city squares.

The protagonist of the poem is in reality the masses, as in another work of this time, the play *Mystery-bouffe*,

and in many other works by Mayakovsky. This tendency of the poet to lose himself behind the anonymity of collectivism runs alongside an equally strong tendency to place himself in the center of the universe and to have an inflated opinion of himself, as shown in "An Extraordinary Adventure," where he invites the sun to a tea as an equally important partner in the process of creativity.

SUPPORTING THE REVOLUTION

After the Revolution, Mayakovsky continued to help the regime establish itself, to contribute to the new literature in his country, and to feud with other literary groups. With the introduction of the New Economic Policy (NEP), however, which allowed a return to a modified, small-scale capitalism, Mayakovsky was among many supporters of the Revolution who felt that the ideals for which so much had been sacrificed were being betrayed. His opposition was somewhat muted; instead of attacking directly, he found a surrogate in the ever-growing bureaucracy. He also detected a resurgence of bourgeois and philistine habits, even among the party members and supporters of the regime, who, "callousing their behinds from five-year sittings,/ shiny-hard as washbasin toilets," worried more about their raises and ball attire than about society's welfare. In the poem "In Re Conferences," he lashes out at the new malaise in the Russian society—incessant conferences, actually an excuse to evade work. At the same time, in "Order No. 2 to the Army of the Arts," he exhorts artists to "give us a new form of art." When Vladimir Ilich Lenin died in 1924, Mayakovsky wrote a long poem eulogizing the great leader, using this opportunity to reaffirm his loyalty to pure communism as personified by Lenin.

ABOUT THAT

During this period, along with poetry on political themes, Mayakovsky wrote poems of an excruciatingly personal nature. The best illustration of this dichotomy in his personality, and one of the most dramatic and disturbing love poems in world literature, *About That*, reveals the poet's unhappiness in his love affair with Lili Brik. More important, however, it lays bare his "agony of isolation, a spiritual isolation," in the words of Helen Muchnic. Belaboring the nature of love, which he does on numerous occasions, the poet is forced to conclude that he is destined to suffer defeat after defeat in love, for reasons he cannot understand. He calls for help, he considers suicide, and he feels abandoned by all, even by those who are closest to him. In retrospect, one can see in these expressions of loneliness and despair signs of what was to come several years later.

BEYOND THE SOVIET UNION

For the time being, however, Mayakovsky found enough strength to continue his various activities and skirmishes with many enemies. A fateful decision was put off during his several trips abroad in the mid-1920's. In poems resulting from these journeys, he was remarkably objective about the world outside the Soviet Union, although he never failed to mention his pride in being a Soviet citizen. In addition to predictable criticism of the evils of capitalist societies, he expressed his awe before the technical achievements of Western urban centers:

> Here
> stood Mayakovsky,
> stood
> composing verse, syllable by syllable.
> I stare
> as an Eskimo gapes at a train,
> I seize on it
> as a tick fastens to an ear.
> Brooklyn Bridge—
> yes . . .
> That's quite a thing!

It was easy for Mayakovsky to voice such unrestrained praise for the "wonders" of the modern world, for he always believed that the urban life was the only way of life worth living.

The trips abroad, however, troubled Mayakovsky more than he acknowledged. In addition to another unhappy love affair, with the beautiful young Russian émigré Tatyana Yakovleva, he was disturbed by his firsthand experience of the West. After his return, he wrote several poems affirming his loyalty to the Soviet regime in a manner suggesting that he was trying to convince himself of his orthodoxy. It is difficult to ascertain, however, whether Mayakovsky was fully aware at this time of the depth of his obsequiousness and, if he was, why he wrote that way. Several

years later, in *At the Top of My Voice*, which was written only three months before his suicide, he would admit the true nature of his submission: "But I/ subdued/ myself,/ setting my heel/ on the throat/ of my own song."

FINE!

Another long poem, *Fine!*, written to celebrate the tenth anniversary of the October Revolution, shows not only Mayakovsky's compulsive optimism but also the signs that his poetic power was diminishing: "Life/ was really/ never/ so good!" he exclaims unabashedly.

> In the cottages
> —farmer lads
> Bushy-beards
> cabbages.
> Dad's rest
> by the hearth.
> All of them
> crafty.
> Plough the earth,
> make
> poetry.

Such idyllic gushing may have reflected truthfully the poet's feelings and observations in 1927, but it is remarkable that only a year or two later he would unleash in his plays a scathing criticism of the same land where "gladness gushes." It is more likely that Mayakovsky wanted to believe what he had written or, more tragically, that he was writing in compliance with an order for a certain kind of poem.

DEPRESSION AND SUICIDE

Mayakovsky's suicide in 1930 showed that everything was not all right, either in his personal life or in his country. Although the act surprised many people, even those professing to have been very close to him, keen observers had felt that Mayakovsky was riddled with morbid pessimism throughout his mature life, his loud rhetoric notwithstanding. Indeed, one could go as far back as 1913 to find, in his very first poem, words such as these: "I am so lonely as the only eye/ of a man on his way to the blind." As early as 1916, in *The Backbone Flute*, he wondered whether he should end his life with a bullet. On another occasion at about that time, in "Chelovek" ("Man"), he stated bluntly:

The heart yearns for a bullet
while
the throat raves of a razor
. . . The soul shivers;
she's caught in ice,
and there's no escape for her.

In a poem discussed earlier, *About That*, he debates with himself whether he should follow the example of a member of the Communist Youth League who had committed suicide. In his last completed poem, *At the Top of My Voice*, he addresses his "most respected comrades of posterity" to explain what he had wanted to achieve in poetry, not trusting contemporary literary critics and historians to tell the truth. Among the incomplete poems found in his apartment after his death, there was a quatrain that may have been intended by Mayakovsky as a suicide note:

And, as they say, the incident is closed.
Love's boat has smashed against the daily grind.
Now you and I are quits. Why bother then
to balance mutual sorrows, pains, and hurts.

The word "love" in the second line was changed to "life" by Mayakovsky in a handwritten version of this stanza.

Whatever the reasons for his suicide, Mayakovsky's death brought to an end a promising career that symbolized for a long time the birth of the new spirit in Russian literature. The eminent literary critic Roman Jakobson saw in his death the work of an entire generation that had squandered its poets. Boris Pasternak brought into focus a virtue of many Soviet writers, both well known and unsung, when he speculated that Mayakovsky "shot himself out of pride because he had condemned something in himself or around himself with which his self-respect could not be reconciled." Placing the heavy hand of officialdom on the memory of the poet who had spent half of his life fighting insensitive officials, Joseph Stalin praised him belatedly: "Mayakovsky was and remains the best and most talented poet of our Soviet epoch. Indifference to his memory and his work is a crime."

VERSIFICATION AND NEOLOGISMS

The work of this great poet will survive both his human weaknesses and the vagaries of the time and place in which he had to create. Although Mayakovsky was not the first in Russian poetry to use free verse, he wrote it with a verve unequaled before or after him. He rhymes sparingly and unconventionally. He seldom divides verses into stanzas; instead, he breaks them into units according to their inner rhythm, producing a cascading effect.

Another strong feature of Mayakovsky's verse is the abundant use of neologisms; there is an entire dictionary of expressions created by him. Mayakovsky also used slang with abandon, deeming any expression acceptable if it suited his purpose; he is credited with bringing the language of the street into Russian poetry. The sound of his verse is richly textured—indeed, his poems are better heard than read.

When this richness of style is added to his original approach to poetry and to his thought-provoking subject matter, the picture of Mayakovsky as one of the most important and exciting poets of the twentieth century is complete.

OTHER MAJOR WORKS

PLAYS: *Vladimir Mayakovsky: Tragediya*, pr. 1913 (*Vladimir Mayakovsky: A Tragedy*, 1968); *Misteriya-buff*, pr., pb. 1918, 1921 (*Mystery-bouffe*, 1933); *A chto y esli? Pervomayskiye grezy v burzhuaznom kresle*, pr. 1920; *Chempionat vsemirnoy klassovoy borby*, pr. 1920 (*The Championship of the Universal Class*, 1973); *Pyeska pro popov, koi ne pobnimayut, prazdnik chto takoye*, pr. 1921; *Kak kto provodit vremya, prazdniki prazdnuya*, pr. 1922; *Radio-Oktyabr*, pr. 1926 (with Osip Brik); *Klop*, pr., pb. 1929 (*The Bedbug*, 1931); *Banya*, pr., pb. 1930 (*The Bathhouse*, 1963); *Moskva gorit*, pr. 1930 (*Moscow Is Burning*, 1973); *The Complete Plays*, 1968.

SCREENPLAYS: *Baryyshyna i khuligan*, 1918; *Ne dlya deneg rodivshiisya*, 1918 (adaptation of Jack London's novel *Martin Eden*); *Serdtse kino*, 1926; *Dekadyuvkov i Oktyabryukhov*, 1928.

NONFICTION: "Kak rabotaet respublika demokraticheskaya," 1922; "Kak delat' stikhi?," 1926 (*How Are Verses Made?*, 1970); *Moye Otkrytiye Ameriki*, 1926 (*My Discovery of America*, 2005).

BIBLIOGRAPHY

Aizlewood, Robin. *Two Essays on Maiakovskii's Verse*. London: University College London Press,

2000. Two short studies of selected poetic works by Mayakovsky.

Almereyda, Michael, ed. *Night Wraps the Sky: Writings by and About Mayakovsky*. New York: Farrar, Straus and Giroux, 2008. Filmmaker Almereyda gathers translations of Mayakovsky's poetry, along with memoirs, artistic appreciations, and eyewitness accounts to produce a profile of a man.

Brown, Edward J. *Mayakovsky: A Poet in the Revolution*. Princeton, N.J.: Princeton University Press, 1973. Discussion of Mayakovsky in his times and in relationship to artists, poets, critics, and revolutionaries including Vladimir Ilich Lenin and Joseph Stalin. Shows how Mayakovsky's work was shaped by events of his life and discusses his relationship to the Soviet state and Communist Party.

Cavanaugh, Clare. "Whitman, Mayakovsky, and the Body Politic." In *Rereading Russian Poetry*, edited by Stephanie Sandler. New Haven, Conn.: Yale University Press, 1999. Discusses the influence of the American poet Walt Whitman on Mayakovsky and the ways in which Mayakovsky sought to overcome this influence or to displace Whitman as a poet of the people and of self-celebration. This fresh, postmodern perspective emphasizes the body and sexuality in the work of Mayakovsky, in terms both literal and symbolic.

Stapanian, Juliette R. *Mayakovsky's Cubo-Futurist Vision*. Houston, Tex.: Rice University Press, 1986. Examines Mayakovsky from the perspective of the artistic movements of cubism and Futurism. Places Mayakovsky not simply within the social and political revolutionary movements of his day but also within the aesthetics of literary and artistic modernism.

Woroszylski, Wiktor. *The Life of Mayakovsky*. New York: Orion Press, 1970. The life of Mayakovsky as told through a variety of records, testimonies, and recollections, which are then arranged in accordance with the author's understanding of their place in Mayakovsky's life. Recollections include that of Boris Pasternak, Ilya Ehrenberg, Lily Brik, and Ivan Bunin. Includes copious illustrations and passages from Mayakovsky's poetry.

Vasa D. Mihailovich

MENG HAORAN

Born: Xianyang, China; 689
Died: Xianyang, China; 740
Also known as: Meng Hao-jan

PRINCIPAL POETRY

Meng Haoran shi ji, 745-750 (collected poems)
Meng Hao-jan, 1981 (Paul Kroll, translator)
The Mountain Poems of Meng Hao-jan, 2004 (David Hinton, translator)

OTHER LITERARY FORMS

Meng Haoran (muhng how-rahn) is known only for his poetry; no other literary works by him are known to exist.

ACHIEVEMENTS

Meng Haoran is considered the first great poet of the Tang Dynasty (618-907) in China. His poetry influenced later writers and affected Chinese poetic sensibilities for centuries to come, securing Meng lasting literary fame in China. Meng's contemporaries and later Chinese poets have admired his keen eye for specific features of the natural landscape, particularly mountains and rivers, and the personal emotion infused in his poems, which are rich in literary allusions. These allusions are not surprising; a classical Chinese poet would be expected to demonstrate mastery of earlier literary traditions.

Meng has been credited with invigorating Chinese poetry by bringing a carefully shaped measure of originality to the conventions of Chinese lyrics established in the fourth and fifth centuries. His poetry inspired his friends and subsequent Tang poets to attempt more innovative work and launched a great flowering of Chinese poetry. Even though only 270 of his poems have survived, in part because he destroyed many poems he deemed faulty, Meng's poems were widely anthologized in various collections after his death. His most famous poems were continuously read, appreciated, and studied by subsequent generations of Chinese poets and scholars.

BIOGRAPHY

Meng Haoran was born in 689 during the Tang Dynasty. His birthplace was his parent's family estate, South Garden, just outside the Chinese city of Xianyang in what is now Hubei province. His parents were small landowners, and he had two or three younger brothers and a sister. Meng's family claimed to be the descendants of the fourth century B.C.E. philosopher Mencius (also known as Mengzi or Meng-tzu), and his parents named the boy Haoran, meaning vast, boundless, or great, after a famous passage written by Mencius.

As landowners, Meng's parents could afford a classical education, stressing philosophy and literature, for the boy. This gave Meng the tools to create his poetry. In the fashion of the day, Meng exchanged his poems with fellow literate men. Meng married and had at least two sons.

At around the age of thirty, Meng started to write poetry to Tang Dynasty officials asking for an official appointment, as was usual for a young educated man. A surviving poem of that time makes reference to Meng's aging mother, for whom the son cannot provide enough food. Scholars doubt that Meng's mother really suffered from hunger and view this passage as a conventional way to justify Meng's request for a job out of filial duty.

At this time, Meng started to travel. First, he visited Luoyang, the eastern capital of the Tang Dynasty, where he made many literary friends but failed to gain employment. His many further travels in China inspired Meng to write poems to his appreciative friends about his impressions of the natural sights he encountered. At the age of thirty-nine, in 728, Meng finally tried to pass the *jinshi* exam for an imperial appointment. He failed.

Returning to Xianyang, Meng fashioned himself as a poet recluse who renounced the bustle of the world, and he took up temporary residence at famous Lumen Shan (Deer Gate Mountain), outside his estate. Meng's poetry impressed friends such as Zhang Jiuling, who secured for Meng the only position he ever held, as assistant investigator supporting Zhang. Friends commented that while Meng was employed, from late 737 until his resignation in the summer of 738, he and Zhang wrote poetry together while traveling on official business.

In 740, in Xianyang, Meng's back became infected. He died either from the infection or from eating spoiled raw fish after recovering from the infection. After Meng's death, from 745 to 750, Wang Shiyuan (Wang Shih-yüan), a local Daoist from nearby Icheng (I-ch'eng) shrine, and Meng's younger brother Meng Xiran (Meng Hsi-jan) collected, edited, and published 218 of Meng's poems. Later additions brought Meng's surviving poems to 270. The oldest known surviving copy of Meng's poetry is preserved through a 1935 facsimile of a Song Dynasty (960-1279) woodblock edition.

ANALYSIS

A key characteristic of Meng Haoran's poetry is his attention to the nuances of natural landscapes together with his concrete images of the animals, plants, and people and buildings inhabiting these geographic regions. Critics have praised Meng for the variety of terms he uses for specific mountain features and his detailed descriptions of flora and fauna. His mountain poems are never generic but tied to very specific scenes.

Scholars have noted that Meng's poetry describes nature as perceived by the specific consciousness of the poet, thereby adding an individual vigor to his poems that distinguishes them. Meng's poems balance successfully the evocation of the persona's feelings, such as longing for home and friends or celebrating friendship, with the natural setting in which they take place. There is a social context to Meng's poems even when set in remote places.

Religion and spirituality enter Meng's poems whenever their setting encompasses a temple, shrine, or monastery. When this is a Buddhist place, Meng's poems show a keen perception of Buddhist teachings and history and successfully allude to them, tying a concrete location to a spiritual theme. When Meng's poems address Daoist themes, they tend to become less concrete. This more general reflection corresponds to Daoism's concern with the transcendent, extraterrestrial aspects of human consciousness.

A reader of Meng's poems in English translation should remember that, as with any translation, particularly of poetry, the translator has had to make difficult decisions as to how to render Meng's verse in accessible English. In the original Chinese, 254 of Meng's poems have only five characters (and therefore five syllables) per line. This means that any English translation cannot be both literal and poetic because English requires more than five syllables to capture the meaning that Meng's five syllables per line created for a Chinese reader. This means that translations of Meng's poems will vary depending on the translator.

MENG HAO-JAN

In his accessible 1981 book-length study of Meng's poetry, Paul Kroll offers his translations of many of Meng's most important poems. Kroll's translation uses a traditional, elevated diction to render the mood evoked by Meng's original Chinese syllables into poetic lines in English. As a result, Meng's poems sound somewhat like late nineteenth century English poetry, yet Kroll still manages to capture the central themes and concerns of Meng's poetry very well. For example, "I Pass the Night at My Teacher's Mountain Dwelling, Expecting Lord Ting Who Does Not Arrive," opens thus: "Evening's sunglow has crossed the west ridge;/ The serried straths suddenly, now, are dark-cast." Meng's attention to the effects of the light of early evening, as well as his detailed rendition of the natural features observed, emerges very well in this translation.

A key concern of Kroll's selection is to show how Meng's poetry goes beyond closely observed natural landscapes and covers a wide range of subjects. "Spring-time Complaint" features a young woman worrying about whom she may love, a query symbolized by her uncertainty over to whom she may give a blossom she has plucked by a pond reflecting her made-up features. "Drinking at the Official Residence in Hsiang-yang" celebrates the occasion of an official banquet in Meng's hometown of Xianyang (Hsiang-yang) and ends with the persona exclaiming exuberantly, "Pleasure and joy, we should preserve together."

Kroll groups his translations and analyses of Meng's poems by theme. He begins with the poems set around Meng's hometown, then those inspired by his travels and his interactions with his friends. Kroll convincingly challenges the traditional view of Meng as a mountain recluse, demonstrating that this image is more

a poetic fabrication than historical reality. Meng's poems with a Buddhist theme are compared with those with a Daoist theme. Buddhist poems focus on concrete images, whereas Daoist ones favor the abstract. "Inscribed at the Aranya of Lord Jung," referring to the Buddhist teacher's dwelling, describes in detail how "A flowing fountain wraps around its steps./ Caltrop and waterlily scent your teaching mat." In contrast, "The Water Pavilion of the Taoist Adept Mei," comments on the presence of the master, even in his absence: "Dwelling hidden, he is not to be seen;/ His lofty discourse no one is able to requite." Kroll closes his book with an evaluation of the lasting power of Meng's poems.

THE MOUNTAIN POEMS OF MENG HAO-JAN

The Mountain Poems of Meng Hao-jan, translated and edited by David Hinton, presents sixty-six of Meng's poems centering on mountain landscapes. Some of Meng's best and most widely admired poems are captured in this work. Hinton's translation emphasizes Meng's interest in Zen Buddhism and Daoist cosmology and tends to evoke the voice of a meditative persona rendering keen perceptions of the world around him. For example, in "Spring Dawn," one of Meng's most famous and widely anthologized poems, the persona appears surprised by the advent of dawn: "In spring sleep, dawn arrives unnoticed." He ends up wondering who can really know what happened during the night, in particular, how "few or many" blossoms were torn down by the night's storm. This demonstrates the persona's observant nature, which is nevertheless limited by the bounds of human perception and knowledge about natural and cosmic events.

Hinton captures well the atmosphere suffusing Meng's key poem, "Year's End, on Returning to Southern Mountains," which helped make the poet known as a mountain recluse. Written most likely after Meng failed the imperial exam at age thirty-nine, the first couplet establishes the persona's decision to quit trying for imperial employment:

> No more hope of advising high ministers,
> I return to my hut in southern mountains

There is a sense of pain and regret as the persona states that he is unworthy of imperial employment, but he does not say if his failure to gain employment is because of an objective reason or a capricious judgment by the authorities. He also laments sickness, the absence of friends, and the advent of white hair before reaching some sort of comfort in the light of the moon through the pines at his home.

Overall, Hinton's selection of poems gives the reader a fine sense of how Meng combines a detailed rendition of natural landscapes with the persona's various feelings. The social quality of Meng's poetry becomes apparent as so many of his poems are addressed to friends and acquaintances or describe visits to them. At times, Meng's poetry also contains wonderful renditions of the emotions of the traveler. In "Overnight on Abiding-Integrity River," the second line spells it out explicitly: "It's dusk, time a traveler's loneliness returns"; dusk is a favorite time of day in Meng's poetry. Hinton's translation gives the reader a good sense of the key themes and the beauty of Meng's mountain poems.

BIBLIOGRAPHY

Hinton, David, trans. and ed. *Mountain Home: The Wilderness Poetry of Ancient China*. New York: New Directions, 2005. This collection of poetry contains an introduction to Meng's poetry and a representative selection in translation. Places Meng in the context of Tang and Song Dynasty poets with similar poetic interests. Map, introduction, notes, and bibliography.

Kroll, Paul W. *Meng Hao-jan*. Boston: Twayne, 1981. Full-length study of the poet and his works; offers translations of many of Meng's most famous poems. Relates Meng's poetry to his native place, his friends, culture, society, and religion, and illustrates his wide range of subjects. Illustrations, notes, bibliography, and index.

Levy, Andre. *Chinese Literature, Ancient and Classical*. Translated by William H. Nienhauser, Jr. Bloomington: Indiana University Press, 2000. Chapter 3, "Poetry," briefly discusses the achievement of Meng and indicates his place within the poetry of the Tang Dynasty, an era that had a lasting effect on Chinese poetry. Index.

Meng Haoran. *The Mountain Poems of Meng Hao-jan.*

Translated and edited by David Hinton. New York: Archipelago Books, 2004. Contains a translation of sixty-six poems by Meng. Hinton's introduction places the poet in the context of Tang Dynasty culture and poetry, focusing on Meng's association with Zen Buddhism and explaining how this and Daoism inform the content and form of his poetry. Map, notes, and bibliography.

R. C. Lutz

GABRIELA MISTRAL
Lucila Godoy Alcayaga

Born: Vicuña, Chile; April 7, 1889
Died: Hempstead, New York; January 10, 1957

PRINCIPAL POETRY
Desolación, 1922
Ternura, 1924 (enlarged 1945)
Tala, 1938
Antología, 1941
Lagar, 1954
Selected Poems of Gabriela Mistral, 1957
Poesías completas, 1958
Poema de Chile, 1967
A Gabriela Mistral Reader, 1993

OTHER LITERARY FORMS

Although the poems published in the three main collections of Gabriela Mistral (mee-STROL) are the principal source for her recognition, she was active until her death as a contributor of prose to newspapers and journals throughout Latin America. She also wrote for newspapers whenever she was abroad, and her translated articles appeared frequently in the local press. The quality of this extensive and continuous journalistic effort is not consistent, though Mistral's prose style has been recognized for its personal accent and spontaneity. Her articles were extremely varied in theme. Much of what she wrote supported principles espoused in her poetry. Though less introspective, the prose, like the poetry, relates closely to the author's life and derives

Gabriela Mistral (Library of Congress)

from episodes that left a profound mark on her. It is combative, direct, and abrupt while revealing her sincerity and ceaseless search for truth and justice.

ACHIEVEMENTS

Latin America's most honored woman poet, Gabriela Mistral was awarded the 1945 Nobel Prize in Literature. The first Latin American writer to be so honored, she was selected as the most characteristic voice of a rich literature that had until then been denied that coveted award. The intrinsic merits of her work, described as lyricism inspired by vigorous emotion, were representative of the idealism of the Hispanic American world.

Mistral's popularity was keen throughout her adult life, during which she received the National Award for Chilean Literature and honorary doctorates from the University of Florence, the University of Chile, the University of California, and Columbia University.

Neither a disciple of Rubén Darío nor a contributor

to the poetic revolution of the vanguard movements (though there are elements of both in her work), Mistral maintained independence from literary groups, preferring to consider herself an outsider. Nevertheless, her personal effort was a ceaseless labor toward unity, in which she pressed her genius into the service of brotherhood among nations, responsibility in professional activity, regard for future generations, appreciation for native American culture, effective education, love for the weak and oppressed, and a yearning for social justice.

All these endeavors are rooted in the principal sentiment of Mistral's poetry—her unsatisfied desire for motherhood. This emotion is in Mistral both a feminine instinct and a religious yearning for fulfillment. She elevates her great feminine anguish to the heights of art; this is her originality.

BIOGRAPHY

Gabriela Mistral was born Lucila Godoy Alcayaga, the child of Chilean parents of Spanish heritage, probably mixed with Indian ancestry. She was said to be part Basque, owing to her mother's last name, and part Jewish, only because her paternal grandmother possessed a Bible and schooled the eager child in its verses. The poet accepted this presumed inheritance, attributing to herself the energy of the Basque, the tenacity of the Jew, and the melancholy of the Indian. When she was three years old, her father left home and never returned. The task of rearing Mistral was shared by her mother and her half sister, Emelina. Both women were teachers and provided the child with primary instruction and a thirst for additional knowledge. Timid and reserved, the young girl had few friends. During her last year of primary instruction, she was falsely accused of wasting classroom materials. Unable to defend herself against this accusation and further victimized when classmates threw stones at her, she was sent home and was taught by Emelina. This first encounter with injustice and human cruelty left a profound impression on the future poet, who became determined to speak out for the rights of the defenseless, the humble, and the poor.

The family moved to La Serena on Chile's coast in 1901. Three years later, the fourteen-year-old Mistral's prose began to appear in local periodicals. These writings seemed somewhat revolutionary in a provincial town and probably accounted for the poet's admission to, and then expulsion from, the normal school. Undeterred, the family continued tutoring her while she finished her studies. In 1905, she began to work as a teacher's assistant. For the next five years, she taught in the primary grades, while nurturing her early work as a writer. This initial poetry possessed a melancholy flavor in tune with poets with whom she was familiar. Certified as an educator in 1910, she began a career as a high school teacher that took her throughout her native country. All during her life, she would characterize herself as a simple rural teacher, and she liked to be remembered as such, more than as a diplomat or a poet. She taught for more than twenty years, assuming the role of spiritual guide for many who approached her. Near the end of her career as an educator, Chile named her Teacher of the Nation. A good portion of her literary work, which has an educational motive, is directed toward young people. Behind the writer is the teacher who desires to encourage moral and spiritual awareness and aesthetic sensitivity.

With the publication of her first book in 1922, the poet's literary name, Gabriela Mistral, definitively replaced her birth name. The name Gabriela was chosen for the archangel Gabriel, one who brings good tidings, and Mistral was chosen for the dry wind that blows in the Mediterranean area of Provence. Also in 1922, Mistral left Chile for Mexico, where she had been invited by José Vasconcelos, secretary of education in Mexico, to participate in a national program of educational reform. Intending at first to stay for six months, she remained in Mexico for two years. This sabbatical began a lifetime of travel during which the poet occupied diplomatic posts, represented her country in international and cultural gatherings, and participated in numerous intellectual endeavors.

In 1932, Mistral became a member of the consular corps of the Chilean government, fulfilling various diplomatic assignments in Spain, Portugal, France, Brazil, and the United States. At the same time, she continued a life of writing and intellectual pursuits. She taught Latin American literature at the University of Puerto Rico and at several institutions in the United States. In 1953, she became the Chilean delegate to the United Nations, where she served until poor health forced her to retire.

ANALYSIS

Through a poetry that is at times deliberately crude and prosaic, Gabriela Mistral distinguished herself as an artist of tenderness and compassion. Her themes are nourished by her personal sorrow, which she ably elevates to the realm of the universal. Maternity, children, love, God, the fight against instinct, the soul of things, are voiced in anguish and in reverence by this most feminine of poets, whose vigor belies her femininity and whose high concept of morality is always present but never militant.

Mistral's three major collections of poems, *Desolación*, *Tala*, and *Lagar*, were published at sixteen-year intervals. They contain a selection of poems from among the many that the poet produced in newspapers during the intervening years. Each volume comprises material that was written at different times and under changing circumstances; thus, a strict topical unity is not to be expected. Each volume was published in response to an external stimulus that affected the life of the poet.

DESOLACIÓN

Desolación was compiled through the initiative of Federico de Onís, professor of Spanish at Columbia University and founder of the Hispanic Institute. Onís had selected the poet's work as the theme for a lecture that he gave at the institute in 1921. The participants, primarily Spanish teachers from the United States, were deeply impressed by the depth and beauty of this vigorous new voice in Hispanic American poetry, and when they discovered that the poet had not yet published a book, Onís insisted on publishing the collection under the auspices of the Hispanic Institute.

The unity of the book is the body of moving, impassioned poems that were inspired by two painful experiences in the life of the youthful poet. While a teacher in La Cantera, Mistral became romantically involved with an employee of the railroad company, but because of bitter differences, they ended the relationship. When the young man later committed suicide for reasons unrelated to his association with the poet, Mistral was deeply affected. Several years later, she met a young poet from Santiago with whom she fell passionately in love. When he rejected her in favor of someone from Santiago's wealthy elite, Mistral was crushed. Shortly thereafter, she requested a transfer to Punta Arenas in Chile's inhospitable southland.

Inasmuch as the poems inspired by these devastating episodes do not appear in chronological order, one reads them as if the poet were relating the history of a single painful love. With great lyrical strength, she expresses the awakening of love, the joy and self-consciousness, the boldness, timidity, hope, humiliation, and jealousy. The poems that deal with suicide of the beloved reveal the poet's anguish and her petition to God concerning his salvation. She wonders about his afterlife and expresses her loneliness, remorse, and obsession to be with him still. The poet is pained and in torment, yet in her vigor, she displays jealousy, revenge, and hate, all of which are employed to combat the demanding powers of an enslaving, fateful love. God is petitioned in her own behalf as well. The agony is tempered at intervals by tenderness, her disillusionment nurtured by hope, her pain anointed with pleasure, and the hunger for death soothed by a reverence for life. In her moments of rapture, there is sorrow and loneliness, identified with the agony of Christ, from whom the poet seeks rest and peace in his presence.

The language of these poems is natural, simple, and direct. It is the realism of one who has lived close to the earth, who eschews delicate subtleties in favor of frankness. Mistral's love is expressed with passion and wrath; her words are coarse, bordering on crudity. This is chaste poetry, nevertheless, inasmuch as its fundamental longing for motherhood and the spiritual yearning for God reject the possibility of eroticism or immodesty.

Mistral lifts her spirit up though it is weighed down in anguish. It is suffering that does not destroy, but brings the spirit to life. The lyrical roots of *Desolación* are not a product of imagination: They are a lived tragedy. When Mistral begins to regard her lost youth, foreseeing the seal of fate in her sterility, condemned to perpetual loneliness, she raises a prolonged, sharp moan. Her entire being protests, argues, and begs at the same time. Overcome, the poet mourns her desolation, her martyrdom in not being able to be the mother of a child from the man she loved. This maternal yearning is not simply the impulse toward the preservation of the race. It is the tender cry of one who loves, who lives in agony over the loss of that which is closest to the ultimate joy of her soul.

Mistral's poetry employs a great variety of verse forms. She freely used sonnets, tercets, quatrains, the five-line stanza, sextains, ballads, and other forms, with little regard for the conventional patterns. She favored the Alexandrine, the hendecasyllabic line, and the nine-syllable line, which gradually became her preferred form; the latter seems to blend well with the slow pace of much of her poetry. The poems in *Desolación* do not follow classical models. Mistral toys with new rhymes, in which her consonants are imperfect or are interspersed with assonances. The artist has been accused of an inability to deal properly with metric forms. It is true that she lacked a musical sense. Her images, too, are frequently grotesque, too close to death and violence. Together with poems of rough, unpolished form in *Desolación*, there are others that are flawless in construction. Mistral reworked many of her poems repeatedly, the result generally being a refinement, although at times it was a disappointment. Her major objective was the power of the word rather than the meter of the lines.

Mistral concludes *Desolación* with the request that God forgive her for this bitter book, imploring men who consider life as sweetness to pardon her also. She promises in the future to leave her pain behind and to sing words of hope and love for others.

TALA

Tala fulfilled this promise sixteen years later. She compiled these poems as a concrete gesture to relieve the suffering of the children of Spain who had been uprooted from their homes during the Spanish Civil War (1936-1939). Mistral was disappointed and ashamed that Latin America had not appeared to share her grief for the plight of these homeless children, and the proceeds from the sale of this volume alleviated the difficulties in the children's camps. The title of the book refers to the felling of trees and applies to both the poems themselves and the purpose for which the author compiled them. The limbs are cut from the living trunk and offered as a gift, a part of oneself, a creation. From within the poet who has made her offering, there remains the assumption of the growth of a new forest. *Tala* has its pain (with allusions to the death of the poet's mother), but this volume is more serene than its predecessor. Mistral controls her emotions to a degree, and happiness, hope, and peace flow in her songs. *Tala* speaks of the beauties of America, as the poet humanizes, spiritualizes, and orders the creatures of the continent around the presence of humankind. Mistral gathers all things together, animate and inanimate, nourishes them like children, and sings of them in love, wonder, thanksgiving, and happiness. Far from America, she has felt the nostalgia of the foreigner for home, and she desires to stimulate the youth of her native soil to complete the tasks that are ahead.

Mistral sees Hispanic America as one great people. She employs the sun and the Andes Mountains as elements that bind the nations geographically, and she calls for a similar spiritual kinship. She believed that governments should be born of the needs of nations; they should emphasize education, love, respect for manual labor, and identification with the lower classes. Like José Vasconcelos, she believed that American man has a mission to discover new zones of the spirit that harmonize with the new civilization in which he lives. The poet treats this subject with great enthusiasm, declaring also that there is much in the indigenous past that merits inclusion in the present. She invokes the pre-Columbian past with nostalgia, feeling remorse for the loss of the Indian's inheritance and his acceptance of destiny.

The maternal longing of the poet is the mainspring of Mistral's many lullabies and verses for children that appear in this and other volumes. The other constant, implicitly present in all the poems of *Tala*, is God. She approaches God along paths of suffering, self-discipline, and a deep understanding of the needs of her fellow people. In God, she seeks peace from her suffering, comfort in her loneliness, and perfection. Her ability to humanize all things grows from her desire to find God everywhere. Thus these objects and the wonder derived from them infuse the religious into the poet's creation. Her metaphors and images derive from the contemplation of nature and its relationship with the divine. More objective than the poetry of *Desolación*, this work retains its personal, lyrical quality.

TERNURA

Ternura (tenderness) is a collection of Mistral's children's poems. First published in 1924, it consisted of the children's verses that had appeared in *Desolación*. The 1945 edition added more poems for children that the author had written up to that date. The principal emotion is depicted in the title. The poet sings lullabies, rounds, and games, following traditional Spanish verse forms, especially the ballad. The poems generally teach a moral lesson, such as love and respect for others, development of one's sense of right and beauty, reverence for nature, country, and the creations of God. In Mistral's later children's verses, she sought to create a distinctly American atmosphere. Her vocabulary and background reflect regional and local material, drawing generously from Indian culture and beliefs.

The unique relationship between mother and child is felt in Mistral's soft, unhurried lullabies, in which the mother tenderly gives herself to the peace of her offspring, softly engendering in the child a reverence for Earth and all its creatures. She expresses the inner wounds of her heart, but in a tender fashion that does not disturb her baby. The only father in these verses is God, who becomes the source toward whom the yearning mother directs the child.

LAGAR

Lagar (wine press) was published less than three years before Mistral's death. Together with the lack of world peace, the years brought new personal tragedies in the suicide of two of Mistral's closest friends and the devastating suicide of her nephew, Juan Miguel Godoy, whom she had reared like a son. Her health declined, and she became preoccupied with thoughts of death. Restless, Mistral moved frequently during this period. *Lagar* tells of the imprint of these experiences on her soul. The wine press of life and death, ever draining her heart, has left her weak and exhausted. In theme, *Lagar* refers back to *Desolación*, though Mistral no longer regards death with the anger of her frustrated youth. She bids it come in silence in its own due time. She is more confident of herself, eliminating the prose glosses that accompanied earlier collections. Her simple, prosaic verses are austere and purified. They beckon to the world beyond the grave in a poetic atmosphere that is as spiritual as it is concrete. Fantasy, hallucination, and dreams all contribute to an ethereal environment governed by imagination and memory.

Like Mistral's other published collections, *Lagar* lacks topical harmony. Mistral delights the reader with playful songs, revels in her creativity, and feels at one with God; yet the pain and weariness of the ever-draining wine press constitute the dominant mood.

The suicide of her nephew, at seventeen, again brought to Mistral's poetry the agony, the terrible emptiness, and the liberation available only when one has renounced earthly life. The young Juan Miguel had been the poet's constant companion, sensitive and helping, the strongest motive for Mistral's own bond with life. With the passing of this last close relative, the poet's will to live became associated more with life beyond the grave than with earthly cares.

Other verses demonstrate the poet's concern with the effects of war. Mistral protests against injustice and identifies with those who suffer through no fault of their own. Religion, not according to a prescribed dogma but rather in a sense of spiritual communication between the living and the dead, along with the ever-present identification with nature, continues as an important theme. In *Lagar*, the fusion of these two motifs is more complete than in the poet's earlier work. Nature is viewed in a spiritual sense. There appears a need to be in contact with the earth and the simplicity of its teaching to maintain spiritual harmony with the divine. This thought comforts the poet, who searches for a spiritual state of knowledge and intelligence. By preceding her nouns with the first-person possessive, she assumes a personal stance not found in her work before, as if she were participating more completely in the process of creation. Indeed, she begins to overuse the adjective, not so much to describe physical attributes as to personify the inanimate and to engender a mood. The mood thus created generally drains or destroys. Past participles used as adjectives (burned, crushed, pierced) fortify this effort, thus strengthening the theme of the title and suggesting the travail of life on Earth as parallel to the crushing of grapes in the wine press.

POEMA DE CHILE

During her last years, Mistral worked intensely on correcting and organizing her numerous unedited and incomplete compositions. Her posthumous *Poema de Chile* is a collection of poems united by one theme, her native country, in which she carries on an imaginary dialogue with a child, "my little one," showing him the geography and the flora and fauna of Chile as they travel together.

BIBLIOGRAPHY

Arce de Vázquez, Margot. *Gabriela Mistral: The Poet and Her Work.* Translated by Helene Masslo Anderson. Ann Arbor: University of Michigan Press, 1990. Biography and critical study of Mistral and her work. Includes bibliographical references.

Castleman, William J. *Beauty and the Mission of the Teacher: The Life of Gabriela Mistral of Chile, Teacher, Poetess, Friend of the Helpless, Nobel Laureate.* Smithtown, N.Y.: Exposition Press, 1982. A biography of Mistral and her life as a teacher, poet, and diplomat. Includes a bibliography of Mistral's writing.

Horan, Elizabeth. *Gabriela Mistral: An Artist and Her People.* Washington, D.C.: Organization of American States, 1994. This biography of Mistral examines her life in Chile and the effect that the social conditions in her native land had on her poetry.

Marchant, Elizabeth. *Critical Acts: Latin American Women and Cultural Criticism.* Gainesville: University Press of Florida, 1999. This refreshing reevaluation of Latin American women writers during the first half of the twentieth century recognizes their overlooked contributions to the public sphere. The critic reconsiders some representative poems, focusing on the dichotomy between Mistral's theories and practices and the female intellectual's alienation from the public sphere. Although Mistral refused a traditional societal role for herself, she advocated it for her readership.

Peña, Karen. *Poetry and the Realm of the Public Intellectual: The Alternative Destinies of Gabriela Mistral, Cecília Meireles, and Rosario Castellanos.* Leeds, England: Legenda, 2007. The author compares and contrasts the poetic works of three Latin American women writers, including Mistral.

Alfred W. Jensen

KENJI MIYAZAWA

Born: Hanamaki, Japan; August 27, 1896
Died: Hanamaki, Japan; September 21, 1933

PRINCIPAL POETRY

Haru to shura, 1924 (*Spring and Asura*, 1973)
The Back Country, 1957
Miyazawa Kenji: Selections, 2007 (Hiroaki Sato, translator)
Strong in the Rain: Selected Poems, 2007 (Roger Pulvers, translator)

OTHER LITERARY FORMS

In addition to a substantial body of free verse and many *tanka* (the *tanka* is a fixed form of thirty-one syllables in five lines), Kenji Miyazawa (mee-yah-zah-wah) wrote children's stories, often in a fantastic vein. He also wrote a limited number of essays, the most important one of which outlines his ideas for an agrarian art. The children's stories have proved popular in Japan, and some of them are available along with the major poems in English translation. It should also be noted that Miyazawa drafted and reworked his poems in a series of workbooks over the course of his creative life; while the notebooks are not publications in a formal sense, they might be considered part of the Miyazawa canon. In any case, they are commonly utilized by scholars investigating the sources of the poet's art.

ACHIEVEMENTS

A poet of unique gifts, Kenji Miyazawa spent his relatively brief life in almost total obscurity. Living in a primitive rural area, writing virtually as a form of religious practice, Miyazawa published only one volume of stories and one of poetry during his life. Neither work attracted attention at the time of its publication.

Shortly after Miyazawa's death, however, his work began to be noticed. His utilization of scientific, religious, and foreign terms became familiar, and the striking images and energy of his verses seemed exciting alongside the generally restrained modes of Japanese poetic expression.

Most surprising of all, Miyazawa started to attain the prominence and affection he still enjoys among the general public. Almost any literate Japanese would know one poem that he jotted down in his notebook late in life. Sketching the portrait of Miyazawa's ideal selfless person, the poem begins with the lines, "Neither to wind yielding/ Nor to rain."

Miyazawa began composing *tanka* poems while still a middle school student. His principal works are in free verse, however, and these he composed mostly during the decade of the 1920's. Throughout these years, various forms of modernism—Futurism and Surrealism, for example—were being introduced to Japan, and certain native poets experimented with these new styles of writing. Miyazawa, however, worked in total isolation from such developments. This is not to say that his work is sui generis in any absolute sense. Assuredly a religious poet, Miyazawa worked out a cosmology for certain of his poems that, according to one Western scholar, resembles in a general way the private cosmologies of such poets as William Blake and William Butler Yeats.

BIOGRAPHY

Kenji Miyazawa was born on August 27, 1896, in the town of Hanamaki in the northern prefecture of Iwate. Iwate has a cool climate, and the farmers of the region led a precarious existence. Miyazawa's father ran a pawnshop, a business that prospered in part because of the poverty of the local farmers.

As the oldest son, Miyazawa would normally have succeeded his father as head of the family business. Uneasy at the thought of living off the poverty of others, however, Miyazawa neglected the task of preparing himself to succeed his father in the family business. Instead, he immersed himself in the study of philosophy and religion. An exemplary student in grade school, Miyazawa's record became worse from year to year in middle school as he pursued his own intellectual interests. Some of this independence is also discernible in occasional escapades during his youth, one of which led to his expulsion from the school dormitory.

By 1915, Miyazawa had decided to find work outside the family business. In this year, he entered the Morioka College of Agriculture and Forestry. Along with his studies in such areas as chemistry and soils, Miyazawa formulated various plans for his future, plans whereby he could utilize his knowledge to contribute to the amelioration of the harsh conditions of rural life. For a time, he even hoped to turn the resources of the family business to some new venture that might be of general economic benefit—producing industrial chemicals from the soil of the area, for example.

A new dimension was added to Miyazawa's differences with his father during these years. Initially he had followed his father's religious preference as a believer in the Jōdo Shin sect of Buddhism. Eventually, however, Miyazawa decided that ultimate truth resided in the militant Nichiren sect, especially in its intense devotion to the Lotus Sutra. In January, 1921, he took the extraordinary step of fleeing the family home in Hanamaki to join a Buddhist organization in Tokyo known as the State Pillar Society. Miyazawa returned home late that same year, partly because of the serious illness of his younger sister Toshiko and partly to take a teaching position at the two-year Hienuki Agricultural School.

Toshiko died in November, 1922, an event that the poet commemorated in a number of impressive elegies. Miyazawa continued to teach until March, 1926. In his spare time, he took his students for long treks in the countryside, writing incessantly in the notebooks that he took on these excursions. The poet made his first and only attempt at publishing his work in 1924. In addition to a volume of children's stories, he brought out at his own expense a volume of sketches in free verse, *Spring and Asura*.

Miyazawa gave up teaching from a sense of guilt. How could he accept a regular wage, no matter how small, when the average farmer was often destitute? Miyazawa decided, therefore, to become a farmer himself. A bachelor his entire life, he lived by himself raising vegetables for his own table and several small cash crops. Using the knowledge he had acquired over the years, he attempted to serve as an informal adviser to the farm community. In addition, he tried to instill in the rural populace a desire for culture.

Miyazawa had never possessed a strong constitution. He was ill on a number of occasions, and around 1928, unmistakable signs of tuberculosis began to ap-

pear. During the final years of his life, Miyazawa seems to have lost his creative urge—or, perhaps, sensing the imminence of death, he simply tried to rework the poems he had already written. The poet spent his last two years, from 1931 to 1933, as an invalid at the family home in Hanamaki. He and his father put aside their religious differences as death came closer for the son. Just before he died, on September 21, 1933, Miyazawa pointed toward a bookshelf and remarked that his unpublished manuscripts lying there had been produced out of a delusion.

ANALYSIS

Like the American poet and physician William Carlos Williams, Kenji Miyazawa absorbed himself in ceaseless service to other people, whether his students or the local farmers. Like the American, Miyazawa, too, would jot down poems in the spare moments available to him. Unlike Williams, however, Miyazawa never seems to have considered a poem finished. With only one volume of poems published in his lifetime, Miyazawa worked steadily at revising and reworking his drafts. Three different sets of poems are titled *Spring and Asura*, a fact that suggests a common ground for a number of seemingly disparate works.

SPRING AND ASURA

The first volume of *Spring and Asura* contains the title poem, a crucial poem that describes the poet caught up in intense visions of his own making. The persona narrates the vision from the viewpoint of an asura, that is, a being that ranks between humans and beasts in the six realms of existence in the Buddhist cosmology. (The six realms are devas, humans, asuras or demons, beasts, hungry ghosts, and dwellers in hell.) Despite the Buddhist references, the world of this asura is one of the poet's own making. A close study of Miyazawa's visionary poems by the American scholar Sarah Strong has uncovered a structure of levels—from a kind of Vacuum at the highest level (with the possibility of other worlds beyond) to the realm of the Western Marshes at the lowest. In between are various levels, with the Radiant Sea of Sky being the most complicated. The asura of Miyazawa's poems rushes about in this universe, finding "ecstasy" and "brightness" at the upper levels while encountering "unpleasantness" and "darkness" toward the bottom. This "structure," it must be noted, is not an immediately obvious feature of the poem. Indeed, to the untutored reader, many of Miyazawa's poems will seem mystifying and kaleidoscopic. For many, the effect of reading such works will surely be dizzying.

Miyazawa's visionary poems are difficult, but the poet has inserted passages that point the way to understanding. Preceding the Japanese text of "Spring and Asura," for example, he has entered these words in English that indicate the nature of the work to follow: "mental sketch modified." The initial volume of *Spring and Asura* also has an introductory poem or "Proem" preceding the title poem of the collection. In "Proem," Miyazawa includes lines and phrases that appear to point quite definitely at his intentions. For example, the poet says that the sketch to follow represents the workings of his imagination over the past twenty-two months. His way of putting the matter may be unusual (each piece on paper is a "chain of shadow and light," linked together "with mineral ink"), but the difficulty is more with the oddity of expression than with the meaning.

ELEGIES FOR TOSHIKO

Another set of poems by Miyazawa, the famous elegies composed upon the death of his sister Toshiko, also shows the imaginative energy of the poet. In this instance, however, the persona tends to stay within the normal and identifiable bounds of nature. The poet races outdoors to collect snow for comforting his dying sister or, after her death, wanders far beyond the region of the home in search of her whereabouts. The reader, however, knows exactly where the action is occurring. Bound to a specific and easily identifiable situation, these works seem more accessible than the aforementioned works from *Spring and Asura*.

Miyazawa's elegies on Toshiko exhibit an idiosyncrasy of vocabulary and image equal to that of "Spring and Asura." In contrast to the thematic uniqueness of this visionary poem, however, the elegies actually fit into a venerable tradition of Japanese poetry. Indeed, the elegy goes back to almost the beginnings of Japanese poetry in the *Manyōshū* (mid-eighth century; *The Collections of Ten Thousand Leaves*; also as *The Ten Thousand Leaves*, pb. 1981, and as *The Manyoshu*,

1940). Admittedly, the grief expressed by Miyazawa over the death of his sister seems more private and concentrated than the emotion found in certain of *The Manyoshu* elegies—in the partly ritualistic works by Kakinomoto no Hitomaro, which mourn the deaths of the high nobility, to mention a celebrated example. At the same time, Miyazawa follows Hitomaro and other elegists of *The Manyoshu* in his search for a trace of the deceased in nature and in his refusal to be satisfied with encountering anything less than the actual person.

DIDACTIC POEMS

If Miyazawa had written only visionary and elegiac poems, he probably would not have attained popularity except as a writer of children's tales. At the very least, his frequent use of foreign terms, whether Chinese or Sanskrit, German or Esperanto, would have made the poetry difficult for the average reader. Aside from the poems in which Miyazawa addresses his private concerns, however, certain works reflect the desire to instruct the common people. In the most celebrated of these didactic works—invariably printed as recorded in a notebook, that is, in the *katakana* syllabary understandable even to a beginning schoolchild—the poet sketches a portrait of the ideal person he wishes to be. That person lives a life of extreme frugality and of selfless devotion to others. Like the Bodhisattva of Buddhist doctrine, Miyazawa's ideal person is totally compassionate—caring for the sick, alleviating hunger, patching up quarrels, and carrying out other works of charity.

"DROUGHT AND ZAZEN"

Miyazawa was very much involved in the everyday life of the common people. This, in conjunction with his high ideals, occasionally elicited from him at least a partly satiric response. A work in this vein, titled "Kanbatsu to zazen" ("Drought and Zazen"), seems to belittle the Zen practice of meditation (zazen)—either for ignoring a pressing practical problem or for deluding its adherents into a false sense of religion's sphere of efficacy. The poem begins by describing some frogs as a Zen chorus anxiously trying to solve those perplexing puzzles known as koans. After this comic opening, Miyazawa depicts himself intently calculating the sequential phases through which the rice seedlings must pass before ripening. The contrast between religious petition on one hand and this primitive sort of scientific calculation on the other is striking.

LIGHTER POEMS

To claim that Miyazawa is satirizing Zen or meditation in this poem might well be an overstatement. If satire is at work, it is certainly good-humored. In fact, the lighthearted side of the poet needs special emphasis in view of the fact that his central works, especially a poem such as "Spring and Asura" and the elegies on Toshiko, are so somber and brooding.

On occasion, the poet will enjoy a lighter moment by himself—when, for example, in a poem titled "Shigoto" ("Work") he momentarily worries about the manure he threw from a cart and left on a hillside. More often, he will jest with the farmers and peasants of the region. In one poem, he pokes fun at a farmer named Hosuke for getting upset when a manure-carrying horse proves unruly; in another instance, he counsels a hard-working farmer to leave off bundling rice at midnight for the sake of the weary wife who is doing her best to assist him. In most of these works, the poet seems a carefree observer and counselor. Since Miyazawa is normally a somber poet, though, and the farmers, even in his lighthearted poems, are always hard at work, one might surmise that the poet regarded humor principally as a way for the farmer to cope with his burdens.

In any event, this playful side of Miyazawa is present in many different poems. Sometimes, the poet simply observes an appealing scene. His poem on an Ayrshire bull is a good example. The animal, seen at night against the light of a pulp factory, enjoys itself by rubbing its horns in the grass and butting a fence. At other times, Miyazawa seems to play with language in an extravagant manner. A certain horse in another poem is said to "rot like a potato" and "feel the bright sun's juice." A second horse meets a dire fate by running into a high-voltage wire in its stable, the funeral taking place with the human mourners shedding "clods of tears" upon the "lolling head" of the dead animal. Hosuke's manure horse engages in some impressive acrobatics, rearing up with "scarlet eyes" on one occasion as if to "rake in blue velvet, the spring sky."

The poem on the Ayrshire bull depicts a casual encounter, the sort of event that happens often in Miyazawa's playful poems about people. Running into an

acquaintance, the poet engages this other in a little drama. These poems, most of them brief, present simple emotions and often contain some deft humor. Certain works employ the same techniques but pursue more ambitious aims. Among them is a fascinating piece titled "Shita de wakareta sakki no hito" ("The Man I Parted from, Below"). The man in question is a somewhat disembodied image that remains in the memory of the poet after the meeting to which the title alludes has taken place. Defined mainly as a smoker, the man has been leading a horse somewhere, possibly to another group of horses visible in the distance. At least this thought occurs to the poet as he surveys the scene before him and composes his appreciation of it. Certain of Miyazawa's typical concerns manifest themselves in the course of the work—the identification and naming of places, for example, or the sense of things happening in a kind of space-time continuum. Occasionally, an odd turn of phrase, too, reminds the reader of the poet's identity—the "aquamarine legs of winds," for example, or the highlands spread out "like ten or more playing cards." The horses on those highlands originally looked to the poet like "shining red ants." Such language, hardly startling to the Miyazawa aficionado, helps to elevate parts of the poem above mere plain description.

Indeed, "The Man I Parted from, Below" might seem tame alongside the coruscating images of "Spring and Asura" and the vibrating language of "Proem." The poem has certain compensations, however, even as a somewhat atypical work of Miyazawa. It shows that the poet could be at home in the calmer modes of Japanese lyricism and could deftly lay out a pattern of relationships involving himself, nature, and his fellow men.

Having parted from the poet, the smoker is now observed together with his horse moving off toward the distant herd. Though abandoned by the smoker as surely as he had once been by Toshiko, Miyazawa does not seem bereft in this poem. All about him are the familiar mountains and valleys for which, at this moment, he feels an "oddly helpless love." All the men in the poem—the keeper of the distant herd, the man with his sole horse, and the poet, too—seem related to one another, and to the animals as well, by their mere presence in the scene. Slightly idiosyncratic, moderately optimistic, entirely understandable, "The Man I Parted from, Below" shows the poet submitting his vision to the requirements of realism on a human scale.

OTHER MAJOR WORKS

SHORT FICTION: *Ginga tetsudo no yoru*, 1922 (*Night of the Milky Way Railway*, 1991); *Chūmon no ōi ryōriten*, 1924 (*The Restaurant of Many Orders, and Other Stories*, 2001); *Winds and Wildcat Places*, 1967; *Night Train to the Stars, and Other Stories*, 1987; *Once and Forever: The Tales of Kenji Miyazawa*, 1993.

MISCELLANEOUS: *Miyazawa Kenji zenshū*, 1967-1968 (12 volumes); *Kohon Miyazawa Kenji zenshū*, 1973-1977 (15 volumes); *A Future of Ice: Poems and Stories of a Japanese Buddhist*, 1989.

BIBLIOGRAPHY

Bester, John. Foreword to *Once and Forever: The Tales of Kenji Miyazawa*. Tokyo: Kodansha International, 1993. The preeminent translator of Miyazawa provides insights into the poet and his poetics.

Miyazawa, Kenji. *Miyazawa Kenji: Selections*. Edited by Hiroaki Sato. Berkeley: University of California Press, 2007. This collection of Miyazawa's poetry includes an introduction by the editor that examines the poet's significance and legacy and his place in Japanese literature. Includes several other essays on the poet.

Mori, Masaki. *Epic Grandeur: Toward a Comparative Poetics of the Epic*. Albany: State University of New York Press, 1997. Argues that the epic genre can be discerned in the twentieth century in works promoting peace as opposed to war. Considers Miyazawa's *Night of the Milky Way Railway* as a "transitional epic."

Pulvers, Roger. "Miyazawa Kenji, Rebel with a Cause." *Japan Quarterly* 43, no. 4 (October-December, 1996): 30-42. Pulvers, who published a translation of Miyazawa's poetry in 2007, describes the life and works of Miyazawa, noting his respect for nature. He discusses the poet's surge in popularity in the mid-1990's.

Ueda, Makoto. *Modern Japanese Poets and the Nature of Literature*. Stanford, Calif.: Stanford University Press, 1983. Summaries of modern Japanese poets, including Miyazawa.

Watson, Burton. Introduction to *Spring and Asura*. Chicago: Chicago Review Press, 1973. An overview of Miyazawa's work.

James O'Brien

N

PABLO NERUDA
Neftalí Ricardo Reyes Basoalto

Born: Parral, Chile; July 12, 1904
Died: Santiago, Chile; September 23, 1973

PRINCIPAL POETRY

Crepusculario, 1923

Veinte poemas de amor y una canción desesperada,
1924 (*Twenty Love Poems and a Song of
Despair*, 1969)

Tentativa del hombre infinito, 1926

El hondero entusiasta, 1933

Residencia en la tierra, 1933, 1935, 1947 (3
volumes; *Residence on Earth, and Other Poems*,
1946, 1973)

España en el corazón, 1937 (*Spain in the Heart*,
1946)

Alturas de Macchu Picchu, 1948 (*The Heights of
Macchu Picchu*, 1966)

Canto general, 1950 (partial translation in *Let the
Rail Splitter Awake, and Other Poems*, 1951;
full translation as *Canto General*, 1991)

Los versos del capitán, 1952 (*The Captain's Verses*,
1972)

Odas elementales, 1954 (*The Elemental Odes*,
1961)

Las uvas y el viento, 1954

Nuevas odas elementales, 1956

Tercer libro de odas, 1957

Estravagario, 1958 (*Extravagaria*, 1972)

Cien sonetos de amor, 1959 (*One Hundred Love
Sonnets*, 1986)

Navegaciones y regresos, 1959

Canción de gesta, 1960 (*Song of Protest*, 1976)

Cantos ceremoniales, 1961 (*Ceremonial Songs*,
1996)

Las piedras de Chile, 1961 (*The Stones of Chile*,
1986)

Plenos poderes, 1962 (*Fully Empowered*, 1975)

Memorial de Isla Negra, 1964 (5 volumes; *Isla
Negra: A Notebook*, 1981)

Arte de pájaros, 1966 (*Art of Birds*, 1985)

Una casa en la arena, 1966 (*The House at Isla
Negra: Prose Poems*, 1988)

La barcarola, 1967

Las manos del día, 1968

Aún, 1969 (*Still Another Day*, 1984)

Fin de mundo, 1969 (*World's End*, 2009)

La espada encendida, 1970

Las piedras del cielo, 1970 (*Stones of the Sky*,
1987)

Selected Poems, 1970

Geografía infructuosa, 1972

New Poems, 1968-1970, 1972

*Incitación al Nixonicidio y alabanza de la
revolución chilena*, 1973 (*Incitement to
Nixonicide and Praise of the Chilean
Revolution*, 1979; also known as *A Call for the
Destruction of Nixon and Praise for the Chilean
Revolution*, 1980)

El mar y las campanas, 1973 (*The Sea and the
Bells*, 1988)

La rosa separada, 1973 (*The Separate Rose*, 1985)

2000, 1974 (English translation, 1992)

El corazón amarillo, 1974 (*The Yellow Heart*,
1990)

Defectos escogidos, 1974

Elegía, 1974 (*Elegy*, 1983)

Jardín de invierno, 1974 (*Winter Garden*, 1986)

Libro de las preguntas, 1974 (*The Book of
Questions*, 1991)

El mal y el malo, 1974

*Pablo Neruda: Five Decades, a Selection (Poems,
1925-1970)*, 1974

El río invisible: Poesía y prosa de juventud, 1980

The Poetry of Pablo Neruda, 2003 (Ilan Stavans,
editor)

OTHER LITERARY FORMS

Pablo Neruda (nay-REW-duh) was an essayist, translator, playwright, and novelist as well as a poet. His
memoirs, *Confieso que he vivido: Memorias* (1974;
Memoirs, 1977), are a lyric evocation of his entire life,

its final pages written after the coup that overthrew Salvador Allende. Neruda's translations include works by Rainer Maria Rilke, William Shakespeare, and William Blake. The volume *Para nacer he nacido* (1978; *Passions and Impressions*, 1983) includes prose poems, travel impressions, and the speech that Neruda delivered on his acceptance of the Nobel Prize. He has written a novel, *El habitante y su esperanza* (1926); a poetic drama, *Fulgor y muerte de Joaquín Murieta* (pb. 1967; *Splendor and Death of Joaquin Murieta*, 1972); and essays on Shakespeare, Carlo Levi, Vladimir Mayakovsky, Paul Éluard, and Federico García Lorca, as well as several works of political concern.

ACHIEVEMENTS

Winner of the Nobel Prize in 1971, Pablo Neruda is one of the most widely read poets in the world today. His most popular book, *Twenty Love Poems and a Song of Despair*, has more than a million copies in print and, like much of his work, has been translated from Spanish into more than twenty languages. Neruda was so prolific a writer that nine of his collections of poems have been published posthumously.

Neruda's goal was to liberate Spanish poetry from the literary strictures of the nineteenth century and bring it into the twentieth century by returning verse to its popular sources. In *Memoirs*, written just before his death, Neruda congratulates himself for having made poetry a respected profession through his discovery that his own aspirations are representative of those shared by men and women on three continents. Writing on the rugged coast of southern Chile, Neruda found passion and beauty in the harshness of a world that hardens its inhabitants, strengthening but sometimes silencing them. His purpose was to give others the voice they too often lacked.

BIOGRAPHY

Pablo Neruda was born Neftalí Ricardo Reyes Basoalto in the frontier town of Parral in the southern part of Chile on July 12, 1904. His mother died of tuberculosis a few days after his birth, and Neruda lived with his stepmother and father, a railroad conductor, in a tenement house with two other families. Hard work and an early introduction to literature and to the mysteries of

manhood distinguished his first seventeen years. In school, the famous Chilean educator and poet Gabriela Mistral, herself a Nobel Prize winner, introduced the young Neruda to the great nineteenth century Russian novelists. In the fall of his sixteenth year, while he was assisting in the wheat harvest, a woman whom he was later unable to identify first introduced the young man to sex. A wide-ranging, voracious appetite for books and the wonders of love are memories to which Neruda continually returns in his work, as well as to the harsh Chilean landscape and the problems of survival that confronted his countrymen.

His father's determination that Neruda should have a profession took the young poet to Santiago, where he intended to study French literature at the university. He had learned French and English in Temuco from his neighbors, many of whom were immigrants. His affiliation as contributor to the journal *Claridad*, with the politically active student group Federación de Estu-

Pablo Neruda (Library of Congress)

diantes, and the attractions of life in a large city, where Neruda quickly made friends with many influential people, served to expand his original plans. While living with the widow of a German novelist, Neruda tried repeatedly to gain access to the offices of the Ministry of External Affairs, hoping to obtain a diplomatic post in Europe. More important, he had begun to write his first serious poetry during his evenings alone in a boardinghouse at 513 Maruri Street.

Neruda's hatred of political oppression became firmly established when the students of a right-wing group attacked the officers of *Claridad* and the Santiago police freed the attackers and arrested the editors, one of whom died in jail. Thus, after a year and a half in Santiago, Neruda abandoned his university career and dramatically declared himself a poet and political activist, taking the pen name Pablo Neruda from the Czech writer Jan Neruda (1834-1891) to conceal his activities from his father.

In 1923, to publish his first book of poems, *Crepusculario*, Neruda sold his furniture and borrowed money from his friends; favorable critical reviews validated his decision. The similarity of his verse to that of the Uruguayan poet Sabat Erscaty forced Neruda to turn from inspirational and philosophical themes back to a more intimate poetry based on personal experience. The result in 1924 was *Twenty Love Poems and a Song of Despair*, Neruda's most popular book, in which he sings of the joy and pain of casual affairs with a student from Santiago and the girl he left in Temuco.

Neruda's abandonment of his university career to write for *Claridad* coincided with his moving to Valparaíso. The port city immediately won his favor. He had not abandoned his goal of a diplomatic post, and finally, through the influence of the Bianchi family, he succeeded in meeting the Minister of External Affairs, who was persuaded to allow Neruda to pick his post. Neruda chose the one city available about which he knew nothing: Rangoon, Burma (now Myanmar), then a province of India.

After a short stay in Burma, Neruda obtained a new post in Ceylon (now Sri Lanka), setting the pattern of his life for the next twenty-five years. During this period, Neruda was abroad most of the time, usually under the auspices of the Chilean government—although on occasion he would flee government arrest. Returning to Chile from the Far East, he was quickly off to Argentina, then to Spain (during the Spanish Civil War), then to France, where he had stopped en route to Rangoon and to which he returned a number of times. During the early years of World War II, Neruda held a diplomatic post in Mexico; he resigned in 1943 to return to Chile, where he became active in politics as a member of the Chilean Communist Party.

Neruda's Communist sympathies (which had their origin in the Spanish Civil War) hardened into an uncritical acceptance of Stalinism, which ill accorded with his genuine populist sentiments. He became a frequent visitor to the Eastern bloc in the 1950's and 1960's, even serving on the committee that met annually in Moscow to award the Lenin Peace Prize, which he himself had won in 1950.

From 1960 until his death in 1973, Neruda worked tirelessly, publishing sixteen books of poetry and giving conferences in Venezuela (1959), Eastern Europe (1960), Cuba (1960), the United States (1961, 1966, and 1972), Italy and France (1962), England (1965), Finland (1965), and the Soviet Union (1967). He was named president of the Chilean Writers Association, correspondent of the Department of Romance Languages of Yale University, doctor *honoris causa* at Oxford, and Nobel Prize winner in 1971. In 1969, he was nominated for the presidency of Chile; he rejected the nomination in favor of Salvador Allende, who named Neruda ambassador to France. Neruda's health, however, and his concern about a civil war in Chile, precipitated his return in 1973. His efforts to prevent a coup d'état proved fruitless, and Neruda died a few days after Allende. He had just finished his *Memoirs*, writing that he enjoyed a tranquil conscience and a restless intelligence, a contentment derived from having made poetry a profession from which he could earn an honest living. He had lived, he said, as "an omnivore of sentiments, beings, books, happenings and battles." He would "consume the earth and drink the sea."

ANALYSIS

Pablo Neruda stated in a prologue to one of four editions of *Caballo verde*, a literary review he had founded in 1935 with Manuel Altalaguirre, that the poetry he was seeking would contain the confused impurities that people leave on their tools as they wear them down with the sweat of their hands. He would make poems like buildings, permeated with smoke and garlic and flooded inside and out with the air of men and women who seem always present. Neruda advocated an impure poetry whose subject might be hatred, love, ugliness, or beauty. He sought to bring verse back from the exclusive conclave of select minorities to the turmoil from which words draw their vitality.

CREPUSCULARIO

Neruda's work is divided into three discernible periods, the turning points being the Spanish Civil War and his return to Chile in 1952 after three years of forced exile. During the first phase of his work, from 1923 to 1936, Neruda published six rather experimental collections of verse in which he achieved the poetic strength that carried him through four more decades and more than twenty books. He published *Crepusculario* himself in 1923 while a student at the University of Santiago. *Crepusculario* is a cautious collection of poems reflecting his reading of French poetry. Like the Latin American *Modernistas* who preceded him, he consciously adhered to classical forms and sought the ephemeral effects of musicality and color. The poem that perhaps best captures the message indicated by the title of the book is very brief: "My soul is an empty carousel in the evening light." All the poems in *Crepusculario* express Neruda's ennui and reveal his experimentation with the secondary qualities of language, its potential for the effects of music, painting, and sculpture.

There are several interesting indications of Neruda's future development in *Crepusculario* that distinguish it from similar derivative works. Neruda eventually came to see poetry as work, a profession no less than carpentry, brick masonry, or politics; this conception of poetry is anticipated in the poem "Inicial," in which he writes: "I have gone under Helios who watches me bleeding/ laboring in silence in my absent gardens." Further, in *Crepusculario*, Neruda occasionally breaks logical barriers in a manner that anticipates much of his later Surrealistic verse: "I close and close my lips but in trembling roses/ my voice comes untied, like water in the fountain." Nevertheless, *Crepusculario* is also

characterized by a respect for tradition and a humorous familiarity with the sacred that Neruda later abandoned, only to rediscover them again in the third phase of his career, after 1952: "And the 'Our Father' gets lost in the middle of the night/ runs naked across his green lands/ and trembling with pleasure dives into the sea." Linked with this respect for his own traditions is an adulation of European culture, which he also abandoned in his second phase; Neruda did not, however, regain a regard for Western European culture in his mature years, rejecting it in favor of his own American authenticity: "When you are old, my darling (Ronsard has already told you)/ you will recall the verses I spoke to you."

In *Crepusculario*, the first stirrings of Neruda's particular contribution to Spanish poetry are evident— themes that in the early twentieth century were considered unpoetic, such as the ugliness of industrialized cities and the drudgery of bureaucracies. These intrusions of objective reality were the seeds from which his strongest poetry would grow; they reveal Neruda's capacity to empathize with the material world and give it a voice.

TWENTY LOVE POEMS AND A SONG OF DESPAIR

One year after the publication of *Crepusculario*, the collection *Twenty Love Poems and a Song of Despair* appeared. It would become the most widely read collection of poems in the Spanish-speaking world. In it, Neruda charts the course of a love affair from passionate attraction to despair and indifference. In these poems, Neruda sees the whole world in terms of the beloved:

> The vastness of pine groves, the sound of beating wings,
> the slow interplay of lights, a solitary bell,
> the evening falling into your eyes, my darling, and in you
> the earth sings.
> Love shadows and timbres your voice in the dying
>   echoing
> afternoon
> just as in those deep hours I have seen
> the field's wheat bend in the mouth of the wind.

Throughout these twenty poems, Neruda's intensity and directness of statement universalize his private experiences, establishing another constant in his work:

the effort to create a community of feeling through the expression of common, universal experience.

TENTATIVA DEL HOMBRE INFINITO

In 1926, Neruda published *Tentativa del hombre infinito* (venture of infinite man), his most interesting work from a technical point of view. In this book-length poem, Neruda employed the "automatic writing" espoused by the Surrealists. The poem celebrates Neruda's discovery of the city at night and tests the capacity of his poetic idiom to sound the depths of his subconscious. Ignoring the conventions of sentence structure, syntax, and logic, Neruda fuses form and content.

The poem opens in the third person with a description of the poet asleep in the city of Santiago. It returns to the same image of the sleeping man and the hearth fires of the city three times, changing person from third to second to first, creating a circular or helical structure. The imagery defies conventional associations: "the moon blue spider creeps floods/ an emissary you were moving happily in the afternoon that was falling/ the dusk rolled in extinguishing flowers."

In the opening passages, Neruda explores the realm between wakefulness and sleep, addressing the night as his lover: "take my heart, cross it with your vast pulleys of silence/ when you surround sleep's animals, it's at your feet/ waiting to depart because you place it face to face with/ you, night of black helixes." In this realm between motive and act, Neruda's language refuses to acknowledge distinctions of tense: "a twenty-year-old holds to the frenetic reins, it is that he wanted to follow the night." Also, the limits that words draw between concepts disappear, and thoughts blend like watercolors: "star delayed between the heavy night the days with tall sails."

The poem is a voyage of exploration that leads to a number of discoveries. The poet discovers his own desperation: "the night like wine enters the tunnel/ savage wind, miner of the heavens, let's wail together." He discovers the vastness of the other: "in front of the inaccessible there passes by for you a limitless presence." He discovers his freedom: "prow, mast, leaf in the storm, an abandonment without hope of return impels you/ you show the way like crosses the dead." Most important, he discovers wonder: "the wind leaving its egg

strikes my back/ great ships of glowing coals twist their green sails/ planets spin like bobbins." The abstract becomes concrete and hence tractable: "the heart of the world folds and stretches/ with the will of a column and the cold fury of feathers." He discovers his joy: "Hurricane night, my happiness bites your ink/ and exasperated, I hold back my heart which dances/ a dancer astonished in the heavy tides which make the dawn rise."

When the poet finds his beloved, he begins to acquire a more logical grasp of objective reality, but when he realizes that he is still dreaming, his joy becomes despair. He gradually awakens; his senses are assaulted by the smell of the timber of his house and the sound of rain falling, and he gazes through the windows at the sky. Interestingly, his dream visions do not abandon him at once but continue to determine his perceptions:

> birds appear like letters in the depths of the sky
> the dawn appears like the peelings of fruit
> the day is made of fire
> the sea is full of green rags which articulate I am the sea
> I am alone in a windowless room
> snails cover the walk
> and time is squared and immobile.

In this experimental work, Neruda mastered the art of tapping his subconscious for associative imagery. Although he never returned to the pure Surrealism of *Tentativa del hombre infinito*, it is the union of strikingly original and often surreal imagery with earthly realism that gives Neruda's mature poetry its distinctive character.

RESIDENCE ON EARTH, AND OTHER POEMS

In the poems of *Residence on Earth, and Other Poems*, Neruda first achieved that mature voice, free of any derivative qualities. One of the greatest poems in this collection, "Galope muerto" ("Dead Gallop"), was written in the same year as *Tentativa del hombre infinito*, 1925, although it was not published in book form until 1933. "Dead Gallop" sets the tone for the collection, in which Neruda repeatedly expresses a passionate desire to assimilate new experiences: "Everything is so fast, so living/ yet immobile, like a mad pulley spinning on itself." Many of the poems in *Residence on Earth, and Other Poems* begin in the same manner, recording those peripheral and secondary sensations that reside on the fringe of consciousness. They work toward the same end, resolving the new into understandable terms. As the poems come into focus, the reader participates in the poet's assimilation of his new world. For example, the significance of his vague memories of saying goodbye to a girl whom he had left in Chile gradually becomes clear in one poem:

> Dusty glances fallen to earth
> or silent leaves which bury themselves.
> Lightless metal in the void
> and the suddenly dead day's departure.
> On high hands the butterfly shines
> its flight's light has no end.
> You kept the light's wake of broken things
> which the abandoned sun in the afternoon throws at the
>   church steps.

Here, one can see Neruda's gift for surreal imagery without the programmatic irrationality and dislocation of the Surrealists.

In *Residence on Earth, and Other Poems*, too, there are magnificent catalogs in the manner of Walt Whitman: "the angel of sleep—the wind moving the wheat, the whistle of a train, a warm place in a bed, the opaque sound of a shadow which falls like a ray of light into infinity, a repetition of distances, a wine of uncertain vintage, the dusty passage of lowing cows."

Like Whitman, Neruda in *Residence on Earth, and Other Poems* opens Spanish poetry to the song of himself: "my symmetrical statue of twinned legs, rises to the stars each morning/ my exile's mouth bites meat and grapes/ my male arms and tattooed chest/ in which the hair penetrates like wire, my white face made for the sun's depth." He presents uncompromising statements of human sensuality; he descends into himself, discovers his authenticity, and begins to build a poetic vision that, although impure, is genuinely human. He manages in these sometimes brutal poems to reconcile the forces of destruction and creation that he had witnessed in India in the material world of buildings, work, people, food, weather, himself, and time.

Although Neruda never achieved a systematic and internally consistent poetic vision, the balance between resignation and celebration that informs *Residence on Earth, and Other Poems* suggests a philosophical acceptance of the world. "Tres cantos materiales" ("Three Material Songs"), "Entrada a la madera" ("Entrance to Wood"), "Apoges del apio" ("Apogee of Celery"), and "Estatuto del vino" ("Ordinance of Wine") were a breakthrough in this respect. In "Entrance to Wood," the poet gives voice to wood, which, though living, is material rather than spiritual. Neruda's discovery of matter is a revelation. He introduces himself into this living, material world as one commencing a funereal journey, carrying his sorrows with him in order to give this world the voice it lacks. His identification with matter alters his language so that the substantives become verbs: "Let us make fire, silence, and noise,/ let us burn, hush and bells."

In "Apogee of Celery," the poet personifies a humble vegetable, as he does later in *The Elemental Odes*. Neruda simply looks closely and with his imagination and humor reveals a personality—how the growth of celery reflects the flight of doves and the brilliance of lightning. In Spanish folklore, celery has humorous though obscene connotations which Neruda unflinchingly incorporates into his poem. The resultant images are bizarre yet perfectly descriptive. Celery tastes like lightning bugs. It knows wonderful secrets of the sea, whence it originates, but perversely insists on being eaten before revealing them.

Popular wisdom also finds its way into the poem "Ordinance of Wine." Neruda's discovery of the wonders of matter and of everyday experience led him to describe the Bacchanalian rites of drunkenness as laws, the inevitable steps of intoxication. In the classical tradition, Neruda compares wine to a pagan god: It opens the door on the melancholy gatherings of the dishonored and disheartened and drops its honey on the tables at the day's edge; in winter, it seeks refuge in bars; it transforms the world of the discouraged and overpowers them so that they sing, spend money freely, and accept the coarseness of one another's company joyfully. The celebrants' laughter turns to weeping over personal tragedies and past happiness, and their tears turn to anger when something falls, breaks, and abruptly ends the magic. Wine the angel turns into a winged Harpy taking flight, spilling the wine, which seeps through the ground in search of the mouths of the dead. Wine's statutes have thus been obeyed, and the visiting god departs.

In "Ordinance of Wine," "Apogee of Celery," and "Entrance to Wood," Neruda reestablished communion between humans and the material world in which they live and work. Since work was the destiny of most of his readers, Neruda directed much of his poetry to this reconciliation between the elemental and the social, seeking to reintroduce wonder into the world of the alienated worker.

Neruda was writing the last poems of *Residence on Earth, and Other Poems* in Madrid when the Spanish Civil War erupted. The catastrophe delayed the publication of the last book of the trilogy by twelve years. More important, the war confirmed Neruda's stance as a defender of oppressed peoples, of the poor. Suddenly, Neruda stopped singing the song of himself and began to direct his verse against the Nationalists besieging Madrid. The war inspired the collection of poems *Spain in the Heart*, a work as popular in Eastern Europe as is *Twenty Love Poems and a Song of Despair* in the West. These poems, such as Neruda's 1942 "Oda a Stalingrad" ("Ode to Stalingrad"), were finally published as part of *Residence on Earth, and Other Poems*. They were written from the defensive point of view of countries fighting against the threat of fascism. In them, the lyric element almost disappears before the onslaught of Neruda's political passion. Indeed, from 1937 to 1947, Neruda's poetry served the greater purpose of political activism and polemics:

You probably want to know: And where are the lilies?
the metaphysics covered with poppies?
And the rain which often struck
his words filling them
with holes and birds?
I'm going to tell you what has happened.
I lived in a neighborhood in Madrid
My house was called
the House of Flowers . . .
And one evening everything was on fire
. . . Bandits with planes and with Moors
bandits with rings and duchesses
bandits with black friars giving blessings
came through the sky to kill children.

More than ten years had to pass before Neruda could reaffirm his art above political propaganda.

CANTO GENERAL

During the 1940's, Neruda worked by plan on his epic history of Latin America, *Canto General*. Beginning with a description of the geography, the flora, and the fauna of the continent, the book progresses from sketches of the heroes of the Inca and Aztec empires through descriptions of conquistadores, the heroes of the Wars of Independence, to the dictators and foreign adventurers in twentieth century Latin America. Neruda interprets the history of the continent as a struggle toward autonomy carried on by many different peoples who have suffered from one kind of oppression or another since the beginnings of their recorded history.

THE CAPTAIN'S VERSES

Neruda, however, did not disappear entirely from his work during these years. He anonymously published *The Captain's Verses* to celebrate falling in love with the woman with whom he would spend the rest of his life, Matilde Urrutia. Unlike his previous women, Matilde shared Neruda's origins among the poor of southern Chile as well as his aspirations. These poems are tender, passionate, and direct, free of the despair, melancholy, and disillusionment of *Twenty Love Poems and a Song of Despair* and of *Residence on Earth, and Other Poems*.

LAS UVAS Y EL VIENTO

While working in exile for the European Peace Party, Neruda recorded in *Las uvas y el viento* (the grapes and the wind) impressions of new friends and places, of conferences and renewed commitments made during his travels through Hungary, Poland, and Czechoslovakia. Neruda warmly remembers Prague, Berlin, Moscow, Capri, Madame Sun Yat-sen, Ilya Ehrenburg, Paul Éluard, Pablo Picasso, and the Turkish poet Nazim Hikmet. The most interesting works in the collection re-create Neruda's return to cities from which he had been absent for more than thirty years.

THE ELEMENTAL ODES

Neruda's travels through the East assured his fame. His fiftieth year signaled his return to Chile to fulfill the demand for his work that issued from three continents. In 1954, he built his house on Isla Negra with Matilde Urrutia and published the first of three remarkable collections, *The Elemental Odes*, followed by *Nuevas odas elementales* (new elemental odes) and *Tercer libro de odas* (third book of odes). In these books, Neruda returned to the discoveries made in the "Material Songs" of *Residence on Earth, and Other Poems*. In the odes, Neruda's poetry again gained ascendancy over politics, although Neruda never ignored his political responsibilities.

The elemental odes reflect no immediately apparent political concern other than to renew and fulfill the search for an impure poetry responsive to the wonder of the everyday world. Neruda writes that earlier poets, himself included, now cause him to laugh because they never see beyond themselves. Poetry traditionally deals only with poets' own feelings and experiences; those of other men and women hardly ever find expression in poetry. The personality of objects, of the material world, never finds a singer, except among writers such as Neruda, who are also workers. Neruda's new purpose is to maintain his anonymity, because now "there are no mysterious shadows/ everyone speaks to me about their families, their work, and what wonderful things they do!"

In the elemental odes, Neruda learns to accept and celebrate the common gift of happiness, "as necessary as the earth, as sustaining as hearth fires, as pure as bread, as musical as water." He urges people to recognize the gifts they already possess. He sings of such humble things as eel stew, in which the flavors of the Chilean land and sea mix to make a paradise for the palate. Against those who envy his work and its unpretentious message of common humanity, Neruda responds that a simple poetry open to common people will live after him because it is as unafraid and healthy as a milkmaid in whose laughter there are enough teeth to ruin the hopes of the envious.

Indeed, the language of the elemental odes is very simple and direct, but, because Neruda writes these poems in such brief, internally rhyming lines, he draws attention to the natural beauty of his Spanish, the measured rhythm of clauses, the symmetry of sentence structure, and the solid virtues of an everyday vocabulary. In the tradition of classical Spanish realism, the elemental odes require neither the magic of verbal pyrotechnics nor incursions into the subconscious to achieve a fullness of poetic vision.

LATER WORK

After the collection *Extravagaria*—in which Neruda redirected his attention inward again, resolving questions of his own mortality and the prospect of never again seeing places and people dear to him—the poet's production doubled to the rate of two lengthy books of poems every year. In response partly to the demand for his work, partly to his increased passion for writing, Neruda's books during the last decade of his life were often carefully planned and systematic. *Navegaciones y regresos* (navigations and returns) alternates a recounting of his travels with odes inspired by remarkable people, places, and events. *One Hundred Love Sonnets* collects one hundred rough-hewn sonnets of love to Matilde Urrutia. *Isla Negra* is an autobiography in verse. *Art of Birds* is a poetic ornithological guide to Chile. *Stones of the Sky*, *Ceremonial Songs*, *Fully Empowered*, and *The House at Isla Negra* are all-inclusive, totally unsystematic collections unified by Neruda's bold style, a style that wanders aimlessly and confidently like a powerful river cutting designs in stone. *Las manos del día* (the hands of the day) and *La espada encendida* (the sword ignited), written between 1968 and 1970, attest Neruda's responsiveness to new threats against freedom. *Geografía infructuosa* (unfruitful geography) signals Neruda's return again to contemplate the rugged coast of Chile. As Neruda remarks in his *Memoirs* concerning his last decade of work, he gradually developed into a poet with the primitive style characteristic of the monolithic sculptures of Oceania: "I began with the refinements of Praxiteles and end with the massive ruggedness of the statues of Easter Island."

OTHER MAJOR WORKS

LONG FICTION: *El habitante y su esperanza*, 1926.

PLAYS: *Romeo y Juliet*, pb. 1964 (translation of William Shakespeare); *Fulgor y muerte de Joaquín Murieta*, pb. 1967 (*Splendor and Death of Joaquin Murieta*, 1972).

NONFICTION: *Anillos*, 1926 (with Tomás Lago); *Viajes*, 1955; *Comiendo en Hungría*, 1968; *Cartas de amor*, 1974 (letters); *Confieso que he vivido: Memorias*, 1974 (*Memoirs*, 1977); *Lo mejor de Anatole France*, 1976; *Cartas a Laura*, 1978 (letters); *Para nacer he nacido*, 1978 (*Passions and Impressions*, 1983); *Correspondencia durante "Residencia en la tierra,"* 1980 (letters; with Héctor Eandi).

BIBLIOGRAPHY

Agosin, Marjorie. *Pablo Neruda*. Translated by Lorraine Roses. Boston: Twayne, 1986. A basic critical biography of Neruda.

Dawes, Greg. *Verses Against the Darkness: Pablo Neruda's Poetry and Politics*. Lewisburg, Pa.: Bucknell University Press, 2006. Dawes examines how Neruda's poetry was affected by his political views during the Cold War. Examines the moral realism in "España en el corazon" (*Spain in the Heart*).

Feinstein, Adam. *Pablo Neruda: A Passion for Life*. New York: Bloomsbury, 2004. The first authoritative English-language biography of the poet's life. Thoroughly researched and indexed.

Longo, Teresa, ed. *Pablo Neruda and the U.S. Culture Industry*. New York: Routledge, 2002. A collection of essays examining the process by which Neruda's poetry was translated into English and the impact of its dissemination on American and Latino culture.

Méndez-Ramírez, Hugo. *Neruda's Ekphrastic Experience: Mural Art and "Canto General."* Lewisburg, Pa.: Bucknell University Press, 1999. This research focuses on the interplay between verbal and visual elements in Neruda's masterpiece *Canto General*. It demonstrates how mural art, especially that practiced in Mexico, became the source for Neruda's ekphrastic desire, in which his verbal art paints visual elements.

Nolan, James. *Poet-Chief: The Native American Poetics of Walt Whitman and Pablo Neruda*. Albuquerque: University of New Mexico Press, 1994. A comparative study of Whitman and Neruda, and the influence on them of both the theme of Native American culture and the practice of oral poetry.

Sayers Pedén, Margaret. Introduction to *Selected Odes of Pablo Neruda*, by Pablo Neruda. Translated by Sayers Pedén. Berkeley: University of California Press, 2000. Sayers Pedén is among the most highly regarded translators of Latin American poetry. Here her introduction to the translations in this bilingual edition constitutes an excellent critical study as well as providing biographical and bibliographical information.

Teitelboim, Volodia. *Neruda: A Personal Biography*. Translated by Beverly J. DeLong-Tonelli. Austin: University of Texas Press, 1991. A biography written by a close friend and fellow political exile.

Wilson, Jason. *A Companion to Pablo Neruda: Evaluating Neruda's Poetry*. Rochester, N.Y.: Tamesis, 2008. Wilson provides a guidebook to Neruda's numerous poetical works, furthering the readers' understanding.

Woodbridge, Hensley Charles. *Pablo Neruda: An Annotated Bibliography of Biographical and Critical Studies*. New York: Garland, 1988. Reflects the growing interest in Neruda following the translations of his works into English in the 1970's.

Kenneth A. Stackhouse

O

CHRISTOPHER OKIGBO

Born: Ojoto-Uno, Nigeria; August 16, 1932
Died: Ekwegbe, near Nsukka, Biafra (now in Nigeria); August, 1967
Also known as: Christopher Ifekandu Okigbo

PRINCIPAL POETRY
"On the New Year," 1958
"Debtor's Lane," 1959
"Moonglow," 1960
"Four Canzones," 1962
Heavensgate, 1962
"Love Apart," 1962
Silences, 1963
Distances, 1964
Limits, 1964
"Lament of the Drums," 1965
Path of Thunder: Poems Prophesying War, 1968
Labyrinths, with Path of Thunder, 1971
Collected Poems, 1986

OTHER LITERARY FORMS
Christopher Okigbo (oh-KIHG-boh) is known primarily for his poetry.

ACHIEVEMENTS
During his short lifetime, Christopher Okigbo produced a small but significant body of work that stands as a legacy for poetry, particularly Nigerian poetry. His work has been celebrated by critics, discussed at university campuses, and examined in scholarly journals. His poetry is often included in Commonwealth poetry anthologies, and an annual poetry award, the All-Africa Okigbo Prize for Poetry, was created in his honor. In 2007, his work was included in *Crossroads*, an anthology marking the fortieth anniversary of his death and containing verses from more than one hundred Nigerian poets. That same year, an international

conference discussing Okigbo's life and works was held in Boston.

In 1966, Okigbo was awarded the Langston Hughes Award for African Poetry by a panel of judges at the Festival of Black African Arts in Dakar. The award was refused by the poet on the grounds that it was awarded based on race. Okigbo was also recognized posthumously with the National Order of Merit of Biafra for his defense of the nation, an effort that cost him his life.

BIOGRAPHY
Christopher Nixton Ifekandu Okigbo was born in 1932, when the British ruled Nigeria as a colony. Although Okigbo received a colonial education and was raised in the Roman Catholic faith, he also followed many Igbo traditions in his childhood. These traditions included the familial worship of the goddess Idoto. Okigbo's grandfather was a priest at the Idoto shrine, which is associated with the river that flows through Ojoto. Much of Okigbo's poetry speaks directly to Idoto, the river goddess, or prominently features or references her.

Okigbo was educated at the University of Ibadan, where he began his studies as a medical student. He switched to a concentration on Greek and Latin classics and graduated in 1956. Okigbo married an Igbira princess, Judith Sefi Attah, daughter of the Attah of Igbiraland. Together, they had a daughter, Obiageli Ibrahmat Okigbo, born in 1964.

Okigbo held a number of jobs in business, politics, publishing, and academia. He served in significant roles, including manager of Cambridge University Press for West Africa and organizer for the Mbari Club, a group of musicians, artists, and writers (including Wole Soyinka). Okigbo, also an accomplished pianist, played with Soyinka on stage. With Chinua Achebe, Okigbo created the publishing house Citadel Press. He eventually dedicated himself full-time to his poetry, until the onset of the civil war in Nigeria.

The war, which was based on ethnic tensions, saw the secession of the Igbo people in Nigeria, leading to the Republic of Biafra in 1967. Many crimes against humanity were committed during the war, and more than three million Igbo Biafrans died of starvation. Okigbo took up arms in defense of the Biafran cause, and was given the title of major. In July, his lodgings in Enugu, where much of his unpublished writing was held, were destroyed in a Nigerian-run bombing campaign. That fall, he led his troops to the front lines of the battle and was killed in action in Ekwegbe, near Nsukka, sometime in August. He was buried in an Igbo grave near Nsukka, but the precise location is unknown. In 2007, a commemorative stone was placed on an empty plot at the Okigbo burial ground in Ojoto.

Shortly after Okigbo's death, Ali Al' Amin Mazrui wrote *The Trial of Christopher Okigbo* (1971). This novel depicts Africa as an afterworld, where Okigbo is on trial for putting personal politics before his own creative potential. The novel addresses age-old questions regarding the responsibility of the artist in a social context.

ANALYSIS

A general discussion of African literature during the 1950's and 1960's would invariably involve themes of oppression, identity in crisis, and the rejection of native culture in favor of the colonizing culture. Although Christopher Okigbo wrote against colonialism, he also disassociated himself from the negritude movement, choosing to be known for his poetry and not for his skin color. Okigbo's work is often described as modernist. His influences range from Yoruba *oriki* (praise poems) to Igbo lamentation songs. In addition, Stéphane Mallarmé, T. S. Eliot, Leopold Senghor, and Vergil and other writers of classic Greek and Latin poetry, whose work Okigbo knew well, also figure into his poetry. Okigbo raises the question of social consciousness in his poems, which were written during a time of social upheaval throughout Africa and much of the world. The Biafran crisis was an especially potent topic for the poet, who devoted much of his later work to Biafra and to freedom movements around the world.

Okigbo's poems are peppered with references to and anecdotes from his Igbo upbringing. Much of his work is highly lyrical and reflects the oral tradition of the Igbo people. His prose is deeply mystic and reflects an ethereal, sometimes foreboding quality. He often refers to the "Prodigal" and the river goddess Idoto, suggesting a structuralist hero on a quest for a higher connection to his roots—the fertile soil, the nationalism

connected to the land, and the ancestors buried in it. Okigbo's family believed him to be the reincarnation of his grandfather; therefore they expected him to continue the worship of Idoto in the role of priest, as his grandfather had. Okigbo believed that in his poetry, he found a way to fulfil his duties as a priest to Idoto.

Because of the lyrical quality of Okigbo's work, it is believed that to truly grasp one of his poems, one must listen to it being spoken aloud. Some of Okigbo's poems were specially written for accompaniment to rhythms played on the drums.

HEAVENSGATE

Heavensgate contains five sections that describe the journey of the Prodigal: "The Passage," "Initiations," "Watermaid," "Lustra," and "Newcomer." The two most renowned poems from this work are "The Passage" and "Watermaid." "The Passage" is probably the most often quoted of Okigbo's poems. In the opening lines, the Prodigal pays homage to Idoto and waits before her to receive recognition and possibly a blessing before beginning his journey.

The Prodigal returns in "Watermaid," where he waits on an island for a white queen. Since he is sitting by the water, he may be waiting for Idoto, but the watermaid who answers him abandons him in the end. The tone of the poem is like that of a love poem, but it ends listlessly, when the Prodigal fails to attain anything but a reflection from the sea. The poem finishes with the starless sky staring down at the Prodigal, sitting alone on his island, struggling to understand a monody. Here, Okigbo displays his musical sensibilities as well as his understanding of Greek literature, for in Greek tragedies, one character would often lament another's death in a monody (ode for one actor or voice). The white queen seems to have been an illusion, one that the Prodigal is unable to attain; therefore, he laments not only her death but also the death of the very idea of her. In this sense, Okigbo may be using allegory to represent the death of the ideals of the colonizers at a time when Nigeria was becoming more and more independent. The Prodigal, whose name suggests "one who returns" to one's roots, may have been mourning, but not necessarily the departure of the British (the white queen) but the ideals for which they claimed to stand—justice, civility, and purity. There is a sense of conflict between the ideals and the white queen who claims to bear them; the Prodigal, who returns to his own roots and sense of self in the following poems, discovers this.

PATH OF THUNDER

Path of Thunder was published posthumously in 1968. The collection is a series of politically explosive poetry, in which Okigbo passes judgment on the Nigerian government and its treatment of the Igbo people. This work is considered to be more accessible and less mystical than Okigbo's previous poetry.

War is the dominant theme of the poems in this work; "Elegy for Alto," one of the most-quoted poems of this collection, is filled with the weapons of war, including detonators, howitzers, bayonets, and cannons. "Elegy for Alto" was written to be accompanied by traditional Igbo funerary and war drumming. It has elements of a Byronic poem in that it is melodic and speaks of a dream state, with the dreamer looking on war and ravage.

Okigbo used the first person in "Elegy for Alto," and it reads as if he were in the poem, imploring Mother Earth to allow him to be the Prodigal, a sacrificial ram led to slaughter. The poem has been thought to be prophetic in that Okigbo foreshadowed his own death and the downfall of the Biafran nation. He describes onlookers as avoiders of truth and says that while people slumber, a dream is dying. In the final lines of the poem, Okigbo describes the loss of an old star, followed by the appearance of a new star. The poem also includes many references to eagles, which descend as thieves. Eagles are often referred to throughout literature, including in the Bible, as an allegory for a more powerful enemy preying on the weaknesses of its opponent, who is often caught unaware. The repetitious references to theft create a sense of anxiety in the poem, making apparent Okigbo's conviction that he is called to serve, to protect his peoples' right to a land under siege, and their very right to exist.

The poem was most likely written very near the time of the poet's death, and it was published soon after. Elegiac poetry is a main staple of the oral form of Igbo literature. Elegies, also called "dirges" in Igboland, are a traditional way to commemorate a death or to honor a fallen hero. Many dirges have since been written in honor of Okigbo.

BIBLIOGRAPHY

Echeruo, Michael J. C. *A Concordance to the Poems of Christopher Okigbo: With a Complete Text of the Poems, 1957-1967*. Lewiston, N.Y.: Edwin Mellen Press, 2008. This is a comprehensive tool for anyone interested in Okigbo's work, as it provides not only access to all of Okigbo's poems in one volume but also a concordance of his imagery and style.

Egudu, Romanus. "Christopher Okigbo and the Growth of Poetry." In *European-Language Writing in Sub-Saharan Africa*, edited by Albert S. Gerard and György M. Vajda. Vol. 2. Budapest, Hungary: Coordinating Committee of a Comparative History of Literatures in European Languages, 1986. Egudu seeks to explain Okigbo's poetry and its modernist components in the wake of the Biafran war.

Mazrui, Ali Al'Amin. *The Trial of Christopher Okigbo*. London: Heinemann, 1971. Mazrui's novel imagines Okigbo on trial for neglecting to put his art before all else.

Nwakanma, Obi. *Christopher Okigbo, 1930-1967: Thirsting for Sunlight*. London: James Currey, 2010. A modern biography of the poet's life and overall contribution to literature.

Nwonga, Donatus Ibe. *Critical Perspectives on Christopher Okigbo*. Washington, D.C.: Three Continents Press, 1984. Although this is an older book, it is quite comprehensive and discusses many of Okigbo's poems individually.

Okafor, Dubem. *The Dance of Death: Nigerian History and Christopher Okigbo's Poetry*. Trenton, N.J.: Africa World Press, 1998. A historical look at Nigeria at the time of the Biafran crisis. Okigbo's poetry is discussed in depth, especially the later poems.

Shannon Oxley

OMAR KHAYYÁM

Born: Nishapur, Persia (now in Iran); May 18, 1048(?)

Died: Nishapur, Persia (now in Iran); December 4, 1123(?)

PRINCIPAL POETRY

Rubā'īyāt, twelfth century (*True Translation of Hakim Omar Khayyam's "Robaiyat*," 1994; commonly known as *Rubáiyát of Omar Khayyám*)

OTHER LITERARY FORMS

Omar Khayyám (OH-mor ki-YOM) is remembered primarily for his *Rubáiyát*.

ACHIEVEMENTS

Omar Khayyám's contemporaries spoke of his mathematical, scientific, and scholarly achievements with immense respect, heaping upon him such epithets as Sage of the World, Philosopher of the Universe, Lord of the Wise Men, and Proof of the Truth—but none mentioned his poetic achievement. One reason for the omission is obvious: Omar Khayyám's quatrains were not published (at least by the regular mode then prevailing) during his lifetime, but only gradually came to light in various citations and manuscripts during the following centuries. Meanwhile, apparently, the quatrains were circulating, either orally or in clandestine written versions, with potent effect. So much may be gathered from the backhanded compliment of a successor, one Abu'l-Hasan Ali Qifti (1172-1248), a defender of the faith who wrote in *Tarikh al-Hukama* (thirteenth century) that the Sufis, a mystical Islamic sect, had been corrupted by Omar Khayyám's quatrains: ". . . these poems are like beautiful snakes, outwardly attractive, but inwardly poisonous and deadly to the Holy Law." Qifti's remarks indicate why the *Rubáiyát* could not be published during Omar Khayyám's lifetime, but, ironically, the religious critics' citation of offending quatrains was one way they were circulated and preserved.

Omar Khayyám's ranking alongside the snake in the Garden of Eden is certainly a tribute to his poetic power; nevertheless, the opposition of religious zealots and the embrace of the mystical Sufis finally did him in. As Persian poets with more substantial *divans* (collections) came to the fore—such as Jalāl Al-Dīn Rūmī, Saʿdi, Hafiz, and Jami—the amateur Omar Khayyám and his one hundred or so quatrains faded into obscurity. The dilution of his achievement through transmission (sometimes by unfriendly hands) and through eventual attribution to him of hundreds of repetitious, inferior quatrains did not help his reputation. Omar Khayyám continued to be thought a very minor poet until suddenly, in Victorian England, his *Rubáiyát* blazed forth again like a literary comet. The cause was Edward FitzGerald's English version, one of the most successful translations of all time, a translation which FitzGerald polished through five editions (the first published in 1859, the fifth in 1889). To the Pre-Raphaelites and others, the *Rubáiyát* gave expression to a whole sad *Weltanschauung*, and as such the work has continued through many editions and translations into the world's major languages. For some time after FitzGerald's translation, Omar Khayyám the poet remained without recognition in his own country, aside from illustrated editions of his quatrains produced for the tourist trade, but in recent decades, Iranian literary scholars have also been giving him their serious attention.

For scholars of the *Rubáiyát*, simply establishing what Omar Khayyám wrote has been, and remains, the biggest problem. One theory is that he produced no quatrains at all, another that he produced thousands. There are numerous competing manuscripts (a few forged) from copyists. Comparing manuscripts endlessly, scholars conservatively accept no more than one hundred or so quatrains as authentic (though differing on which quatrains). Based on a fourteenth century manuscript considered as reliable as any, FitzGerald's translation (fifth edition) is used in this essay for purposes of quotation.

Despite his limited production, Omar Khayyám was no literary lightweight, certainly not the shallow Epicurean condemned by early religious fanatics and sought after by modern sensualists. Worthy of Jean-Paul Sartre or Albert Camus, these thoughts have an amazingly modern flavor that is not merely the result of Fitz-Gerald's translation. Although Qifti considered them venom, they are really the wine distilled from a life in the harsh desert soil of an old Muslim land. That such freethinking could proceed from the midst of such repressive conditions as those surrounding Omar Khayyám is one indication of his achievement, and certainly an encouragement to the human race. This freedom of tone gives the *Rubáiyát* a paradoxically uplifting quality despite Omar Khayyám's pessimism about the human condition.

BIOGRAPHY

Just as it is difficult (if not impossible) to say exactly what Omar Khayyám wrote, so also it is difficult, except in the broadest outline, to establish the facts of his life. The scanty information available on Omar Khayyám is embroidered by romantic legend, attempts to discredit him (or to show him repenting), and idle speculation. One source, for example, calls him inhospitable and bad-tempered, but this characterization is not borne out by other information. Another source maintains that Omar Khayyám believed in metempsychosis, then tells the following story to prove it: One day when Omar Khayyám and his students were walking about the college, they came across a donkey too stubborn to move with its load of bricks. Omar Khayyám explained that the donkey was inhabited by the soul of a former lecturer at the college, whose beard had transmigrated to the donkey's tail, and he got the donkey to move by improvising a quatrain on it. Such is the nature of most of the information on Omar Khayyám.

The poet's full name was Ghiyasoddin Abolfath Omar ibn Ebrahim Khayyámi, the name Khayyám meaning "tent-maker," probably referring to the trade of one of his ancestors. His family had lived in Nishapur for generations before he was born. After attending school at Nishapur, he continued his studies at Balkh, distinguishing himself especially in geometry and astronomy. Following his schooling, he worked for the magistrate of Samarkand, the ruler of Bokhara, and eventually the grand Sultan Ma-

lekshah (reigned 1072-1092). Among the projects he worked on were the construction of an observatory and the creation of a more accurate calendar.

During the first half of his life, Omar Khayyám's growing prominence and powerful patrons seem to have shielded him from the religious fanatics, while also attracting their attention. When Sultan Malekshah died, Omar Khayyám appears to have suffered setbacks. Apparently he had to leave Nishapur in 1095, staying away for several years, during which time he made his pilgrimage to Mecca and visited Baghdad. The ruler of the province that included Nishapur was Malekshah's son Sanjar, whom, the story goes, Omar Khayyám alienated with an offhand remark when Sanjar was a child. In 1117, Sanjar became sultan. It may have been from his own experience of political re-

Omar Khayyám (©Bettman/CORBIS)

verses that Omar Khayyám was speaking when, in the *Rubáiyát*, he advocated the simple life in the wilderness, "where name of Slave and Sultan is forgot."

ANALYSIS

A noteworthy coincidence in intellectual history is that Edward FitzGerald's translation of Omar Khayyám's *Rubáiyát* came out the same year as Charles Darwin's *On the Origin of Species by Means of Natural Selection: Or, The Preservation of Favoured Races in the Struggle for Life* (1859). Despite their obvious differences, the two works show remarkable similarities: Both are inimical to religion and evince a thoroughgoing empiricism. Like Omar Khayyám, Darwin thought God was cruel, and both authors espouse a deterministic view of the world. Both authors had sharpened their minds through years of scientific investigation, enabling them to cut through the fat of human illusion to the heart of things. Taking their stand as rebels and empiricists, both authors were precursors of modern Existentialism, with its doctrine of the absurd. Sticklers for facts will point out that Omar Khayyám lived eight to nine centuries before Existentialism. Precisely—his quatrains had to wait all those centuries before they finally found a responsive audience in Victorian England, an alien society that nevertheless had much in common with the Muslim world in which Omar Khayyám lived.

If Darwin's *On the Origin of Species by Means of Natural Selection* marked the triumph of science over religion in the Christian world, the suppression of Omar Khayyám's quatrains symbolized religion's triumph over science in the Muslim world. The centuries preceding Omar Khayyám had seen a great flowering of scientific achievement in Muslim lands, but by his time, religious reaction had set in. In near hysteria over losing control, the religious authorities had hardened their attitudes, sometimes to the point of fanaticism. In Persia, the religious authorities regained control with the rise of the Seljuq rulers, nomadic Turks from central Asia only recently converted to Islam. Both parties found a political alliance convenient. The pursuit of knowledge, except for knowledge with immediate practical applications, became suspect. Rationalism was attacked as a foreign import (from the Greeks), and the study of logic was banned; only those words and thoughts which ran

within the circumscribed patterns set by the Qur'ān and its interpreters were allowed—and even there, any ambiguity could be fatal. For example, the great religious scholar Abu Hamed Mohammed Ghazali, a friendly opponent and contemporary of Omar Khayyám (both taught at Nishapur for a time), was charged with apostasy and his books burned because he said "There cannot be anything better than what is," which he took as a statement of God's power but others took as a statement of God's weakness (he had also made enemies by favoring logic and by publicly criticizing another religious authority). Other religious leaders who misspoke were crucified or burned at the stake. Indeed, aside from powerful friends, only the factionalism of the fanatics themselves offered any precarious safety.

THE RUBA'I STANZA

In this repressive atmosphere, what mode of expression remained for the independent, rational thinker who wished to retain his sanity? For Omar Khayyám, it was apparently the quatrain (*ruba'i*), a literary form especially suited to guerrilla tactics. In quantitative meter (translated by FitzGerald as iambic pentameter), rhyming *aaba* and occasionally *aaaa*, the *ruba'i* is like a haiku or epigram—or, even better, a combination of haiku and epigram, of image and pointed, witty remark. The unrhymed third line causes the rhyming fourth line to fall with particular force. Each *ruba'i*, it should be stressed, is a separate poem, not a stanza in a longer work (in Persian, a collection of *rubáiyát* is arranged alphabetically, according to the final rhyming letter of each *ruba'i*). Thus, the *ruba'i* is not long enough to be taken too seriously; it can be delivered orally, perhaps as a humorous aside or innocuous rhyme; and it is easy to remember.

How Omar Khayyám safely transmitted his *rubáiyát* is unknown—whether individually and orally to trusted students and friends, or collected in circulating manuscripts, or in a secret manuscript discovered after his death—but their underground nature can be easily seen when they are compared with his public utterances. Treating many of the same issues as the quatrains, Omar Khayyám's philosophical commentaries are models of evasiveness: brief, vague, and noncommittal, sketching out the issues without taking a stand (unlike the quatrains, which assert heretical positions on everything from God to wine).

CRITIQUING GOD

Omar Khayyám's conception of God represents a critique of the orthodox idea of a personal God. From orthodox teachings, Omar Khayyám deduces a God who is either cruel or incompetent. Only a cruel God would make man weak, beset his path with sin, and then punish him for falling. Not even "a peevish Boy" would take such perverse delight in destroying his creation. From this point of view, men are only God's playthings: "a moving row/ Of Magic Shadow-shapes" presented "by the Master of the Show"; "helpless Pieces of the Game He plays/ Upon this Chequer-board"; the "Ball" that "the Player" tosses onto "the Field" and strikes with his mallet. Or, if this view seems too extreme, then God must at least be incompetent, a potter who mars his pots. In either case, God is placed in the position of needing human forgiveness, rather than vice versa.

THE RUBÁIYÁT

If anyone is cruel or incompetent, it is the theologians, whose efforts to define God Omar Khayyám is really attacking. Their definitions tend to be circular: They define God in their own image. At other times, they contradict themselves by trying to reconcile a perfect Creator with an imperfect creation, or merely slip into wishful thinking. In the *Rubáiyát*, some of this mushy logic is exemplified in the conversation among the "Pots":

> Whereat some one of the loquacious Lot—
> I think a Súfi pipkin—waxing hot—
> "All this of Pot and Potter—Tell me then,
> Who is the Potter, pray, and who the Pot?"
> "Why," said another, "Some there are who tell
> Of one who threatens he will toss to Hell
> The luckless Pots he marred in making—Pish!
> He's a Good Fellow, and 'twill all be well."

None of this confusion stands up under the scrutiny of Omar Khayyám, who considers theological speculation a waste of time.

Instead, Omar Khayyám constructs an empirical worldview based strictly on available evidence. Admittedly, evidence is in short supply—"Into this Universe, and *Why* not knowing/ Nor *Whence*, like Water willynilly flowing. . . ." Still, the Universe exists, hence a

Creator. From what Omar Khayyám can see, however, the Creator pays little attention to humans, but is only an impersonal force rather like Fate:

> The Moving Finger writes; and, having writ,
> Moves on: nor all your Piety nor Wit
> Shall lure it back to cancel half a Line,
> Nor all your Tears wash out a Word of it.

There is no Heaven and no Hell (except of humanity's own making), hence no afterlife. All that remains is this life, wherein the fate of humans is defined by the limitations of their nature: "With Earth's first Clay They did the Last Man knead,/ And there of the Last Harvest sow'd the Seed. . . ."

The salient facts of humanity's fate are a transitory life and a certain death, dust to dust. Death takes the good and the bad, the great and the small indifferently; all that remains of the departed is the dust beneath one's feet or the grass along the riverbank. Therefore, seek neither "the Glories of This World" nor "the Prophet's Paradise to come"; instead, "take the Cash, and let the Credit go," seize the day, live like the blooming rose:

> Come, fill the Cup, and in the fire of Spring
> Your Winter-garment of Repentence fling:
> The Bird of Time has but a little way
> To flutter—and the Bird is on the Wing.

Like any good teacher, Omar Khayyám instructs not only by his advice but also by his example. He confesses that he once spent his time in trifling scholarly pursuits—improving the calendar ("'Twas only striking from the Calendar/ Unborn To-morrow, and dead Yesterday"), and conducting scientific and philosophical investigations ("Of all that one should care to fathom, I/ Was never deep in anything but—Wine"). Eventually, however, Omar Khayyám repented such a sorry existence and "made a Second Marriage": He "divorced old barren Reason" from his bed and "took the Daughter of the Vine to Spouse."

Whether or not Omar Khayyám found happiness with wine, his example and advice need not be taken literally. In the *Rubáiyát*, wine is also important as a symbol, the central symbol wherein the two main lines of thought, the antireligious sentiment and the empiricism, converge. In traditional Islamic law, one sip of wine is worth eighty lashes, so Omar Khayyám's description of the tavern as a temple indicates his scorn for religious teachings, for the prohibitions and illusions that cut people off from seizing life while they can. It is also appropriate that what is prohibited by religion should, as so frequently happens, symbolize the heart's desire, for empiricism shows that, even if life is absurd, some people do not know any better than to be happy. In the *Rubáiyát*, wine symbolizes the possibility of seizing happiness, in whatever form. Happiness does not necessarily have to take the form of spending one's day in taverns:

> A book of Verses underneath the Bough,
> A jug of Wine, a Loaf of Bread—and Thou
> Beside me singing in the Wilderness—
> Oh, Wilderness were Paradise enow!

It is to be hoped that, with his wine, his Sákí (the girl who serves the wine), and his quatrains, Omar Khayyám did manage to find happiness even in old Persia.

OTHER MAJOR WORKS

NONFICTION: *Maqalat fi al-Jabr wa al-Muqabila*, 1070 (*The Algebra of Omar Khayyam*, 1931); *The Nectar of Grace: Omar Khayyám's Life and Works*, 1941 (includes *The Measure of Philosophy* and other essays); *Mizan al-Hikma*, eleventh century (*The Measure of Philosophy*, 1941).

BIBLIOGRAPHY

Bloom, Harold, ed. *Edward FitzGerald's the "Rubáiyát of Omar Khayyám."* Philadelphia: Chelsea House, 2004. Presents an introduction to FitzGerald's infamous study and chapters that consider the "fin de siècle cult" of FitzGerald's work, comparisons with poets such as Tennyson, "forgetting" FitzGerald's study, and more. Bibliography, index.

Dashti, Ali. *In Search of Omar Khayyám*. Translated by L. P. Elwell-Sutton. London: Allen and Unwin, 1971. A very reliable study of Omar Khayyám, which includes a review of his age and the known facts of his life, a collection of seventy-five quatrains that the author argues can be attributed with some confidence to Omar Khayyám, and a sympathetic and sensitive identification of themes in the poems.

FitzGerald, Edward. *Rubáiyát of Omar Khayyám*. 4th ed. London: Bernard Quaritch, 1879. This is the last edition the author saw to press and thus the official, final version of the poem.

_____. *Rubáiyát of Omar Khayyám: A Critical Edition*. Edited by Christopher Decker. Charlottesville: University Press of Virginia, 1997. Decker provides a scholarly critique of Omar Khayyám's life, FitzGerald's translations of the *Rubáiyát*, and the merits of the various editions of this famous set of poems. Decker's book is a useful tool for serious students looking for the definitive edition of FitzGerald's *Rubáiyát of Omar Khayyám*.

Heron-Allen, Edward. *Edward FitzGerald's "Rubáiyát of Omar Khayyám" with Their Original Persian Sources*. Boston: L. C. Page, 1899. A study of FitzGerald's stanzas paralleled with the Persian texts of possible sources, demonstrating that, although FitzGerald was inspired by Khayyamic and other Persian quatrains, *Rubáiyát of Omar Khayyám* is an original English poem and not a translation.

Naini, Bahram Baghaie. *The Genuine Face of Omar Khayyám*. London: Parsees Arts, 2007. This biography attempts to portray the actual man behind the myths and legends.

Nasr, Seyyed Hossein. *The Islamic Intellectual Tradition in Persia*. Edited by Mehdi Amin Razavi. Richmond, Surrey, England: Curzon Press, 1996. Presents a chapter exploring Omar Khayyám as a philosopher, poet, and scientist. Bibliography, index.

Rashed, Rushdei, and Bijan Vahabzadeh. *Omar Khayyám: The Mathematician*. New York: Bibliotheca Persica Press, 2000. An exploration of Omar Khayyám's work in mathematics. Part of the Persian Heritage series. Bibliography, index.

Razavi, Mehdi Amin. *The Wine of Wisdom: The Life, Poetry, and Wisdom of Omar Khayyám*. Oxford, England: Oneworld, 2006. This biography of the poet discusses his works and places him in the world of Persian poetry.

Teimourian, Hazhir. *Omar Khayyám: Poet, Rebel, Astronomer*. Stroud, England: Sutton, 2007. Biography that examines the various roles of Omar Khayyám, as well as his writings.

Harold Branam

P

DAN PAGIS

Born: Radautsi, Romania; October 16, 1930
Died: Jerusalem, Israel; July 29, 1986

PRINCIPAL POETRY

Shaon ha-hol, 1959
Sheut mauheret, 1964
Gilgul, 1970
Poems by Dan Pagis, 1972
Moah, 1975
Points of Departure, 1981
Milim nirdafot, 1982
Shneim asar panim, 1984
Shirim aharonim, 1987
*Variable Directions: The Selected Poetry of
    Dan Pagis*, 1989
Col ha-shirim, 1991

OTHER LITERARY FORMS

Although Dan Pagis (pah-GEE) is internationally known as a poet, he has written a children's book in Hebrew, *ha-Beitzah she-hithapsah* (1973; the egg that tried to disguise itself). As a professor of medieval Hebrew literature at Hebrew University, he has published important studies on the aesthetics of medieval poetry, including expositions of Moses Ibn Ezra, Judah ha-Levi, Ibn Gabirol, and the other great poets of the eleventh and twelfth centuries who celebrated the colors and images of worldly existence in elegant, formal verse. Pagis's own poems, more understated and conversational than the medieval texts he studied, have been translated into Afrikaans, Czech, Danish, Dutch, Estonian, French, Hungarian, Italian, Japanese, Polish, Portuguese, Romanian, Serbo-Croatian, Swedish, Vietnamese, and Yiddish.

ACHIEVEMENTS

The first generation of Israeli poets often used a collective identity to write poetry of largely ideological content. However, the reaction to previous ideological values that arose in the late 1950's and the 1960's has been described by Hebrew critic Shimon Sandbank as "the withdrawal from certainty." Poets Yehuda Amichai and Natan Zach were at the forefront of this avant-garde movement, a "new wave" that included Dan Pagis, Tuvia Ruebner, Dahlia Ravikovitch, and David Rokeah. These poets of the 1950's turned away from the socially minded national poets, believing in the poet as an individual and using understatement, irony, prosaic diction, and free verse to express their own views.

Most of all, the revolution in Hebrew verse that Pagis, Amichai, and Zach brought about was the perfection of a colloquial norm for Hebrew poetry. Pagis and Amichai especially made efforts to incorporate elements of classical Hebrew into the colloquial diction, with Pagis often calling on a specific biblical or rabbinical text. His poems have appeared in major American magazines, including *The New Yorker* and *Tikkun*.

BIOGRAPHY

Dan Pagis was born in Radautsi, Romania, and was brought up in Bukovina, speaking German in a Jewish home in what was once an eastern province of the Austro-Hungarian Empire. He spent three years in Nazi concentration camps, from which he escaped in 1944. After he arrived in Palestine in 1946, Pagis began to publish poetry in his newly acquired Hebrew within only three or four years, and he became a schoolteacher on a kibbutz.

He settled in Jerusalem in 1956, where he earned his Ph.D. from Hebrew University and became a professor of medieval Hebrew literature. Pagis also taught at the Jewish Theological Seminary in New York, Harvard University, and the University of California, at both San Diego and Berkeley. During his life, he was the foremost living authority on the poetics of Hebrew literature of the High Middle Ages and the Renaissance. He was married and had two children. Pagis died of cancer in Jerusalem in 1986.

ANALYSIS

Reflecting the geographic and linguistic displacements of his life, displacement is a governing concept in Dan Pagis's poetry, in the sense that to "displace" is to remove or put out of its proper place. Although there is a great deal of horror in his poetry, the historical record of that horror is so enormous that Pagis uses displacement to give it expression without the shrillness of hysteria or the bathos of melodrama. Instead, he cultivates a variety of distanced, ventriloquist voices that become authentic surrogates for his own voice. Pagis survived one of the darkest events in human history and managed to set distance from it through the medium of his art. Pagis is a playful poet as well, sometimes using humor and whimsy to transform the displacement of his life from a passively suffered fate into an imaginative reconstruction of reality.

POEMS BY DAN PAGIS

In *Poems by Dan Pagis*, it is apparent why many discussions of Pagis's poems tend to pigeonhole him as a "poet of the Holocaust." The first poem is titled "The Last Ones," and the first-person speaker in the poem speaks for all the Jews left after the Holocaust. Ironically, he states that "For years I have appeared only here and there/ at the edges of this jungle." Nevertheless, he is certain that "at this moment/ someone is tracking me. . . . Very close. Here." The poem ends with the line "There is no time to explain," indicating a collective consciousness that is still running in fear for its life.

A section of the book called "Testimony" contains six Holocaust poems, among them "Europe, Late," the brilliant "Written in Pencil in the Sealed Railway-Car," and the chilling "Draft of a Reparations Agreement." In "Europe, Late," the speaker betrays his innocence by asking what year it is, and the answer is "Thirty-nine and a half, still awfully early." He introduces the reader to the life of the party, dancing the tango and kissing the hand of an elegant woman, reassuring her "that everything will be all right." However, the voice stops mid-sentence at the end of the poem, "No it could never happen here,/ don't worry so—you'll see—it could."

Often Holocaust themes are placed in an archetypal perspective, as in the widely known poem "Written in Pencil in the Sealed Railway-Car." The speaker is "eve" traveling with her son "abel," and she means to leave a message for her other son. "If you see my other son/ cain son of man/ tell him i"; here the poem ends abruptly, leaving the reader to meditate on the nature of evil.

In "Draft of a Reparations Agreement," the speaker is again a collective voice, the voice of the perpetrators of the Holocaust. The agreement promises that "Everything will be returned to its place,/ paragraph after paragraph," echoing the bureaucratic language in which the whole Nazi endeavor was carried out. In a kind of mordant displacement the draft writer promises "The scream back into the throat./ The gold teeth back to the gums." Also,

> . . . you will be covered with skin and sinews and you
>   will live,
> look, you will have your lives back,
> . . . .
> Here you are. Nothing is too late.

The exquisite irony exposes the absurdity of reparations as well as the lunacy of the speaker.

POINTS OF DEPARTURE

In *Points of Departure*, Pagis's voice runs the gamut from horrifying to deceptively whimsical. In "End of the Questionnaire," he creates a questionnaire to be filled out posthumously, with questions including "number of galaxy and star,/ number of grave." "You have the right to appeal," the questionnaire informs the deceased. It ends with the command, "In the blank space below, state/ how long you have been awake and why you are surprised." Ironically, this poem provokes the reader to meditate on the great finality of death.

"The Beginning" is a poem about "the end of creation." Pagis envisions the end as "A time of war," when "distant fleets of steel are waiting." The shadow of the Holocaust hovers over all, as "High above the smoke and the odor of fat and skins hovers/ a yellow magnetic stain." The poet seems to be saying that the Holocaust is the beginning of the end, when "at the zero-hour/ the Great Bear, blazing, strides forth/ in heat."

In a charming cycle in which five poems are grouped under the heading "Bestiary," each poem is rich with humor and whimsy. In the first, "The Elephant," Pagis writes of the pachyderm who ties on sixteen "marvelously accurate wristwatches" and "glides forth smoothly/ out of his elephant fate." Armchairs also become animals in this bestiary: "The slowest animals/ are the soft large-eared leather armchairs" that "multiply/ in the shade of potted philodendrons." Balloons also are animate, as they "fondle one another" and cluster at the ceiling, humbly accepting their limit. However, what is playful suddenly becomes ominous, as

> The soul suddenly leaks out
> in a terrified whistle
> or explodes
> with a single pop.

The darkest poem in this group is the one titled "The Biped." Pagis points out that though he is related to other predatory animals, "he alone/ cooks animals, peppers them,/ he alone is clothed with animals," and he alone "protests/ against what is decreed." What the poet finds strangest is that he "rides of his own free will/ on a motorcycle." "The Biped" becomes an existential comedy through this odd mixture of traits Pagis chooses to juxtapose, including the last three lines of the poem, which state "He has four limbs,/ two ears,/ a hundred hearts."

"BRAIN"

The highly intellectual poetry of Pagis treats each subject in a style which seems most appropriate. In "Brain" (from *Points of Departure*), he uses several different styles to illustrate the tortured life of this brain in exile, or, what the reader might imagine, Pagis himself. Typical of his later poetry, "Brain" is concerned with the ambivalence of the poet's experience of the world and employs images from the laboratory, popular culture, the Hebrew Bible, and medicine. The poem begins with a reference to religious life, although the "dark night of the soul" here becomes ironically "the dark night of the skull," during which "Brain" discovers "he" is born. In part 2, in a biblical reference, "Brain hovers upon the face of the deep," yet he is not a deity when his eyes develop, he discovers the world complete.

Brain first suspects that he is the whole universe, as an infant is aware only of itself, but then suspects he embodies millions of other brains, all "splitting off from him, betraying him from within." In a sudden shift of tone in part 4, Pagis gives us an image of Brain, looking exactly as one would picture him: "grayish-white convolutions,/ a bit oily, sliding back and forth." Brain sets out to explore the world and makes a friend, with

whom he communicates over radio sets in the attic. He questions the friend to find out if they are alike, and when they become intimate Brain asks, "Tell me, do you know how to forget?"

When his life is half over, Brain finds his "bush of veins" enveloping him, snaring him, and in a fit of existential despair, he wonders why he ever spoke, to whom he spoke, and if there is anyone to listen to him. Part 9 is an encyclopedic entry describing the brain, and Brain is embarrassed by so much praise; he commands "Let there be darkness!" and closes the encyclopedia. Brain metamorphoses throughout the poem and starts to think about outer space.

Toward the end of this remarkable poem, Brain is receiving signals from light years away and makes contact with another world, which may be a heart. The discovery is cloaked in the language of science fiction; Brain is both a microcosm and a macrocosm, and he is astounded to find that

> There is a hidden circle somewhere
> whose center is everywhere
> and whose circumference is nowhere;
> . . . so near
> that he will never
> be able
> to see it.

With his new knowledge, his old sarcasm and jokes desert him, along with his fear. Finally, he achieves what he desires; "he no longer has to remember."

"INSTRUCTIONS FOR CROSSING THE BORDER"

The second line of "Instructions for Crossing the Border," "You are not allowed to remember," is typical of the preoccupation with memory that haunts this poet. The advice is positive, almost upbeat: "you are a man, you sit in the train./ Sit comfortably./ You've got a decent coat now." This is sinister advice, considering that the last line is a direct contradiction of the second: "Go. You are not allowed to forget." The voice is that of an official speaking, addressing "Imaginary man." It is a dehumanized voice, one that cannot recognize the man to whom it is speaking; the addressee is only present in the speaker's imagination. Although it is an early poem, using the stripped and spare vocabulary of his early work, "Instructions for Crossing the Border" forecasts the later "Brain" in its preoccupation with obliterating memory.

"Harvests"

"Harvests" starts with a deceptively benign image, that of "The prudent field-mouse" who "hoards and hoards for the time of battle and siege." Other benign images follow until an ironic twist in the sixth line, "the fire revels in the wheat," hints at what is ahead. What waits, of course, is the hawk, against whom the mouse's prudence and marvelously tunneled home is no protection at all. To darken the image further, the hawk is both "sharp-eyed" and "punctual," implying that the time of the mouse's demise is determined and no matter how canny he is, the hawk will appear at the appointed time. "Harvests" is a small parable in which Pagis, typically, uses animals to make a statement about the human condition, similar to his whimsical poem "Experiment of the Maze."

Other major works

NONFICTION: *The Poetry of David Vogel*, 1966, fourth edition, 1975; *The Poetry of Levi Ibn Altabban of Saragossa*, 1968; *Secular Poetry and Poetic Theory: Moses Ibn Ezra and His Contemporaries*, 1970; *Hindush u-mascoret be-shirat-ha-hol ha-'Ivrit, Sefarad ve-Italyah*, 1976.

CHILDREN'S LITERATURE: *ha-Beitzah she-hithapsah*, 1973.

Bibliography

Alter, Robert. "Dan Pagis and the Poetry of Displacement." *Judaism* 45, no. 80 (Fall, 1996). This article places the poet among his peers, primarily Yehuda Amichai and Natan Zach, illuminating Pagis's similarities and differences.

_____. Introduction to *The Selected Poetry of Dan Pagis*. Translated by Stephen Mitchell. Berkeley: University of California Press, 1996. Alter examines the life of Pagis and offers some literary criticism in this introduction to a translation of selected works. Originally published as *Variable Directions* in 1989.

Burnshaw, Stanley, T. Carmi, and Ezra Spicehandler, eds. *The Modern Hebrew Poem Itself*. New York: Holt, Rinehart and Winston, 1989. This book offers a stunning explication of Pagis's poem "The Log Book" and an afterword covering Hebrew poetry from 1965 to 1988. Provides a detailed discussion of the literary world Pagis inhabited and places him securely in the poetic movement of his generation. Each poem is presented in the original Hebrew, in phonetic transcription, and in English translation.

Keller, Tsipi, ed. *Poets on the Edge: An Anthology of Contemporary Hebrew Poetry*. Introduction by Aminadav Dykman. Albany: State University of New York Press, 2010. Contains a selection of poems by Pagis as well as a brief biography. The introduction discusses Pagis and Hebrew poetry in general, placing him among his fellows.

Omer-Sherman, Ranen. "In Place of the Absent God: The Reader in Dan Pagis's 'Written in Pencil in a Sealed Railway Car.'" *Cross Currents* 54, no. 2 (Summer, 2004): 51-61. Discusses teaching Pagis's well-known poem to students and their reactions and understandings. He also briefly outlines Pagis's life and provides analysis of the poem itself.

Sheila Golburgh Johnson

Nicanor Parra

Born: San Fabián de Alico, near Chillán, Chile; September 5, 1914

Principal poetry

Cancionero sin nombre, 1937
Poemas y antipoemas, 1954 (*Poems and Antipoems*, 1967)
La cueca larga, 1958
Versos de salón, 1962
Canciones rusas, 1967
Obra gruesa, 1969
Los profesores, 1971
Artefactos, 1972
Emergency Poems, 1972
Antipoems: New and Selected, 1985
Nicanor Parra: Biografía emotiva, 1988

Poemas para combatir la calvicie: Muestra de antipoesia, 1993

Discursos de sobremesa, 1997, 2006 (*After-Dinner Declarations*, 2009; bilingual edition)

Nicanor Parra en breve, 2001

Antipoems: How to Look Better and Feel Great, 2004

OTHER LITERARY FORMS

Nicanor Parra (PAH-rah) and Pablo Neruda co-authored *Pablo Neruda y Nicanor Parra: Discursos* (1962; Pablo Neruda and Nicanor Parra: speeches), which celebrated the appointment of the latter as an honorary member of the faculty of the College of Philosophy and Education of the University of Chile. The volume includes the speech of presentation by Parra, in which he proffers his point of view regarding Neruda's work, and that of acceptance by Neruda. Parra has been active on an international scale in poetry readings, seminars, conferences, and informal gatherings. Many of his poems composed since the publication of *Cancionero sin nombre* (untitled songs) are available in English through the two bilingual volumes published by New Directions—*Poems and Antipoems* and *Emergency Poems*—and one bilingual volume, *After-Dinner Declarations*, published by Host.

ACHIEVEMENTS

Nicanor Parra is the originator of the contemporary poetic movement in Latin America known as antipoetry. The antipoet, as this Chilean calls himself, is the absolute antiromantic, debasing all, even himself, while producing verses that are aggressive, wounding, sarcastic, and irritating. He has plowed new terrain in Latin American poetry using a store of methods that traditional poetry rejects or ignores. Parra's work is attacked as boring, disturbing, crude, despairing, ignoble, inconclusive, petulant, and devoid of lyricism. The antipoet generally agrees with these points of criticism, but begs the reader to lay aside what amounts to a nostalgic defense of worn-out traditions and join him in a new experience. Parra has established himself firmly in a prominent position in Hispanic American literature, influencing both his defenders and detractors.

BIOGRAPHY

Nicanor Parra Sandoval, one of eight children in a family plagued by economic insecurity, grew up in Chillán, in the south of Chile. His father was a schoolteacher whose irresponsibility and alcoholism placed considerable strain on the life and order of the family, which was held together by Parra's mother. Parra was in his early teens when his father died. The earlier antipathy he felt toward his father then turned toward his mother, and he left home. He began a process of identification with his father, toward whom he felt both attraction and repulsion, and to whom he attributes the basic elements of his inspiration for antipoetry.

During his youth, Parra composed occasional verses, so that when he went to the University of Chile in Santiago in 1933, he felt that he was a poet in addition to being a student of physics. He associated with the literary leaders at the student residence where he lived, and a year prior to graduating in 1938, he had published his first volume of poetry, *Cancionero sin nombre*.

After completing studies in mathematics and physics at the Pedagogical Institute of the university, Parra

Nicanor Parra (Andre Sanchez/Courtesy, New Directions)

taught for five years in secondary schools in Chile. Between 1943 and 1945, he studied advanced mechanics at Brown University in the United States. Returning home in 1948, he was named director of the School of Engineering at the University of Chile. He spent two years in England studying cosmology at Oxford, and upon his return to South America he was appointed professor of theoretical physics at the University of Chile.

The publication of Parra's second collection of poetry, *Poems and Antipoems*, formally introduced the antipoetry with which his name is associated. This new poetry shook the foundation of the theory of the genre in Latin America, winning for its author both condemnation and praise. In 1963, Parra visited the Soviet Union, where he supervised the translation into Spanish of an anthology of Soviet poets, and then traveled to the People's Republic of China. He visited Cuba in 1965, and the following year served as a visiting professor at Louisiana State University, later holding similar positions at New York University, Columbia, and Yale.

ANALYSIS

Nicanor Parra avoids the appearance of didacticism, claiming that he is not a preacher and that he is suspicious of doctrines, yet his purpose is to goad the reader with his corrosive verses, caustic irony, and black humor until the poet's response to human existence is shared. Satiric rather than political, antipoetry's sad, essentially moralizing, verse of hopelessness contains a strange and infinite tenderness toward humanity in its fallen condition. Neither philosophical nor theoretical poetry, it is intended to be an experience that will elicit a reaction and simulate life itself.

Even though he is a mathematician and a physicist, Parra does not consider life to be governed by a logical system of absolutes that, when harnessed, can direct humans toward organization and progress. On the contrary, he believes that the poet's life is absurd and chaotic, and the world is in the process of destruction and decay. Humans either accept this fact, together with their own powerlessness, or they deceive themselves by inventing philosophical theories, moral standards, and political ideologies to which they

cling. Parra views his own role as that of obliging humanity to see the falsity of any system that deceives one into believing in these masks that hide the grotesque collective condition in a chaotic universe. Parra makes fun of love, marriage, religion, psychology, political revolutions, art, and other institutions of society. They are rejected as futile dogmas that attempt to ennoble or exalt humans above the reality of their insignificance.

Poetry too comes under attack by this anarchist who claims he has orders to liquidate the genre. As the antipoet, Parra resists defining his own poetic structure, knowing that in such an event it too must be destroyed. Thus, he searches continually for new paths, his own evolution, a revolution.

The prefix notwithstanding, antipoetry, however unconventional, is poetry, and Parra himself willingly explains his concept of the form. It is, he says, traditional poetry enriched by Surrealism. As the word implies, the "antipoem" belongs to that tradition that rejects the established poetic order. In this case, it rebels against the sentimental idealism of Romanticism, the elegance and the superficiality of the *Modernistas*, and the irrationality of the vanguard movement. It is not a poetry of heroes, but of antiheroes, because humans have nothing to sing to or celebrate. Everything is a problem, including the language.

Parra eschews what he considers the abuse of earlier poetic language in favor of a direct, prosaic communication using the familiar speech of everyday life. He desires to free poetry from the domination of figures and tropes destined to accommodate a select group of readers who want to enjoy an experience in poetry that is not possible in life itself. He has declared his intent to write poems that are experiences. He is hostile to metaphors, word games, or any evasive power in language that helps to transpose reality. Parra's task is to speak to everyone and be understood by all. The antipoet recreates or reproduces slang, jargon, clichés, colloquialisms, words of the street, television commercials, and graffiti. He does not create poetry; he selects and compiles it. The genius of the language is sought in the culture of each country as reflected in the language of life. It is poetry not for literature's sake, but for humanity's sake. Its sentiments are the frustrations and hysteria of modern existence, not the anguish and nostalgia of Romanticism. Inasmuch as poetry is life, Parra also utilizes local or national peculiarities in language to underscore a specific social reality.

The destruction of the traditional poetic language is the first step in stimulating readers to be torn from the sacred myths that soothe them. Parra avoids so-called poetic words or uses them in unfamiliar contexts (the moon, for example, is poison). His images astonish readers with their irreverence, lack of modesty, grotesqueness, and ambiguity. They inherit the oneiric and unusual qualities of the Surrealists. Placed in the context of daily life, they equate the sublime with the ridiculous, the serious with the trivial, the poetic with the prosaic. Comic clichés and flat language are used by the protagonists in the antipoems to express their hurt and despair. The irony thus created by these simultaneous prosaic and tragic elements charges the work with humor and pathos. The reader laughs, though the protagonist, or antihero, suffers. The antihero's ineptitudes, failures, and foolishness are viewed with pity, scorn, and amusement. Parra's placement of familiar language and everyday failures in the life of the antihero, however, catches up with readers and compounds the irony, reducing the initial distance between readers and the protagonist. Readers become uncomfortable as this distance closes, their laughter not far from sadness.

The antihero in Parra's poetry is a rebel, disillusioned with all aspects of life, who suffers and is alone. He is a wanderer, distrustful and doubting, obsessed with suicide and death. Too insignificant, too ridiculous and nihilistic to be a tragic hero, he is merely the caricature of a hero. In need of communication, he undermines himself at every turn, belittling all of his efforts at self-expression. The grotesque inhabitants of the antipoetic world, comedians in an absurd play, unfulfilled in love and in their potentialities, suffer the passage of time, the agonizing problems of aging, and the inevitable confrontation with death. They are incapable of heroic gestures in any realm because their environment, habits, and nature make them ridiculous. The antipoet holds nothing sacred. The serious, the traumatic, is presented in a casual and burlesque fashion. Life is absurd and death is trivial.

The antihero's self-destruction and demoralization are simply mirrors of the malaise of contemporary society. Antipoetry views the world as a sewer in which humans, reduced to the level of vermin, live and multiply. Any effort to alter the situation is destined to failure. Humans nurture their own importance and worth, self-centered creatures obsessed with the need to possess and to consume. Love is false, friendship insincere, and social justice neither exists nor is desired; the environment becomes more and more artificial at the expense of nature and beauty. Political revolutions are deceits that benefit the new leaders but alter nothing. Love is viewed as an egotistical pursuit to fulfill sexual desire; spiritual bonds are denied. Although a few of Parra's poems present women as fragile, innocent beings who are invariably abused by men, the majority of the antipoet's female characters are aggressive rivals who threaten and humiliate men. Yet man, who fears woman, desires and seeks her as a sexual object. Finally, Parra mocks a corrupt Catholic Church; greedy, lascivious priests; a hypocritical pope; and an omni-impotent God.

CANCIONERO SIN NOMBRE

Parra's first collection of poems, *Cancionero sin nombre*, was inspired by the gypsy ballads of Federico García Lorca. The poems are stylized versions of traditional Spanish folkloric ballads, but in Parra's volume the action remains a dreamlike illusion without taking form. This volume had more attackers than defenders, and although some of the elements of his later work are evident, Parra himself calls this work a sin of his youth, better forgotten.

Parra attributes the roots of antipoetry to an independent response to human circumstances, not to any traditions in literature. Nevertheless, he recognizes those writers who have influenced his own literary development. After the publication of his first collection, Parra became enthusiastic about the poetry of Walt Whitman. He delighted in the metric freedom; the relaxed, loose, unconventional language; the narratives and descriptions; and the passionate vehemence that characterized Whitman's verse. When Parra returned to Chile from the United States in 1946, he came to know and appreciate the works of Franz Kafka. Kafka showed Parra the alienation and neurosis of modern culture, the comic deformation, the ironic treatment of the absurd in the human condition, the peculiar importance of atmosphere, the distortions and deformations that entrap the helpless protagonist. Parra was much more comfortable with Kafka's struggling protagonists than with Whitman's heroic vision of humanity. The Chilean's developing poetic style, new to the Spanish-speaking world, was antiromantic, antirhetorical, antiheroic, and antipoetic.

Parra's two-year stay in England beginning in 1949 crystallized this style into that of the antipoet. He was moved by the poetry of John Donne, W. H. Auden, Cecil Day Lewis, Stephen Spender, and especially T. S. Eliot. Parra appreciated Eliot's radical transformation of poetic diction and his inclusion of prosaic and colloquial language in his poems. These English-language poets inspired Parra in their observation of contemporary humanity and of humanity's environment, politics, manners, and religion and the didactic opportunities they exploited in treating these themes.

LA CUECA LARGA AND VERSOS DE SALÓN

Parra's third collection, *La cueca larga* (the *cueca* is a native dance of Chile), exalts wine. Written in the popular tradition of marginal literature, the book is anti-intellectual and vulgar, a frivolous contribution to Chilean folklore akin to antipoetry in preference for the masses and its position on the periphery of established literature.

In *Versos de salón* (salon verses), Parra returns to the antipoetic technique, but with some significant differences. The ironic attack on the establishments of society remains (the collection should be titled "Antisalon Verses"), but these poems are shorter than the earlier ones. They are fragments whose images follow one another in rapid fashion and mirror the absurd chaos of the world. The reader, forced to experience this confusion at first hand, is left restless, searching for a meaning that is not to be found. The chaotic enumeration of the Surrealists, a favorite technique with Parra, abounds, while the anecdotal poetry of *Poems and Antipoems*, with its emphasis on dialogue, all but disappears. The sense of alienation is sharper, the bitterness and disillusion more deeply felt, the humor more pointed. The antihero changes from a victim into an odd creature who flings himself at the world in open

confrontation. His introverted suffering is now a metaphysical despair.

CANCIONES RUSAS

Canciones rusas (Russian songs) was a product of the antipoet's visit to the Soviet Union. These poems are gentle, serene, lyrical, serious, a bit optimistic. The caustic spirit of the antipoet is not entirely absent, and the poet is not enthusiastic, but there is an expression of hope. The Soviet experience, not a political doctrine but a hope for underdeveloped nations symbolized by the progress of a people, is responsible for the change in tone. This is visual poetry, simple, stripped of images. The title notwithstanding, however, there is no music in these verses.

ADDRESSING SOCIAL ILLNESSES

In *Obra gruesa* (basic work), Parra returned once again to antipoetry. The Soviet Union is no longer an ideal, and hope for humankind is extinguished. This volume includes all the poetry Parra had published to 1969, with the exception of his first collection. *Los profesores* is a parody of the world of education, in which overly serious teachers fill the minds of their students with worthless information unrelated to human needs. Parra overwhelms the reader with lists of stifling questions, and the pedagogical idiom of the teachers contrasts with the picturesque colloquialisms of the students. *Emergency Poems* is a reprinting of the verses that appeared in "Straight Jacket," a section of *Obra gruesa*, as well as thirty-one new poems. These titles both refer to symptoms of a social illness that is becoming epidemic. A state of emergency is declared (hence the title) as inflation, pollution, and crime increase; wars exist in crisis proportion while people are controlled by the very monsters they invented to protect themselves from reality. Society has placed humans in straight jackets, and the antihero, an old person, is reduced to waiting for death; the sum of the antihero's life equals zero.

Parra's cynicism allows for no program of hope; the symptoms are not accompanied by a proposed remedy. The author uses himself as an example of the critical state of things. These poems enjoy a greater coherence than the author's most recent verses. Anecdotes again begin to appear. Parra's poetry becomes more aggressive and more social, with the appearance of a host of frustrated, unhappy characters, including beggars, drug addicts, and revolutionaries.

ARTEFACTOS

In *Artefactos*, Parra moved to a new poetic form. The antipoem had become fashionable in Latin America, and with the imitators came the risk that Parra's creation might become a mere formula. *Artefactos*, not in truth a book but a box of postcards on which each "artifact" appears, along with a brief illustration, approximates antipoetry in purpose and spirit. If some of the lines of poetry from the author's more recent collections were isolated from the poem, they would become artifacts. Indeed, Parra defines them as the result of the explosion of the antipoem, which became so filled with pathos it had to burst. The brief and self-sufficient artifact reduces the antipoem to its essential element, its strength resulting from its brevity and freedom from poetic context. Thus, the once complex antipoem has evolved into the most basic of fragments while still retaining its essence.

AFTER-DINNER DECLARATIONS

In *After-Dinner Declarations*, Parra uses the mundane and boring after-dinner speech as the foundation for his poems—what could be more ordinary, more "antipoetic," than an after-dinner speech? The book is made up of five long speech-sequences, each consisting of a number of short poems. In "There Are Different Types of Speeches," he writes " . . . the reader will agree with me/ That all kinds of speeches/ Come down to two possible types:/ Good speeches and bad speeches." The book's translator, David Oliphant, writes in the introduction that Parra's book is a "book of antipoetic homilies, maxims, jeremiads, homages, mathematical puns, and literary histories" that nevertheless take things very seriously, however playful the poet's style and method.

OTHER MAJOR WORKS

NONFICTION: *Pablo Neruda y Nicanor Parra: Discursos*, 1962; *Discursos de sobremesa*, 1997; *Pablo Neruda and Nicanor Parra Face to Face*, 1997.

TRANSLATION: *Lear, Rey and Mendigo*, 2004 (of William Shakespeare's *King Lear*).

MISCELLANEOUS: *Obras completas and algo [más]*, 2006.

BIBLIOGRAPHY

Carrasco, Iván. *Para leer a Nicanor Parra*. Santiago, Chile: Editorial Cuarto Propio, 1999. An insightful analysis of the perception of Parra's work as antipoetry. An expert on Parra's work analyzes the evolution of his poetry from its rejection of thematic and syntactic structures to the development of a unique yet mutable voice that responds to its social and political environment. In Spanish.

Neruda, Pablo. *Pablo Neruda and Nicanor Parra Face to Face*. Lewiston, N.Y.: Edwin Mellen Press, 1997. This is a bilingual and critical edition of speeches by both Neruda and Parra on the occasion of Neruda's appointment to the University of Chile's faculty, with English translations and a useful introduction by Marlene Gottlieb. Bibliographical references.

Parra, Nicanor. *Antipoems: New and Selected*. Translated by Frank MacShane, edited by David Unger. New York: New Directions, 1985. This bilingual anthology focuses on representative antipoems in an attempt to demonstrate how Parra's poetry has revolutionized poetic expression globally as well as within the sphere of Latin American poetry. Notes by the editor enhance understanding for English-speaking readers.

Parrilla Sotomayor, Eduardo E. *Humorismo y sátira en la poesía de Nicanor Parra*. Madrid: Editorial Pliegos, 1997. This study identifies and discusses the elements of humor and satire in Parra's antipoetry. It analyzes the poet's technique as well as unique antirhetorical style and language that creates a direct link to contemporary Latin American society. In Spanish.

Rowe, William. "Latin American Poetry." In *The Cambridge Companion to Modern Latin American Culture*, edited by John King. New York: Cambridge University Press, 2007. Rowe's chapter in this collection on Latin American culture in modern times includes discussion of the life and work of Parra.

Rudman, Mark. "A Garland for Nicanor Parra at Ninety." *New England Review* 26, no. 2 (2005): 204-213. Rudman, in this article celebrating Parra's life at the age of ninety in 2005, remembers meeting the Chilean poet for the first time in 1973. An intimate perspective on Parra and his life and work.

Sarabia, Rosa. *Poetas de la palabra hablada: Un estudio de la poesía hispanoaméricana contemporánea.* London: Tamesis, 1997. This study analyzes the oral nature of the literary production of several representative contemporary Latin American writers with roots in oral literature. In her chapter titled "Nicanor Parra: La antipoesía y sus políticas," the author explores the origins and consequences of antipoetry in its political and social milieus in contemporary Latin America, especially the *Cono Sur,* Chile, and Argentina. In Spanish.

Taylor, John. Review of *After-Dinner Declarations,* by Nicanor Parra, and *Before Saying Any of the Great Words,* by David Huerta. *Antioch Review* 67, no. 3 (Summer, 2009): 594-601. Taylor compares and contrasts the works of these two authors.

Alfred W. Jensen

BORIS PASTERNAK

Born: Moscow, Russia; February 10, 1890
Died: Peredelkino, near Moscow, Soviet Union (now in Russia); May 30, 1960

PRINCIPAL POETRY

Bliznets v tuchakh, 1914
Poverkh barierov, 1917 (*Above the Barriers,* 1959)
Sestra moia zhizn': Leto 1917 goda, 1922 (*My Sister, Life,* 1964; also known as *Sister My Life*)
Temy i variatsii, 1923 (*Themes and Variations,* 1964)
Vysokaya bolezn', 1924 (*High Malady,* 1958)
Carousel: Verse for Children, 1925
Devyatsot pyaty' god, 1926 (*The Year 1905,* 1989)
Lyutenant Shmidt, 1927 (*Lieutenant Schmidt,* 1992)
Spektorsky, 1931
Vtoroye rozhdeniye, 1932 (*Second Birth,* 1964)
Na rannikh poezdakh, 1943 (*On Early Trains,* 1964)
Zemnoy prostor, 1945 (*The Vastness of Earth,* 1964)

Kogda razgulyayetsa, 1959 (*When the Skies Clear,* 1964)
Poems, 1959
The Poetry of Boris Pasternak, 1917-1959, 1959
Poems, 1955-1959, 1960
In the Interlude: Poems, 1945-1960, 1962
Fifty Poems, 1963
The Poems of Doctor Zhivago, 1965
Stikhotvoreniya i poemy, 1965, 1976
The Poetry of Boris Pasternak, 1969
Selected Poems, 1983

OTHER LITERARY FORMS

Besides poetry, Boris Pasternak (PAS-tur-nak) composed several pieces of short fiction. They include "Pisma iz Tuly" (1922; "Letters from Tula," 1945), "Detstvo Luvers" (1923; "The Childhood of Luvers," 1945), and *Rasskazy* (1925; short stories). He wrote two autobiographical works: *Okhrannaya gramota* (1931; *Safe Conduct,* 1949) and *Avtobiograficheskiy ocherk* (1958; *I Remember: Sketch for an Autobiography,* 1959). His novel *Doktor Zhivago* (*Doctor Zhivago,* 1958) was first published in Italy in 1957. An unfinished dramatic trilogy, *Slepaya krasavitsa* (*The Blind Beauty,* 1969), was published after his death, in 1969.

Among Pasternak's many translations into Russian are several of William Shakespeare's plays, including *Romeo and Juliet* (pr. c. 1595-1596) in 1943 and *Antony and Cleopatra* (pr. 1606-1607) in 1944. Most of these translations were published between 1940 and 1948. He also translated into Russian the works of several Georgian lyric poets, especially those works of his friends Titian Tabidze and Paolo Iashvili. His translation of Johann Wolfgang von Goethe's *Faust: Eine Tragödie* (pb. 1808, 1833; *The Tragedy of Faust,* 1823, 1838) appeared in 1953, and Friedrich Schiller's *Maria Stuart* (1800) in 1957. Other authors whose works he translated include Heinrich von Kleist, Lord Byron, and John Keats.

The best English editions of Pasternak's prose works are found in *Selected Writings*—which includes the short prose works, *Safe Conduct,* and selected poems—translated by C. M. Bowra et al.; *I Remember,* translated with preface and notes by David Magarshack;

and *Doctor Zhivago,* translated by Max Hayward and M. Harari, with the poems translated by Bernard G. Guerney.

ACHIEVEMENTS

Known in the West mainly as the author of *Doctor Zhivago*, Boris Pasternak established his reputation as a poet in the Soviet Union in 1922 with the publication of *My Sister, Life*. He is regarded as a "poet's poet," and his contemporary Anna Akhmatova referred to him simply as "the poet," as if there were no other in his time. Indeed, Pasternak ranks as one of the foremost Russian poets of the twentieth century, if not the greatest. At the turn of the century, Symbolism, as in the works of Andrey Bely and Aleksandr Blok, dominated Russian poetry, and in the years before the Revolution more daring innovation and verbal experimentation occurred in the Futurist movement, as in the poetry of Vladimir Mayakovsky and Sergei Esenin. Pasternak inherited from both movements and yet was a part of neither. Like the Symbolists, he is able to see life in images; like the Futurists, he uses daring verbal combinations, intricate sound patterns, and a relaxed conversational vocabulary. In his verses, there is a simplicity and clarity that goes back to Alexander Pushkin, together with a freshness and originality that are timeless.

Pasternak's early poetry, especially *My Sister, Life*, is his most innovative and enigmatic. In these "rimes and riddles," as Robert Payne observes, Pasternak seemed to send the reader "in search of the key, until he realized that no key was necessary." Pasternak creates pure poetry, and the creation itself is the message. His poetry is music, like that of Paul Verlaine, whom he greatly admired; it is a search and a discovery, like Paul Valéry's; it is a perpetual celebration of the senses, as in Mikhail Lermontov; above all, it is a cosmic apotheosis of nature. It had a message of newness for the years of hope and optimism following the Revolution, and as Lydia Pasternak-Slater writes: "each reader discovered individually and for himself that these poems were the spontaneous outbursts of genius, of a 'poet' by the grace of God."

Pasternak was not a political poet. He seldom wrote of the Revolution or of reform. At first glance, he seems to be unaware of events, as he states in the poem "About These Verses": "Dear friends . . . what millennium is it out there?" A. Lezhnev states that these lines might be considered the epigraph of Pasternak's entire work. Yet the throbbing rhythm of *My Sister, Life* incarnates the Revolution, as *The Year 1905* sounds an ominous yet hopeful note, and as the poems of the 1940's speak of the desolation of the war years. Contemporary events are both present and absent in Pasternak's verse. Their absence angered Soviet officials, yet Joseph Stalin himself spared Pasternak.

Pasternak's greatest poetry, *The Poems of Doctor Zhivago* and the poems of his last years, sheds the excessive imagery and startling verbal play of his earlier works. These poems reach a sublime simplicity in perhaps a single transparent image, and the music and the message are one. Such is "Winter Night," perhaps one of the greatest poems in all Russian literature. Into these later works, Pasternak has injected a profound Christian symbolism, very much evident in the *The Poems of Doctor Zhivago*, more subtle in *When the Skies Clear*. Many of these poems are probably among the best-known modern poems in the entire world for their simplicity, universality, and lyricism.

BIOGRAPHY

Boris Leonidovich Pasternak was born in Moscow on February 10, 1890 (January 29, Old Style). He was the first and most illustrious of four children born to the painter Leonid Osipovich Pasternak and the pianist Rosa Isidorovna Kaufman. A close family relationship and a deeply cultured atmosphere marked his childhood. The influence of the Russian Orthodox religion came to this child of predominantly Jewish roots through his nurse Akulina Gavrilovna and was to reappear during his later years. Leonid Pasternak's literary associations, particularly with Leo Tolstoy and Rainer Maria Rilke, were to prove very important to Pasternak's development, although perhaps the most powerful influence on him was exerted by the composer Aleksandr Scriabin. Scriabin was his idol from 1903 to 1909, when Pasternak also began composing. Disillusioned in 1909, he abandoned the pursuit of a musical career and turned to philosophy. A trip to Marburg in 1912, then the philosophical center of Germany, where he was to study under Professor Hermann Cohen,

Boris Pasternak (Time & Life Pictures/Getty Images)

When the Revolution broke out, he returned to Moscow enthusiastically, only to be disillusioned. This famous summer of 1917 is immortalized in the volume of poetry *My Sister, Life*, which was published in 1922, immediately assuring his reputation as a poet.

In 1922, Pasternak married Evgenia Vladimirovna Lourié, and their son Evgeny was born in 1923. The marriage, however, was not a happy one, and in 1930, he became enamored of Zinaïda Nikolaevna Neuhaus, whom he married in 1934. Their son Leonid was born in 1937. Although his second wife was to remain faithful to him until his death, their relationship was greatly strained by Pasternak's liaison with Olga Vsevolodovna Ivinskaya, which began in 1946. Ivinskaya showed a sensitive appreciation of Pasternak's literary works and aided him in much of his secretarial work. For her association with him, she was imprisoned and deported to Siberia twice, from 1949 until Stalin's death in 1953 and after Pasternak's death in 1960 until 1964. Pasternak himself was spared—miraculously, since the 1930's and 1940's saw the exile, death, or suicide of many of Russia's most gifted writers. Never hostile to the regime, he also never wrote according to the tenets of Socialist Realism and thus was in constant jeopardy.

During the difficult years of World War II and afterward, Pasternak supported himself and his family principally by translating, which he resumed later when he was unable to receive royalties from the West. After Stalin's death, he began working seriously on *Doctor Zhivago*, which he regarded as his most important work. Its refusal by the journal *Novy Mir* and subsequent publication in Italy by Petrinelli in 1957 placed him in a very dangerous position. When awarded the Nobel Prize in Literature in 1958, official pressures caused him to refuse. He died on May 30, 1960, at Peredelkino, the writers' village where he had spent almost all his summers and many of his winters since 1936.

ANALYSIS

Although Boris Pasternak would refuse to equate music with poetry, his verse is inseparable from the music it embodies. D. L. Plank has studied the music of Pasternak in great detail and speaks of his "sound sym-

seemed to be the ultimate fulfillment of his dreams. Then a sentimental crisis, Ida Vysofskaya's refusal of his proposal of marriage, led him to abandon philosophy and to turn to poetry—without, however, his losing altogether the musical gift and the philosophical preoccupations that are evident in his works.

Upon his return to Moscow, Pasternak became involved in literary circles and devoted himself completely to poetry. The wife of his early protector, the Lithuanian poet Jurgis Baltrushaitis, rightly warned him that he would later regret the publication of his first volume, pretentiously called *Bliznets v tuchakh* (a twin in the clouds). Its title suggested the Futurist movement, which Pasternak was unable to integrate into his work. Exempted from the military draft because of a childhood leg injury, he tutored and worked at a chemical plant in the Urals from 1914 to 1917. The beauty of the Urals, which so impressed him, colors many of his works, from "The Childhood of Liuvers" to his poetry.

bolism" and "phonetic metaphors." With its unusual rhythms and internal rhymes, alliteration, and evocative word patterns, Pasternak's poetry has a resonance that most translators have despaired of capturing. At all times he uses classical patterns and regular meters, never attempting the free verse of the Futurists, whose daring use of vocabulary, however, he does share. Perhaps one of the best examples of Pasternak's sound patterns is "Oars at Rest," brilliantly analyzed by Plank and Nils Nilsson.

It is not surprising that Pasternak's last work should be called *Zhivago*, which means "life," for his entire literary creation is a celebration of life. In *My Sister, Life*, he wrote, "In all my ways let me pierce through into the very essence. . . ." Although his sensitive nature suffered greatly during the personal and national upheavals in which he participated, he was basically positive and optimistic, a poet of hope and exultation. He frequently wrote of birth; one of his volumes of verse is titled *Second Birth*; the sight of the Urals for the first time is the vision of the great mountains in the pangs of childbirth and joy of new life. He frequently wrote of the change of seasons, implying life and death, growth and change. The religious poems of the Zhivago cycle lead to the Resurrection, the ultimate symbol of life and hope.

NATURE

Nature is the subject of the majority of Pasternak's poems. Poet Marina Tsvetaeva said: "We have written about nature, but Pasternak has written nature." Nature is the actor in his poems, the doer, the hero. Traditional roles are reversed: the garden comes into the house to meet the mirror ("Mirror"); "Dust gulps down the rain in pellets" ("Sultry Night"); young woods climb uphill to the summit ("Vision of Tiflis"). Pasternak became the river or the mountain or the snow. He captured nature on the move. For him, says Payne, "All that happened was eternally instantaneous."

Pasternak lived in a world of linden trees and grasses, lilacs and violets, herbs and nettles. They were personified and became the poet and time and life. "Today's day looks about with the eyes of anemones" ("You in the Wind . . ."); "The storm, like a priest, sets fire to the lilacs" ("Our Thunderstorm"). Lilacs and linden trees seemed to have a mysterious but definite significance

for him. Most of nature entered his works through rain or snow. Poet Tsvetayeva said that the entire book *My Sister, Life* swims. The mere titles of the poems reveal this love of rain: "Rain," "Spring Rain," "The Weeping Garden." The same theme is evident in *When the Skies Clear*, but here snow dominates. There are blizzards, blinding snow, like the passing of the years, but also "Flowers covered with surprise;/ Corners where the crossroads rise," for Pasternak was essentially a poet of hope, and for him drenching rains and snowy winters were signs of life and growth.

LOVE

Life for Pasternak was inseparable from love. *My Sister, Life* evokes a tumultuous love affair. *Second Birth* is the story of his love for Zinaïda Nikolaevna, with regrets and admiration for Evgenia Vladimirovna. The poems of the Zhivago cycle probably refer to Ivinskaya in the person of Lara. Pasternak seldom wrote of love in explicit terms but used rhythm and metonomy: the sleepy breast, elbows, willows ("Oars at Rest"); crossed arms and legs ("Winter Night"). Like Stéphane Mallarmé, Pasternak frequently combined love and artistic creation, especially in his earlier works.

IMAGERY

Pasternak's early method is associative and linear. Many brief themes follow in rapid succession, with only a tenuous link, if any. Lezhnev observes that Pasternak, like an Impressionist painter, was a better colorist than draftsman. In the early works, images cascade and overwhelm one another and the reader. "Definition of Poetry" moves from the crescendo of a whistle to a ringing icicle to a duel between nightingales. Andrei Sinyavsky notes that for Pasternak, the poet does not compose or write images; he gathers them from nature. The young Pasternak was overwhelmed by all that he saw in nature, and his early works are saturated with such imagery.

SPIRITUALITY

The religious theme is barely present in Pasternak's earlier works, which seem like a pantheistic celebration of nature. Even in *When the Skies Clear*, humanity's creative power is seen in the might of the elements ("Wind"). In the Zhivago cycle, however, the spiritual element dominates, corresponding to a maturing and broadening of Pasternak's talent as well as to an inner conversion. This development has been interpreted as a poetic conversion to another set of images, but it is evident that Pasternak's values have moved to another sphere. He reaches a metaphysical and spiritual plane that uplifts the reader and draws him into an atmosphere of hope and immortality.

MY SISTER, LIFE

My Sister, Life (or *Sister My Life*, as Phillip Flayderman prefers in his translation) consists of fifty short lyrics written by Pasternak in a single burst of creative energy in the summer of 1917. It was his third volume of verse, and his first really great poetic achievement, immediately establishing his reputation. In it, Pasternak writes of life, love, and nature in a cosmic yet a very personal sense. The book is dedicated to Mikhail Lermontov, the great nineteenth century Russian poet whom Pasternak greatly admired, and the first poem recalls Lermontov's magnificent *Demon* (1841; *The Demon*, 1875). Pasternak himself states that in the summer of 1917, Lermontov was to him "the personification of creative adventure and discovery, the principle of everyday free poetical statement." The book is broken up by twelve subtitles, such as "Isn't It Time for the Birds to Sing," "Occupations of Philosophy," "An Attempt to Separate the Soul," and "Epilogue," which give only a slight indication of the contents of the respective sections.

The summer of 1917 was unlike any other in Pasternak's lifetime or in Russian history. It was the summer between the February and October revolutions, when Pasternak returned to Moscow, near which, at the family *dacha* at Molodi, he composed the poems of this cycle. There is scarcely an echo of revolutionary events in the whole volume, yet Pasternak calls it "A Book of the Revolution." Tsvetayeva discerned "a few incontrovertible signs of 1917" in "The Sample," "Break-up," "The Militiaman's Whistle," "A Sultry Night," and the poem to Aleksandr Kerensky, "Spring Rain." Robert Payne sees the entire volume as poems "filled with the electric excitement of those days." The rhythm begins softly, as in "The Weeping Garden," and ends in stifling heat and thunderstorms, as in "Summer," "A Momentary Thunderstorm Forever," and "At Home."

Many of the poems refer directly to a love affair:

stormy, tumultuous, and at times tender. Pasternak does not reveal the person or the circumstances but simply portrays the emotional impact. He does this mostly through images of nature and sonorous evocations that defy translation. The significance of the images is intensely personal, and although the sensitive reader can feel the emotion and identify with it, he cannot interpret it. There are playful and sensual images ("Your lips were violets") as well as serious ones: "You handed me life from the shelf,/ And blew the dust away" ("Out of Superstition"). The love affair seems to end on a note of farewell, like a song that has been sung and a moment immortalized in poetry.

As is usual in Pasternak's early poetry, images of nature saturate each poem. Gardens (especially drenched in rain), lilac branches, summer storms, and starry skies run through most of the poems. Pasternak does not create them; he gathers them up from the universe in a net as a fisherman gathers his fish. He does not evoke them; he becomes the river or the storm or the rain. There is a cosmic quality about his nature imagery which excites and exalts. At the same time, Pasternak uses simple conversational language. He writes of mosquitoes and cafés and trolleys along with more exotic themes. The short prose work "The Childhood of Liuvers" has been considered to be a companion piece to *My Sister, Life* and thus helps to clarify some of the more enigmatic images that many critics, including Pasternak's sister Lydia, see as "too complicated, too cryptic, with too many escapes into the brilliance of sound and word."

If there is a philosophical message in these early works, it is the absolute value of freedom. Pasternak remains above political involvement and above conventional images. Like Lermontov, he seeks sensual freedom as well. He expresses freedom in language as he creates new melodies independent of ordinary vocabulary and syntax. Although Pasternak had not yet achieved the realism of Pushkin's imagery, with its universal application, his subjective boldness stands out in *My Sister, Life* as a new and fresh voice in Russian poetry.

HIGH MALADY

Pasternak's greatest achievement is in lyric poetry, but in the 1920's, he attempted four longer poems of epic scope dealing with the Revolution. They are *High Malady, The Year 1905, Lieutenant Schmidt,* and *Spektorsky*—the latter was left unfinished. Although all these poems have the narrative quality that Pasternak was to develop in his prose works, they are colored predominantly by his lyricism and emotional response.

High Malady is the only epic directly connected with the Revolution. It is a debate about the nature of poetry, "the high malady that is still called song," and Moscow under Bolshevik rule. Under the shadow of the siege of Troy, Pasternak speaks of the suffering in Moscow during the early 1920's: the cold winter, the lack of food, the imminence of death. Into this somber atmosphere, he introduces Vladimir Lenin (Vladimir Ilich Ulyanov), whose "living voice pierced [us] with encircling flames like jagged lightning." He grows taller, his words are like the thrust of a sword, as alone "he ruled the tides of thought." Lenin is one with history and brings hope to the suffering people.

THE YEAR 1905

The Year 1905 is retrospective of twenty years, written by Pasternak in 1925 to 1926. As a young student, he had participated in some of the Moscow demonstrations in 1905, and the recollection remained with him all his life. The poem consists of six parts, of unequal lengths and varying meters. The first part, "Fathers," goes back to the roots of the Revolution in the 1880's, grouping together such diverse people as the anarchist Sergey Nechayev and the great novelist Fyodor Dostoevski. Part 2, "Childhood," is partially autobiographical and contains reminiscences of Pasternak's own student days, his father's study, and the music of Aleksandr Scriabin. Against a background of snow, Pasternak fuses and confuses events in both St. Petersburg (or Petrograd) and Moscow, as he is spiritually present in both. The third part, "Peasants and Factory Workers," short and perhaps the least successful, describes the Polish insurrection at Lodz.

"PRINCE POTEMKIN"

Part 4 describes the mutiny at sea aboard the *Prince Potemkin*. With classical overtones recalling Homer, Pasternak salutes the sea. With classical reticence, he avoids the direct description of violence. The hero, Afanasy Matushenko, is described in larger-than-life

proportions, and as the section ends, the ship sails away "like an orange-colored speck." Part 5, "The Students," tells of the funeral procession of Nikolai Baumann, killed by an agent of the secret police. In the tone of a lament, Pasternak writes: "The heavens slept plunged in a silver forest of chrysanthemums." The last part, "Moscow in December," speaks of the famous strike of the railwaymen. Pasternak himself was very moved by this event and, perhaps in memory of it, frequently used the image of railways in his poetry. The entire poem is powerful in its lyricism, but, as J. W. Dyck observes, it is too diffuse and lacks a central focus.

LIEUTENANT SCHMIDT

Lieutenant Schmidt remedies this problem by evoking a single subject. Lieutenant Schmidt was a historical personage who led a mutiny among the sailors at Sebastopol and almost single-handedly seized one battleship. Ten other ships had already joined him when he was captured and condemned. His famous "Testament," in which he speaks about cherishing his country's destiny and sees himself as "happy to have been chosen," is one of the most sublime parts of the entire poem.

SPEKTORSKY

Spektorsky was never completed, but Pasternak planned it as a novel in verse. It is highly autobiographical and tells of the unsuccessful love affair of Olga and Spektorsky and his later meeting with her while she was a revolutionary. A second love affair, with the poetess Maria Ilyna, is equally disappointing. The poem is also symbolic of the spiritual submission of the poet, not yet characteristic of Pasternak. It reflects independence in the face of any given ideology. The handling of plot in *Spektorsky* is unsure, but the poem does present a very modern character and shows the development of Pasternak's lyric gifts.

THE POEMS OF DOCTOR ZHIVAGO

Although the epic poems do not constitute the highest form of Pasternak's literary expression, they pleased the general public because of their accessibility. They also show the fusion of Pasternak's lyric and narrative skills, anticipating the achievement of *Doctor Zhivago*. In his *I Remember*, Pasternak describes *Doctor Zhivago* as "my chief and most important work, the only one I am not ashamed of and for which I can answer with the utmost confidence, a novel in prose with a supplement in verse." The essential connection between the poetry and prose is evident to the sensitive reader, for Pasternak intended the poems to constitute the seventeenth and final chapter of his work. Donald Davie, Dmitri Obolensky, and George Katkov, among others, have provided valuable commentaries in English that help to interpret the poems and show their link with the novel.

The Poems of Doctor Zhivago represents the most mature phase of Pasternak's poetry. The musical quality is important here, as in all his works. The poems are inherently religious, a fact recognized by the editors of *Novy Mir*, who refused to print them. They speak of life and death, love and immortality, within a framework of the four seasons. The year begins in March, with a promise of spring, and ends with Holy Thursday and the hope of resurrection. The cycle begins and ends with Gethsemane and emphasizes the mission of Christ, of Hamlet, and of the poet "to do the will of him who sent me."

Obolensky divides the poems into three basic categories or themes: nature, love, and the author's views on the meaning and purpose of life. Although each of the twenty-five poems fits one of these categories better than the others, they overlap and the division is not absolute. The nature poems speak of all the seasons, but spring predominates: "March," "Spring Floods," "In Holy Week," "The Earth," and the religious poems that conclude the cycle. The nightingale, so frequent in Pasternak's poetry, is present here, and appears as the Robber-Nightingale of Russian folklore in "Spring Floods." The poems of spring point to the Resurrection, where "death finds its only vanquishing power."

The love poems are among the most intense in modern literature, yet they are remarkable for their restraint. The many women whom Pasternak knew and loved in his lifetime inspired the poems, yet there is a universality that applies to all human love, sublimated in the divine. The erotic "Intoxication," the tender "Meeting," and the mysterious "White Night" speak variously of the poet's passion. Perhaps the most successful is "Winter Night," which, by delicate repetitions of words and sounds (especially the letter *e*), by metonymic suggestions, and by the central image of the candle burning in a window, suggests the fateful passion and the consuming possession of love.

The love poems move imperceptibly into the religious cycle and form a part of it, underlining the deeply spiritual aspect of love and the ultimate meaning of life for Pasternak. "Christmas Star" introduces the series and recalls a medieval Russian icon and a Russian version of the Dutch *Adoration of the Magi* alluded to in *Safe Conduct*, Pasternak's first autobiography. "Daybreak" is addressed to Christ and emphasizes the importance of the New Testament to Pasternak, like a dawn in his own life. The other religious poems refer to the liturgical texts used in the Holy Week services in the Orthodox Church. They end with Christ in the Garden of Gethsemane and complete the cycle of death and resurrection, destruction and creation, sin and redemption—for Zhivago is a sinful man, yet one who has faith in life.

The Poems of Doctor Zhivago is a work of extraordinary simplicity. The use of religious imagery raises the poems above the purely personal symbols of *My Sister, Life*. Although Pasternak makes no effort to repeat the verbal brilliance and intricate sound patterns of his early years, the rhythm is clear and resonant. Each poem has a central focus around which the images converge. The cycle itself centers on the person of Hamlet, whom Pasternak considers to be a heroic figure, symbolizing Christ and, ultimately, resurrection. Pasternak's basic optimism, his celebration of life and exaltation of love, have their finest expression in this cycle of poems.

OTHER MAJOR WORKS

LONG FICTION: *Doktor Zhivago*, 1957 (*Doctor Zhivago*, 1958).

SHORT FICTION: "Pisma iz Tuly," 1922 ("Letters from Tula," 1945); "Detstvo Liuvers," 1923 ("The Childhood of Luvers," 1945); *Rasskazy*, 1925; *Sochineniya*, 1961 (*Collected Short Prose*, 1977).

PLAY: *Slepaya krasavitsa*, pb. 1969 (*The Blind Beauty*, 1969).

NONFICTION: *Okhrannaya gramota*, 1931 (autobiography; *Safe Conduct*, 1945 in *The Collected Prose Works*); *Avtobiograficheskiy ocherk*, 1958 (*I Remember: Sketch for an Autobiography*, 1959); *An Essay in Autobiography*, 1959; *Essays*, 1976; *The Correspondence of Boris Pasternak and Olga Freidenberg, 1910-*

1954, 1981; *Pasternak on Art and Creativity*, 1985; *Pis'ma k gruzinskim*, n.d. (*Letters to Georgian Friends by Boris Pasternak*, 1968).

TRANSLATIONS: *Hamlet*, 1941 (of William Shakespeare); *Romeo i Juliet*, 1943 (of Shakespeare); *Antony i Cleopatra*, 1944 (of Shakespeare); *Othello*, 1945 (of Shakespeare); *King Lear*, 1949 (of Shakespeare); *Faust*, 1953 (of Johann Wolfgang von Goethe); *Maria Stuart*, 1957 (of Friedrich Schiller).

MISCELLANEOUS: *The Collected Prose Works*, 1945; *Safe Conduct: An Early Autobiography, and Other Works by Boris Pasternak*, 1958 (also known as *Selected Writings*, 1949); *Sochinenii*, 1961; *Vozdushnye puti: Proza raz nykh let*, 1982; *The Voice of Prose*, 1986.

BIBLIOGRAPHY

Barnes, Christopher. *Boris Pasternak: A Literary Biography*. New York: Cambridge University Press, 1989-1998. A two-volume comprehensive biography, scholarly but also accessible.

Ciepiela, Catherine. *The Same Solitude: Boris Pasternak and Marina Tsvetaeva*. Ithaca, N.Y.: Cornell University Press, 2006. Ciepiela examines the ten-year love affair between Pasternak and Tsvetayeva, whose relationship was primarily limited to long-distance letters. Included in this volume is the correspondence between the two authors along with letters from Rainer Maria Rilke, who completed the couple's literary love triangle. Ciepiela reveals the similarities between Pasternak and Tsvetayeva by painting a portrait of their lives and personalities. She scrutinizes their poetry and correspondence, finding significant links between them. This volume is written clearly and succinctly, making it easily accessible to all readers.

Conquest, Robert. *The Pasternak Affair: Courage of Genius*. London: Collins and Harvill, 1961. A detailed account of Pasternak's conflict with the state on his reception of the Nobel Prize. Conquest provides much valuable information about Pasternak as a man and a writer.

De Mallac, Guy. *Boris Pasternak: His Life and Art*. Norman: University of Oklahoma Press, 1981. An extensive biography of Pasternak. The second part is devoted to De Mallac's interpretation of the most important features of Pasternak's works. A detailed chronology of his life and an exhaustive bibliography complete this beautifully illustrated book.

Erlich, Victor, ed. *Pasternak: A Collection of Critical Essays*. Englewood Cliffs, N.J.: Prentice-Hall, 1978. This skillfully arranged collection of essays covers all important facets of Pasternak's work, including short fiction, although the emphasis is on his poetry and *Doctor Zhivago*.

Fleishman, Lazar. *Boris Pasternak: The Poet and His Politics*. Cambridge, Mass.: Harvard University Press, 1990. An extensive study of Pasternak's life and works written under the oppressive political system. A must for those who are interested in nonliterary influences upon literary creations.

Ivinskaya, Olga. *A Captive of Time*. Garden City, N.Y.: Doubleday, 1978. Ivinskaya, Pasternak's love in the last years of his life, the model for Lara in *Doctor Zhivago*, and a staff member at the influential Soviet literary magazine *Novy Mir*, provides a wealth of information about Pasternak, his views and works, and Russia's literary atmosphere in the 1940's and 1950's.

Pasternak, Boris, Rainer Maria Rilke, and Marina Tsvetayeva. *Letters: Summer 1926*. New York: New York Review Books, 2001. The selected correspondence between the great Russian writers, scattered in the wake of the Bolshevik Revolution. This poignant record of a dreadful year for all three writers reveals their views on art, love, and sorrow.

Rudova, Larissa. *Understanding Boris Pasternak*. Columbia: University of South Carolina Press, 1997. A general introduction to Pasternak's work, including both his early poetry and prose and his later work; provides analyses of individual novels and stories.

Sendich, Munir. *Boris Pasternak: A Reference Guide*. New York: Maxwell Macmillan International, 1994. This indispensable reference contains a bibliography of Pasternak editions with more than five hundred entries, a bibliography of criticism with more than one thousand entries, and essays on topics including Pasternak's poetics, relations with other artists, and influences.

Irma M. Kashuba

OCTAVIO PAZ

Born: Mexico City, Mexico; March 31, 1914
Died: Mexico City, Mexico; April 19, 1998

PRINCIPAL POETRY

Luna silvestre, 1933
Bajo tu clara sombra, y otros poemas sobre España, 1937
Raíz del hombre, 1937
Entre la piedra y la flor, 1941
Libertad bajo palabra, 1949, 1960
Águila o sol?, 1951 (*Eagle or Sun?*, 1970)
Semillas para un himno, 1954
Piedra de sol, 1957 (*Sun Stone*, 1963)
La estación violenta, 1958
Agua y viento, 1959
Libertad bajo palabra: Obra poética, 1935-1957, 1960, 1968
Salamandra, 1962 (*Salamander*, 1987)
Selected Poems, 1963
Blanco, 1967 (English translation, 1971)
Discos visuales, 1968
Topoemas, 1968 (*Topoems*, 1987)
La centena, 1969
Ladera este, 1969 (*East Slope*, 1987)
Configurations, 1971
Renga, 1972 (in collaboration with three other poets; *Renga: A Chain of Poems*, 1972)
Early Poems, 1935-1955, 1973
Pasado en claro, 1975 (*A Draft of Shadows, and Other Poems*, 1979)
Vuelta, 1976 (*Return*, 1987)
Poemas, 1979
Selected Poems, 1979
Airborn = Hijos del Aire, 1981 (with Charles Tomlinson)
Arbol adentro, 1987 (*A Tree Within*, 1988)
The Collected Poems of Octavio Paz: 1957-1987, 1987 (includes the translation of several poetry collections)
Obra poetica (1935-1988), 1990
Stanzas for an Imaginary Garden, 1990 (limited edition)

Viento, agua, piedra / Wind, Water, Stone, 1990 (limited edition)
"Snapshots," 1997
A Tale of Two Gardens: Poems from India, 1952-1995, 1997
Figuras y figuraciones, 1999 (*Figures and Figurations*, 2002)

OTHER LITERARY FORMS

If Octavio Paz (pahz) excelled at poetry, he is no less respected for his writings in a multitude of other humanistic disciplines. Perhaps his best-known prose work is *El laberinto de la soledad: Vida y pensamiento de México* (1950, rev. and enlarged 1959; *The Labyrinth of Solitude: Life and Thought in Mexico*, 1961), which is a discussion of Mexican culture and the Mexican psyche. *El arco y la lira* (1956; *The Bow and the Lyre*, 1971) is an outstanding study in the field of poetics. His literary criticism includes *Los hijos del limo: Del romanticismo a la vanguardia* (1974; *Children of the Mire: Modern Poetry from Romanticism to the Avant-Garde*, 1974); the Charles Eliot Norton lectures for 1971-1972; *The Siren and the Seashell, and Other Essays on Poets and Poetry* (1976); and *Corriento alterna* (1967; *Alternating Current*, 1973). He edited a number of important anthologies, including *Antología poética* (1956; *Anthology of Mexican Poetry*, 1958) and *New Poetry of Mexico* (1970), and he wrote one short play.

ACHIEVEMENTS

Octavio Paz was Mexico's outstanding man of letters, the "leading exemplary intellectual of Latin America," as Ivar Ivask notes. His diverse output included poetry, literary criticism, philosophy, anthropology, art history, and cultural, social, and political commentary. As early as the mid-1960's, J. M. Cohen, in his influential study *Poetry of This Age, 1908-1965*, cited Paz with Pablo Neruda as "two of the chief Spanish-American poets." Carlos Fuentes has described Paz as "certainly the greatest living poet of the Spanish language," while Kenneth Rexroth declared Paz to be "without any question the best poet in the Western Hemisphere. There is no writer in English who can compare with him." Although some may disagree with

Rexroth, all agree that Paz was one of the finest poets of the twentieth century.

Paz's accomplishments were recognized from the outset of his career. In 1944, he was awarded a Guggenheim Fellowship, which allowed him to study and travel in the United States. In 1963, he received the prestigious Belgian Grand Prix International de Poésie. He gave the Charles Eliot Norton lectures at Harvard during the 1971-1972 academic year. In 1977, three honors were bestowed on him: the Jerusalem Prize, the Premio National de Letras, and the Premio Crítico de Editores de España. The Golden Eagle Prize (Nice, France) followed a year later. The Ollin Yoliztli Prize, Mexico's richest literary honor, was conferred in 1980. The Miguel de Cervantes Prize, "the Spanish-speaking world's highest award," came in 1981. In 1982, Paz was the recipient of the Neustadt International Prize for Literature, one of the literary world's most important awards, often a prelude to the Nobel Prize. Indeed, just eight years later, Paz received the 1990 Nobel Prize in Literature. Other accolades included the German Book Trade Peace Prize (1984), the T. S. Eliot Award for Creative Writing (1987), and the Alexis de Tocqueville Prize (1989). The University of Mexico and Boston, Harvard, and New York Universities conferred honorary degrees on Paz.

Octavio Paz (©The Nobel Foundation)

BIOGRAPHY

Octavio Paz was born on March 31, 1914, in Mexico City. His mother, Josephina Lozano, was of Spanish extraction, while the family of his father, Octavio, was both Mexican and Indian. Paz was a precocious youngster, influenced by his politically active grandfather, a journalist and writer, whose twelve-thousand-volume library provided the necessary material for his intellectual development. Paz's father was a lawyer who joined Emiliano Zapata during the 1910 Mexican Revolution and represented him in America. After secondary school, Paz studied from 1932 to 1937 at the National University of Mexico. In 1931, he founded *Barandal*, the first of his many journals. He also began to publish his poetry, and in 1933, *Luna silvestre*, his first collection, appeared; in the same year, he also founded his second journal, *Cuadernos del valle de Mexico*. In 1937, Paz attended a conference in Spain;

after the conference, he decided to remain there for a year. His allegiance was, naturally, to the Republican cause during the Spanish Civil War. In 1938, he passed through Paris, where he met Alejo Carpentier and Robert Desnos; Paz's firsthand encounter with the Surrealists was particularly decisive, and their profound influence on his subsequent work cannot be overestimated.

In 1938, Paz returned to Mexico, where he worked with Spanish political refugees, wrote on political matters for *El popular*, and founded *Taller*. A fourth journal, *El hijo pródigo*, followed in 1943. For these literary periodicals, he translated many French, German, and English works. Receipt of a Guggenheim Fellowship enabled him to spend the 1944-1945 academic year in the United States studying poetry. It was in the United States that he encountered the writings of T. S. Eliot, Ezra Pound, William Carlos Williams, Wallace Stevens, and E. E. Cummings, poets whose impact on Paz's work equaled that of the Surrealists some years before. When he ran out of money in New York in 1946, he decided to join the Mexican diplomatic service; he was sent to Paris, where he met Jean-Paul

Sartre, Albert Camus, Jules Supervielle, and many other writers. During the next twenty-three years, his diplomatic work allowed him to spend extended periods in many countries, including Switzerland, the United States, Japan, and India. Asia opened a new world to Paz, and after his first trip in 1952, his writings begin to display many Asian characteristics. He then returned to Mexico and spent the period from 1953 to 1958 writing in his usual prolific fashion.

In 1962, Paz was appointed Mexico's ambassador to India, and it was there that he met Marie-José Tramini, whom he married in 1964; they had one daughter. Although Paz's political interests had waned over the years, he resigned his ambassadorship in 1968 in protest against the Mexican government's overreaction to the student riots. During the 1970-1971 academic year, Paz was the Simón Bolívar Professor of Latin American Studies at Cambridge University, and during the following academic year, he held the Charles Eliot Norton Professorship of Poetry at Harvard. He also taught at the universities of Texas, Pittsburgh, and California, San Diego. In 1971, he founded yet another journal, *Plural*, a political and literary review, which lasted until 1976, when he founded his last literary-cultural periodical, *Vuelta*. Early in 1982, King Juan Carlos of Spain presented Paz with the Miguel de Cervantes Prize, and some months later, he received the Neustadt International Prize for Literature at the University of Oklahoma. The Nobel Prize in Literature followed in 1990. He died in Mexico City on April 19, 1998.

ANALYSIS

Any poet whose worldview has a chance to develop and mature over an extended period of time will create different types of poetry. Eliot, for example, began with short lyrics, moved toward longer and deeper pieces such as *The Waste Land* (1922), and concluded with the powerfully philosophical *Four Quartets* (1943). Eliot provides an especially germane analogue, since Octavio Paz was influenced by his work and is often compared to him thematically and stylistically; as J. M. Cohen remarked, "With the exception of T. S. Eliot, Octavio Paz is the only contemporary poet capable of feeling his metaphysics, and calling them to life."

Paz, too, began his career writing short lyrics, advanced to longer, surrealistic pieces, reworked the prose poem, and finally, after more than a quarter of a century of creative activity, began to experiment with collagelike texts and assemblages that bear little relation to poetry as traditionally defined. Such experiments follow the logic of Paz's stylistic evolution; he has always been a self-conscious poet and he has written many poems about poetry and the nature of the creative process. Indeed, Paz's conception of poetry is philosophical: Poetry alone permits humans to comprehend their place in the universe.

"POETRY"

In "Poesía" ("Poetry"), for example, Paz personifies this power of language to engage reality: "you burn my tongue with your lips, this pulp,/ and you awaken the rages, the delights,/ the endless anguish. . . ." The creative act is perceived as a struggle and the poet as a vehicle through whom words are spoken, comparable to a Greek oracle: "You rise from the furthest depth in me. . . ." Paz's references to images as "babblings" and to "prophets of my eyes" confirm the implication of oracular utterance. The poet is a seer, and only his articulation can defeat the ubiquitous silence of the universe.

"THE BIRD"

It is silence against which Paz battled most consistently, beginning with his early lyric pieces. Silence can be neutral, but it also represents Camus's indifferent cosmos, offering neither help nor solace. "El Pájaro" ("The Bird") presents the neutral form of silence, a natural scene broken by a bird's song. Ironically, articulation is not a palliative; here, it merely reminds the poet of his mortality. There is the silence of lovers, the silence of solitude, and the silence of death—silences that can be broken only by the poet. Other thematic threads that run through Paz's poetry—recurring images and motifs such as light, lightning, women, transparency, mirrors, time, language, mysticism, cycles, the urban wasteland, and various mythic perceptions—all can be related to his conception of the nature of poetry.

"STARS AND CRICKET"

Many of Paz's poems fall within traditional lengths, ranging from roughly ten to thirty lines, but he has not hesitated to publish the briefest haiku-like outbursts. Consider "Estrellas y grillo" ("Stars and Cricket") in its cryptic entirety:

> The sky's big.
> Up there, worlds scatter.
> Persistent,
> Unfazed by such a night,
> Cricket:
> Brace and bit.

SUN STONE

At the same time, Paz also experimented with the long poem. His *Sun Stone* consists of 584 eleven-syllable lines of abstruse rumination:

> I search without finding, I write alone,
> there's no one here, and the day falls,
> the year falls, I fall with the moment,
> I fall to the depths, invisible path
> over mirrors repeating my shattered image. . . .

"INTERRUPTED ELEGY"

One of Paz's most moving poems is "Elegía interrumpida" ("Interrupted Elegy"), a philosophical description of a number of people whose deaths affected the poet. Each of the poem's five stanzas begins with the same incantation: "Now I remember the dead of my own house." From this point, Paz muses on first impressions, those who take their leave quickly, those who linger, those who are forgotten—and all this in subdued, sparsely imagistic language. The poem itself is a metaphysical quest, and the dead whom it memorializes are brought to life. Despite the cathartic nature of the elegy, however, Paz's concluding couplet is despairing: "The world is a circular desert,/ heaven is closed and hell is empty."

EAGLE OR SUN?

Eagle or Sun?, a collection of short prose poems, the first book of its kind in Spanish, has been extremely influential. Part 1, "Trabajos del poeta" ("The Poet's Works"), consists of sixteen brief sections, each of which elaborates a narrative line, but usually in strongly imagistic and even surrealistic language. The surface concerns of these poems mask Paz's underlying interest: the poet's relationship with his creation. This is not allegory, which is read on one level and interpreted on

another: Here, the reader perceives the two levels simultaneously. The ubiquitous silence is interrupted by a tapping ("it is the sound of horses' hooves galloping on a field of stone . . ."); these are the words appearing, demanding articulation. They pour out uncontrollably, this "vomit of words":

> The thistle whistles, bristles, buckles with chuckles. Broth of moths, charts of farts, all together, ball of syllables of waste matter, ball of snot splatter, ball of the viscera of syllable sibyls, chatter, deaf chatter. I flap, I swing, smashdunguided I flap.

Here, Paz conveys what it is like to be an artist, always at the mercy of competing inner voices, of spontaneous creative demands.

The second part of *Eagle or Sun?*, "Arenas movedizas" ("Shifting Sands"), consists of nine sections; each is a self-contained account couched in mundane, imageless prose with occasional dialogue interspersed. Some of the sections, such as "El ramo azul" ("The Blue Bouquet"), recall the manner of Jorge Luis Borges; others, such as "Un aprendizaje difícil" ("A Difficult Apprenticeship"), are Kafkaesque; still others, such as "Mi vida con la ola" ("My Life with the Wave"), have the flavor of André Breton: Together, they resemble a collection of very short stories more than they do a series of prose poems.

The concluding part of *Eagle or Sun?*, the title section, contains twenty-one pieces. Divided between investigations into the poetics of creation and metaphysical narratives—Paz thus attempts to combine the methodologies developed in parts 1 and 2—these pieces are abstract and are therefore less accessible than the earlier ones in the volume, but they are not meant to be hermetic conundrums. The opening sentences of "Mayúscula" ("Capital") exemplify this final mode:

> The screaming crest of dawn flames. First egg, first peck, decapitation and delight! Feathers fly, wings spread, sails swell, and wing-oars dip in the sunrise. Oh unreined light, first light rearing.

It is clear that *Eagle or Sun?* is a multifaceted volume, the three parts of which are tenuously connected only through their formal similarities, with each part functioning autonomously.

SURREALISTIC IMAGERY

One of the most pervasive stylistic elements in Paz's poetry is a finely controlled Surrealism. Unlike many programmatic Surrealists, Paz never allows his work to degenerate into a series of unrelated, bizarre images. Rather, he inserts potent incongruities into his lyric or metaphysical sequences, where they are most effective. Consider "Semillas para un himno" ("Seeds for a Psalm"), a relatively traditional fifty-four-line poem, imagistic to be sure, but in a subdued and striking fashion, as in the line "Even the blind decipher the whip's writing." This, however, is followed immediately by "Clusters of beggars are hanging from the cities." The power of this image—by far the most radical in the poem—derives precisely from the fact that it is not merely another in a string of bizarre, surreal tropes.

If surrealistic imagery is Paz's most pervasive rhetorical device, mythic experience is his favored structuring principle. Indeed, Paz believes that in the modern age, poetry has supplanted myth as a redemptive force, a revealer of truth as the poet perceives it. Rachel Phillips has observed that what she terms the mythic mode allows Paz "to clothe his epistemological anxieties in comfortably familiar garb. . . ." This is certainly true for the traditional mythology with which most Western readers are acquainted, but many readers of Paz's work, even Latin Americans, will be confused and at times alienated by the complex indigenous Mexican myths that play such an important role in some of his poetry, especially in "Salamandra" ("Salamander") and the long and difficult *Sun Stone*, to which Cohen refers as "one of the last important poems to be published in the Western world. . . ." The same caveat obtains for Paz's poems that revolve around the history, philosophy, and myths of India.

BLANCO

Here and there throughout his oeuvre, Paz has experimented with unusual poetic forms. Until the mid-1960's, this tendency was generally limited to eccentric page layout and syntactical sparsity; *Blanco* is the epitome of this phase. Here, the poem emerges from a multifaceted layout and, in its original publication, in the format of a scroll; one is reminded of *Un Coup de dés jamais n'abolira le hasard* (1897; *A Dice-Throw*, 1958; also as *Dice Thrown Never Will Annul Chance*,

1965) by Stéphane Mallarmé, a poet whose influence on Paz is often noted. An extremely complex poem with its three simultaneous lines, *Blanco* has met with a mixed critical response: Rachel Phillips calls it a masterpiece, while poet-translator Robert Bly regards the poem as a disaster.

DISCOS VISUALES AND RENGA

Paz followed *Blanco* with more extreme formal experiments. In *Discos visuales*, for example, sets of concentric and overlapping disks spin on axes; as the top disk revolves, different words appear in its little windows. One thus "creates" a variety of poems by turning the upper disk. Another of Paz's forays into the unconventional is the collaborative *Renga*, a poem in which the four stanzas of each section have been individually composed by four different poets in four different languages.

"SNAPSHOTS"

In 1997, a year before he died, Paz published "Snapshots" in a literary review. These eleven disconnected couplets are prosaic, metaphorical, surreal, and progressive. They are the desperate and sometimes depressing thoughts of an old man who may already be aware that he is ill: Reminiscences, premonitions, and recollections scrupulously articulated indicate that Paz never stopped observing, thinking, and experimenting. This powerful echo of the past concludes,

> swarm of reflections on the page, yesterday confused
>   with today, the seen,
> entwined with the half-seen, inventions of memory,
>   gaps of reason;
>
> encounters, farewells, ghosts of the eye, incarnations
>   of touch unnamed
> presences, seeds of time: at the wrong time.

Paz's work is a fecund source of inspiration for his readers. His thematic and structural diversity, linguistic mastery, and philosophical commitment have produced an astonishing and replete body of poetry and prose. He drew on both indigenous and international material to provide readers with a universally comprehensible message: Plurality and diversity are positive objectives. The result is that Paz was the premiere man of letters in Mexico and Hispanic America and one of the outstanding literary and cultural figures of the twentieth century.

OTHER MAJOR WORKS

PLAY: *La hija de Rappaccini*, pb. 1990 (dramatization of a Nathaniel Hawthorne story; *Rappacini's Daughter*, 1996).

NONFICTION: *Voces de España*, 1938; *Laurel*, 1941; *El laberinto de la soledad: Vida y pensamiento de México*, 1950, 1959 (*The Labyrinth of Solitude: Life and Thought in Mexico*, 1961); *El arco y la lira*, 1956 (*The Bow and the Lyre*, 1971); *Las peras del olmo*, 1957; *Rufino Tamayo*, 1959 (*Rufino Tamayo: Myth and Magic*, 1979); *Magia de la risa*, 1962; *Cuatro poetas contemporáneos de Suecia*, 1963; *Cuadrivio*, 1965; *Poesía en movimiento*, 1966 (*New Poetry of Mexico*, 1970; translated and edited by Mark Strand); *Puertas al campo*, 1966; *Remedios Varo*, 1966; *Claude Lévi-Strauss: O, El nuevo festín de Esopo*, 1967 (*Claude Lévi-Strauss: An Introduction*, 1970); *Corriento alterna*, 1967 (*Alternating Current*, 1973); *Marcel Duchamp*, 1968 (*Marcel Duchamp: Or, The Castle of Purity*, 1970); *Conjunciones y disyunciones*, 1969 (*Conjunctions and Disjunctions*, 1974); *México: La última década*, 1969; *Posdata*, 1970 (*The Other Mexico: Critique of the Pyramid*, 1972); *Las cosas en su sitio*, 1971; *Los signos en rotación y otros ensayos*, 1971; *Traducción: Literatura y literalidad*, 1971; *Apariencia desnuda: La obra de Marcel Duchamp*, 1973 (*Marcel Duchamp: Appearance Stripped Bare*, 1978); *El signo y el garabato*, 1973; *Solo a dos voces*, 1973; *La búsqueda del comienzo*, 1974; *Los hijos del limo: Del romanticismo a la vanguardia*, 1974 (*Children of the Mire: Modern Poetry from Romanticism to the Avant-Garde*, 1974); *El mono gramático*, 1974 (*The Monkey Grammarian*, 1981); *Teatro de signos/transparencias*, 1974; *Versiones y diversiones*, 1974; *The Siren and the Seashell, and Other Essays on Poets and Poetry*, 1976; *Xavier Villaurrutia en persona y en obra*, 1978; *In/mediaciones*, 1979; *México en la obra de Octavio Paz*, 1979, expanded 1987; *El ogro filantrópico: Historia y política 1971-1978*, 1979 (*The Philanthropic Ogre*, 1985); *Sor Juana Inés de la Cruz: O, Las trampas de la fé*, 1982 (*Sor Juana: Or, The Traps of Faith*, 1989); *Sombras de obras: Arte y literatura*, 1983; *Tiempo nublado*, 1983 (*One Earth, Four or Five Worlds: Reflections on Contemporary History*, 1985); *Hombres en su siglo y otros ensayos*, 1984; *On Poets and Others*, 1986; *Convergences: Essays on Art and Literature*, 1987; *Primeras letras, 1931-1943*, 1988 (Enrico Mario Santi, editor); *Poesía, mito, revolución*, 1989; *La búscueda del presente/In Search of the Present: Nobel Lecture, 1990*, 1990; *La otra voz: Poesía y fin de siglo*, 1990 (*The Other Voice: Essays on Modern Poetry*, 1991); *Pequeña crónica de grandes días*, 1990; *Convergencias*, 1991; *Al paso*, 1992; *One Word to the Other*, 1992; *Essays on Mexican Art*, 1993; *Itinerario*, 1993 (*Itinerary: An Intellectual Journey*, 1999); *La llama doble: Amor y erotismo*, 1993 (*The Double Flame: Love and Eroticism*, 1995); *Un más allá erótico: Sade*, 1993 (*An Erotic Beyond: Sade*, 1998); *Vislumbres de la India*, 1995 (*In Light of India*, 1997).

EDITED TEXTS: *Antología poética*, 1956 (*Anthology of Mexican Poetry*, 1958; Samuel Beckett, translator); *New Poetry of Mexico*, 1970.

MISCELLANEOUS: *Lo mejor de Octavio Paz: El fuego de cada dia*, 1989; *Obras completas de Octavio Paz*, 1994; *Blanco*, 1995 (facsimiles of manuscript fragments and letters).

BIBLIOGRAPHY

Bloom, Harold, ed. *Octavio Paz*. Philadelphia: Chelsea House, 2002. A collection of essays examining the poetry of Paz, looking at motifs and Surrealistic aspects, among other topics.

Chiles, Frances. *Octavio Paz: The Mythic Dimension*. New York: Peter Lang, 1987. Discusses the use of myth in Paz's poetry.

Durán, Manuel. "Remembering Octavio Paz." *World Literature Today* 73, no. 1 (Winter, 1999): 101-103. A reminiscence and critical commentary on Paz's work. Tributes to, critical essays on, and an interview with Paz. (Reprinted with additions from *Books Abroad*, Autumn, 1972.)

Fein, John M. *Toward Octavio Paz: A Reading of His Major Poems, 1957-1986*. Lexington: University Press of Kentucky, 1986. A critical analysis of six of the longer works.

Grenier, Yvon. *From Art to Politics: Octavio Paz and the Pursuit of Freedom*. Lanham, Md.: Rowman &

Littlefield, 2001. Focuses on the ways in which Paz's social and political views surface in his poetry.

Hozven, Roberto, ed. *Otras voces: Sobre la poesía y prosa de Octavio Paz.* Riverside: University of California Press, 1996. A collection of critical essays in both English and Spanish. Includes bibliographical references.

Lutes, Todd Oakley. *Shipwreck and Deliverance: Politics, Culture, and Modernity in the Works of Octavio Paz, Gabriel García Márquez, and Mario Vargas Llosa.* Lanham, Md.: University Press of America, 2003. A comparative study of modernism in three Latin American authors.

Quiroga, José. *Understanding Octavio Paz.* Columbia: University of South Carolina Press, 1999. A critical study of selected poems by Paz. Includes a bibliography of the author's works, an index, and bibliographical references.

Underwood, Leticia Iliana. *Octavio Paz and the Language of Poetry: A Psycholinguistic Approach.* New York: Peter Lang, 1992. Includes illustrations and bibliographical references.

Williamson, Rodney. *The Writing in the Stars: A Jungian Reading of the Poetry of Octavio Paz.* Toronto, Ont.: University of Toronto Press, 2007. Williamson interprets Paz's poetry through the lens of the thought of Carl Jung, paying attention in particular to the concept of the archetype.

Wilson, Jason. *Octavio Paz.* Boston: Twayne, 1986. A solid introduction in Twayne's World Authors series. Contains a bibliography and an index.

Robert Hauptman

ALEXANDER PUSHKIN

Born: Moscow, Russia; June 6, 1799
Died: St. Petersburg, Russia; February 10, 1837

PRINCIPAL POETRY

Ruslan i Lyudmila, 1820 (*Ruslan and Liudmila*, 1936)
Gavriiliada, 1822 (*Gabriel: A Poem*, 1926)

Kavkazskiy plennik, 1822 (*The Prisoner of the Caucasus*, 1895)
Bratya razboyniki, 1824
Bakhchisaraiskiy fontan, 1827 (*The Fountain of Bakhchisarai*, 1849)
Graf Nulin, 1827 (*Count Nulin*, 1972)
Tsygany, 1827 (*The Gypsies*, 1957)
Poltava, 1829 (English translation, 1936)
Domik v Kolomne, 1833 (*The Little House at Kolomna*, 1977)
Skazka o mertvoy tsarevne, 1833 (*The Tale of the Dead Princess*, 1924)
Skazka o rybake ir rybke, 1833 (*The Tale of the Fisherman and the Fish*, 1926)
Skazka o tsare Saltane, 1833 (*The Tale of Tsar Saltan*, 1950)
Skazka o zolotom petushke, 1834 (*The Tale of the Golden Cockerel*, 1918)
Medniy vsadnik, 1837 (*The Bronze Horseman*, 1899)
Collected Narrative and Lyrical Poetry, 1984
Epigrams and Satirical Verse, 1984

OTHER LITERARY FORMS

Often considered the founder of modern Russian literature, Alexander Pushkin (POOSH-kuhn) was a prolific writer, not only of poetry but also of plays, novels, and short stories. His *malenkiye tragedii*, or "little tragedies"—brief, dramatic episodes in blank verse—include *Skupoy rytsar* (pr. 1852; *The Covetous Knight*, 1925), *Kamyenny gost* (pb. 1839; *The Stone Guest*, 1936), *Motsart i Salyeri* (pr. 1832; *Mozart and Salieri*, 1920), and *Pir vo vryemya chumy* (pb. 1833; *The Feast in Time of the Plague*, 1925).

Boris Godunov (pb. 1831; English translation, 1918) is Pushkin's famous historical tragedy constructed on the Shakespearean ideal that plays should be written "for the people." A story set in late sixteenth century Russia—a period of social and political chaos—it deals with the relationship between the ruling classes and the masses; written for the people, it, not surprisingly, gained universal appeal.

Pushkin's most important prose work, *Kapitanskaya dochka* (1836; *The Captain's Daughter*, 1846), is a historical novel of the Pugachev Rebellion. *Pikovaya dama* (1834; *The Queen of Spades*, 1858) is another well-known prose work, which influenced Fyodor Dostoevski's novels.

With its emphasis on civic responsibility, Pushkin's works have been translated into most major languages. His letters have been collected and annotated in English by J. Thomas Shaw as *The Letters of Alexander Pushkin* (1963).

ACHIEVEMENTS

Alexander Pushkin was the first poet to write in a purely Russian style. Aleksandr Tvardovsky calls him "the soul of our people." Considered as one of Russia's greatest poets, if not the greatest, he does not hold the same place in foreign countries, because his greatest achievement is in his use of the Russian language, with a flavor impossible to capture in translation. His verses continue to be regarded as the most natural expression of Russian poetry. After a lengthy period of stiff classicism and excessive sentimentality in eighteenth century literature, as seen in Konstantine Batyushkov, Vasily Zhukovsky, and Nikolai Karamzin, Pushkin breathed freshness and spontaneity into Russian poetry. Zhukovsky, the acknowledged dean of Russian letters, recognized this new spirit when, after the publication of *Ruslan and Liudmila* in 1820, he gave Pushkin a portrait of himself with the inscription: "To the victorious pupil from the vanquished master on that most important day on which he completed *Ruslan and Liudmila*."

It was Pushkin who brought the Romantic spirit to Russia, although it is impossible to categorize him as a pure Romantic. Pushkin's Byronic heroes in *The Prisoner of the Caucasus* and Aleko in *The Gypsies* introduced a new type of character, proud, disillusioned, and in conflict with himself and society, which greatly appealed to the Russia of the 1820's. Pushkin also introduced a love for the primitive and the exotic, which he found especially in southern Russia, and a deep and personal appreciation of nature. In the Romantic spirit, Pushkin showed a fond appreciation of Russia's past, her heroes, her folklore, and her people, which Soviet critics saw as *narodnost.*

Pushkin was also a realist who maintained a certain detached objectivity and distance, never quite penetrat-

ing beneath the surface of his heroes or completely identifying with them. He documents even his most Romantic poems. Pushkin's last post permitted him access to the imperial archives, a privilege that he deeply cherished. His interest in history led him to works on Peter the Great, on the Pugachev Rebellion, and into his own family history in *Arap Petra velikogo* (1828-1841; *Peter the Great's Negro*, 1896).

Although Pushkin was primarily a lyric poet, he was accomplished in all genres. *Evgeny Onegin* (1825-1832, 1833; *Eugene Onegin*, 1881), the only Russian novel in verse, lacks the richness of plot and social commentary that Honoré de Balzac, Leo Tolstoy, and Fyodor Dostoevski were later to develop, but it does contain humor, satire, and tender lyricism, all presented in poetry of incomparable assurance and grace. The work was acclaimed by the great nineteenth century critic Vissarion Belinsky as "an encyclopedia of Russian life."

Pushkin aimed at revitalizing the Russian theater and saw William Shakespeare as a better model than Jean Racine or Molière. Although his major play *Boris Godunov* falls short of dramatic intensity in its failure to realize the tragic fate of the hero, it is a lyric masterpiece and a profound study of ambition and power. Never a success on the stage, Pushkin's play was the inspiration for operas by Modest Mussorgsky and Sergei Prokofiev. The "little tragedies" are models of concision and true classical concentration. Each highlights one main theme: covetousness (*The Covetous Knight*), envy (*Mozart and Salieri*), passion (*The Stone Guest*, on the Don Juan theme), and pleasure before death (*Feast in Time of the Plague*). These plays rank among Pushkin's finest achievements.

Pushkin's later years were devoted more to prose than to poetry, with the exception of *The Bronze Horseman*, the folktales in verse, and several lyric poems. Pushkin did for Russia what the Brothers Grimm did for Germany in folk literature. Although many of his sources were not specifically Russian, such as *The Tale of the Dead Princess*, Pushkin transformed them into authentic national pieces by his unaffected use of folk expressions, alliteration, and real feeling for the people. In all his work, his effortless rhymes, easy and varied rhythms, natural speech, and true identification with the spirit of his time make him beloved by the Russian people and the founder of all Russian literature.

Biography

Alexander Sergeyevich Pushkin was born in Moscow on June 6, 1799, the second of three children. His mother, Nadezhda Osipovna Hannibal, was of African descent through her grandfather, Abram Hannibal, who was immortalized by Pushkin in *Peter the Great's Negro*. His father, Sergei Lvovich, and his uncle, Vasily Lvovich, were both writers. His father frequently entertained literary friends and had an excellent library of French and Russian classics, in which Pushkin by the age of twelve had read widely but indiscriminately. Pushkin's childhood was marked by the lack of a close relationship with his parents, although he formed lasting ties with his maternal grandmother, Marya Alexeyevna, and his nurse, Arina Rodionovna, who was responsible for his love of folklore. The fam-

ily could boast of very ancient aristocratic roots but suffered from a lack of money.

In 1811, Pushkin was accepted into the newly founded *lycée* at Tsarskoe Selo, designed by the czar to give a broad liberal education to aristocrats, especially those destined for administrative posts in the government. He remained there until his graduation in 1817, where he distinguished himself less by diligence than by natural ability, especially in French and Russian literature. Always of uneven temperament, he was not the most popular student in his class, but he did form lasting friendships with schoolmates Ivan Pushchin, Wilhelm Küchelbecker and Baron Anton Delvig; he also formed ties with such great literary figures as Zhukovsky and Karamizin, as well as bonds with the hussar officers, notably Pyotr Chaadayev. Pushkin began writing his earliest verses in French but soon turned to Russian.

After completing the *lycée*, Pushkin was appointed to the Ministry of Foreign Affairs in St. Petersburg. From 1817 to 1820, he led a dissipated life in the capital, much like that of Onegin in chapter 1 of *Eugene Onegin*. He became involved in liberal causes, though not as a member of the more revolutionary secret societies, and began to circulate his liberal verses. This alarmed the authorities, who proposed exile in Siberia, but because of the intercession of prominent personalities, among them Zhukovsky and the former principal of the *lycée*, Egor Englehardt, Pushkin was simply transferred to the south under the supervision of the paternal General I. N. Inzov.

Pushkin's first months in the south were spent traveling with the family of General Nikolai Raevsky through the Caucasus and the Crimea. Overwhelmed by the beauty of nature and the simplicity of the people, it was here that he wrote most of his so-called southern poems. The Raevskys introduced him to an appreciation of Lord Byron, which was reflected in his works of this period. Their daughters, especially Marya, were among Pushkin's many passions. Between 1820 and 1823, a productive literary period, he remained mostly in Kishinev. This peaceful existence was to end when Pushkin was transferred to Odessa under the stern General Vorontsov,

Alexander Pushkin (Library of Congress)

whose wife, Elisa, became the object of Pushkin's attentions after Amalia Riznich. For this and other offenses, Pushkin was dismissed from the service in 1824 and sent to his mother's estate at Mikhailovskoe near Pskov. Here he was placed under the direct supervision of his father and the local authorities. He quarreled constantly with his family, so that all of them withdrew and left him alone from 1824 to 1826. He had few companions other than the aged nurse Arina Rodionovna. This enforced isolation proved very productive, for it was here that he composed a great deal of *Eugene Onegin*, wrote *Boris Godunov* and many short poems, and drew his inspiration for later *skazki* (tales).

The death of Alexander I in 1825 provoked the Decembrist Revolt on December 26 of the same year. Pushkin's sympathies were with the revolutionaries, but his exile fortunately prevented him from participating. He took the opportunity of the new czar's accession to the throne, however, to make a successful plea for liberation. After 1826, he was permitted to travel to Moscow and, with reservations, to the capital, although his supervisor, Count Benkendorf, was not amenable to his requests. The years between 1826 and 1830 were a period of maturing and searching; they were also rich in literary output, especially of lyric poetry and the "little tragedies."

In 1830, Pushkin became engaged to the Moscow beauty Natalia Nikolayevna Goncharova, whom he married in 1831. It was an unsuccessful match, though not a completely disastrous marriage. Pushkin's wife had no interest in literature and had social aspirations far beyond either her or her husband's means. Four children were born to them, but Natalia's dissipation and Pushkin's jealousy eventually led him to melancholy and resentment. Financial worries and lack of advancement added to his problems. When Baron Georges d'Anthès, a young Alsatian, began paying undue attention to Pushkin's wife and the entire affair became a public scandal, Pushkin challenged d'Anthès to a duel. Pushkin was mortally wounded and died on February 10, 1837.

ANALYSIS

Alexander Pushkin's first verses were written in the style of French classicism and sentimentalism. His models were Voltaire and Evariste Parny, Gavrila Derzhavin, Zhukovsky, and Batyushkov. He wrote light, voluptuous verses, occasional pieces, and epigrams. Even in his early works, of which the most important is *Ruslan and Liudmila*, he shows restrained eroticism, always tempered by his classical training, which led him from the very beginning into excellent craftsmanship, brevity, and simplicity.

WIT, HUMOR, AND SATIRE

The lively wit, humor, and satire that were evident from the first continued to characterize Pushkin's work. *Ruslan and Liudmila* is a mock-epic, and the same strain appears in chapters 1 and 2 of *Eugene Onegin*. *Gabriel*, a parody on the Annunciation, which caused Pushkin a great deal of embarrassment with the authorities, has many witty passages, such as Satan's ensnarement of Adam and Eve by love. Pushkin achieves his humor by the use of parody, not hesitating to use it in dealing with the greatest authors such as Shakespeare and Voltaire, and with his friend and master Zhukovsky. Like Molière, however, he never really offends; his satire and dry irony produce a generally good-natured effect.

POLITICAL POEMS

Pushkin first became known in St. Petersburg as a writer of liberal verses, and this—coupled with charges of atheism—made him a constant target of the imperial censors. His famous "Vol'nost': Oda" ("Ode to Freedom") is severe on Napoleon and condemns the excesses of the French Revolution, yet it reminds monarchs that they must be subservient to the law. In "Derevnya" ("The Countryside"), he longs for the abolition of serfdom, yet looks to the czar for deliverance. Pushkin did not conceal his sympathy for the Decembrists, and in his famous "Vo glubine sibirskikh rud" ("Message to Siberia"), he reminds the exiled revolutionaries that "freedom will once again shine, and brothers give you back your sword." His later poems address more general issues, and in 1831 during the Polish Uprising, he speaks out clearly in favor of the czar in "Klevetnikam Rossii" ("To the Slanderers of Russia"). Finally, *The Bronze Horseman* addresses the very complex theme of the individual in conflict with the state.

HEROINES AND LOVE POETRY

Pushkin knew many passions in his brief lifetime, and several women inspired both his life and poetry.

Marya Raevskaya became the model for many of his heroines, from the Circassian girl in *The Prisoner of the Caucasus* to Marya in *Poltava*. Amalia Riznich, destined to die in Italy, reappears in "Dlya beregov otchizny dal'noy" ("Abandoning an Alien Country") in 1830. Elisa Vorontsova, the wife of Pushkin's stern superior in Odessa, was a powerful influence who haunted the poet long after his return to the north. The ring she gave him is immortalized in "Khrani menya, moy talisman" ("Talisman") and "The Burned Letter," where the ashes recall her memory. Anna Kern was the inspiration for the almost mystical "Ya pomnyu chudnoye mgnoven'ye" ("I Remember a Wonderful Moment"). Natalya Goncharova, while still Pushkin's fiancé, likewise assumes a spiritual role in "Madona" ("Madonna"). Pushkin's love poetry, while passionate, is also delicate and sensitive, and even the most voluptuous evocations concentrate on images such as those of eyes and feet.

NATURE

In Romantic fashion, Pushkin was one of the first to introduce nature into his works. First inspired by the trip to the south, where the beauty of the Caucasus overwhelmed him, he sees freedom in the wide expanses and steep mountains. Later, on a second trip—as described in "Kavkazsky" ("The Caucasus")—he evokes the playful rivers, the low clouds and the silver-capped mountains. He feels that the sight of a monastery brings him to the neighborhood of Heaven. The north also has its charms, particularly the Russian winter. There are exquisite verses on winter in the fifth chapter of *Eugene Onegin*, and in his lyrics about the swirling snowstorm in "Zinniy Vecher" ("Winter Evening") or the winter road that symbolizes his sad journey through life. Both city and country come alive in the crisp cold of winter in the prologue to *The Bronze Horseman*.

MELANCHOLY

Despite ever-recurring wit, irony, and gentle sensitivity, Pushkin's poetry is fundamentally melancholy and often tragic. This dichotomy corresponds to the division of his personality: dissipated yet deep. The southern poems all end tragically, his plays are all tragedies, and *Eugene Onegin* ends with the death of Lensky and the irremediable disappointment of Tatyana and

Onegin. Pushkin frequently writes of the evil and demoniac forces of nature (as in Tatyana's dream), of madness (Eugene in *The Bronze Horseman*), and of violence (in "Zhenikh," "The Bridegroom"). A melancholy vein permeates his lyrics as well. Like the Romantics, Pushkin speaks frequently of death, perhaps foreseeing his own. The hour of parting from a loved one, a frequent subject of his lyrics, foreshadows death. As early as 1823, in "Telega zhizni" ("The Wagon of Time"), he sees the old man as the one who calmly awaits eternal sleep. Pushkin's tragic vision is complicated by the absence of a Christian worldview with a belief in life after death. Unlike Dostoevski, Pushkin writes of unmitigated, not of redemptive, suffering. S. M. Frank, who does admit a spiritual dimension in Pushkin, compares his work to Mozart's music, which seems gay but is in fact sad. Yet it is this very sadness which puts him in the tradition of Russian literature, anticipating Nikolai Gogol's "laughter through tears."

RUSLAN AND LIUDMILA

Pushkin's first major work, *Ruslan and Liudmila*, was published in 1820. It is now usually placed in a minor category, but it was important at the time as the first expression of the Russian spirit. Witty and ironic, the poem is written in the style of a mock-epic, much in the tradition of Ariosto's *Orlando Furioso* (1516, 1521, 1532; English translation, 1591). It also echoes Voltaire, and the fourth canto parodies Zhukovsky's "Spyaschaya carevna" ("Twelve Sleeping Maidens"). In fact, the whole plot resembles Zhukovsky's projected "Vladimir." It consists of six cantos, a prologue added in 1828, and an epilogue. Pushkin began the poem in 1817 while still in school, and he was already in exile in the south when it was published.

Ruslan and Liudmila, in Walter Vickery's words, transports the reader to the "unreal and delightful poetic world of cheerful unconcern," returning to the legendary days of ancient Kiev, where Prince Vladimir is giving a wedding feast for his daughter Liudmila. The fortunate bridegroom Ruslan is about to enjoy the moment he has so voluptuously awaited, when a clap of thunder resounds and his bride is snatched away from him by the dwarf enchanter Chernomor. Prince Vladimir promises half of his kingdom and Liudmila as a bride to the man who rescues her, Ruslan sets off with his three rivals, Ratmir, Rogdai, and Farlaf. Ratmir eventually chooses a pastoral life, Rogdai is slain, and Farlaf reappears at the moment when Ruslan is about to return with Liudmila. In true knightly fashion, Ruslan saves Kiev from an attack by the Pechenegs, kills his last rival, and marries the princess.

Pushkin's poem captures many exaggerated scenes from the *byliny* or heroic tales, such as the death of the giant head, and ends with a full-scale epic battle. It is a gentle mockery of chivalry, sorcery, and love. Critics from Zhukovsky to the Soviets hailed it as a true folk-epic in the spirit of *narodnost* (nationalism) although many of Pushkin's contemporaries were shocked at his unfaithfulness to classical antiquity and his trivial subject. The public, however, welcomed it, seeing in it a new inspiration for the times. The prologue, especially, captures the popular spirit with its learned cat on a green oak who recites a folktale when he turns to the left and a song when he moves to the right.

As in all of Pushkin's works, the language is the most important feature, offsetting the many flaws of Pushkin's still immature talent. His choice of vocabulary is very Russian, even popular, and his rhythms and rhymes are graceful and effortless. Henri Troyat refers to him as "a virtuoso of rime" and says that this talent alone announced possibilities for the future.

EUGENE ONEGIN

Eugene Onegin, Pushkin's novel in verse, was begun in 1823 in Kishinev and completed in 1830. It is composed of eight cantos or chapters, as Pushkin preferred to call them. There are projects and fragments for two other parts, including Onegin's journey. Each chapter contains forty to fifty-four stanzas of fourteen lines each, in four-foot iambic, and with a special rhyme scheme called the "Onegin stanza": *AbAbCCdd-EffEgg* (small letters indicating masculine and capitals feminine rhymes). Pushkin did not return to this stanza form and it has rarely been used since. The novel itself resembles sentimental types such as Jean-Jacques Rousseau's *La Nouvelle Héloïse* (1761; *Julia: Or, The New Eloisa*, 1773) and Benjamin Constant's *Adolphe* (1815; English translation, 1816). It is also a type of bildungsroman or the *éducation sentimentale* of Tatyana and Onegin. It is in reality a combination of several genres: novel, comic-epic, and above all poetry, for it is inseparable from the verse in which it is written.

The first two chapters, the product of Pushkin's youth, show the greatest absence of structure. They abound in digressions and poetic ruminations ranging from the ballet to women's feet. They introduce us to the hero Eugene Onegin, a St. Petersburg dandy, who spends his life in boredom until an inheritance brings him to an equally boring life in the provinces. Here he meets the dreamy poet Lensky, in love with a neighbor, Olga Larin. It is at this point that the tone of the poem changes, as Olga's older sister, Tatyana, immediately develops an intense passion for Onegin, and in her simplicity reveals her love for him in her famous letter. Onegin politely refuses her and continues his aimless existence, interrupted by a flirtation with Olga, thus provoking a duel with Lensky in which the poet is killed.

Years pass, and Tatyana is married against her will to an elderly and unattractive general. Onegin meets her in Moscow and falls passionately in love with her. He declares his love, but this time it is Tatyana in her mature serenity who informs him: "I love you . . . but I have become another's wife; I shall be true to him through life." Here the poem ends abruptly yet fittingly as Tatyana emerges as the tragic heroine in this tale of twice-rejected love.

The poem maintains an internal unity through the parallel between Onegin's rejection of Tatyana and her refusal of him. *Eugene Onegin* is, however, essentially a lyric poem about the tragic consequences of love rather than a pure novel with a solid substructure. Pushkin draws poetry out of a samovar, the wrinkled nanny who is modeled on Arina Rodionovna, and the broken-hearted resignation of Tatyana. The changing of the seasons indicates the passage of time as Pushkin sings of the beautiful Russian countryside. He likewise enters into his characters, and makes of Onegin a realistic hero and the first of a long line of "superfluous men" to appear in Mikhail Lermontov, Ivan Goncharov, and Ivan Turgenev. Tatyana is perfectly consistent as her youthful naïveté changes into a controlled maturity. She has often been described as the purest figure in the whole of Russian literature, and has become the prototype of Russian womanhood. Pushkin's contemporaries read his poem with enthusiasm, and today it is still one of the great classics of Russian literature. Foreign readers may know it better through Pyotr Ilich Tchaikovsky's opera; again, this results from the fact that it is essentially a poem, defying translation.

POLTAVA

Pushkin always showed a great deal of interest in Peter the Great, and refers to him in his lyric poetry, in longer poems, and in his prose (*Peter the Great's Negro*). It is in *Poltava* and *The Bronze Horseman* that he reaches his height. *Poltava*, written in three weeks in 1828, has an epic quality but also draws on the ballad, ode, and oral tradition. It recalls Sir Walter Scott's *Marmion* (1808), since it places historical characters in a Romantic background. Lord Byron in *Mazeppa* (1819), drew on the same sources but used instead an apocryphal account of the hero's youth.

The main focus of *Poltava* is the battle of 1709, in which the Russians under Peter the Great defeated the Swedes under Charles XII. Poltava was the turning point in the Russo-Swedish War. Against this historical backdrop is set the romance of the aged Ukrainian Cossack hetman Mazepa with the young and beautiful Marya, daughter of Kochubey, who refuses to allow the marriage. The two marry in spite of him, and Kochubey seeks revenge by revealing, to Peter, Mazepa's plan of revolt against him. His project miscarries, however, when Peter believes Mazepa's denials. Kochubey is taken prisoner by Mazepa and is about to be executed when Marya learns about her husband's treachery against her father. Arriving too late to save him, she leaves, returning to her husband only briefly as a madwoman before Mazepa's flight with Charles XII after leading an unsuccessful revolt against the victorious Peter.

Although Pushkin has interwoven much historical material into his tale, he has been charged with excessive melodrama by critics from Belinsky to the present day, who see in Mazepa a kind of Gothic villain. Pushkin is likewise charged with unsuccessfully fusing the historical and the Romantic, and more recently, by John Bayley, for the gap "between two kinds of romance, the modern melodrama and the traditional tragic ballad." Mazepa is one of Pushkin's few dark and villainous characters, but Marya has been acknowl-edged as truly *narodnaya* by Belinsky and Soviet critics. Peter is the all-pervading presence, larger than life, who symbolizes the growing importance of Russia.

THE BRONZE HORSEMAN

In *The Bronze Horseman*, Peter reappears in retrospect. Pushkin wrote *The Bronze Horseman* in 1833 partially in response to the Polish poet Adam Mickiewicz, who had attacked the Russian autocracy. It consists of an introduction and two parts, 481 lines in all, and is rightly considered one of Pushkin's greatest masterpieces. It combines personal lyricism and political, social, and literary themes and raises philosophical questions in paradoxical fashion. The title refers to the equestrian statue of Peter the Great by E. M. Falconet that still stands along the Neva River. The historical incident that inspired the poem was the devastating flood that struck St. Petersburg on November 7, 1824.

In the introduction, Peter the Great stands looking over the Neva, then a deserted swamp with a few ramshackle huts. He plans to build a city there, which will open a window to the West and terrify all his enemies. A hundred years pass, and the young city is the pride of the north, a cold sparkling gem of granite and iron, the scene of royal balls, military reviews, and winter sports. Suddenly, the picture changes as Pushkin begins his sad tale. Eugene, a poor government clerk (whose last name is not important), is making plans to marry Parasha. That very night, the Neva whirls and swirls and rages like an angry beast; the next day Parasha's home is destroyed, and she is lost. Eugene visits the empty spot, and goes mad from the shock. Life continues as usual, but poor Eugene wanders through the city until one day he shakes his angry fist at the Bronze Horseman, who gallops after him down the streets of St. Petersburg. Later, a dilapidated house is washed up on one of the islands; near it Eugene's corpse is found.

Pushkin's poem shows complete mastery of technique. In lines starkly terse yet rich with onomatopoeic sounds, Pushkin conjures up the mighty flood, the proud emperor, and the defenseless Eugene. In the last scene, Peter and Eugene come face to face, and seemingly the emperor wins, yet Pushkin is far from being reconciled to the notion that individual destiny must be sacrificed to historical necessity. Indeed, Eugene is the first of a long line of downtrodden Russian heroes, such as Akakiy Akakyevich and Makar Devushkin, possessing dignity and daring to face authority. Peter is the human hero, contemplating greatness; he is also the impassive face of destiny. The poem itself poses the problem of Pushkin's own troubled existence as well as the ambiguous and cruel fate of all human beings.

Other major works

LONG FICTION: *Evgeny Onegin*, 1825-1832, 1833 (*Eugene Onegin*, 1881); *Arap Petra velikogo*, 1828-1841 (*Peter the Great's Negro*, 1896); *Kirdzhali*, 1834 (English translation, 1896); *Kapitanskaya dochka*, 1836 (*The Captain's Daughter*, 1846); *Dubrovsky*, 1841 (English translation, 1892); *Yegipetskiye nochi*, 1841 (*Egyptian Nights*, 1896); *Istoriya sela Goryukhina*, 1857 (*History of the Village of Goryukhino*, 1966).

SHORT FICTION: *Povesti Belkina*, 1831 (*Russian Romance*, 1875; better known as *The Tales of Belkin*, 1947); *Pikovaya dama*, 1834 (*The Queen of Spades*, 1858).

PLAYS: *Boris Godunov*, pb. 1831 (wr. 1824-1825; English translation, 1918); *Motsart i Salyeri*, pr. 1832 (*Mozart and Salieri*, 1920); *Pir vo vryemya chumy*, pb. 1833 (*The Feast in Time of the Plague*, 1925); *Rusalka*, pb. 1837 (*The Water Nymph*, 1924); *Kamyenny gost*, pb. 1839 (wr. 1830; *The Stone Guest*, 1936); *Skupoy rytsar*, pr. 1852 (wr. 1830; *The Covetous Knight*, 1925); *Stseny iz rytsarskikh vryemen*, pr., pb. 1937 (wr. 1835); *Little Tragedies*, 1946 (includes *The Covetous Knight*, *The Stone Guest*, *Mozart and Salieri*, and *The Feast in Time of the Plague*).

NONFICTION: *Istoriya Pugacheva*, 1834 (*The Pugachev Rebellion*, 1966); *Puteshestviye v Arzrum*, 1836 (*A Journey to Arzrum*, 1974); *Dnevnik, 1833-1835*, 1923; *Pisma*, 1926-1935 (3 volumes); *The Letters of Alexander Pushkin*, 1963 (3 volumes); *Pisma poslednikh let 1834-1837*, 1969.

MISCELLANEOUS: *The Captain's Daughter, and Other Tales*, 1933; *The Poems, Prose, and Plays of Pushkin*, 1936; *The Works of Alexander Pushkin*, 1936; *Polnoye sobraniye sochineniy*, 1937-1959 (17 volumes); *The Complete Prose Tales of Alexander Pushkin*, 1966; *A. S. Pushkin bez tsenzury*, 1972; *Pushkin Threefold*, 1972; *Polnoye sobraniye sochineniy*, 1977-1979 (10 volumes); *Alexander Pushkin: Complete Prose Fiction*, 1983.

Bibliography

Bethea, David M. *Realizing Metaphors: Alexander Pushkin and the Life of the Poet*. Madison: University of Wisconsin Press, 1998. Bethea illustrates the relation between the art and life of Pushkin and shows how he speaks to modern times.

_____, ed. *The Pushkin Handbook*. Madison: University of Wisconsin Press, 2005. A collection of essays by Pushkin scholars in the Soviet Union and North America that looks at his life and legacy. Includes essays on his poetic works.

Binyon, T. J. *Pushkin: A Biography*. New York: Knopf, 2004. An extensive biography of Pushkin, Russia's national poet.

Debreczeny, Paul. *Social Functions of Literature: Alexander Pushkin and Russian Culture*. Stanford, Calif.: Stanford University Press, 1997. Debreczeny divides his study into three parts: the first is devoted to selected readers' responses to Pushkin; the second explores the extent to which individual aesthetic responses are conditioned by their environment; and the third concerns the mythic aura that developed around Pushkin's public persona.

Evdokimova, Svetlana. *Pushkin's Historical Imagination*. New Haven, Conn.: Yale University Press, 1999. An examination of the range of Pushkin's fictional and nonfictional works on the subject of history. Evdokimova considers Pushkin's ideas on the relation between chance and necessity, the significance of great individuals, and historical truth.

Feinstein, Elaine. *Pushkin: A Biography*. London: Weidenfeld & Nicolson, 1998. Drawing on newly discovered documents, Feinstein explores the life of one of nineteenth century Russia's greatest writers.

Kahn, Andrew, ed. *The Cambridge Companion to Pushkin*. New York: Cambridge University Press, 2006. Looks at his works and their legacy. Contains several chapters on his poetry.

Ryfa, Juras T., ed. *Collected Essays in Honor of the Bicentennial of Alexander Pushkin's Birth*. Lewiston, N.Y.: Edwin Mellen Press, 2000. A selection of scholarly essays devoted to various works by Pushkin and his influence on his literary descendants.

Shaw, J. Thomas. *Pushkin's Poetics of the Unexpected: The Nonrhymed Lines in the Rhymed Poetry and the Rhymed Lines in the Nonrhymed Poetry.* Columbus, Ohio: Slavica, 1993. This is a highly specialized study of Pushkin's poetic technique that will be of most use to specialists.

Vitale, Serena. *Pushkin's Button.* Translated by Ann Goldstein and Jon Rothschild. New York: Farrar, Straus and Giroux, 1999. A cultural history and narrative of the last months of Pushkin's life before his fatal duel. Vitale brings to life the world of St. Petersburg in the 1830's using her own research with information gleaned from secondary literature and the memoirs and letters of Pushkin's contemporaries.

Irma M. Kashuba

R

ALFONSO REYES

Born: Monterrey, Mexico; May 17, 1889
Died: Mexico City, Mexico; December 27, 1959

PRINCIPAL POETRY

Huellas, 1923
Ifigenia cruel, 1924
Pausa, 1926
Cinco casi sonetos, 1931
Romances del Rio de Enero, 1933
A la memoria de Ricardo Güiraldes, 1934
Golfo de Mexico, 1934 (*Gulf of Mexico*, 1949)
Yerbas del Tarahumara, 1934 (*Tarahumara Herbs*, 1949)
Infancia, 1935
Minuta, 1935
Otra voz, 1936
Cantata en la tumba de Federico García Lorca, 1937
Poema del Cid, 1938 (modern version of *Cantar de mío Cid*)
Villa de Unión, 1940
Algunos poemas, 1941
Romances y afines, 1945
La vega y el soto, 1946
Cortesía, 1948
Homero en Cuernavaca, 1949
Obra poética, 1952

OTHER LITERARY FORMS

Alfonso Reyes (RAY-yays) was an essayist, short-story writer, and critic as well as a poet. Indeed, the bulk of the more than twenty volumes of his *Obras completas* (1955-1967; complete works)—an ongoing project undertaken by the Mexican Fondo de Cultura Económica to make accessible the seemingly inexhaustible archive of manuscripts and papers that he left behind—is criticism rather than poetry. Spanning cul-

tures and disciplines, the breadth of his knowledge was truly astounding. His *Grata compañía* (1948; pleasing company), for example, includes essays on Robert Louis Stevenson, G. K. Chesterton, Marcel Proust, Jean-Jacques Rousseau, René Descartes, Jakob Burckhardt, José Maria de Eça de Queiróz, Hermann Alexander Keyserling, Graça Aranha, Leopoldo Lugones, Miguel de Unamuno y Jugo, Antonio Caso, and Pedro Henríquez Ureña. In the fourteen issues of his personal newsletter, *Monterrey*, sent from Rio de Janeiro and Buenos Aires, he particularly liked to focus on the relationship of great European intellectual figures to the American experience: Johann Wolfgang von Goethe and the United States, Giuseppe Garibaldi and Cuba, Ramón María del Valle-Inclán and Mexico, Luis de Góngora y Argote and New Spain, Paul Morand and Brazil, and so on.

Reyes's masterpiece, *Visión de Anáhuac* (1917; *Vision of Anáhuac*, 1950)—its title referring to the Aztec name for the Valley of Mexico, the site of the mighty Aztec capital, Tenochtitlán (later Mexico City)—written in Madrid in 1915, is a brilliant prose poem of some twenty-five pages depicting the Indian civilization on the eve of the Spanish conquest. *Cartones de Madrid* (1917; sketches of Madrid) is a collection of impressionistic essays. Reyes's essays are always lyric—even when they treat philosophical themes—and are often laced with humor. Some of his finest short stories, such as "La cena" (the dinner) and "La mano del comandante Aranda" ("Major Aranda's Hand"), blend a lyric realism with supernatural or fantastic elements, while others, such as "El testimonio de Juan Peña" (the testimony of Juan Peña) and "Silueta del indio Jesús" (silhouette of the Indian Jesus), treat indigenous themes. Among his best literary criticism are the essays of *La experiencia literaria* (1942; literary experience) and "Sobre la estética de Góngora" (on the aesthetics of Góngora), an essay which contributed significantly to the modern reappraisal of the Baroque poet. In *El deslinde: Prolegómenos a la teoría literaria* (1944; the boundary line: prolegomenon to literary theory), he addressed a wide range of aesthetic questions, drawing on semantics, philology, and the philosophy of language.

Reyes was an avid translator. He rendered several of Chesterton's works, including a volume of his detective stories, *El candor de Padre Brown* (1921), into Spanish. He also translated *Olalla* (1922), by Stevenson, and *A Sentimental Journey* (1768), by Laurence Sterne (*Viaje sentimental por Francia e Italia*, 1919). Reyes's translation of the first nine books of Homer's *Iliad* (c. 750 B.C.E.; English translation, 1611) as *La Ilíada de Homero* is considered the best available in Spanish, and he also produced a modern prose version of the *Cantar de mío Cid* (early thirteenth century) as *Poema del Cid*. He translated poems by Stéphane Mallarmé, José-Maria de Heredia, Robert Browning, Oliver Goldsmith, Dante, and Goethe, and, in conjunction with N. Tasin, a story by Anton Chekhov. Finally, Reyes produced Spanish versions of C. M. Bowra's *Ancient Greek Literature* (1933) as *Historia de la literatura griega* (1948), and Gilbert Murray's *Euripides and His Age* (1913) as *Eurípides y su época* (1949).

Achievements

Alfonso Reyes strove indefatigably to draw the literature and culture of Latin America into the Latin cultural sphere of Spain, France, and Italy, and to effect a reconciliation between Spain and its former colonies. Indeed, his cosmopolitan spirit did much to internationalize a hitherto parochial Latin American literature. In his own country, he cast the light of Vergil and Goethe upon the Mexican landscape. Reyes assimilated a great deal from contemporary French writers such as André Gide, Paul Valéry, and Valery Larbaud, and he maintained lifelong friendships and correspondences with the most influential Spanish intellectuals of his time—Unamuno, Valle-Inclán, José Ortega y Gasset, Juan Ramón Jiménez, and Ramón Gómez de la Serna. Reyes, by his own example, was able to disprove to the Spaniards the widely held opinion that Spanish American writers were capable of nothing more inspired than exaggerated stylistic flourishes. As Mexican ambassador to Brazil, he worked to improve cultural relations between the Spanish-speaking countries and Brazil. He opened so many channels of communication with the outside world that Octavio Paz (quoting a phrase used in another context by Reyes himself) called him "the horseman of the air," and Xavier Villaurrutía dubbed him "the man of the roads."

Considering the unique nature of Reyes's literary contributions, he has neither direct antecedents nor direct successors in the Hispanic tradition, yet many have learned from his example. Paz has cited *La experiencia literaria* and *El deslinde* as works of particular value to him. Gabriela Mistral described *Vision of Anáhuac* as the best single piece of Latin American prose, and Larbaud and Juan José Domenchina have suggested that the work exercised an influence on the *Anabase* (1924; *Anabasis*, 1930) of Saint-John Perse.

In the realm of poetry, Reyes stands out as one of the first Latin American writers to incorporate into Spanish verse the casual tradition of the English lyric, with its alternations of delicacy with diversion and seriousness with whimsy. As a critic working under the tutelage of Ramón Menéndez Pidal, Reyes wrote important analyses of past writers; in particular, he was instrumental in refurbishing the image of the seventeenth century poet Góngora, a rediscovery of great importance to Spanish literature.

The University of California, the University of Michoácan, and the University of Mexico, as well as Tulane University, Havana University, Harvard University, and Princeton University, awarded honorary degrees to Reyes. He received the Premio Nacional de Ciencias y Artes (National Prize for Arts and Sciences) in 1945 and was named president of the Mexican Academy in 1957, after having been a member for nearly forty years.

Biography

Alfonso Reyes Ochoa was born in Monterrey, Nuevo León, Mexico, the ninth of twelve children born to General Bernardo Reyes and Aurelia Ochoa, both of whom were from the environs of Guadalajara in the state of Jalisco. General Reyes, the author of an array of military manuals, brochures, and histories, was an enlightened and efficient governor of the state of Nuevo León and was largely responsible for the progressive spirit which obtains in Monterrey even in the twenty-first century. Of his early years, Reyes wrote in "Sol de Monterrey" ("Monterrey Sun"), "I knew no shadow in my childhood,/ only the brilliance of the sun"; a sun that followed at his heels "like a Pekinese." Reyes entered the Escuela Nacional Preparatoria in Mexico City in 1905, and went on to the Escuela Nacional de Altos

Estudios. Mexico at that time was in the tight grip of the dictator Porfirio Díaz, and although the positivist milieu that Díaz encouraged was not favorable to the study of the humanities, Reyes immersed himself in the study of the classics.

Reyes married Manela Mota in 1911, and their only child, Alfonso, was born in 1912. The following year, Reyes received a law degree from the University of Mexico. He became the youngest member of the Centennial Generation (which included Pedro Henríquez Ureña, Antonio Caso, and José Vasconcelos), a group dedicated to changing the official modes of thought in Mexico. Reyes also helped found the Ateneo de la Juventud (Athenaeum of Youth), an institution for young intellectuals that flourished until 1940.

When Díaz was ousted by Francisco Madero in 1910, Mexico was thrown into a welter of revolt and banditry. Before dawn on February 9, 1913, rebel troops tried to install General Reyes, long viewed as Díaz's successor, as head of state. General Reyes was shot to death in street fighting at the Zocalo in Mexico City; seventeen years later, his son honored his father—that "tower of a man"—in a prose elegy, "Oración del 9 de febrero de 1913" ("Prayer of the Ninth of February"), giving Reyes the opportunity to observe in himself a "presentiment of an obscure equivocation in the moral clockwork of our world." There is also a four-stanza poem on the same subject, "+9 de febrero de 1913," in which the poet asks, "Where are you, man of seven wounds,/ blood spurting at midday?" and proceeds to promise that "if I have continued to live since that day,/ it is because I carry you with me, where you are inviolable."

In August of 1913, Reyes went to Paris as second secretary of the Mexican legation. The following year, he gravitated to Madrid, where he earned a meager living from journalism. He soon became associated with the famous Center of Historical Studies in Madrid, directed by Pidal, and made valuable contributions to the *Revista de filología española*. He worked in the company of such scholars as Américo Castro, Federico de Onís, Tomás Navarro Tomás, and Antonio Solalinde, all of whom Reyes called "the princes of Spanish philology" and into whose society he was readily admitted. Reminiscing years later about those days in

Alfonso Reyes (©Alberto Dallal)

Madrid, Reyes wrote that literature had been everywhere—in the air, in the cafés, and in the streets.

In 1927, Reyes returned to Mexico and became the Mexican ambassador to Argentina, where he remained until 1930, when he went to Rio de Janeiro as ambassador to Brazil. In 1939, he returned to Mexico to stay, after nearly twenty-five years of almost continuous diplomatic service. He proceeded to establish two great educational institutions: the group of scholars called El Colegio Nacional and the graduate school of the humanities, El Colegio de México. His home in Mexico City included a magnificent library that became for Reyes a sanctuary of the muses; the library was dubbed "Capilla Alfonsina" (Alfonsine Chapel) by his friend, Enrique Díez-Canedo, a Spanish poet.

At the age of seventy, Reyes succumbed to the last of a series of heart attacks and was buried in the Rotonda de los Hombres Ilustres in the Panteón Civil de Dolores in Mexico City. His wife was killed in an accident in 1965, and their granddaughter, Alicia Reyes, directs the Alfonsine Chapel, used as a research center and sponsored by the Mexican government.

ANALYSIS

Like his contemporaries, the Argentine Ricardo Güiraldes, the Chilean Pedro Prado, and the Colombian José Eustasio Rivera, Alfonso Reyes was above all a writer of prose, yet at no time in his life did he cease to write poetry. He began to write verse at an early age, and his first poems appeared in print when he was sixteen. The poems reflect his love for ancient Greece and for the sculptures of Phidias and Praxiteles. Reyes's first book of verse, *Huellas* (footprints), containing pieces from the years 1906 to 1919, appeared in 1923. These poems reveal a Parnassian influence evident in the works of other Latin American poets of the time, yet they already showed some of Reyes's characteristic variety of subject matter, mood, and style. Later, he would make use of realism (especially in his descriptions of Mexico) and Surrealism in *Gulf of Mexico*.

There is something of the dilettante about Reyes the poet; chatting with or about his friends, musing over feminine beauty, worrying about death, reworking the *ubi sunt* commonplace, or simply delighting in intellectual silliness. "I prefer to be promiscuous/ in literature," Reyes wrote in the poem "Teoría prosaica" ("Prose Theory"), claiming further that he preferred the antiquated measurements of the *almud*, the *vara*, and the *cuarterón* to the metric system. Reyes kept his poetic sanity by alternating "the popular ballad/ of my neighbor/ with the rare quintessence/ of Góngora and Mallarmé."

EXHAUSTIVE VOCABULARY

A traveler and an explorer in different worlds, Reyes made use of everyday speech, the Greek chorus, the monologue of Mallarmé, the Spanish of the Golden Age, and names from the Tarahumara pharmacopoeia. Reyes exhausted all sources of Spanish vocabulary. In his poems, there are Latin expressions, Greek words, and obscure Arabisms not normally used in conversational language—*alcatraz* (cornucopia), *almirez* (brass mortar), *alquitara* (still)—yet none of these occurs in such profusion or within such complicated syntax as to overwhelm the reader. Reyes delighted in place-names, in words peculiar to certain countries that gave his work local color—*ñañigo* (member of a secret Cuban society of blacks), *tamanco* (Brazilian sandal)—and in chatty words—*corretón* (gadding about), *copetín* (little goblet). He frequently repeated synonymous or near-synonymous words in the same line, as if searching for maximum precision—*curuja, buho* (both meaning "owl"); *alfónsigo, pistacho* (both meaning "pistachio"); and *tierra, terrena, terruño* (all meaning "land").

EPITHETS

Reyes was also fond of epithets. His father is the "ruddy lion," Benito Juárez is the "master of the bow" whose arrows "fastened in the heavens' red meteors," and the American Hispanist Sylvanus Griswold Morley is the "California Quijote." Occasionally, Reyes embedded in his poetry significant lines from Dante or Mallarmé in the original Italian or French. Nothing was alien to Reyes, and the world that he inhabited is "our" world rather than "the" world. The statue of David in Florence is "my" David, the street in Rio de Janeiro where he lived is "my" rua de Laranjeiras, and his native city, Monterrey, was so much his that he marveled at why he had never attached its name to his own. He sometimes spoke of himself as Alfonso in his poems and especially delighted in words or neologisms that resembled his name, such as *alfónsigo* (pistachio), *alfonsecuente* (on the model of *consecuente*, coherent, or "Alfonso-coherent").

HELLENISM

Reyes considered even the humblest subject matter worthy of poetry, and much of his charm stems from his ability to popularize intellectual material. He demonstrated his love of Greek mythology and Hellenism in his verse play, *Ifigenia cruel* (cruel Iphigenia), which is crafted in the simplest language. Here, he converted the Euripidean heroine into a formidable Amazon torn between her career as a sacrificial priestess and her desire for her home. Eventually, she opts for the former; as Barbara Bockus Aponte observes, the Iphigenia who prefers her liberty to the tradition of her home in Greece is the Reyes who left behind the strife of Mexico and abjured thoughts of vengeance in the search for his own freedom.

Reyes's Hellenism is evident as well in *Homero en Cuernavaca* (Homer in Cuernavaca), comprising thirty sonnets that are sometimes romantic but just as often satirical (as in "De Helena"). In these poems, as well as in *Ifigenia cruel*, the language is kept simple.

"JACOB" AND "LAMENTACIÓN DE NAVIDAD"

While the Bible did not inspire Reyes as much as did the *Iliad*, a biblical influence is nevertheless apparent in his poetry. His "Lamentación de Navidad" (Christmas lament) ends with a prayer that the poet be given works to accomplish or be made to fly like the seeds to settle eventually on fertile ground. He utilized the theme of Jacob wrestling with the angel (his "white enemy") in "Jacob," which Reyes narrates in the first person, and this poem, too, ends with a prayer that the angel win the match. Reyes used the same theme in his essay "Jacob o la idea de la poesía" (Jacob or the idea of poetry), in which he describes the artistic process as a struggle with "lo inefable" (the unutterable).

"SOPA"

Typical of Reyes's mixture of learning and playfulness are his poems titled *Minuta* (menu)—poems about such "unpoetic" subjects as soup, bread, salad, a plate of almonds. His two-stanza poem "Sopa" (soup), for example, is introduced by an epigraph from Saint Theresa ("between the soup pots walks the Lord"). In a simple four-line poem, Reyes honored the aperitif: "Exquisite collaboration/ of host and hostess;/ the ice of the visit is broken/ in the glass that brings good cheer." Elsewhere, Reyes reminded his readers that gastronomic concerns have always occupied an important place in Hispanic literary tradition, citing Fernando de Rojas's play *Comedia de Calisto y Melibea* (1499; commonly known as *La Celestina*; *Celestina*, 1631), Miguel de Cervantes's *El ingenioso hidalgo don Quixote de la Mancha* (1605, 1615; *The History of the Valorous and Wittie Knight-Errant, Don Quixote of the Mancha*, 1612-1620; better known as *Don Quixote de la Mancha*), and Francisco Delicado's *Retrato de la loçana andaluza* (1528; *Portrait of Lozana: The Lusty Andalusian Woman*, 1987).

Reyes was clearly one of the most brilliant and versatile writers in modern Spanish, yet his great gifts never produced the masterpieces that his readers expected from him. His most lasting contribution to Latin American culture lies in his example as an international man of letters, a lover of literature, and a tireless cultural activist.

OTHER MAJOR WORKS

SHORT FICTION: *El plano oblicuo*, 1920; *Quince presencias*, 1955; *Alfonso Reyes: Prosa y poesía*, 1977 (includes "Major Aranda's Hand," "Silueta del indio Jesús," and "El testimonio de Juan Peña").

NONFICTION: *Cuestiones estéticas*, 1911; *Cartones de Madrid*, 1917; *Visión de Anáhuac*, 1917 (*Vision of Anáhuac*, 1950); *Retratos reales e imaginarios*, 1920; *Simpatías y diferencias*, 1921-1926; *Cuestiones gongorinas*, 1927; *Discurso por Virgilio*, 1933; *Capítulos de literatura española*, 1939; *La crítica en la edad ateniense*, 1941; *La experiencia literaria*, 1942; *Ultima Thule*, 1942; *El deslinde: Prolegómenos a la teoría literaria*, 1944; *Grata compañía*, 1948; *The Position of America, and Other Essays*, 1950 (includes *Vision of Anáhuac*); *Arbol de pólvora*, 1953; *Parentalia: Primer libro de recuerdos*, 1954; *Albores: Segundo libro de recuerdos*, 1960; *Mexico in a Nutshell, and Other Essays*, 1964.

TRANSLATIONS: *Viaje sentimental por Francia e Italia*, 1919 (of Laurence Sterne's *A Sentimental Journey*); *El candor de Padre Brown*, 1921 (of G. K. Chesterton's detective stories); *Olalla*, 1922 (of Robert Louis Stevenson's stories); *Historia de la literatura griega*, 1948 (of C. M. Bowra's *Ancient Greek Literature*); *Eurípides y su época*, 1949 (of Gilbert Murray's *Euripides and His Age*); *La Ilíada de Homero*, 1951 (of Homer's *Iliad*).

MISCELLANEOUS: *Obras completas*, 1955-1967.

BIBLIOGRAPHY

Aponte, Barbara Bockus. *Alfonso Reyes and Spain: His Dialogue with Unamuno, Valle-Inclán, Ortega y Gasset, Jiménez, and Gómez de la Serna*. Austin: University of Texas Press, 1972. The author explores the dialogues that Reyes maintained with Spanish literary contemporaries. Their correspondence sheds light upon the lives and works of all these writers. Reyes relied upon this form of communication to maintain friendships and share ideas. As a member of the Mexican intellectual elite, Reyes recognized that his Spanish contacts were vital to his literary development.

Carter, Sheila. *The Literary Experience*. Mona, Jamaica: Savacou, 1985. A critical analysis of *El deslinde*, with bibliographic references.

Conn, Robert T. *The Politics of Philology: Alfonso Reyes and the Invention of the Latin American Literary Tradition*. Lewisburg, Pa.: Bucknell University Press, 2002. Conn examines Reyes and his legacy in the context of Latin American and Spanish intellectual life.

Robb, James W. "Alfonso Reyes." In *Latin American Writers*, edited by Carlos A. Solé. Vol. 2. New York: Charles Scribner's Sons, 1989. A thorough article from the Scribner writers series.

_____. *Patterns of Image and Structure*. New York: AMS Press, 1969. Critical analysis of the essays of Reyes.

Jack Shreve

RUAN JI

Born: Weishi, China; 210
Died: China; 263
Also known as: Juan Chi

PRINCIPAL POETRY

Poetry and Politics: The Life and Works of Juan Chi, A.D. 210-263, 1976 (includes translations of his *yonghuai* verses, *fu* rhyme-prose, and essays; Donald Holzman, translator)

Ruan Ji shi xuan = The Poems of Ruan Ji, 2006 (Wu Fusheng and Graham Hartill, translators)

OTHER LITERARY FORMS

Several of the rhyme-prose works—quasi-poetic compositions incorporating rhyme and rhythm—of Ruan Ji (ron jee) are lengthy effusions, extending to many hundreds of lines, and are celebrated for their novel profundity of thought in their treatment of such themes as "The Doves," "The Monkey," "Biography of the Great Man," and "Essay on Music." Other essays discuss philosophical issues in the Daoist tradition—critical interpretations of Laozi, Zhuangzi, and the *Yijing* (eighth to third century B.C.E.; English translation, 1876; also known as *Book of Changes*, 1986).

ACHIEVEMENTS

Together with his senior, Cao Zhi, Ruan Ji stands at the head of a new era in Chinese poetics. His verse provides a link between the earlier epoch of Han and pre-Han forms, and the post-Han tradition of lyric poetry. His diction and imagery often recall the canonic odes (1000-600 B.C.E.), the mid- to late-Zhou (600-221 B.C.E.) philosophical writings, and the rhetoric of the southern *Sao* anthology; in his hands, the new pentameter form becomes an acceptable and established vehicle for the expression of political and social anguish. Furthermore, in the long tradition in which courtly pomposities too frequently usurped genuine thought, Ruan Ji's poetry is admired to this day for its complexity of Confucian and Daoist ideals, its passionate concern for contemporaneous worldly ills, and the poet's own moral dilemmas, all expressed in a deceptively artless diction (characteristics for which the poetry of Tao Qian is also greatly admired). Indeed, so perplexing and perilous was Ruan Ji's political situation that his necessarily allusive satire became enigmatic, and his contemporaries, as much as later scholars, admitted difficulty in penetrating his precise import. Nevertheless, his quasi-religious mysticism has exerted a perennial fascination upon scholar-poets, and Ruan Ji's verse is among the most commonly cited and imitated in the Chinese literary heritage.

BIOGRAPHY

Ruan Ji, a member of the Daoist-inspired Seven Sages of the Bamboo Grove, was the son of Ruan Yu, himself a member of the celebrated coterie of poets known as the Seven Masters of the Jienan Era (the terminal period of the Han Dynasty, 196-220). Ruan Ji was ten years old at the time of the Caowei usurpation of the Han throne, and the latter half of his life was dominated by the decline of the Cao monarchs and the eventual usurpation of their power by the Sima clan.

Cao Cao overthrew the Han, and in 220, his son Cao Pei acceded to the throne as the emperor of the Caowei regime. He was succeeded at his death in 226 by Cao Rui, who squandered his patronage and oppressed the people. No direct offspring survived his death in 239, and a child successor was enthroned under the regency of Cao Shuang and an elderly general, Sima Yi. At first outmaneuvered by Cao Shuang, Sima Yi engineered a coup in 249 during which Cao Shuang, his relatives, and his supporters were massacred, so that the "number of famous men in the empire was reduced by half." Sima Yi himself died in 251 and was succeeded by his son Sima Shi, who executed still more of the Cao and their clique and in 254 deposed the twenty-year-old Cao Fang in favor of Cao Mao, seven years Fang's junior. Cao Mao was assassinated by the Sima in 260; Ruan Ji died in 263; and in 265 the Sima extinguished the Caowei and established the Jin Dynasty.

Ruan Ji's personal and political dilemma lay in his sense of obligation to serve in public office, his distaste for the degeneracy of his liege lords, the Cao rulers, to whom he was bound in loyalty, and his antipathy toward the cruel ambition of the Sima usurpers, into whose service he had become trapped. Actually a devout Confucianist, he turned to Daoist mysticism—the quasi religion available to third century Chinese—and the unconventional *ziran* (unrestrained spontaneity in behavior) and *qingtan* (pure discussion—that is, metaphysical speculation, rather than practical, political affairs) much in vogue among the politically disappointed and disillusioned intellectuals of his time. Such pursuits were typified by the activities of his coterie, the Seven Sages of the Bamboo Grove, among whom Ruan Ji gained a reputation for his skill as a cittern player.

Ruan Ji seems from his youth to have tried to avoid involvement in public affairs, however much this may have tormented his conscience. An anecdote relates how, at an interview with a provincial governor, the young Ruan Ji remained silent throughout—to the admiration of the officer, who deemed him extraordinary and "unfathomable." He must have resisted other summons, because it was not until 239, after the death of Cao Rui, that he was finally drafted, and he joined the entourage of regent Sima Yi. Ruan Ji was never thereafter able to retire from Sima employ and could only watch with dismay and passive resistance while the Sima furthered their own fortunes against the legitimate Cao, whom they ostensibly served.

In 242, Ruan Ji reluctantly accepted another post in the central government, but only after the composition of a now-celebrated letter to his patron, begging to be relieved. In any case, he later pleaded illness and returned home. In the late 240's, Cao Shuang's faction enlisted him, but again he soon resigned on the pretext of illness. He refused yet another post with Cao Shuang on the same pretense and retired to the countryside. When Cao Shuang was killed by Sima Yi in 249, Ruan Ji's reputation for political foresight was much enhanced.

With Sima Yi's death in 251, Ruan Ji was retained by Sima Shi, while all those who had been associated with Cao Shuang were executed. Three years later, upon the accession of Cao Mao, Ruan Ji was awarded an honorary knighthood, an official sinecure, and a substantive administrative position in the imperial secretariat—by then dominated by the Sima. Sima Shi died soon after Cao Mao's installation, and his son and successor, Sima Zhao, drafted Ruan Ji into his military headquarters.

The following year, in 256, Ruan Ji was promoted to the office from which he derived his sobriquet, *bubingxiaowei* (colonel of infantry, hence "Infantry Ruan"). The reason traditionally given for his acceptance of the post may be apocryphal: He is supposed to have been attracted by the skillful brewing and the quantity of fine wine boasted by the official kitchens. Tradition further relates that he became deeply intoxicated while on the job and abandoned his official duties. Greatly favoring him, nevertheless, Sima Zhao attempted to wed his own daughter to him, but Ruan Ji again remained drunk (for two months) so that no arrangements could be made. Stories are also told of how, in a grotesque sign of his displeasure, he would roll his eyes so that only the whites showed. He was finally granted a post in the countryside, away from the intrigues and perils of the capital; his descriptions of his new environment indicate his disgust with the general poverty of body and spirit among the population there.

The assassination of the puppet emperor Cao Mao in 260 brought Ruan Ji back into the center of politics, writing apparently in support of the Sima. Confucianist commentators, however, have taken pains to explain away his change of heart: It was his official responsibility to write such commendations, he was deliberately drunk at the time of writing, and other, satirical compositions from his pen at the time represent his true desire for noninvolvement. He died in office at the age of fifty-three.

ANALYSIS

The works of Ruan Ji were mentioned in a sixth century imperial catalog that mentions Ruan Ji's collected works in fourteen folios (including a table of contents in one folio). A century later, they are listed as ten folios, and by the eleventh century, they are reduced to five. In the fourteenth century, however, they appear again as ten folios. Extant editions of his works include considerably fewer: about twenty essays and *fu* rhyme-prose, official letters, and poetry.

Ruan Ji eschewed the traditional *yuefu* (music bureau songs—that is, new lyrics set to old tunes and titles) that were in great vogue before, during, and after his time, but he espoused the pentameter verse form established during the preceding Han era (207 B.C.E.-220 C.E.). Indeed, his eighty-two enigmatic verses under the general designation *yonghuai shi* (poems singing of my emotions) are among the most assiduously studied and imitated poems in this genre. They vary from eight to twenty lines, the majority being of ten or twelve lines, in the traditional *abcbdb* rhyme scheme.

In view of the dominating political influences upon Ruan Ji and the oblique style in which he expressed his moral conflicts, commentaries on his work have, reasonably, followed two interests: line-by-line interpretation, whereby political targets are identified and his satiric references and allusions are explicated, and appreciation of the genuine personal torment he expressed in attractive poetic form. Near-contemporaneous texts reflect these attitudes. For example, the fifth century court poet Yan Yazhi says: "During the administration of Sima Zhao, Ruan Ji was ever fearful of catastrophe, and thus composed his verses." Yan Yazhi notes, again:

> Ruan Ji personally served in a chaotic regime and was ever fearful of being slandered and encountering disaster. Thus he composed his verses; and so, whenever he sighed, saddened for his life, although his situation lay in satire and ridicule, yet his writings contain enigma and obscurity. A hundred generations hence it will be difficult to fathom his sentiments. Thus I roughly clarify the overall meaning and outline the remote resonances.

During the sixth century, Zhong Hong completed one of the first and greatest canons of Chinese literary theory and criticism, the *Shipin* (classification of poets). Herein, Ruan Ji is included in the top rank of three classifications, Zhong Hong saying that his poetic heritage was the minor odes (a section of the Confucian *Canon of Poetry*, 1000-600 B.C.E., traditionally associated with political satire) and commenting:

> He made no effort at worm-whittling [that is, intricate, superfluous embellishment], yet his poems on expressing his emotions shape one's spirit, and inspire one's innermost thoughts. His words lie within ordinary sight and sound, but his sentiments lodge beyond universal bounds.

The necessity for obscure allegory and the obscurity itself are undisputed. In setting a scene, Ruan Ji typically makes reference, itself disguised, to a similar situation in ancient history, his allusions cleverly enhanced by synonymous location or other nomenclature. For example, he will "hitch up a carriage and go forth from the Wei capital." Here he exploits the fortuitous existence of an ancient state of Wei during the Zhou Dynasty (1066-221 B.C.E.), synonymous with his own regime. The "Wei capital" may then refer either to the ancient Daliang or to the Caowei metropolis at Loyang. Elsewhere, he will say, "In the past I wandered in Ta-liang" and, again, "I gaze back toward Ta-liang" for the same effect. Other references, revealing Ruan Ji's exceptional scholarship in a milieu in which vast erudition was a mere *modus vivendi*, recall in similarly recognizable and pertinent allegory scenes of splendor long since turned to dust, sounding the familiar theme of the transience of mortal glory and warning against the excesses of current rulers.

"THE DOVES"

The decline of society and political morality also features prominently in Ruan Ji's satire. Political aspirations, he suggests, were the cause of the pollution of original innocence. Ruan Ji's principal villains are not identified directly, but commentators have been in general agreement in their speculations. For example, the lines "Reckless extravagance bringing decline to worldly custom./ How could one say he'd make eternal his years!" refer to Cao Rui, while in "The Doves" (traditional symbols of honest government), Sima Yi is lampooned as a "ravening dog" which in a rage destroyed the "doves"—that is, Cao Shuang and his brother Cao Xi.

Court officers as a class are also pilloried for their hypocritical Confucianism. They are "perfumed herbs" that exist "East of Liang," blooming twice or thrice in a single morn ("morning" being an ancient pun on "court"—held in the early morn); their doubtful "achievements" and influence will disappear with the moment. In other complex imagery, the lush decay of a southern scene is to be understood as representing the decline of Cao Fang and his clique. At the conclusion of yet another tirade against the hypocrisies of court life—courtesies, decorum, frugality, and virtue in public, but venal petty-mindedness in private—Ruan Ji flatly avows that the posturing of his colleagues sickens him to the heart.

As much as such plaints fill the pages of Ruan Ji's verse, it is his own toil and suffering that attract the sympathy of the reader. His ideal was honorable public administration in the service of a legitimate, stable, and righteous sovereign—that is to say, the ideal of the sincere Confucian who sought to combine literary and scholarly pursuits with a career of public service. Ruan Ji was to live out his life, however, in fear of slander, entrapment, and disaster. Unable to achieve his Confucian ideal, he turned to an uneasy and conscience-stricken espousal of Daoist retreat, abandoning his public career for the safety and nourishment of his inner, eternal spirit.

"MONKEY"

Much of the rhetoric of this plaint derives from the *Chu ci* (*Ch'u tz'u: The Songs of the South, an Ancient Chinese Anthology*, 1959), an anthology ranging from the fourth to the first century B.C.E., in which the lengthy poem "Li sao" (*The Li Sao, an Elegy on Encountering Sorrows*, 1929) mourns a career destroyed by sycophantic court rivals. Such slander had brought about the demise of many of Ruan Ji's more illustrious colleagues, whom he mourns, and thus he writes that he fears not the naked sword, but rather the words of some insinuating tongue. Like Qu Yuan (343?-290? B.C.E.) of *The Li Sao*, Ruan Ji feels that his sincerity, probity, and steadfastness—"a tall pine that does not wither in

the bitter adversity of winter"—are not appreciated, but indeed are the source of jealousy and backbiting. In his "Monkey" rhyme-prose, he sees himself as an amusing pet, in captive service; at the same time, the animal may represent the empty ritual, the monkey tricks, of the lesser courtiers. In famous Daoist parlance, the poet recognizes that it is the useful who perish while the useless live out their vain lives.

MOUNT SHOUYANG

Under such circumstances, even traditional Confucianism sanctioned retreat. Ruan Ji's lines frequently summon forth the spirit of Mount Shouyang; indeed, he composed a forty-six-line rhyme-prose on the subject at the time of Cao Fang's removal in November, 254. This location was associated with the brothers Bo Yi and Shu Qi, who secluded themselves and died of hunger rather than serve the new Zhou Dynasty at the fall of the Shang (twelfth century B.C.E.).

One may give credence to Ruan Ji's own indifference to wealth and glory acquired during shameful times as he "northward gazed toward Shouyang's peak, below which those men gathered brambles." In Ruan Ji's mind, the argument of even this celebrated precedent was attenuated by his own very real potential, amply demonstrated by the favor shown to him by both the Cao and the Sima rulers.

LIFE IN RETREAT

Even when a long-sought posting to the countryside offered Ruan Ji relief from metropolitan involvements, he found nothing of the bucolic idyll for which he yearned. Rather, his works describing his observations there became veritable models for misanthropic rhetoric. His rhyme-proses on the locations Kangfu and Dongping (in a marshy region of the modern northeastern province of Shandong), a total of three hundred lines, report that only inedible vegetables grow in the cold, wet climate there, and the peasantry are dull clods, for whom no civilization is possible.

Thus, neither circumstances nor venue permitted Ruan Ji the opportunity for either Confucian loyal service or the innocent simplicity of Daoist eremitism. Within this failure lie the tensions and paradoxes of Ruan Ji's thought, which have continued to intrigue Chinese intellectuals. Ruan Ji reveals contempt and shame for the corrupted Confucianism of his day, and he pines for settled times when moral virtue such as his can shine forth in worthy employment. Turning to Daoist principles, he despises himself for his fearful retreat. In his works, there appears only justification for temporary retirement, and none of the ridicule for Confucian precepts that marks the committed Daoist. The swift passage of time enters as a motif, defeating, says Ruan Ji, any strategy for patiently waiting out current alarms.

Daoist mysticism

In the end, Ruan Ji's philosophical preoccupations led him into a profound, if quasi-religious, Daoist mysticism—quasi-religious because the concept of divinity was foreign to the Chinese at that time. True freedom, writes Ruan Ji in some of the most difficult and obscure poetry in Chinese literature, lies in abandoning attachment to the world and its values, to the emotions which trap mortals in the snares of passion, and eventually to the self, at which point utter tranquillity is attained. This mystical rapture had been expressed in the fourth century B.C.E. by the Daoist Zhuangzi and would reappear centuries later in the Chinese Buddhist ethic. In the third century, however, Ruan Ji's sincerity of belief, born of his disillusionment with the social world, led him to strikingly original formulations. His search for a transcendent immortal, again made ambiguous by his rational Confucian disbelief in immortality, led him to what amounted to a concept of a deity, described in a vast effusion about a "Great Man" who would exemplify the ideal of sage-like aloofness from the dusty world while yet being of the world, and of service to it.

In summary, Ruan Ji favored the pentameter lyric poetry and rhyme-prose genres of his time, and while he added nothing to the development of these forms, he endowed them with a distinctive political, social, philosophical, and religious content, whose complexity of scholarship, allusion, and allegory has by turns bewildered and awed his audiences. He enlivened poems of dark political enigma and unfathomable mystical experience with profoundly sincere personal concern, and to the present day he remains one of the most admired and beloved of Chinese poets.

Bibliography
Cai, Zong-qi. *The Matrix of Lyric Transformation: Poetic Modes and Self-Presentation in Early Chinese Pentasyllabic Poetry*. Ann Arbor: Center for Chinese Studies, University of Michigan, 1996. Includes an insightful study of Ruan Ji in the course of lyric genre transformation and poetic expression of the self and cultural identity.

Criddle, Reed Andrew. "Rectifying Lasciviousness Through Mystical Learning: An Exposition and Translation of Ruan Ji's Essay on Music." *Asian Music* 38, no. 2 (Summer, 2007): 44-72. While this article focuses on an essay on music written by Ruan Ji, it also provides background information and a context for understanding Ruan Ji's poetry.

Holzman, Donald. *Chinese Literature in Transition from Antiquity to the Middle Ages*. Brookfield, Vt.: Ashgate, 1998. Covers roughly the period from 221 B.C.E. through 960 C.E., placing Ruan Ji in context. Generous bibliographic references.

_____. *Immortals, Festivals, and Poetry in Medieval China: Studies in Social and Intellectual History*. Brookfield, Vt.: Ashgate, 1998. Excellent for understanding Ruan Ji's poetry in context. Includes bibliographical references and index.

_____. *Poetry and Politics: The Life and Works of Juan Chi, A.D. 210-263*. New York: Cambridge University Press, 1976. A full-length critical study of Ruan Ji's life and literary achievements. An extension of his 1953 publication on Ruan Ji.

Watson, Burton, ed. *The Columbia Book of Chinese Poetry*. New York: Columbia University Press, 1984. An excellent anthology. As no special collections of Ruan Ji's poems in English translation are available, this is a good place to locate his poems in English and discussions of the Chinese poetry of retreat.

Yu, Pauline. "The Poetry of Retreat." In *Masterworks of Asian Literature in Comparative Perspective*, edited by Barbara Stoler Miller. Armonk, N.Y.: M. E. Sharpe, 1994. A thoughtful discussion of Ruan Ji in the Chinese poetic tradition of the recluse, along with other poets such as Tao Qian and Xie Lingyun. Includes provocative comments on Ruan Ji's eighty-two "Poems Singing My Thoughts" and the conflict between his fidelity to Confucian principles of service and his interest in Daoist mysticism.

John Marney

JALĀL AL-DĪN RŪMĪ

Born: Balkh (now in Afghanistan); c. September 30, 1207
Died: Konya, Asia Minor (now in Turkey); December 17, 1273

PRINCIPAL POETRY

Dīvan-e Shams-e Tabrīz, 1244-1273 (*Selected Poems from the Divani Shamsi Tabrīz*, 1898; better known as *The Sufi Path of Love: The Spiritual Teachings of Rumi*, 1983)
Ma'navī-ye Ma'navī, 1259-1273 (*The Mathnavī of Jalālu'ddīn Rūmī*, 1925-1940)
Mystical Poems of Rūmī, 1968
The Love Poems of Rumi, 1998

OTHER LITERARY FORMS

Among the prose works of Jalāl al-Dīn Rūmī (REW-mee), a collection of transcribed talks titled *Fīhī mā fihi* (early 1200's; *Discourses of Rumi*, 1961) deserves special mention. While in its spiritual messages and reflections this book is no less dense and subtle than *The Mathnavī of Jalālu'ddīn Rūmī*, its free and informal prose style—in its original Persian as well as in the English translation by A. J. Arberry—provides a suitable introduction to the poet's teachings. A book of correspondences (*Maktubāt*, 1335; *Letters*, 1983) and a collection of seven sermons, *Majāles-e Sab'a* (1315-1319; *Seven Sessions*, 1983), are also attributed to Rūmī.

ACHIEVEMENTS

Speaking of Jalāl al-Dīn Rūmī and *The Mathnavī of Jalālu'ddīn Rūmī*, the well-known fourteenth century Persian Sufi poet Jami said, "He is not a prophet and yet he has given us a Holy Book." The British Orientalist R. A. Nicholson, after having devoted much of his life to the study and translation of Rūmī's works, wrote,

Today the words I applied to the author of the *Mathnawi* thirty-five years ago, "the greatest mystical poet of any age," seems to me no more than just. Where else shall we find such panorama of universal existence unrolling itself through Time and Eternity?

The American author and psychoanalyst Erich Fromm praised Rūmī as "a man of profound insight into the nature of man."

These are but a few examples of countless tributes bestowed on the venerated Persian poet, who is also well known for having laid the foundations of what came to be known as the Order of Whirling Dervishes. All the same, Rūmī himself made no claims to any poetic accomplishments. Of writing poetry, he once said, "I do it for the sake of these people who come to see me and hope that I'd gladden their hearts a little bit. So I recite a poem or two for them. Otherwise what do I care for poetry?" (from *Discourses of Rumi*). This was no false modesty but the expression of the genuine feeling of a man who wanted, first and foremost, to unburden his listeners and readers of the sorrow that comes with ignorance and to awaken them to what Søren Kierkegaard called "possibility of life." In the long run, Rūmī's greatest achievement has been just that—at least in the case of those readers who have found him, in the words of the celebrated Urdu and Persian poet Muḥammad Iqbāl, an opener of the doors: "What do I need of logicians' long polemics or professors' tedious lectures/ When a couple of lines from Rūmī or Jami open the closed doors?"

A Rūmī revival, even if on a small scale, in the United States inspired poets such as Robert Bly, Jack Marshall, and W. S. Merwin to produce modern renditions of some of the Persian poet's works.

BIOGRAPHY

Jalāl al-Dīn Rūmī, also known as Maulānā (our master), was born on or near September 30, 1207, in the city of Balkh (in modern northern Afghanistan). When he was five years old and shortly before the onset of the Mongol invasion, his father, who was a religious scholar of renown, left his native land in the company of his family and, traveling westward, finally settled in Konya, a city of Asia Minor (modern Turkey). After his father's death, Rūmī succeeded him as a religious leader and scholar and soon gathered a large following.

The arrival in Konya of the wandering dervish Shams al-Dīn of Tabrīz was an event of radical consequence in Rūmī's life. The details of the meeting between the two are rather sketchy and at times contradictory. The account that seems to be more reliable than others belongs to the chronicler Dowlatshāhi and can be summarized as follows. One day, the peripatetic Shams—who, in search of a kindred soul, had arrived in Konya and had taken lodgings in the Caravansarai of Sugar Merchants—saw a man riding on a mule while his disciples followed him on foot. The man was Rūmī, who after the death of his father had become Konya's most distinguished religious scholar, enjoying a large following. Walking up to him, Shams said, "Tell me, what is the purpose of all the discipline and study of books and recitation of knowledge?" "To know the religious laws and precepts, of course," the scholar answered. "That is too superficial," the Sage of Tabrīz countered. Taken aback, the man of learning asked, "What else is there beyond these?" "True knowledge is that which leads you to the real, to the source," Shams replied and quoted a line from the Sufi poet Sanāʾi: "Ignorance is far superior to that knowledge which does not free you of you." So profound was the impact of the exchange that Rūmī dismounted his mule and right there and then decided to turn his back on a life of secondhand knowledge and academic disputation.

The details of what followed are scanty, veiled in hagiographical embellishments. What is certain is that the result of the communion that took place between the two was nothing short of life changing for the thirty-seven-year-old Rūmī: Soon, the respectable professor of religious studies turned into a poet of love and wisdom, and he altogether abandoned sermons and the seminary.

Utterly perplexed by the change in their master, Rūmī's disciples directed their ire at the stranger from Tabrīz and plotted against him. Shams fled to Damascus. Rūmī dispatched his son and passionate poems of entreaty, asking the dervish to return. Shams complied and returned to Konya, only to find his enemies' anger and jealousy surging anew. Finally sensing that a plot against his life was imminent, Shams disappeared, in about 1247, never to be seen again.

Shams's disappearance caused further upheaval in the poet's consciousness and released torrents of rapturous *ghazals* (lyrics), whose themes ranged from the sorrow of separation and the longing to be reunited with the ecstasy of the perception of the unity of love. Soon Rūmī was to realize that Shams was, like himself, a mind re-flecting the Supreme. Mirrors have no "content," therefore no separate entities. "While there was you I turned around you/ Once I became you, around myself I turn."

Two of Rūmī's later disciples became, in succession, the recipients of a similar proffering of love. The second, Husāmuddin Chalabi, who asked the Master to compose *The Mathnavī of Jalālu'ddīn Rūmī*, was the transcriber of most of that monumental work and, in a way, its very raison d'être.

ANALYSIS

In one of the *ghazals* of *The Sufi Path of Love*, Jalāl al-Dīn Rūmī cries out,

> I have had it with the canons of measure, meter, rhyme
>   and ghazal
> May floods come and take them away
> Paper-crowns deserving of poets' heads.
> A mirror am I and not a man of letters
> You read me if your ears become eyes.

The lines are indicative of how "the greatest mystical poet of any age" was at odds with the artifices of poetry and, in fact, with the entrapments of language itself. "I banish the word and thought/ And, free of those intruders, commune with thee." *Khāmush* (Persian for "silent") was the poetic pen name he used for many of his *ghazals*.

In a similar way, Rūmī the thinker was a persistent negator of philosophical speculations of every kind. In fact, a recurrent theme of some twenty-seven thousand couplets that make up his magnum opus, *The Mathnavī of Jalālu'ddīn Rūmī*, is the inadequacy of logic and reason. "The feet of logicians are of wood," and wooden legs cannot be trusted. To be sure, he attests the necessity of clear thinking and reasoning, but in the same breath he points to the paralyzing limitations of "partial intelligence" (*aql-e jozʿi*) which, anchored in knowledge, is in conflict with the wholeness of life:

> Partial intelligence is not the intelligence of discovery.
> It yields skill, and no insight.
> It is clear, but it is a thing.
> Nothing it has never been.
> Caught between losing and gaining it totters.
> Total intelligence soars high and is safe—come what
>   may.

The Mathnavī of Jalālu'ddīn Rūmī

As can be seen from this small sample, *The Mathnavī of Jalālu'ddīn Rūmī* is not an easy book to read. Even though it has been revered through the ages, few people have the patience to carry on a sustained reading of even two or three pages of it. In part, its difficulty can be attributed to the author's multifarious nature.

The Rūmī of *The Mathnavī of Jalālu'ddīn Rūmī* is at once a serious spiritual teacher, a love-intoxicated poet, an entertaining raconteur, a learned man familiar with most of the current knowledge of his time, and a Menschen-kenner of profound psychological insights. To give an example of the interplay of all these facets would not be possible in a limited space. To illustrate the point, however, here is how, in the middle of a moral discourse, one word leads by association to another, and the poet continues:

> Once again I have become a madman. . . . And I have not
> a speck of reason left in me, see?
> So don't expect ceremonies and polite words, for
> Heaven's sake. Once again I have become a madman . . .
> Otherwise, how do you account for this erratic
> Babble, O sober ones?

On another occasion, when he is telling the story of Ayaz—the beautiful, pure-hearted, righteous serf of Sultan Mahmoud—the poet suddenly abandons the ongoing narrative. "O Ayaz! The tale of your anguish and ecstasy made me so weak./ I stop. *You* tell *my* story." In the course of another discourse, having used the analogy of the sun, the word reminds him of its synonym *Shams*, and that in turn unleashes feelings about the vanished "king of love" Shams al-Dīn of Tabrīz.

Such stream-of-consciousness interruptions and interpolations, which are found throughout *The Mathnavī of Jalālu'ddīn Rūmī*, are responsible for its difficulty and for its unparalleled richness and density, as well as its unique stylistic features. It should be mentioned, however, that in no way is Rūmī composing self-conscious literary work, much less giving discourses according to any design or for any motive such as self-expression. Rather, he creates as he goes along, with the utter freedom and felicity of love. When at the end of the sixth and final book of *The Mathnavī of Jalālu'ddīn Rūmī* he stops, even the promptings of his son Bahā al-Dīn Valad are of no avail, because as the latter quotes his father, "The camel of my speech is now laid to rest and not until doomsday will it raise its head."

Like any book of and on truth, *The Mathnavī of Jalālu'ddīn Rūmī* is full of seemingly contradictory statements: "Don't strive after water, seek thirst/ Waters will then spring aplenty, head to toe"; "So long as you haven't died [to yourself] the agony of dying will go on"; "Let go of your ears, then be all ears!/ Abandon your consciousness, then be conscious!" Paradoxes of this kind are scattered through *The Mathnavī of Jalālu'ddīn Rūmī*. Paradoxical also is the fact that the poet is consistently absent from and ubiquitously present in the book. Often, it is difficult to tell whether it is the character in a story who is speaking or whether it is Rūmī with one of his innumerable interpolations or poetic flights.

Scattered throughout the book are stories, ranging from anecdotes a sentence or two in length (such as the story of the ugly Negrito who rejoiced because others, not himself, saw his face) to elaborate tales. Some of the longer stories (such as the moving "Umar and the Harp Player" and "The Prophet and the Gluttonous Arab") are literary masterpieces and, at the same time, moral allegories with "epiphanies" at once ripe and hard-hitting. Seldom are the stories governed by the conventional demands of artistic unity; rather, their form is determined by the spontaneity borne of love, which "like life comes, in timeless moments, afresh."

The Sufi Path of Love

If love is the creative propeller of *The Mathnavī of Jalālu'ddīn Rūmī*, it is for the most part, the substance and subject matter of *The Sufi Path of Love*. Except for a limited number of Rubaiyat stanzas, *The Sufi Path of Love* is a collection of *ghazals* of mixed chronology (grouped alphabetically according to the last letters of end-rhymes). The word *ghazal*, which etymologically is related to love, lovemaking, and courting, denotes a lyric consisting of between six and seventeen lines, the last line containing the poet's *takhallos* (pen name). (For his *takhallos*, in most of the *ghazals* of *The Sufi Path of Love*, Rūmī uses Shams's name, a token of love's undoing of separateness.) Originally an amatory lyric of mainly aesthetic significance, the *ghazal* underwent a transformation of intent and import in the hands of such Sufi-inspired poets as Arāqi, Sanāʾi, and Attār, who found in the form a vehicle for the expression of the ineffable feelings of transcendent love.

It is, however, in the pages of Rūmī's *The Sufi Path of Love* that the *ghazal* achieves an ecstatic quality unexampled by any other Persian poet, not even by such masters as Hafiz or Saʿdi (the two names well known to Western readers, thanks in part to the efforts of such luminaries as Johann Wolfgang von Goethe and Ralph Waldo Emerson). What distinguishes Rūmī's poems from those of other lyricists cannot be elaborated here. Suffice it to mention that at their best the poems of *The Sufi Path of Love* throb with the raptures of a religious self-abandonment—religion not in the conventional sense of organized religion or of dogma, sect, or ritual but, in Rūmī's own words, a "religion beyond all religions" (the complete line is: "The lover's religion is beyond all religions"). It is primarily the religion of lovers and love that permeates the pages of the poem. Here, to try to define the nature of love—as sacred, profane, personal, universal, divine, mystical and so on—or to identify the object of the poet's love (Shams? God? an "earthly" beloved such as a woman?)—to try to circumscribe love with such distinctions would be the result of thought's projections about love, whereas, as Rūmī tries to drive home again and again, not only can thought not fathom the mystery of love, but also it is in fact an obstacle to it:

> Thought says, I have measured; all sides end in walls.
> Love says, I have travelled beyond these walls many
>   times.
> Thought says, Beware! Don't step! the unknown is
>   full of thorns.
> Love says, look better, you're the maker of those
>   thorns . . .
> Love saw a corner market and erected its little shop
> Love saw many a variegated bazaar beyond . . .

By now it may be fairly clear why in many poems of *The Sufi Path of Love*, the poet speaks in praise of wine, of taverns and tavern dwellers.

SOUND AND SENSE

The importance of the auditory aspect of the Rūmī *ghazal*, and that which is responsible for the difficulty of translating it into English, cannot be overempha-

sized. The poet, who was the founder of the Order of Whirling Dervishes, is believed to have composed most of his lyrics during *samāʿ* (sessions of listening to music, mostly of primitive instruments such as the reed in the case of *The Mathnavī of Jalālu'ddīn Rūmī*, or the drum and tambourine in the case of *The Sufi Path of Love*; ambulatory dances were part of the latter). Often, the lyric so seems to ride on the tidal wave of ecstatic rhythms that the poet refuses to bother about words as carriers of meaning. In one of the poems of *The Sufi Path of Love*, for example, the repetition of the refrain *tananāhā yāhou* spills over into an entire couplet and becomes nothing more than a nonsense cluster of prosodic syllables: "Tatatantan tatatantan tatatatan tatatan/ Tatatantan tatatantan tatatantan tatatan." It is important to point out that there is not the slightest indication of poetic mannerism in *ghazals* of this kind; rather, the interplay of the sound with the sense comes naturally, as if inevitably, creating rare spiritual lyrics of rhapsodic beauty.

As was mentioned earlier, the matrix of the poetry of Rūmī, in *The Mathnavī of Jalālu'ddīn Rūmī* and *The Sufi Path of Love* alike, is love, and love does not permit the extraneousness of the word. "I think of rhymes and the beloved taunts/ Don't ever think of aught but seeing me!" It may now be understood why the author of two hefty volumes of poetry spoke so often and so rapturously of silence: With the lifting of the veil of words and their mental associations, the face of the Real is revealed in all its splendor, and "The pen [that] was running so swift and smooth/ Shatters when it comes to love, and stops."

OTHER MAJOR WORKS

NONFICTION: *Fīhī mā fīhi*, early 1200's (*Discourses of Rumi*, 1961); *Majāles-e Sab'a*, 1315-1319 (*Seven Sessions*, 1983); *Maktubāt*, 1335 (*Letters*, 1983); *The Essential Rumi*, 1995.

MISCELLANEOUS: *A Rumi Anthology*, 2000.

BIBLIOGRAPHY
Baldock, John. *The Essence of Rūmī*. London: Arcturus, 2006. A compact biography of the poet that examines his life and his poetry and how they are interrelated.

Lewis, Franklin. *Rūmī, Past and Present, East and West: The Life, Teachings, and Poetry of Jalāl al-Dīn Rūmī.* Rev. ed. Oxford, England: Oneworld, 2008. A comprehensive study of Rūmī's life and times, using primary sources by and about Rūmī to draw pictures of his legacy and to discuss his continuing significance. Looks also at *The Sufi Path of Love*, Rūmī's children, Rūmī and the Muslim and Western worlds, mythology, and media representation. Maps, bibliography, index.

Mannani, Manijeh. *Divine Deviants: The Dialectics of Devotion in the Poetry of Donne and Rūmī.* New York: Peter Lang, 2007. Compares and contrasts the poetry of Rūmī and John Donne, both of whom were religious poets, examining topics such as religious duty and mystical transcendence.

Moyne, John A. *Rūmī and the Sufi Tradition.* 1998. Reprint. Costa Mesa, Calif.: Mazda, 2009. The well-known translator of Rūmī offers this brief monograph analyzing the mystical roots and expression of Rūmī in the context of Sufism. Glossary, bibliographical references.

Schimmel, Annemarie. *As Through a Veil: Mystical Poetry in Islam.* 1982. Reprint. Oxford, England: Oneworld, 2001. In five densely annotated essays (originally lectures), the author demonstrates the centrality of Rūmī to all subsequent Sufistic literary expression. The chapter on Rūmī reviews his life, suggests a chronology of his lyrics, and describes images and symbols for love in his verse.

_____. *Rūmī's World: The Life and Work of the Great Sufi Poet.* 1992. Reprint. Boston: Shambala, 2001. A biography by the leading Rūmī scholar. Examines the relationship between his poetry and Sufi beliefs.

Tourage, Mahdi. *Rūmī and the Hermeneutics of Eroticism.* Boston: Brill, 2007. Explores the bawdy tales and eroticism included in Rūmī's poetry, which was used to convey mystical knowledge.

Zweig, Connie. *A Moth to the Flame: The Life of the Sufi Poet Rūmī.* Lanham, Md.: Rowman & Littlefield, 2006. Written in an accessible style, this biography is meant to entertain while informing.

Massud Farzan

S

SAʿDI

Mosharrif Al-Dīn ibn Moṣliḥ al-Dīn
Born: Shīrāz, Persia (now in Iran); c. 1200
Died: Shīrāz, Persia (now in Iran); c. 1291
Also known as: Shaykh

PRINCIPAL POETRY

Bustan, 1257 (*The Orchard*, 1882)
Gulistan, 1258 (*The Rose Garden*, 1806)
Kolliyat Saʿdi, 1963
Ghazals, thirteenth century
Khabisat, thirteenth century
Qasidas, thirteenth century
Rubáiyát, thirteenth century

OTHER LITERARY FORMS

Saʿdi (SAH-dee) wrote a number of prose tracts of minor significance, and *The Rose Garden* and the *Khabisat* are part prose. The prose of *The Rose Garden* has long been considered a model of Persian writing, while three scandalous mock-homilies in the *Khabisat* exhibit another side of Saʿdi.

ACHIEVEMENTS

One of Persia's great poets, sometimes called the greatest, Saʿdi is venerated as almost a saint in his homeland, where his works are read alongside the Qurʾān and where he is fondly referred to as Shaykh Saʿdi or, for short, the Shaykh. Saʿdi is also the best-known Persian poet in the West, except possibly for Omar Khayyám, whose one work (*Rubāʿīyāt*, twelfth century; *True Translation of Hakim Omar Khayyam's "Robaiyat,"* 1994; commonly known as *Rubáiyát of Omar Khayyám*) hardly compares with Saʿdi's extensive and varied output. The English-speaking world became acquainted with Saʿdi before it did with Omar Khayyám: Persian was the official language of India when the British arrived, and British officials used

Saʿdi's *The Rose Garden* as a language text. *The Rose Garden* was translated repeatedly into English during the nineteenth century—in expurgated versions still read as accurate texts (the Victorians were especially shocked by Saʿdi's casual acceptance of pederasty, a common, albeit illegal, practice in the Persia of his day). Unfortunately, Saʿdi has not found his own Edward FitzGerald, the superb English translator of the 1859 edition of Omar Khayyám. Probably the best English translation of Saʿdi is Edward Rehatsek's version of *The Rose Garden*, published in a limited edition for the Kama Shastra Society in 1888 and reissued in 1965.

As a battered survivor of difficult times, when the Muslim world was beset by Mongols on one side and Crusaders on the other (not to mention rulers at home), Saʿdi still has some wisdom to offer the modern world. Saʿdi's politics of survival is not the same pious wisdom he offered the Victorians, and his expedient advice might not be altogether pleasing. The literary historian Edward G. Browne called *The Rose Garden* "one of the most Machiavellian works in the Persian language" (whether he was admiring or condemning is not clear). However, a survivor who came out singing, as Saʿdi did, has something worth hearing on how to retain one's humanity through it all. Saʿdi's humanity reverberates most strongly in *The Orchard* and *The Rose Garden*—even if, in translation, the singing is rather faint.

BIOGRAPHY

There are numerous entertaining stories about Saʿdi's life, many from his own works, but their accuracy is uncertain. A few miraculous stories are obviously saints' legends, while others have a suspiciously legendary cast, such as the symmetrical division of his life into thirty years of study, thirty years of travel, and thirty years of writing (some versions stretch this last period out to forty, fifty, or sixty years). In the preface to *The Rose Garden*, Saʿdi says that he took stock of his wasted life and settled down around the age of fifty, but he also says that his fame as a writer was already widespread. The unembellished truth about Saʿdi is hard to establish, but what follows is a compendium of generally accepted information.

Saʿdi's real name was apparently Mosharrif Al-Dīn

ibn Moṣliḥ al-Dīn, Saʿdi being a *takhallus* (pen name) adopted from the Atabeg rulers of Fars Province, Saʿd ibn Zangī, his son Abū Bakr ibn Saʿd, and his grandson Saʿd ibn Abū Bakr. Effusive flattery of rulers then was commonplace, even necessary for survival, since, as *The Orchard* and *The Rose Garden* show, these rulers were as capricious as they were powerful. Saʿdi also perhaps had reason to feel genuine gratitude. Apparently Saʿdi's father, a minor court official, died when Saʿdi was a child, and Saʿd ibn Zangī supported Saʿdi's education, first at Shīrāz and then at the Nizamiya College in Baghdad. According to *The Orchard*, Saʿdi also held a fellowship at the Nizamiya College that required him to slave away at instructing. Possibly it was such an existence that encouraged him to become a mendicant dervish and trust his fortunes to the open road, although the invasion of the Mongol hordes in the 1220's might have influenced his decision to travel.

During his wanderings, Saʿdi traveled to North Africa, Ethiopia, Palestine, Syria, Armenia, Arabia, India, and throughout the provinces of Persia. His adventures and the resulting lore are documented in *The Orchard* and *The Rose Garden*. In Palestine, he was captured by the Crusaders and put to work fortifying Tripoli (now in Lebanon). He was ransomed by an Aleppo friend, whose shrewish daughter he married (it proved to be a bad trade). Later Saʿdi also married a woman in Arabia, who bore him a child who died. He made several pilgrimages to Mecca (the legendary number is fourteen).

In the early 1250's, Saʿdi returned to Shīrāz to settle down alone, impelled by a sense of urgency: His own life was slipping away, and the eastern Muslim world was crumbling under another Mongol invasion. Before either event occurred, Saʿdi wanted to write what he knew, so in relative seclusion at Shīrāz, he sat down to compose *The Orchard* and *The Rose Garden*. Shīrāz was somewhat safe from the Mongol invasion, since the Fars rulers had made peace by bowing down and kissing the feet of the invaders. Baghdad, the political and cultural center of the eastern Muslim world, had no such luck; in 1258, the Mongols overran the city, slaughtering a million and a half inhabitants. Saʿdi wrote a famous lament on the occasion. At approximately the same time, he brought out *The Orchard* and *The Rose Garden*.

ANALYSIS

In his best-known writings, *The Orchard* and *The Rose Garden*, Saʿdi is clearly working within a long and distinguished tradition, an Eastern tradition of didactic literature wherein the poet is also a teacher. Drawing on both literary and folk sources, and forming a symbiotic relationship with religion, this tradition usually brings forth a conventional product. Such is not the case with Saʿdi. He is entertaining because he is able to draw on an additional source, his own nomadic experiences that he somehow survived. Thus, Saʿdi is able to infuse his conventional wisdom with lively examples. At the same time, there is this danger involved: The examples set up a tension with the conventional wisdom, sometimes undercutting it and resulting not in morality but in expediency. The same result can be observed in his language and tone, which occasionally verge on parody, Saʿdi getting carried away and letting a devilish streak emerge.

In his writing as well as in his travels, Saʿdi liked to live dangerously. He obviously managed to satisfy the conventional expectations of his contemporaries, but for the modern reader the tension between the pious and the politic Saʿdi forms the main attraction of his work.

THE ORCHARD

Written in epic meter throughout, *The Orchard* is divided into ten sections. Each section illustrates a particular public or private virtue—for example, good government, generosity, humility, resignation, contentment, gratitude—through a collection of brief stories, mostly exempla but occasionally parables and fables. Otherwise disconnected, the stories do provide a variety of content, including the author's own purported experiences.

In the few stories where he figures, Saʿdi does not hesitate to make himself a hero. For example, at a dinner put on by a *cadi* (a Muslim judge), Saʿdi is forced to sit among the inferior guests because of his impoverished appearance. In the legal disputations that follow, Saʿdi dominates, and the *cadi* takes off his fine turban, offers it to Saʿdi, and invites Saʿdi to sit among the lawyers and other guests of honor. Saʿdi turns down both offers and leaves, telling the *cadi* that it is what one has inside one's head rather than what one wears on it that matters. There is a further irony, directed at himself, in Saʿdi's references to the *cadi*'s big head, for Saʿdi was not modest about his own gifts; in the tag on a story advocating reticence (one of his favorite virtues), he advises the reader either to speak like Saʿdi or to remain silent.

Even Saʿdi opens his mouth once too often in another story set in India. In the midst of a temple crowd worshiping an idol, Saʿdi comments to a friend concerning the crowd's naïve superstition. The friend, however, proves to be a true believer himself, and he angrily denounces Saʿdi to the assembly. The crowd falls on Saʿdi, and he saves himself only through fast talking and dissimulation. Pleading that he is an ignorant foreigner, he asks to be initiated into the true meaning of the worship. The chief Brahmin forces him to spend the night weeping, praying, and kissing the statue. In the morning, the statue rewards him and other worshipers by raising its hand. Several days later, when he is trusted, Saʿdi goes into the temple, slips behind the scenes, and discovers the chief Brahmin working the levers that operate the statue's hands. Saʿdi then kills the Brahmin by throwing him down a well and dropping a rock onto his head. The moral is: Once one exposes a villain, one must destroy him; if not, he will destroy you.

Similar advice is available for dealing with one's enemies. The general drift of Saʿdi's urgings is to remain quiet and not to make enemies, especially of people with power or wagging tongues. If, despite all one's caution, an enemy arises, one should take the first good opportunity to dash out his brains; such dealings improve not only one's predicament but also one's disposition. Saʿdi does warn, however, against lowering oneself to the level of one's enemy. Lastly, if a dangerous enemy is too powerful to handle, one should flee.

A number of Saʿdi's stories contain not only irony but also what would today be called black humor. The fortunes of a rich man and a beggar are reversed; a doctor who predicts a patient's imminent death dies himself instead, and the patient lives to a ripe old age; a haughty prince is ungrateful to a physician who cures him, so the physician returns him to his former state. In a cat fable, a discontented cat learns contentment by leaving home and becoming a target for archers. The

wages of gluttony are illustrated by a fat man who climbs a date tree, falls out, and dies. A sultan, who feels pity for a shivering night watchman standing in the rain and snow, promises to send his fur coat out to the watchman. The sultan returns inside to the warm arms of his favorite harem girl and promptly forgets his promise. Repentance is demonstrated by the story of a man who rejoices over the death of his enemy—until he tears open the enemy's grave and sees the decaying corpse.

Aside from Saʿdi's slightly warped wisdom, part of the appeal of *The Orchard* is the apparently random juxtaposition of stories, offering not only variety but also contrast. Irony and black humor alternate with heavy moralizing. Stories of pleasant comedy about a polite but stingy host, for example, or about a newly groomed warrior who gets ashes dumped on his head and reflects that he deserved the fire, alternate with stories of sorrow or tragedy—for example, about a strong warrior whose will is broken, or about the death of Saʿdi's child. If the mood of one story does not satisfy, the reader may go on to the next. If Saʿdi seems to be laying on the conventional wisdom too heavily, then he is probably preparing a surprise. The random juxtaposition of material gives *The Orchard* the rough, unplotted texture of experience itself. Thus, there is wisdom embodied in the form as well as the content of *The Orchard*.

THE ROSE GARDEN

The Rose Garden is the same type of work as *The Orchard* and is organized along the same lines, with collections of anecdotes supposedly illustrating certain virtues or topics. There are eight chapters in all. A number of the headings overlap those in *The Orchard*, and, as in *The Orchard*, some of the stories do not particularly fit their headings. There, however, similarities of form end. *The Rose Garden* is written partly in prose, partly in verse of various kinds, mostly in Persian but containing passages of Arabic (including quotations from the Qurʾān). *The Rose Garden* has a larger element of conventional lore, often displayed in striking comparisons, and is more heavily interlarded with commentary, usually taking the form of a pungent verse or two. The final chapter consists not of anecdotes but entirely of maxims and admonitions. If *The*

Orchard offers an entertaining variety of content, *The Rose Garden* offers a delightful hodgepodge of content and form.

Some of the content recalls *The Orchard*. There is a long chapter on the behavior of kings, another long chapter on the behavior of dervishes, and contentment and silence are again treated. The morality likewise resembles that of *The Orchard*. For example, Saᶜdi gives some familiar advice on revenge: One should take it at the first good opportunity, even if that means biding one's time for a while. In chapter 1, a brutal soldier hits a dervish on the head with a rock. The pious dervish saves the rock until the soldier falls out of favor with the king and is imprisoned in a well, then throws the rock down onto the soldier's head. The first story of *The Rose Garden* endorses well-intentioned lying; other stories warn against trusting one's friends too much.

In general, however, the tone of *The Rose Garden* is lighter than that of *The Orchard, The Rose Garden* containing more humor. An example is the story of Saᶜdi's capture by the Crusaders. A friend from Aleppo ransoms Saᶜdi for ten dinars, then pays Saᶜdi a dowry of a hundred dinars to marry his daughter. Later, the woman turns shrewish and spitefully reminds Saᶜdi of his rescue by her father. Saᶜdi replies that, yes, it cost her father ten dinars to free him from the Crusaders but one hundred dinars to bind him to her. Besides male-female relationships, another source of humor is the bad voices of singers and muezzins. One muezzin who performs his office gratis is paid to go elsewhere, and a singing dervish cures Saᶜdi of the frivolous desire to attend dervish parties. Aphorisms, epigrams, and folk sayings are still another source of humor; the following saying is typical: When the scorpion was asked why he did not come out in winter, he replied, "What renown do I have in summer that I should also come out in winter?"

A number of stories contain a combination of humor and irony, particularly a group stressing the relativity of everything. A boy afraid of being aboard a ship learns to love it after he is thrown into the ocean; after seeing a man without feet, Saᶜdi feels happier about not having shoes; he also concludes it is better to beg than to have your hand cut off for stealing. A long story about a young man who sets off to make his fortune, but

runs into numerous misfortunes, is reminiscent of the discontented cat fable in *The Orchard*; the young man returns home much more contented.

There is nothing funny, however, about many of the stories in *The Rose Garden*, including those in which Saᶜdi's attempts at humor are askew, as in his bigotry toward Jews and blacks. Such bigotry is a reminder that Saᶜdi lived in a harsh age when people could be, and often were, disposed of as objects. This attitude appears in a number of stories, as in the one in which a drunken king, whose advances were refused by a Chinese slave girl, turns her over to a black slave to ravish (after which the king wants to kill them both). In a time when the Mongols could raze the city of Baghdad and butcher its million and a half inhabitants, it is not surprising that Saᶜdi should occasionally share such an attitude. What is surprising is that he should so often rise above it. While the Christians were mounting crusades to tame the infidels, Saᶜdi, in *The Orchard* and *The Rose Garden*, was helping his age and subsequent ages define once again what it means to be human.

BIBLIOGRAPHY

Arberry, A. J. *Classical Persian Literature*. 1994. Reprint. New York: RoutledgeCurzon, 2004. One of the leading introductions to Iran's greatest period of literature (ninth through fifteenth centuries). The chapter on Saᶜdi gives an excellent idea of his range. Includes generous quotations of his lyrical poetry in translation, a bibliography, and an index.

Barks, Coleman. *The Hand of Poetry: Five Mystic Poets of Persia*. New Lebanon, N.Y.: Omega, 1993. Translations of Sufi poetry, including that of Saᶜdi. Also contains lectures on Persian literature by Inayat Khan.

Ernst, Carl W. *The Shambhala Guide to Sufism*. Boston: Shambhala, 1997. A reference guide to classical and modern Sufi poetry and Sufism. Includes a summary of Saᶜdi's work on the morals of the dervishes from *The Rose Garden* to show the various characteristics of an Islamic mystic in the classical sense. Glossary.

Katouzian, Homa. *Saᶜdi: The Poet of Life, Love, and Compassion*. Oxford, England: Oneworld, 2006. Part of the Makers of the Muslim World series, this biography looks at the life of the poet and relates it to his poetry.

Motaghed, Ehsan. *What Says Saadi*. Tehran, Iran: 1986. An eighty-six-page book collecting translated quotations and explanations that shed light on Saʿdi's philosophical themes embedded in his poetry.

Yohannan, John D. *The Poet Saʿdi: A Persian Humanist*. Lanham, Md.: University Press of America, 1987. A critical appraisal of Saʿdi as a Sufi poet, reminding the reader to avoid reading Saʿdi's narrative tales as didactic Aesopian fables because that would strip them of the multifaceted complexities of Sufi poetry. Bibliography, index.

Harold Branam

LÉOPOLD SENGHOR

Born: Joal, Senegal; October 9, 1906
Died: Verson, France; December 20, 2001

PRINCIPAL POETRY

Chants d'ombre, 1945
Hosties noires, 1948
Chants pour Naëtt, 1949
Chants d'ombre—Hosties noires, 1956
Éthiopiques, 1956
Nocturnes, 1961 (English translation, 1969)
Poèmes, 1964
Selected Poems, 1964
Élégie des Alizés, 1969
Selected Poems of Léopold Sédar Senghor, 1977
Oeuvre poétique, 1990 (*The Collected Poetry*, 1991)

OTHER LITERARY FORMS

Léopold Senghor (sehn-GAWR) was a poet and a politician, a combination of professions unusual in the Anglo-Saxon world but not uncommon in French literary history. As one of the leaders of the emerging nationalism of the former French African colonies and later, as president of Senegal, Senghor was called on to make speeches, prepare reports, and write articles in newspapers, reviews, and periodicals. These many arti-

cles deal with a variety of topics: political, cultural, economic, judicial, and social, as well as literary. In 1948, Senghor edited *Anthologie de la nouvelle poésie nègre et malgache de langue française*, with a preface by Jean-Paul Sartre titled "Orphée noir." Among Senghor's prose works are *Congrès constitutif du P.F.A.: Rapport sur la doctrine et le programme du parti* (1959; *Report on the Principles and Programme of the Party*, 1959) and *La Préhistoire et les groupes éthniques* (1960; prehistory and ethnic groups). Senghor's interest in socialism and its application in Africa was expressed in *Nation et voie africaine du socialisme* (1961; as volume 2 of *Liberté*, 1971; *Nationhood and the African Road to Socialism*, 1962; abridged as *On African Socialism*, 1964) and *Théorie et pratique du socialisme sénégalais* (1964). In the works of the Catholic thinker Pierre Teilhard de Chardin, Senghor found a synthesis of Catholicism and socialism that fit his personal beliefs, reflected in *Pierre Teilhard de Chardin et la politique africaine* (1962). *Liberté: Négritude et humanisme*, 1964 (*Freedom I: Negritude and Humanism*, 1974) collects a wide range of Senghor's articles and lectures.

ACHIEVEMENTS

As a result of his multitude of activities, Léopold Senghor presented a problem for critics assessing his poetic works. Does the fact that he was a black African make him a mouthpiece of black African peoples, or should he be judged only as a poet who happened to be black? Does the fact that Senghor wrote in French mean that he must be judged as a French poet or as an African—more specifically, a Senegalese poet—who happened to write in French? Must the fact that Senghor was a successful politician interfere with the way his poetry is judged?

There are no easy answers to these questions. Senghor himself was torn between the various worlds he inhabited, and—as is obvious in his poetry—he was not always successful in separating his different interests or in properly synthesizing them. As an educated, intelligent young Senegalese—he was the first African to receive the very competitive French *agrégation* (the equivalent of a doctorate for teachers) and thereby able to teach French in French *lycées*—Senghor became one of the leaders of the expatriate blacks in Paris during the 1930's. With Aimé Césaire and Léon Damas, he founded the magazine *L'Étudiant noir*. After the war, he published his first collection of poems, *Chants d'ombre*, and three years later, his second, *Hosties noires*. It was not, however, until he edited an anthology of black poetry that same year, *Anthologie de la nouvelle poésie nègre et malgache de langue française*, that he attracted the attention of French critics, and even then it was probably the preface by Sartre, then at the height of his career, that earned the book notice.

In 1960, he was elected president of Senegal, a post he held until 1981. The demands of political office kept the poet too busy to be prolific. As president of Senegal, Senghor encouraged the study of African literature at the University of Dakar, which he was instrumental in founding, and made Dakar, the capital of Senegal, the intellectual capital of Africa. During his presidency, Senghor also initiated an ambitious campaign to eradicate illiteracy and promote books and reading in his country.

Senghor's honors and awards are almost too numerous to mention, flowing from institutions around the world and acknowledging his many accomplishments, both literary and political. He received the Peace Prize of the German Book Trade Association (1968), the Knokke Biennial International Poetry Grand Prix (1970), the Grenoble Gold Medal (1972), the Haile Selassie African Research Prize and the Cravat of Commander of Order of French Arts and Letters (both in 1973), the Apollinaire Prize for Poetry (1974), the Prince Pierre of Monaco's Literature Prize (1977), the Prix Eurafrique (1978), the International Book Award sponsored by UNESCO's International Book Committee (1979), the Alfred de Vigny Poetry Prize and the Aasan World Prize (both in 1981), the Jawaharlal Nehru Award (1984), and the Athinai Prize (1985). Senghor became a member of the Academy of Overseas Sciences and the Black Academy of Arts and Sciences, both in 1971, and was elected to the French Academy in 1983. He also received the Grand Cross of the French Legion of Honor, was named Commander of Academic Palms, and received the Franco-Allied Medal of Recognition. He was the recipient of many honorary doctorates from academic institutions the world over.

Léopold Senghor

BIOGRAPHY

Léopold Sédar Senghor was born on October 9, 1906, in Joal, a small coastal village south of Dakar, in Senegal. The Serer tribe to which Senghor's family belongs is a Roman Catholic enclave in a predominantly Muslim region; the name Léopold is Senghor's Catholic name, while Sédar is his Serer name. Senghor's father, Basile Diogoye Senghor, and mother, Nyilane Senghor, were a well-to-do couple. Until the age of seven, Senghor was allowed to grow up wild and free in lush nature, which he recalls fondly as the kingdom of childhood in *Chants d'ombre*. At seven, Senghor was plucked from his kingdom and—to the chagrin of his mother, who thought he was much too young—sent to a Catholic mission school at Ngazobil, a few miles north of Joal. There, Senghor was still close to the nature he loved, but for the first time, the future socialist and politician became aware of the poverty of many black Africans. In 1922, Senghor was sent to the Catholic seminary in Dakar, where he hesitated between becoming a priest and becoming a professor. Told that he lacked the dedication to be a priest, he prepared for a career as a professor. Upon graduation in 1928, he left Senegal for the first time and traveled to Paris, where he entered the Lycée Louis-le-Grand. There, he met such future French luminaries as Paul Guth and Georges Pompidou, as well as fellow black expatriates from Africa and the West Indies, including Césaire and Damas.

In Paris, a whole new world opened up for Senghor. For the black expatriates of the 1930's, France was both an adopted mother and an enemy. Blacks living in France did not face the legalized discrimination that existed at that time in the United States; instead, they were the victims of a polite, unofficial policy of segregation. In response, the expatriates banded together to analyze their situation; one product of such analysis was the concept of negritude, a word coined by Césaire and adopted by Senghor.

It was during these years in Paris that Senghor began developing his talents as a poet, writing the poems that were later to be published in *Chants d'ombre*. In 1932, Senghor received his *diplôme d'études supérieures* (the equivalent of the master's degree) with a thesis on exoticism in the works of Charles Baudelaire, and in 1935, he took French citizenship to be able to receive his *agrégation*, which allowed him to teach French to French children. After his military service, Senghor began his career as a teacher at the Lycée Descartes in Tours, a city important to the Popular Front; the children he taught were workers' sons. In this atmosphere, Senghor's socialist inclinations were reinforced. After Tours, Senghor taught at the Lycée Marcelin Berthelot at Saint-Maur des Fossés. Just before the war, he participated with Jacques Roumain and others in compiling a special edition for Editions Plon devoted to ethnic subjects. In 1939, Senghor was drafted; taken prisoner by the Germans in 1940, he was released in 1942 because of frequent illness. He returned to teaching and joined the Resistance. These unhappy times of war and suffering were the inspiration for his second volume of poetry, *Hosties noires*.

After the French liberation, Senghor's political activities intensified. Besides becoming professor of African language and civilization at the École Nationale de la France d'Outre-mer in Paris, he was elected to the French National Assembly. In 1946, he married Ginette Eboué, daughter of the governor of French Equatorial Africa. He was accused by some of marrying to enhance his career. In 1948, Senghor left the Socialist Party and created a new party, the Bloc Démocratique Sénégalais. In the 1950's, Senghor's political career continued to advance. He was part of the Edgar Fauré Cabinet and later a member of the Constitutional Assembly of Senegal. Finally, on September 5, 1960, he became the first president of the new, independent country of Senegal.

During the years between the war and his election, Senghor had traveled widely and had made many trips back to Serer country, where he participated in village feasts, the inspirations for several of his poems. When, in 1956, Senghor's first marriage failed, he married Colette Hubert, a white Frenchwoman who had been secretary to his first wife.

In 1981, Senghor voluntarily retired as president of Senegal, a rare act for an African head of state, to devote himself to writing and to promoting the Socialist International Organization, of which he has been vice president.

It is a testament to his preeminence as a politician, a poet, and a philosopher that, on October 18, 1996, UNESCO organized a three-day ceremony in Paris to honor Senghor on his ninetieth birthday. The celebration consisted of art exhibits and tributes by world dignitaries such as French president Jacques Chirac, Hassan II of Morocco, Pope John Paul II, and winner of the 1986 Nobel Prize in Literature Wole Soyinka of Nigeria. Unable to attend in person, Senghor opened the festivities with a videotaped message pleading for solidarity among peoples and universal synthesis of cultures, a note that echoes his enduring dream of reconciling French-language culture and its humanism with negritude, the embodiment of the values of the black world.

As creator of the Organization of African Unity, Senghor was a champion of pan-Africanism, and as a pivotal architect in the creation of the International Francophone Community, he bolstered his vision of a cultural community. Senghor died in late 2001, but many biographies of this man of uncommon destiny have appeared, and his poetry lives on in the many reprintings of his works, which have been translated into some thirty languages. His poetry has strongly influenced the literary world.

ANALYSIS

Léopold Senghor was at once a politician and a poet, a combination that he regarded as a logical marriage because, as he stated in an interview with Armand Guibert, culture—of which poetry is the highest expression—is the foundation and at the same time the ultimate goal of politics. When he was a student in the 1930's, Senghor, unlike his West Indies friends, believed that a cultural revolution should precede a political one. He wanted to be the *dyali* (Sengalese troubadour) of his country. In Senghor's experience, however, other dichotomies were not as easy to resolve. These dichotomies are expressed in his poems; indeed, they are the heart of many of them. During his years in France, Senghor was torn between his love for his native land (his "sister," as he sometimes calls it in his verses) and his love for his adopted country (his "foster sister"). He was caught between two very dissimilar civilizations, each with its own merits and faults. Repelled by French colonialism and by the racial prejudice that he encountered at first hand, he nevertheless admired French culture and the French language. When he was in Paris, he missed Senegal, and when he was back in Serer country, he missed "la douce France." He was a black man in a white world, and while many of his poems reflect his sensuous admiration of the black woman, who for him symbolizes Africa, several other poems express his love of a white woman (his first wife was black; his second, white). Finally, Senghor's poetry, especially his first volume, *Chants d'ombre*, is marked by nostalgia for the magic kingdom of his childhood, associated with a mythical, primeval Africa.

One of the major influences on Senghor's poetry was the Serer poet Maronne, whose songs introduced Senghor to the traditional literature of his native area. Even earlier, as a child, he had listened to the *gymnique* poets, whose songs accompany the wrestling matches so popular in Senegal and serve as work songs and lullabies as well. Senghor was also familiar with the poetry of the *griots*, professional and learned oral poets. Music was another major influence on Senghor's poetry. Under the titles of most of his poems, Senghor indicated the African musical instruments that should be used to provide accompaniment. In an interview with Guibert, Senghor stated that there is a double reason for this: Musical accompaniment both enhances the effect of the poetry and revives the African oral tradition, in which poetry was song. Images of music abound in Senghor's poetry. He referred, for example, to the rhythm of the world, and a beloved is described as a flute. Senghor's French education was inevitably an influence also. From poets such as Baudelaire and his successors Arthur Rimbaud, Paul Verlaine, and Stéphane Mallarmé, Senghor learned to use Symbolism "to express complex sensations," as Abiola Irele observes in her introduction to *Selected Poems of Léopold Sédar Senghor*. Paul Claudel's influence is evident in Senghor's religious poems extolling the mysteries of the Catholic faith. Irele believes that Senghor took up Claudel's distinctive verse form, the *verset*, and infused it with elements of African oral tradition. There are also affinities between Senghor and Saint-John Perse, but Senghor said that he first read Perse only after his own style was formed; thus, the similarities between them reflect a convergence rather than the influence of one on the other.

When Senghor started writing poetry, Surrealism was in full bloom. The 1930's were marked by a renaissance of black awareness in Europe while the Surrealist revolt against Cartesian rationalism glorified the so-called primitive civilizations; thus, Senghor's proclamation of the purity of the black race—a purity that the white race had lost—was perfectly in accord with Surrealist dogma. What André Breton sought in the subconscious, Senghor sought by going back to his African roots. The European Surrealist had to delve deep into his subconscious to find his instincts and natural desires, but the black African had only to be himself. While Surrealist poets such as Paul Éluard tried to merge the real and the fantastic to avoid paranoia, Senghor saw no need for this synthesis. It already characterized the bushman, who knew neither insanity nor psychosis and in whom the body and the mind were one. Even in methods of composition, Senghor and the

Surrealists followed the same path: The poetry of the Senegalese *griots* was spoken thought, a practice stemming from an oral tradition, a sort of psychic automatism. Describing the process he followed to write his poetry, Senghor said that he begins with an expression that is whispered in his ear like a leitmotif; when he began to write, he did not know what form the poem would take.

This new view of the black African corresponded to Senghor's definition of the term negritude, meaning the entire cultural heritage of the black civilizations of Africa. In Senghor's view, the black man, as a result of his heritage, enjoys a greater capacity for feeling and a closer relationship with the natural world than that bequeathed to the white man by European civilization. In general, Anglophone African writers have rejected the concept of negritude; the Nigerian poet, playwright, and novelist Soyinka has observed that a tiger does not speak of its *tigritude*. Indeed, in recent decades, during which Africa has achieved independence from the colonial powers, the notion of negritude has lost much of its appeal in Francophone regions as well.

CHANTS D'OMBRE

More than any other African poet, Senghor was classical in his poetic style. The first poem of *Chants d'ombre* has a Latin title, and many of his poems contain classical allusions; for this he was criticized by other African writers. On the other hand, French critics have objected to African elements in his verse, ranging from his frequent use of repetition (a legacy of the oral tradition) to his sentence structure and his diction. Senghor liked to use words drawn from the two major languages of Senegal, Wolof and Serer. In an interview with Guibert, Senghor defended this practice, saying that he did not indulge in exoticism but had merely drawn on the vocabulary used by the French-speaking Senegalese and even by the French living in Senegal.

According to Senghor, rhythm is the key element of African art. He quoted American jazz great Duke Ellington to describe his own poetry: "popular Negro music." Senghor used several devices to achieve rhythm, including alternation of accented and atonal syllables instead of long and short, as well as more conventional devices, such as alliteration and assonance. Another quality of Senghor's poetry which marked him as an African poet is his imagery. He has been called the Poet of the Night because of his many references to night and darkness as symbols of good. Like many other black writers, especially the black American poets, Senghor reversed the solar hierarchy of white poets, who glorify the sun and the color white as good and depict night and black as evil.

Chants d'ombre, a collection of poems written during Senghor's early years in Paris, reflects the poet's nostalgia for his African home and his childhood, as well as his growing awareness of his own alienation in a country whose duplicity as a colonizer he could not ignore. The first poem in the collection, "In memoriam," is written in the form of a prayer. Despite the poet's religious fervor, however, his alienation is obvious. He feels set apart from the people with whom he goes to church in Paris; his prayer is to the dead, to his ancestors, as is the custom in his native land. He is further distinguished from the other churchgoers by his color. They, whom he calls his brothers, have blue eyes and "hard hands," a term that, in Africa, is a metaphor for hate, meanness, and inhospitality. "In memoriam" sets the tone of the entire collection. What follows is reminiscence. In "Tout le long du jour" (all day long), as the poet travels on the European train, he remembers his native land, the little uniform railroad stations, and the chatty, nubile young black girls. In these reminiscences, he seeks to forget Europe, and in so doing he idealizes his homeland. "Joal" reflects the same theme. Eight times, the words "I remember" are used, and what the poet remembers is an innocent Africa whose rhythm of life is simple and whose awareness of the divine presence in the universe is unique. The sacrifices to the gods, the pagan singing of the *Tantum ergo*, and the little parish church complement rather than oppose one another. The style of the poem is simple, as befits the subject matter; it ends, however, with a return to reality and the poet's awareness of his exile.

"FOR KORAS AND BALAFONG"

"For Koras and Balafong" is a long poem, a solemn chant in nine stanzas embracing all the themes of the collection. The poet examines the conflicts that tear at him, celebrating the African past and mourning its passing at the hands of the colonizers. The title immediately sets the African mood. The *kora* is a musical instrument similar to the harp, while the *balafong* is an African xylophone. The poem is dedicated to René Maran, a French West Indian writer whose novel *Batouala* (1921) dealt for the first time in literature with French colonial policy. "For Koras and Balafong" was written when Europe was on the brink of World War II. Stanza 1 is an idyllic description of Europe and of the poet's childhood. In stanzas 2, 3, and 4, the poet remembers his French schooling and the beginnings of his alienation, leading him to make comparisons between old France and young Africa. Stanzas 5, 6, and 7 celebrate Africa before the white man altered it; Senghor compares his continent to a black princess. In stanza 8, the socialist Senghor views the future as a solemn procession of seven thousand peasants carrying the riches of his race, no longer slaves as in the days of colonialism. Stanza 9, a lyric paean to Africa, is dominated by the color black. Africa is a dark beauty, a black night. Night delivers the poet from the arguments and sophistries of salons, from the butchery rationalized by the colonizers. In "For Koras and Balafong," the language is French, but the poet is undeniably African.

"PARIS IN SNOW"

The dominant color of "Paris in Snow" is white—here, the color of death: the white of the snow on the roofs of Paris, white sheets, and the white hands that whipped the slaves and cut down the forests of Africa. An indictment of Western civilization, "Paris in Snow" establishes a bitter contrast between the message of peace of the Christmas season and the rumbles of war presaged in the destruction of Spain and the persecution of the Jews. Ultimately, however, the theme of the poem is religious. In the first line, the speaker addresses Christ ("Lord, you visited Paris on the day of your birth"), and the entire poem is cast in the form of a prayer. The speaker's ambivalence and spiritual torment are revealed in contrasting images of white: Christ's "snow of peace" and the "white cold" of his demanding love versus the brutal "white hands" of the colonizers. The paradoxical images of Christ recall the poetry of John Donne and George Herbert: Senghor's Christ is dark (the Saras, a people from Chad, are "beautiful like the first men that were created by your brown hands"), yet the speaker of the poem,

seeking to overcome his hatred of the white colonizers, concludes:

> My heart, oh Lord, has melted like the snow on the
> roofs of Paris
>
> In the sun of your Goodness,
>
> It is kind to my enemies, my brothers with the snowless
> white hands. . . .

"BLACK WOMAN"

The most impressionistic and most sensuous poem of the volume is "Femme noire" ("Black Woman"). Senghor observed that in black Africa, the woman holds a particularly high standing: She is both the giver of life and the repository of tradition, and she assures the clan's future. When a woman marries in Africa, she does not renounce her clan to become integrated into her husband's family; she continues to belong to her own clan. She also runs the household and has her own property. In 1950, in an article on African American poetry, Senghor wrote that American blacks have a cult of the black woman, who symbolizes negritude. The woman more than the man is sensitive to the mysteries of life and the cosmos; she is also more sensitive to joy and pain. "Black Woman" is not about a particular woman but about a generic woman: a lover, a mother, and finally Africa herself. The poem is a succession of images; the black woman is a promised land, a savannah, a tom-tom, and a gazelle. Mezu compares Senghor's poem to Breton's *L'Union libre* (1931; *Free Union*, 1982), in which Breton appropriates the manner of the litany. Senghor's "Black Woman" is also faithful to the tradition of the African praise poem.

HOSTIES NOIRES AND ÉTHIOPIQUES

Hosties noires, Senghor's second volume of poems, was written as a result of Senghor's experiences as a prisoner of war. With this volume, Senghor moved from personal to collective poetry and from lyric and nostalgic to nationalistic poetry. Two recurring themes in *Hosties noires* are the sacrifices of black soldiers and the poet's ambivalent relation to France and the European tradition. The title, with its religious overtones—*hostie* refers to the Host in the Catholic Mass—unequivocally designates the most important theme of the volume, the black soldiers who died for France as sacrificial victims.

In *Éthiopiques*, Senghor adopted a more Hermetic style displaying strong affinities with Surrealism. The four major long poems of the volume are "Chaka," "Letters to the Princess," "Congo," and "To New York." Chaka, an early nineteenth century Zulu chieftain, was an effective but ruthless soldier and leader who quickly rose to power and was driven insane by the nightmares of his crimes. He was finally assassinated by his brothers. Thomas Mofolo had written a novel on Chaka, and Senghor, in his poem, takes up where Mofolo left off— that is, at the end of Chaka's regime. In "Chaka," Senghor concentrates on the conflict between Chaka's political love and his personal love; the Zulu leader had to sacrifice his beloved Noliwe for his people. Senghor the African expresses his admiration for Chaka's nationalism and resistance to oppression, but Senghor the educated politician speaks as the "White Voice" in the poem and expresses his hatred of fanaticism and extremism. The White Voice calls Chaka the provider of hyenas and vultures. Nevertheless, what followed Chaka's regime was even more barbaric: colonialism.

"Letters to the Princess" deals with the conflict between love and politics; unlike Chaka, Senghor does not sacrifice his love to his political ambitions. The title figure of the poem is called "the Princess of Belborg," denoting a northern woman of noble blood, possibly an illicit love, since, as Mezu surmises, in chivalrous literature, the conventions of which this poem imitates, passion is usually illicit. Senghor wrote "Letters to the Princess" in the period during which he divorced his first wife, a black West Indian, and married a white Frenchwoman. Senghor, writing in Senegal, addresses letters to his distant love; he expresses nostalgia for Paris, for the neighborhoods where he once lived and which he associates with her. The bitterness he once felt toward Europe is assuaged; he feels the pain of the war-devastated continent. He hopes that his loved one will come to be with him in the land of his mother, "where the soil is black and the blood is dark and the oil is thick." The sensuality that prevails in "Black Woman" is repeated here when Senghor describes Lilanga, who symbolizes Africa:

Lilanga, her feet are two reptiles, hands that gather the pestles that

beat the males that till the earth

And from the earth wells up the rhythm, sap and sweat, wave and smell

of the damp earth

That shudders the legs of the statue, the thighs that open to the secret

Flows over the buttocks, hollows the loins stretched the belly gorges and

hills

Prows of drums. . . .

The same sensual and female images occur in "Congo." The Congo of the title is the river which Senghor calls "Queen over Africa." This queen has tamed "Phalli of mountains" and is the mother of all things. The Congo is another variation of the feminine archetype dear to the son of a matriarchal regime. In "To New York," perhaps the finest poem in the collection, Senghor distinguishes between two New Yorks: Manhattan, the white section—which is male, sterile, and livid, and where there is no child's laughter, no mother's breast—and Harlem, the black section—which is female, alive with sounds and color. New York's only hope is to allow the black blood to flow into the white. In this poem, as he did in "Paris in Snow," Senghor refers to the blackness of God: "God who with a burst of saxophone laughter created the heavens and the earth in six days./ And on the seventh day, he slept his great negro sleep." Similarly, in the second stanza of the poem, he proclaims that "there is more truth in the Night than in the day."

NOCTURNES

Nocturnes was published one year after Senghor became president of Senegal; the volume is made up of two parts: "Chants pour Signare" ("Songs for Signare") and "Élégies" ("Elegies"). The former is a group of love poems originally published in 1949 under the title

Chants pour Naëtt. Written with Senghor's first wife in mind, they were revised for the later publication, and the name Naëtt was changed to Signare in deference to Senghor's second wife. (In Senegal, *signare*, from the Portuguese *senhora*, designates a woman of quality.) Among other revisions, Senghor substituted African words for French words, omitted some secondary words (such as articles), and changed the punctuation to give his poems a more African rhythm. The "Songs for Signare" are no longer concerned with the conflicts that tormented the poet in his earlier volumes. They are primarily love poems wherein the poet addresses an unnamed beloved and seeks her solace to soothe his weariness. The loved one is, as in previous poems, the archetypal woman, the nurturer and the giver of life; she is black and she is white, she is alive and she is abstract. The poet is now in his native land, but he longs for earlier, simpler days of childhood, and the woman symbolizes for him not only Africa but also the Africa of his childhood. If the conflicts seem to be resolved, the contrasts remain. The key words for the entire collection are "night" and "light," beginning with the first line of the first poem: "A hand of light caressed my eyelids of darkness." The title of the collection, *Nocturnes*, indicates night for Senghor is peaceful, a time to be with his beloved; light is associated with the white man and political duties. In these poems, the contrasts of light and dark are set against a multitude of colors: the green smell of rice fields, the trees with golden leaves, the red African soil, and the blue city of the dead.

In "Elegies," the second part of the volume, the poet is more self-confident, more conscious of being a leader. As John Reed and Clive Wake point out in their introduction to their translation of *Nocturnes*, even though the "Elegies" recall some of the early conflicts, they incorporate a more recent viewpoint which recognizes the importance of the creative act and of reconciliation. "Élégie de minuit" ("Elegy of Midnight") begins with the poet's discontent with what fame has brought him. The third stanza of the poem depicts in very erotic terms the despair that not even the music of love can calm. In the last stanza, the poet asks to be born again in the Kingdom of Childhood, to be shepherd to his shepherdess, to dance like the athlete, but then he calms

down and accepts the fact that peace will come, that "I shall sleep the sleep of death by which the Poet is fed." "Élégie de l'eau" ("Elegy of Water"), as Reed and Wake observe, is Senghor's "supreme poem of reconciliation." Here, fire and water are symbols of purification; Chicago and Moscow are burning, and the poet calls for rain, on New York, on Pompidou, on Paris: ". . . China— four hundred thousand Chinese are drowned, twelve million Chinese are saved. . . ." Finally, he calls for rain "on straw heads and wool heads./ And life is born again color of whatever is."

OTHER MAJOR WORKS

NONFICTION: *Congrès constitutif du P.F.A.: Rapport sur la doctrine et le programme du parti*, 1959 (*Report on the Principles and Programme of the Party*, 1959); *La Préhistoire et les groupes éthniques*, 1960; *Nation et voie africaine du socialisme*, 1961 (as volume 2 of *Liberté*, 1971; *Nationhood and the African Road to Socialism*, 1962; abridged as *On African Socialism*, 1964); *Pierre Teilhard de Chardin et la politique africaine*, 1962; *Liberté: Négritude et humanisme*, 1964 (*Freedom I: Negritude and Humanism*, 1974); *Théorie et pratique du socialisme sénégalais*, 1964; *Les Fondements de l'Africanité: Ou, Négritude et arabité*, 1967 (as *Négritude, arabisme, et francité: Réflexions sur le problème de la culture*, 1967; *The Foundations of "Africanité": Or, Négritude and "Arabité,"* 1971); *La Parole chez Paul Claudel et chez les négro-africains*, 1973; *Pour une relecture africaine de Marx et d'Engels*, 1976; *Liberté: Négritude et civilisation de l'universel*, 1977; *Liberté: Socialisme et planification*, 1983; *Liberté: Le Dialogue des cultures*, 1993.

EDITED TEXT: *Anthologie de la nouvelle poésie nègre et malgache de langue française*, 1948.

MISCELLANEOUS: *Prose and Poetry*, 1965.

BIBLIOGRAPHY

Bâ, Sylvia W. *The Concept of Negritude in the Poetry of Léopold Sédar Senghor*. Princteon, N.J.: Princeton University Press, 1973. Examines issues of race identity in Senghor's works. Includes translations of selected poems. Bibliography.

Harney, Elizabeth. *In Senghor's Shadow: Art, Politics,*

and the Avant-garde in Senegal, 1960-1995. Durham, N.C.: Duke University Press, 2004. Re-examines Senghor's views of modernism, his loyalties to France and Africa, and his legacy.

Hymans, Jacques. *Leopold Sédar Senghor: An Intellectual Biography*. Edinburgh: Edinburgh University Press, 1971. This full biography pays particular attention to Senghor's philosophical and literary development. Considers, among other things, the influence of Pierre Teilhard de Chardin, Paul Claudel, Marc Chagall, and Jacques Maritain. Bibliography.

Kluback, William. *Léopold Sédar Senghor: From Politics to Poetry*. New York: Peter Lang, 1997. A book of imagined conversations based on Senghor's philosophy regarding humanity's moral evolution.

Markovitz, Irving Leonard. *Leopold Sédar Senghor and the Politics of Négritude*. New York: Atheneum, 1969. A penetrating consideration of Senghor's philosophy of leadership and issues of race identity.

Mezu, Sebastian Okechukwu. *The Poetry of Leopold Sédar Senghor*. Rutherford, N.J.: Fairleigh Dickinson University Press, 1973. A rare monograph focusing on Senghor's poetry.

Rasmussen, R. Kent. *Modern African Political Leaders*. New York: Facts On File, 1998. Covers leaders, including Senghor, representative of the major regions of Africa during a period when many African nations moved from colonial rule to independence.

Spleth, Janice. *Léopold Sédar Senghor*. New York: Macmillan Library Reference, 1985. A detailed overview of Senghor's poetry, his development as poet and statesman, and the conflicts of those two roles. This discussion involves the author in extending her coverage beyond Senghor to examine the relationship between French and francophone African literature in general.

_____, ed. *Critical Perspectives on Léopold Sédar Senghor*. Washington, D.C.: Three Continents Press, 1993. A collection of critical essays on Senghor's writings.

Vaillant, Janet G. *Black, French, and African: A Life of Leopold Sédar Senghor*. Cambridge, Mass.: Harvard University Press, 1990. A biography that adds to previous literature an extended examination of

Senghor's childhood, including interviews with his extended Senegalese family. More material on his poetry than on his presidency of Senegal. The first major biography in English.

Monique Nagem
Updated by Nagem

VIKRAM SETH

Born: Calcutta, West Bengal, India; June 20, 1952

PRINCIPAL POETRY
Mappings, 1981
The Humble Administrator's Garden, 1985
The Golden Gate: A Novel in Verse, 1986
All You Who Sleep Tonight, 1990
Beastly Tales from Here and There, 1992
The Poems, 1981-1994, 1995

OTHER LITERARY FORMS

Vikram Seth (sayt) is best known for his novels. *A Suitable Boy* (1993), a family epic set in postcolonial India, is a monumental 1,349-page work that received mixed reviews but that became one of Seth's best-known works. *An Equal Music* (1999), set in contemporary London, is a love story about the members of a string quartet. Seth wrote a prizewinning travel book, *From Heaven Lake: Travels Through Sinkiang and Tibet*, published in 1983, and translated Chinese poetry in *Three Chinese Poets: Translations of Poems by Wang Wei, Li Bai, and Du Fu* (1992). *Arion and the Dolphin* (1995), written as the libretto for an opera, was also published as a children's book.

ACHIEVEMENTS

Vikram Seth won the Thomas Cook Travel Book Award in 1983 for *From Heaven Lake*; the Quality Paperback Book Club New Voice Award and a Gold Medal from the Commonwealth Club of California, both in 1986, for *The Golden Gate*; the W. H. Smith Award in 1994 for *A Suitable Boy*; and the Commonwealth Writer's Prize in 1994. He received an Ingram

Merrill Fellowship in 1985-1986, a Guggenheim Fellowship in 1986-1987, and the Order of the British Empire in 2001. In 2005, he received India's Pravasi Bharatiya Samman award for exceptional work in literature and in 2007 received India's Padma Shri award for his contributions to education and literature.

BIOGRAPHY

Vikram Seth was born in Calcutta, India, in 1952, the oldest of three children. His father, Prem Seth, was a shoe company executive and his mother, Laila Seth, served as a judge. Seth left India to study at Oxford University in England, earning degrees in philosophy, economics, and politics. He enrolled at Stanford University in California, intending to complete a Ph.D. in economics. While at Stanford, Seth was a Wallace Stegner Fellow in creative writing. He wrote the poems collected in *Mappings* during this time. From 1980 to 1982, Seth was in China for two years of travel and economic research. While there, he studied classical Chinese poetry and language at Nanjing University. He wrote an account of a hitchhiking journey to India during this time, published as *From Heaven Lake*.

Seth's works present a variety of subjects based on his experiences and travels. The poetry collections *The Humble Administrator's Garden* and *All You Who Sleep Tonight* (1990) merge Chinese, Indian, and Californian influences; *From Heaven Lake* details the hitchhiking trip through Nepal and Tibet that Seth took while a student in China; and *The Golden Gate* is about young professionals in San Francisco, searching for love and identity.

Translation has played an important part in Seth's life, reflecting the multicultural sources of his material. His earliest book of poetry includes works translated from Chinese and Hindi. In 1992, *Three Chinese Poets* was published, illustrating again the deep understanding of Chinese culture that critics appreciated in *From Heaven Lake*. In the introduction to *Three Chinese Poets*, Seth acknowledges his debt to works in translation, particularly Russian, French, and Greek, and presents the book as an offering of thanks to other translators.

After publishing *The Golden Gate* in 1986, Seth returned to India to live with his family and work on his major epic, *A Suitable Boy*. This novel, published in 1993, propelled him into the public spotlight. The book launched Seth into a series of interviews, talk shows, and book signings. However, critical reviews were mixed, and the public and his publishers were dismayed when the book was not considered for the Booker Prize in 1993.

After *A Suitable Boy*, Seth returned to London, where he was commissioned by the English National Opera to write a libretto based on the Greek legend of Arion and the dolphin. His 1999 novel, *An Equal Music*, was also set in London, and in 2001 he was awarded the Order of the British Empire for his achievements.

ANALYSIS

Vikram Seth is a versatile writer who is at ease in a variety of genres. He is known for his clear and readable style, joyful use of language, irony, and technical mastery. He has made a place for himself as an Indian writing in the English language. Though his published works reflect his versatility, set in London, San Francisco, and China, as well as India, his best-known work is his epic of Indian culture, religion, family life, and postcolonial politics, *A Suitable Boy*.

Seth's work can be analyzed in terms of several distinctive factors. One is his multicultural identity. His books of poetry contain material influenced by his residence and familiarity with the literature of Eastern and

Vikram Seth (Getty Images)

Western countries and cultures. He is further influenced by literature in translation from Russia and Greece. This cultural diversity is reflected in the variety of his themes and material. Nevertheless, Seth remains ultimately an Indian writer.

A second distinctive factor in Seth's poetry is his technical mastery of traditional forms of rhyme and meter, unusual in a poet of the modern age. Seth has written that since his academic training was in economics rather than English, he followed his own inclinations and tastes in his own poetry. Verse "in form" is what he reads and recalls, and therefore writes.

Critics have noted the simplicity of style and unassuming tone of his poetry. The sheer joy of some of his use of language; his sense of humor, ease, and fun; his joy in small daily moments; and his strong sense of irony characterize the best of his work. While Seth's form is traditional, he is thematically a postmodernist. Coming through the irony and humor is a theme of the loneliness of late twentieth century life, the difficulty of forming relationships, the ultimate failure of love as a bond. His familiarity with contemporary idiom and culture further reflects his time and place. He has a postmodern self-consciousness as well, transparently revealing his writing technique and his presence as narrator throughout his work.

MAPPINGS

Seth's first published book of poetry reflects mixed feelings of nostalgia for India after studying for years in England and the United States. The book includes translations of poems from Hindi, German, and Chinese. His original work expresses youthful restlessness, the sadness of unfulfilled love, and ambivalent feeling toward family. These lines from "Panipat" show the poet's sense of being caught between two cultures:

> Family, music, faces,
> Food, land, everything
> Drew me back, yet now
> To hear the koyal sing
>
> Brings notes of other birds,
> The nightingale, the wren,
> The blackbird; and my heart's
> Barometer turns down.

THE HUMBLE ADMINISTRATOR'S GARDEN

This book is divided into three sections—"Wutong," "Neem," and "Live-Oak"—that identify their influences: Chinese, Indian, and Californian. As in *Mappings*, Seth reports on surfaces and the trivia of life while using the traditional forms of the sonnet, quatrain, and epigrammatic couplet. Critics liked the book for Seth's unassuming tone and technical discipline. Themes of the poems include a refusal to look inward and a celebration of the simple pleasures of life. The California poems refer to loneliness and the dangers of a superficial life. Seth sometimes uses a deceptively simple form to mock emotion, as these lines from "Love and Work": "There is so much to do/ There isn't any time for feeling blue./ There isn't any point in feeling sad./ Things could be worse. Right now they're only bad." Although some of the poems appear so offhand as to be trivial, Seth's irony, humor, and ease with language express the ethic of an unromantic and eclectic contemporary mind.

THE GOLDEN GATE

The Golden Gate, widely reviewed and critically well received, established Seth's reputation as a poet and popular writer. The "novel" is a 307-page series of nearly six hundred sonnets of iambic tetrameter. The long narrative poem is loosely modeled on Russian poet Alexander Pushkin's *Evgeny Onegin* (1825-1832, 1833; *Eugene Onegin*, 1881).

The novel is driven by the lives and entanglements of its characters John, a self-controlled white Anglo-Saxon Protestant yuppie computer designer; Phil, a sensitive Jewish intellectual; Janet, a Japanese feminist rock musician; Liz, a career-driven Italian corporate lawyer; and her brother Ed, a troubled gay Roman Catholic. Each character is a part of a subculture of San Francisco life, and through them Seth demonstrates his thorough familiarity with the setting, the coffee houses, singles bars, and bookshops of 1980's San Francisco.

As in *The Humble Administrator's Garden*, central themes are loneliness, the failure of romantic love to resolve the need for others, and the significance of ordinary life. The narrative is witty and amusing and demonstrates Seth's skill and flexibility with language and mastery of verse form. While some critics found it unusual to depict 1980's yuppies through narrative verse, many found the form's unconventionality appropriate for a work that is both lightly comic and reflective. Despite the traditional model and form, *The Golden Gate* employs techniques of postmodernism, in which the act of writing is self-consciously present, as the author comments upon himself and his technique and employs unexpected coincidences and interweaving of plots.

ALL YOU WHO SLEEP TONIGHT

The poems in this volume continue the Seth hallmarks of rhyme and traditional form. The book is divided into several distinct thematic sections, reflecting Seth's diversity of material. The section "Romantic Residues" reinforces some of the themes of *The Golden Gate*: the quality of love and the reluctance to make commitments and take risks. The second section, "In Other Voices," brings a new element of high seriousness to Seth's poetry, including poems about the Holocaust, the atomic destruction of Hiroshima, and acquired immunodeficiency syndrome (AIDS). "In Other Places" is a series of vignettes about varied places including China; "Quatrains" is a series of clever presentations of Seth's perspective on life; and the final section, "Meditations of the Heart," while also witty, presents a perspective that is saddened by death, loss, and solitude. The final section includes the title poem: "Know that you aren't alone./ The whole world shares your tears,/ Some for two nights or one,/ And some for all their years."

BEASTLY TALES FROM HERE AND THERE

This 1992 book is a collection of animal fables retold by Seth in lively tetrameter couplets. Once again Seth reveals his versatility and multicultural influences, including two tales each from India, China, Greece, and Ukraine, along with two original tales. The tales are characterized by their fluent storytelling and combination of the comic and the tragic. On one level, these are children's tales, but they are more than simple retellings, as Seth gives the fables a moral twist all his own. The reader is left with a sense of ambiguity. What is the true moral?

The final story in the volume is Seth's original "The Elephant and the Tragopan." This fable has a thoroughly contemporary feel, as its theme is the protection of the environment, and the head of the council,

Bigshot, is more concerned with money and votes than with saving Bingle Vale. The resolution is left open:

> And so I'll end the story here.
> What is to come is still unclear.
> Whether the fates will smile or frown,
> And Bingle Vale survive or drown,
> I do not know and cannot say;
> Indeed, perhaps, I never may.

OTHER MAJOR WORKS

LONG FICTION: *The Golden Gate: A Novel in Verse*, 1986; *A Suitable Boy*, 1993; *An Equal Music*, 1999.

PLAY: *Arion and the Dolphin*, pr., pb. 1994 (libretto; music by Alec Roth).

NONFICTION: *From Heaven Lake: Travels Through Sikiang and Tibet*, 1983; *Two Lives*, 2005.

TRANSLATION: *Three Chinese Poets: Translations of Poems by Wang Lei, Li Bai, and Du Fu*, 1992.

CHILDREN'S LITERATURE: *Arion and the Dolphin*, 1995.

BIBLIOGRAPHY

Agarwalla, Shyam S. *Vikram Seth's "A Suitable Boy": Search for an Indian Identity*. New Delhi: Prestige Books, 1995. A scholarly, book-length source on Seth. Employing the techniques of literary criticism, the book includes general cultural information and discussion of Seth's role as an Indian writer.

Corey, Stephen. Review of *All You Who Sleep Tonight*. *Ohio Review*, no. 47 (1991): 132-139. Critical review of the volume. Corey's conclusion is that the poetry is often trivial, singsongy, and oversimplified.

Gopal, Priyamvada. *The Indian English Novel: Nation, History, and Narration*. New York: Oxford University Press, 2009. An introduction to the Indian novel in English, now considered "a fixture on the international literary scene." Major writers covered include Seth, Rabindranath Tagore, Salman Rushdie, and Arundhati Roy.

Mohanty, Seemita. *A Critical Analysis of Vikram Seth's Poetry and Fiction*. New Delhi: Atlantic, 2007. A thorough study of Seth's writing, including both his poetry and his fiction, and the ways he approaches the writing process. Intended for scholars and general readers alike.

Perloff, Marjorie. "Homeward Ho! Silicon Valley Pushkin." Review of *The Golden Gate. American Poetry Review* 15, no. 6 (November/December, 1986): 37-46. Perloff asserts that Seth's concern with rhyme weakens the novel's characterization, plot, and satirical force. A scholarly article, with detailed analysis and extensive references to poetic form and poets in history.

Perry, John Oliver. "World Literature in Review: India." Review of *All You Who Sleep Tonight. World Literature Today* 65, no. 3 (Summer, 1991): 549-550. Perry discusses the content and form of several specific poems and concludes, "It is a tribute to the poems . . . that often they can sound a bit like Frost or Hardy."

Seth, Vikram. Introduction and foreword to *The Poems, 1981-1994.* New York: Viking Penguin, 1995. A primary source, the poet's foreword reprinted in a volume of selected poems. Seth discusses his poetry and influences and reveals themes and insight into his priorities and thought processes.

Woodward, Richard B. "Vikram Seth's Big Book." *The New York Times Magazine* 142 (May 2, 1993): 32-36. A profile of Seth that includes biographical and background information on the author, his writing, and his career.

Susan Butterworth

WOLE SOYINKA

Born: Ijebu Isara, Nigeria; July 13, 1934

PRINCIPAL POETRY

Idanre, and Other Poems, 1967
Poems from Prison, 1969
A Shuttle in the Crypt, 1972
Ogun Abibiman, 1976
Mandela's Earth, and Other Poems, 1988
Early Poems, 1998
Samarkand and Other Markets I Have Known, 2002

OTHER LITERARY FORMS

Wole Soyinka (shaw-YIN-ka) is primarily known as a playwright. His first play *The Invention* (pr. 1955), is a satire based on the hypothetical situation resulting from South African blacks suddenly becoming white. *A Dance of the Forests* (pr. 1960) warns his countrymen to avoid the violence and the pettiness of their past, and *The Lion and the Jewel* (pr. 1959) critiques the effect of Western modernization on traditional African culture. A prolific writer, Soyinka's first novel *The Interpreters* (1965) describes Nigeria after it gained independence from Great Britain. *"The Man Died": Prison Notes of Wole Soyinka* (1972) discusses his own imprisonment as well as the results of the Nigerian Civil War. It provides a context for the imagery and political and personal references in his poetry, as does his autobiography *Aké: The Years of Childhood* (1981). Soyinka's *You Must Set Forth at Dawn: A Memoir* (2006) describes his exile from Nigeria and his continuing battle for human rights. His essay collection *Myth, Literature, and the African World* (1976) is helpful in understanding his poetry.

ACHIEVEMENTS

In 1986, Wole Soyinka became the first African to win the Nobel Prize in Literature. He has received numerous grants and won a variety of prizes, including the Enrico Mattei Award for the Humanities, the Léopold Sédar Senghor Award for the Arts, the John Whiting Drama Prize (1966), the Benson Medal of the Royal Society for Literature, the Premio Grinzane Cavour, the Premio Litterario Internazionalle Mondello (Italy), the UNESCO Medal for the Arts, the Anisfield-Wolf Book Award (1983), and the Agip Prize for Literature (1986). In 1994, he was named the UNESCO Goodwill Ambassador for the promotion of African culture. He is a fellow of the Royal Society of Literature of the United Kingdom, the French Académie Universelle des Cultures, the German Academy of Arts and Letters, the American Academy of Arts and Science, the Pan-African Writers Association, and the Association of Nigerian Authors. He has received honorary degrees from numerous educational institutions, including the University of Leeds, Harvard University, Princeton University.

BIOGRAPHY

Wole Soyinka was born Akinwande Oluwole Soyinka, the second child of Soditan (Samuel) Akinyiode, headmaster of the Abeokuta Grammar School, a Christian primary school established by the British, and Grace Eniola (Grace) Soyinka, a shopkeeper. Soyinka grew up in western Nigeria and attended his father's school. His father was an agnostic and his mother a devout Christian. Soyinka's grandfather introduced him to tribal mythologies and had him secretly initiated into Yoruba manhood. Soyinka began writing in high school; he attended University College at Ibadan, studying literature with an emphasis on drama. There he began to investigate Yoruba and Greek mythology and published several poems in the literary magazine *Black Orpheus*. Soyinka left Africa to study drama at Leeds University in England. In 1955, his first play, *The Invention*, was staged. In 1960, Soyinka returned to the University of Ibadan as a Rockefeller Research Fellow in drama.

Soyinka taught English literature at the University of Ife, traveled, and directed plays. However, politics began to intrude, and in 1964, he was arrested by the Nigerian government; he was released after three months. In 1967, Soyinka became chair of the department of theater arts at the University of Ibadan, but his stand against the Nigerian Civil War (1967-1970) resulted in his arrest. He spent two years in Kaduna Prison. After his release in 1969, Soyinka left Nigeria and did not return until after the government had changed in 1975. He worked as a professor of comparative literature at the University of Ife, but further involvement in politics resulted in his leaving the country in 1994 before being charged with treason. After changes in the government as well as its personnel and policies, Soyinka returned to Nigeria in 1998, becoming professor emeritus at the University of Ife. Soyinka has taught at numerous institutions and has served as the Elias Ghanem Professor of Creative Writing at the University of Nevada, Las Vegas, and the President's Marymount Institute Professor in Residence at Loyola Marymount University.

ANALYSIS

Wole Soyinka's poetry reflects the contradictions in his heritage. His religious beliefs are tribal, specifically

Wole Soyinka (©The Nobel Foundation)

the Yoruba pantheon of gods, and Christian, and his cultural upbringing draws from African traditions, opposed to modernization, and Western traditions. Although he celebrates the complexities that are Africa, he does not romanticize his native land. He writes about the beauty of the land and the value of the African traditions and myths, and he condemns Africans for their materialism and politicians for their corruption. His poetry ranges from lyrical to satiric, from sad to humorous. He writes in English and is known for his complicated syntax and often unusual word choices. Much like T. S. Eliot, Soyinka uses allusions from mythology and history as key elements in his poetry. Some critics state that Soyinka's poetry is unnecessarily complex, often obscure, and unreadable. However, his poetry embraces a wider world beyond Africa and speaks about the human condition, of triumph and despair, of cruelty and compassion.

EARLY POETRY

While a student at Ibadan, Soyinka began writing poetry. His first poem, published in 1962, was "Telephone Conversation," a humorous, yet savage satire on racism. It details the conversation between an English landlady and an African student looking to rent a room. The speaker, the student, has almost completed a transaction over the telephone to rent a room, but realizes he must reveal he is African. The announcement is met with silence; finally the landlady asks, how dark. His reply "West African sepia" is meaningless to her. The rudeness of the landlady elicits a respectful yet detailed reply from the student that includes the fact that his bottom is "raven black." Soyinka's message concerning racism and its absurdity is concealed in humor. Other early satiric poems include "The Immigrant" and "The Other Immigrant," which creates a portrait of a sharply dressed black student who dons dignity with his suit. The poem is an ironic statement about imitation and social pretension. Soyinka's early poetry was not restricted to satire. "Requiem" introduces ideas developed in later poems: the sadness of death and the fragility of life.

IDANRE, AND OTHER POEMS

Soyinka's first book of poetry, *Idanre, and Other Poems*, introduces the Yoruban god Ogun, a reoccurring figure in his poetry. Ogun is the god of iron and metallurgy, of exploration and artistic skill. He is a hunter and embodies the creative spirit. Ogun is also a god of destruction, of war and death. Ironically, modern Yurubans worship Ogun as the guardian of highways. The first section of the book focuses on the theme of the road, which is used to convey sudden death as well as the cost exacted by technical progress in Africa. The concept of creativity and violence are reflected in the poems, such as "Death in the Dawn," which ties the death of a white cock, hit by a speeding car, to a dead man. The much-discussed "The Hunchback of Dugbe" portrays a lonely man who lives on the fringe of society, yet his apartness points out the weakness of a modernizing world. "Abiku" is based on the Yoruba belief of the changeling child "who dies and returns again and again to plague the mother." The poem can be viewed as a metaphor on the unchanging nature of pain and the continuous cycle of suffering and death.

"Idanre," the title poem, interweaves the legend of Ogun, Yoruba god of violence and harvest, with that of Sango, the god of lightning and thunder. The poem

shows how something creative can come from destruction. Although written before the Nigerian Civil War (Biafran War), it reflects Nigeria's experience of bloodshed and hate. Despite the violence, the poem ends hopefully, with a new dawn "of bright processions" and harvests, as corn, eggs, and fruit "burst over throngs of golden gourds."

A SHUTTLE IN THE CRYPT

Soyinka was a suspected sympathizer of the Biafrans, who attempted to separate from Nigeria and form their own country. He was arrested in 1967, and although he was not charged with any crime, he was imprisoned for more than two years. He smuggled two poems out of prison: "Live Burial" and "Flowers for My Land." "Live Burial" describes his situation, as he measures his cell and strives to maintain his sanity. "Flowers" compares floral images to the nation's soldiers, sacrificed in a civil war. Soyinka looks at what is lost and a loss of hope, "I do not/ Dare to think these bones will bloom tomorrow." These two poems were published in the pamphlet *Poems from Prison* and later included in *A Shuttle in the Crypt*.

The image of the shuttle represents the poetic imagination in its relentless movement, weaving a tapestry from the experience of the imprisoned poet, as well as the struggle of the poet, looking to create meaning from his experience. In "O Roots!" the poet asks for roots to be his anchor, to keep him from despair, and to find in the earth "new sustaining draughts." Another poem with the comic title "Conversation at Night with a Cockroach" reflects his isolation; Soyinka spent much of his prison time in solitary confinement.

"Four Archetypes," the second section of the book, portrays the visionary, the exile, and the intellectual, through the characters of Hamlet, Joseph, Gulliver, and Ulysses. Their plights reflect Soyinka's; like him all are lonely seekers of truth and ideals. Like Soyinka, Joseph and Gulliver are imprisoned. Ulysses experiences a number of difficulties in his travels, echoing Soyinka's hardships during the Nigerian crisis, and Hamlet reflects treachery against innocent individuals. The characters speak of false accusations, reflecting Soyinka's situation. Joseph has been falsely accused by Potiphar's wife. In "Gulliver," Soyinka compares Lilliput to Nigeria and Blesfusca to Biafra. Like Gulliver, the poet tried arbitration to solve difficulties between the two "countries," but the Lilliputians, like the Federalists of Nigeria, were committed to wiping out the enemy.

The section "Chimes of Silence" is central to the book and to Soyinka's witnessing the death of five fellow prisoners. "The Processional" details the hanging of these men, whose "hands are closed on emptiness." Soyinka, shut in his cell, able to see only through a small chink in the door, is there for the men, "Pallbearer to hereafter." Like other poets, he is a recorder of their deaths and must live to reanimate these men through his words.

OGUN ABIBIMAN

Ogun Abibiman was inspired by the acts of Samora Machel, president of Mozambique who stood against the minority white regime of Rhodesia (now Zimbabwe) before the war of liberation. Ogun is the Yoruban god, and Abibiman stands for "the Black (Abibi) Nation (man), the land of the Black People." In the first section, Ogun leads his people to battle to destroy white racist power in southern Africa. The second section shifts from the gods' involvement to that of the Zulu king, Shaka, a warlord who never lost a battle. Together Ogun and Shaka lead black Africans against the colonial regimes in southern Africa. The final section affirms that war is not to promote vengeance or hate, but to create justice and hope for long-oppressed people.

MANDELA'S EARTH, AND OTHER POEMS

Mandela's Earth, and Other Poems contains poems expressing Soyinka's continuing concerns: the abuse of power in postcolonial Africa, the continuation of poverty and atrocities, and the persistence of hope. The first section focuses on Nelson Mandela and his long imprisonment. Soyinka marvels at Mandela's strength and questions whether he is more a symbol than a man. The fourth section, "New York, U.S.A.," takes the form of a travelogue, as the poet travels though the airport and is faced with the reality of racism, rigid immigration controls, and lurid but deceptive advertising. Soyinka compares American society with that of the ancient Roman Empire and details the corruption of the American Dream through references to the Ku Klux Klan, genocide, slavery, and capitalism. Poems range from a discussion of the trivialization of events in "The

Most Expensive Anchorman in U.S.A" to the life of the junkie in "Columbia Circle, N.Y."

SAMARKAND AND OTHER MARKETS I HAVE KNOWN

Samarkand and Other Markets I Have Known includes poems of mourning as well as outrage, and beneath the satire is a persistent sadness as Soyinka comments on the situation in Nigeria. Poems in the first section, "Outsiders," protest Nigerian dictator Sani Abacha. The Abacha regime (1993-1998) was responsible for the hanging of world-famous writer Ken Saro-Wiwa and eight other activists. The book also reflects on Nigeria's return to Islamic fundamentalism. "Elegy for the Nation" states that "our nation is not dead, not clinically/ Yet." Soyinka writes about the past, when "our gazes roamed the land, godlike," but the past is dead, and "hate clerics" evoke the "murdering tyranny of Creed." He describes a "cairn of stones" in the public square, ready for "a female scapegoat" to be sacrificed to keep woman "obedient to the laws of man." "Vain Ransom" is a memorial for African victims of the 1998 al-Qaeda bombings. Soyinka comments that the "price their forebears paid" was not enough, reflecting back to those sold into slavery, the "manhood of a continent/ Lost to white knives in a Brave New World." This, according to Soyinka is not enough, and the "rage of blood" continues.

OTHER MAJOR WORKS

LONG FICTION: *The Interpreters*, 1965; *Season of Anomy*, 1973.

PLAYS: *The Invention*, pr. 1955; *The Swamp Dwellers*, pr. 1958; *The Lion and the Jewel*, pr. 1959; *A Dance of the Forests*, pr. 1960; *The Trials of Brother Jero*, pr. 1960; *Five Plays*, 1963; *The Strong Breed*, pb. 1963; *Three Plays*, 1963; *Kong's Harvest*, pr. 1964; *The Road*, pr., pb. 1965; *Madmen and Specialists*, pr. 1970, revised pr., pb. 1971; *The Bacchae of Euripides: A Communion Rite*, pr., pb. 1973 (adaptation of Euripides' play); *The Jero Plays*, pb. 1973; *Jero's Metamorphosis*, pb. 1973; *Collected Plays*, 1973-1974 (2 volumes); *Death and the King's Horseman*, pb. 1975; *Opera Wonyosi*, pr. 1977 (adaptation of Bertolt Brecht's play *The Three-Penny Opera*); *Requiem for a Futurologist*, pr. 1983; *A Play of Giants*, pr., pb. 1984;

Six Plays, 1984; _Form Zia, with Love_, pr., pb. 1992; _The Beatification of Area Boy: A Lagosian Kaleidoscope_, pr. 1996; _Plays: Two_, 1999.

RADIO PLAYS: _Camwood on the Leaves_, 1960; _A Scourge of Hyacinths_, 1990.

NONFICTION: _"The Man Died": Prison Notes of Wole Soyinka_, 1972 (autobiography); _Myth, Literature, and the African World_, 1976; _Aké: The Years of Childhood_, 1981 (autobiography); _Art, Dialogue, and Outrage: Essays on Literature and Culture_, 1988; _Ìsarà: A Voyage Around "Essay,"_ 1989; _The Credo of Being and Nothingness_, 1991; _Orisha Liberated the Mind: Wole Soyinka in Conversation with Ulli Beier on Yoruba Religion_, 1992; _Wole Soyinka on "Identity,"_ 1992; _"Death and the King's Horseman": A Conversation Between Wole Soyinka and Ulli Beier_, 1993; _Ibadan: The Penkelemes Years: A Memoir, 1946-1965_, 1994; _The Open Sore of a Continent: A Personal Narrative of the Nigerian Crisis_, 1996; _The Burden of Memory, the Muse of Forgiveness_, 1999; _Seven Signposts of Existence: Knowledge, Honour, Justice, and Other Virtues_, 1999; _Conversations with Wole Soyinka_, 2001 (Biodun Jeyofo, editor); _Climate of Fear: The Quest for Dignity in a Dehumanized World_, 2005; _You Must Set Forth at Dawn: A Memoir_, 2006.

TRANSLATION: _Forest of a Thousand Daemons: A Hunter's Saga_, 1968 (of D. O. Gaunwar's novel _Ogbo Ode Ninu Igbo Irunmale_).

BIBLIOGRAPHY

Jeyifo, Biodun. _Wole Soyinka: History, Poetics, and Postcolonialism._ New York: Cambridge University Press, 2009. A scholarly discussion of five volumes of Soyinka's poetry.

Msiska, Mpalive-Hangson. _Postcolonial Identity in Wole Soyinka._ New York: Rodopi, 2007. Notes how Soyinka's upbringing influenced his sense of identity and discusses his universalism, which has been criticized by other African writers.

Ogunyemi, Yemi D. _The Literary Political Philosophy of Wole Soyinka._ Baltimore: PublishAmerica, 2009. Examines Yoruba literature and philosophy as revealed in the writings of Soyinka.

Tucker, Martin. "African Genesis." Review of _Idanre._ _The Nation_ 10 (November, 1969): 510-512. This review provides commentary on the title poem, "The Hunchback of Dugbe," and "Abiku."

Wright, Derek. _Wole Soyinka Revisted._ New York: Twayne, 1993. Although Wright proclaims that Soyinka is "not a great poet," his criticism of individual poems is detailed and insightful.

Marcia B. Dinneen

T

Rabindranath Tagore

Born: Calcutta, India; May 7, 1861
Died: Calcutta, India; August 7, 1941
Also known as: Rabindranath Thakur

Principal poetry

Saisab sangit, 1881
Sandhya sangit, 1882
Prabhat sangit, 1883
Chabi o gan, 1884
Kari o komal, 1887
Mānashi, 1890
Sonār tari, 1893 (*The Golden Boat*, 1932)
Chitra, 1895
Chaitāli, 1896
Kanika, 1899
Kalpana, 1900
Katha o kahini, 1900
Kshanikā, 1900
Naivedya, 1901
Sisu, 1903 (*The Crescent Moon*, 1913)
Smaran, 1903
Utsarga, 1904
Kheya, 1905
Gitānjali, 1910 (*Gitanjali Song Offerings*, 1912)
The Gardener, 1913
Gitali, 1914
Balāka, 1916 (*A Flight of Swans*, 1955, 1962)
Fruit-Gathering, 1916
Gan, 1916
Stray Birds, 1917
Love's Gift, and Crossing, 1918
Palataka, 1918 (*The Fugitive*, 1921)
Lipika, 1922
Poems, 1922
Sisu bholanath, 1922
The Curse at Farewell, 1924
Prabahini, 1925

Purabi, 1925
Fifteen Poems, 1928
Fireflies, 1928
Mahuya, 1929
Sheaves: Poems and Songs, 1929
Banabani, 1931
The Child, 1931
Parisesh, 1932
Punascha, 1932
Vicitrita, 1933
Bithika, 1935
Ses saptak, 1935
Patraput, 1936, 1938 (English translation, 1969)
Syamali, 1936 (English translation, 1955)
Khapchada, 1937
Prantik, 1938
Senjuti, 1938
Navajatak, 1940
Rogsajya, 1940
Sanai, 1940
Arogya, 1941
Janmadine, 1941
Poems, 1942
Sesh lekha, 1942
The Herald of Spring, 1957
Wings of Death: The Last Poems, 1960
Devouring Love, 1961
A Bunch of Poems, 1966
One Hundred and One, 1967
Last Poems, 1973
Later Poems, 1974
Final Poems, 2001

Other literary forms

Besides more than fifty collections of poetry, Rabindranath Tagore (tuh-GOHR) wrote thirteen novels, ten collections of short stories, more than sixty plays, and numerous volumes of literary criticism, letters, translations, reminiscences, lectures, sermons, travel sketches, philosophy, religion, and politics. In addition, he translated a considerable amount of his own work from its original Bengali into English.

Tagore's drama, which generally tends to be more lyric than dramatic, is best represented by *Visarjan* (pb. 1890; *Sacrifice*, 1917), *Chitrāngadā* (pb. 1892; *Chitra*,

1913), *Prayaschitta* (pr. 1909; atonement), *Rājā* (pb. 1910; *The King of the Dark Chamber*, 1914), *Dākghar* (pb. 1912; *Post Office*, 1914), and *Raktakarabi* (pb. 1924; *Red Oleanders*, 1925). Examples of later plays— *Muktadhārā* (pb. 1922; English translation, 1950), *Natir Pujā* (pb. 1926; *Worship of the Dancing Girl*, 1950), and *Chandālikā* (pr., pb. 1933; English translation, 1938)—were translated by Marjorie Sykes in *Three Plays* (pb. 1950).

Tagore's fiction, which also reflects his lyric bent, sometimes seems to prefigure the "open form." Including some of his best work, his short stories have been compared to those of Guy de Maupassant. Some of his short stories have been translated in *The Hungry Stones, and Other Stories* (1916), *Mashi, and Other Stories* (1918), and *The Runaway, and Other Stories* (1959). *Gora* (1910; English translation, 1924) is usually considered his best novel, but others of interest are *Chokher bāli* (1902; *Binodini*, 1959), *Ghare bāire* (1916; *Home and the World*, 1919), *Chaturanga* (1916; English translation, 1963), *Jogajog* (1929; cross currents), *Shesher kabita* (1929; *Farewell My Friend*, 1946), and *Dui bon* (1933; *Two Sisters*, 1945).

Tagore's nonfictional prose, some of which was originally written as lectures in English, is represented by *Jivansmriti* (1912; *My Reminiscences*, 1917), *Personality* (1917), *Nationalism* (1919), *Creative Unity* (1922), *The Religion of Man* (1931), and *Towards Universal Man* (1961).

ACHIEVEMENTS

Few writers have achieved such fame as came to Rabindranath Tagore when he was awarded the 1913 Nobel Prize in Literature. The first Asian to receive the award, he was viewed in the West as the embodiment of Eastern mystical wisdom. Indian critics at the time, however, often attacked his work, usually for political reasons, even though he did more than any other writer to establish Bengali as a flexible literary language (he was experimenting with it to the end of his life). Perhaps needing money for the school he had established at Santiniketan, Tagore took advantage of his fame to churn out English translations. Although he admitted his limited skill in English, he was shrewd enough to satisfy the sentimental streak in his English-speaking

audiences. The combination of modest skill and banality was devastating for his poetry. His so-called prose poems—usually paraphrases, though they occasionally break into Whitmanesque free verse—are noteworthy examples of what is lost in the translation of poetry. Eventually, these translations caught up with his reputation, which began sinking in the West about the time that graduates of Santiniketan began producing books on their *Gurudev*. One of these former students, Aurobindo Bose, has produced the best English translations of Tagore's poetry now available.

As Jane Addams (of Hull House) noted, Tagore was "at once a poet, a philosopher, a humanitarian, an educator," and as Hermann Hesse said, Tagore's reputation was built in part on "the rich heritage of ancient Indian philosophy." Similarly, Tagore's work reflects certain native literary traditions, such as Indian drama and the *Baul* folk songs, which are alien to the West. Finally, where his poetry is concerned, it should be borne in mind that Tagore was a songwriter (he composed about two thousand songs), that he set some of his poems to music, and that in Bengali his poetry has rich musical qualities—rhythm, rhyme, alliteration, assonance—that accompany the words, images, and ideas. All these factors must be carefully weighed in evaluating Tagore's overall achievement.

Otherwise, each individual work must be considered separately. Tagore wrote too much, so there is repetition and wide variation in quality, especially in his poetry. (Apparently he needed a critical audience off which to bounce his poems, but he found it neither in his Indian milieu nor in the adulatory West.) For example, the same period that produced *Gitanjali Song Offerings* and *A Flight of Swans* also produced the soppy poems in *The Crescent Moon*. Besides *Gitanjali Song Offerings* and *A Flight of Swans*, perhaps his finest works are the short stories translated in *The Hungry Stones, and Other Stories*. Readers of English would also do well to rediscover his lectures, wherein Tagore speaks for peace, internationalism, and understanding—themes prominent in his literary work.

BIOGRAPHY

Rabindranath Tagore was born into a wealthy, influential, and culturally active Brahmin family. The name

Tagore is an English corruption of the title *Thakur* (that is, Brahmin), and the name Rabindranath means "lord of the sun" (*rabi* means "the sun"). Tagore's father was Maharishi (Great Sage) Devendranath Tagore, an important religious writer and leader of Brahmo Samaj (Society of God), a new monotheistic religion founded on a return to the Upanishads and progressive political ideas. A response both to orthodox Hinduism (characterized by idolatry, the caste system, suttee, and similar oppressive practices) and to Western culture (especially Christianity), the reformist Brahmo Samaj virtually defined the development of Tagore's own thought.

Despite his apparent advantages, Tagore, the youngest of fourteen children, had a difficult childhood. His father was involved with his activities as a maharishi, and Tagore's mother was sickly (she died when he was thirteen). The infant Rabi was turned over to the care of servants, who simplified their duties by confining him within rooms and chalk circles. He did not last long in any of the several schools he attended, consequently receiving little formal education. He was saved by his father and family activities. At the age of twelve, he accompanied his father, whom he idolized, on an extended journey to Santiniketan (his father's rural retreat, about one hundred miles west of Calcutta), Amritsar, and the Himalayas, where they lived in a mountain hut and where his father instructed him. On his return to Calcutta, the young Tagore gradually became involved in family activities.

The family was ostracized by orthodox Hindus, thus leaving the Tagores free to do as they pleased. As a result, the family home, Jorasanko Palace, was the cultural center of Calcutta, buzzing with more than a hundred inhabitants as well as a steady flow of distinguished visitors—reformist religious leaders, nationalist politicians, writers, artists, and musicians. The evenings were filled with musical performances, plays, readings, and discussions that lasted far into the night. Even the women were involved, further scandalizing the neighbors, who still practiced purdah (the formal seclusion of women from public view). The lively teenage Tagore plunged into this activity, contributing songs, readings, and critical observations. When, in 1877, the family started its own monthly magazine, *Bharati*, the sixteen-year-old Tagore helped edit it and

Rabindranath Tagore (©The Nobel Foundation)

was a main contributor. What better education could one find for Tagore the writer (not to mention Tagore the singer, songwriter, actor, critic, politician, philosopher, and artist)?

One more try at formal education occurred in 1878, when Tagore was sent to Great Britain to prepare to study law, first at a school in Brighton, then at University College, London. He continued to make contributions to *Bharati*, expressing his dislike for the British people and his love for British literature (especially William Shakespeare and the Romantics). After two years, Tagore returned home, and in 1883, a marriage was arranged for him with Mrinalini Devi (then only nine years old), whom he called Nalini. In 1891, they settled down in Shelidah, where Tagore's father assigned him to manage the family estates and where Tagore for the first time came into direct contact with the Indian countryside and peasant life. This period was an eye-opener for Tagore, providing him with some of his best material for short stories. (For example, he rescued a tenant's wife who was being swept down a flooding river, but did she thank him? No, she was trying to commit suicide.) Sympathy for the conditions of peasant life also deepened his involvement in the growing Indian Nationalist movement, for which he wrote and made speeches. When the Nationalist movement eventually became violent, however, he broke off his involvement and withdrew to Santiniketan (which, appropriately, means "abode of peace"). Later, he would come to believe that nationalism is one of the great evils of the modern world.

In 1901, Tagore began his career as an educator, starting a school at Santiniketan. It is ironic, but understandable, that the dropout should become the educator; some of his five children were of school age, and, recalling his school experience, he had his own ideas about how to teach them. These ideas he put into practice at Santiniketan. He was also responding to the conditions around him, seeking to uplift his countrymen in a way that did not involve violence. Besides, there was always something of the teacher in Tagore, as shown by his campaign to enlighten first his own countrymen and later the West. The teacher comes out frequently (though indirectly) in his poetry, in which he sometimes seems to adopt the stance of the Great Sage. Above all, Tagore was interested in seeing certain ideas prevail, as proclaimed by the motto of Santiniketan: "Santam, sivam, advaitam" (peace, good, union).

The early years at Santiniketan were marred for Tagore by great personal loss: In 1902 his wife died, in 1904 his eldest daughter, in 1905 his father, and in 1907 his youngest son. However, the deepening process of meditating on these losses produced his best poetry, *Gitanjali Song Offerings* and *A Flight of Swans*. The school was also in constant need of money, which eventually required him to make several fund-raising and lecture trips to the United States, Great Britain, and the European Continent. These journeys established him as an ambassador to the West—a role he found much easier to fill after he won the 1913 Nobel Prize in Literature. Everywhere he went, he was received as the Great Sage, and he was awarded numerous honors (such as a British knighthood in 1915). He visited the Soviet Union and Japan, both of which he admired, but he crit-

icized Communist suppression of individual rights and the militant nationalism of the Japanese. He was especially appalled by Japanese efforts to conquer China.

Tagore's last years were spent in traveling, in expanding the Santiniketan complex, in practicing a new art (painting), and in pointing the world toward peace. In 1922, he established Sriniketan (abode of grace), an institute for agriculture and rural reconstruction, and Visva-Bharati (universal voice), an international university for bringing the message of the East to the West. His paintings were exhibited in Europe to favorable reviews. He was disappointed in his work for peace, thinking that nations that had endured one world war would not want another. The 1930's were increasingly depressing for him, and he died in 1941, just as World War II was reaching its full incarnation.

ANALYSIS

The main theme of Rabindranath Tagore's poetry is the essential unity (or continuity) of all creation, which is also the main theme of the ancient Hindu Upanishads. Indeed, a brief summary of Hindu belief provides a useful introduction to Tagore's work. According to Hindu thought, the only absolute, unchanging, eternal thing is Brahman, the supreme being or world soul who forms the essence of everything. In living things, the essence of Brahman is known as Atman, or soul. Brahman operates through three aspects: Brahma, the creator; Siva, the destroyer; and Vishnu, the preserver or renewer. Brahma's work is finished, but Siva and Vishnu are necessary for change, and change is necessary so that living things may grow toward union with Brahman, a perfect, changeless state, nirvana. Few, if any, achieve nirvana in one lifetime, so reincarnation is necessary. In each successive incarnation, one improves one's status in the next through good karma or deeds (broadly interpreted as actions, thoughts, or faith).

The questions raised by Hindu belief may be ignored here (for example, why would Brahman create something imperfect in the first place?); so also may certain negative social implications (such as the potential for inaction, the caste system, and unconcern for the individual human life). Instead, what should be noticed is the positive emphasis of Hinduism, in contrast to Western thought as characterized by the old Germanic notion that everything is moving toward *Götterdämmerung*; the Christian emphasis on Original Sin, evil, and Hell; the masked versions of human sacrifice. It is the positive implications of Hindu belief that Tagore develops in his poetry. For example, his imagery—dwelling on sunrises and sunsets, flowers and their scents, songs and musical instruments, the beautiful deodar tree (*deodár* meaning "divine wood"), the majestic Himalayas—is a constant reminder that creation is charged with divinity: Beauty and majesty are concrete manifestations of Brahman. Change, natural disasters, and death are necessary for renewal, which will come. All people have divine souls, so they should tolerate, respect, and love one another. The advantaged should help the disadvantaged; thereby, they both rise toward Brahman. The individual should strive to live in such a way as to throw off impurities and achieve the essence of divinity within the self. The development of these and related themes can be traced throughout Tagore's oeuvre.

GITANJALI SONG OFFERINGS

Published in 1910, *Gitanjali Song Offerings* is Tagore's most popular work. The English edition, published in 1912, includes translations not only from the original *Gitānjali* but also from other collections, particularly *Naivedya* (offerings). As light work to keep his mind occupied, Tagore did the translations himself while he was convalescing from an illness at Shelidah and on board a ship for Great Britain. He showed them to British friends who wanted to read his work. They in turn showed the translations to William Butler Yeats, and the result was English publication followed by the 1913 Nobel Prize in Literature. Aware of the undistinguished quality of his translations, Tagore himself could never understand why he was rash enough to do them or why they created such a sensation.

Sometimes compared to the Book of Psalms, *Gitanjali Song Offerings* explores the personal relationship between the poet and divinity. This divinity he calls Jivandevata, which he often translates as "Lord of my life" or "life of my life" but also refers to as "my God," "King," "Father," "Mother," "lover," "friend," and "innermost one." The range of terms here suggests the varied associations of Jivandevata and also the conventional metaphors Tagore generally uses to develop his relationship with Jivandevata. Perhaps the most nu-

merous poems are those in which, like John Donne or Saint Teresa of Ávila, Tagore speaks of the deity as a lover with whom he longs to be united. In Song 60 (numbers refer to the English edition), Tagore varies the formula somewhat. He describes a woman who dwells in purdah within his heart. Many men have come asking for her, but none has seen her face, because she waits only for God. The woman represents the spark of divinity in Tagore which longs to be reunited with its source, and the purdah suggests its loneliness and purity. The divinity within inspires Tagore's songs and motivates him to lead a pure life, but he confesses that involvement in commonplace events sometimes creates a smoke screen that obscures the divinity within and without. The commonplace, however, also has its divinity. God is to be found not only in the temple but also with the workers in the fields. Because divinity runs through everything, even the metaphors that Tagore uses to describe God have an element of literal truth.

The most interesting poems in *Gitanjali Song Offerings* are a group dealing with death. Songs 86 and 87 are about a family member—probably the poet's wife—whom death has taken. Although heartbroken by her death, Tagore welcomes the visit of God's "servant" and "messenger," and seeking her in the oneness of the universe has brought Tagore closer to God. Thus reconciled, Tagore welcomes his own death as "the fulfillment of life." His dying will be like a bride meeting her bridegroom on the wedding night or like a feeding babe switching from the right breast to the left breast of its mother. Meanwhile, his soul is like "a flock of homesick cranes," on the wing day and night to reach "their mountain nests."

A FLIGHT OF SWANS

Perhaps Tagore's best work, *A Flight of Swans*, takes its title from the image on which *Gitanjali Song Offerings* ends. Thematically, *A Flight of Swans* also takes up where *Gitanjali Song Offerings* ends. Although *A Flight of Swans* continues to develop the personal relationship between the poet and divinity, there is a new emphasis on the impersonal workings of divinity throughout creation. The dual emphasis can be seen in the opening poem of the English edition, the title poem, wherein the flight of swans breaking the silence of the evening symbolizes not only the aspiration of the human soul but also the yearning of inanimate nature for "the Beyond." Even the mountains and deodar trees long to spread their wings like the "homeless bird" inside the breast of Tagore and "countless others." The images of movement and yearning here also serve to introduce the theme of change so prominent in *A Flight of Swans*.

For Tagore, the abstract notion of change is embodied in the dance of Siva, the destroyer, who is featured in several poems. Sometimes called Rudra (the terrible one), Siva brings violence, destruction, and death. To scholars of Sigmund Freud, Tagore's worship of Siva might sound like an Eastern version of the death wish, and his reveling in "the sea of pain" and "the sport of death" might repel squeamish readers. Nevertheless, there is a reason for Tagore's embrace of resounding agony. The dance of Siva purges the cosmological systems. It prevents the flow of "gross Matter" from backing up and putrefying, "renews and purifies" creation in "the bath of death," and speeds souls onward toward nirvana. The only thing which survives Siva's dance is immortal art, as represented by the Taj Mahal. Becoming Siva's partner, Tagore aligns himself with the young rather than the old, with the unknown rather than the known, with wandering rather than home, with movement rather than stagnancy.

With its focus on movement and change, on the cyclic nature of things, *A Flight of Swans* breathes the same spirit as Percy Bysshe Shelley's "Ode to the West Wind": If Siva comes, can Vishnu be far behind? Indeed, Tagore hoped that Vishnu, the preserver and renewer, would come soon. Tagore wrote *A Flight of Swans* at the outset of World War I, and the poems reflect his awareness of the war's catastrophic violence. Once the war started, he hoped that it would at least bring about some good results—that it would clean out the evils of the old world system and bring about a new order of peace and brotherhood.

PATRAPUT

Patraput means "a cup of leaves." The poems in this collection are the leaves shed by the poet's tree of life during his old age. *Patraput* is also a reminder that Tagore wrote poetry on subjects other than religion. He was a love poet, especially in his early career, a nature poet (*Banabani*) concentrating on trees and plants, and he even wrote a collection of humorous poems that he

called *Khapchada* (a little offbeat). *Patraput* represents not only the mellowness of Tagore's old age but also the variety of his subjects. There are even a few love poems from the seventy-five-year-old poet.

Many of the poems in *Patraput* celebrate subtle effects. With humor and sensitivity, two poems (2 and 7) explore the idleness of holidays. At home by himself in the countryside (probably Santiniketan), the poet has trouble adjusting to doing nothing but feels himself better off than vacationers scrambling through railway stations. In the surrounding scenes of nature that Tagore pauses to observe, God provides him with a "change of air" and a visit to "the eternal ocean" for free. Meanwhile, he knows his "return ticket" will soon expire and he will have to return to the workaday world, "to return here from here itself." These two poems and others contain some attractive descriptions of nature. Another excellent example is Poem 9, which traces the coming and passing of a storm. A number of the poems also trace shifts of mood, from one season to another, from one time of day to another, from one scene to another. In some of these small effects, there are suggestions of bigger themes. For example, there are intimations of the poet's coming death ("return ticket") in the description, as though he is sinking slowly into the placid Indian countryside. The epiphany in Poem 1, where the poet climbs a mountaintop to see the sun setting on one hand and the moon rising on the other, is reminiscent of William Wordsworth's topping of Mount Snowdon in *The Prelude: Or, The Growth of a Poet's Mind* (1850).

Another interesting group of poems in *Patraput* consists of those containing social commentary. In Poem 6, Tagore urges the reader ("O thou hospitable") to invite in the destitute pilgrim so that the poor fellow can rise above his mere struggle for existence. In Poem 15, Tagore, himself ostracized when a child, identifies with the untouchables who are prohibited from entering temples, and with the itinerant *Baul* singers, who sing that God is "the Man of my heart." Like them, Tagore has no caste, no temple, no religion except the religion of Man. Poem 16 is a lament for Africa, ransacked for slaves by the purveyors of Christian "civilization." Their phony belief in religion is duplicated in the modern era by the militarists who seek Buddha's blessings for their killing (apparently a slap at Japanese aggression in Manchuria).

CRITICISM OF FORMAL RELIGION

As the unflattering references to Hindus, Christians, and Buddhists indicate, Tagore had no more enthusiasm for formal religion than he had for formal education. Nevertheless, along with such figures as Gerard Manley Hopkins and T. S. Eliot, Tagore is a leading religious poet of the modern era. The social commentary in *Patraput* marks the final stage of his spiritual journey. In *Gitanjali Song Offerings*, he is concerned with his personal fate, his individual relationship to God. In *A Flight of Swans*, he explores the impersonal workings of divinity through the terrible dance of Siva; and in *Patraput*, he shows that religious belief must ultimately be expressed through concern (and action) for one's fellow men. With his "religion of Man," Tagore ends up in a position very similar to Western Humanism, but it is a position that retains its ties to ancient religious belief, belief summed up in the teaching of the humble *Baul* singers that God is "the Man of my heart."

OTHER MAJOR WORKS

LONG FICTION: *Bau-Thakuranir Hat*, 1883; *Rajarshi*, 1887; *Chokher bāli*, 1902 (*Binodini*, 1959); *Naukadubi*, 1906 (*The Wreck*, 1921); *Gora*, 1910 (English translation, 1924); *Chaturanga*, 1916 (English translation, 1963); *Ghare bāire*, 1916 (*Home and the World*, 1919); *Jogajog*, 1929; *Shesher kabita*, 1929 (*Farewell My Friend*, 1946); *Dui bon*, 1933 (*Two Sisters*, 1945).

SHORT FICTION: *The Hungry Stones, and Other Stories*, 1916; *Mashi, and Other Stories*, 1918; *Stories from Tagore*, 1918; *Broken Ties, and Other Stories*, 1925; *The Runaway, and Other Stories*, 1959; *Selected Short Stories*, 1991 (translated with an introduction by William Radice).

PLAYS: *Prakritir Pratishodh*, pb. 1884 (verse play; *Sanyasi: Or, The Ascetic*, 1917); *Rāja o Rāni*, pb. 1889 (verse play; *The King and the Queen*, 1918); *Visarjan*, pb. 1890 (verse play; based on his novel *Rajarshi; Sacrifice*, 1917); *Chitrāngadā*, pb. 1892 (verse play; *Chitra*, 1913); *Prayaschitta*, pr. 1909 (based on his novel *Bau-Thakuranir Hat*); *Rāja*, pb. 1910 (*The King of the Dark Chamber*, 1914); *Dākghar*, pb. 1912 (*The Post Office*, 1914); *Phālguni*, pb. 1916 (*The Cycle of Spring*, 1917); *Arupratan*, pb. 1920 (revision of his play *Rāja*); *Muktadhārā*, pb. 1922 (English translation, 1950); *Raktakarabi*, pb. 1924 (*Red Oleanders*, 1925); *Chirakumār Sabhā*, pb. 1926; *Natir Pujā*, pb. 1926 (*Worship of the Dancing Girl*, 1950); *Sesh Rakshā*, pb. 1928; *Paritrān*, pb. 1929 (revision of *Prayaschitta*); *Tapati*, pb. 1929 (revision of *Rāja o Rāni*); *Bānsari*, pb. 1933; *Chandālikā*, pr., pb. 1933 (English translation, 1938); *Nritya-natya Chitrāngadā*, pb. 1936 (revision of his play *Chitrāngadā*); *Nritya-natya Chandālikā*, pb. 1938 (revision of his play *Chandālikā*); *Three Plays*, 1950.

NONFICTION: *Jivansmriti*, 1912 (*My Reminiscences*, 1917); *Sadhana: The Realisation of Life*, 1913; *Nationalism*, 1917; *Personality*, 1917; *Glimpses of Bengal*, 1921; *Greater India*, 1921; *Creative Unity*, 1922; *Talks in China*, 1925; *Lectures and Addresses*, 1928; *Letters to a Friend*, 1928; *The Religion of Man*, 1931; *Mahatmaji and the Depressed Humanity*, 1932; *The Religion of an Artist*, 1933; *Man*, 1937; *Chhelebela*, 1940 (*My Boyhood Days*, 1940); *Sabhyatar Samkat*, 1941 (*Crisis in Civilization*, 1941); *Towards Universal Man*, 1961.

MISCELLANEOUS: *Collected Poems and Plays*, 1936; *A Tagore Reader*, 1961.

BIBLIOGRAPHY

Das Gupta, Uma. *Rabindranath Tagore: A Biography*. New York: Oxford University Press, 2004. A biography of Tagore, based largely on his letters, that reveals him as a poet and writer with a social conscience.

_____, ed. *The Oxford India Tagore: Selected Writings on Education and Nationalism*. New York: Oxford University Press, 2009. An examination of Tagore's views on education and nationalism and his relationship with Oxford.

Dutta Gupta, Reeta. *Rabindranath Tagore: The Poet Sublime*. New Delhi: Rupa, 2002. A biography that examines the life and works of Tagore, with emphasis on his poetry.

Ghosh, Dipali, comp. *Bengali Works of Rabindranath Tagore into English: A Bibliography*. Calcutta: Firma KLM, 2008. A bibliography of the works written by Tagore in Bengali and translated into English.

Ivbulis, Viktors. *Tagore: East and West Cultural*

Unity. Calcutta: Rabindra Bharati University, 1999. The author looks at the influence of both the West and the East in Tagore's work. Bibliography.

Nandī, Sudhīrakumāra. *Art and Aesthetics of Rabindra Nath Tagore.* Calcutta: Asiatic Society, 1999. Nandī analyzes the Tagore's aesthetics as expressed in his writings. Bibliography and index.

Nandy, Ashis. *The Illegitimacy of Nationalism: Rabindranath Tagore and the Politics of Self.* New York: Oxford University Press, 1994. This study focuses on the political and social views of Tagore as demonstrated by his life and writings. Bibliography and index.

_____. *Return from Exile.* New York: Oxford University Press, 1998. An analysis of Tagore's political writing which puts him in the context of India's move in the 1920's toward nationalism. This, in turn, illuminates some of the philosophy and themes in his other writing.

Saha, Panchanan. *Tagore and USA.* Calcutta: Biswabiksha, 2009. An account of Tagore's life that focuses on his travels in the United States and relations with Americans.

Sen Gupta, Kalyan. *The Philosophy of Rabindranath Tagore.* Burlington, Vt.: Ashgate, 2005. A comprehensive introduction to Tagore's poetry and essays and the way they relate to his philosophy, politics and religion.

Harold Branam

TAO QIAN

Born: Xinyang (now in Henan), China; 365
Died: Xinyang (now in Henan), China; 427
Also known as: T'ao Ch'ien; T'ao Yüan-ming; Tao Yuanming

PRINCIPAL POETRY

T'ao the Hermit: Sixty Poems by T'ao Ch'ien (365-427), 1952 (William Acker, translator)
The Poems of T'ao Ch'ien, 1953 (Lily Pao-hu Chang and Marjorie Sinclair, translators)

The Poetry of T'ao Ch'ien, 1970 (James Robert Hightower, translator)
Complete Works of Tao Yuanming, 1992
Selected Poems, 1993

OTHER LITERARY FORMS

Tao Qian (tow chee-EHN) is known primarily as a poet. Among his extant works are two *fu* rhyme-prose compositions (that is, rhythmic and occasionally rhymed prose), the renowned "Return" in *ci* form (another quasi-poetic genre), a letter to an acquaintance, prefaces, seven *can* collophons (*envois*), a biographical note on an official colleague, several essays, obituaries, and the celebrated "Record of the Peach Grove."

ACHIEVEMENTS

Probably more has been written about Tao Qian, in whatever language, than about any other Chinese poet. Studies by Japanese scholars alone, to whom Tao Qian most strongly appealed, run into many hundreds of titles. Tao Qian is primarily associated with the foundations of the *tianyuan*, or "pastoral" (literally, "cultivated fields and orchards") school of poetry (as opposed to the rugged *shanshui* "mountains and waters" landscapes of his contemporary, the celebrated nobleman Xie Lingyun, 385-433). The unadorned directness of his poetic diction and the innocent, touching sentiment of his anchorite forbearance have perennially appealed to the oversophisticated Chinese bureaucrat-litterateur. Writing in the prevailing pentameter line of his day, Tao Qian was the first to exploit the *shi* lyric form extensively for such topics as wine (which he tirelessly celebrated) and the idiosyncrasies of his own children. These eventually became favorite themes in Tang and later poetry. As James Robert Hightower has observed in *The Poetry of T'ao Ch'ien*, "even the shortest and most selective list of famous Chinese poets would have to find a place for Tao Qian," and his poetry above that of all others appears the most frequently in anthologies of Chinese verse.

BIOGRAPHY

Biographies in the Chinese dynastic histories are principally concerned with their subject's official career and influence on national politics. Since Tao Qian's service career was minimal, and grudging at that, little contemporaneous record was kept, and the few remarks about him were included in the section on hermits, rather than in the "literati" category. His various sobriquets, too, reflect his preference for eremitic life. Later efforts to construct, or contrive, a respectable account befitting the life of a universally beloved poet relied largely on anecdote and on Tao Qian's autobiographical self-evaluations, such as "Biography of Mr. Five Willows" (a nom de plume describing his rustic environment). By his own account, Tao Qian was a quiet, unassuming man. He enjoyed scholarship but took no pleasure in pedantic obscurities. He would have his readers believe that he was a great drunkard, and indeed the greater part of the official record consists of stories illustrating his love of tippling, noting, for example, his insistence on cultivating brewing grain rather than food, however destitute his family. Even the memoir bringing him into friendly association with the then-ascendant court poet Yan Yazhi focuses on wine, relating how Tao Qian had deposited a large sum of money given him by Yen in a local wine shop.

Tao Qian lived during the decline of the Eastern Jin regime (317-420) of the Sima clan on a small farm south of the Yangzi River. His forebears had once been eminent officials, but the family had fallen on hard times, and Tao Qian lacked the all-important connections at court that would have secured for him, at the outset, an entrée into higher echelons of the administration. He was assigned various minor provincial posts, but he became disgusted with the pervasive corruption of the regime and with the petty drudgery of local officers and resigned rather than "crook his back for a five-peck salary." Thus, for most of his life he was a sort of gentleman farmer, living in relative poverty but wryly content with his wife and children, wine, chrysanthemums, friends, stringless lute, and poetry.

ANALYSIS

Scholars of Chinese literature and literati throughout the ages have unanimously admired Tao Qian's poetry. Some eighty-eight of his poems survive. These are of varying length and in tetrasyllabic or pentasyllabic lines. Many are prefaced by an introduction explaining the circumstances under which they were composed.

Tao Qian found no place for the artificial *yuefu* ("music bureau") compositions popular in his time—lyrics written to ancient tunes and titles which dictated theme, mood, and style. He did, however, on his own terms produce a set of poems "imitating" or "in the style of" earlier compositions.

Typical rhetoric describes Tao Qian's moral sentiments as "far-reaching waves, and lofty soaring clouds." Other famous poet-critics were drawn to imitate Tao Qian's style, notably the eleventh century poet Su Dongpo (also known as Su Shi), who wrote a set of 120 matching verses. A focus of controversy to this day is the dissenting judgment of the sixth century Zhong Hong, who, in his *Shipin* ("classification of poets"), placed Tao Qian in the second of three categories of poets because, in an age of florid ornamentation, Tao Qian's work disdained empty embellishments.

In the development of Chinese literature, Tao Qian is most securely associated with the flourishing of the *dianyuan* ("pastoral") genre, the embryonic origins of which stem from the tetrasyllabic odes of the great eleventh to seventh century B.C.E. canon. Poetry, thereafter, particularly during the Tang (618-907) and the Song (960-1279) dynasties, was imbued with his influence.

Although unwilling to compromise his principles for a corrupt regime, Tao Qian was acutely aware of the Confucian moral obligation of the literate gentleman to make his abilities available to the state. A number of his poems recall this duty, and they laud members of his own clan and other eminent bureaucrats who contributed their energies to public administration: "In hearing lawsuits he is just/ A hundred miles enjoy his help." He had had no taste for office as a youth, he says, but he too had tried to be of service, "fallen by mischance into the dusty net/ And thirteen years away from home." Such occupation was intolerable for him "in a time of decadence, when one longs for the ancient kings." Far too long, he had been a "caged prisoner." In the end, he was "not one to volunteer his services" and would "not be bound by love of rank," "scorning the role of opportunist." On the topic of posthumous fame, he was ambivalent. He asks, Daoist-like, what is the use of an honored name if it costs a lifetime of deprivation, yet he also suggests that fame may endure as an inspiration for a thousand years. Seeking solace for what he considered his own lifetime of failure, however, he stresses the transience of fame rather than its inspirational legacy.

DESTITUTION

In versifying the destitution to which he was reduced, Tao Qian indulged in no bleak self-pity. Virtually all his poems and many of his famous prose works mention his poverty, but he counts his blessings—and by Chinese standards, then and now, he must have been relatively self-sufficient. He owned a few acres of land and an ill-thatched cottage with "four or five" rooms (sometimes interpreted "as four plus five" rooms), shaded by elms and willows at the back, and with peaches and plums stretching out in front. He cultivated (or, more likely, oversaw the farming of) hemp, mulberry, and beans, and daily extended the area under his plow, delighting in the pleasures of the woods and fields.

Occasionally resorting to hyperbole, he claims in his poems that when his crops did badly, hunger drove him to begging, knocking on doors and fumbling for words. His house burned down several times, pests decimated his stock of grain, and even in winter, his family slept without covers, longing for the dawn. On a more cheerful note, his hut is repaired; plowing and spinning supply his needs; and if he is diligent in the fields, he will not be cheated. In fact, two poems specifically praise the farmer's lot, describing how new shoots enfold new life, and how labor, too, gives joy. Another dozen or so verses laud the "impoverished gentleman" along with other humble but principled men of ancient days. A long lament mourns "gentlemen born out of their times," who relinquished glory and took pleasure in poverty and low condition.

WINE

One consolation in Tao Qian's rustic plight was wine. A major part of his official biography and of his autobiographical comments focuses on his tippling, and some critics complain that his poetry revolves around little else. Certainly, no other poet before him had ever sung the praises of alcohol so prolifically and insistently, and in this, Tao Qian set a precedent for a subgenre that was to catch the imagination of later poets, notably Li Bo in the eighth century and Su Dongpo in the eleventh. Like poverty, wine is mentioned in virtually every one of Tai Qian's poems: Twenty poems

were written "after drinking wine"; another describes "drinking alone in the rainy season"; yet another long poem gives "an account of wine"; and there is a rather pathetic poem in which Tao Qian confides that he wishes he could stop drinking—though the pathos of this admission is attenuated by the form of the verse, a game wherein the word "stop" appears in each of the twenty lines.

However undesirable Tao Qian's apparent alcoholism may seem to the modern Western reader, no odium attached itself to the poet in his time. The Chinese heritage better appreciated the spiritual liberation achieved by mild inebriation and credited much of the innocent genius of Tao Qian's poetry to this condition. Later critics, too, have defended Tao Qian by arguing that such drunkenness was a timeworn ploy in China (the antics of the poet Ruan Ji in the third century constitute a formidable example), to a large extent feigned to avoid the jeopardy of involvement in political machinations.

CHRYSANTHEMUMS

Almost as much as with wine, Tao Qian was fascinated by the chrysanthemum, a flower that has come to be associated with his poetry. The chrysanthemum bloom survives the blight of autumn; as the last flower of the year, it represented for Tao Qian his own fortitude in adversity. So too appear in his lines the cypress and the pine—evergreens that symbolize Confucian moral steadfastness.

Tao Qian found great comfort in his family. He was the first Chinese poet to record his feelings about his children so freely, and in doing so he left to posterity some of the most appealing lines in the Chinese literary heritage. In "Finding Fault with My Sons," the poet complains about the laziness and self-indulgence of his five boys: The nine-year-old, for example, wants only pears and chestnuts, and the thirteen-year-olds cannot even count to their age. It is Tao Qian's ability to capture casual moments from childhood, however—the toddler peeking through a crack in the door, anticipating his father's return from the fields—that has given his poems on children a timeless appeal.

RURAL DELIGHTS

Tao Qian's pastoral poetry typified the *dianyuan* genre. Rather than tramping in climbing boots among the wooded peaks and precipices of a Jiangsu-Zhejiang estate, as did Xie Lingyun, Tao Qian would sit quietly at his casement window in his tumbledown thatched cottage and contemplate the passing scene, sip his wine, think of old and absent friends, and muse on his approaching old age. Gentle delight in the rural community fills his verse, rather than the wonder of nature's vast power and magnificence that erupts from Xie Lingyun's nature poetry. Noteworthy, too, is the absence from Tao Qian's diction of the color, glitter, mysticism, classical obscurantism, and pedantic reference and allusion of the overrefined, overembellished poetry then in vogue—in particular the unctuous congratulatory court verse of his friend, Yan Yanzhi.

In the most simple, natural language, Tao Qian writes about the dense, hovering clouds, and the fine rain at dusk that settles on the road, making it impassable. These, typically, are static images, reinforced by the absence of boat or carriage that might bring visiting friends. Movement lies more in the new blossoms springing forth, eliciting the emotions of a sensitive observer. Still-life landscapes depict new grains and the waters of a wide lake stretching endlessly into the distance. Herbs and flowers grow in rows, over which trees and bamboo cast their shade. "Interior" scenes show a cittern (stringed instrument) across a bench and a jug half-filled with muddy wine.

Time passes in the pell-mell revolution of the seasons. Blossoms are dead by morning; the cicada's mournful chirp heralds the fading of summer's heat; plum and peach of springtime give way to autumn's chrysanthemum; one sees migrating geese and notes the morning cockcrow. Frosts wither the crops, and evening dew soaks the poet's gown. His years slip away, his hair turns gray, and his children mature. As the sun sets, a torch serves in place of a costly candle, and if the company is congenial, dawn arrives too soon. Thousand-year cares may be forgotten; tomorrow need not concern a person in his or her enjoyment of the moment.

Tao Qian's poems further adumbrate a kind of farmer's almanac, detailing the activities of his daily life. There is habitual drinking, but the poet also writes of hitching up his wagon at early dawn and starting along the road to his plowing and weeding. He dis-

cusses with the locals the prospects for the harvest of mulberry and hemp. Tired, staff in hand, he returns home by a path twisting through the bushes, pausing to bathe his feet in a mountain stream. He digs a well for water, and plucks a wild chrysanthemum by a bank. For leisure, there are books wherein to discover heroic models from the past who may inspire him in his adversity. As a series of thirteen poems reveals, he especially delights in the fantasies and adventures of the imaginative *Shan hai jing* (date unknown; *The Classic of Mountains and Seas*, 2000) and the magic and marvels of *Mu Tianzi zhuan* (c. fourth century B.C.E.; travels of King Mu). Always he sings of his contentment, however poor: how neat his garden is, and how glad he is to have relinquished worldly affairs.

CLASSICAL PHILOSOPHICAL VIEWS

The philosophical views that Tao Qian espoused were entirely classical. Although he lived within the shadow of Mount Lu, the great monastic seat of Hui Yuan's White Lotus sect of Buddhism, to which Xie Lingyun and other intellectual literati had been massively attracted, Tao Qian's works exhibit no interest in the newly introduced faith—celibacy and abstention were hardly characteristic of him. The popular Daoism of the time, too, with its mysticism and dilettante metaphysical speculation and searches for elixirs of immortality seems to have touched him but little, and he both doubts and eschews the labors and regimens recommended for the attainment of transcendent sagehood.

DEATH

In addition, death itself did not seem to frighten Tao Qian. He concludes his long discourse on "Substance, Shadow, and Spirit" with the simple attitude, "When it is time to go, then we shall simply go—there is nothing, after all, that we can do about it." Life, he explains, is nothing but a shadow play, which in the end reverts to nothingness: There is no immortality, no afterlife, no rebirth. Indeed, the primitive concepts he expresses smack most strongly of the early Daoism of Laozi (sixth century B.C.E.) and Zhuangzi (third century B.C.E.).

If frequency of citation is a criterion, then Tao Qian's favorite source of classical philosophical reference were the Confucian *Lunyu* (later sixth-early fifth centuries B.C.E.; *The Analects*, 1861) a collection of aphorisms attributed to Confucius and compiled some two centuries after his death. Tao Qian was especially observant of passages wherein the Master sanctioned retirement from officialdom during the administration of a corrupt and unworthy regime, doubtless to assuage his own pangs of conscience. The heroes who appear in his "Impoverished Gentlemen," drawn from philosophies and histories through the third century Han Dynasty, also exemplify the person of pure principle, who, like himself, would rather eke out an existence in humble obscurity than strive for empty glories in sycophantic court service.

One often anthologized verse exemplifies these various elements of Tao Qian's work and thought. The poem is dated in the ninth month of the year 410, after the rice harvest, and located in some "western field":

> Man's life may conform to the Way,
> But clothing and food are indeed fundamental.
> If no provision be made for them,
> How can one seek peace?
> At the opening of springtime, I took care of
> the ordinary jobs,
> And the harvest has turned out considerable.
>
> . . . .
>
> My four limbs in truth so weary,
>
> . . . .
>
> Far, far though the mind of Chü and Ni be,
> A thousand years I still sense affinity with them.
> Would that things be forever thus:
> It is not plowing the fields that I complain of!

Tao Qian affirms that mortal life is bound by morality, but, echoing the Confucian rationalist, Mencius, he realizes that the basis of ethical behavior is material sustenance. The life of the producer of these essential commodities is not an easy one, subject as it is to wearisome toil and the exigencies of the natural world. Well enough he appreciates the attitudes of the plowmen Zhangzhu and Jie, who rejected the overtures of Confucius and his disciple Zilu to engage them in discourse (a clever closure balancing the Confucian sentiments of the opening). Indeed, it is not the productive plowing of which Tao Qian complains. Rather, he implies, he grieves over the political situation, for the men of power and status have reneged on their mandate of moral leadership.

UTOPIA

Tao Qian describes his vision of utopia in his renowned "Peach Blossom Spring," the story of a fisherman who loses his way, enters a flowering peach grove, and comes upon a lost society—refugees from the rapacious Qin regime (221-206 B.C.E.). He remains there for several days, entertained by the inhabitants, and although enjoined to secrecy, upon his return home he reports his experience to the authorities. Searches, however, fail to rediscover the location of the peach grove.

As described in the narrative, Tao Qian's perfect society enjoys broad plains of rich fields and ponds and substantial dwellings. Well-tended paths traverse the fields, where mulberry and bamboo grow. Courtyards are stocked with domestic animals; the people dress unpretentiously and are happy and carefree. They till the soil in mutual contract, and at sunset cease from their toil. No taxes are extorted for imperial indulgences; roads remain untraveled by the king's officers. No calendar regulates the natural progression of the seasons; artful machines are not needed.

Such is the nature of Tao Qian's views as presented in his poetry. His wistful forbearance in the adversity of humble poverty—when riches and honor, however tainted by dishonorable service, could have been his—his cheerful self-consolation and his sincere attachment to the life of farmer and peasant that he intimately chronicled, his love of family, his high morality tempered by human failings, his doubts as to the rectitude of his retirement from admittedly evil times, and his refuge in quiet inebriation have endeared him and his work to Asian and Western readers irrespective of era, class, or aspiration.

BIBLIOGRAPHY

Davis, A. R. *T'ao Yüan-ming: His Works and Their Meaning.* 1983. Reprint. 2 vols. New York: Cambridge University Press, 2009. This thorough study consists of a volume of translation and commentary, and a second volume of commentary, notes, and a biography of the poet.

Field, Stephen L. "The Poetry of Tao Yuanming." In *Great Literature of the Eastern World,* edited by Ian P. McGreal. New York: HarperCollins, 1996. A brief teaching guide with an analysis of Tao Qian's three poems "A Returning to Live in the Country," "Return Home!" and "Peach Blossom Found."

Kwong, Charles Yim-tze. *Tao Qian and the Chinese Poetic Tradition: The Quest for Cultural Identity.* Ann Arbor, Mich.: Center for Chinese Studies, 1994. One of the few English-language literary studies of Tao Qian's work. Discusses the poet in his cultural and literary contexts, comparing his work to that of both Chinese and Western poets.

Lin, Pauline. "Rediscovering Ying Qu and His Poetic Relationship to Tao Qian." *Harvard Journal of Asiatic Studies* 69, no. 1 (June, 2009): 31. Lin argues that Tao Qian was influenced by the earlier poet Ying Qu. She compares their poetry, finding similarities, and discusses why Ying Qu is not as famous.

Rusk, Bruce. "An Interpolation in Zhong Hong's *Shipin*." *Journal of the American Oriental Society* 128, no. 3 (July-September, 2008): 553-558. Examines the part of *Shipin* in which the author assigns a "middle" grade to Tao Qian as a poet and argues that the text may be corrupt.

Swartz, Wendy. *Reading Tao Yuanming: Shifting Paradigms of Historical Reception (427-1900).* Cambridge, Mass.: Asia Center, Harvard University, 2008. This critical analysis of Tao Qian's work looks at how his poetry was received in various time periods. Dismissed as a minor poet after his death, his reputation later grew to the point where he is considered one of China's major poets.

Tao Qian. *The Poetry of T'ao Ch'ien.* Translated and edited by James Robert Hightower. Oxford, England: Clarendon Press, 1970. The standard edition in English. The translations themselves are not noticeably superior to those of his predecessors, but Hightower's notes make the book an essential reference for anyone doing serious work on Tao Qian. It is by far the best guide to its subject's use of traditional elements of the Chinese literary tradition.

Tian, Xiaofei. *Tao Yuanming and Manuscript Culture: The Record of a Dusty Table.* Seattle: University of Washington Press, 2006. This analysis of Tao Qian's works examines how transmission of manuscripts has affected the poems. Editors and scholars along the way made changes to many of the poems. The author discusses the reliability of the texts used by Chinese scholars.

Yu, Pauline. "The Poetry of Retreat." In *Masterworks of Asian Literature in Comparative Perspective*, edited by Barbara Stoler Miller. Armonk, N.Y.: M. E. Sharpe, 1994. A thoughtful discussion of Tao Qian in the Chinese poetic tradition of the recluse, along with other poets such as Ruan Ji and Xie Lingyun.

John Marney

MARINA TSVETAYEVA

Born: Moscow, Russia; October 8, 1892
Died: Yelabuga, Tatar Autonomous Soviet Republic, Soviet Union (now in Russia); August 31, 1941
Also known as: Marina Tsvetaeva

PRINCIPAL POETRY

Vecherny albom, 1910
Volshebny fonar, 1912, 1979
Iz dvukh knig, 1913
Razluka, 1922
Versty I, 1922
Stikhi k Bloku, 1922, 1978
Psikheya, 1923
Remeslo, 1923
Posle Rossii, 1928 (*After Russia*, 1992)
Lebediny stan, 1957 (*The Demesne of the Swans*, 1980)
Selected Poems of Marina Tsvetayeva, 1971
Poem of the End: Selected Narrative and Lyrical Poetry, 1998

OTHER LITERARY FORMS

Marina Tsvetayeva (tsvih-TAH-yuh-vuh) wrote a number of plays, including *Konets Kazanovy* (pb. 1922; the end of Casanova), *Metel* (pb. 1923; the snowstorm), *Fortuna* (pb. 1923; fortune), *Priklyuchenie* (pb. 1923; an adventure), *Tezey* (pb. 1927; Theseus), and *Fedra* (pb. 1928; Phaedra). Several of these were later expanded or combined and reissued under different titles. Tsvetayeva's prose is extensive. Parts of her diaries and her many memoirs have appeared in journals and newspapers, mostly abroad. Some of these prose pieces, together with literary portraits, critical essays, and letters, were collected in *Proza* (1953). A prose collection in English, *A Captive Spirit: Selected Prose*, appeared in 1980. Tsvetayeva also translated poetry, prose, and drama into French, and from French into Russian. Some of her letters, notes, and individual poems remain unpublished and unlocated, but émigré publishers continue to search for material. A modest number of plays and prose pieces have been printed in Soviet journals.

ACHIEVEMENTS

Recognition came to Marina Tsvetayeva late in life, following decades of critical neglect, official Soviet os-

Marina Tsvetayeva (The Granger Collection, New York)

tracism, and émigré hostility. Her suicide during World War II, not known to the world for a long time, engendered critical fascination with the details of her life, eventually followed by publication, republication, and scholarly evaluation of her work. The creative variety and quality of Russian writing in the first quarter of the twentieth century created a situation in which many talented poets, among them Tsvetayeva, escaped public attention. Her adherence to the old orthography and to pre-Revolutionary values, cast into unconventional, awkward-seeming syntax, caused her work to appear disjointed. Only the subsequent careful study of her form and language has revealed the verbal and stylistic brilliance of a unique poetic voice. Political events forced Tsvetayeva to live in exile with artistically conservative Russians who did not understand her poetic experiments. She courageously developed her style, despite exclusion from émigré publishing houses and Soviet rejection of new forms, proudly suffering the ensuing material deprivation. Many of her themes are so closely linked to events in her life that it is difficult to comprehend them without biographical information; the publication of several critical and biographical studies has made her verse more accessible. Translations into English have appeared, and literary scholars now acknowledge her as a major Russian poet.

BIOGRAPHY

Marina Ivanovna Tsvetayeva's birth on October 8, 1892, into an educated, artistic family, augured well for her poetic future. Her mother, a talented amateur pianist, instilled in her an appreciation for the fine arts and insisted on rigorous musical training, while her father's respected position as a professor of art at Moscow University provided exposure to the creative community in Russia. Nicolas II himself, with his family, attended the opening of Professor Tsvetayeva's lifelong project, the Moscow Fine Arts Museum. This august event impressed Tsvetayeva and is reflected in both her poetry and prose, possibly contributing to the unswerving loyalty she displayed toward the imperial family, even when the expression of such sympathies proved dangerous. At age six, Tsvetayeva performed at a public piano recital and tried her hand at versification. Her mother's illness in 1902 necessitated a four-year stay abroad, during which Tsvetayeva developed her interest in literature at Swiss and German boarding schools. After the death of her mother in 1906, she reluctantly entered the Moscow *gimnaziya*, where she treated her courses rather casually. No longer attracted to music, she drifted in and out of schools, devoting all her time to the writing of poetry. She barely managed to complete secondary education, lagging two years behind her graduating class. A collection of poems written in her teens, *Vecherny albom* (evening album), was privately published in 1910 in an edition of five hundred copies. Several critics generously noted artistic promise in the volume, and the poet-painter Max Voloshin introduced Tsvetayeva to Moscow's literary world.

Tsvetayeva's independent, sometimes provocative demeanor—she smoked, bobbed her hair, traveled alone abroad—coupled with a budding literary reputation, brought a measure of local fame. At Voloshin's Crimean house, which served as an artists' colony, she met and shortly thereafter, in 1912, married the eighteen-year-old Sergey Efron, member of a prominent Jewish publishing family. In the same year, she issued her second book of verse, *Volshebny fonar* (the magic lantern), dedicated to her new husband. Neither this collection nor her third, *Iz dvukh knig* (from two books), caused much of a critical stir, with public attention diverted by an abundance of other talented writers and the imminent war. When Tsvetayeva's daughter Ariadna was born in 1912, she immediately became a frequently mentioned star in her mother's verse. Tsvetayeva's writings during the next ten years, disseminated primarily through public readings and occasional journal printing, also failed to receive critical acclaim. These pieces saw publication only in 1922 under the title *Versty I* (milestones I).

The Bolshevik Revolution found the poet in Moscow, nursing her second daughter, Irina, while Efron fought with the White Army in the south. Tsvetayeva coped poorly with the hardships of the Civil War. Unwilling to waste time at nonliterary jobs, she lived on the edge of starvation, and Irina died of malnutrition in a government orphanage in 1920. These years, however, were poetically Tsvetayeva's most productive. Between 1917 and 1921, she completed work that was eventually assembled into "Versty II" (unpublished),

The Demesne of the Swans, *Razluka* (separation), and *Remeslo* (craft), and she developed friendships with the foremost poets of the time, among them Aleksandr Blok, Vladimir Mayakovsky, Osip Mandelstam, and Boris Pasternak. By 1921, Efron had made his way to Prague, where Tsvetayeva joined him with their surviving daughter a year later. During the following years, much of her work was printed by émigré houses in Berlin, Paris, and Prague. In 1925, having expanded her range to epic poems and plays, and following the birth of her son Georgy, Tsvetayeva set up residence in Paris, where a large colony of anti-Communist Russians had gathered. While her contact with foreign writers remained limited, she corresponded regularly with Marcel Proust and Rainer Maria Rilke. The latter, deeply impressed by her talent, addressed a long elegy to her in 1926.

Tsvetayeva's poetic style developed in exile, heavily reflecting Futurist trends. Its experimental nature did not find favor with conservative émigré writers or the public, and her 1928 collection, *After Russia*, largely escaped notice. Reluctantly, Tsvetayeva turned to prose to support herself but never managed a comfortable existence. Her romantic involvements testify to a growing estrangement from Efron, who changed his political outlook in the 1930's and became a Soviet agent. This step had disastrous consequences for the poet. In 1937, her daughter, a confirmed Communist, returned to the Soviet Union. Later that year, Efron was implicated in several political murders, but he escaped to the Soviet Union before he could be brought to trial. Tsvetayeva, now ostracized by fellow exiles and in desperate financial straits, decided to follow her family back to the Soviet Union in 1939. Before her departure, she wisely left her manuscripts in several safe places. This collection later facilitated a Tsvetayeva revival by Western researchers.

The poet returned home to a chilly reception. Tsvetayeva's émigré status and well-known pre-Revolutionary sympathies precluded publication of her work. Only one poem appeared in print after her return, and no record of subsequent work exists or has been made public. Instead, a series of tragic events—the aftermath of Joseph Stalin's purges—drove her to record thoughts of suicide in her diary. Within months of her arrival,

Ariadna was sent to a labor camp, where Tsvetayeva's sister, Anastasia, also spent the last decade of Stalin's rule. Efron disappeared and was executed some time later. Fellow Russians, fearing political contamination, shunned Tsvetayeva. By 1941, wartime evacuation found her with her teenage son in the Tartar Autonomous Republic, east of Moscow. The village of Elabuga could offer the penniless poet only a job as kitchen maid. Proud and stubborn as always, she insisted on a more dignified occupation. When an appeal to establishment writers quartered nearby failed, she hanged herself. The villagers, unaware of her artistic credentials, buried her without ceremony in an unmarked grave. Her son Georgy joined the army and is presumed to have been killed in action. When the "Thaw" began after Stalin's death, Ariadna returned from prison and, with the aid of no-longer-silent poets, devoted herself to promoting her mother's literary heritage. In 1956, a Soviet edition of selected poems appeared, followed by public readings and further publication, always in moderate proportion, carefully chosen to avoid anti-Soviet allusions. In 1980, the Moscow Excursion Bureau instituted a tour of places associated with Tsvetayeva, during which the guide recites generous excerpts of her poetry. This revival, accompanied by an intense interest in her remarkable life, has led to a Tsvetayeva cult in the Soviet Union and a lively black market in her work, finally giving her the recognition so long withheld.

ANALYSIS

Marina Tsvetayeva's poetry is notable for its stylistic innovations, peculiarity of language, political sympathies, and autobiographical intensity. She did not immediately achieve mastery of style. Her early work shows that she was searching for a voice of her own, recreating the language of Moscow's high society in a rather stilted, overly elegant fashion, punctuated by allusions to childhood and romantic longings that do not always mesh with her aristocratic tone. By the time she composed the poems collected in *Versty I*, the ornate phrasing had developed into a simpler language, but one reflecting old, already archaic Russian usage, thus evoking the poetic diction of earlier centuries. At the same time, Tsvetayeva destroyed this historic illusion by incorporating deliberately incongruous colloquialisms and by placing sacred Church Slavonic phrases in coarse contexts. This stylistic violence is redeemed by the expressive, sometimes whimsical quality of her language, which became the trademark of her later work. She selects significant words, often creating new ones by building on familiar roots, which can evoke extended images or form connections to the next phrase without any grammatical links. One of her favorite devices is the verbless stanza: She achieves the necessary cohesion by clever juxtaposition of sharply delineated nouns, producing a brittle, succinct, almost formulaic precision of line. Her lexical and phonetic experiments, especially her neologisms, evoke the work of Mayakovsky and other Futurists, but she manages to maintain a voice peculiarly her own, which is partially the result of her skill in combining archaisms with colloquialisms to produce an incongruous but striking blend of tradition and novelty.

In much of Tsvetayeva's later work, she also shifts the stress within the poetic line, carefully selecting her vocabulary to accommodate such prosodic deformation. Depending on the desired effect, Tsvetayeva drops unstressed syllables, adds dashes to represent syllables, or adds syllables to words, occasionally generating such awkward sequences that she feels it necessary to give intonation or pronunciation information in footnotes. Intensely interested in language expansion, she delighted in pushing poetic devices beyond existing limits. When employing enjambment, she broke the very word in half, creating odd, internal rhymes. These metric innovations, combined with her highly unusual diction, were responsible in part for the relative neglect that Tsvetayeva's work suffered for some time.

Theoretically, Tsvetayeva favored lost causes and failures. The most prominent example is *The Demesne of the Swans*, a cycle of mourning for the defeated White Army. The same compassion appears in the 1930 cycle on Mayakovsky, following his suicide, and in the poems condemning the German invasion of Czechoslovakia. Her loyalty to and love for the past led her again and again to reinterpret motifs from classical literature, with a particular emphasis on Russia's old epics and folklore.

A knowledge of Tsvetayeva's life does not merely

enhance an understanding of her work; it is vital to it. Her poetry is a kind of diary in verse, a chronological account of her experiences, often inaccessible without further elucidation. When preparing her work for safekeeping before returning to Russia, she recognized the hurdles facing the reader and provided explanatory footnotes for many pieces. Even so, her verse demands time and attention before it yields its richness, and she is generally considered to be a difficult poet. The phonetic and semantic interplay that characterizes much of her work poses formidable challenges to the translator. Her inability or unwillingness to exist harmoniously with her surroundings—she continually stressed her otherness—led to a crippling isolation long before political exigencies forced her to extremes. While this withdrawal from the general community nourished her talents, it also lost her publishers, readers, friends, and family. In a December 30, 1925, letter to A. Tesková, she confessed that she had no love for life as such, caring only for its transformation into art. When that was no longer possible, she chose to end her existence.

VECHERNY ALBOM

Tsvetayeva's first book of verse, *Vecherny albom*, already shows the talent and originality of the later perfectionist, although it is still dominated by the immature, conventionally romantic confessions of a young girl. The poems are grouped around two thematic centers: hero worship and childhood feelings. She admires those who achieve a measure of exaltation and personal glory despite handicaps and mundane origin, among them Napoleon, Sarah Bernhardt, and Huck Finn. A special series is devoted to the doomed nobles featured in Edmond Rostand's works. When Tsvetayeva treats her early family life, she is equally idealistic, expressing impatience with the ways of the world: "I thirst for miracles/ Now, this minute, this very morning." The nursery verses also contain a fairy-tale dimension, filled with endearing diminutives, storytelling, the figure of her mother, and her own fear of leaving this shelter for adulthood. The metrical line and strophe are still traditional, although occasionally enlivened by flashes of lexical innovation.

VOLSHEBNY FONAR

Tsvetayeva's second collection, *Volshebny fonar*, dedicated to her bridegroom, does not differ signifi-

cantly in theme and style. The desire to linger in the safe haven of childhood remains strong. She implores Efron to honor these sentiments: "Help me to remain/ A little girl, though your wife," so that the marriage will proceed "From one fairytale into another." Family, friends, and husband are celebrated in sad and joyful verses. While a few snatches of brisk dialogue point to her later telegraphic style, rhyme and meter are strictly conventional. Forty-one poems from her first two volumes were collected in *Iz dvukh knig*, concluding Tsvetayeva's idealistic, romantic period.

VERSTY I

Versty I (milestone I) represents the maturing of Tsvetayeva's poetry—hence the title. In this collection, she trims her lexical material to a minimum, focusing on sharply delineated images to produce an aphoristic style, and her rigid metrical design gives way to the more contemporary mixed meter, called *dolniki*, with which she had begun to experiment. The book serves as a poetic chronicle of 1916. Its unifying theme is the city of Moscow, to which she pays homage in every group of poems. She connects writers, friends, and family with various places in town, and employs diverse poetic personae (tavern queens and beggars) and a range of colorful, lower-class expressions. Among those poets singled out are Anna Akhmatova, Blok, and Mandelstam. In cycles dedicated to the first two, Tsvetayeva cleverly rephrases the artists' own poetic idiom and adapts their metrical peculiarities to her own compositions, giving the reader the strange impression of two simultaneous poetic voices. A brief infatuation with Mandelstam resulted in an exchange of dedications. Finally, there are personal poems, walks around the city with Ariadna, and the poet's first separation from her daughter. In one striking composition, she envisions her own grand funeral procession winding through the streets of Moscow, quite unlike the pauper's burial for which she was destined. The voice of alienation, of being out of place, so dominant in her later verse, already prevails in a number of poems in this volume.

THE DEMESNE OF THE SWANS

The Demesne of the Swans, Tsvetayeva's most controversial book, saw its first publication only in 1957, with a later edition in 1980 featuring English translations facing the original. The printings in the West evoked protest in the Soviet Union, where the work has never been published. Although Tsvetayeva's expressionistic technique and verbal brilliance are particularly evident in these cycles, the provocative theme of a noble, courageous White Army overrun by vile Bolshevik hordes dominates the book. Tsvetayeva's outrage at the destruction of venerated tradition by reincarnated Tartar hordes screams from almost every page. In chronicling the downfall of czarism, starting with Nicolas II's abdication and ending with the Communist victory in 1920, the poet reaches into Russia's epic past for motifs. She compares the White Army to the doomed troops of Prince Igor's campaign, whose defeat at the hands of looting Asiatics foreshadowed Russia's long suffering under the Tartar yoke. Conversely, the Red Army is depicted as an unseemly mob, stampeding all that is sacred and precious into the dust. Tsvetayeva's anguish concerning the unknown fate of Efron is evident but is overshadowed by the national tragedy, which she describes in dramatic effusion: "White Guard, your path is destined to be high/ . . . Godlike and white is your task/ And white is your body that must lie in the sands." Even the more personal poems in the volume are saturated with her hatred of the new regime. The intensity attending Tsvetayeva's treatment of the Civil War is in marked contrast to the poet's customary nonpolitical, disinterested stance and continues to affect her standing in Russia.

The remainder of Tsvetayeva's lyric output continues the driving rhythm, the aphoristically compressed line, and the discordant sound patterns introduced in *Versty I*. Rejection of the environment and notes of despair appear ever more frequently in her verse. Following the Revolution, she also produced epic narratives, adding new dimensions to her style but still basing the narrative on private experience or reaching into Russian history to re-create its heroic legacy.

Tsvetayeva's verse is part of the general poetic flowering and experimentation of the early twentieth century. Her approaches reflect the innovations of Russian Futurists, but she manages to preserve a voice of her own. Despite isolation and hardship in exile, she continued to explore new means of poetic expression, maintaining an artistic link with developments in the

Soviet Union. When her extensive output was finally collected and published, she began to emerge as a major Russian poet.

OTHER MAJOR WORKS

PLAYS: *Konets Kazanovy*, pb. 1922; *Fortuna*, pb. 1923; *Metel*, pb. 1923; *Priklyuchenie*, pb. 1923; *Tezey*, pb. 1927 (also known as *Ariadna*); *Fedra*, pb. 1928.

NONFICTION: *Proza*, 1953; *Izbrannaia Proza v Dvukh Tomakh, 1917-1937*, 1979; *A Captive Spirit: Selected Prose*, 1980; *Art in the Light of Conscience: Eight Essays on Poetry*, 1992.

MISCELLANEOUS: *Izbrannye proizvedeniya*, 1965 (selected works).

BIBLIOGRAPHY

Ciepiela, Catherine. *The Same Solitude: Boris Pasternak and Marina Tsvetaeva*. Ithaca, N.Y.: Cornell University Press, 2006. Ciepiela examines the ten-year love affair between Boris Pasternak and Tsvetayeva, whose relationship was primarily limited to long-distance letters. Included in this volume is the correspondence between the two authors along with letters from Rainer Maria Rilke, who completed the couple's literary love triangle. Ciepiela reveals the similarities between Pasternak and Tsvetayeva by painting a portrait of their lives and personalities. She scrutinizes their poetry and correspondence, finding significant links between them. This volume is written clearly and succinctly, making it easily accessible to all readers.

Cixous, Hélène. *Readings: The Poetics of Blanchot, Joyce, Kafka, Kleist, Lispector, and Tsvetayeva*. Translated by Verena Andermatt Conley. Minneapolis: University of Minnesota Press, 1991. A comparative analysis of a variety of innovative writers, including Tsvetayeva, by a noted French feminist thinker, geared toward a scholarly audience.

Feiler, Lily. *Marina Tsvetaeva: The Double Beat of Heaven and Hell*. Durham, N.C.: Duke University Press, 1994. This psychological biography draws on both classical and postmodernist psychoanalytic theory—Sigmund Freud's notion of pre-Oedipal narcissism and Julia Kristeva's concept of depression as "the hidden face of Narcissus"—to explain the contradictory impulses evident throughout Tsvetayeva's work.

Feinstein, Elaine. *A Captive Lion: The Life of Marina Tsvetayeva*. London: Hutchinson, 1987. A popular biography with annotation and a selected bibliography, this work draws on material from scholars and presents Tsvetayeva as a humanist and feminist interested in art, not politics.

Karlinsky, Simon. *Marina Tsvetaeva: The Woman, Her World, and Her Poetry*. New York: Cambridge University Press, 1985. A revised, updated, and definitive biography based on the poetry and prose of Tsvetaeva as well as the memoirs of her relatives. Material about her life and her writing are integrated in the text. Includes an excellent bibliography and notes.

Kudrova, Irma. *The Death of a Poet: The Last Days of Marina Tsvetaeva*. Translated by Mary Ann Szporluk. Woodstock, N.Y.: Overlook Press, 2004. A harrowing look at the conclusion of Tsvetayeva's life, pieced together using KGB documents.

Makin, Michael. *Marina Tsvetaeva: Poetics of Appropriation*. Oxford, England: Clarendon Press, 1993. Eschewing biographical interpretation, Makin stresses Tsvetayeva's reliance on literary antecedents. The text is well documented, contains a comprehensive source list, and provides original translations of the poetry discussed.

Pierpont, Claudia Roth. *Passionate Minds: Women Rewriting the World*. New York: Knopf, 2000. A collection of evocative interpretive essays on the life paths and works of twelve women, including Tsvetayeva.

Proffer, Ellendea, ed. *Tsvetaeva: A Pictorial Biography*. Translated by J. Marin King. Introduction by Carl R. Proffer. Ann Arbor, Mich.: Ardis, 1980. An excellent collection of annotated photographs of Tsvetayeva throughout her life.

Schweitzer, Viktoria. *Tsvetaeva*. Translated by Robert Chandler and H. T. Willetts. New York: Farrar, Straus and Giroux, 1992. This biography portrays Tsvetayeva as alienated from the world since early childhood by her poetic sensibilities. The author argues that a compulsive "need to be needed" kept Tsvetaeva grounded in events of the real world. Includes bibliography, chronology, index, and biographical notes.

Margot K. Frank

V

CÉSAR VALLEJO

Born: Santiago de Chuco, Peru; March 16, 1892
Died: Paris, France; April 15, 1938

PRINCIPAL POETRY

Los heraldos negros, 1918 (*The Black Heralds*, 1990)

Trilce, 1922 (English translation, 1973)

España, aparta de mí este cáliz, 1939 (*Spain, Take This Cup from Me*, 1974)

Poemas en prosa, 1939 (*Prose Poems*, 1978)

Poemas humanos, 1939 (*Human Poems*, 1968)

Obra poética completa, 1968

César Vallejo: The Complete Posthumous Poetry, 1978

Poesía completa, 1978

Selected Poems, 1981

The Complete Poetry: A Bilingual Edition, 2007 (Clayton Eshleman, editor)

OTHER LITERARY FORMS

César Vallejo (vah-YAY-hoh) wrote fiction, plays, and essays, as well as lyric poetry, although his achievement as a poet far outstrips that in any other genre. His short stories—many of them extremely brief—may be found in *Escalas melografiadas* (1923; musical scales). A longer short story, "Fabla salvaje" (1923; primitive parlance), is a tragic idyll of two rustic lovers, and *Hacia el reino de los Sciris* (1967; toward the kingdom of the Sciris) is set in the time of the Incas. *El tungsteno* (1931; *Tungsten*, 1988), is a proletarian novel with an Andean setting that was written in 1931, the year Vallejo joined the Communist Party. Another story, *Paco Yunque* (1969), is about the mistreatment of a servant's son by a classmate who happens to be the master's son.

Vallejo became interested in the theater around 1930, but he destroyed his first play, "Mampar." Three others, *Entre las dos orillas corre el río* (pb. 1979; the river flows between two banks); *Lock-Out* (pb. 1979), and *Colacho hermanos: O, presidentes de América* (pb. 1979; Colacho brothers), never published during the poet's lifetime, are now available in *Teatro completo* (1979; complete theatrical work). His long essay, *Rusia en 1931: Reflexiones al pie del Kremlin* (1931; reissued in 1965), was followed by *Rusia ante el segundo plan quinquenal* (1965); *Contra el secreto profesional* (1973); and *El arte y la revolución* (1973). His master's thesis, *El romanticismo en la poesía castellana*, was published in 1954.

ACHIEVEMENTS

Finding an authentic language in which to write has always represented a fundamental problem for Latin American writers, since it became evident that the language inherited from the Spanish conquerors could not match Latin American reality. The problem of finding such a language goes hand in hand with that of forging a separate cultural identity. An important attempt at renovating poetic language was made by the Spanish American *Modernistas* around the turn of the century, but their verse forms, imagery, and often exotic subject matter were also becoming obsolete by the time César Vallejo reached maturity. It was thus up to him and his contemporaries to find a language that could deal with contemporary concerns involving war, depression, isolation, and alienation. Although hardly recognized in his lifetime, Vallejo did more than perhaps any other poet of his generation to provide an idiom that would at once reflect the Spanish tradition, his own Peruvian heritage, and the contemporary world. Aware of his heritage from Spain's great writers of the past, he blended traditional poetic vocabulary and tropes with homely Peruvian idioms and even the language of children. Where the result was still inadequate, he made up new words, changed the function of old ones, and incorporated a lexicon never before seen in poetry, often savaging poetic convention.

Vallejo's gradual conversion to Marxism and Communism is of great interest to those attempting to understand how collectivist ideals may shape poetry. The evolution of his ideology continues to be studied intensively by many individuals committed to bettering the conditions of poverty and alienation about which Vallejo wrote so eloquently—conditions that still exist in Latin America and other parts of the world. His unflinchingly honest search for both linguistic and moral solutions to the existential anguish of modern human beings gives his poems universal validity, while their density and complexity challenge critics of the most antithetical modes.

BIOGRAPHY

César Abraham Vallejo was born in Santiago de Chuco, a primitive "city" of some fourteen thousand inhabitants in Peru's northern mountains that could only be reached by a rail trip and then several days ride on mule or horseback. Both of his grandfathers had been Spanish priests and both of his grandmothers native Peruvians of Chimu Indian stock. His parents were literate and of modest means; his father was a notary who became a subprefect in the district. Francisco de Paula Vallejo and María de los Santos Mendoza were an upright and religious pair whose marriage produced twelve offspring and who were already middle-aged when their youngest child, César, was born. In his writings, Vallejo was often to remember the security and warmth of his childhood home—games with three of his older siblings, and particularly with his mother, who might have been especially indulgent with her sensitive youngest child.

At age thirteen, Vallejo left Santiago de Chuco to attend high school in Huamachuco, another mountain village, where he received an introduction to literature and began scribbling verses. Economic difficulties prevented him from continuing the university studies that he had begun in the larger coastal cities of Trujillo and Lima in 1911. The young man first went to work in a nearby tungsten mine—an experience that he would later draw upon for his Socialist Realist novel *Tungsten*—and then on a coastal sugar plantation. While there, he observed the tightly structured hierarchy that kept workers in misery while the

middle class, to which he himself belonged, served the needs of the elite. In 1913, he returned to the University of Trujillo and graduated two years later, having written a master's thesis titled *El romanticismo en la poesía castellana*. For the next few years, he studied law in Trujillo, supporting himself by becoming a first-grade teacher. One of his pupils, Ciro Alegría, later to become an important novelist, described Vallejo in those days as lean, sallow, solemn, and dark skinned, with abundant straight black hair worn somewhat long, brilliant dark eyes, a gentle manner, and an air of sadness.

During these years, Vallejo became familiar with the writings of Ralph Waldo Emerson, José Rodó, Friedrich Nietzsche, Miguel de Unamuno y Jugo, Walt Whitman, and Juan Ramón Jiménez. Vallejo also read the poems of two of the leading Spanish American *Modernistas*, Rubén Darío and Julio Herrera y Reissig, as well as those of Peruvian poets of the day. Vallejo

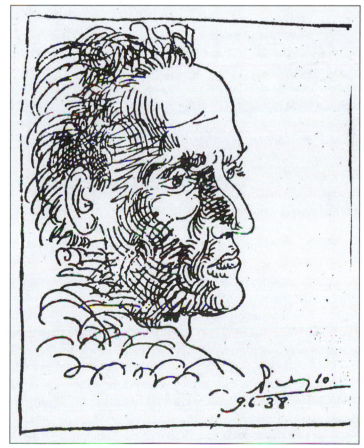

César Vallejo, as drawn by Picasso in 1938. (The Granger Collection, New York)

declaimed his own poems—mostly occasional verse—at various public ceremonies, and some of them appeared in Trujillo's newspapers. Critical reception of them ranged from the cool to the hostile, since they were considered to be exaggerated and strange in that highly traditional ambience. Vallejo fell in love with a young Trujillo girl, Zoila Rosa Cuadro, the subject of several poems included in *The Black Heralds*. The breakup of this relationship provided one motive for his departure, after he had obtained a law degree, for Lima in 1918. There he found a position teaching in one of the best elementary schools and began to put the finishing touches on his first volume of poems.

Vallejo was soon in love with the sister-in-law of one of his colleagues, a woman identified only as "Otilia." A number of the *Trilce* poems, which he was writing at the time, deal with this affair. It ended when the poet refused to marry the woman, resulting in the loss of his job. This crisis was compounded by the death of his mother, a symbol of stability whose loss made him feel like an orphan. For some time, Vallejo had thought of going to Paris, but he decided to return first to his childhood home in Santiago de Chuco. During a national holiday, he was falsely accused of having been the instigator of a civil disturbance and was later seized and imprisoned for 112 days despite the public protests of many Peruvian intellectuals. The experience affected him profoundly, and the poems that he wrote about it (later published in *Trilce*) testify to the feeling of solidarity with the oppressed that he voiced for the first time. While in prison, he also wrote a number of the sketches to appear in *Escalas melografiadas*. In 1923, he sailed for Europe, never again to return to Peru.

While Vallejo's days in Lima had often been marked by personal problems, in Paris, he experienced actual penury, sometimes being forced to sleep in the subway. Eventually, he found employment in a press agency but only after a serious illness. He began to contribute articles to Lima newspapers, made friends with a number of avant-garde artists, and journeyed several times to Spain, where he was awarded a grant for further study. Increasingly concerned with injustice in the world, he made his first trip to Russia in 1928 with the intention of staying. Instead, he returned within three weeks, liv-ing soon afterward with a Frenchwoman, Georgette de Philippart, who was later to become his wife. With some money that had come to her, the pair set out on a tour by train through Eastern Europe, spending two weeks in Moscow and returning by way of Rome. As Vallejo's enthusiasm for Marxism became increasingly apparent in his newspaper articles, he found them no longer welcome in Lima, and in 1930, he was ordered to leave France because of his political activity. Once again in Spain, he wrote several plays and the novel *Tungsten* and published *Rusia en 1931*, the only one of his books to sell well. No publisher could be found for several other works. After a third and final visit to Russia as a delegate to the International Congress of Writers, he wrote *Rusia ante el segundo plan quinquenal* (Russia facing the second five-year plan) and officially joined the Communist Party.

In 1932, Vallejo was permitted to return to Paris, where he tried unsuccessfully to publish some new poems. In 1936, the Spanish Civil War broke out, and Vallejo became an active supporter of the Republic, traveling to Barcelona and Madrid to attend the Second International Congress for the Defense of Culture. He visited the battlefront and learned at first hand of the horrors suffered by the Spanish people in the war. Returning to Paris for the last time, he poured his feelings into his last work, *Spain, Take This Cup from Me*. In March, 1938, he became ill. Doctors were unable to diagnose his illness, and Vallejo died a month later on Good Friday, the day before the troops of Francisco Franco won a decisive victory in Spain.

ANALYSIS

One of the unique qualities of César Vallejo's poetry—one that makes his work almost impossible to confuse with that of any other poet writing in the Spanish language—is his ability to speak with the voice and sensibility of a child, whether as an individual orphaned by the breakup of a family or as a symbol of deprived and alienated human beings everywhere. Always, however, this child's voice, full of expectation and hope, is implicitly counterposed by the adult's ironic awareness of change and despair. Inseparable from these elements is the poet's forging of a language capable of reflecting the register and the peculiarly elliptical reasoning of a child and, at the same time, revealing the Hermetic complexity of the adult intellectual's quest for security in the form of truth. The poetry that is Vallejo's own answer to these problems is some of the most poignant and original ever produced.

THE BLACK HERALDS

The lines of Vallejo's subsequent development are already evident in his first volume, *The Black Heralds*, a collection of sixty-nine poems grouped under various subtitles. As critics have observed, many of these poems reflect his involvement with Romantic and *Modernista* poetry. They are conspicuous in many cases for their descriptions of idyllic scenes in a manner that juxtaposes words of the Peruvian Sierra and the vocabulary of Symbolism, including religious and erotic elements. Vallejo did not emphasize rhyme and rhythm to the extent that some *Modernistas* did, but most of these early poems are framed in verse forms favored by the latter, such as the Alexandrine sonnet and the *silva*. While demonstrating his impressive mastery of styles already worked out by others, he was also finding his own voice.

This originality is perhaps most evident in the last group of poems in *The Black Heralds*, titled "Canciones de Hogar" ("Home Songs"), poems dealing with the beginning of Vallejo's sense of orphanhood. In "A mi hermano Miguel in memoriam" ("To My Brother Miguel in Memoriam"), the poet relives a moment of the childhood game of hide-and-seek that he used to play with his "twin heart." Speaking to his brother, Vallejo announces his own presence in the part of the family home from which one of the two always ran away to hide from the other. He goes on to remind his playmate of one day on which the latter went away to hide, sad instead of laughing as he usually was, and could not be found again. The poem ends with a request to the brother to please come out so as not to worry "mama." It is remarkable in that past and present alternate from one line to the next. The language of childhood, as well as the poet's assumed presence at the site of the events, lends a dramatic immediacy to the scene. At the same time, the language used in the descriptive passages is clearly that of the adult who is now the poet. Yet in the last verse, the adult chooses to accept literally the explanation that the brother has remained in hiding

and may finally respond and come out, which would presumably alleviate the mother's anxiety and make everything right once more. The knowledge that the poet is unable (or refuses) to face the permanent alteration of his past may elicit feelings of tragic pathos in the reader.

"Los pasos lejanos" ("The Distant Steps") recalls the poet's childhood home in which his parents, now aged, are alone—the father sleeping and the mother walking in the orchards. Here, the only bitterness is that of the poet himself, because he is now far away from them. He in turn is haunted by a vision of his parents as two old, white, and bent roads along which his heart walks. In "Enereida," he imagines that his father has died, leading to a regression in time so that the father can once again laugh at his small children, including the poet himself, who is again a schoolboy under the tutelage of the village priest.

Many of the poems in *The Black Heralds* deal with existential themes. While religious imagery is pervasive, it is apparent that the poet employs it to describe profane experiences. Jean Franco has shown that in speaking of "the soul's Christs" and "Marías who leave" and of Communions and Passions, Vallejo trivializes religious language rather than attempting to inflate the importance of his own experiences by describing them in religious terms. As well as having lost the security and plenitude of his childhood home, the poet has lost the childhood faith that enabled him to refer in words to the infinite.

In the title poem, "Los heraldos negros" ("The Black Heralds"), Vallejo laments life's hard blows, harder sometimes than humans can stand. He concludes that these blows come from the hatred of God, that they may be the black heralds sent by Death. In "Los dados eternos" ("The Eternal Dice"), God is a gambler throwing dice and may as easily cast death as life. In fact, Earth itself is his die. Now worn to roundness, it will come to rest only within the sepulchre. Profane love is all that is left; while the beloved may now be pure, she will not continue to be so if she yields to the poet's erotic impulses. Love thus becomes "a sinning Christ," because humankind's nature is irrevocably physical. Several poems allude to the poet's ideal of redeeming himself through brotherly love, a thematic constant in Vallejo's work, yet such redemption becomes difficult if not impossible if a person is lonely and alienated. In "Agape," the poet speaks of being alone and forgotten and of having been unable therefore to "die" for his brother. "La cena miserable" ("The Wretched Supper") tells of the enigma of existence in which humans are seen, as in "Agape," as waiting endlessly for spiritual nurture, or at least for some answer concerning the meaning of life. Here, God becomes no more than a "black spoon" full of bitter human essence, even less able than humans to provide needed answers. The lives of humans are thus meaningless, since they are always separated from what they most desire—whether this be the fullness of the past, physical love, God's love, or brotherly love.

Even in the poems most laden with the trappings of *Modernismo*, Vallejo provides unusual images. In "El poeta a su amada" ("The Poet to His Beloved"), he suggests that his kiss is "two curved branches" on which his beloved has been "crucified." Religious imagery is used with such frequency that it sometimes verges on parody, and critics agree that in playing with language in this way Vallejo is seeking to highlight its essential ambiguity, something he continues to do in *Trilce* and *Human Poems*, even while totally abandoning the imagery of *Modernismo*. Such stripping away of excess baggage is already visible in *The Black Heralds*. Antitheses, oxymorons, and occasional neologisms are also to be noted. While the great majority of the poems are elegantly correct in terms of syntax—in marked contrast to what is to become the norm in *Trilce*—there are some instances of linguistic experimentation, as when nouns are used as adjectives. In "The Distant Steps," for example, the mother is described as being "so soft, so wing, so departure, so love." Another device favored by the poet in all his later poems—enumeration—is also present. Finally, traditional patterns of meter and rhyme are abandoned in "Home Songs," with the poetic emotion being allowed to determine the form.

TRILCE

Despite these formal adumbrations and although *The Black Heralds* is not a particularly transparent work, there is little in it to prepare the reader for the destruction of language in the Hermetic density of *Trilce*,

which came along only three years later. These were difficult years for the poet, in which he lost his mother, separated from Otilia, and spent what he was later to refer to as the gravest moments of his life in the Trujillo jail. All the anguish of these events was poured into the seventy-seven free-verse poems of his second major work. If he suffered existentially in *The Black Heralds* and expressed this suffering in writing, it was done with respect for traditional verse forms and sentence structure, which hinted at an order beyond the chaos of the poet's interior world. In *Trilce*, this order falls. Language, on which "logical assumptions" about the world are based, is used in such a way as to reveal its hollowness: It, too, is cut loose and orphaned. Abrupt shifts from one metaphorical sphere to another make the poems' internal logic often problematic.

A hint of what is to come is given in the title, a neologism usually taken to be a hybrid of *tres* (three) and *dulce* (sweet), an interpretation that is in accord with the poet's concern about the ideal number expressed in several poems. It is not known, however, what, if any, concrete meaning the poet had in mind when he coined the word; it has become a puzzle for readers and critics to solve. It is notable that in "interpreting" the *Trilce* poems, critics often work out explications that seem internally consistent but that turn out to be related to a system diametrically opposed to the explication and system of some other critic. It is possible, however, to say with certainty that these poems deal with a struggle to do something, bridge something, and say something. Physical limits such as the human body, time, space, and numbers often render the struggle futile.

Two of the thematic sets of *Trilce* for which it is easiest to establish concrete referents are those dealing with the poet-as-child and those dealing with his imprisonment. In poem III, the poet once again speaks in the voice of a child left at home by the adults of the family. It is getting dark, and he asks when the grown-ups will be back, adding that "Mama said she wouldn't be gone long." In the third stanza, an ironic double vision of years full of agonizing memories intrudes. As in "To My Brother Miguel in Memoriam," the poet chooses to retain the child's faith, urging his brothers and sisters to be good and obey in letter and spirit the instructions left by the mother. In the end, it is seen that the "leaving" is without remedy, a function of time itself; it eventually results in the poet's complete solitude without even the comfort of his siblings. In poem XXIII, the mother, the only symbol of total plenitude, is seen as the "warm oven" of the cookies described as "rich hosts of time." The nourishment provided by the mother was given freely and naturally, taken away from no one and given without the child's being obliged. Still, the process of nurturing leads to growing up and to individuation and alienation. Several poems mythicize the process of birth but shift so abruptly to demythicize human existence that the result is at first humorous. In poem XLVII, a candle is lighted to protect the mother while she gives birth, along with another for the babe who, God willing, will grow up to be bishop, pope, saint, "or perhaps only a columnary headache." Later, in *Human Poems*, there is a Word Incarnate whose bones agree in number and gender as it sinks into the bathtub ("Lomo de las sagradas escrituras"/"Spine of the Scriptures").

In poem XVIII, the poet surveys the four walls of the cell, implacably closed. He calls up a vision of the "loving keeper of innumerable keys," the mother, who would liberate him if she could. He imagines the two longer walls as mothers and the shorter ones as the children each of them is leading by the hand. The poet is alone with only his two hands, struggling to find a third to help him in his useless adulthood. In poem LVIII, the solid walls of the cell seem to bend at the corners, suggesting that the poet is dozing as a series of jumbled thoughts produce scenes in his mind that follow no easy logical principle of association. The poet sees himself helping the naked and the ragged, then dismounting from a panting horse that he also attempts to help. The cell is now liquid, and he becomes aware of the companions who may be worse off than he. Guilt suddenly overwhelms him, and he is moved to promise to laugh no more when his mother arises early to pray for the sick, the poor, and the prisoners. He also promises to treat his little friends better at play, in both word and deed. The cell is now boundless gas, growing as it condenses. Ambiguously, at the end, he poses the question, "Who stumbles outside?" The openness of the poem is similar to that of many others in *Trilce*, and it is difficult to say what kind of threat to the poet's resolutions is posed by the figure outside. Again, the poetic voice has

become that of a child seeking to make all that is wrong in the world right once more by promising to be "a good boy." Of course, he is not a child at all, as the figure outside may be intended to remind both him and the reader. The result is once again a remarkable note of pathos tinged with poignant irony.

Many of *Trilce*'s poems deal with physical love and even the sexual act itself. "Two" seems to be the ideal number, but "two" has "propensities of trinity." Clearly, the poet has no wish to bring a child into the world, and sex becomes merely an act of organs that provides no solution to anything. While the poet seems to appreciate the maternal acts performed by his lover, he fails to find any transcendental satisfaction in the physical relationship, even though he is sad when it is over.

An important theme that emerges in *Trilce* and is developed more fully in *Human Poems* and *Spain, Take This Cup from Me* is that of the body as text. In poem LXV, the house to which the poet returns in Santiago seems to be his mother's body. Parts of the body—the back, face, shoulder, eyes, hands, lips, eyelashes, bones, feet, knees, fingers, heart, arms, breasts, soles of the feet, eyelids, ears, ribs—appear in poem after poem, reminding the reader of human and earthly functions and the limitations of human beings.

In many ways, *Trilce* resembles the poetry of such avant-garde movements as Surrealism, Ultraism, and Creationism in the boldness of its images, its unconventional vocabulary, and its experimentation with graphics. Vallejo did have very limited exposure to some of this poetry after he reached Lima; his critics, however, generally agree that *Trilce* was produced independently. While Vallejo may have been encouraged to experiment by his knowledge of European literary currents, his work coincides with them as an original contribution.

HUMAN POEMS

As far as is known, the poems after *Trilce* were written in Europe; with very few exceptions, none was published until 1939, a year after the poet's death, when they appeared under the title *Human Poems*. While Vallejo's life in Peru was far from affluent, it must have seemed easy in comparison with the years in Paris, where he often barely subsisted and suffered several illnesses. In addition, while he did see a new edition of *Trilce* published through the intervention of friends in 1931 and his *Rusia en 1931* did go into three editions during his lifetime, he could never count on having his writings accepted for publication.

Human Poems, considered separately from *Spain, Take This Cup from Me*, is far from being a homogeneous volume, and its final configuration might have been different had it been Vallejo who prepared the final edition rather than his widow. Generally speaking, the poems that it includes deal with ontological anguish whose cause seems related to physical suffering, the passage of time, and the impossibility of believing that life has any meaning. In fact, *Human Poems* examines suffering and pain, with their corollaries, poverty, hunger, illness, and death, with a thoroughness that few other works can match. At times, the anguish seems to belong only to the poet, now not only the orphan of *Trilce* but alienated from other people as well. In "Altura y pelos" ("Height and Hair"), the poet poses questions: "Who doesn't own a blue suit?/ Who doesn't eat lunch and board the streetcar . . . ?/ Who is not called Carlos or any other thing?/ Who to the kitty doesn't say kitty kitty?" The final answer given is "Aie? I who alone was solely born." At least two kinds of irony seem to be involved here. The activities mentioned are obviously trivial, but neither is it easy to be alone. In the well-known "Los nueve monstruos" ("The Nine Monsters"), the poet laments the abundance of pain in the world: "Never, human men/ was there so *much* pain in the chest, in the lapel, in the wallet/ in the glass, in the butcher-shop, in arithmetic!" and "never/ . . . did the migraine extract so much forehead from the forehead!" Pain drives people crazy "in the movies,/ nails us into the gramophones,/ denails us in bed . . ." The poem concludes that the "Secretary of Health" can do nothing because there is simply "too much to do."

"The Nine Monsters" is representative of several features of *Human Poems*. The language is extremely concrete, denoting things that are inseparable from everyday existence. Much of the poem consists of lists, continuing a device for which the poet had already shown a disposition in his first work. Finally, the logic of the systems represented by the items named is hard to pin down, so that it is somewhat reminiscent of child

logic in its eccentricity. Again and again, Vallejo's remarkable sensibility is demonstrated beyond any preciosity or mere posturing.

One reason for the poet's alienation is that he sees people as engaged in trivial occupations and as being hardly more advanced on the evolutionary scale than pachyderms or kangaroos, whereas he himself aspires to rise above his limitations. In "Intensidad y altura" ("Intensity and Height"), he tells of his desire to write being stifled by his feeling "like a puma," so that he might as well go and eat grass. He concludes, "let's go, raven, and fecundate your rook." He thus sees himself condemned not to rise above the purely mundane. Religion offers no hope at all. In "Acaba de pasar el que vendrá . . ." ("He Has Just Passed By, the One Who Will Come . . ."), the poet suggests that "the one who will come"—presumably the Messiah—has already passed by but has changed nothing, being as vague and ineffectually human as anyone else.

While the majority of these posthumously published poems convey utter despair, not all of them do. Although the exact dates of their composition are generally unknown, it is natural to associate those that demonstrate growing concern for others with Vallejo's conversion to Marxist thought and eventually to Communism. In "Considerando en frío . . ." ("Considering Coldly . . ."), speaking as an attorney at a trial, the poetic voice first summarizes the problems and weaknesses of humanity (he "is sad, coughs and, nevertheless,/ takes pleasure in his reddened chest/ . . . he is a gloomy mammal and combs his hair . . .") Then, however, he announces his love for humanity. Denying it immediately, he nevertheless concludes, "I signal him,/ he comes,/ I embrace him, moved./ So what! Moved . . . Moved. . . ." Compassion thus nullifies "objectivity." In "La rueda del hambriento" ("The Hungry Man's Wheel"), the poet speaks as a man so miserable that his own organs are pulled out of him through his mouth. He begs only for a stone on which to sit and a little bread. Apparently ignored, aware that he is being importunate, he continues to ask, disoriented and hardly able to recognize his own body. In "Traspié entre dos estrellas" ("Stumble Between Two Stars"), the poet expresses pity for the wretched but goes on to parody bitterly Christ's Sermon on the Mount ("Beloved be the one with bedbugs,/ the one who wears a torn shoe in the rain"), ending with a "beloved" for one thing and then for its opposite, as if calling special attention to the emptiness of mere words. It is possible to say that in these poems the orphan has finally recognized that he is not alone in his orphanhood.

SPAIN, TAKE THIS CUP FROM ME

Although first published as part of *Human Poems*, *Spain, Take This Cup from Me* actually forms a separate, unified work very different in tone from the majority of the other posthumous poems—a tone of hope, although, especially in the title poem, the poet seems to suspect that the cause he has believed in so passionately may be lost. In this poem, perhaps the last that Vallejo wrote, the orphan—now all human children—has found a mother. This mother is Spain, symbol of a new revolutionary order in which oppression may be ended. The children are urged not to let their mother die; nevertheless, even should this happen, they have a recourse: to continue struggling and to go out and find a new mother.

Another contrast is found in the odes to several heroes of the Civil War. Whereas, in *Human Poems*, humans are captives of their bodies and hardly more intelligent than the lower animals, *Spain, Take This Cup from Me* finds people capable of true transcendence through solidarity with others and the will to fight injustice. A number of poems commemorate the battles of the war: Talavera, Guernica, Málaga. Spain thus becomes a text—a book that sprouts from the bodies of an anonymous soldier. The poet insists again and again that he himself is nothing, that his stature is "tiny," and that his actions rather than his words constitute the real text. This may be seen to represent a greatly evolved negation of poetic authority, first seen in *The Black Heralds* with the repeated cry, "I don't know!"

Nevertheless, *Spain, Take This Cup from Me* rings with a biblical tone, and the poet sometimes sounds like a prophet. James Higgins has pointed out certain images that recall the Passion of Christ and the New Jerusalem, although religious terminology, as in all Vallejo's poetry, is applied to humans rather than to divinity. While Vallejo continues to use techniques of enumeration—which are often chaotic—and to use concrete nouns (including many referring to the body), he also employs abstract terms such as peace, hope, martyrdom, harmony, eternity, and greatness. The sense of garments, utensils, and the body's organs stifling the soul is gone and is replaced by limitless space. In Vallejo's longest poem, "Himno a los voluntarios de la República" ("Hymn to the Volunteers for the Republic"), a panegyric note is struck.

One of Vallejo's most immediately accessible poems, "Masa" ("Mass"), tells almost a parable of a dead combatant who was asked by one man not to die, then by two, and finally by millions. The corpse kept dying until surrounded by all the inhabitants of Earth. The corpse, moved, sat up and embraced the first man and then began to walk. The simplicity of the story and of its narration recalls the child's voice in *Trilce*, promising to cease tormenting his playmates in order to atone for the world's guilt. In this piece, as well as in all Vallejo's last group of poems, however, the irony is gone.

POETIC CYCLE

It is thus possible to see the completion of a cycle in the four works. Disillusionment grows in *The Black Heralds*, and then alienation works its way into the language itself in *Trilce*. *Human Poems* is somewhat less Hermetic than *Trilce*, but life is an anguished nightmare in which the soul is constrained by the ever-present body that seems to be always wracked with pain. Only in *Spain, Take This Cup from Me*, with the realization that men are brothers who can end their common alienation and suffering by collective action, does the poet regain his lost faith and embark upon a positive course. The orphan relocates the lost mother, whom he now sees to be the mother of all, since all men are brothers. The true significance of Vallejo's poetry, however, surely lies in his honesty in questioning all established rules of poetic expression, as well as the tradition of poetic authority, in order to put poetry fully in touch with the existential prison house of twentieth century humanity.

OTHER MAJOR WORKS

LONG FICTION: *Fábula salvaje,* 1923 (novella); *El tungsteno,* 1931 (*Tungsten,* 1988).

SHORT FICTION: *Escalas melografiadas,* 1923; *Hacia el reino de los Sciris,* 1967; *Paco Yunque,* 1969.

PLAYS: *Colacho hermanos: O, presidentes de América*, pb. 1979; *Entre las dos orillas corre el río*, pb. 1979; *La piedra cansada*, pb. 1979; *Lock-Out*, pb. 1979; *Teatro completo*, 1979.

NONFICTION: *Rusia en 1931: Reflexiones al pie del Kremlin*, 1931, 1965; *El romanticismo en la poesía castellana*, 1954; *Rusia ante el segundo plan quinquenal*, 1965; *Contra el secreto profesional*, 1973; *El arte y la revolución*, 1973.

BIBLIOGRAPHY

Britton, R. K. "Love, Alienation, and the Absurd: Three Principal Themes in César Vallejo's *Trilce*." *Modern Language Review* 87 (July, 1992): 603-615. Demonstrates how Vallejo's poetry expresses the anguished conviction that humankind is simply a form of animal life subject to the laws of a random, absurd universe.

Dove, Patrick. *The Catastrophe of Modernity: Tragedy and the Nation in Latin American Literature*. Lewisburg, Pa.: Bucknell University Press, 2004. This discussion of the theme of modernity as a catastrophe contains a chapter on Vallejo's *Trilce*.

Hart, Stephen M. *Stumbling Between Forty-six Stars: Essays on César Vallejo*. London: Centre of César Vallejo Studies, 2007. A collection of essays on various aspects of the poet.

Hart, Stephen M., and Jorge Cornejo Polar. *César Vallejo: A Critical Bibliography of Research*. Rochester, N.Y.: Boydell and Brewer, 2002. A bibliography collecting works of Vallejo. Invaluable for researchers.

Hedrick, Tace Megan. "Mi andina y dulce Rita: Women, Indigenism, and the Avant-Garde in César Vallejo." In *Primitivism and Identity in Latin America: Essays on Art, Literature, and Culture*, edited by Erik Camayd-Freixas and José Eduardo González. Tucson: University of Arizona Press, 2000. Relates the indigenism of "Dead Idylls" from *The Black Heralds* to the "avant-garde concerns and practices" of *Trilce*, often considered Vallejo's most brilliant work.

Higgins, James. *The Poet in Peru: Alienation and the Quest for a Super-Reality*. Liverpool, England: Cairns, 1982. Contains a good overview of the main themes of Vallejo's poetry.

Lambie, George. "Poetry and Politics: The Spanish Civil War Poetry of César Vallejo." *Bulletin of Hispanic Studies* 69, no. 2 (April, 1992): 153-170. Analyzes the presence of faith and Marxism in *Spain, Take This Cup from Me*.

Niebylski, Dianna C. *The Poem on the Edge of the Word: The Limits of Language and the Uses of Silence in the Poetry of Mallarmé, Rilke, and Vallejo*. New York: Peter Lang, 1993. In the context of the language "crisis" of modern poetry and the poet's dilemma in choosing language or silence, Niebylski examines the themes of time and death in Vallejo's *Human Poems*.

Sharman, Adam, ed. *The Poetry and Poetics of César Vallejo: The Fourth Angle of the Circle*. Lewiston, N.Y.: Edwin Mellen Press, 1997. Collection of essays examining Vallejo's work from the perspectives of Marxism, history, the theme of the absent mother, and postcolonial theory.

Lee Hunt Dowling

VĀLMĪKI

Born: Ayodhya(?), India; fl. c. 500 B.C.E.
Died: India; fl. c. 500 B.C.E.

PRINCIPAL POETRY

Rāmāyaṇa, c. 500 B.C.E. (*The Ramayana*, 1870-1874)
Yoga Vāsiṣṭha, c. 500 B.C.E. (*The Supreme Yoga: A New Translation of the Yoga Vasistha*, 1976, two volumes)

OTHER LITERARY FORMS

Vālmīki (vol-MEE-kee) is not known for anything other than his poetry.

ACHIEVEMENTS

Indian tradition credits Vālmīki with having invented poetry. Particularly in the Punjab section of India, the Vālmīki sect of Hinduism worships him as divine and considers his writings to be scriptures; he is, at minimum, revered throughout the Indian community. *The Ramayana* has been extraordinarily popular for millennia, helping to establish cultural ideals. Its stories have been staples of Southeast Asian dance, drama, and painting. Adaptations of it in the major languages of Southeast Asia, such as Thailand's *Ramakien*, have themselves become influential classics. *Ramayan* (1987-1988), a television series based on *The Ramayana* and produced by Ramanand Sagar, was the most-watched series in Indian history. American adaptations of *The Ramayana* include Virgin Comics' *Ramayan 3392 a.d.* (2006), written by the best-selling author Deepak Chopra and the filmmaker Shekhar Kapur. *The Ramayana* has inspired video games, action figures, and such animated films as the Indo-Japanese anime *Ramayana: The Legend of Prince Rama* (1992). Among the classics of Yoga and Advaita Vedanta (monistic Hindu philosophy), Vālmīki's *The Supreme Yoga* is the longest and possibly the most prestigious.

BIOGRAPHY

According to one Hindu tradition, Vālmīki was an incarnate god who wrote in 867,000 B.C.E. Western scholarship argues that if a person named Vālmīki actually existed, he probably lived around 500 B.C.E. In the first century C.E., the Buddhist author Ashvagosha praised Vālmīki in a manner that establishes that some portion of *The Ramayana* had already been written. There are, however, many passages in *The Ramayana* that were composed in the very elaborate *kāvya* style, of which Ashvagosha's writings are the first known example. Therefore, the *kāvya* passages in *The Ramayana* most likely were composed in the first century C.E. or later. The standard version of *The Ramayana* states that Vālmīki is its author, although these attributions are made in sections written in third person that appear to be later additions and not written by Vālmīki himself. Similarly, in its standard version, *The Supreme Yoga* has a third-person account that attributes its writing to Vālmīki, but attempted reconstructions of the original text presume that it (and its use of characters from *The Ramayana*) come from the first century C.E. or later, when *The Ramayana* perhaps was adapted to changes in Indian religion and literary taste.

According to the *Adhyatma Rāmāyaṇa* (c. four-

teenth century C.E.; *The Adhyatma Ramayana*, 1913), Vālmīki supported his family through highway robbery, but when his family members were asked whether they were willing to share his karmic sufferings for his sins, they declined. Shocked by this, Vālmīki sought salvation. Repeating the sacred syllables *ma* and *rā*, he remained immobile for years until termites formed a nest around him (the name Vālmīki being derived from the Sanskrit word for these insects). Eventually, he achieved a total reformation. Because *The Adhyatma Ramayana* emphasizes the divinity of Rāma (the protagonist of *The Ramayana*), it shows that even a thief can rise to holiness and eminence by repeating the name Rāma. However, devotees of Vālmīki, who see him as divine, consider this story slanderous.

The Ramayana begins with the sage Vālmīki complaining that the period in which he lives lacks an exemplar of morality. To contradict him, his companion Nārada (possibly a personification of the music associated with poetry) summarizes the story of Rāma. Subsequently, Vālmīki sees two cranes mating. A hunter kills the male of the pair, and Vālmīki curses the hunter. Vālmīki's words spontaneously assume a metric form—the first poem. The god Brahmā appears to Vālmīki and suggests that he compose an epic life of Rāma, following the meter of that curse. In the poem that Vālmīki then writes, however, he relates that he had already met Rāma and helped to raise the latter's twin sons. This contradiction—Vālmīki's apparent lack of knowledge about Rāma in the introductory section and his mention of an encounter with Rāma in the poem written after the crane's death—may indicate that these sections were written by different authors. Indeed, *The Ramayana*'s earliest written version may not have been the work of a single poet, but rather an accumulation of lines recited by oral bards over centuries.

ANALYSIS

Underlying the poems ascribed to Vālmīki is the idea of poetry as magic. Verse began as Vālmīki's curse, which shortened the hunter's life. Both *The Ramayana* and *The Supreme Yoga* mention numerous effective spells. For example, both poems allude to a myth about the chief god Indra, who commits adultery with the wife of a holy man and is castrated by the man's words, then healed by another ritual. A major portion of the narratives in each of the poems concerns the characters' efficacious prayers, liturgies, chanting of mantras (magical words), and incantations. Near the conclusion of *The Ramayana*, the chief sacrifice (that of a horse) is part of a ceremony in which Rāma's two sons recite the entire Ramayana from memory—24,000 verses of thirty-two syllables each. The performance lasts for twenty-five days. The enormous length of the work suggests that memorizing (or even sitting through it all) involves an act of *tapas*: psychic energy obtained in altered states of consciousness induced, for example, by prolonged immobilization while magic words are spoken. The experience is associated even more closely with the supernatural, when Rāma and the rest of the audience hear their listening to it described in that epic and their future predicted. Vālmīki's style (in both poems) subtly contributes to this eeriness by depending less on detailed description than on metaphor. In classical Greek poetry, detail makes a narrated setting seem more solid and real, but Vālmīki's metaphors tend to compare the human world to mythological exemplars, increasing fantasy. Rāma's royal father, for example, is habitually likened to Indra, ruler of the gods.

THE RAMAYANA

Although shorter than the other great Indian epic (*Mahābhārata*, c. 400 B.C.E.-200 C.E.; *The Mahabharata*, 1834), *The Ramayana* may contain sections that predate it, if one judges by depiction of social customs. It has seven *kandas* (books), yet Western scholars tend to consider the first and last *kandas* to be later additions. The first book, for example, makes Rāma an incarnation of the god Vishnu—an identification not mentioned in the passages deemed oldest (since devotion to Vishnu grew in Hinduism).

The basic plot is a love story, albeit one that runs quite counter to modern Western notions of romance. Rāma wins his wife Sītā by drawing a great bow no one else can string, comparable to Odysseus in Homer's *Odyssey* (c. 725 B.C.E.; English translation, 1614). Whereas Odysseus's abilities, however, only slightly exaggerate human possibility, Rāma is a more extreme (and stranger) idealization, from his blue skin to his superhuman feats of strength, moving mountains and forests. His father, King Daśaratha, decides to abdicate in his favor, but owes two favors to Kaikeyi (one of the king's three queens). She insists that Rāma be banished and that her son, his half-brother Bharata, rule in his place for fourteen years. Daśaratha cannot take back the words he has spoken to Kaikeyi. While Rāma is in the forest, his father's old enemy, the demon king Rāvaṇa kidnaps Sītā. With the aid of the talking monkey Hanumān, Rāma rescues her, but false rumors that the demon seduced her cause her to prove her innocence through a trial by fire. The rumors, nonetheless, persist. Since, in this epic, words have a supernatural power that cannot be ignored, Rāma banishes her. She kills herself, and he is inconsolable.

Some Western interpretations have presumed that the story is an allegory of the conquest of India by Aryans, with Rāma personifying them, the monkeys being their racist depiction of southern Indians, and the demons being their equally racist portrait of Sri Lankans. In its present form, though, the allegory is less political than cultural, characterized by extreme stereotypes. Kaikeyi, being royal, would not have thought on her own of any scheme so evil as exiling Rāma, so she is persuaded by a hunchbacked maid. No clear motivation beyond the latter's being hunchbacked is needed. If her body is crooked, then she must be so in character, as Rāma's physically embodying the Indian ideal signifies his absolute virtue. In *The Ramayana*, evil tends to have a female origin, for example, the maid, or a female demon who arranges for Sītā's kidnapping, or Sītā's own complicity in it by greedily insisting that Rāma leave her to bring her a pet deer. This stereotyping, however, is consistent with a magical conception of language as embodying eternal archetypes—mythic patterns that give it power and conserve a static social structure.

THE SUPREME YOGA

For more than a decade, the Moksopaya Project Research Group led by Walter Slaje has been arguing that a brief Kashmir version of *The Supreme Yoga* is much closer to the original than the longer one, previously considered standard. Whereas the longer version is a series of parables told to Rāma to enlighten him, the shorter one (the *Mokṣopāya*) is a lecture delivered to an audience. Slaje's group tends to prefer the Kashmir version. Even if his historical argument is correct, however, one might praise the longer version as vastly enriched with stories within stories, connecting it to *The Ramayana* as well as to the growing worship of Vishnu.

Less sexist than *The Ramayana*, the longer *The Supreme Yoga* contains such charming tales as that of Queen Cūḍālā. Being enlightened herself, she tries to counsel her foolish husband against seeking enlightenment in the forest, when he could better attain it at home. While he is wasting his time in the wild, she rules. She visits him in male guise, eventually managing to enlighten him. He learns from her what each of the stories within *The Supreme Yoga* repeat: that the world is an illusion, the dream of the divine Brahman, the one reality. Suffering comes from having forgotten this primal unity. Enlightenment is best achieved by combining this knowledge with an active life rather than (like the foolish king) abandoning one's duties for *tapas* in the wilderness. This belief that Brahman alone exists is also the argument of those Hindu scriptures the Upanishads, some of which contain sections from the longer *The Supreme Yoga*. Ironically, if this doctrine is correct, then Vālmīki indeed is merely a fiction, since the whole world is.

BIBLIOGRAPHY

Bose, Mandakranta, ed. *"The Ramayana" Revisited.* New York: Oxford University Press, 2004. This collection of essays both documents and engages in many facets of the reinterpretation of *The Ramayana* throughout Southeast Asia, particularly concerning the epic's attitudes toward gender and caste.

Chatterjee, Asim Kuma. *A Historical Introduction to the Critical Edition of the Rāmāyaṇa.* Calcutta: Rajyashree Bhattacharya, 2007. This valuable supplement to the 1960-1973 critical edition not only examines the historical context of *The Ramayana*, but also the history of its influence.

Khan, Benjamin. *The Concept of Dharma in Valmiki Ramayana.* Delhi: Munshi Ram Manohar, 1965. In addition to its main subject (the epic's presentation of ethics), Khan also summarizes considerable scholarship on Vālmīki and the epic.

Leslie, Julia. *Authority and Meaning in Indian Religions: Hinduism and the Case of Valmiki.* Burlington, Vt.: Ashgate, 2003. Beginning with a twenty-first century controversy in the United Kingdom between Hindu worshipers of Vālmīki and Hindus criticizing him, Leslie searches for roots of the conflict through an analysis of works traditionally attributed to Vālmīki and their historical development.

Sena, Nabanītā Deba. *Alternative Interpretations of the Rāmāyaṇa: Views from Below.* New Delhi: Centre for Women's Development Studies, 2001. Part of the J. P. Naik Memorial Lecture Series, this volume exemplifies a feminist approach to *The Ramayana* in modern India.

Vālmīki. *The Rāmāyaṇa of Vālmīki.* 6 vols. Princeton, N.J.: Princeton University Press, 1990-2009. A multivolume translation of most of the epic. Contains background information, scholarly introductions, and copious notes. Translators and editors include R. P. Goldman, S. S. Goldman, R. Lefeber, S. I. Pollock, and B. A. van Nooten.

Yardi, M. R. *"The Rāmāyaṇa," Its Origin and Growth: A Statistical Study.* Poona, India: Bhandarkar Oriental Research Institute, 1994. This examination of changes in the writing style comes to similar (but slightly more conservative) conclusions than the consensus view of *The Ramayana*'s textural history. For example, Yardi considers part of the first book to have been written by someone other than the poet who wrote the epic's earliest version.

James Whitlark

ANDREI VOZNESENSKY

Born: Moscow, Soviet Union (now in Russia); May 12, 1933

Died: Moscow, Russia; June 1, 2010

PRINCIPAL POETRY
Mozaika, 1960
Parabola, 1960

Treugol'naya grusha, 1962

Antimiry, 1964 (*Antiworlds*, 1966)

Akhillesovo serdtse, 1966

Voznesensky: Selected Poems, 1966

Antiworlds and the Fifth Ace, 1967

Stikhi, 1967

Ten' zvuka, 1970 (*The Shadow of Sound*, 1975)

Dogalypse, 1972

*Little Woods: Recent Poems by Andrei
    Voznesensky*, 1972

Nostalgia for the Present, 1978

Soblazn, 1978

Stikhotvoreniia: Poemy, 1983

An Arrow in the Wall: Selected Poetry and Prose,
    1987

Rov, 1987 (*The Ditch: A Spiritual Trial*, 1987)

On the Edge: Poems and Essays from Russia, 1991

Gadanie po knige, 1994

OTHER LITERARY FORMS

Andrei Voznesensky (voz-nuh-SEHN-skee) is known primarily for his lyric poetry; however, he produced a body of experimental work that challenges the borders between literary forms. For example, his long work "Oza" (1964) is a literary montage alternating verse with prose passages and incorporating several points of view. *Avos* (1972; *Story Under Full Sail*, 1974), based on the life of the Russian diplomat and explorer Nikolai Petrovich Rezanov, is sometimes classified as poetry, sometimes as prose. Voznesensky's prose writings include a short memoir, "I Am Fourteen," which sheds light on his friendship with the famed Russian writer Boris Pasternak; "O" (about), which appears in *An Arrow in the Wall*, a critical commentary on art and literature; and "Little Crosses," an essay on spirituality. In addition, he wrote a play, *Save Your Faces* (pr. 1971), and collaborated on musical and theatrical pieces such as the "rock opera" *Iunona i Avos* (pr. 1983; Juno and Avos).

ACHIEVEMENTS

During the early 1960's, Andrei Voznesensky, like his contemporary Yevgeny Yevtushenko, enjoyed enormous popularity in what was then the Soviet Union. His books sold hundreds of thousands of copies as soon as

they were published, and fans flocked to public readings held in athletic stadiums to accommodate audiences of ten thousand and more.

His poetry, which is intellectually demanding, drew critical acclaim internationally as well as within the Soviet Union. His literary awards spanned three decades. *Antiworlds* was nominated for the Lenin Prize in literature in 1966, and "The Stained Glass Panel Master" won the State Literature Prize in 1978. He was awarded the International Award for Distinguished Achievement in Poetry in 1972, and his collection *An Arrow in the Wall*, edited by William Jay Smith and F. D. Reeve, received the *New York Times* Editor's Choice Award in 1987.

BIOGRAPHY

Born in Moscow in 1933 to a well-educated family, Andrei Andreyevich Voznesensky was exposed to art and literature at an early age. His mother, a teacher, read him poetry and inspired his interest in major Russian writers. His father, a professor of engineering, introduced him to the work of the Spanish artist Francisco de Goya, which would later inspire "I Am Goya," one of Voznesensky's best-known poems. While growing up, Voznesensky pursued interests in the arts, especially painting, but he did not focus on poetry until 1957, the year he completed a degree from the Moscow Institute of Architecture. Then, in a strange twist of fate, a fire at the institute destroyed his thesis project. For Voznesensky, this was a sign that his future lay not in architecture but in poetry.

In the same year, he met the famed Russian writer Boris Pasternak, with whom he had been corresponding. Pasternak served as a mentor for Voznesensky, but the younger poet quickly found his own voice. The similarities between the work of the two authors lie in their moral vision and their goals as writers to revive Russian literature after years of oppression under the dictatorship of Joseph Stalin. An essential difference is in their fates. In spite of an easing of government censorship following Stalin's death in 1953, Pasternak was expelled from the powerful Soviet Writers' Union for the 1957 publication of *Doktor Zhivago* (*Doctor Zhivago*, 1958). The novel's free-thinking protagonist criticizes Soviet Communism. However, in the changing literary-political climate of the time, Voznesensky quickly became one of the best-known poets in the Soviet Union. In 1960, his first collection, *Mozaika* (mosaic), appeared in print, and he published a number of collections in rapid succession, as audiences responded enthusiastically to the freshness of his work.

The success of Voznesensky, his contemporary Yevtushenko, and other "liberal" writers created a backlash within the Writers' Union. By 1963, Voznesensky had come under attack from the more orthodox literary establishment, the government-controlled press, and Soviet premier Nikita Khrushchev. Unlike Pasternak, who was censored for the content of his writing, Voznesensky was denounced for his innovative style, which critics claimed produced a decadent, superficial art, devoid of meaning. Charges of formalism and obscurantism resurfaced throughout the 1960's and into the following decade.

In response, Voznesensky addressed his critics directly in his poetry, and he began to produce verse on the subject of creative freedom and the nature of art. He defended the complexity and ambiguity of his work, asserting, "if the poems are complicated, why then, so is life." He also spoke out against government censorship. In 1967, he openly supported fellow writer Aleksandr Solzhenitsyn, who had been expelled from the Writers' Union and later exiled from the Soviet Union for his attack on Soviet censorship. In 1979, Voznesensky participated in the publication of an independent literary journal.

In spite of recurring conflicts with government and the conservative literary establishment, Voznesensky incurred only minor punishment. Throughout his career, he was able to travel abroad, live comfortably, and publish regularly. He remained committed to innovative and experimental art forms, producing a body of work that challenges conventional classification. Married to the writer and critic Zoya Boguslavskaya, he had one son. He died in Moscow, at the age of seventy-seven, on June 1, 2010.

ANALYSIS

The American poet W. H. Auden remarked that Andrei Voznesensky is a writer who understands that "a poem is a verbal artifact which must be as skillfully and solidly constructed as a table or a motorcycle." Voznesensky was well known for his technical virtuosity and structural innovation. His metric and rhyme schemes varied, often determined by the aural and visual aspects of the work. He paid close attention to surface patterning and sound play—assonance, alliteration, shaped text, stepped lines, palindromes—and often startled the reader with shifts in perspective, incongruous juxtaposition of images, and unexpected rhyme created by inserting slang or colloquial language into a line. He confronted the reader with a staggering array of metaphor, historical reference, and cultural allusion. Evidence of his early training in painting and architecture abounds in his work, which has been described as cubist, Surrealist, and Futurist. Voznesensky acknowledged, "As a poet I have been more profitably influenced by ancient Russian churches and by the works of Le Corbusier than by other poets."

Voznesensky's concern with technique and experi-

Andrei Voznesensky (©Arkady Hershman)

mentation related directly to the content of his writing and his central concern with human destiny, which he viewed as dependent on interconnectedness. For him, without a sense of connection to one another, to culture and tradition, and to the planet, humanity might fall into a destructive spiral. In a mechanized, technological world, the potential for fragmentation and alienation is great. The responsibility of the artist is to expose relationships, to "peel the skin from the planet."

Voznesensky sought to achieve his goal by breaking away from habitualized methods of seeing, from routines that limit and fragment vision. His wordplay, his seemingly bizarre selections of imagery, his multiple perspectives, and his blurring of genres were all designed to defamiliarize the world, allowing the reader to discover the spiritual ecosystem of existence. While Voznesensky's themes are universal, his innovativeness, particularly his sound play, makes his work difficult to translate. Effective English versions of his work are the Haywood/Blake 1967 edition *Antiworlds and the Fifth Ace* and the award-winning collection *An Arrow in the Wall*, edited by Smith and Reeve.

"I AM GOYA"

One of the earliest and best-known of his poems, "I Am Goya" (1959), exemplifies Voznesensky's skill in creating new forms to examine broad themes. He framed the poem by opening and closing with the same line, "I am Goya." In identifying with Goya, a nineteenth century Spanish painter known for his harsh depictions of war, Voznesensky established an immediate link across time, space, and artistic genres. He reinforced these links in each of the four stanzas with an eclectic range of images and allusions and by the repetition of the first line. The horrors of war belong to all ages, and the artist's role is to transcend the immediate and speak to the universal, "hammer[ing] stars into the unforgetting sky—like nails."

Voznesensky composed "I Am Goya" aloud rather than writing it on paper in order to develop fully the aural qualities of the verse. He described it as "picking the words, so that they would ring out" like the bells of an ancient monastery playing "the music of grief." To this end, Voznesensky combined repetition of sounds with an uninterrupted beat that tolls throughout the poem. The rhythms of the poem anticipate the powerful image "of a woman hanged whose body like a bell/ tolled over a blank square," then embed it in a synesthetic format.

"PARABOLIC BALLAD"

Voznesensky considered "Parabolic Ballad" (1960) one of his best poems. Citing the career of the French painter Paul Gauguin as a model, Voznesensky justifies the ambiguity and experimental nature of his own work and reasserts his aesthetics. Like Gauguin, who "To reach the royal Louvre,/ Set his course/ On a detour via Java and Sumatra," the poet must not take the direct route, choose the ready-made symbol, or speak in clichés. Rather, the artist must follow the trajectory of a rocket, a parabola, to escape "the earth's force of gravitation" and explore the far side of the universe.

"OZA"

Written in 1964, a year after Voznesensky was denounced for formalism and obscurity, "Oza" was a bold response to his critics. This complex narrative poem contemplates the fate of humanity in a technological society and continues the poet's experiments with poetic structure. Sections of prose alternate with poetry, themes intersect, and point of view shifts. The work is rich in literary and historical allusion. One section parodies Edgar Allan Poe's poem "The Raven"; another satirizes former Soviet dictator Stalin.

Introduced as a diary found in a hotel in Dubna, the site of a Soviet nuclear research facility, "Oza" describes a world rearranged by technology. The protagonist, Zoia, is a well-meaning scientist transformed through her own arrogance and complacency into an automaton named Oza. Zoia means "life" in Russian, but in the rearrangement of letters of her name, the "I" has been lost, suggesting the loss of self in a rigidly mechanized culture. Like Zoia/Oza, the poet risks losing his identity. In a scene described sometimes comically from the perspective of a ceiling mirror, the poet is invisible, immune to the inversion of the reflecting surface, and alienated from his fellow beings. Although unseen, he makes himself heard, proclaiming "I am Andrei; not just anyone/ All progress is regression/ If the progress breaks man down."

THE DITCH

This long narrative poem explores human greed. The actual ditch is the site of a massacre near Simferopol, a city on the Crimean Peninsula, where in 1941, twelve thousand Jews were executed by Nazis. In the 1980's, grave robbing occurred at the site. Although several men were convicted and received prison sentences in 1985—and it is to this event that the "trial" of the subtitle alludes—the looting continued. On a visit to the site two years after the trial, Voznesensky observed skulls that had been excavated and smashed for the bits of gold in the teeth.

As in earlier works, Voznesensky employed contrasting imagery, shifts in perspective, and inversions. A prose "afterword" introduces the work, suggesting an inversion of values. The mixture of voices and genres and the range of references take the subject beyond the specific crime into an examination of human nature.

GADANIE PO KNIGE

Inspired by traditional Russian fortune-telling, *Gadanie po knige* (telling by the book) examines the interconnectedness of chance and design. In this collection, Voznesensky took his wordplay to a new level, creating complex, multilingual meanings. Like a fortune-teller, he shuffled language and laid it out in patterns: circles, palindromes, anagrams. At times, he mixed English words with Russian ones, switching between the Cyrillic and Roman alphabets as well; he fragmented words from both languages and rearranged the syllables. What may initially appear random, pointless, or merely amusing surprisingly yields meaning, as when he exploited phonetically MMM, the name of a financial institution involved in a costly scandal. He connected MMM with the English word "money," the Russian word for "mania," and finally, the Russian slang for "nothing."

OTHER MAJOR WORKS

LONG FICTION: *Avos*, 1972 (*Story Under Full Sail*, 1974).

PLAYS: *Save Your Faces*, pr. 1971; *I Am Goya*, pr. 1982 (music by Nigel Osborne); *Iunona i Avos*, pr. 1983 (music by Alexei Rybnikov).

BIBLIOGRAPHY

Airaudi, Jesse T. "Hard to Be a God: The Political Antiworlds of Voznesensky, Sokilov, and the Brothers Strugatsky." In *Visions of the Fantastic: Selected Essays from the Fifteenth International Conference on the Fantastic in the Arts*, edited by Allienne R. Becker. London: Greenwood Press, 1996. Airaudi provides a sound rationale for Voznesensky's use of the fantastic to escape from the false, primary world imposed by governments and ruled by ideologies. Airaudi places Voznesensky in the tradition of the Russian writer Nikolai Gogol, yet suggests Western readers can best understand Voznesensky in terms of Surrealism.

Anderson, Raymond. "Andrei Voznesensky, Russian Poet, Dies at Seventy-seven." *The New York Times*, June 1, 2010, p. A23. Obituary of Voznesensky recalls his experimental poetry, his problems with the Soviet authorities, and his popularity as a poet.

Brown, Deming. *Soviet Russian Literature Since Stalin*. New York: Cambridge University Press, 1978. This well-documented literary history provides a good overview of the complex and ever-fluctuating relationship between literature and politics in the two decades following the death of dictator Joseph Stalin. Voznesensky is referred to throughout the book and is a key figure in the fifth chapter, "The Younger Generation of Poets."

Carlisle, Olga. *Poets on Street Corners: Portraits of Fifteen Russian Poets*. New York: Random House, 1968. In this collection of biographical sketches, Carlisle, the granddaughter of noted Russian writer Leonid Andreyev, has included poets who write about and for ordinary Russians living ordinary lives. Her chapter on Voznesensky features lengthy quotations from interviews with the poet between 1963 and 1967. Voznesensky's comments on the significance of poetry and the role of the poet are particularly illuminating.

Jason, Philip K., ed. *Masterplots II: Poetry Series*. Rev. ed. Pasadena, Calif.: Salem Press, 2002. This set contains summaries and analyses of the Voznesensky poems "Foggy Street" and "The Last Train to Malkhovka."

Plimpton, George, ed. *Beat Writers at Work: "The Paris Review."* New York: Random House, 1999. Conversations between Voznesensky and American poets Allen Ginsberg and Peter Orlovsky provide an entertaining, behind-the-scenes look at the writers as they discuss the poet's craft.

Porter, Robert, ed. *Seven Soviet Poets*. London: Gerald Duckworth, 2000. Porter's slender collection provides a thoughtful introduction, bibliographies, a historical reference guide, annotations, and biographical time lines for Voznesensky as well as other twentieth century Russian poets. These sections are in English, but the poetry is in Russian. For readers who are new to the language, the collection provides a good starting point with a supplemental vocabulary.

K Edgington

DEREK WALCOTT

Born: Castries, St. Lucia, West Indies; January 23, 1930

PRINCIPAL POETRY

Twenty-five Poems, 1948
Poems, 1951
In a Green Night: Poems, 1948-1960, 1962
Selected Poems, 1964
The Castaway, and Other Poems, 1965
The Gulf, and Other Poems, 1969
Another Life, 1973, expanded, 2004
Sea Grapes, 1976
The Star-Apple Kingdom, 1979
The Fortunate Traveller, 1981
Midsummer, 1984
Collected Poems, 1948-1984, 1986
The Arkansas Testament, 1987
Omeros, 1990
Poems, 1965-1980, 1992
The Bounty, 1997
Tiepolo's Hound, 2000
The Prodigal, 2004
Selected Poems, 2007 (Edward Baugh, editor)
White Egrets, 2010

OTHER LITERARY FORMS

Derek Walcott has written many plays, published in *Dream on Monkey Mountain, and Other Plays* (1970), *The Joker of Seville and O Babylon! Two Plays* (1978), *Remembrance and Pantomime: Two Plays* (1980), and *Three Plays* (1986), as well as *The Odyssey* (1993); *The Capeman*, a musical with music by Paul Simon (1998); and *The Haitian Trilogy* (2001). His nonfiction includes his Nobel Prize lecture, *The Antilles: Fragments of Epic Memory* (1993); a collaboration with Joseph Brodsky and Seamus Heaney, *Homage to Robert Frost* (1996); and a collection of essays, *What the Twilight Says* (1998).

ACHIEVEMENTS

Derek Walcott's work is infused with both a sacred sense of the writer's vocation and a passionate devotion to his island of birth, St. Lucia, and the entire Caribbean archipelago. A cultural dichotomy supplies the major tensions in his writing: He combines native French Creole and West Indian dialects with the formal, high structures of English poetry. His mystic sense of place and eruptive imagination are poised against a highly controlled metrical form. As a lyrical and epic poet he has managed to encompass history, culture, and autobiography with an intensely aesthetic and steadily ironic vision. Walcott is arguably a major poet in his ability to dramatize the myths of his social and personal life, to balance his urgent moral concerns with the ideal of a highly polished, powerfully dense art, and to cope with the cultural isolation to which his mixed race sadly condemns him.

The Dream of Monkey Mountain, Walcott's most highly lauded play, won the 1971 Obie Award. His book *Another Life* received the Jock Campbell/New Statesman Prize in 1974. He received the Los Angeles Times Book Prize for poetry in 1986 for *Collected Poems*. In 1972, he received not only an honorary doctorate of letters from the University of the West Indies but also an O.B.E. (Officer, Order of British Empire), and he was named an honorary member of the American Academy of Arts and Letters in 1979. Other awards and fellowships include a Guggenheim Fellowship in 1977, the American Poetry Review Award in 1979, the International Writer's Prize of the Welsh Arts Council in 1980, a John D. and Catherine T. MacArthur Foundation "genius" grant in 1981, the Queen Elizabeth II Gold Medal for Poetry in 1988, and the St. Lucia Cross in 1993. Walcott received the 1992 Nobel Prize in Literature. In 2010, he became Professor of Poetry at the University of Essex, where he was awarded an honorary degree in 2008.

BIOGRAPHY

Derek Alton Walcott was born in Castries, the capital of St. Lucia, to a civil servant, Warwick, and to Alix, the head of a Methodist grammar school. St. Lucia is a volcanic island of 238 square miles in the Lesser Antilles, halfway between French Martinique to the north

Derek Walcott (Virginia Shendler)

West Indies, since they link Columbus and Robinson Crusoe, Africa and America, slavery and colonialism, exploitation and emancipation. Curiously, he even compartmentalizes his writing, stressing oral tales and folk language in his plays while suffusing most of his poems with an Elizabethan richness and Miltonic dignity of diction.

In *Another Life* Walcott has rendered an autobiographical narrative of his childhood and early career. This long narrative poem unfolds the evolution of a poet who will always consider himself "the divided child." At school he was taught European art, history, and literature, but his mother insisted on connecting him to the Africa-based culture of the black St. Lucian majority. A landscape painter and teacher, Harry Simmons, and a drawing and drinking friend, Dunstan St. Omer, sought to fashion him in their images. Walcott discovered, however, that "I lived in a different gift,/ its element metaphor" and abandoned the canvas for the printed page.

In part 3, "A Simple Flame," he falls in love with Anna, but her golden body cannot long compete with his passion for poetry,

> which hoped that their two bodies could be made
> one body of immortal metaphor.
> The hand she held already had betrayed
> them by its longing for describing her.

He mythicizes his Anna, dissolving her into all the literary Annas he has adored: Eugene O'Neill's Anna Christie, Leo Tolstoy's Anna Karenina, and the great modern Russian poet Anna Akhmatova. He leaves for study abroad.

In part 4, "The Estranging Sea," he returns home, "one life, one marriage later" (to Fay Moston, from 1954 to 1959). He encounters Dunstan, called "Gregorias," and finds him alcoholic, unable to hold a job, painting poorly, failing even at suicide. He learns that Simmons has killed himself, with his body lying undiscovered for two days. Walcott then scathingly denounces ill-wishers who condemn their promising artists to an early grave. He finds comfort and hope in the sea, wishes a peaceful rest to his friends and loves, and dedicates himself to literature, his fury spent:

and English St. Vincent to the southeast. It was discovered by Christopher Columbus in 1502, then contested for generations by the French and British, until the latter gained legal control in 1803, to yield their colonial hold only in 1959. Still, the Gallic influence remains, insofar as the population of about 100,000, largely of black African descent, speaks a Creole patois.

Because Walcott is descended from a white grandfather and black grandmother on both sides of his family, he has found himself ineluctably suspended between loyalties, resentments, fears, and fantasies. He has referred in essays to a schizophrenic boyhood, split between two lives: the interior pull toward poetry and the exterior push toward the world of action, as well as the raw spontaneity of his native argot opposed to the syntactical sinews of formal English. Inescapably, he has been both victim and victor of his divided culture, a kind of Caribbean Orestes who shuttles between the legends and folklore of his upbringing and the formal traditions of the cosmopolitan West. In his work Walcott has made much of the bridging geography of the

> for what else is there
> but books, books and the sea,
> verandahs and the pages of the sea,
> to write of the wind and the memory of
>
> wind-whipped hair
> in the sun, the colour of fire?

Walcott made his debut as a writer in 1948, with *Twenty-Five Poems*, privately printed in Barbados with a two-hundred-dollar loan from his mother and hawked by the author through the streets of Castries. In 1951, he published his second collection, *Poems*, while studying at the Mona campus of the University of the West Indies. During the 1950's he taught at secondary schools and colleges in St. Lucia, Grenada, and Jamaica. In 1958, he moved to Trinidad and there founded, in 1959, the Trinidad Theatre Workshop, with which he remained associated as both playwright and director until 1976, seeking to blend Shakespearean drama and calypso music, Bertolt Brecht's stage craft with West Indian folk legends. Crucial in his development as a dramatist were several months he spent in New York City in 1958, studying under José Quintero on a Rockefeller grant, learning how to incorporate songs and dances into a dramatic text.

For many years Walcott has divided his time between a home in Trinidad and teaching positions in the United States, including visiting professorships at Columbia and Harvard universities and lectureships at Yale and Rutgers. In 1985, he became a visiting professor at Boston University. His career has been both prolific and versatile, not only as poet and playwright but also as producer, set designer, painter, critic, and cultural commentator. He has been married three times, each marriage ending in divorce, and has one son from his first marriage and two daughters from his second.

ANALYSIS

Derek Walcott's first important volume of verse, *In a Green Night*, was a landmark in the history of West Indian poetry, breaking with exotic native traditions of shallow romanticism and inflated rhetorical abstractions. In such entries as "A Far Cry from Africa," "Ruins of a Great House," and "Two Poems on the Passing of an Empire," he began to confront the complex personal fate that would dominate all of his work—his identity as a transplanted African in an English-organized society. In "A Far Cry from Africa" he concludes,

> I who am poisoned with the blood of both,
> Where shall I turn, divided to the vein?
> I who have cursed
> The drunken officer of British rule, how choose
> Between this Africa and the English tongue I love?
> Betray them both, or give back what they give?
> How can I face such slaughter and be cool?
> How can I turn from Africa and live?

Using the English tongue he loves does not preclude Walcott from feeling outrage at the degradation to which the British Empire has subjected his people, "the abuse/ of ignorance by Bible and by sword." He calls "Hawkins, Walter Raleigh, Drake,/ Ancestral murderers and poets." Yet this rage-filled poem ends on a note of compassion, as the speaker recalls that England was also once an exploited colony subject to "bitter faction." The heart dictates anger, but the intelligence controls and mellows feelings, perceiving the complexity of human experience.

IN A GREEN NIGHT

In the initial poem, "Prelude," the young poet looks down on his island and sees it beaten into proneness by indifferent tourists who regard it as insignificant. Yet he knows that his poetry is a means of transcending his land's triviality "in accurate iambics." He thus sets the stage and plot for his personal odyssey as an artist, which he would undertake over and over again in his career. With the duplicity of a guerrilla and the self-conscious stance of T. S. Eliot's J. Alfred Prufrock, he plans to "straighten my tie and fix important jaws,/ And note the living images/ Of flesh that saunter through the eye."

In the poem's concluding stanza, the speaker states that he is "in the middle of the journey through my life," as Dante was at the opening of his *Inferno* (in *La divina commedia*, c. 1320; *The Divine Comedy*, 1802). He encounters the same animal as the Florentine poet— a leopard, symbolizing self-indulgence. Walcott thus merges his identity as an islander with his mission as a poet, his private self becoming a public metaphor for art's affirmation.

In "Origins," Walcott composes a creation myth of his native place, finding in the cosmogonic conditions of his landscape a protean identity as an individual and an epic consciousness of his culture, akin to that of Walt Whitman and Pablo Neruda. The sonic boom of the first two lines—"The flowering breaker detonates its surf./ White bees hiss in the coral skull"—is reminiscent of the acoustical flamboyance present in such Hart Crane poems as "Voyages" and "O Carib Isle." The warm Caribbean waters become an amniotic bath for the poet, who sees himself as "an infant Moses" envisioning "Paradise as columns of lilies and wheat-headed angels." In sections 3 and 4 of his long poem Walcott pays homage to his island's language, laying out undulating strings of images in the manner of Aimé Césaire, another West Indian poet and dramatist, with the roll of surrealistic phrases imitating the roll of the surf.

In a Green Night exhibits Walcott's remarkable formal virtuosities. He can compose rhyming quatrains of iambic tetrameter, as in the title poem, or a traditional sonnet sequence, such as in "Tales of the Islands," which combines subtle metrical music with exuberant energy. He can chant like Dylan Thomas ("A City's Death by Fire"), be as astringent as W. H. Auden ("A Country Club Romance"), or indulge in Creole language ("Parang"). Like Andrew Marvell, whose Metaphysical poetry was an influential model for the early Walcott, he is caught between the pull of passion and his awareness of its futility.

THE CASTAWAY, AND OTHER POEMS

In *The Castaway, and Other Poems*, Walcott's focus on the artist's role becomes more overt, as he describes the poet as the archetypal artist-in-exile, thus a castaway, symbolizing also West Indians in general as historical discard from other cultures. He perceives the poet, paradoxically, as both the detached observer of society and its centrally located, living emblem. Walcott adopts the protean Robinson Crusoe image for this purpose, dramatizing him as Adam, Columbus, Daniel Defoe, even God, as the first inhabitant of a second Paradise, as discoverer and ruler of the world he has made. He insists on a complex relationship between the creative, exploring artist and a largely imperceptive community that tends to isolate and ignore him, yet that the poet nonetheless persists in representing. Sometimes he finds art inadequate in trying to order inchoate life, as in "Crusoe's Island": "Art is profane and pagan,/ The most it has revealed/ Is what a crippled Vulcan/ Beat on Achilles' shield."

THE GULF, AND OTHER POEMS

The next collection, *The Gulf, and Other Poems*, deepens the theme of isolation, with the poet extending his sense of alienation to the world of the 1960's: John Kennedy's and Che Guevara's killings ("The Gulf" and "Che," respectively), racial violence in the United States ("Blues"), the Vietnam War ("Postcards"), the civil war in Nigeria ("Negatives"). The gulf, then, is everywhere, with divisions mocking people's best efforts at unity, intimacy, order, harmony, and happiness. Despite his disappointments, Walcott employs the gulf image ambivalently. To be sure, it encompasses the moral wasteland that the world has largely become; more optimistically, however, it stands for a healing awareness of separateness whereby the castaway, Crusoe-like artist understands his identity and place in the world. In the last analysis, Walcott insists, it is the poet's art that endures: "some mind must squat down howling in your dust,/ some hand must crawl and recollect your rubbish,/ someone must write your poems." The poet's apartness does not, then, result in his total alienation—he still commits his art to the world's experiences.

ANOTHER LIFE AND SEA GRAPES

In *Another Life*, Walcott avoids self-centered egotism as he mythologizes his island life, reimagining the *Iliad* (c. 750 B.C.E.; English translation, 1611) in the context of his own land and culture and using the odyssey motif to sustain this long poem. He even envisages his islanders as Homeric archetypes (Ajax, Cassandra, Helen, and others), engaged in an intense quest for their national identity. The poet's journey becomes a microcosm of the West Indian's, indeed the New World's, search for wholeness, acceptance, and fulfillment. As the young Walcott is taught by Gregorias, the peasant-painter-pal, he develops his talent—though for letters rather than the visual arts—within the context of an artistic tradition that articulates the dreams and needs of his people. He ends the superbly sustained narrative by celebrating both the painter's and the poet's mission:

"Gregorias, listen, lit,/ we were the light of the world!/ We were blest with a virginal, unpainted world/ with Adam's task of giving things their names."

Sea Grapes is a quieter, more austere book than *Another Life*, a calm after the storm, with many of its poems elegiac, elegant, sparely constructed, and sad. The prevailing mood of the volume is one of middle-age acceptance, maturation, and resignation: "why does my gift already look over its shoulder/ for a shadow to fill the door/ and pass this very page into eclipse?" ("Preparing for Exile"). Again, Walcott rehearses the tensions of his divided heritage as a West Indian trying to accommodate his African instincts to the formalities and calculations of European modes. In the title poem he equates himself to the sea-wandering Odysseus, longing for Nausicaa while duty-bound for his home and family, torn between obsession and responsibility, and poignantly concludes, "The classics can console. But not enough." A five-part, long work, "Sainte Lucie," is a psalm to St. Lucia, mixing French Creole with English, vernacular speech with stately diction.

THE STAR-APPLE KINGDOM

The Star-Apple Kingdom is a lyrical celebration, studded with vivid images. Its most ambitious poem, "The Schooner Flight," features a seaman-poet, Shabine, a fleeing castaway from his island; Shabine is clearly a Walcott double, with "Dutch, nigger and English" in him so that "either I'm nobody, or I'm a nation." Shabine's ordeal is the allegory of Everyman. He loves his wife and children but also desires the beautiful Maria Concepcion. Like Odysseus, he encounters terrors and defeats them; unlike Odysseus, he often runs away from his duties rather than toward them. He does manage to escape a web of corruption and betrayal, however, and matures into a waterfront Isaiah whose vision embraces his people's history, learning to appreciate nature's simplicities, "satisfied/ if my hand gave voice to one people's grief."

The protagonist of "The Star-Apple Kingdom" is more sophisticated, satirical, and astute than Shabine, with his reflections more acerbic and cerebral. The poem begins as he peruses a photograph album dating from the Victorian era, featuring such subjects as "Herefords at Sunset in the Valley of the Wye." Then he pon-

ders the miseries of blacks excluded from the joys of the plantation aristocracy, "their mouths in the locked jaw of a silent scream." A dream possesses him. In it he plunges into a nightmare procession of Caribbean injustices, both during and after the rule of colonialism. Awakening at dawn, he feels rejuvenated and serene. His eye falls on an elderly, black cleaning woman who now represents to him his people's strength and endurance, with a "creak of light" evoking the possibility of a better future for both her and them.

THE FORTUNATE TRAVELLER

In *The Fortunate Traveller*, Walcott largely removes his pulsating sensibility from his home turf, focusing on New England, Manhattan, the American South, Chicago, London, Wales, and Greece. In "Old New England" he apprentices himself to the American vernacular, sounding somewhat like Robert Lowell in such statements as "Old Glories flail/ the crosses of green farm boys back from 'Nam." Yet no one can successfully assume a new idiom overnight, and Walcott's pentameters usually retain their British, Yeatsian cadences: "The crest of our conviction grows as loud/ as the spring oaks, rooted and reassured/ that God is meek but keeps a whistling sword."

Some of Walcott's many virtues are evident in this collection: He is deeply intelligent, keeps enlarging his range of styles and reach of subjects, has a fertile imagination, and often commands precise, sonorous eloquence. In "Hurucan," he compellingly summons the god of hurricanes, "havoc, reminder, ancestor," who stands allegorically for the world's oppressors. In "The Hotel Normandie Pool," he masters both his social topic and personal memories. At the pool Walcott imagines a fellow exile, Ovid, banished from Rome to a Black Sea port, facing the rigors of a harsher climate yet continuing to compose his verses, epitomizing the predicament of an educated colonial poet writing in the language of an empire.

The book's best poem is its last, "The Season of Phantasmal Peace." It begins at twilight, as migrating birds lift up the net of the shadows of the earth, causing a "passage of phantasmal light/ that not the narrowest shadow dared to sever." These singers unify the earth's various dialects and feel "something brighter than pity" for creatures that remain below, wingless, in their dark holes and houses. The birds close the poem by undertaking an act of brief charity, lifting their net above betrayals, follies, and furies. The poem thereby lifts whatever darkness exists for an instant of peace, constituting a transcendent surge of song beyond the implied darkness of the world's wars and hatreds.

MIDSUMMER

Midsummer is a gathering of fifty-four poems, a number that corresponded to Walcott's age when the book was published. These lyric poems give the sense of their author noting his preoccupations during the course of a year. He equates midsummer with boredom, stasis, middle age, midcareer, and the harsh glare of self-examination, as he tries to fix the particular tone and texture of his inner life from one summer to the next. He turns ethnographer, chronicling hotel and motel life in Rome, Warwickshire, New York, Boston, and Chicago. Two-thirds of the sequence is set, however, in the tropics of Central America and his Caribbean islands.

As always, Walcott is nowhere comfortably at home. In the West Indies, he sees that "our houses are one step from the gutter," with "the doors themselves usually no wider than coffins." Once more, he plays Odysseus-in-exile: "And this is the lot of all wanderers, this is their fate,/ that the more they wander, the more the world grows wide." Writing to a friend in Rome, he contrasts its ancient heritage with the Caribbean area's sand-weighted corals, its catacombs with "silver legions of mackerel." In Boston, he mocks the stale air of cobblestoned streets and Transcendentalist tradition, feeling self-consciously black amid New England's white spires, harbors, and filling stations, with pedestrians, moving like "pale fishes," staring at him as though he were a "black porpoise."

Unable to resolve his dilemma of perpetual uprooting, Walcott is graceful enough to parody his wanderings among cultures and his position as a prodigal son who cannot arrive at any home or rest. In "LI," he tells himself, half-mockingly, "You were distressed by your habitat, you shall not find peace/ till you and your origins reconcile; your jaw must droop/ and your knuckles scrape the ground of your native place."

In poem 27, Walcott sardonically describes the American impact on the West Indies, such as a chain-

link fence separating a beach from a baseball field. "White, eager Cessnas" dot an airstrip in St. Thomas; fences separate villas and their beaches from illegal immigrants; "bulldozers jerk/ and gouge out a hill, but we all know that the dust/ is industrial and must be suffered." Even a pelican "coasts, with its engine off." No wonder that he feels "the fealty changing under my foot."

COLLECTED POEMS, 1948-1984

In 1986, Walcott's American publisher issued his *Collected Poems, 1948-1984*, a massive 516-page tome that includes selections from all of his previous books and the entirety of *Another Life*. Critical reception was largely laudatory, particularly welcoming Walcott's lyrical gifts, the extraordinary variety of his styles and settings, the sensuous eloquence and freshness of his language, the intensity of his tone, and his talent for uniting power with delicacy. Some reviewers, however, complained of inflated rhetoric, a penchant for grandiose clichés, diction that is overly ornamental, and a tendency to propagandize at the expense of authentic feeling.

THE ARKANSAS TESTAMENT

Walcott resumes his doomed search for a homeland in *The Arkansas Testament*. In the work's first section, "Here," he again inspects the society of his native island but finds only incomplete connections, fragmented friendships. In the moving "The Light of the World," set in a minibus in St. Lucia, the speaker segues from social intimacy to abandonment. He leaves the vehicle, concluding, "They went on in their transport, they left me on earth./ . . . / There was nothing they wanted, nothing I could give them but this thing I have called 'The Light of the World.'" The "light" is Walcott's talent for writing—to which his fellow passengers are largely oblivious.

In the "Elsewhere" section, the poet searches for fulfillment in other countries, praying "that the City may be just/ and humankind be kind." In the title poem, consisting of twenty-four segments of sixteen lines each, the speaker wanders from a motel in Fayetteville, Arkansas, to an all-night cafeteria, then returns to his motel, noting the exploitation of black Americans and calling the American flag "the stripes and the scars." His conclusion is, as usual with Walcott, bleak:

"Bless . . . / these stains I cannot remove/ from the self-soiled heart."

Images of dislocation and disharmony pervade the book, inducing a melancholy mood. Walcott refers to the Sphinx, to sirens and satyrs—all of them half-human, half-animal. Doors are unhinged, telephone calls are unanswered, poetry goes unread; justice and mercy are usually unmet. *The Arkansas Testament* is a musical chant mourning the world's many woes.

OMEROS

Omeros is a colossal modern epic, Walcott's most ambitious achievement, which universalizes his persistent themes of displacement, isolation, exploitation, estrangement, exile, and self-division. He merges the island chain of his Caribbean with the Mediterranean island chain now called Greece, where the *Iliad* (c. 750 B.C.E.; English translation, 1611) and *Odyssey* (c. 725 B.C.E.; English translation, 1614) are conventionally attributed to an Achaean bard, Homer, whose name is Omeros in modern Greek form. Omeros/Homer makes several appearances in the poem, most frequently as Seven Seas, a poor, blind fisherman, but also as an African tribal singer and as a London bargeman, thus helping to internationalize this narrative of more than eight thousand lines.

The links between the ancient Greeks and modern Antilleans are plausible enough: Both societies were and are seafaring, and both inhabit islands rife with legends, ghosts, and natural spirits. Walcott takes an audacious gamble when he assumes that the Caribbean patois, with its linguistic uncertainties, is capable of occasionally declaiming in classically patterned verse; he uses three-line stanzas in a salute to Dante's terza rima. He safeguards his venture, however, by minimizing the Creole argot and having most of the action related by a patently autobiographical, polished narrator: a displaced poet living in Boston and Toronto, visiting the Great Plains and the sites of American Civil War battles and encountering Omeros in both London and St. Lucia.

Walcott likens his squabbling, scrounging fishermen to the ancient Greeks and Trojans, and projects Homeric counterparts in his modern Caribbean Helen, Achille, Hector, Circe, and Philoctete. Helen works as a housemaid in the home of Major and Mrs. Plunkett.

As in Greek mythology, she is beautiful, proud, lazy, shallow, selfish, and magnetically irresistible to men. When she is fired by Mrs. Plunkett, she goes to work (occasionally) as a waitress, exciting the libidos of two fishermen friends, Hector and Achille. Walcott likens her to Judith and Susannah, Circe and Calypso, with her body creating a stirring drama out of every appearance.

Walcott's Hector differs drastically from Homer's, who had an ideal marriage to Andromache and was the Trojans' indispensable hero. This Hector abandons, at Helen's behest, his dignified but poorly paying work as a fisherman for the degrading but more lucrative job of taxiing tourists, hustling passengers at the wharf and airport. Paralleling Homer, Achille kills Hector in a fight over Helen, she settles down with him, and they will be parents to her expected child—Hector is the father.

The poem's focus expands further as it deals with Major Plunkett. At first he seems a stereotypical British colonial, with his "pensioned moustache" and Guinness-drinking taste. Walcott associates him, however, with not only the end of the Empire but also Montgomery's World War II victories in the Middle Eastern desert, and further with American Caucasian settlers displacing the American Indians. Undertaking genealogical research, the major discovers an ancestor who took part in the victory of the British navy's Admiral George Brydges Rodney over Admiral François-Joseph-Paul de Grasse's French fleet, acquiring St. Lucia as part of the British West Indies.

Then there is Philoctete, a fisherman disabled by a festering sore on his thigh. The link with the Greek myth is evident. Philoctetes, listed as one of the Greek Helen's many suitors, wanted to lead a flotilla of seven ships against Troy, but never reached it. Bitten on the foot by a snake on the island of Lemnos, he was ostracized by the other Achaean chieftains because the stench of his infected, rotting flesh nauseated them. Walcott's Philoctete is wounded by a rusty anchor and is also abandoned by his fellows while Achille undertakes a journey to Africa.

In the end, Philoctete is cured by a native healer and rejoins the island's fishing community. Yet the only cure Walcott offers is the palliative of his poem: "Like Philoctete's wound, this language carries its cure,/ its radiant affliction." *Omeros* holds much woe and desolation in its complex web, but Walcott's epic is a magnificent feat of cultural interweaving.

The Bounty

Some critics have discerned in Walcott's post-Nobel poetry a slow coming to acceptance of his colonial and colonized identity. The poems of *The Bounty* reflect not only the bounty of nature but also of the ship, H.M.S. *Bounty*, which first brought breadfruit from the Pacific to the Caribbean islands. This fruit is a staple foodstuff, but the conjunction of a Pacific fruit and an African population only occurred as the result of European colonization and exploration. As always, abundance and oppression go ironically hand in hand. Perhaps as a result of winning the Nobel—certainly the archetypal mark of international acceptance—Walcott's poems seem to show the poet more at peace with his colonial heritage. Being neither one thing nor another can create the permission to be anything and everything. The Carribean's "lack of history," which has so bedeviled Walcott at times, becomes a state of grace in which the evils of history can be overcome, or simply ignored.

Tiepolo's Hound

Tiepolo's Hound marks Walcott's return to the autobiographical narrative poetic form. Walcott interweaves his own life with meditations on the life of Camille Pissarro, the Caribbean-born Sephardic Jew who emigrated to France and became a noted Impressionist painter. The poem revisits Walcott's longstanding interest in the visual arts and is illustrated with several of the poet's own paintings.

The poem is marked by shifts in direction and focus, although its uncertainties are justified by its underlying autobiographical core: Walcott's wrestling with his own problems of cultural identity, which gives a tension both to his meditations on Pissarro and to the quest, driven by the intensity of his memory of a brush stroke representing a hound's thigh in an eighteenth century Venetian painting—by Giovanni Battista Tiepolo, or possibly by Paulo Veronese; the uncertainty is one of the driving forces of the poem—seen long ago in a museum.

In a densely tangled passage late in the poem, the original vision of the hound, its revelation "so exact in

its lucency" of art's power, is the event that has led Walcott in his own development as an artist and has brought him to a point where he is both a Theseus searching through labyrinths for the Minotaur beast that is "history," and the beast itself, "a beast// that was my fear, my self, my craft,/ not the white elegant wolfhound at the feast." He continues: "If recognition was the grace I needed/ to elevate my race from its foul lair/ by prayer, by poetry, by couplets repeated/ over its carcase, I was both slain and slayer."

Both recrimination and nostalgia threaten to surface in *Tiepolo's Hound* as he describes his journey to Venice—the museum Europe to which he had been introduced in childhood by his father's art books—to look for Veronese and Tiepolo, and struggles to reconcile his deep admiration for Pissarro with the feeling that Pissarro somehow betrayed his origins.

What resolves this emotional tangle, and makes the book finally a moving whole of which "Tiepolo's hound" can be the triumphant concluding image, is the combination of Walcott's homage to Pissarro's persistence as an artist in France through experiences of alienation and recurrent self-doubt, and Walcott's own poetic and painterly love of the Caribbean landscape that, in childhood, they shared. Walcott imagines Pissarro's discovery that the monumental works of European tradition that he finds in the Louvre are not where he can find himself, and imagines his discovery of his own vision outside the museum, in the streets of Paris and the modern, secular, myth-erasing art of the nineteenth century, with its new understanding of light. Walcott's account of Pissarro dwells especially on the years Pissarro spent in Pontoise, painting its landscapes and buildings again and again in changing lights and weathers, never getting it "right," suffering poverty and repeated rejection by the academy, and always trying again.

The loose yet carefully structured poetic form Walcott uses is a satisfying medium for a meditative art that in some respects is an equivalent of Pissarro's. Like Pissarro, he circles, comes back again and again to the same subjects, the same problems, the same images, though always with a difference. His fundamental verse form here is couplets, arranged so that the end sounds of one couplet rhyme, sometimes very loosely, with the end sounds of the next, a malleable *ab ab* form that lends itself to a discourse that makes distinctions, draws boundaries, only to let them blur again (as, for instance, with the similarities and differences between himself and Pissarro). The rhymes allow sharply pointed effects, linking "St. Thomas" and "Pontoise," for example, and "Pissarro" and "sorrow," but are usually less obtrusive. Walcott likens his couplets to Pissarro's brush strokes; he also gets a flowing and sliding effect with syntactical slips and with words whose meanings point in two directions (Pissarro, newly in Pontoise, is "an immigrant/ prodigal with confirmations," both the prodigal runaway from his native place and the artist prodigal with talent and discovery).

Loose forms and long, circling poems that evade tight narrative structure are liable to overinclusiveness, to long passages that lose poetic intensity, and *Tiepolo's Hound* does not avoid these failings. The intensity of the moment, the moment of artistic revelation, however, is the center of the poem and the justification, paradoxically, of its meanderings:

> . . . in the tints of Tiepolo's sky,
> in the yellowing linen of a still life by Chardin,
> in that stroke of light that catches a hound's thigh,
> the paint is all that counts, no guilt, no pardon,
> no history, but the sense of narrative time
> annihilated in the devotion of the acolyte,
> as undeniable as instinct, the brushstroke's rhyme
> and page and canvas know one empire only: light.

Light dominates Walcott's Caribbean landscapes, and Tiepolo's hound, metaphorically the inspiration for Walcott's fiction of Pissarro, finally points him back to the black Caribbean hound that is "the mongrel's heir," an abandoned puppy: "we set it down in the village to survive/ like all my ancestry. The hound was here." Coming near the end of the poem, this passage makes sense of the inconclusiveness of Walcott's search for the Venetian painting that has haunted his memory; his pilgrimage has a conclusion after all in his return home and the voyage into self that the poem has created. In its last lines, the poet looks to the constellations, reformed by his book: "the round// of the charted stars, the Archer, aiming his bow,/ the Bear, and the studded collar of Tiepolo's hound."

OTHER MAJOR WORKS

PLAYS: *Henri Christophe: A Chronicle*, pr., pb. 1950; *The Sea at Dauphin*, pr., pb. 1954; *The Wine of the Country*, pr. 1956; *Ione*, pr., pb. 1957; *Ti-Jean and His Brothers*, pr. 1957 (music by Andre Tanker); *Drums and Colours*, pr. 1958; *Malcochon: Or, Six in the Rain*, pr. 1959; *Dream on Monkey Mountain*, pr. 1967; *In a Fine Castle*, pr. 1970; *The Charlatan*, pr. 1974; *The Joker of Seville*, pr. 1974 (adaptation of Tirso de Molina's *El burlador de Sevilla*; music by Galt MacDermot); *O Babylon!*, pr. 1976; *Remembrance*, pr. 1977; *"The Joker of Seville" and "O Babylon!":* *Two Plays*, 1978; *Pantomime*, pr. 1978; *Marie LaVeau*, pr. 1979; *"Remembrance" and "Pantomime,"* 1980; *Beef, No Chicken*, pr. 1981; *The Isle Is Full of Noises*, pr. 1982; *The Last Carnival*, pr. 1982; *A Branch of the Blue Nile*, pr. 1983; *The Haitian Earth*, pr. 1984; *Three Plays*, 1986; *To Die for Grenada*, pr. 1986; *Ghost Dance*, pr. 1989; *Viva Detroit*, pr. 1990; *Steel*, pr. 1991 (music by MacDermot); *The Odyssey*, pr. 1992; *Walker*, pr. 1992; *The Capeman: A Musical*, pr. 1997 (music by Paul Simon); *The Haitian Trilogy*, 2001.

NONFICTION: "Meanings: From a Conversation with Derek Walcott," 1970 (in *Performing Arts*); *The Antilles: Fragments of Epic Memory*, 1993 (Nobel lecture); *Homage to Robert Frost*, 1996 (with Joseph Brodsky and Seamus Heaney); *What the Twilight Says: Essays*, 1998.

BIBLIOGRAPHY

Bloom, Harold, ed. *Derek Walcott*. Philadelphia: Chelsea House, 2003. A collection of essays intended to provide an overview of the critical reception of Walcott's work.

Bobb, June D. *Beating a Restless Drum: The Poetics of Kamau Brathwaite and Derek Walcott*. Trenton, N.J.: Africa World Press, 1998. Examines the influence of colonization and slavery on the Caribbean's most important anglophone poets, linking them to a specifically Caribbean tradition rooted in African mythologies and other influences. Bibliography, index.

Burnett, Paula. *Derek Walcott: Politics and Poetics*. Gainesville: University Press of Florida, 2001. Sees the drama and poetry together designed to create a legacy for modern Caribbean society, incorporating myth, identity, and aesthetics. Notes, bibliography, index.

Davis, Gregson, ed. *The Poetics of Derek Walcott*. Durham, N.C.: Duke University Press, 1997. A collection of critical essays on the poetry. The cornerstone essay is one in which Walcott reflects on poetics, illuminating his masterpiece *Omeros*. Other contributors focus on central thematic concerns as well as modes of expression.

Figueroa, Víctor. *Not at Home in One's Home: Caribbean Self-fashioning in the Poetry of Luis Palés Matos, Aimé Césaire, and Derek Walcott*. Madison, N.J.: Fairleigh Dickinson University Press, 2009. The chapter "Roads Taken yet Not Taken: Derek Walcott's 'Ethical Twist'" focuses on Walcott's poetry, namely *Omeros*, as it relates to his ideas on home, identity, and representation.

Hamner, Robert D. *Derek Walcott*. New York: Twayne, 1993. Hamner conducts a thorough exploration of Walcott's plays, poems, and critical articles, ending with *The Star-Apple Kingdom*. The text is supplemented by a selected bibliography of both primary and secondary sources and an index.

King, Bruce. *Derek Walcott: A Caribbean Life*. New York: Oxford University Press, 2000. The first literary biography, with reference to letters, diaries, uncollected and unpublished writings, and interviews in the Caribbean, North America, and Europe.

_____. *Derek Walcott and West Indian Drama*. Oxford, England: Clarendon Press, 1995. This thoroughly researched study of the development of Walcott's Trinidad Theatre Workshop is valuable for its historical data, illustrations, and calendar of performances from the 1950's through 1993.

Ross, Robert L., ed. *International Literature in English: Essays on the Major Writers*. New York: Garland, 1991. Robert D. Hamner contributes an essay on Walcott. Counts fourteen books of poetry (to *The Arkansas Testament*) and four volumes of plays, and discusses the chiaroscuro of Walcott's aesthetic choices, which "creates the illusion of bulk and depth for three-dimensional objects in a two-dimensional plane."

Terada, Rei. *Derek Walcott's Poetry: American Mimicry*. Boston: Northeastern University Press, 1992. Terada discusses Walcott's creative use of ideas and elements assimilated from the many cultural strands running through the New World.

Thieme, John. *Derek Walcott*. New York: St. Martin's Press, 1999. An introductory biography and critical interpretation of selected works. Includes bibliographical references and index.

Walcott, Derek. *"Another Life": Fully Annotated*. Boulder, Colo.: L. Rienner, 2004. Valuable notes and a critical essay by Edward Baugh and Colbert Nepaulsingh greatly enhance the reader's understanding of this work.

_____. *Conversations with Derek Walcott*. Edited by William Baer. Jackson: University Press of Mississippi, 1996. Collection of previously published interviews, spanning 1966 to 1993.

_____. "An Interview with Derek Walcott." Interview by J. P. White. *Green Mountain Review* 4, no. 1 (Spring-Summer, 1990): 14-37. A comprehensive interview with Walcott.

Gerhard Brand; Anne Howells
Updated by Leslie Ellen Jones

WANG WEI

Born: District of Qi, Taiyuan Prefecture, Shanxi Province, China; 701
Died: Changan (now Xian), Jingzhao Prefecture, China; 761
Also known as: Wang Mojie; Wang Youcheng; Wang Yu-ch'eng

PRINCIPAL POETRY

Wang Wei: New Translations and Commentary, 1980 (Pauline Yu, translator)
Laughing Lost in the Mountains: The Poems of Wang Wei, 1991 (Willis Barnstone, Tony Barnstone, and Shu Haixin translators)
The Selected Poems of Wang Wei, 2006 (David Hinton, translator)

OTHER LITERARY FORMS

Although known primarily for his poetry, Wang Wei (wong way) was also the author of several important writings pertaining to various traditions in Tang Dynasty Buddhism, in particular his funeral inscription for the *stēlē* of the Sixth Chan (Zen) Patriarch, Huineng. In addition, Wang was an accomplished musician and painter, acquiring considerable renown for the latter talent after his death. No painting authentically attributable to him is extant, but numerous copies of several of his works were executed over a period of centuries. One of the best known of these is the long scroll depicting his country estate on the Wang River. From the Song Dynasty onward, when only copies of his works survived, he became glorified as the preeminent Chinese landscape painter, with his work honored as the prototype of *wen ren hua* (literati painting)—amateur rather than academic, intuitive and spontaneous rather than formalistic and literal.

ACHIEVEMENTS

Wang Wei is generally acknowledged to be one of the major poets of the Tang Dynasty (618-907), the most brilliant period in the long history of Chinese poetry; he was probably the most respected poet of his own time. In one of the many classificatory schemes of which traditional Chinese critics were particularly fond, he was labeled the "Poet Buddha," ranked with the two poets of the era who were to exceed him in fame, Li Bo, the "Poet Immortal," and Du Fu, the "Poet Sage." This appellation reflects Wang's association with Buddhism, which flourished in eighth century China, but it is important to note that very few of his poems are overtly doctrinal or identifiable solely with any one of the many traditions or lineages of Buddhism active during the Tang.

Like those of most men of letters of the time, Wang's life and works reflect a typically syncretic mentality, integrating yet exploring the conflicts among the goals and ideals of Confucian scholarship and commitment to public service, Daoist retreat and equanimity, and Buddhist devotion. Such issues, however, are not dealt with directly or at length in his works. His poetry relies on suggestion rather than direct statement, presenting apparently simple and precise visual imagery drawn from nature which proves elusive and evocative at the same time. He eschews definitive closure for open-endedness and irresolution, leaving the reader to attempt to resolve the unanswered questions of a poem. His best poems rarely include any direct expression of emotion and frequently suppress the poet's own subjective presence, yet this seeming impersonality has become the hallmark of a very personal style.

Because Wang's poems embody what Stephen Owen has called the artifice of simplicity, they were frequently imitated, both by the coterie of court contemporaries at whose center he stood and by later poets, followers of the "Wang Wei school." Although many of the imitators were able to replicate the witty understatement, the stark imagery, and the enigmatic closure of Wang's work, none—by general critical agreement—succeeded in probing to the same extent depths of emotion and meaning beneath a deceptively artless surface.

BIOGRAPHY

Wang Wei (also known by his cognomen, Wang Mojie, and his courtesy name, Wang Youcheng) was the eldest child of a prominent family in Shanxi Province. He became known for his precocious poetic, musical, and artistic talents and was well received by aristocratic patrons of the arts in the two capital cities of the empire. After placing first in his provincial examinations at the age of nineteen, Wang went on to pass the most literary of the three main types of imperial civil-service examinations in 721, one of the thirty-eight successful candidates that year. (Typically, only 1-2 percent of the thousands of candidates recommended each year for this highly competitive examination would pass.) He received the *jinshi* (presented scholar) degree and began his slow but steady rise through government ranks.

Like all Chinese scholar-bureaucrats, Wang moved from post to post and to various parts of the empire, most of which appear in his poetry. From his position as a court secretary of music in the western capital of Changan, he was sent to the east in Shandong (720's), back to the capital (734), to the northwest frontier (737), south to the Yangzi River area (740), and back to the capital (742). His career was interrupted at intervals by temporary losses of favor, factional intrigues, and various infractions, the most serious of which was his collaboration—though forced—in the puppet government of the rebel general An Lushan, whose armies overran the capitals and forced Emperor Xuanzong into exile from 755 to 757. Only the intercession of Wang's younger brother, Wang Jin, who had fought valorously with the loyalist forces, secured a pardon for the poet in 758. The next year, he attained the high-ranking sinecure of *shangshu youcheng* (undersecretary of state) and is thus frequently referred to as Wang Youcheng. In this respect, his career differed markedly from that of his two most famous poet contemporaries, Li Bo and Du Fu, neither of whom passed the imperial examinations or enjoyed Wang's considerable family connections. Unlike them, Wang never suffered severe financial hardship (despite the posing of some of his poems), maintaining a relatively secure position in the social and cultural center of what was later to be perceived as the golden age of the Tang Dynasty itself, the reign of Emperor Xuanzong (713-755).

The date of Wang's marriage has not been recorded, nor the number and names of any children he may have had. His wife died around 730, however, and Wang remained celibate thereafter—somewhat unusual for the times and an index of his devotion to Buddhist principles. It was in fact around the time of his wife's death that he began a serious study of Buddhism. In addition to the several essays and inscriptions connected with issues and figures in Tang Buddhism that are included in Wang's collected works, the most illuminating evidence of his religious commitment is his choice of cognomen, Mojie. Combined with his given name, Wei, these syllables form the Chinese transliteration (Weimojie) of one of the Buddha's best-known contemporaries, Vimalakīrti, said to have preached a sutra that became especially popular in China, not only for its doctrines but also because he himself remained a layman throughout his life. Vimalakīrti also espoused such central Confucian social ideals as filial piety and loyalty to the ruler and demonstrated to the Chinese that the good Buddhist did not necessarily have to leave his family and retreat to a monastery.

This example was an important one for Wang, for his religious beliefs never led him to abjure totally his political and social relationships. Popular legend has long held Wang to have been but a reluctant bureaucrat, and his poetry speaks frequently of a desire for reclusion. Wang did spend much of his time on retreat in various locations, particularly at his country estate at Lantian on the Wang River, which he acquired around 750 and where he eventually built a monastery. All the same, he remained officially in office until his death.

ANALYSIS

The poems of Wang Wei were first collected by his brother, Wang Jin, at imperial request and presented to the throne in 763. The number of poems that can be attributed definitively to him is small—371, compared with the thousand or more each of Li Bo and Du Fu. The official dynastic history records his brother as telling the emperor that there were once ten times that many, the rest having been lost during the turmoil of the An Lushan Rebellion.

Whatever the case, the poems for which Wang is best remembered have fostered an image of him as a private, contemplative, self-effacing observer of the natural scene. In fact, however, despite references in several poems to his solitude behind his "closed gate" at home, many of his poems were inspired by social occasions—visits from or to friends, journeys of fellow bureaucrats to distant posts, his own departures to new offices—and by official occasions as well. Wang was a highly successful court poet, the master of a graceful, formally regulated style whose patterns had been perfected during the seventh century.

The ability to write poetry on any occasion was expected of all government officials and was in fact tested on the civil-service examination. Several of Wang's poems bear witness by their titles to having been written "to imperial command" on some formal court occasion—an outing to the country, an important birthday, the construction of a new building, the presentation of some gift—and often "harmonize respectfully" with the rhymes of a model poem composed by the emperor himself. Most of these poems were written in a heptasyllabic eight-line form with rigidly regulated rules of tone, parallelism, and rhyme. Poets in attendance would vie with one another to complete their poems first, and there was often some official evaluation of literary quality. Other poems in Wang's corpus arose out of less formally decorous contexts but reveal nevertheless the demands on the Tang poet to be able to respond to the stimulus of an occasion in an apparently spontaneous and sincere, appropriate, economical, and witty manner.

"LADY XI"

A good example of Wang's mastery of the literary and contextual demands of the poem written on command is his early work "Xi furen" ("Lady Xi"). He is said to have composed this poem at the age of twenty (nineteen by Western reckoning), when he was preparing for the imperial examination and in residence at the court of the emperor's half brother, Li Xian, prince of Ning. It is one of several poems in Wang's collection for which was noted his supposed age at composition—unverifiable, but attesting the recognition of his early prowess. An anecdote recorded in a collection of stories attached to poems compiled in the ninth century provides the necessary explanation of the background of the poem. The prince, it seems, had been attracted by the wife of a pastry vendor and had purchased her as his concubine. After a year had passed, he asked her if she still thought of her husband, but she did not reply. The prince then summoned the vendor, and when his wife saw him, her eyes filled with tears. Ten or so people were present at the time, including Wang, and their patron commanded them to write a poem on the subject. Wang's quatrain was the first completed, and everyone else agreed that none better could be written. The prince then returned the pastry vendor's wife to her husband.

In the poem itself, there are, surprisingly, no overt references to the couple in question. The first two lines express a simple and general denial—that loves of the past can be forgotten because of present affections. The last two lines conclude with an allusion, but not to the pastry vendor and his wife; they refer to a text, a story in the Zuo commentary on the "Spring and Autumn Annals" (722-481 B.C.E.) of the *Chunqiu* (sixth to fifth century B.C.E.), one of the Confucian classics. There it is recorded that the king of Chu defeated the ruler of Xi and took the latter's wife as his own. Though she bore him children, Lady Xi never spoke to her new spouse, and when finally asked why, she is said to have an-

swered: "I am but one woman, yet it has been my fate to serve two husbands. Although I have been unable to die, how should I dare to speak?"

This poem illustrates concisely Wang's typical "artifice of simplicity," his ability to charge the briefest of poems—twenty syllables in all—with a considerable burden. Typically, denials open and close the poem, revealing Wang's penchant for the open-ended quality of negation as opposed to assertion. What could have been a merely sentimental episode becomes dignified here through the link made to the moral dilemma of a historical ruler's wife and by the poet's choice not to mention the contemporary protagonists at all. Typically effective, also, is the poet's refusal to make any direct comment. Understatement and allusion work hand in hand here to make a point that is no less clear for not being stated explicitly.

THE WANG RIVER COLLECTION

These same methods of indirection and evocation, of using objects and events to suggest something lying beneath the surface, distinguish Wang's most famous poems, his limpid and apparently selfless depictions of natural scenes. These works are not, as a rule, devoid of people, and much of their impersonal quality derives simply from the general tendency of the classical Chinese language to avoid the use of subjective pronouns and to remain uninflected for person, tense, number, gender, and case. Wang does, however, exploit the inherent potential of the language to create indeterminate or multiple meanings more than do most other traditional poets. This is true, for example, of several poems in his well-known sequence, the Wang River collection. As Wang's preface explains, this group of twenty pentasyllabic quatrains, each of which names a site on Wang's country estate, was written in the company of one of his closest friends, a minor official named Pei Di (born 716). Pei wrote twenty poems to match those of his host, and these are also included in standard collections of Wang's poetry.

As Owen has noted in his history of poetry in the High Tang, Wang's quatrains as a whole probably represent his most significant contribution to generic development, particularly because of his substitution of enigmatic understatement for the epigrammatic closure more common at the time. The Wang River collection is informed by some of the key modes of consciousness of the poet's entire oeuvre: an emphasis on perceptual and cognitive limitations, a transcendence of temporal and spatial distinctions, and a sense of the harmony of the individual and nature. This is especially true of the fifth and probably most famous poem in the sequence, "Lu zhai" ("Deer Park").

"DEER PARK"

This poem exemplifies typical quatrain form, narrowing its focus from the massiveness of a mountain to a ray of the setting sun entering a mossy grove. Each line presents a perception that is qualified or amplified by the next. What is given in the first line as an "empty mountain," where no people are seen, reverberates with echoes of human voices in the second line. Whether these echoes signify that other people are actually present on the mountain at some distance or are intended metaphorically, to suggest the poet's memories of friends in an altogether different location, however, remains unspecified. The third line places the plot in a specific place and time—toward sunset, when "returning" (*fan*) light sends a "reflected" (also *fan*) glow through an opening into a glade. The fourth line suggests that the poet has been in the grove that same morning, or perhaps all day, and thus knows that the light is shining on the blue-green moss "again."

More than a brief nature poem, "Deer Park" links keenly observed and deceptively simple perceptions with far-ranging Buddhist implications. Scholar Marsha L. Wagner has made some important observations about the title: that "Deer Park" was the name of the site near Benares where the Buddha preached his first sermon after becoming enlightened, that it was an alternate name for the monastery Wang built on his Wang River estate, and that the deer not caught in a trap was a conventional Buddhist symbol for the recluse. Within the poem itself, the crucial word is *kong* (empty), on which hinges more than the question about the unpopulated state of the mountain. *Kong* is also the translation of the Sanskrit word *śūnyatā*, which was a key term in the Buddhist traditions with which Wang was familiar, denoting the illusory or "empty" nature of all reality and the ultimate reality, therefore, of "emptiness." *Kong* is one of the most frequently recurring words in Wang's poetic vocabulary—translated some-

times as "empty," at other times meaning "merely" or "in vain," in each case with the same powerful resonance. Moreover, the vision of the light entering the grove, the counterpart of beams of moonlight in other poems, provides a concrete image of the experience of enlightenment itself. The poem as a whole, then, encapsulates key Buddhist notions about the nature of reality and human perception of it.

"Deer Park" provides a good example of how Wang suggests religious and philosophical doctrines and attitudes in an indirect manner. Even in poems that treat Buddhist subjects more directly, doctrinal elements are generally merely implicit. Many of his accounts of journeys to monasteries, for example, are by convention metaphorical from the outset: Since temples were frequently located high in the mountains, visiting them required an effort that represented the physical counterpart to the progress toward enlightenment. Several of Wang's poems on this topic emphasize the spiritual implications of the physical ascent, among which "Guo Xiangji si" ("Visiting the Temple of Gathered Fragrance") is particularly well known.

"VISITING THE TEMPLE OF GATHERED FRAGRANCE"

Wang opens "Visiting the Temple of Gathered Fragrance" with a profession of ignorance. He does not "know" the temple, and this at once suggests several possibilities: He does not know of its existence, of its location, or of its significance—or perhaps he has discarded a rational, cognitive kind of "knowing" for an intuitive, nondifferentiating awareness more conducive to true spiritual knowledge. In any event, this special kind of ignorance sets the tone for the description of the journey up the mountain, each stage of which contains images of extreme ambiguity and vagueness. The second line speaks of "entering cloudy peaks," but the verb can refer either to the action of the speaker or to the location of the monastery, thus deliberately blurring the distinction between the traveler and his destination, or subject and object. The obscurity of these cloudy peaks is frequently associated in Wang's poetry with temples and transcendent realms and suggests the inadequacy of merely sensuous perception on such a journey of the spirit.

The poem continues to reinforce this sense of linguistic and perceptual ambiguity. The phrase "paths without people" in the third line can also be read as "no paths for people," thus further suggesting the speaker's venture into unknown territory, untraveled by others; this experience must be undertaken in absolute solitude. This sense of mystery is evoked again in the question of the following line: "Where is the bell?" As in the opening couplet, Wang reveals here a distrust of visual perception and purely intellectual cognition. Presumably the sound of a bell from somewhere deep in the mountains confirms the existence of the monastery, at least, if not its precise location. Has he heard the bell himself, though? He does not say. Thus, he must continue his ascent without the comforting knowledge of where he is or where he is going.

In the third couplet, the images appear to be more concrete than those in the preceding lines, but they are in fact equally ambiguous. In each line of the third couplet, the verb can be read either actively or passively, suggesting that the processes occurring cannot be subjected to rational analysis; they can be apprehended only intuitively as one total experience in which subject and object are indistinguishable. Furthermore, Wang's diction also undermines the sensuous precision of the couplet. Rather than focusing on the concreteness of the nouns—"stream" and "sun"—he speaks of the former's "sound" and the latter's "color," so that in each case he is describing an abstraction rather than a concrete object.

The final couplet of the poem in no way diminishes the mysterious quality of the journey. Wang has reached a pond—perhaps at the monastery, though he does not say—whose bends and curves continue to recall the winding paths of other spiritual journeys. What does it mean for the pond to be "empty"? Is it dried up, deserted, illusory, or an image of ultimate reality? In the last line, Wang simply presents a process without specifying the subject or the precise nature of the object. The "peaceful meditation" may be that of a monk from the temple or the poet himself, or it may not refer to an individual at all but rather to an intangible atmosphere of the place. The "poison dragons" tamed by the meditation are traditionally interpreted as passions or illusions that may stand in the way of enlightenment, and many possible sources in Buddhist texts have been sug-

gested. They are controlled and not eliminated, present by virtue of their very mention, thus suggesting Wang's awareness, in this poem, at least, of the effort required to attain the tranquil and selfless union with the world that, in so many of his poems, he seems to possess.

This harmony is one that transcends boundaries between subject and object and those of language as well; hence Wang's reliance on understatement and what he does not say. One well-known poem, however, flirts briefly with the possibility that perhaps words are not inadequate after all. "Chou Chang shaofu" ("In Response to Vice-Magistrate Chang") opens quite discursively with an observation that occurs frequently in Wang's poetry on the contrast between past and present priorities. The profession that only age has enabled him wisely to reject worldly involvement is familiar also to readers of the poetry of Tao Qian, the poet of the past with whom Wang most strongly identified and in whose eighth century revival he played an instrumental role. Like Tao Qian, who left office early on matters of principle, Wang claims also to be rejecting the "long-range plans" associated with governmental policy. He now "only" (or "emptily"—*kong* again) knows "to return to the old forest," and the word "return" recalls the importance of the same word for Tao Qian, who employed it frequently for the implications it possessed in early Daoist literature of getting back to one's original nature, uncorrupted by civilization and its trappings.

The third couplet of "Visiting the Temple of Gathered Fragrance" provides images of Wang's newfound freedom. Pine winds blow loose the belt of his robe, and the moon provides congenial companionship as he plays the zither, the instrument traditionally associated with scholar-recluses. The penultimate line turns to a question posed by the addressee of the poem and suggests that Wang will finally put into words the wisdom he has gained, the "reasons for success and failure" or the "principles of universal change." His response in the last line, however, provides no easy answer, only an enigmatic image of a fisherman's song that can be read in a number of ways.

In the first place, the last line in the third couplet may be regarded as a nonanswer in the tradition of the Chan or Zen koan, by means of which a Buddhist master attempts to bring a student to enlightenment by answering a rational question with a non sequitur, thus jolting the latter out of conventional, logical, categorical modes of thinking, and liberating his mind to facilitate a sudden, intuitive realization of truth. Wang's answer, then, would deliberately bear no relationship to Chang's query, seeking instead to reject such cognitive concerns or indeed denying the validity of his question.

There is a second possibility. Because the fisherman, along with the woodcutter, was a favorite Daoist figure representing the rustic, unselfconscious life in harmony with nature, this final line may be read as a simple suggestion to change to follow the example of such recluses and escape from official life to the freedom and serenity of country living. This is a realm, moreover, where the vicissitudes of the world and such distinctions as failure and success will have no meaning.

A third interpretation of the line hinges on a possible reference to a specific fisherman's song, the "Yufu" ("Fisherman"), included in the southern anthology, the *Chu ci* (songs of Chu), compiled during the Han Dynasty. In the earlier poem, a wise fisherman converses with the fourth century B.C.E. poet Qu Yuan, who had been a loyal minister to the king of Chu and committed to the Confucian ideal of service but who was slandered by others at court and banished. He remained self-righteous about his inflexible moral purity and later chose suicide rather than compromise his principles. In this song, when Qu Yuan meets the fisherman, he explains the reasons behind his exile; the fisherman suggests that it might have been more circumspect to adapt to the circumstances, but Qu Yuan insists that he would rather drown than do so. The fisherman departs with a gentle mocking reply, singing that if the waters are clean, he will wash his hat-strings in them, and if they are dirty, he will wash his feet. Unlike the self-righteous Qu Yuan, the fisherman can adjust to the conditions he finds and paradoxically remains freer of their influence. Ultimately, perhaps, he realizes that, when seen from a higher perspective, the waters are all the same.

If Wang's use of this allusion is to be granted, then he is certainly affirming the kind of unifying vision and transcendence of distinctions that underlies his poetry as a whole. Perhaps the more important point, however,

is Wang's failure to allow a definitive resolution to the question at all. The conclusion to this poem, as to so many of his poems, is purposely inconclusive and open-ended, leaving the reader to puzzle out what answers there may be.

BIBLIOGRAPHY

Chou, Shan. "Beginning with Images in the Nature Poetry of Wang Wei." *Harvard Journal of Asiatic Studies* 42 (June, 1982): 117-137. Chou proposes that the solution to the problem of meaning in Wang's nature poetry is to be found in understanding the Buddhist influence.

Owen, Stephen. "Wang Wei: The Artifice of Simplicity." In *The Great Age of Chinese Poetry: The High T'ang*. New Haven, Conn.: Yale University Press, 1981. Owen supplies an excellent short overview of Wang as poetic technician and relates the poet's work to his life and historical context.

Wagner, Marsha L. *Wang Wei*. Boston: Twayne, 1982. Part of the Twayne World Authors series, this scholarly, well-written account of Wang's life provides a balanced, perceptive appraisal of his contributions as poet, painter, and government official. Includes fine translations.

Wang Wei. *Laughing Lost in the Mountains: Poems of Wang Wei*. Translated by Tony Barnstone, Willis Barnstone, and Xu Haixin. Hanover, N.H.: University Press of New England, 1991. Excellent translation of 171 poems. The critical introduction, "The Ecstasy of Stillness," by the Barnstones provides insights into these poems.

_____. *The Poetry of Wang Wei: New Translations and Commentary*. Translated by Pauline Yu. Bloomington: Indiana University Press, 1980. This study provides excellent, scholarly translations and notes as well as knowing critical appraisals of Wang's poems.

_____. *The Selected Poems of Wang Wei*. Translated by David Hinton. New York: New Directions, 2006. A translation of Wang's poems, with an introduction providing critical analysis and a biography.

Wang Wei, Li Bo, and Du Fu. *Three Chinese Poets: Translations of Poems by Wang Wei, Li Bai, and Du Fu*. Translated by Vikram Seth. Boston: Faber and

Faber, 1992. A collection of poems by Wang, Du Fu, and Li Bo. Commentary by translator Seth provides useful information.

Weinberger, Eliot. *Nineteen Ways of Looking at Wang Wei*. Mount Kisco, N.Y.: Moyer Bell, 1987. This short book offers insights into the art of translating Chinese poems. Includes commentary by both Weinberger and writer Octavio Paz.

Yang, Jingqing. *The Chan Interpretations of Wang Wei's Poetry: A Critical Review.* Hong Kong: Chinese University Press, 2007. Looks at Chan (Zen) Buddhism and how it relates to Wang's poetry.

Young, David, trans. *Five T'ang Poets: Wang Wei, Li Po, Tu Fu, Li Ho, Li Shang-yin*. Oberlin, Ohio: Oberlin College Press, 1990. Provides an opportunity for appreciating Wang along with contemporary poets during the Tang Dynasty.

Pauline Yu

X

XIE LINGYUN

Born: Zhejiang Province, China; 385
Died: Canton, Nanhai, China; June 26, 433
Also known as: Hsieh K'ang-lo; Hsieh Ling-Yün;
Xie Kanglo

PRINCIPAL POETRY

*The Murmuring Stream: The Life and Works of
Hsieh Ling-yün*, 1967 (2 volumes; J. D.
Frodsham, editor)

OTHER LITERARY FORMS

The official biography of Xie Lingyun (sheh lihng-YUHN), compiled during the early sixth century, records his collected works in twenty folios and notes that Xie compiled a history of the Jin Dynasty, elements of which still survive. Also extant are fourteen *fu* rhyme-prose compositions (that is, prose poetry, with rhythm and occasional rhyme) and twenty-eight items of official prose, letters, prefaces, eulogies, *in memoriams*, and Buddhist essays totaling four folios.

ACHIEVEMENTS

Important critics from the sixth century to the eighteenth century have been unanimous in attributing to Xie Lingyun both the founding of the *shanshui* (literally "mountains and waters") or "nature" poetry, popular in his own day, and its highest development. His travels in mountain retreats, for which he invented special climbing boots with reversible studs, and which inspired his tumultuous landscape descriptions, further brought him into contact with newly introduced Buddhist ideals, and his profound philosophical speculations added dimensions to the religious debates of his time and to the evolution of Buddhist sectarian thought. A member of the most aristocratic of the Southern Dynasties' families, his great intellectual abilities and skill as a calligrapher and painter attracted the notice of em-

perors of two regimes, and he was involved—fatally, as it was to transpire—in the most serious matters of state. Locations in his native Jiangsu and Zhejiang provinces are still named after him.

BIOGRAPHY

Following the flight of the Jin aristocracy in 317, south across the Yangzi River to escape the invading Topa tribes from central Asia, the Xie clan came to prominence among the handful of cultured land barons who dominated the ensuing Southern Dynasties era (317-589). Their eminence stemmed from successive generations of extraordinary political and intellectual brilliance. Xie Lingyun's own direct forebears included the distinguished poet Xie Kun (280-322) and the statesman Xie An (320-385). On Xie's mother's side, he was descended from the great calligraphers Wang Xizhi (321-379) and his son Wang Xianzchi (344-388).

The young Xie Lingyun was intellectually precocious and, presuming on his wealthy estate as a duke of the realm (the duke of Kangle), became notorious for his personal excesses and extravagances (even for the times) and for his sharp, critical wit. These tendencies and his later consort with rebellious peasantry and ruffians eventually brought about his downfall.

Near-contemporaneous records mention that as a child, Xie Lingyun was sent for safety to live with the Du family, esoteric Daoists associated with fine calligraphy, in Hangzhou (hence his sobriquet Little Guest Xie). These philosophical and artistic influences were ever to remain with Xie. Then, in 399-400, when Xie was fifteen, an uprising brought the Daoist-inspired rebel Sun En into Xie territories in Zhejiang and Jiangsu, and many of their clan, and the related Wang, were killed, including Xie Lingyun's father. The boy was transferred to the capital at Jiankang (modern Nanking) and lodged with his uncle, Xie Hun (who was married into the Sima royal family). Here, he acquired his first official appointment, in the service of a Sima prince, but in 406, with great political consequences, Xie was transferred into the entourage of a rival faction of the ascendant Liu clan.

At that time, Xie Lingyun's new patron, Liu Yi, headed the dominant clique at court, and he enjoyed the backing of the powerful Xie. By 410, however, the general Liu Yu had outmaneuvered supporters and contenders alike, so that Liu Yi, with Xie Lingyun in tow, found himself rusticated to a posting in Hubei. This chance circumstance brought about Xie Lingyun's first contact with the great Buddhist institution at Mount Lu, founded by the epoch-creating cleric Huiyuan (334-416). Here emerged the White Lotus sect of Buddhism, which, appealing as it did to the educated aristocratic laity, quickly attracted a coterie of extraordinary minds. The combination of religious intellectualism, the breathtaking mountain scenery, and release from court intrigue and official drudgery exerted incalculable affect on Xie Lingyun's literary endeavors.

The idyll, however, did not last long. In the provinces, Liu Yi attempted a coup but was suppressed by Liu Yu's forces. Xie Lingyun was captured; Liu Yi hanged himself. Luckily, Liu Yu appreciated Xie Lingyun's talents, bringing him back to the capital and installing him in an administrative post. For the next half-decade, Xie Lingyun was in and out of trouble, including a charge of murder; larger events, however, were to shape his future: In January, 419, Liu Yu strangled the idiot Emperor An and replaced him with Sima Dewen. In the spring of 420, Dewen was deposed and later assassinated. Liu Yu then ascended to the throne as the first emperor of the Liu Song regime (420-479).

The Xie clan found favor with the new emperor, but in the intrigues over the succession, Xie Lingyun was again caught on the wrong side. Liu Yu died on June 26, 422, and Xie Lingyun's clique was exiled to Yongjia (modern Wenzhou, in Zhejiang Province). The way was long and perilous, and Xie Lingyun had become ill from tuberculosis and leg ulcers. He made a detour via the family estates at Shining (modern Shangyu) and finally arrived in Yongjia in October that year. He remained bedridden for the winter months, contemplating Daoist and Buddhist thought; during this time, he produced a major contribution to the Buddhist tradition in China ("Discussion of Essentials"). Well enough by the spring of 423 to resume his duties, he nevertheless neglected official affairs and passed his time wandering in the hills until 424, when he resigned altogether, departed from Yongjia, and retired to an anchorite life at Shining. He devoted himself to costly repairs of the estate, damaged during the Sun En incursions; his monumental rhyme-prose "Dwelling in the Mountains" describes his labors and the wondrous beauties of the wilderness scene. His understanding of Buddhism, too, deepened at Shining, as witnessed by the four dozen or so poems he wrote there.

Another political upheaval occurred in August, 424, with the assassination of the emperor and the accession of Emperor Wen (reigned 424-453). Xie Lingyun was moved to write of his sorrows, and again he fell ill, but soon he was recalled to "illumine" an undistinguished court. He declined twice on account of problems with his legs but eventually accepted. His was the classic dilemma facing a Chinese bureaucrat: His duty was to serve, but he was disillusioned by the frustrations of public life. A scion of the highest aristocracy, he was yet denied consummate power by the upstart Sima and Liu monarchs and their minions. Nevertheless, he was assigned a congenial occupation—the compilation of an official history of the preceding Jin Dynasty, and an imperial bibliography. His verse and calligraphy had earned the royal epithet "twin gems," but his erratic behavior and unauthorized absences brought impeachment and disgrace. On April 1, 428, he found himself packed off once more to Shining, ostensibly on sick leave.

There, Xie Lingyun found his beloved cousin, the poet Xie Huilian, also in disgrace, and their mutual inspiration produced some of the most celebrated verse in the Chinese literary heritage. Dismissed from all offices in November of 428, he retired to his Daoist and Buddhist preoccupations, improvements to his estate, mountain climbing, and the assembling of a vast library. Some eighteen months later, Xie Huilian was pardoned; his departure for the capital occasioned yet more perennially admired verse.

Xie Lingyun's intellectual and literary brilliance and his high-born status and wealth had thus far protected him from greater harm than mere rustication, but his arrogance and lack of political acumen had provoked serious enmities. Slander, deriving from friction over the mutual encroachments of public and private lands at Shining, intensified, and to defend himself, Xie Lingyun presented an eloquent appeal at the imperial court. Meanwhile, the emperor's forces returned from a disastrous defeat in the North, in 431, and a bitter controversy over Buddhist doctrine was resolved in Xie Lingyun's favor. Xie Lingyun was found innocent of the charges against him, but was granted office-in-exile in distant Kiangsi, where, still contemptuous of his duties, he was arrested by local officials. Driven to the limits of his uncertain patience, he seized the arresting officers and declared an uprising for the restoration of the Jin. His unpremeditated coup was easily put down, but even then, the emperor overlooked his indiscretions, and instead of being sentenced to death, Xie Lingyun was merely reduced to the status of a commoner and was banished to the malarial southlands of Canton. There, his influence gone, and the Sima loyalists dangerously active, he was again accused of sedition. Although unconvinced by the weak evidence, the emperor ordered Xie Lingyun's execution.

ANALYSIS

Early literary critics in China, particularly the sixth century Zhong Hong and Liu Xie, concerned themselves with the evolution of literary styles and forms. Their evaluations of Xie Lingyun's work therefore were concerned chiefly with placing him in the stream of literary history. According to Zhong Hong, Xie Lingyun's "talents were lofty and his diction flourishing, rich in charm and difficult to emulate," so that as "the master of the Yüan-chia period (424-453)" he transcended the literary giants who preceded him. Placing Xie Lingyun in the top rank of three categories of poets, Zhong Hong remarked that Xie Lingyun's poetry was derived from that of the politically minded Cao Zhi (192-232) and interspersed with elements of the florid Zhang Xie (flourished 295).

EARLY INFLUENCES

By the seventeenth or eighteenth century, in spite of evidence to the contrary, Xie Lingyun was firmly ensconced in Chinese literary history as the founder of *shanshui* ("nature" or "landscape") verse. J. D. Frodsham demonstrates that landscape and nature themes were prominent from the earliest beginnings of Chinese poetry. In particular, Frodsham points out, Xie Lingyun's early landscape verse appears to have been molded by the instruction of his uncle Xie Hun. In the end, however, it matters less that Xie Lingyun was the inventor of the genre than that he was its most qualified exponent.

Among the various influences that enhanced Xie Lingyun's native literary genius were his childhood Daoist studies and his later association with the most advanced Buddhist intellectuals of his day, his personal involvement in the perilous political life of his times, and his travels in the course of official postings, exiles, and banishments in the forested mountains and rivers of South China—in the fifth century, still mostly virgin territory.

Unlike his predecessor Ruan Ji (210-263), for example, Xie Lingyun wrote very little poetry satirizing political evils. Occasionally he quotes from the Confucian canon, saying that when government is in decay, it is proper to retire. Otherwise, he criticizes his own disinterest in mundane administration, apologizing to his liege-lord and eulogizing him rather than remonstrating with him. He admits that he is idle and stupid, his administration far from ideal, quite unworthy of the honors bestowed on him. The emperor, on the other hand, is perfectly sincere and excels in the Way. Such was the accepted rhetoric of the time, and no great political or satirical construction should be placed on these worn lines.

Daoist anchorite escapism abounds in the poetry of Xie Lingyun, usually expressed in admiration for the sages of ancient tradition. Within the space of a few lines in a single poem, one reads both of his ambivalence toward an official career ("Throughout my life I'd have preferred distant solitude") and of the seductive appeal of a steady government salary. Free at last—involuntary retirement—in bucolic tranquillity, he shakes off the dust of the world of affairs and chooses the simple life, strolling about his tumbleweed dwelling. After all, not for him the fret and frustration of mortal renown. No doubt he was sincere enough, but one always bears in mind that his immense wealth and nobility afforded him the easy choices of a glamorous life at the metropolitan court or gentlemanly retirement to his vast and lavish estates.

BUDDHIST THEMES

Overt expression of Buddhist affiliation also appears frequently in Xie Lingyun's verse, although it is in his prose works that his important dissertations on controversial doctrine lie. In his poetry, Buddhist themes such as the ephemeral and insubstantial nature of the world are generally introduced into larger concerns of scene and circumstance. The brevity and lyricism of the references in their contexts preclude theological exposition, but even so, one catches glimpses of the essence of Xie Lingyun's arguments: "Seeing all this, mortal thoughts vanish, In an instant of enlightenment, one attains to abandonment." Xie Lingyun's proposition that transcendental wisdom derived from sudden enlightenment, eventually vindicated by new textual evidence arriving from the troubled North, clashed with prevailing views in the South and earned for him the enmity of court favorites who subscribed to the current ritualistic and pedantic practices of gradual accumulation of Buddhistic merit by which enlightenment was thought to be attained. (It is interesting, however, that religious persecution did not exist per se in Xie Lingyun's society; while religious conflicts may have exacerbated tensions, his rivals brought only civil charges against him.)

GROWING OLD

Anguish over political uncertainties seems to have troubled Xie Lingyun less than his enforced partings from friends and dear relatives, his peregrinations and illnesses, and his awareness of approaching old age. "Mindful of old friends, I was loath to depart," he writes. "A wanderer come upon the eventide, I cherish old [friends]." He describes how his hair has begun to show streaks of gray in the mirror and how his girdle hangs loosely about his shrunken girth. Pursuit of pay as a bureaucrat has brought him to his sickbed in exile, and he misses his friends as time and the seasons whirl by. The most celebrated expression of these concerns occurs in the set of five stanzas he wrote in matching reply to his cousin Xie Huilian, with whom he shared some eighteen months of banishment on the family estate at Shining. Prosodically, they feature an unusually developed anadiplosis in the last line of one stanza and the first line of the next.

LANDSCAPE THEMES

While these elements certainly feature conspicuously in Xie Lingyun's verse, it is overwhelmingly his *shanshui* content, the treatment of landscape themes, for which he is renowned. Buddhist and Daoist ideas,

and his own sensitive humanity and love of the wild countryside, ubiquitously inform the tumultuous scenes he observes with a more profound contemplation of humanity in the universe. Nevertheless, it is the torrential cascade of crags and crevices, ranges and ridges that block out half the sky, peaks and precipices winding circuitously to bewilder the traveler's sense of direction, torrid summer forests, sunset birds in the trees of a riverbank, flying mists in abysmal ravines, the hooked moon among the autumn stars, pale willows murmuring in a breeze, crystal eddies in a bouldered stream— these things and more—that enrapture and awe the reader. The traveler may delight in the myriad creations and transformations of scene and season, but people are travelers in time, too. They pass on, politician and poet, sorrowed by partings, wearied, sickened, and aged by the vexations of their paths.

Xie Lingyun sees in grand nature the permanence of renewal and never tires of encountering these transformations. Thrusting up and growing, new bamboo is clad in spring-green shoots; tender reeds wear their purple blossoms. Each miracle further endears his world to the poet, ever responsive as he is to the beauties he sees all about him. The grandeur of the rugged mountains of his domain, traditionally the abode of divinities and sages, was a reminder to him of the insignificance and transience of social goals. Their neutrality and silence reinforced Xie Lingyun's Buddhist and Daoist notions of relativity and quiescence. If saddened and disappointed in his political fortunes, he was able to identify his own mortality in the passing seasons and ever-changing scene and with composure await his end.

BIBLIOGRAPHY

Cai, Zong-qui, ed. *How to Read Chinese Poetry: A Guided Anthology*. New York: Columbia University Press, 2008. Contains a chapter on landscape poems that has three sections on poetry by Xie Lingyun. It takes a step-by-step approach to the poetry, explaining wording and references. Contains English translations, Chinese originals, and romanizations of the Chinese.

Chang, Kang-i Sun. *Six Dynasties Poetry*. Princeton, N.J.: Princeton University Press, 1986. The second chapter provides a scholarly discussion of Xie Lingyun's life and poems.

Cheng, Yü-yü. "Bodily Movement and Geographic Categories: Xie Lingyun's 'Rhapsody on Mountain Dwelling' and the Jin-Song Discourse on Mountains and Rivers." *American Journal of Semiotics* 23, nos. 1-4 (2007): 193-222. Examines Xie Lingyun's "Dwelling in the Mountains" and his other work and argues that the poet's landscape poetry was not a static observation of his surroundings but a bodily engagement with them, thus creating a new geographical discourse.

Feng, Youlan. *A History of Chinese Philosophy*. Translated by Derk Bodde. 2 vols. 1973. Reprint. Princeton, N.J.: Princeton University Press, 1983. Chapter 7 of the second volume of this excellent scholarly work carefully examines various aspects of Buddhism and Xie Lingyun's role and influence in its interpretations. Splendid comparative chronological tables of the period of classical learning; informative notes throughout; superb bibliography; fine index.

Frodsham, J. D. *The Murmuring Stream: The Life and Works of the Chinese Nature Poet Hsieh Ling-yun (385-433), Duke of K'ang-Lo*. 2 vols. Kuala Lumpur: University of Malaya Press, 1967. Definitive scholarly study; eminently readable. Volume 1 is largely biographical; volume 2 translates and examines Lingyun's poetry extensively. Helpful footnotes throughout. Adequate appendices and index.

Hargett, James M. "The Poetry of Xie Lingyun." In *Great Literature of the Eastern World*, edited by Ian P. McGreal. New York: HarperCollins, 1996. Guide to the themes and style of Xie Lingyun's po-

ems. Includes both biographical and bibliographical information.

Lewis, Mark Edward. *China Between Empires: The Northern and Southern Dynasties*. Cambridge, Mass.: Harvard University Press, 2009. This cultural history discusses, among many other topics, the importance of gardens and describes Xie Lingyun's country villa as well as his poem "Dwelling in the Mountains" and its meaning.

Williams, Nicholas Morrow. "A Conversation in Poems: Xie Lingyun, Xie Huilian, and Jiang Yan." *Journal of the American Oriental Society* 127, no. 4 (October-December, 2007) 491-506. Examines poetry between Xie Lingyun and his cousin Xie Huilian as well as the poetry Jiang Yan wrote in response to the Xie cousins' work. Williams says the poems between the cousins were meant to preserve their friendship against separation. Likewise, Jiang states that poetry and language can conquer physical barriers.

Xie, Lingyun. *The Mountain Poems of Hsieh Ling-Yün*. Translated by David Hinton. New York: New Directions, 2001. A translation that includes introduction, notes, a map, a list of key terms intended to outline the poet's worldview, and a bibliography. The poems are divided into three sections, from his first exile, his time in Shining, and his final exile.

Yang, Xiaoshan. *Metamorphosis of the Private Sphere: Gardens and Objects in Tang-Song Poetry*. Cambridge, Mass.: Harvard University Press, 2003. Notes in its discussion that in his poems, Xie Lingyun included the doors and windows from which he viewed the mountains and gardens.

John Marney

Y

YEVGENY YEVTUSHENKO

Born: Stantsiya Zima, Siberia, Soviet Union (now in Russia); July 18, 1933

PRINCIPAL POETRY

Razvedchicki gryadushchego, 1952

Tretii sneg, 1955

Shossye entuziastov, 1956

Stantsiya Zima, 1956 (*Zima Junction*, 1962)

Obeshchaniy, 1957

Luk i lira, 1959

Stikhi raznykh let, 1959

Yabloko, 1960

Nezhnost, 1962

Vzmakh ruki, 1962

Selected Poetry, 1963

Bratskaya GES, 1965 (*Bratsk Station, and Other New Poems*, 1966)

The Poetry of Yevgeny Yevtushenko 1953-1965, 1965

Kachka, 1966

Yevtushenko: Poems, 1966

Poems Chosen by the Author, 1967

Idut belye snegi, 1969

Stolen Apples, 1971

Doroga Nomer Odin, 1972

Poyushchaya dambra, 1972

Otsovskiy slukh, 1975

From Desire to Desire, 1976

Ivanovskiye sitsi, 1976

V Polniy Rost, 1977

Golub' v Sant'iago, 1978 (novel in verse; *A Dove in Santiago*, 1983)

Tyazholive zemli, 1978

The Face Behind the Face, 1979

Ivan the Terrible and Ivan the Fool, 1979

Invisible Threads, 1981 (poems and photographs)

The Poetry of Yevgeny Yevtushenko, 1981

Ty na planete ne odin, 1981

Early Poems, 1989

Grazhdane, poslushaite menia, 1989

Stikhotvoreniya i poemy, 1990

The Collected Poems, 1952-1990, 1991

Pre-Morning: A New Book of Poetry in English and Russian, 1995

Walk on the Ledge = Progulki po karnizu: A New Book of Poetry, 2005 (in English and Russian)

Yevtushenko: Selected Poems, 2008

OTHER LITERARY FORMS

The prose works of Yevgeny Yevtushenko (yehv-tuh SHEHNG-koh) include *Primechaniya k avtobiografii* (1963; *A Precocious Autobiography*, 1963), first published in the Paris periodical *L'Express*; *Talant est' chudo nesluchainoe: Kniga statei* (1980; talent is not an accidental wonder), a collection of essays that are mainly on poetry but also on music, film, and prose; *Yagodnye mesta* (1981; *Wild Berries*, 1984), a novel; and *Pod kozhey statuey sbobody* (pr. 1972; under the skin of the Statue of Liberty), a poetic drama. Yevtushenko also published the novel *Ne umirai prezhde smerti* (1993; *Don't Die Before You're Dead*, 1995), which is based on the failed 1991 coup d'etat attempted by old-school communists who opposed the government of Mikhail Gorbachev. Yevtushensko was the compiler and wrote the introduction for a one-thousand-page poetry anthology, *Twentieth Century Russian Poetry: Silver and Steel* (1993). The massive anthology ranges over the entire corpus of Russian poetry in the twentieth century and had to be smuggled out of the country in sections beginning in 1972.

ACHIEVEMENTS

Yevgeny Yevtushenko's appeal to a popular audience began with his first verses, which appeared in a sports magazine, *Sovjetskiy sport*, in 1949. His early publications, full of autobiographical revelations, charmed his audiences by their freshness and sincerity. After Joseph Stalin's death in 1953, Yevtushenko began to address deeper social and political issues and became known as a dissident voice in Soviet literature. During the period of liberalization under Nikita Khrushchev in the late 1950's and early 1960's, Yevtushenko's personal and political poetry appeared in numerous Soviet journals and newspapers, including *Sovjetskiy sport*, *Yunost*, *Komsomolskaya pravda*, *Molodaya gvardiya*, *Literaturnaya gazeta*, *Pravda*, *Znamya*, *Ogonyok*, *Rossiya*, *Novy mir*, and *Oktyabr*. When *Stikhi raznykh let* (poems of various years) appeared in 1959, twenty thousand copies were sold immediately. The 1962 collection *Vzmakh ruki* (a wave of the hand) enjoyed a sale of 100,000 copies.

Not all of Yevtushenko's poetry, however, was so widely appreciated. When the controversial "Babii Yar" was published in *Literaturnaya gazeta* in 1961, many hostile articles appeared in the Soviet press, such as that of D. Starikov in *Literatura i zhizn*. It was during this same period that Yevtushenko wrote the script for Dmitri Shostakovich's moving *Thirteenth Symphony* (1962), a work that uses the Babii Yar incident as its principal motif. As a tribute to the poem's power, "Babii Yar" was inscribed in the Holocaust Memorial Museum in Washington, D.C. The New York Philharmonic made a recording of the Shostakovich work featuring Yevtushensko reciting "Babii Yar." In the early 1960's, Yevtushenko began to travel abroad, to France, England, and the United States. This exposure made him one of the most popular Soviet poets. Articles about him, as well as his poems, appeared in *Paris-Match*, *London Observer*, *Der Spiegel*, *Time*, *Saturday Review*, *Holiday*, *Life*, *Harper's Magazine*, and many others. Known as a dynamic performer and reciter of poetry, Yevtushenko gave many poetry readings both in the Soviet Union and abroad in a vibrant, declamatory style. He claims to have given 250 in 1961 alone.

Yevtushenko has been recognized throughout his career for both his literary and political achievements. He was given the U.S.S.R. Commission for the Defense of Peace award in 1965, the U.S.S.R. state prize in 1984, and an Order of Red Banner of Labor. His novel *Wild Berries* was a finalist for the 1985 Ritz Paris Hemingway award for best novel published in English. He has traveled widely and incorporated his observations and reactions into poetry, photography (*Invisible Threads*), film, drama, essays, and fiction.

BIOGRAPHY

Yevgeny Alexandrovich Yevtushenko was born in Stantsiya Zima, Siberia, in the Soviet Union, on July 18, 1933, of mixed Ukrainian, Russian, and Tartar blood. In his famous poem "Stantsia Zima" ("Zima Junction"), he describes in detail this remote Siberian town on the Trans-Siberian Railway about two hundred miles from Irkutsk and not far from Lake Baikal. Both his grandfathers were victims of Stalinist purges, a fact that helps to explain Yevtushenko's attitude toward Stalin. Yevtushenko's father was a geologist, and between the ages of fifteen and seventeen, young Zhenya, as he was familiarly called, accompanied his father on geological expeditions to Kazakhstan and the Altai. His mother, of modest peasant stock, worked as a singer in Moscow during and after the war. His parents' careers gave Yevtushenko a broad appreciation for common working people and the day-to-day struggles to survive in an authoritarian state.

As a young boy in Moscow, Yevtushenko began to read Russian and foreign classics, familiarizing himself not only with the works of Leo Tolstoy and Anton Chekhov, but also those of Alexandre Dumas, père, Gustave Flaubert, Friedrich Schiller, Honoré de Balzac, Dante, and many other foreign authors. In 1941, he was evacuated to Zima Junction, where he developed his love for the Siberian taiga and his impassioned opposition to war. When his parents were separated in 1944, he returned to Moscow with his mother. His education from 1944 to 1948 was very desultory, and when he was expelled from school at fifteen, he ran off to join his father in Siberia for two years.

Among Yevtushenko's many interests was sports, and it was not accidental that his first verses were published in a sports magazine. He met the editors Tarasov and Barlas, who became his first mentors, although his continued interest in reading led him to other models, especially Ernest Hemingway, Aleksandr Blok, Sergei Esenin, and Vladimir Mayakovsky. Yevtushenko wrote in the style of the times, paying lip service to Stalin until the latter's death in 1953.

The year 1953 was a turning point in Yevtushenko's life, for along with many other Russians, he experienced disillusionment with the Stalinist regime. With the coming of the Khrushchev "Thaw" in 1956, he began to write poetry against the former rulers and, gradually, advocating for human rights and expressive freedom. In 1954, he married Bella Akhmakulina, whom he himself describes as Russia's greatest living woman poet, although the marriage was doomed to failure. Yevtushenko's meeting with Boris Pasternak in 1957 brought him into contact with his greatest mentor.

In 1962, Yevtushenko began to travel abroad. His great success and popularity was temporarily interrupted by the publication in Paris of *A Precocious Autobiography* without the permission of the Soviet authorities, for which infraction his travel was curtailed. He subsequently made trips abroad, however, including one to the United States in 1966, where he gave many poetry readings and charmed audiences with his engaging and dynamic personality. He also visited Cuba, which he admired greatly as exemplary of the revolutionary ideal. Later travels to Rome, Vietnam, Africa, Japan, Alaska, California, and Florida also inspired poems. He lists sixty-four countries that he visited up to 1981. His second marriage, to Galina Semyonovna, and the birth of a son greatly inspired his life and work. He later would marry Jan Butler (1978) and Maria Novika (1986).

Since the 1970's, he has been active in many fields of culture, writing novels and engaging in acting, film directing, and photography. His first novel, *Wild Berries*, was a finalist for the Ritz Paris Hemingway prize in 1985, and his first feature film, *The Kindergarten* (1984), played in the Soviet Union, England, and the United States. Yevtushenko wrote and direced the film *Stalin's Funeral* (1990), which featured Vanessa Redgrave and Claus Maria Brandauer. Yevtusheko was appointed honorary member of American Academy of Arts and Sciences in 1987. He continued to be politically outspoken during this period as well, supporting author Aleksandr Solzhenitsyn and other Russian writers who were exiled or imprisoned.

With the advent of glasnost (a term used to refer to the gradual opening of Soviet culture and politics under Gorbachev) in the late 1980's, Yevtushenko became a leading activist in the struggle to reform Soviet society. In 1989, Yevtushenko became a member of the Congress of People's Deputies, and he was appointed vice president of Russian PEN in 1991. From 1988 to 1991, Yevtushenko worked against censorship and for freedom of expression when he served in the first freely elected Russian Parliament. When the old Soviet stalwarts attempted to derail Gorbachev's new govern-

Yevgeny Yevtushenko (Jean-Claude Bouis)

ment in 1991, Yevtushenko shouted his poetry from the balcony of the Russian White House in front of a huge crowd. In 1993, he received a medal as Defender of Free Russia, which was given to those who took part in resisting the hard-line Communist coup in August, 1991. However, in 1994, Yevtushenko refused to accept President Boris Yeltzin's tribute of The Order of Friendship Between Peoples as an expression of his opposition to the Russian war against Chechen rebels. In 1996, Yevtushenko joined the faculty at Queens College, New York; he later began teaching Russian and European poetry and cinema at the University of Tulsa, Oklahoma. Although critical and popular reception of Yevtushenko's work has mostly depended on the Soviet political climate, critics have generally praised the multicultural quality of his writings and regard Yevtushenko as Russia's premier but unofficial cultural emissary to the world.

ANALYSIS

Although not the most original poet of the post-Stalinist era in the Soviet Union, Yevgeny Yevtushenko has shown himself to be one of the most significant. This is essentially because he has been able to put his finger on the pulse of the times. He became the spokesperson for a new generation, not only in his native land but also all over the world. Unflinchingly honest and sincere, he has spoken with clarity and courage on issues that threaten freedom. He is best known for his poems of protest such as "Babii Yar" and "Stalin's Heirs." In the tradition of Russian poetry, Yevtushensko sees himself invested with a mission and a message, and he proclaims it fearlessly. He directs his criticism not only against the cult of personality, anti-Semitism, and oppression in his own land, but also against the same abuses in other countries, especially in the United States. Images of Martin Luther King, Jr., John and Robert Kennedy, and Allison Krause of Kent State University appeared in his work in the 1970's; the perils of television and advertising, war in Northern Ireland, and the threat of nuclear weapons in poems of the late 1970's. "Freedom to Kill," "Flowers and Bullets," and "Safari in Ulster," among others, explore these themes.

Yevtushenko knows how to combine the social with the personal and how to move effortlessly from one to the other. His poetry is extremely autobiographical, and one can read his life by exploring his verse. He tells whimsically of his Siberian childhood in Zima Junction, in the poem by the same name; of his youth in Moscow; of his travels and disappointment in love; and of his family and children. He reflects on the idealism of youth and the fears of impending old age. He is especially sensitive to childhood and can frequently combine his own experiences, a universal theme of childhood, and social observation. A typical poem is "Weddings," which recounts his folk dancing at ill-fated wartime weddings in Siberia.

A child of the North, Yevtushenko speaks best of nature when evoking the taiga, the lakes, and the rivers of Siberia; or the smell of fresh berries or the blue glow of fresh snow in "Zima Junction," "Monologue of the Fox," and "The Hut." He is close to the sea and often associates it with love ("The Sea"), with women ("Glasha, Bride of the Sea"), and with contemporary problems, as in "Kachka" ("Pitching and Rolling"). Nature, however, is not the most common source of im-

ages for this contemporary poet, who prefers the city with its neon lights, the sound of jazz, and the smell of smog. He is especially fond of New York and records his impressions in many poems such as "New York Elegy," "Smog," and *Pod kozhey statuey sbobody*.

People, more than nature, dominate Yevtushenko's poetry. In the tradition of Fyodor Dostoevski, Anton Chekhov, and Maxim Gorky, the lowly and the downtrodden occupy an important place. Socialist Realism places an emphasis on the "people." Yevtushenko adopts this attitude, but he goes even further, showing genuine sympathy for the worker and the peasant, especially evident in *Bratsk Station, and Other New Poems*, in which he also speaks of the unmarried mother ("Nushka"). While extolling the humble and the poor, he manifests hatred for the cruel overseer, the bully, or the compromiser. Such characters appear in "Babii Yar," "Zima Junction," and "Song of the Overseers" and in *Bratsk Station, and Other New Poems*. He detests hypocrisy and slavery in any form and denounces it loudly in the Soviet Union, the United States, South Africa, and anywhere else in the world.

Women occupy an important place in Yevtushenko's verse. In keeping with his sympathy for the peasant and workers, he dedicates many poems to the hardworking Russian woman, as in "The Hut." Old women in particular are among his favorites, such as the one who brings the red flowers of the taiga to the workers of Bratsk Station. The young innocent girl in love, such as "Masha"; the mothers who work for their young children and are never appreciated; the dancer; the singer: All these are living people who impart to Yevtushenko's works a strong dramatic quality.

The narrative, along with the lyric, is an important feature of Yevtushenko's poetry. He prefers the epic style, and "Zima Junction," *Bratsk Station, and Other New Poems*, and *Ivan the Terrible and Ivan the Fool* illustrate this tendency, although he often falls short of his goals. All his verse is dynamic rather than static. Many of his shorter works have a balladlike quality; among these are "Glasha, Bride of the Sea," "Rhythms of Rome," and "Nushka" in *Bratsk Station, and Other New Poems*. Dialogue occurs frequently and enhances the dramatic effect of his verse. *Pod kozhey statuey sbobody*, partially prose and partially verse, was staged in Moscow as a play in 1972; it satirized Russia as well as the United States.

Yevtushenko claims as his masters Hemingway (to whom he had dedicated one of his finest poems, "Encounter"), Esenin, Mayakovsky, and Pasternak, whom he knew personally and who offered friendly criticism of his early verse. The influence of Esenin and Mayakovsky is not always evident in his style, although at first glance he seems to be an avid disciple of Mayakovsky. Yevtushenko uses the "step lines" of Mayakovsky, but the verbal brilliance, bold speech, and innovation of the older poet are rarely evident. Yevtushenko employs a colloquial style, with many words borrowed from foreign languages. His poetry is filled with vivid twentieth century speech, with frequent sound effects, internal rhymes, and wordplay not always evident in English translations. He uses a wide variety of rhymes and rhythms, as well as free verse. His earlier poems tend to be freer than the poems of the late 1970's and early 1980's, which make use of regular meters and indulge in much less verbal experimentation. At all times he seems to write with ease and facility, although his poems frequently give the impression of too great haste. He is a prolific, spontaneous poet who writes without looking back and sometimes produces profound and startling insights.

Yevtushenko is a poet who wishes to be accessible to as many people as possible. He refuses poetic isolation and an elitist concept of art. In fact, he has chosen photography as a medium because its meaning is immediately obvious and it does not become obscure in translation. Above all, he is an apostle of human brotherhood. He believes in kindness and mutual understanding. *Invisible Threads* captures this theme dramatically. He is satirical, disarmingly frank, yet idealistic and trusting. Images of Christ, the sea, African jungles, and neon lights all serve to highlight his essential optimism and hope for the future.

Yevtushenko's poetry falls into distinct periods. The first, from 1952 to 1960, contains poems of youthful enthusiasm and is extremely autobiographical, as in "Zima Junction," "The Visit," and "Weddings." Memories of war and the child's inability to grasp its impact appear in "Weddings," "Party Card," and "A Companion." Since Yevtushenko had not begun his travels at this time, his inspiration was limited to Russia, centering especially on Moscow, Siberia, and Georgia. Although Yevtushenko was born long after the Revolution and did not know it at first hand, he manifests amazing conviction and enthusiasm for its ideals. "Lies" and "Knights" are among the many typical examples. Lyricism, love, and, above all, human sympathy characterize this early period.

"ZIMA JUNCTION"

Perhaps the best and most important poem of this period is "Zima Junction," first published in the journal *Oktyabr* in 1956. It refers to a visit to his native village in 1953, after the death of Stalin, the Doctors' Plot, and the deposition of Lavrenti Beria. Relatives and friends in far-off Siberia are anxious to learn all the news at first hand from this Moscow visitor, who, they expect, has all the information and has known Stalin personally. He accepts their naïveté with humor and respect for their simple lives, while at the same time noticing how both he and they have changed, and how they too have anxieties beneath the apparent simplicity of their ways.

The return to Zima Junction is the occasion for a retrospective glance at his own past and the past of his ancestors, as he recalls his great-grandfather's trip to Siberia from his peasant village in the Ukraine, and his grandfather's revolutionary idealism. Yevtushenko returns to the place where he was born not only for the past but also for the future, to seek "strength and courage." He realizes that he, like the people of the village, has changed, and that it is difficult to decide wisely on a course of action. He personifies Zima Junction, which speaks to him through the forest and the wheat, in some of his best nature images. The section "Berry-Picking" has frequently been reprinted separately.

Throughout the poem, local color abounds, and Yevtushenko's narrative quality emerges through images of such people as the barefoot berry picker, the garrulous fisherman, and the disappointed wife in the hayloft who complains of her ungrateful and inattentive husband. Yevtushenko's family such as Uncle Volodya and Uncle Andrei, simple laborers, contrast with Pankratov, "the ponderous didactic president." The wheat and the village speak to young Zhenya, who is on the uncertain threshold of manhood, urging him to explore the world over and to love people.

Although the poem consists of many isolated incidents, they are obviously linked by the village and its message of courage and hope. The style is simple and colloquial, interspersed with local Siberian and Ukrainian expressions. The dialogue is suited to the speaker, and the nature imagery is among Yevtushenko's best. Belief in revolutionary ideals is evident, and party ideology, although present, is sincere and unaffected. Yevtushenko began to acquire fame after publishing this poem, where the personal note becomes universal.

"Babii Yar"

Yevheny's second distinct period—the poems of the 1970's—shows a broader scope and is mainly influenced by travel. Yevtushenko writes especially of the United States, Latin America, Cuba, Alaska, Hawaii, and Rome. He speaks out more freely against hypocrisy and loss of freedom, and he addresses social and political abuses, of which "Babii Yar" is the most significant example. At the same time, he professes strong patriotism, as evidenced in the lengthy *Bratsk Station, and Other New Poems*. The North, especially Siberia, is an inspiration for his work, especially *Kachka*. The personal and autobiographical theme returns in poems about love and loss of love. A more serious note is expressed in images of guilt, suffering, and repentance. Poems such as "Twist on Nails" and "Torments of Conscience" (published in English in *Stolen Apples*) express these themes through religious and dramatic imagery, of which one of the most striking examples is that of the pierced hands of the crucified Christ. These are poems of maturity and of considerable depth and sensitivity in both the personal and the social order.

"Babii Yar" was first published in the *Literaturnaya gazeta* in 1961. It is a poetic meditation on the tragic fate of the Jews in Eastern Europe, thirty-three thousand of whom were killed by the Germans in 1941 at Babii Yar, a ravine near the city of Kiev. As an attack on Soviet anti-Semitism, the poem stimulated controversy in the Soviet press and provoked counterattacks from leading journalists, but Yevtushenko continued to publish. In the poem, Yevtushenko deplores the absence of a monument at Babii Yar. One has subsequently been erected, without reference to the specific massacre of 1941.

The poem is not confined to Soviet anti-Semitism; it attacks prejudice against all peoples, but especially against Jews everywhere. In the poem, Yevtushenko, who is not Jewish himself, identifies with all the Jews of the past: those in ancient Egypt, Christ on the Cross, Alfred Dreyfus, and Anne Frank. Amid the harsh indictment of those who killed the Jews, Yevtushenko inserts delicate poetry: "transparent as a branch in April." He emphasizes the need for all people to look at one another and to recognize their responsibility and their brotherhood. By poetic transfer, Yevtushenko sees in himself each of these murderers and accepts responsibility for the terrible massacre. With characteristic optimism, he expresses trust in Russia's international soul, which will shine forth when anti-Semitism is dead.

"Bratsk Station"

"Bratsk Station" was first published in the April, 1965, issue of *Yunost*. It is a long discursive poem of epic proportions: five thousand lines divided into thirty-five unequal and loosely connected parts. The main idea, as expressed by Yevtushenko himself, is a "controversy between two themes: the theme of disbelief expressed in the monologue of the Pyramid and the theme of faith, expressed by Bratsk Station." The Bratsk project was launched in 1958. It is a gigantic hydroelectric station, and it also contains lumber mills and plants for pulp, cardboard, wood by-products, and aluminum. Located in central Siberia along the Angara River, it is one of the largest hydroelectric plants in Russia. Yevtushenko sees it as a monument to free labor and considers the manpower that constructed it and keeps it in operation as a symbol of brotherhood, expressed in the word "bratsk," which means "brotherly."

The essential conflict is expressed in the recurring dialogue between the Egyptian Pyramid and Bratsk Station. Yevtushenko sees the Pyramid as a construction of slaves, and therefore it has no faith in itself. Moreover, it maintains that all men will ultimately turn to slavery and that freedom is only an illusory dream. This naïve interpretation of Egyptian history has provoked much criticism, notably from Andrei Sinyavsky in "In Defense of the Pyramid," where he maintains that Yevtushenko does not understand the significance of Egyptian society. The Bratsk Station, on the other hand, extols the free labor that built it, for it is the daughter of Russia who has attained freedom through centuries of suffering.

To illustrate the quest for freedom in the Russian soul, Yevtushenko evokes a number of events and heroes from Russian history, especially Stenka Razin, the Decembrists, and the followers of Mikhail Petrashevsky. To these he adds Russia's greatest writers; Alexander Pushkin, Tolstoy, Dostoevski, and the modern writers he so admires; Esenin and Mayakovsky, with a poem in the style of the latter. Finally, there are the unsung heroes of the people: Issy Kramer, the Light Controller, who still suffers from anti-Semitism; Sonka and Petka, the concrete pourers; and Nushka, the unwed mother. Yevtushenko relates that when he read his poem to the workers of Bratsk Station, mothers like Nushka held their children up to him, recognizing themselves in his poem.

Themes of socialism and patriotism abound in the poem, frequently exaggerated. Despite its loosely connected parts, the poem moves quickly, with dramatic and lively style and balladlike quality. There are echoes of "Babii Yar" in the Light Controller and of "Zima Junction" in the images of the taiga and the Simbirsk Fair, and the work is autobiographical as well as political and social. It begins and ends with poetry. In the "Prayer Before the Poem," Yevtushenko invokes Pushkin, Mikhail Lermontov, Nikolai Nekrasov, Blok, Pasternak, Esenin, and Mayakovsky and asks for their gifts (mutually exclusive, claims Sinyavsky). The final section, "The Night of Poetry," evokes the Siberian custom of improvising poetry and delivering it to musical accompaniment. In the moment of recitation, Yevtushenko sees before him the great Russian heroes and writers of the past and experiences with them the glory of freedom symbolized by Bratsk Station.

THE 1970'S

The years from 1970 to 1981 show both a return to basic structures in theme and composition and a broadening of scope into various genres: photography, the theater, the novel, and the essay. As the father of a child, Yevtushenko again writes about childhood, as in "Father and Son," "Walk with My Son," and "A Father's Ear." Now approaching middle age, he writes more of death ("A Child's Grave," "Come to My Tomb") and speaks of his desire to live in all lands and be all types of people possible, but to be buried in Russia. The travel theme is still uppermost, with an emphasis on the Far East, where Vietnam becomes an important social and political question. Yevtushenko, always against war, continues to make an appeal to human brotherhood in Northern Ireland, in South Africa, and between the United States and Russia.

IVANOVSKIYE SITSI

Still drawn to the epic theme, Yevtushenko published *Ivanovskiye sitsi* in the journal *Avrora* in 1976. The title means literally "calico from Ivanovo" and refers to Ivanovo-Voznesensk, a large textile center important for the labor movement. In 1905, there was a strike there that led to the establishment of one of the first Soviets of Workers' Deputies. Yevtushenko is always fond of wordplay and thus uses "Ivan" in several contexts. There is Ivan the Terrible, czar of Russia from 1533 to 1584, the symbol of autocracy in constant conflict with the people. Ivan the Fool is an important but composite character from folk epic and represents the growing popular consciousness. The poem glorifies the Revolution and the proletariat and expresses faith in the consciousness of the working class, bearers of the Russian soul. Yevtushenko maintains, however, that the Revolution extols heroes of all nations—Joan of Arc, John Brown, and Anne Frank—and aims for human brotherhood and a real International.

INVISIBLE THREADS

Invisible Threads, published in the United States and composed of poetry and photography, takes its inspiration from Edward Steichen's *Family of Man* exhibit and emphasizes the same theme. It contains poems from the late 1970's and addresses contemporary themes such as the threat of atomic warfare, the conflict in Northern Ireland, and the universal themes of birth and death, the former inspired by the birth of Yevtushenko's son in London. In the poem "Life and Death," a balladlike lyric, Life and Death exchange places. Death realizes that she is respected, if only because of fear, whereas Life is not. Yevtushenko pleads again for human dignity. Religious images are more evident than in the past, although Yevtushenko sees salvation among human beings on earth. He wishes to echo every voice in the world and "dance his Russian dance on the invisible threads that stretch between the hearts of men."

THE COLLECTED POEMS, 1952-1990

The Collected Poems, 1952-1990 reflects Yevtushenko's poetic career in microcosm: vast and ever astonishing in its variety. The title is somewhat misleading, since the volume offers only a selection from Yevtushenko's extensive career, and in addition, several long poems are represented in excerpts only. The translations by twenty-five translators vary in quality: A few are revisions of earlier versions, and because most of Yevtushenko's poems use slant rhyme relying heavily on assonance, few attempts were made to retain this feature in the English translations, or indeed to use rhyme at all.

Yevtushenko's characteristic political criticisms and commentary find a dominant place in this collection. He praises Chile's Salvador Allende and Cuba's Ché Guevara, condemns the Vietnam War, and deplores the situation in Northern Ireland. He also warns against Soviet political abuses, castigating militarists and dishonest bureaucrats. These critical poems range from "Stalin's Heirs" and "Babii Yar," from the early 1960's, to later poems, including "Momma and the Neutron Bomb" and poems about the dissident Andrei Sakharov and the Afghanistan war (with the Soviets) in the 1980's. When one considers that, due to censorship, many of Yevtushenko's poems were not published when they were written in the 1960's, his cynical critique of Soviet politics is understandable. Included in this collection are a number of his censored poems. Among them are verses to fellow Russian poets, "Russian Tanks in Prague," and "The Ballad of the Big," a bawdy tale about castration for the good of the party.

Another thread running through Yevtushenko's work is the importance of poetry and the responsibility of the poet to humankind. He constantly questions his own talent and mission, thus continuing the Russian tradition of meta-poetry. Likewise very Russian is the dialogue between writers living and dead that Yevtushenko carries on, in poems addressed to or evoking Pasternak, Pablo Neruda, and Jack London, along with numerous others. He also blasts modern writers in "The Incomprehensible Poets," in which he admits: "My guilt is my simplicity./ My crime is my clarity." In "I Would Like," he notes: "I would like to belong to all times,/ shock all history so much/ that it would be amazed/ what a smart aleck I was."

Personal accounts, such as "On a Bicycle" and "Flowers for Grandmother," fill several pages in the collection. "Blue Fox" combines his concern for animals with an allegory of the collective state; "Monologue of an Actress" is a witty complaint by an aging actress that no worthwhile roles are left to play. His own experiences are represented here as well, contributing to his range of personal stories. His poetry is a kind of diary that details his extensive travels and especially his many love affairs. Remarkable love poems follow the poet from first love, to the birth of his sons, to the sadness of falling out of love again. The poems contain a rich fabric of quarrels, memories, farewells, and even a conversation with his dog, who shares the poet's grief that his woman has gone. The human breadth that he captures is perhaps the strongest aspect of this collection.

WALK ON THE LEDGE

Walk on the Ledge, despite the subtitle "A New Book of Poetry," contains both new and old poems, including "Babii Yar" and "Fears," which were written more than forty years earlier but appear in new translations alongside the original Russian. A few of the poems, such as "On the Grave of May the First" (1996) and "The City of Yes and the City of No" (1964), were also written earlier. However, the majority of the thirty-seven poems in this book are new and come from the early twenty-first century. Most of these poems were translated and edited by Gracie and Bill Davidson with help from Deborah Taggart. Yevtushenko has continued to tinker with his best-known poems long after they were first published. The 2005 version of "Babii Yar" differs from the 1961 version in significant ways, perhaps due to different translations and continued additions. Yevtushenko's postscript to "Fears" states that ever since Shostakovich based his thirteenth symphony on the poem, the poet had wanted to revise it because some stanzas seemed poetically weak. He attributes the flawed earlier version to his own hurried composition and the censorship standards of the Soviet magazine that first printed it. The predominant themes are by now familiar to Yevtushenko's readers: the expansiveness and generosity of youthful love, alienation from mother Russia, feelings of displacement in foreign countries, cultural conflict between western capitalism and idealistic socialism, Chechen separatists and their battles for ethnic identity, and the effects on people clinging to the failed Soviet socialist system.

Walk on the Ledge follows the modern trend towards bilingual publishing, printing English and Russian language versions on opposite pages. Perhaps Russia's increasing importance as a strategic partner of Western Europe and the United States has increased the attractiveness of Russian language study in schools and colleges.

The title poem, "Walk on the Ledge," describes Yevtushenko's tenuous relationship with his homeland during Stalin's 1950's repressions, when the poet felt as if he were balanced on a precipice with a glass of vodka in his hand, a metaphor for the political balancing act of creative expression in an authoritarian state. The poet confesses his joy of singing and climbing to the rooftops, playing at love and clamoring to escape through the Iron Curtain to the liberties beckoning from Rome or Paris. Much of the appeal of Yevtushenko's poetry comes through his exuberance and desire to thumb his nose at the humorless doctrine of Soviet socialism. Equally joyful are the poet's many effusions dedicated to love of women and relationships such as "My First Woman," "Eyelashes," and "Men Don't Give Themselves to Women." In "Old Photograph," Yevtushenko reflects on a youthful dalliance with a fellow intellectual, a young American woman who left the poet with a photo inscribed with her wish for his future success. As he holds the photo of his old girlfriend, the poet hears her voice admonishing him to keep producing, to keep loving, and to keep living zestfully.

Another of Yevtushenko's favorite themes is the idealism of the early Soviet vision for an egalitarian utopia versus the crumbled reality of a corrupt political system and severe restrictions against artistic freedom. "Tsunami" deals with the disastrous 2004 earthquake and resulting tsunami that claimed thousands of lives in Thailand and across Southeast Asia. The poet recalls hiding in San Francisco during the 1960's with his American girlfriend under the watchful eyes of the Central Intelligence Agency and the KGB. At this time, young people idolized Cuban revolutionary Ché Gue-

vara and admired Fidel Castro's new socialist republic in Cuba, but the reality of Cold War politics became clear. Fashionable "socialists" in Hollywood did not care about the political message as long as profits from films and records kept flowing. Meanwhile, new oil-rich Muscovites cared nothing for political theory as long as they could wear shiny new clothes and ride around in chauffeur-driven stretch limousines. The intensity and loss of life of the tsunami that hit Thailand rendered political discussions meaningless. Political commentary continues in many poems such as "When Will a Man Come to Russia," "Gorbachev in Oklahoma," and "On the Grave of May the First."

In "School in Beslan," the poet reflects on the 2004 hostage crisis when Chechen rebels stormed a school and took children as hostages, demanding that Russia stop the war. Yevtushenko compares Beslan to a place of his youth much like in "Zima Junction" and finds abundant buried reminders of the unconscious powers that shaped his imagination. He feels the jumbled emotions of his expectations for greatness and early fame in his homeland mingled with his strange twenty-first century irrelevance in midwestern America. Yevtushenko looks over the range of twentieth century history with the wreckage of Stalin's purges, dissidents, deportations to Kazakhstan, the war against Chechen rebels, and Yeltsin's egoism. The poet wonders whether the multinamed "gods" of Muhammad, Christ, or Vladimir Ilyich Lenin will together be able to save anyone in the ongoing war between religions, nations, and armies.

The final poem in this collection is "La Corrida" ("The Bullfight"). The long, discursive narrative poem employs a variety of stanza structures, voices, and tones ranging from talking horses to political commentary. The poet discusses seeing the spectacle of sport and savage animal sacrifice in Seville, Spain, which becomes a statement of universal suffering, human hypocrisy, and passions of the moment. The grandiose celebration of toreadors, street parades, and drunken revelry masks the brutality of primitive religion and blood sacrifice. Animals are enslaved for human entertainment much in the same way that power politics views individuals as expendable pawns in a game of conquest. The public spectacle renders brutality into grand theater for the benefit of those in power, the bullfighters or politicians. Murderers are viewed as heroes by the frenzied crowd as blood flows through the streets of Seville, Berlin, or Moscow.

YEVTUSHENKO: SELECTED POEMS

This work pays homage to the importance of Yevtushenko in the revival of the traditional lyric poem in the Soviet Union/Russia of the twentieth century. Translated by British scholars Robin Milner-Gulland and Peter Levi, *Yevtushenko: Selected Poems* is a reissue of the original 1963 Penguin Classic that wound up on many shelves of politically aware college students in the United States and Europe. When first published, *Yevtushenko: Selected Poems* outsold every book of foreign poetry in translation except E. V. Rieu's *Odyssey*. It contains many of Yevtushenko's strongest works, such as "Babii Yar," "Zima Junction," and "Fears," and an assortment of amorous and politically inspired short poems. Levi writes that the appeal of Yevtushenko has to do with the poet's personal sensibilities and his concept of what are acceptable topics, which are far outside the Westerner's experience. The core of Yevtushenko's message is found in honesty, acceptance of what life brings, and a hopefulness about human nature that transcends politics. It destroys the common image of Soviet society as being hostile, impenetrable, and cold-blooded.

OTHER MAJOR WORKS

LONG FICTION: *Yagodnye mesta*, 1981 (*Wild Berries*, 1984); *Ne umirai prezhde smerti*, 1993 (*Don't Die Before You're Dead*, 1995).

PLAY: *Pod kozhey statuey sbobody*, pr. 1972.

NONFICTION: *Primechaniya k avtobiografii*, 1963 (*A Precocious Autobiography*, 1963); *Talant est' chudo nesluchainoe: Kniga statei*, 1980; *Fatal Half Measures: The Culture of Democracy in the Soviet Union*, 1991.

BIBLIOGRAPHY

Brown, Deming. *The Last Years of Soviet Russian Literature: Prose Fiction, 1975-1991*. New York: Cambridge University Press, 1993. History and criticism of late Soviet-era Russian literature. Includes bibliographical references and index.

Brown, Edward J. *Russian Literature Since the Revolution*. Rev. ed. Cambridge, Mass.: Harvard University Press, 1982. A survey and critical analysis of Soviet literature. Includes bibliographic references.

The Economist. "Past, Implacable." 306, no. 7535 (January 30, 1988): 75-76. Draws parallels between Yevtushenko's poetic themes and glasnost, concentrating on "Bukharin's Widow" and "Monuments Not Yet Erected."

Emerson, Caryl. *The Cambridge Introduction to Russian Literature*. New York: Cambridge University Press, 2008. Comprehensive historical essays that cover the range of Russian poetry and prose. Includes thematic essays and index.

Hingley, Ronald. *Russian Writers and Soviet Society, 1917-1978*. New York: Random House, 1979. A history of Russian literature of the Soviet era. Includes a bibliography and index.

Kinzer, Stephen. "A Russian Poet Steeped in America." *The New York Times*, December 11, 2003, p. E1. Deals with the poet's beliefs and his interactions with students.

Milne, Ira Mark, ed. *Poetry for Students*. Vol. 29. Detroit: Thomson/Gale Group, 2009. Contains an analysis of "Babii Yar."

Slonim, Mark. *Soviet Russian Literature*. 2d ed. New York: Oxford University Press, 1977. A historical and critical study of Russian literature.

Vanden Heuvel, Katrina. "Yevtushenko Feels a Fresh Wind Blowing." *Progressive* 24 (April, 1987): 24-31. Addresses Yevtushenko's views on Russian politics, poetry's public service, glasnost, and relations with the West.

Yevtushenko, Yevgeny. "September 11th as Teacher of Teachers." *South Central Review* 19 (Summer/Autumn, 2002): 11-22. Reflective essay by the poet about the emotional reaction to flying on the day of the terrorist attacks in New York city.

Irma M. Kashuba; Sarah Hilbert
Updated by Jonathan Thorndike

Yosano Akiko

Born: Sakai, Japan; December 7, 1878
Died: Tokyo, Japan; May 29, 1942

PRINCIPAL POETRY
Dokusō, 1901
Midaregami, 1901 (*Tangled Hair*, 1935, 1971)
Koōgi, 1904
Koi goromo, 1905
Mai hime, 1906
Yume-no-hana, 1906
Hakkō, 1908
Tokonatsu, 1908
Sabo hime, 1911
Shundeishū, 1911
Seikainami, 1912
Pari yori, 1913
Sakura Sō, 1915
Maigoromo, 1916
Shubashū, 1916
Myōjōshū, 1918
Wakakiotome, 1918
Hinotori, 1919
Tabi-no-uta, 1921
Taiyō-to-bara, 1921
Kusa-no-yume, 1922
Nagareboshi-no-michi, 1924
Ningen ōrai, 1925
Ruriko, 1925
Kokoro no enkei, 1928
Shiro zakura, 1942
The Poetry of Yosano Akiko, 1957
Tangled Hair: Selected Tanka from "Midaregami," 1971
Akiko shukasen, 1996
River of Stars: Selected Poems of Yosano Akiko, 1996

OTHER LITERARY FORMS

Although the married name of Yosano Akiko (yoh-sah-noh ah-kee-koh) was Yosano (placed before her personal name, in the normal Japanese order), she is commonly called Akiko, which is her "elegant name."

Among her many translations and modernizations, the most enduringly popular is her modern Japanese version of the greatest Japanese novel, *Genji monogatari* (early eleventh century; *The Tale of Genji*, 1881), written by Murasaki Shikibu. Akiko's version was published in 1912 and 1939. This monumental work revived general interest in Murasaki and other classical authors; it is included with Akiko's autobiography, novels, fairy tales, children's stories, essays, and original and translated poetry in the standard Japanese edition of her works, *Yosano Akiko zenshū* (1972).

ACHIEVEMENTS

Yosano Akiko is generally admired as the greatest female poet and *tanka* poet of modern Japan, as an influential critic and educator, and as the grand embodiment of Romanticism, feminism, pacifism, and social reform in the first three decades of the twentieth century. She has been called a princess, queen, and goddess of poetry. In fact, Japanese Romanticism in the early twentieth century has been called the age of Akiko. She also influenced feminist writers internationally. She infused erotic and imaginative passion into the traditional *tanka* form (a poem of five lines containing five, seven, five, seven, and seven syllables respectively) at a time when it had grown lifelessly conventional, having lost the personal vitality of ancient times; in the same way, she revived certain classical qualities of the *Manyōshū* (mid-eighth century; *The Collections of Ten Thousand Leaves*; also as *The Ten Thousand Leaves*, 1981, and as *The Manyoshu*, 1940) and other ancient collections, while introducing stunning innovations of style. Projecting her own life and spirit into the form, she insisted that every word be charged with emotion. Such intensity is rarely transmitted through English translations, but Kenneth Rexroth's translations are fine poems in their own right as well as the most expressive renditions of Akiko's strong but subtle art.

Akiko's first book, *Tangled Hair*, was an immediate success and remains her most popular collection. It contains 399 *tanka* about her tempestuous love for the man who became her husband, Yosano Hiroshi (known as Tekkan). Her sequence of poems dramatically reveals the agonizing and sometimes ecstatic interactions among Akiko; Tekkan, his second wife (whom he was divorcing), and Yamakawa Tomiko. Tomiko, a beautiful poet beloved by both Tekkan and Akiko, was the leader of Shinshisha (the new poetry society) and edited its journal, *Myōjō* (the morning star), the chief organ of Japanese Romanticism.

Altogether, Akiko published seventy-five books, of which more than twenty are collections of original poetry. She wrote approximately seventeen thousand *tanka* as well as five hundred poems in free verse, which she devoted primarily to social issues such as pacifism and feminism. One of her outstanding poems of this kind, "Kimi shinitamō koto nakare" ("Never Let Them Kill You, Brother!"), was addressed to her own brother, who participated in the attack on Port Arthur in 1904 during the Russo-Japanese War. Akiko disliked war, observing that it brought nothing but suffering and death. Her rhetorical question—How can the emperor, who does not fight, allow his subjects to die like beasts?—was so outrageously subversive at the time that people stoned her house. It was, in fact, the first criticism of the emperor, aside from political prose, that had been published. She was defended by Mori Ōgai and other writers, and this most famous of all Japanese antiwar poems has been revived periodically by antimilitarists. Akiko also courageously defended radicals who were executed in 1912.

Another often-quoted poem in free verse, "Yama no ugoku hi kitaru" ("The Day When Mountains Move"), was one of twelve of her poems to appear in *Seitō* (bluestocking) when that feminist journal was founded in 1916, establishing Akiko as the leading poet of women's consciousness in Japan. In 1921, with Tekkan, Akiko founded the Bunka Gakuin (culture school) for girls, where she worked as a teacher and dean, while also advancing the cause of women's education and social emancipation in essays in *Taiyō* and other journals. Between 1925 and 1931, with Tekkan and a third editor, she edited and published an authoritative fifty-volume set of Japanese classics, a work that helped to democratize the study of literature and gave her and her husband financial security. Her literary and financial success never interfered with her struggle for justice, which in her view was inseparable from literature. In "Kogan no shi" ("Death of Rosy-Cheeked Youth"), for

example, she mourned the slaughter of Chinese boy-soldiers by the Japanese in Shanghai.

Some conservative critics ruthlessly denounced both Akiko and Tekkan for their scandalous lives and writings, which violated so many conventions, both literary and social. Undeterred by such attacks, Akiko struggled ceaselessly against prejudice and abuse to attain a high place among major Japanese poets of all eras.

BIOGRAPHY

Yosano Akiko was born in Sakai, Japan, December 7, 1878. Her father, Hō Sōshichi, owned a confectionery shop in Sakai, a suburb of Osaka. Both Akiko's father and her mother imposed traditional constraints on her, but she soon developed precocious literary enthusiasms and talents, thanks to the libraries of her great-grandparents; her great-grandfather was called the "master's master" of the town because of his knowledge of Chinese literature and his skilled composition of haiku. Akiko read all the literature that she could find from France and England, as well as from ancient and modern Japan—especially such classics as *The Manyoshu*, Sei Shōnagon's *Makura-no-sōshi* (early eleventh century; *Pillow Book*, 1928), and *The Tale of Genji* (which Akiko eventually translated from the archaic style into modern Japanese).

At age nineteen, Akiko published her first poem in a local journal, and within three years, she became prominent in Kansai-area literary activities. In 1900, Tekkan, the poet-leader of the new Romanticism, discovered Akiko's genius, began teaching her literature, brought her into his Shinshisha in Tokyo, and had her work published in the journal *Myōjō*; Akiko helped to edit the journal from 1901 until its demise in 1908, and again during its revival from 1921 to 1927. In 1901, Tekkan also edited and arranged publication for Akiko's first book, *Tangled Hair*. Her immediate success ensured her impact as a feminist and a pacifist, as well as the popularity of her many other books of poetry and prose, the royalties from which helped to finance Tekkan's three-year trip to France. Akiko was able to join him for six months in 1912, also visiting Germany, Holland, England, and Manchuria. She was inspired by European writers and artists, especially Auguste Rodin. She was also intrigued by the relative freedom of European women, and her tour strengthened her determination to change Japanese life through the power of the creative word. Her husband died in 1935, and two years later, she began working on a collection of others' poetry, *Shin Manyōshū* (1937-1939). In addition to her vigorous cultural activities, she gave birth to thirteen children, rearing eleven of them to adulthood. She died in 1942, of a stroke.

ANALYSIS

Not even the finest translations can fully convey the subtle nuances of tone, the delicacy of imagery, and the great suggestiveness and complex allusiveness of Yosano Akiko's poetry—or indeed of most Japanese literature; English simply does not have the "feel" of Japanese, in sound, diction, grammar, or prosody. For example, there are no English equivalents for poignant sighs at the ends of many poems, or exclamations such as *ya!* and *kana!*

Fortunately, Rexroth's masterful renditions reveal Akiko's sensibility, passion, and imagination in English poems that are themselves enduring works of art. In the selections from her work included in his *One Hundred More Poems from the Japanese* (1974)—in which each English version is followed by the poem in romanized Japanese—Rexroth captures the erotic intensity that shocked Akiko's first readers. Other poems in this selection poignantly foreshadow separation—as a man fondles his lover in the autumn, as lovers gaze at each other without speaking or thinking of the future, or as a woman smells her lover's clothes in the darkness as he says good-bye. In others, the poet remembers writing a poem with her lover before separating from him, looks back on her passion like a blind man unafraid of the dark, contemplates sorrow as if it were hail or feathers falling, and watches cherry blossoms fall as stars go out in a false dawn. Such poems suggest the intricate, heartbreaking love story that comes alive, as in a novel, in hundreds of Akiko's original poems, many of them arranged to be read in a kind of narrative sequence. Most of them, however, are still unavailable in English.

Akiko also wrote many poems that calmly contemplate nature—poems in which, for example, snow and stars shine on her disheveled hair; an old boat reflects the autumn sky; ginkgo leaves scatter in the sunset; the

nightingale sleeps with doubled-up jeweled claws; a white bird flying over the breakers becomes an obsessive dream; and cranes fly crying across Waka Bay to the other shore (an image traditionally suggesting Nirvana).

In his 1977 anthology, *The Burning Heart: Women Poets of Japan*, Rexroth included additional translations of Akiko's poetry. This collection illustrates how Akiko's influence has enabled women poets to speak out in a country whose literary tradition has been dominated by men. Some of Akiko's *tanka* included in the volume concern the love triangle in which Tomiko—Akiko's friend and her husband's lover—appears as a lily or queen in summer fields; Akiko's heart is envisioned as the sun drowned in darkness and rain. One of Akiko's poems in free verse, "Labor Pains," is also included; in it, the birth of her baby is likened to truth pushing outward from inwardness.

Rexroth usually renders Akiko's *tanka* in five lines, and he often approximates the normal syllable count without distorting sound or sense; his cadences, as well as his melodies and imagery, evoke the tone of the Japanese much more reliably than does H. H. Honda's rhymed quatrains, which seem more akin to A. E. Housman's verse than to Akiko's. Honda's *The Poetry of Yosano Akiko* is useful, however, for readers with even an elementary knowledge of Japanese, for the original poem is given in Japanese script as well as in romanized Japanese under each translation; Honda's selections from nineteen of Akiko's books are arranged so the reader can follow the overall development of the poet's work and her growing consciousness of aging, of her children, and of her place in society and in the universe. Although he bypasses the explicitly erotic passages that attracted Rexroth, Honda does convey something of Akiko's sensuousness in poems that show her cherishing her five-foot-long hair after a bath or rain, gazing at herself in a mirror for an hour, caressing herself, and floating like a serene lily in a pond. Some of Honda's best renditions are "The Cherries and the Moon," a snow scene in Kyoto; "Upon the Bridge of Shijo," where twilight hail falls on the brow of a dancer; "Down in the Ocean of My Mind," where fish wave jewel-colored fins; "Like Open-Eyed Fish," in which the fish are compared to the poet, who is unable to sleep; "There Side by Side," about being a slave to love; and the satirical poems "O That I Could," a defiance of Japanese conventionality, and "Naught Knowing the Blissful Touch," in which Akiko teases a youthful Buddhist monk.

Akiko's poetry is characterized by lyric, rhetorical, dramatic, and narrative strength. Each poem expresses an intense feeling of a particular moment in the poet's life, a feeling that is often too subtle, complex, or ambiguous to be fully comprehended by Westerners unfamiliar with the nuances of Japanese sensibility. The rhetorical thrust of many of Akiko's poems can readily be understood, however, especially in those poems concerned with dramatic conflicts between lovers, with the plight of women generally, and with protests against social conventions. The drama of Akiko's stormy life, concentrated in the *tanka*, reveals the intricate story of her romance, marriage, and literary career; thus, a study of her collections as unified works is usually more fruitful than formal analysis of individual poems. The narrative dimension of her work does not unfold chronologically, as a rule, but evolves cyclically from poem to poem, as she returns periodically to the dominant images and themes of her life. Indeed, the details of her life are inseparable from her poems, which require far more biographical knowledge on the part of the reader than is usually required for Western poetry. Such themes as love, jealousy, fear, loneliness, rebellion against oppression, and death are, however, universal, and may be directly and deeply appreciated by any reader.

TANGLED HAIR

The best English translations of Akiko's work, besides Rexroth's, are those by Sanford Goldstein and Shinoda Seishi. Their 1971 translation of *Tangled Hair* (which includes 165 of the 399 *tanka* in the collection, along with the Japanese originals) is supplemented by an excellent biographical introduction and useful notes based in part on the pioneering commentaries by Satake Kazuhiko. Goldstein and Shinoda's free-verse translations (usually in five lines, but without the conventional syllable count) are sensitive, vivid, and faithful to the meaning and feeling of the original, though not as intense. In "Yawahada no" ("You Have Yet to Touch"), the translators convey Akiko's seductive,

sarcastic, teasing tone, as she asks an "Expounder of the Way" if he is not lonely for her blood and flesh. Satake's commentary on this poem identifies the "Expounder" as Tekkan; in Satake's reading, the poem reflects Akiko's impatience with Tekkan before he divorced his second wife and married her. Satake disagreed with Akiko's own interpretation of the poem as a generalized polemic against society, but its attack on hypocritical moralizing is surely as universal as it is personal. Akiko's rival Tomiko also figures in many poems in *Tangled Hair*. In "Sono namida" ("Tears in Your Eyes"), Akiko turns away unsympathetically from Tomiko's tears and gazes at the waning moon (always an image of sadness) reflected in a lake. The poignancy is heightened by knowledge that Akiko has just discovered that Tekkan still loves Tomiko, although he intends to marry Akiko.

Other poems evolve from customs such as the Dolls' Day celebration in "Hitotsu hako ni" ("Laying"), in which Akiko, in adolescence, sighs with some strange sexual awareness after putting the emperor and empress dolls together in a box; in an amazing image, she is afraid of her sigh being heard by peach blossoms. Sometimes Akiko identifies herself with women in ancient times, such as courtesans. In "Nakade isoge" ("Complain Not"), she tells a man to hurry on his way to other women who will undress him. Buddhism enters many of her poems in original ways. In "Wakaki ko no" ("Only the Sculptor's Fame"), she writes that she was attracted to the artist (probably Tekkan) because of his reputation when he was young, but now she is drawn to the face of the Buddha that he has carved (perhaps Tekkan's Buddha nature).

Sakanishi Shio's *Tangled Hair* (1935) includes translations not only from Akiko's first book but from eleven others as well, along with an informative introduction and a sketch of Akiko that might be compared to the photograph in Honda's volume. Sakanishi's versions are much more aesthetically subtle than Honda's and deserve close attention for their suggestively vivid imagery, natural speech rhythms, and artfully controlled syntax, all of which help to convey Akiko's tone. The sensuous and psychological implications of her hair are spun out in a variety of startling images. Her hair, for example, sweeps the strings of her koto, and its breaking strands recall the sound of the koto's strings; elsewhere, nightingales sing in a nest made from her fallen hair. Her discontent with traditional religions is manifest in her turning from the gods toward natural beauties, from the sutras to her own song, to the attractive flesh of a young monk, or to her loving husband. At other times, she prays to bodhisattvas while cherry blossoms fall on them and returns to sutras in bewilderment and despair, or sees the Buddha in the rising sun—a traditional image of Shingon Buddhism. Many of Akiko's poems included in Sakanishi's selection explicitly detail her life with Tekkan—her ambivalence about their original romance, resentful memories, ecstasies, the sadness of separation during his years in France, reunions, the agony of childbirth as three hearts beat in her body and one twin dies there, despair, children burning in volcanic eruptions, and renewed joy in rearing her children, to whom she gives her great-grandmother's prayer beads.

Thus, while the nuances of Akiko's verse remain resistant to translation, much of her artistry is accessible to English-speaking readers, who are now able to appreciate her significant contribution to the development of modern poetry in Japan.

OTHER MAJOR WORKS

LONG FICTION: *Genji monogatari*, 1912, 1939 (modern version); *Akarumi e*, 1913.

NONFICTION: *Nyonin sōzō*, 1920 (essays); *Yushosha to nare*, 1934; *Uta no tsukuriyō*, 1948; *Gekido no naka o yuku*, 1991; *Ai resei oyobi yuki*, 1993; *Travels in Manchuria and Mongolia: A Feminist Poet from Japan Encounters Prewar China*, 2001.

CHILDREN'S LITERATURE: *Watakushi no oitachi*, 1915.

MISCELLANEOUS: *Yosano Akiko zenshū*, 1972.

BIBLIOGRAPHY

Beichman, Janine. *Embracing the Firebird: Yosano Akiko and the Birth of the Female Voice in Modern Japanese Poetry*. Honolulu: University of Hawaii Press, 2002. This book-length biography of Akiko looks at her life, from birth to death, and analyzes her poetry at length, especially *Tangled Hair*. Contains an appendix with the poems in the original Japanese.

Morton, Leith. *The Alien Within: Representations of the Exotic in Twentieth-Century Japanese Literature*. Honolulu: University of Hawaii Press, 2009. Contains two chapters on Akiko: One argues that Akiko adapted ideas drawn from translations of Western poetry in revitalizing the *tanka* form, the other discusses Akiko's descriptions of childbirth in her poems, a subject not previously used in poetry.

_____. "The Birth of the Modern: Yosano Akiko and Tekkan's Verse Revolution." In *Modernism in Practice: An Introduction to Postwar Japanese Poetry*. Honolulu: University of Hawaii Press, 2004. Describes how Akiko and Tekkan helped modernize Japanese poetry.

Okada, Sumie. "The Visit by Hiroshi (1873-1935) and Akiko Yosano (1878-1942) to France and England in 1912." In *Japanese Writers and the West*. New York: Palgrave Macmillan, 2003. Discusses Akiko's impressions of French women and her resulting belief that Japanese women could have a more independent existence.

Rowley, Gillian Gaye. *Yosano Akiko and "The Tale of Genji."* Ann Arbor: University of Michigan Press, 2000. A critical analysis of Akiko's modern Japanese version of *The Tale of Genji*. Includes bibliographical references and index.

Takeda, Noriko. "The Japanese Reformation of Poetic Language: Yosano Akiko's *Tangled Hair* as Avant-Garde Centrality." In *A Flowering Word: The Modernist Expression in Stéphane Mallarmé, T. S. Eliot, and Yosano Akiko*. New York: Peter Lang, 2000. This comparative study of modernism examines Akiko's most famous work for its poetic language.

Morgan Gibson and Keiko Matsui Gibson

Z

DAISY ZAMORA

Born: Managua, Nicaragua; June 20, 1950

PRINCIPAL POETRY

La violenta espuma, 1981 (*The Violent Foam: New
and Selected Poems*, 2002)

En limpio se escribe la vida, 1988 (*Riverbed of
Memory*, 1992)

Clean Slate: New and Selected Poems, 1993
(bilingual edition)

A cada quién la vida, 1989-1992, 1994 (*Life for
Each*, 1994; bilingual edition)

Tierra de nadie, tierra de todos, 2007 (*No-Man's
Land, Everybody's Land*, 2007)

OTHER LITERARY FORMS

Daisy Zamora (zah-MOH-rah) is primarily known
for her poetry. Her words played an important role during her participation in the Sandinista Revolution in
Nicaragua, when she was program director for clandestine Radio Sandino during the final 1979 Sandinista offensive.

ACHIEVEMENTS

Daisy Zamora is a prominent Latin American poet.
Her uncompromising stance on human rights, culture,
women's issues, revolution, history, and art is presented in a manner that beckons to the average reader
and motivates him or her to join in her unquenchable
search for justice via the poetic voice. Her works have
been translated into Bulgarian, Chinese, Czech, Dutch,
English, Flemish, French, German, Italian, Russian,
Slovak, Spanish, Swedish, and Vietnamese. Her poems, essays, and articles have been published in magazines and literary newspapers throughout Latin America, the Caribbean, Canada, Europe, and the United
States. *The Oxford Book of Latin American Poetry: A
Bilingual Anthology* (2009) includes her work.

Zamora received the Mariano Fiallos Gil National

Poetry Prize from the University of Nicaragua in 1977.
In 1995, she was featured in Bill Moyer's Public
Broadcasting Service series *The Language of Life*. In
2002, the California Arts Council awarded her a fellowship for poetry, and the Nicaraguan Writers Center
gave her an award for her valuable contributions to Nicaraguan literature. The National Association of Artists
in Nicaragua named her writer of the year in 2006.
Zamora has given numerous lectures and conducted
many workshops in poetry at prestigious universities in
the United States and Europe.

BIOGRAPHY

Daisy Zamora was born in Managua, Nicaragua, on
June 20, 1950. She grew up in a wealthy and politically
active family. She received her primary education in
Roman Catholic convent schools. Later, she attended
Universidad Centroamericana in Nicaragua and received a degree in psychology. She earned a postgradu-
ate degree at the Instituto Centroamericano de Admin-
istracion de Empresas (INCAE), a Central American
branch of Harvard University. Zamora has also studied at the Academia Dante Alighieri and the Escuela
Nacional de Bellas Artes. During the struggle against
the regime of Anastasio Somoza Debayle in the 1970's,
she joined the Sandinista National Liberation Front
(FSLN) in 1973 and was exiled, living in Honduras,
Panama, and Costa Rica. During the final Sandinista
offensive in 1979, she served as program director for
the clandestine Radio Sandino. After the Sandinista
victory against Somoza, she served as the vice minister of culture and the executive director of the Institute of Economic and Social Research of Nicaragua. In
addition to her political work, Zamora has fought for
women's rights all her adult life.

Zamora has taught poetry workshops at various universities and lectured in the Latin American and Latino
studies department at the University of California, Santa
Cruz. She married the American author George Evans;
the couple has three children. She has been spending
part of the year in San Francisco and part in Managua.

ANALYSIS

Daisy Zamora writes about common, ordinary
women, her lovers, and revolutionaries—both those

whom she encountered in her active role in the Nicaraguan revolution and lesser-known revolutionaries. The focus of her poems is not the repressive elite but rather the proletariat masses. Zamora's work discusses marginal groups in a manner that implores the reader to consciously or unconsciously participate in a form of identity construction of these diverse factions.

The structure, style, and method of Zamora's poetry is an amalgamation of simplicity and eloquence. Using almost simplistic Nicaraguan Spanish, she creates easily understandable and condensed lines that straightforwardly present her eloquent and sensualistic understanding of the issue being presented. The poems seem to be written not just about everyday Nicaraguan citizens, but also for them. Her poems relate the day-to-day activities and experiences of her fellow Nicaraguans and are accessible to the average person. They project an imagery that reflects the passion, emotions, thoughts, and ideas of life and love. She excels in the treatment of women and their issues.

Although they are highly accessible, Zamora's poems are not superficial. The syntactic and symmetrically uncomplicated text presents a gamut of social, gender, and political dilemmas in a manner that is unique to Zamora, a manner that gives the reader pause and permits, even demands, further consideration. Zamora's works are widely read and often memorized and recited in many Spanish-speaking countries, including countries with high rates of poverty, disease, illiteracy, inadequate housing, and domestic violence—the very groups Zamora is seeking to reach with her work. Her works are welcomed in Latin American countries where the reading of poetry and the honoring of poets is much more a part of everyday life than in the more literate, developed world. Zamora's poetry has also found an audience in academic circles and institutions in the United States and Europe, which attests to her poetry's depth.

Zamora writes with a revolutionary zeal. The approachability of her poetry does not, in any manner, limit her impassioned defense of women's causes. She does not hesitate to rail against the poor treatment of women in Nicaragua and other countries. She pulls no punches in her denunciation of the situations in which many women in Latin America find themselves.

Zamora not only movingly exposes the tragic consequences for women trapped in dysfunctional marriages, underpaid and dehumanizing jobs, and other potential-limiting situations, but she also reveals and excoriates the macho cultures that produce and promote limited cultural expectations for women and other disenfranchised groups.

In her poetry, Zamora pays extreme attention to detail. She accentuates seemingly insignificant details in the everyday lives of women and others. Mundane actions such as washing clothes reveal the monotonous toll of the laundrywoman's job. The sensuality of a woman is revealed by means of elaborate depictions of flowers. She uses uncomplicated but detailed images to solicit introspection on the part of the reader in complicated dilemmas.

THE VIOLENT FOAM

Zamora's husband, Evans, translated her first collection, *The Violent Foam*, into English. In this collection, Zamora writes of the struggles of her country and her gender. She compares the realities of the Nicaraguan Revolution to the realities of the fight for women's rights. Her poems often relate to a more subtle but real revolution fought within the bounds of everyday life in Latin America. She includes many astute references to women caught in mundane work and stifling marriages. The women of these poems are captive within a society that limits not only their possibilities, but also their right to express their angst and hopelessness. Her themes include the monotony of life for Nicaraguan women. For example, Zamora describes the tedious world of a seamstress, whose nights are spent dreaming of endless stitching and of repetitive, mindless work that does not allow time for interaction with men. The seamstress laments to her son that his father has ruined her chances to the point where she cannot even imagine what might otherwise have been. In the era in which these poems were penned, many felt the Nicaraguan Revolution was ongoing. Regardless, it is obvious that Zamora felt that the uprising of women in response to the confining patriarchal culture of Nicaragua was an inevitable and ongoing process.

CLEAN SLATE

In *Clean Slate*, Zamora directly and eloquently challenges the patriarchal hegemony of her geographical and temporal space. With a determined but fair approach, she takes on reproduction, family, daily housework, the dual role of woman as angel and whore, work equality, and macho-related issues as they relate to Nicaraguan women. Zamora's unique point of view—that of a woman who actively participated in the Nicaraguan Revolution that eventually brought down the Somoza dynasty, one of the most entrenched and male-dominated regimes in Latin America—is evident in the poems. However, her themes go beyond critiquing the lack of balance between the masculine and feminine in Latin America and embrace the natural physical alliance between the sexes. Her scorn for arrogant male dominance does not preclude the simple but profound exposition of the inherent values of the female body and existence. Zamora embraces the capacity for affection as expressed by both genders. She states that being born a woman in Latin America necessitates unjust and unwarranted devotion to others in terms of service and dedication. Her poems embody a uniquely Nicaraguan feminism, often without the North American and European fervor in opposition to all things male. In "Vision of Your Body," she succinctly articulates how the sight of a lover's body can evoke sentiments as strong as the earth itself being ripped apart.

OTHER MAJOR WORK

EDITED TEXT: *La mujer nicaragüense en la poesía: Anthología*, 1992.

BIBLIOGRAPHY

Balderston, Daniel, and Mike Gonzalez, eds. *Encyclopedia of Latin American and Caribbean Literature, 1900-2003*. New York: Routledge, 2004. Contains a short biographical entry on Zamora. Also contains an introduction that places Zamora in context.

Bowen, Kevin. *Writing Between the Lines: An Anthology on War and Its Social Consequences*. Amherst: University of Massachusetts Press, 1997. This anthology includes an analysis of several of Zamora's poems, including "Surreptitious Encounter with Joaquin Pasos," "Urgent Message to My Mother," and "Testimony: Death of a Guatemalan Village." Includes index and bibliography.

Dawes, Greg. *Aesthetics and Revolution: Nicaraguan Poetry, 1979-1990*. Minneapolis: University of Minnesota Press, 1993. Contains a chapter on feminist and feminine self-representation that features a section on Zamora. Dawes finds her to be a realist rather than an avant-garde poet.

Gioseffi, Daniela, ed. *Women on War: An International Anthology of Writings from Antiquity to the Present*. 2d ed. New York: Feminist Press at the City University of New York, 2003. Contains a brief biography of Zamora and her poems "Song of Hope" and "When We Go Home Again." Gioseffi's introduction provides perspective on Zamora's writings.

Jason, Philip K., ed. *Masterplots II: Poetry Series*. Rev. ed. Pasadena, Calif.: Salem Press, 2002. Contains an in-depth analysis of Zamora's poem "Dear Aunt Chofi."

Zamora, Daisy. "Daisy Zamora." Interview by Margaret Randell. In *Sandino's Daughters: Testimonies of Nicaraguan Women in Struggle*. Rev. ed. New Brunswick, N.J.: Rutgers University Press, 1995. First published in 1981, this work is based on a series of interviews Randell conducted with women involved in the Sandinista Revolution. In the Zamora interview, written like a memoir, she describes her life before, during, and after the war; her political beliefs; and her poetry. Includes a few poems.

_____. "'I Am Looking for the Women of My House': Daisy Zamora." Interview by Margaret Randell. In *Sandino's Daughters Revisited: Feminism in Nicaragua*. New Brunswick, N.J.: Rutgers University Press, 1994. In this interview, Zamora talks about her background, her work during the war, and women's rights in Nicaragua.

Paul Siegrist

RESOURCES

Explicating Poetry

Explicating poetry begins with a process of distinguishing the poem's factual and technical elements from the readers' emotional ones. Readers respond to poems in a variety of ways that may initially have little to do with the poetry itself but that result from the events in their own lives, their expectations of art, and their philosophical/theological/psychological complexion.

All serious readers hope to find poems that can blend with the elements of their personal backgrounds in such a way that for a moment or a lifetime their relationship to life and the cosmos becomes more meaningful. This is the ultimate goal of poetry, and when it happens—when meaning, rhythm, and sound fuse with the readers' emotions to create a unified experience—it can only be called the magic of poetry, for something has happened between reader and poet that is inexplicable in rational terms.

When a poem creates such an emotional response in readers, then it is at least a partial success. To be considered excellent, however, a poem must also be able to pass a critical analysis to determine whether it is mechanically superior. Although twenty-first century criticism has tended to judge poetic works solely on their individual content and has treated them as independent of historical influences, such a technique often makes a full explication difficult. The best modern readers realize that good poetry analysis observes all aspects of a poem: its technical success, its historical importance and intellectual force, and its effect on readers' emotions.

Students of poetry will find it useful to begin an explication by analyzing the elements that poets have at their disposal as they create their art: dramatic situation, point of view, imagery, metaphor, symbol, meter, form, and allusion. The outline headed "Checklist for Explicating a Poem" (see page 360) will help guide the reader through the necessary steps to a detailed explication.

Although explication is not a science, and a variety of observations may be equally valid, these step-by-step procedures can be applied systematically to make the reading of most poems a richer experience for the reader. To illustrate, these steps are applied below to a difficult poem by Edwin Arlington Robinson.

Luke Havergal

Go to the western gate, Luke Havergal,
There where the vines cling crimson on the wall,
And in the twilight wait for what will come.
The leaves will whisper there of her, and some, 4
Like flying words, will strike you as they fall;
But go, and if you listen, she will call.
Go to the western gate, Luke Havergal—
Luke Havergal.   8

No, there is not a dawn in eastern skies
To rift the fiery night that's in your eyes;
But there, where western glooms are gathering,
The dark will end the dark, if anything: 12
God slays Himself with every leaf that flies,
And hell is more than half of paradise.
No, there is not a dawn in eastern skies—
In eastern skies.   16

Out of a grave I come to tell you this,
Out of a grave I come to quench the kiss
That flames upon your forehead with a glow
That blinds you to the way that you must go. 20
Yes, there is yet one way to where she is,
Bitter, but one that faith may never miss.
Out of a grave I come to tell you this—
To tell you this.   24

There is the western gate, Luke Havergal
There are the crimson leaves upon the wall.
Go, for the winds are tearing them away,—
Nor think to riddle the dead words they say, 28
Nor any more to feel them as they fall;
But go, and if you trust her she will call.
There is the western gate, Luke Havergal—
Luke Havergal.

E. A. Robinson, 1897

STEP I-A: *Before reading*

1. "Luke Havergal" is a strophic poem composed of four equally lengthened stanzas. Each stanza is long enough to contain a narrative, an involved description or situation, or a problem and resolution.

2. The title raises several possibilities: Luke Havergal

CHECKLIST FOR EXPLICATING A POEM

I. THE INITIAL READINGS

A. Before reading the poem, the reader should:
   1. Notice its form and length.
   2. Consider the title, determining, if possible, whether it might function as an allusion, symbol, or poetic image.
   3. Notice the date of composition or publication, and identify the general era of the poet.

B. The poem should be read intuitively and emotionally and be allowed to "happen" as much as possible.

C. In order to establish the rhythmic flow, the poem should be re-read. A note should be made as to where the irregular spots (if any) are located.

II. EXPLICATING THE POEM

A. *Dramatic situation.* Studying the poem line by line helps the reader discover the dramatic situation. All elements of the dramatic situation are interrelated and should be viewed as reflecting and affecting one another. The dramatic situation serves a particular function in the poem, adding realism, surrealism, or absurdity; drawing attention to certain parts of the poem; and changing to reinforce other aspects of the poem. All points should be considered. The following questions are particularly helpful to ask in determining dramatic situation:
   1. What, if any, is the narrative action in the poem?
   2. How many personae appear in the poem? What part do they take in the action?
   3. What is the relationship between characters?
   4. What is the setting (time and location) of the poem?

B. *Point of view.* An understanding of the poem's point of view is a major step toward comprehending the poet's intended meaning. The reader should ask:
   1. Who is the speaker? Is he or she addressing someone else or the reader?
   2. Is the narrator able to understand or see everything happening to him or her, or does the reader know things that the narrator does not?
   3. Is the narrator reliable?
   4. Do point of view and dramatic situation seem consistent? If not, the inconsistencies may provide clues to the poem's meaning.

C. *Images and metaphors.* Images and metaphors are often the most intricately crafted vehicles of the poem for relaying the poet's message. Realizing that the images and metaphors work in harmony with the dramatic situation and point of view will help the reader to see the poem as a whole, rather than as disassociated elements.
   1. The reader should identify the concrete images (that is, those that are formed from objects that can be touched, smelled, seen, felt, or tasted). Is the image projected by the poet consistent with the physical object?
   2. If the image is abstract, or so different from natural imagery that it cannot be associated with a real object, then what are the properties of the image?
   3. To what extent is the reader asked to form his or her own images?

4. Is any image repeated in the poem? If so, how has it been changed? Is there a controlling image?
5. Are any images compared to each other? Do they reinforce one another?
6. Is there any difference between the way the reader perceives the image and the way the narrator sees it?
7. What seems to be the narrator's or persona's attitude toward the image?

D. *Words.* Every substantial word in a poem may have more than one intended meaning, as used by the author. Because of this, the reader should look up many of these words in the dictionary and:
   1. Note all definitions that have the slightest connection with the poem.
   2. Note any changes in syntactical patterns in the poem.
   3. In particular, note those words that could possibly function as symbols or allusions, and refer to any appropriate sources for further information.

E. *Meter, rhyme, structure, and tone.* In scanning the poem, all elements of prosody should be noted by the reader. These elements are often used by a poet to manipulate the reader's emotions, and therefore they should be examined closely to arrive at the poet's specific intention.
   1. Does the basic meter follow a traditional pattern such as those found in nursery rhymes or folk songs?
   2. Are there any variations in the base meter? Such changes or substitutions are important thematically and should be identified.
   3. Are the rhyme schemes traditional or innovative, and what might their form mean to the poem?
   4. What devices has the poet used to create sound patterns (such as assonance and alliteration)?
   5. Is the stanza form a traditional or innovative one?
   6. If the poem is composed of verse paragraphs rather than stanzas, how do they affect the progression of the poem?
   7. After examining the above elements, is the resultant tone of the poem casual or formal, pleasant, harsh, emotional, authoritative?

F. *Historical context.* The reader should attempt to place the poem into historical context, checking on events at the time of composition. Archaic language, expressions, images, or symbols should also be looked up.

G. *Themes and motifs.* By seeing the poem as a composite of emotion, intellect, craftsmanship, and tradition, the reader should be able to determine the themes and motifs (smaller recurring ideas) presented in the work. He or she should ask the following questions to help pinpoint these main ideas:
   1. Is the poet trying to advocate social, moral, or religious change?
   2. Does the poet seem sure of his or her position?
   3. Does the poem appeal primarily to the emotions, to the intellect, or to both?
   4. Is the poem relying on any particular devices for effect (such as imagery, allusion, paradox, hyperbole, or irony)?

could be a specific person; Luke Havergal could represent a type of person; the name might have symbolic or allusive qualities. Thus, "Luke" may refer to Luke of the Bible or "Luke-warm," meaning indifferent or showing little or no zeal. "Havergal" could be a play on words. "Haver" is a Scotch and Northern English word meaning to talk foolishly. It is clear from the rhyme words that the "gal" of Havergal is pronounced as if it had two "l's," but it is spelled with one "l" for no apparent reason unless it is to play on the word "gal," meaning girl. Because it is pronounced "gall," meaning something bitter or severe, a sore or state of irritation, or an impudent self-assurance, this must also be considered as a possibility. Finally, the "haver" of "Havergal" might be a perversion of "have a."

3. Published in 1897, the poem probably does not contain archaic language unless it is deliberately used. The period of writing is known as the Victorian Age. Historical events that may have influenced the poem may be checked for later.

STEP I-B: *The poem should be read*

STEP I-C: *Rereading the poem*

The frequent use of internal caesuras in stanzas 1 and 2 contrast with the lack of caesuras in stanzas 3 and 4. There are end-stopped lines and much repetition. The poem reads smoothly except for line 28 and the feminine ending on lines 11 and 12.

STEP II-A: *Dramatic situation*

In line 1 of "Luke Havergal," an unidentified speaker is addressing Luke. Because the speaker calls him by his full name, there is a sense that the speaker has assumed a superior (or at least a formal) attitude toward Luke and that the talk that they are having is not a casual conversation.

In addition to knowing something about the relationship in line 1, the reader is led to think, because of the words "go to the western gate," that the personae must be near some sort of enclosed house or city. Perhaps Luke and the speaker are at some "other" gate, since the western gate is specifically pointed out.

Line 2 suggests that the situation at the western gate is different from that elsewhere—there "vines cling crimson on the wall," hinting at some possibilities

about the dramatic situation. (Because flowers and colors are always promising symbols, they must be carefully considered later.)

The vines in line 2 could provide valuable information about the dramatic situation, except that in line 2 the clues are ambiguous. Are the vines perennial? If so, their crimson color suggests that the season is late summer or autumn. Crimson might also be their natural color when in full bloom. Further, are they grape vines (grapes carry numerous connotations and symbolic values), and are the vines desirable? All of this in line 2 is ambiguous. The only certainty is that there is a wall—a barrier that closes something in and something out.

In lines 1-3, the speaker again commands Luke to go and wait. Since Luke is to wait in the twilight, it is probably now daylight. All Luke must do is be passive because whatever is to come will happen without any action on his part.

In line 4, the speaker begins to tell Luke what will happen at the western gate, and the reader now knows that Luke is waiting for something with feminine characteristics, possibly a woman. This line also mentions that the vines have leaves, implying that crimson denotes their waning stage.

In line 5, the speaker continues to describe what will happen at the western gate: The leaves will whisper about "her," and as they fall, some of them will strike Luke "like flying words." The reader, however, must question whether Luke will actually be "struck" by the leaves, or whether the leaves are being personified or being used as an image or symbol. In line 6, the speaker stops his prophecy and tells Luke to leave. If Luke listens, "she" will call, but if he does not, it is unclear what will happen. The reader might ask the questions, to whom is "she" calling, and from where?

In summarizing the dramatic situation in stanza 1, one can say that the speaker is addressing Luke, but it is not yet possible to determine whether he or she is present or whether Luke is thinking to himself (interior monologue). The time is before twilight; the place is near a wall with a gate. Luke is directed to go to the gate and listen for a female voice to call.

From reading the first line in the second stanza, it is apparent that Luke has posed some kind of question, probably concerned with what will be found at the western gate. The answer given is clearly not a direct answer to whatever question was asked, especially as the directions "east" and "west" are probably symbolic. The reader can expect, however, that the silent persona's response will affect the poem's progress.

Stanza 3 discloses who the speaker is and what his relationship is to Luke. After the mysterious discourse in stanza 2, Luke has probably asked "Who are you?" The equally mysterious reply in stanza 3 raises the issue of whether the voice speaking is a person or a spirit or whether it is Luke's imagination or conscience.

Because the voice says that it comes out of the grave, the reader cannot know who or what it is. It may be a person, a ghost, or only Luke's imagination or conscience. Obviously the answer will affect the dramatic situation.

In line 18, the reader learns that the speaker is on a particular mission: "to quench the kiss," and the reader can assume that when the mission is complete he or she will return to the grave. This information is sudden and shocking, and because of this sharp jolt, the reader tends to believe the speaker and credit him or her with supernatural knowledge.

In stanza 4, it becomes apparent that Luke and the speaker have not been stationary during the course of the poem because the western gate is now visible; the speaker can see the leaves upon the wall (line 26).

The wind is blowing (line 27), creating a sense of urgency, because if all the leaves are blown away they cannot whisper about "her." The speaker gives Luke final instructions, and the poem ends with the speaker again pointing toward the place where Luke will find the female persona.

In summary, one can say that the dramatic situation establishes a set of mysterious circumstances that are not explained or resolved on the dramatic level. Luke has been told to go to the western gate by someone who identifies himself or herself as having come from the grave in order to quench Luke's desire, which seems to be connected with the estranged woman, who is, perhaps, dead. The dramatic situation does not tell whether the commanding voice is an emissary from the woman or from the devil, or is merely Luke's conscience; nor does it suggest that something evil will happen to Luke at the western gate, although other elements in the poem make the reader afraid for him.

The poet, then, is using the dramatic situation to draw the reader into questions which will be answered by other means; at this point, the poem is mysterious, obscure, ambiguous, and deliberately misleading.

STEP II-B: *Point of view*

There are a number of questions that immediately come to mind about the point of view. Is the speaker an evil seducer, or is he or she a friend telling Luke about death? Why is the poem told from his or her point of view?

From a generalized study, readers know that the first-person singular point of view takes the reader deep into the mind of the narrator in order to show what he or she knows or to show a personal reaction to an event.

In "Luke Havergal," the narrator gives the following details about himself and the situation: a sense of direction (lines 1 and 9); the general type and color of the vegetation, but not enough to make a detailed analysis of it (line 2); a pantheistic view of nature (line 4); a feeling of communication with the leaves and "her" (lines 5 and 6); a philosophic view of the universe (stanza 2); the power to "quench the kiss," a sense of mission, and a home—the grave (line 18); special vision (line 20); a sense of destiny (lines 21 and 22); and a sense of time and eternity (lines 27 through 29).

Apparently, the narrator can speak with confidence about the western gate, and can look objectively at Luke to see the kiss on his forehead. Such a vantage point suggests that the speaker might represent some aspect of death. He also knows the "one way to where she is," leaving it reasonable to infer that "she" is dead.

There is another possibility in regard to the role of the speaker. He might be part of Luke himself—the voice of his thoughts, of his unconscious mind—or of part of his past. This role might possibly be combined with that of some sort of spirit of death.

The poem, then, is an internal dialogue in which Luke is attempting to cope with "she," who is probably dead and who might well have been his lover, though neither is certain. He speaks to another persona, which is probably Luke's own spirit which has been deadened by the loss of his lover.

Once it is suggested that Luke is a man who is at the depth of despair, the dramatic situation becomes very important because of the possibility that Luke may be driving himself toward self-destruction.

The dramatic situation, therefore, may not be as it originally seemed; perhaps there is only one person, not two. Luke's psychological condition permits him to look at himself as another person, and this other self is pushing Luke toward the western gate, a place that the reader senses is evil.

If the voice is Luke's, then much of the mystery is clarified. Luke would have known what the western gate looked like, whereas a stranger would have needed supernatural powers to know it; furthermore, Luke had probably heard the leaves whispering before, and in his derangement he could believe that someone would call to him if he would only listen.

Establishing point of view has cleared up most of the inconsistencies in this poem's dramatic situation, but there is still confusion about the grave and the kiss. It is easy to make the grave symbolically consistent with point of view, but the reader should look for other possibilities before settling on this explanation.

In stanzas 1 and 2, there is no problem; the dramatic situation is simple and point of view can be reconciled since there is no evidence to prove that another person is present. If, however, the voice is that of Luke's other self, then why has it come from the grave, and where did the kiss come from? At this point, it is not possible to account for these inconsistencies, but by noting them now, the reader can be on the alert for the answers later. Quite possibly accounting for the inconsistencies will provide the key for the explication.

STEP II-C: *Images and metaphors*

Finding images in poems is usually not a difficult task, although seeing their relation to the theme often is. "Luke Havergal" is imagistically difficult because the images are introduced, then reused as the theme develops.

In stanza 1, the reader is allowed to form his or her own image of the setting and mood at the western gate; most readers will probably imagine some sort of mysterious or supernatural situation related to death or the dead. The colors, the sound of the words, and the particular images (vines, wall, whispering leaves) establish the relationship between the living and the dead as the controlling image of the entire poem.

Within the controlling death-in-life image, the metaphors and conceits are more difficult to handle. Vines clinging crimson on the wall (line 2) and waiting in the twilight for something to come (line 3) are images requiring no particular treatment at this point, but in lines 4 and 5 the reader is forced to contend directly with whispering leaves that are like flying words, and there are several metaphorical possibilities for this image.

First, there is the common image of leaves rustling in a breeze, and in a mysterious or enchanted atmosphere it would be very easy to imagine that they are whispering. Such a whisper, however, would ordinarily require a moderate breeze, as a fierce wind would overpower the rustling sound of leaves; but there is more ambiguity in the image: "The leaves will whisper there for her, and some,/ Like flying words, will strike you as they fall."

Because of the syntactical ambiguity of "some,/ Like flying words, will strike," the reader cannot be sure how close or literal is the similarity or identity of "leaves" and "words." The reader cannot be completely sure whether it is leaves or words or both that will strike Luke, or whether the sight of falling leaves might be forcing him to recall words he has heard in the past. There is a distinct metaphoric connection between leaves and words, however, and these in some way strike Luke, perhaps suggesting that the words are those of an argument (an argument in the past between Luke and "her" before her death) or perhaps meant to suggest random words which somehow recall "her" but do not actually say anything specific.

In stanza 2, the poet forces the reader to acknowledge the light and dark images, but they are as obscure as the falling leaves in stanza 1. The dawn that the reader is asked to visualize (line 9) is clear, but it is immediately contrasted with "the fiery night that's in your eyes"; Luke's smoldering, almost diabolic eyes are imagistically opposed to the dawn.

Line 11 returns to the western gate, or at least to the "west," where twilight is falling. The "western glooms" become imagistic as the twilight falls and depicts Luke's despair. Twilight is not "falling," but dark is "gathering" around him, and glooms not only denotes darkness but also connotes Luke's emotional state.

The paradox in line 12, "The dark will end the dark," beckons the reader to explore it imagistically, but it is tion; the sun is setting in the west, but even though the sun sets, there will not be a dawn in the east to dispel Luke's dark gloom. Traditionally the dark, which is gathering in the west, is symbolic of death (the west is also traditionally associated with death), and only the dark will end Luke's gloom in life, if anything at all can do it.

There is one important allusion in the poem, which comes in stanza 3; the kiss which the speaker is going to quench may be the "kiss of death," the force that can destroy Luke.

In both concept and language, stanza 3 is reminiscent of the dagger scene and killing of Duncan (act 2, scene 1) in William Shakespeare's *Macbeth* (pr. 1606). Just before the murder, Macbeth has visions of the dagger:

> Art thou not, fatal vision, sensible
> To feeling as to sight? or art thou but
> A dagger of the mind, a false creation,
> Proceeding from the heat-oppressed brain?
> I see thee yet, in form as palpable
> As this which now I draw.
> Thou marshall'st me the way that I was going

And a few lines later (act 2, scene 2) Lady Macbeth says:

> That which hath made them drunk hath made me bold;
> What hath quench'd them hath given me fire.

The reversal in point of view in "Luke Havergal" gives the poem added depth, which is especially enhanced by the comparison with Macbeth. The line, "That blinds you to the way that you must go" is almost a word-for-word equivalent of "Thou marshall'st me the way that I was going," except that in "Luke Havergal" whoever is with Luke is talking, while Macbeth himself is talking to the dagger.

The result of the allusion is that it is almost possible to imagine that it is the dagger that is talking to Luke, and the whole story of Macbeth becomes relevant to the poem because the reader suspects that Luke's end will be similar to Macbeth's.

The words of Lady Macbeth strengthen the allusion's power and suggest a male-female relationship that is leading Luke to his death, especially since, in the resolution of *Macbeth*, Lady Macbeth goes crazy and whispers to the spirits.

not easy to understand how darkness relieves darkness, unless one of the two "darknesses" is symbolic of death or of Luke's gloom. With this beckoning image, the poet has created emphasis on the line and teases with images which may really be symbols or paradoxes. The same thing is true for lines 13 and 14, which tempt the reader to imagine how "God slays Himself" with leaves, and how "hell is more than half of paradise."

The beginning of stanza 3 does not demand an image so much as it serves to tell where the narrator comes from, and to present the narrator's method for quenching the kiss. Line 19, however, presents an image that is as forceful as it is ambiguous. The kiss, which may be the kiss of the estranged woman, or "the kiss of death," or both, flames with a glow, which is also paradoxical. The paradox, however, forms an image which conveys the intensity of Luke's passion.

Stanza 4 returns to the imagery of stanza 1, but now the whispering leaves take on a metaphorical extension. If the leaves are whispering words from the dead, and if the leaves are "her" words, then once the wind tears all the leaves away, there will no longer be any medium for communication between the living and the dead. This adds a sense of urgency for Luke to go to the western gate and do there what must be done.

In summary, the images in "Luke Havergal" do more than set the mood; they also serve an important thematic function because of their ambiguities and paradoxical qualities.

STEP II-D: *Words*

Because the poem is not too old, the reader will find that most of the words have not changed much. It is still important, however, for the reader to look up words as they may have several diverse meanings. Even more important to consider in individual words or phrases, however, is the possibility that they might be symbolic or allusive.

"Luke Havergal" is probably not as symbolic as it at first appears, although poems that use paradox and allusion are often very symbolic. Clearly the western gate is symbolic, but to what degree is questionable. No doubt it represents the last light in Luke's life, and once he passes beyond it he moves into another type of existence. The west and the twilight are points of embarka-

364

If the reader accepts the allusion as a part of the poem, the imagery is enhanced by the vivid descriptions in *Macbeth*. Most critics and writers agree that if a careful reader finds something that fits consistently into a poem, then it is "there" for all readers who see the same thing, whether the poet consciously put it there or not. Robinson undoubtedly read and knew Shakespeare, but it does not matter whether he deliberately alluded to *Macbeth* if the reader can show that it is important to the poem.

There is a basic problem with allusion and symbol that every explicator must resolve for himself: Did the poet intend a symbol or an allusion to be taken in the way that a particular reader has interpreted it? The New Critics answered this question by coining the term "intentional fallacy," meaning that the poet's *intention* is ultimately unimportant when considering the finished poem. It is possible that stanza 3 was not intended to allude to *Macbeth*, and it was simply by accident that Robinson used language similar to Shakespeare's. Perhaps Robinson never read *Macbeth*, or perhaps he read it once and those lines remained in his subconscious. In either case, the reader must decide whether the allusion is important to the meaning of the poem.

STEP II-E: *Meter, rhyme, structure, and tone*

Because "Luke Havergal" is a poem that depends so heavily on all the elements of prosody, it should be scanned carefully. Here is an example of scansion using the second stanza of the poem:

No, there/ is not/ a dawn/ in eas/tern skies
To rift/ the fie/ry night/ that's in/ your eyes;
But there,/ where wes/tern glooms/ are gath/ering,
The dark/ will end/ the dark,/ if an/ything:
God slays/ Himself/ with eve/ry leaf/ that flies,
And hell/ is more/ than half/ of par/adise.
No, there/ is not/ a dawn/ in east/ern skies—
In eas/tern skies.

The basic meter of the poem is iambic pentameter, with frequent substitutions, but every line except the last in each stanza contains ten syllables.

The stanza form in "Luke Havergal" is very intri-

cate and delicate. It is only because of the structure that the heavy *a* rhyme (*aabbaaaa*) does not become monotonous; yet it is because of the *a* rhyme that the structure works so well.

The pattern for the first stanza works as follows:

Line	Rhyme	Function
1	a	Sets up ideas and images for the stanza.
2	a	Describes or complements line 1.
3	b	Lines 3, 4, and 5 constitute the central part of the mood and the fears. The return to the a rhyme unifies lines 1-5.
4	b	
5	a	
6	a	Reflects on what has been said in lines 1-5; it serves to make the reader stop, and it adds a mysterious suggestion.
7	a	Continues the deceleration and reflection.
8	a	The repetition and dimeter line stop the stanza completely, and the effect is to prepare for a shift in thought, just as Luke's mind jumps from thought to thought.

Stanza 2 works in a similar manner, except for lines 13 and 14, which tie the stanza together as a couplet. Thus, lines 13 and 14 both unify and reflect, while lines 15 and 16 in the final couplet continue to reflect while slowing down.

Lines	Rhyme	Function
9 and 10	a	Opening couplet.
11 and 12	b	Couplet in lines 11-12 contains the central idea and image.
13 and 14	a	Couplet in 13-14 reflects on that in 11-12, but the autonomy of this third couplet is especially strong. Whereas in stanza 1, only line 5 reflects on the beginning of the stanza to create unity, this entire couplet is now strongly associated with the first, with the effect of nearly equating Luke with God.
15 and 16	a	Final couplet reflects on the first and completes the stanza.

Stanza 3 works in the same manner as stanza 2, while stanza 4 follows the pattern of stanza 1.

Each stanza is autonomous and does not need the others for continuation or progression in plot; each stanza appears to represent a different thought as Luke's mind jumps about.

The overall structure focuses on stanza 3, which is crucial to the theme. Stanzas 1 and 2 clearly present the problem: Luke knows that if he goes he will find "her," and the worst that can happen is that the darkness will remain. With stanza 3, however, there is a break in point of view as the narrator calls attention to himself.

With stanza 4 there is a return to the beginning, reinforced by the repetition of rhyme words; the difference between stanzas 4 and 1 is that the reader has felt the impact of stanza 3; structurally, whatever resolution there is will evolve out of the third stanza, or because of it.

The stanza form of "Luke Havergal" achieves tremendous unity and emphasis; the central image or idea presented in the *b* lines is reinforced in the remainder of the stanza by a tight-knit rhyme structure. There are several types of rhymes being used in the poem, all of which follow the traditional functions of their type. Stanza 1 contains full masculine end rhyme, with a full masculine internal rhyme in line 2 (*There where*). Lines 2 and 3 contain alliteration (*c* in line 2, *t* in line 3) also binding the lines more tightly.

With "go" occurring near the end of stanza 1 and "No" appearing as the first word in stanza 2, this rhyme becomes important in forming associations between lines. Lines 9, 10, 15, 16, and 18 form full masculine end rhyme, with line 14 "paradise" assonating with a full rhyme. Lines 11 and 12 are half falling rhymes; these lines also contain a full internal rhyme ("there," "where") and alliteration (*g* and *w* in line 11). "Dark" in line 12 is an exact internal rhyme. The *l* and *s* in "slays" and "flies" (line 14) create an effect similar to assonance; there is also an *h* alliteration in line 15.

In stanza 3, the plosive consonants *c* and *q* make an alliterative sound in line 18, binding "come" and "quench" together; there is also an *f* alliteration in line 19. All the end rhymes are full masculine in stanza 3 except line 21, which assonates. Stanza 4 contains full masculine end rhyme, with one internal rhyme ("they

say") in line 28, one alliteration in line 29, and consonance ("will call") in line 30.

In addition to its function in developing the stanza, rhyme in "Luke Havergal" has important influence on sound, and in associating particular words and lines.

In lines 1 and 2 of "Luke Havergal," there are a number of plosive consonants and long vowels, in addition to the internal rhyme and *c* alliteration. The cadence of these lines is slow, and they reverberate with "cling" and "crimson." The tone of these lines is haunting (which is consistent with the situation), and the rhythm and sound of the poem as a whole suggest an incantation; the speaker's voice is seductive and evil, which is important to the theme, because if Luke goes to the gate he may be persuaded to die, which is what the voice demands.

Through its seductive sound, the poem seems to be having the same effect on the reader that it does on Luke; that is, the reader feels, as Luke does, that there is an urgency in going to the gate before all the leaves are blown away, and that by hearing "her" call, his discomfort will be relieved. The reader, unable to see the evil forces at work in the last stanza, sympathizes with Luke, and thinks that the voice is benevolent.

Whereas sound can be heard and analyzed, tone is a composite of a number of things that the reader can feel only after coming to know the poem. The poet's attitude or tone may be noncommittal or it may be dogmatic (as in allegory); sometimes the tone will affect the theme, while at other times it comes as an aside to the theme.

Poems that attempt to initiate reform frequently have a more readily discernible tone than poems that make observations without judging too harshly, although this is not always true. "Luke Havergal" is, among other things, about how the presence of evil leads toward death, but the poet has not directly included his feelings about that theme. If there is an attitude, it is the poet's acceptance of the inevitability of death and the pain that accompanies it for the living.

Perhaps the poet is angry at how effectively death can seduce life; it is obvious that Robinson wants the poem to haunt and torment the reader, and in doing so make him or her conscious of the hold death has on humanity.

Luke must meet death part way; he must first go to

the gate before he can hear the dead words, which makes him partly responsible for death's hold over him. The tone of "Luke Havergal" is haunting and provocative.

STEP II-F: *Historical context*

Finished in December, 1895, "Luke Havergal" was in Robinson's estimation a Symbolist poem. It is essential, then, that the explicator learn something about the Symbolist movement. If his or her explication is not in accord with the philosophy of the period, the reader must account for the discrepancy.

In a study of other Robinson poems, there are themes parallel to that of "Luke Havergal." One, for example, is that of the alienated self. If Robinson believes in the alienated self, then it is possible that the voice speaking in "Luke Havergal" is Luke's own, but in an alienated state. This view may add credence to an argument that the speaker is Luke's past or subconscious, though it by no means proves it. Although parallelisms may be good support for the explication, the reader must be careful not to misconstrue them.

STEP II-G: *Themes and motifs, or correlating the parts*

Once the poem has been placed in context, the prosodic devices analyzed, and the function of the poetical techniques understood, they should be correlated, and any discrepancies should be studied for possible errors in explication. By this time, every line should be understood, so that stating what the poem is about is merely a matter of explaining the common points of all the area, supporting it with specific items from the poem, secondary sources, other poems, other critics, and history. The reader may use the specific questions given in the outline to help detail the major themes.

BIBLIOGRAPHY

Coleman, Kathleen. *Guide to French Poetry Explication*. New York: G. K. Hall, 1993.

Gioia, Dana, David Mason, and Meg Schoerke, eds. *Twentieth-Century American Poetics: Poets on the Art of Poetry*. Boston: McGraw-Hill, 2003.

Hirsch, Edward. *How to Read a Poem and Fall in Love with Poetry*. New York: Harcourt Brace, 1999.

Kohl, Herbert R. *A Grain of Poetry: How to Read Contemporary Poems and Make Them a Part of Your Life*. New York: HarperFlamingo, 1999.

Lennard, John. *The Poetry Handbook: A Guide to Reading Poetry for Pleasure and Practical Criticism*. 2d ed. New York: Oxford University Press, 2006.

Martínez, Nancy C., and Joseph G. R. Martínez. *Guide to British Poetry Explication*. 4 vols. Boston: G. K. Hall, 1991-1995.

Oliver, Mary. *A Poetry Handbook*. San Diego, Calif.: Harcourt Brace, 1994.

Preminger, Alex, et al., eds. *The New Princeton Encyclopedia of Poetry and Poetics*. 3d rev. ed. Princeton, N.J.: Princeton University Press, 1993.

Ryan, Michael. *A Difficult Grace: On Poets, Poetry, and Writing*. Athens: University of Georgia Press, 2000.

Statman, Mark. *Listener in the Snow: The Practice and Teaching of Poetry*. New York: Teachers & Writers Collaborative, 2000.

Steinman, Lisa M. *Invitation to Poetry: The Pleasures of Studying Poetry and Poetics*. Walden, Mass.: Wiley-Blackwell, 2008.

Strand, Mark, and Eavan Boland, eds. *The Making of a Poem: A Norton Anthology of Poetic Forms*. New York: W. W. Norton, 2000.

Wolosky, Shira. *The Art of Poetry: How to Read a Poem*. New York: Oxford University Press, 2001.

Walton Beacham

LANGUAGE AND LINGUISTICS

Most humans past the infant stage have a spoken language and use it regularly for understanding and speaking, although much of the world's population is still illiterate and cannot read or write. Language is such a natural part of life that people tend to overlook it until they are presented with some special problem: They lose their sight or hearing, have a stroke, or are required to learn a foreign language. Of course, people may also study their own language, but seldom do they stand aside and view language for what it is—a complex human phenomenon with a history reaching back to humankind's beginnings. A study of the development of one language will often reveal intertwinings with other languages. Sometimes such knowledge enables linguists to construct family groups; just as often, the divergences among languages or language families are so great that separate typological variations are established.

True language is characterized by its systematic nature, its arbitrariness of vocabulary and structure, its vocality, and its basis in symbolism. Most linguists believe that language and thought are separate entities. Although language may be necessary to give foundation to thought, it is not, in itself, thinking. Many psychologists, however, contend that language is thought. An examination of language on the basis of these assertions reveals that each language is a purely arbitrary code or set of rules. There is no intrinsic necessity for any word to sound like or mean what it does. Language is essentially speech, and symbolism is somehow the philosophical undergirding of the whole linguistic process. The French author Madame de Staël (1766-1817) once wrote, in describing her native language, that language is even more: "It is not only a means of communicating thoughts, feeling and acts, but an instrument that one loves to play upon, and that stimulates the mental faculties much as music does for some people and strong drink for others."

ORIGIN OF LANGUAGE

How did language originate? First, the evidence for the origin of language is so deeply buried in the past

that it is unlikely that people shall ever be able to do more than speculate about the matter. If people had direct knowledge of humankind's immediate ancestors, they should be able to develop some evolutionary theory and be able to say, among other things, how speech production and changes in the brain are related. Some linguists maintain that language ability is innate, but this assertion, true though it may be, rests on the assumption of a monogenetic theory of humanity's origin. Few scholars today are content with the notion that the human race began with Adam and Eve.

According to the Bible, Adam is responsible for human speech. Genesis reports:

> And out of the ground the Lord God formed every beast of the field, and every fowl of the air, and brought them unto Adam to see what he would call them; and whatsoever Adam called every creature, that was the name thereof. And Adam gave names to all cattle, and to the fowl of the air, and to every beast of the field.

If the story of Adam and Eve is taken literally, one might conclude that their language was the original one. Unfortunately, not even the Bible identifies what this language was. Some people have claimed that Hebrew was the first language and that all the other languages of the world are derived from it; Hebrew, however, bears no discernible relationship to any language outside the Hamito-Semitic group. Besides, any so-called original language would have changed so drastically in the intervening millennia before the onset of writing that it would not bear any resemblance to ancient Hebrew. Whatever the "original" language was—and there is every reason to believe that many languages sprang up independently over a very long span of time—it could not sound at all like any language that has been documented.

Many theories of the origin of language have been advanced, but three have been mentioned in textbooks more frequently than others. One, the "bow-wow" or echoic theory, insists that the earliest forms of language were exclusively onomatopoeic—that is, imitative of the sounds of animals and nature, despite the fact that the so-called primitive languages are not largely composed of onomatopoeic words. Furthermore, some measure of conventionalization must take place before echoisms become real "words"; individual young children do not call a dog a "bow-wow" until they hear an older child or adult use the term. Another theory, called the "pooh-pooh" or interjectional theory, maintains that language must have begun with primitive grunts and groans—that is, very loose and disjointed utterances. Many have held that such a theory fits animals better than humans; indeed, this kind of exclamatory speech probably separates humans quite clearly from the animals. Still another theory, dubbed the "ding-dong" theory, claims that language arose as a response to natural stimuli. None of these theories has any strong substantiation. Some linguists have suggested that speech and song may have once been the same. The presence of tones and pitch accent in many older languages lends some plausibility to the idea; it is likely that language, gestures, and song, as forms of communication, were all intertwined at the earliest stages.

Is it a hopeless task to try to discover the origin of language? Linguists have continued to look into the question again, but there is little chance that more than a priori notions can be established. It has been suggested, for example, that prehumans may have gradually developed a kind of grammar by occasionally fitting together unstructured vocal signals in patterns that were repeated and then eventually understood, accepted, and passed on. This process is called compounding, and some forms of it are found in present-day gibbon calls.

THE HISTORY OF LANGUAGE STUDY

In the history of language study, a number of signposts can be erected to mark the path. The simplest outline consists of two major parts: a prescientific and a scientific period. The first can be dispensed with in short order.

The earliest formal grammar of any language is a detailed analysis of classical Sanskrit, written by the Indian scholar Pānini in the fourth century B.C.E. He called it the Sutras (instructions), and in it, he codified the rules for the use of proper Sanskrit. It is still an authoritative work. Independently of Pānini, the ancient Greeks established many grammatical concepts that strongly influenced linguistic thinking for hundreds of years. Platonic realism, although by today's standards severely misguided in many respects, offered a number of useful insights into language, among them the basic division of the sentence into subject and predicate, the recognition of word stress, and the twofold classification of sounds into consonants and vowels. In the third century B.C.E., Aristotle defined the various parts of speech. In the next century, Dionysius Thrax produced a grammar that not only improved understanding of the sound system of Greek but also classified even more clearly the basic parts of speech and commented at length on such properties of language as gender, number, case, mood, voice, tense, and person. At no time, though, did the Hindu and Greek scholars break away from a focus on their own language to make a comparison with other languages. This fault was also largely one of the Romans, who merely adapted Greek scholarship to their own needs. If they did any comparing of languages, it was not of the languages in the Roman world, but only of Latin as a "corrupt" descendant of Greek. In sum, the Romans introduced no new concepts; they were, instead, content to synthesize or reorganize their legacy from ancient Greece. Only two grammarians come to mind from the fourth and fifth centuries of the Roman Empire—Priscian and Donatus, whose works served for centuries as basic texts for the teaching of Latin.

The scientific period of language study began with a British Sanskrit scholar, Sir William Jones, who headed a society organized in Calcutta for the exploration of Asia. In 1786, he delivered a paper in which he stated that

> the Sanskrit language . . . [was] more perfect than the Greek, more copious than the Latin, and more exquisitely refined than either; yet [bore] to both of them a stronger affinity . . . than could possibly have been produced by accident; so strong, indeed, that no philologer could examine them all three without believing them to have sprung from some common source, which, perhaps, no longer exists.

He went on to say that Germanic and Celtic probably had the same origin. His revolutionary assertion that Sanskrit and most of the languages of Europe had descended from a single language no longer spoken and never recorded first produced considerable scholarly opposition, but shortly thereafter set the stage for comparative analysis. He insisted that a close examination of the "inner structures" of this family of languages would reveal heretofore unsuspected relationships.

Franz Bopp, a German born in 1791 and a student of Oriental languages, including Sanskrit, was the founder of comparative grammar. In his epochmaking book *Über das Conjugationssystem der Sanskritsprache in Vergleichung mit jenem der griechischen, lateinischen, persischen und germanischen Sprache* (1816), he demonstrated for all time what Jones and Friedrich von Schlegel and other researchers had only surmised. A young Danish contemporary named Rasmus Rask corroborated his results and established that Armenian and Lithuanian belong to the same language group, the Indo-European. The tool to establish these relationships was the "comparative method," one of the greatest achievements of nineteenth century linguistics. In applying this method, linguists searched in the various languages under investigation for cognates—words with similar spelling, similar sound, and similar meaning. They then set up sound correspondences among the cognates, much like looking for the lowest common denominator in a mathematical construction, from which the original linguistic forms could be constructed.

The German linguist Jakob Grimm (one of the Brothers Grimm known for books of fairy tales) took Rask's work one step further and, in a four-volume work published between 1819 and 1822, showed conclusively the systematic correspondences and differences between Sanskrit, Greek, and Latin, on one hand, and the Germanic languages, on the other hand. The formulation of this system of sound changes came to be known as Grimm's law, or the First Sound Shift, and the changes involved can be diagramed as follows:

Proto-Indo-European: *bh dh gh b d g p t k*
Proto-Germanic: *b d g p t k f Ө h*

Where the Indo-European, as transmitted through Latin or Greek, had a *p* sound (as in *piscis* and *pēd*), the German-based English word has an *f* ("fish" and "foot");

the Latinate *trēs* becomes the English "three." In addition to the changes described above, another important change took place in the Germanic languages. If the *f Ө h* resulting from the change of *p t k* stood after an unaccented vowel but before another vowel, they became voiced fricatives, later voiced stops, as in the pair *seethe : sodden*. This change also affected *s*, yielding *z*, which later became *r* (Rhotacism) and explains, for example, the alternations in *was : were*. It was described by Karl Verner, a Danish linguist, and is known appropriately as Verner's law. There are one or two other "laws" that explain apparent exceptions to Grimm's law, illustrating the basic regularity of Grimm's formulations. At the very end of the nineteenth century, the neo-Grammarians, led by Karl Brugmann, insisted that all exceptions could be explained—that, in fact, "phonetic laws are natural laws and have no exceptions." Even those studying the natural sciences do not make such a strong assertion, but the war cry of the neo-Grammarians did inspire scholars to search for regularity in language.

The German language itself underwent a profound change beginning probably in the far south of the German-speaking lands sometime during the fifth century, causing a restructuring of the sounds of all of the southern and many of the midland dialects. These became known, for geographical reasons, as High German, while those dialects in the north came to be known as Low German. Six consonants in various positions were affected, but the most consistently shifted sounds were the Indo-European *b*, which in English became *p* and in German *pf*, and the *d* to *t* and *ts*. For example, the Latin *decim* became the English "ten" and the German *zehn*.

In the course of the nineteenth century, all such changes were recognized, and scholars were enabled to identify and diagram the reflex languages of Indo-European into five subgroups known as *satem* languages and four known as *centum* languages. This division is significant both geographically—the *satem* languages are located clearly to the east of where the original home of the Indo-Europeans probably was—and linguistically—the *satem* languages have, among other characteristics, *s* sounds where the *centum* languages have *k* sounds (the word *centum* is pronounced

THE *SATEM* LANGUAGES

Indo-Iranian	Earliest attested form, Sanskrit; modern languages include Hindi, Bengali, and Persian.
Albanian	Spoken by a small number of Balkan people.
Armenian	Spoken by a small number of people in that country.
Slavic	Divided into East Slavic (Great Russian, the standard language; Little Russian or Ukrainian; White Russian, spoken in the region adjacent to and partly in modern-day Poland); West Slavic (Czech, Slovak, Polish); South Slavic (Slovenian and Serbo-Croatian; Bulgarian).
Baltic	Lithuanian and Lettic, spoken in the Baltic states.

with an initial hard *c*). The very words *satem* and *centum*, meaning "hundred" in Avestan (an Indo-Iranian language) and Latin, respectively, illustrate the sound divergence.

INDO-EUROPEAN LANGUAGES

The original home of the Indo-Europeans is not known for certain, but it is safe to say that it was in Europe, and probably close to present-day Lithuania. For one thing, the Lithuanians have resided in a single area since the Neolithic Age (2500-2000 B.C.E.) and speak a language of great complexity. Furthermore, Lithuania is situated on the dividing line between *centum* and *satem* languages. One would also assume that the original home was somewhere close to the area where the reflex languages are to be found today and not, for example, in Africa, Australia, or North or South America. For historical and archaeological reasons, scholars have ruled out the British Isles and the peninsulas of southern Europe. Last, there are indications that the Indo-Europeans entered

India from the northwest, for there is no evidence of their early acquaintanceship with the Ganges River, but only with the Indus (hence "Indo-"). Certain common words for weather conditions, geography, and flora and fauna militate in favor of a European homeland.

Scholars have classified the Indo-European languages as a family apart from certain other languages on the basis of two principal features: their common word stock and their inflectional structure. This type of classification, called genetic, is one of three. Another, called geographical, is usually employed initially. For example, if nothing whatsoever was known about American Indian languages, one might divide them into North American and South American, Eastern North American and Western North American, and perhaps some other geographical categories. A third variety of classification, called typological, is possible only when a good deal is

THE *CENTUM* LANGUAGES

Greek (Hellenic)	Attic, Ionic, and Doric, formerly spoken throughout the eastern areas around the Mediterranean; modern Greek.
Italic	Latin; modern Italian, French, Spanish, Portuguese, Catalan, Sardinian, Romanian, and Rhaeto-Romanic.
Celtic	Modern Welsh, Cornish, Breton, Irish, and Scots Gaelic.
Germanic (Teutonic)	East Germanic (Gothic, now extinct); North Germanic (Danish, Norwegian, Swedish, Icelandic); West Germanic (Low German: English, Dutch, Frisian, Plattdeutsch; High German: standard German).
In addition	Several extinct Indo-European languages, such as Tocharian and the Anatolian languages, especially Hittite.

known about the structure of a language. The four main types of languages arrived at through such classification are inflectional, meaning that such syntactic distinctions as gender, number, case, tense, and so forth are usually communicated by altering the form of a word, as in English when -*s* added to a noun indicates plurality but, when added to a verb, singularity; agglutinative, meaning that suffixes are piled onto word bases in a definite order and without change in phonetic shape (for example, Turkish *evlerimden*, "house-s-my-from"); isolating, meaning that invariable word forms, mostly monosyllabic, are employed in variable word order (for example, Chinese *wŏ*, meaning, according to its position in the utterance, "I," "me," "to me," or "my"); and incorporating or polysynthetic, meaning that a sentence, with its various syntactic features, may be "incorporated" as a single word (for example, Eskimo /a: wlisa-utiss?ar-siniarpu-na/, "I am looking for something suitable for a fish-line").

OTHER LANGUAGES

Although the Indo-European languages have been studied in more detail than other language families, it is possible to classify and describe many of the remaining language families of the world, the total comprising more than twenty-seven hundred separate languages. In Europe and Asia, relatively few languages are spoken by very large numbers of people; elsewhere many distinct languages are spoken by small communities. In Europe, all languages are Indo-European except for Finnish, Estonian, Hungarian, and Basque. The last-named is something of a mystery; it appears to predate Indo-European by such a long period that it could conceivably be descended from a prehistoric language. The first three belong to the same family, the Finno-Urgic. Sometimes Turkish is added to the group, and the four are called the Ural-Altaic family. All are agglutinative.

The most extensive language family in eastern Asia is the Sino-Tibetan. It consists of two branches, the Tibeto-Burman and Chinese. Mandarin is the language of the northern half of China, although there are three different varieties—northern, southwestern, and southern. In the south, there is a range of mutually unintelligible dialects. All are isolating in structure.

In other parts of Asia are found the Kadai family, consisting of Thai, Laotian, and the Shan languages of Burma, and in southern Asia, the Munda languages and Vietnamese. The latter has a considerable number of speakers.

Japanese and Korean are separate families, even though cultural relationships between the two countries have produced some borrowing over the years. Japanese is essentially agglutinative.

On the continent of Africa, the linguistic family of prime importance is the Hamito-Semitic family. Hebrew, Arabic, and some of the languages of Ethiopia make up the Semitic side. There are four Hamitic languages: Egyptian, Berber, Cushitic, and Chad. All exhibit some inflectional characteristics. In addition to these languages, Hausa, an important trade language, is used throughout the northern part of the continent.

In central and southern Africa, the Niger-Congo language family is dominant. The largest subgroup of this family is Bantu, which includes Swahili in central and eastern Africa, Kikuyu in Kenya, and Zulu in the south. Most appear to be either agglutinative or polysynthetic.

The Malayo-Polynesian languages are spoken as original tongues all the way from Madagascar to the Malay Peninsula, the East Indies, and, across the Pacific, to Hawaii. Many seem to be isolating with traces of earlier inflections.

The Indian languages of the Americas are all polysynthetic. Until recently, these Indian languages were classified geographically. Many of the North American languages have been investigated, and linguists group them into distinct families, such as Algonquian, Athabaskan, Natchez-Muskogean, Uto-Aztecan, Penutian, and Hokan.

MODERN LANGUAGES

In addition to the distinction between prescientific and scientific periods of language study, there are other divisions that can help clarify the various approaches to this vast topic. For example, the entire period from earliest times until the late nineteenth century was largely historical, comparative at best, but scarcely truly scientific in terms of rigor. Beginning with the neo-Grammarians Brugmann and Delbrück, the stage was set for what may be called a period of general or descriptive linguistics. Languages were examined not only diachronically—that is, historically—but also synchronically, where a segment or feature of language was scrutinized without regard to an earlier stage. The most important names associated with this descriptive school are those of N. S. Trubetzkoy and Roman Jakobson. Strongly influenced by the theories of the Swiss linguist Ferdinand de Saussure, they examined each detail of language as a part of a system. In other words, they were ultimately more interested in the system and the way it hung together than in each individual detail. These scholars were members of the European school of linguistic thought that had its origin in Jakobson's Prague circle. Across the Atlantic, their most important counterpart was Leonard Bloomfield, who, in 1933, published his classic linguistics text, *Language*. Like his contemporary, Edward Sapir, Bloomfield began as a comparativist in Germanic linguistics, then studied American Indian languages, and finally became an expert in the general principles of language. Bloomfield's theory of structuralism has been criticized for its resemblance to the psychological theory of behaviorism, which restricts itself to the observable and rejects the concept of mind.

Since the 1930's, there has been a steady procession of American linguists studying and reporting on the sounds and grammatical features of many different languages, in some sense all derivative from the foundation laid by the phonemicists beginning with Saussure and Bloomfield. Kenneth Pike's tagmemics, in part an attempt to present language behavior empirically through a description at each level of grammatical form, evolved directly out of descriptive linguistics. In 1957, Noam Chomsky launched transformational-generative grammar, concerned at first only with syntax, but later also with phonology. Considerable tension has developed between structuralists and transformational-generative grammarians, concerning not only syntactic analysis but also the representation of sounds. For some, stratificational grammar provides a connection, through strata or levels of description, among descriptive, tagmemic, and computational analyses.

THE TECHNICAL SIDE OF LANGUAGE

A language is made up of its sound system, grammar, and vocabulary. The former two may differ considerably from language family to language family, but there is a workable range in the extent and type of sounds and grammatical functions. The inventory of significant sounds in a given language, called phonemes, extends from about twenty to about sixty. English has forty-six, including phonemes of pitch, stress, and juncture. If the grammatical facts of a complicated language can be written out on one or two sheets of paper, the grammar of English can be laid out on the back of an envelope. In short, some languages are simpler phonologically or grammatically than others, but none is so complicated in either respect that every child cannot learn his or her language in about the same time.

The study of the sounds of which speech is made up became scientific in method by the end of the nineteenth century, when Paul Passy founded the International Phonetic Association. Down to the present day, articulatory phonetics has borne a close relationship to physiology in the description of the sounds of speech according to the organs producing them and the position of these organs in relation to surrounding structures.

By the mid-1920's, phoneticians realized that the unit of description of the phonology of a language had to be a concept rather than some physical entity. The term phoneme was chosen; it designates a minimally significant sound unit, an abstraction around which cluster all the phonetic realizations of that generalized sound. Thus, the English phoneme /p/ represents all recognizably similar pronunciations of [p], with more or less or no aspiration depending on position within a word or the speech habits of a given speaker. In other words, it designates a class of sounds distinct from others in the language. It carries no meaning as such, but it serves to distinguish one sound from another and, together with other phonemes, produces morphemic, or meaning, differences. Thus /p/, /i/, and /n/ are separate phonemes, but, taken together, make up a morpheme— the word *pin*—which is distinct, by virtue of a single phoneme, from, say, /bin/, "bin," or /tin/ "tin." Sometimes, morphemes show relations between words, as when -*s* is added to a noun to indicate plurality or possession or to a verb to indicate singularity.

The sound system and grammar of a language are thus closely related. Grammar, at least for Indo-European languages and many others, can be defined as consisting of a morphology and syntax, where, expressed simply, the former refers to the words and their endings and the latter to the order of words. Accompanying the words are, however, other features of language that can alter meaning. It matters, for example, whether the stress occurs on the first or second syllable of the word *pervert* or *permit*. If the stress falls on the first syllable, the word is a noun; if on the second, it is a verb. It matters whether the last few sounds of an utterance convey an upturn or a downturn and trail-off, for a question or a statement may result. It matters also what the pitch level is and whether juncture is present. These features, too, are phonemic.

To function in a language, one must have control of close to 100 percent of the phonology and 75 percent or more of the grammar, but a mere 1 percent of the vocabulary will enable the speaker to function in many situations. For a speaker of a language the size of English, a vocabulary of six thousand words will suffice. Possessing a vocabulary implies an unconscious knowledge of the semantic relationship to the phonology and grammar of the language. One theory of the word regards the word as a compound formed of two components: a physical element, the sequence of sounds of speech; and a semantic element, the amount of meaning expressed by the segment of speech. The first is called the formant, the second the morpheme. The word "cook" /kuk/ is one morpheme expressed by one formant—the formant consisting of one syllable, a sequence of three phonemes. In the plural of "cook," *-s* is a formant that is not even a syllable. In fact, a formant is not even necessarily a phoneme, but can be the use of one form instead of another, as in "her" instead of "she." There is no reason that the same formant, such as *-s*, cannot express more than one morpheme: "cooks" (noun) versus "cook's" versus "cooks" (verb). The same morpheme can also be expressed by more than one formant; there are, for example, many different formants for the plural, such as basis/bases, curriculum/curricula, datum/data, ox/oxen, child/children, man/men, woman/women, cherub/cherubim, monsignore/monsignori.

The distinction in morphology made above between words and their endings needs further amplification. An examination of a stanza from Lewis Carroll's "Jabberwocky" (from *Alice's Adventures in Wonderland*, 1865) illustrates the manner in which the poet uses formants with no evident meaning to the average speaker:

> 'Twas brilling, and the slithy toves
> Did gyre and gimble in the wabe;
> All mimsy were the borogoves,
> And the mome raths outgrabe.

Alice herself remarks that the words fill her head with ideas, but she does not know what they are. There is a rightness about the way the poem sounds because the endings, the structural morphemes, are correctly placed. When the message is of primary importance and the speaker knows the language only imperfectly, the structural morphemes may be incorrect or missing and a string of pure message morphemes may be the result: Her give man bag money.

Message morphemes have their own peculiar properties, limiting their use to certain contexts, regardless of the accuracy of the combined structural morphemes. To illustrate this principle, Chomsky composed the sentence "Colorless green ideas sleep furiously." The subject is "colorless green ideas"; the predicate, "sleep furiously." This sentence has the same structure as any sentence of the shape: adjective/adjective/noun/intransitive verb/adverb. However, there is something semantically troubling. How can one describe something green as colorless? Can ideas be green? How can an intransitive verb that describes such a passive activity be furiously involved in an action?

Chomsky's example was designed to combine structural familiarity with semantic impossibility. It is possible to devise similar sentences that, though semantically improbable, could conceivably be used by an actual speaker. The sentence "Virtue swims home every night" attributes to an abstract noun an action performed by animate beings, and poses other difficulties as well (in what setting can one swim home?), yet such strange semantic violations, given a meaningful context, are the stuff of poetry.

Indeed, semantic change actually occurs with a

measure of frequency in the history of a language. It is usually of two types. Words that are rather specific in meaning sometimes become generalized; for example, Latin *molīna* (gristmill) originally meant "mill" but expanded to cover "sawmill," "steel mill," even "diploma mill." Many words in English of very broad meanings, such as "do," "make," "go," and "things," derive from words of more specific notions. At the same time, the opposite often happens. Words that once were very general in meaning have become specific. Examples include *deer*, which formerly meant merely "animal" (compare German *Tier*), and *hound*, "dog," now a particular kind of dog. Sometimes, words undergo melioration, as in the change in *knight*, meaning originally a "servant," to "king's servant," or pejoration, as in the change in *knave*, meaning "boy" (compare German *Knabe*), to "rascal."

Perhaps the most significant force for change in language is analogy. It is occasioned by mental associations arising because of similarity or contrast of meaning and may affect the meaning or the form of words or even create new words. Most verbs in English are regular and form their preterit and past participles by the addition of *-ed* (or *-t*), as "dream, dreamed, dreamt," and not by vowel change, as in "drink, drank, drunk." New words taken into the language, as well as some of the irregular ones already in use, will usually become regular. It is by no means unusual to hear a child use analogy in forming the past of, say, "teach" or "see" as "teached" and "see'd" instead of "taught" and "saw." Since most English nouns form their plural by the addition of *-s*, it is to be expected that unfamiliar words or words with little-used, learned plural forms will be pluralized in the same way: for example, "memorandums" (or "memos") for *memoranda*, "stadiums" for *stadia*, "gymnasiums" for *gymnasia*, "prima donnas" for *prime donne*, and "formulas" for *formulae*. Sometimes a resemblance in the form of a word may suggest a relationship that causes a further assimilation in form. This process is known as folk etymology and often occurs when an unfamiliar or foreign word or phrase is altered to give it a more meaningful form. There are many examples: "crayfish" comes from Old French *crevisse* (crab), but *-visse* meant nothing and thus was changed to the phonetically similar *-fish*; a hangnail is not a (fin-

ger)nail that hangs, but one that hurts (from Old English *ang*); the second element of "titmouse" has nothing to do with a mouse, but comes from Middle English *mose*, the name for several species of birds.

There are many other processes in language by which changes are brought about. Among them are several of great importance: assimilation, dissimilation, conversion, back formation, blending, and the creation of euphemisms and slang.

Assimilation causes a sound to change in conformance with a neighboring sound, as in the plural of "kit" with [-s] (/kits/), as opposed to the plural of "limb" with [-z] (/limz/), or in the preterit and participial forms of regular verbs: "grazed" [greyzd], but "choked" [čowkt].

Dissimilation is the opposite process, whereby neighboring sounds are made unlike, as in "pilgrim" from Latin *peregrīnus*, where the first *r* dissimilates.

Conversion is the change of one part of speech or form class into another, as the change from noun to verb: The nouns "bridge," "color," and "shoulder" are converted to verbs in "to bridge a gap," "to color a book," and "to shoulder a load."

A back formation occurs when a word is mistakenly assumed to be the base form from which a new word is formed, as in "edit" from "editor," "beg" from "beggar," "peddle" from "pedlar."

Some words are blends: "flash" + "blush" = "flush"; "slight" (slim) + "tender" = "slender"; "twist" + "whirl" = "twirl"; "breakfast" + "lunch" = "brunch."

Euphemisms are words and expressions with new, better-sounding connotations—for example, to "pass away" or "breathe one's last" or "cross the river" for "to die"; "lingerie" or "intimate wear" for "underwear"; "acute indigestion" for "bellyache."

Slang consists of informal, often ephemeral expressions and coinages, such as "turkey" for "stupid person," "blow away" for "to kill," and "kook," meaning "odd or eccentric person," from "cuckoo."

All three constituents of language change over a long period of time—sounds, structure, and vocabulary—but each language or dialect retains its distinctiveness. The most durable and unchanging aspect of language is writing, of which there are two major varieties: picture writing, also called ideographic writing, and alphabetic writing. The former kind of writing began as actual pictures and developed gradually into ideograms linked directly to the objects or concepts and having no connection with the sounds of the language. The latter variety began as symbols for syllables, until each symbol was taken to represent a single spoken sound. Although alphabetic writing is much more widespread and easier to learn and use, ideographic writing has the advantage of maintaining cultural unity among speakers of dialects and languages not mutually intelligible. An alphabetic writing system can, over time, act as a conservative influence on the spoken language as well as provide valuable etymological clues. Ideographic writing can be, and often is, seen as art capable of conveying messages separate from speech. Both systems are vehicles for the transmission of history and literature without which civilization would falter and perish.

THE SOCIAL SIDE OF LANGUAGE

The social side of language is inextricably linked to behavior. It is concerned with the use of language to create attitudes and responses toward language, objects, and people. For example, certain overt behaviors toward language and its users can create unusual political pressures. The insistence by the Québecois on French as the primary, if not sole, language of their province of Canada has led to near secession and to bitter interprovincial feelings. The creation of modern Hebrew has helped to create and sustain the state of Israel. The Irish are striving to make Irish the first language of that part of the British Isles. The Flemish urge full status for their variety of Dutch in the Brussels area. African Americans sometimes advocate clearer recognition of black English. Frisians, Bretons, Basques, Catalans, and Provençals are all insisting on greater acceptance of their mother tongues.

Within a language or dialect, there can be specialized vocabulary and pronunciation not generally understood. The term "dialect" is commonly taken to mean a regional variety of language or one spoken by the undereducated, but, strictly speaking, it is differentiated from language as such, being largely what people actually speak. Some dialects differ so substantially from standard, national tongues that, to all intents and

purposes, they are languages in their own right. The term "vernacular" is similar in that it designates everyday speech as opposed to learned discourse. "Lingo" designates, somewhat contemptuously, any dialect or language not readily comprehended. "Jargon" is specialized or professional language, often of a technical nature; in this context, the term "cant," as in "thieves' cant," is virtually synonymous with "jargon." Closely related to these two terms is the term "argot," referring to the idiom of a closely knit group, as in "criminal argot." Finally, "slang," discussed above, refers to the colorful, innovative, often short-lived popular vocabulary drawn from many levels of language use, both specialized and nonspecialized.

Words, like music, can produce moods. They can raise one's spirits or lower them. They can stir up discontent or soothe human anger. They can inspire and console, ingratiate and manipulate, mislead and ridicule. They can create enough hatred to destroy but also enough trust to overcome obstacles. While a mood may originate in physical well-being or physical discomfort and pain, language can express that mood, intensify it, or deny it. Language can be informative (emotionally neutral), biased (emotionally charged), or propagandistic (informatively neutral).

Language is informative when it states indisputable facts or asks questions dealing with such facts, even though those facts are very broad and general. One can also inform with misstatements, half-truths, or outright lies. It does not matter whether the statement is actually true or false, only that the question can be posed.

Language often reflects bias by distorting facts. Frequently, the substitution of a single derogatory term is sufficient to load the atmosphere. Admittedly, some words are favorably charged for some people, unfavorably for others. Much depends on the context, word and sentence stress, gestures, and former relationship.

Language can be propagandistic when the speaker desires to promote some activity or cause. The load that propaganda carries is directly proportional to the receiver's enthusiasm, bias, or readiness to be deceived. Almost invariably, propaganda terms arise out of the specialized language of religion, art, commerce, education, finance, government, and so forth. Propaganda is a kind of name calling, using words from a stock of esoteric and exclusive terms. Not many people are thoroughly familiar with the exact meanings of words such as "totalitarian," "fascist," "proletarian," and "bourgeois," but they think they know whether these words are good or bad, words of approval or disapproval. The effect is to call forth emotions as strong as those prompted by invectives.

The language of advertising achieves its effectiveness by conveniently combining information, bias, and propaganda. A good advertisement must gain immediate attention, make the reader or listener receptive to the message, ensure its retention, create a desire, and cause the person to buy the product without setting up resistance. Advertising must, moreover, link the product to "pleasant" or "healthy" things. In advertising circles, there is no widespread agreement as to which is more important: the avoidance of all associations that can create resistance or the creation of desire for a particular object. Even if the latter is regarded as the prime objective, it is still important to avoid resistance. The most powerful tools of the advertiser are exaggeration and cliché. The words generally used in ads deal with the basic component and qualities of a product, while the qualifiers are hackneyed and overblown: lather (rich, creamy, full-bodied); toothpaste (fights cavities three ways, ten ways, tastes zesty); cleanser (all-purpose, powerful, one-step); coffee (full of flavor buds, brewed to perfection, marvelous bouquet). The danger of advertising is evident when its pathology carries over into other areas of life. Every culture must be on guard against the effect of advertising on the health of its citizenry and the shaping of its national image. Even foreign policy can be the victim of advertising that stresses youth over maturity, beauty of body over soundness of mind, physical health over mental serenity, or the power of sex appeal over everything else.

In the latter part of the twentieth century, language began to be closely examined by certain groups aiming to rid it of inherent prejudice. Of all of these groups, perhaps feminists have had the greatest effect on the vocabulary, and even the structure, of languages that differentiate along sex lines. A vociferous contingent of women contend that the symbols of perception—words—give both meaning and value to the objects they define and that many of these words are loaded with a male-chauvinist aspect. For example, words with the affix *-man* are being avoided or paired with *-woman* or *-person*: "congressman"/"congresswoman," "chairman"/"chairwoman"/"chairperson." In some instances, gender is eliminated altogether: "humankind" for "mankind," "chair" for "chairman" or "chairwoman." There are many more techniques employed to desexualize English; some even involve tampering with personal pronouns, a much less likely area for success. Nevertheless, any language can cope with any pressing linguistic problem. The impetus for a solution begins with the individual or a small group, but the community as a whole often applies brakes to change that is too rapid or drastic, dramatizing the fact that language exists not for the individual alone but for the community as a whole.

APPLICATIONS

Almost everybody is intimately acquainted with at least one language. Everybody can produce the sounds and sound combinations of his or her language and understand the meanings of the sounds produced by other speakers. Everybody knows which sounds and sound combinations are allowable and which do not fit the language. Sentences that are grammatically or semantically unacceptable or strange are easily recognized. Despite this intuitive or unconscious knowledge of one's language, the average native speaker cannot comment authoritatively on the sound system or the structure of his or her language. Furthermore, there are no books containing the complete language of English or Arabic or Mandarin Chinese in which all possible sentences and sound combinations are listed. Instead, people must rely largely on dictionaries for a list of words and on grammars and linguistic texts for a statement of rules dealing with sounds, morphology, and syntax. To study one's language as an object or phenomenon is to raise one's consciousness of how language functions.

Some people have a professional need to know a lot about a language as opposed to simply being able to use it. Some of the more obvious examples include language teachers, speech therapists, advertising writers, communications engineers, and computer programmers. Others, such as the anthropologist or the historian, who often work with documents, employ their knowledge as an ancillary tool. The missionary may have to learn about some very esoteric language for which there is no grammar book and perhaps even no writing. The psychologist studies language as a part of human behavior. The philosopher is often primarily interested in the "logical" side of language. Students of foreign languages can benefit greatly from linguistic knowledge; they can often learn more efficiently and make helpful comparisons of sounds and structures between their own and the target language.

Translation and interpretation are two activities requiring considerable knowledge about language. Strictly speaking, the terms are not interchangeable; translation refers to the activity of rendering, in writing, one language text into another, whereas interpretation is oral translation. Translation is of two kinds, scientific and literary, and can be accomplished by people or machines. In general, machine translation has been a disappointment because of the grave difficulties involved in programming the many complexities of natural language. Interpretation is also of two kinds: legal and diplomatic. Whereas the legal interpreter requires a precise knowledge of the terminology of the court and must tread a thin line between literal and free interpretation, the diplomatic interpreter has the even more difficult task of adding, or subtracting, as circumstances dictate, allusions, innuendos, insinuations, and implications. Interpretation is accomplished in two ways: simultaneously with the speaker, or consecutively after a given segment of speech.

One of the important questions before linguistics is: Does linguistics aid in the study and appreciation of literature? Many would automatically assume that the answer is an unqualified yes, since the material of which literature is made is language. There are others, however, who find linguistic techniques of analysis too mechanical and lacking in the very feeling that literature tries to communicate. Probably most thoughtful people would agree that linguistics can make a contribution in tandem with more traditional analytical approaches, but that alone it cannot yet, if ever, disclose the intrinsic qualities of great literary works.

By one definition at least, literature consists of texts constructed according to certain phonological, morpho-

logical, and syntactic restrictions, where the result is the creation of excellence of form and expression. For poetry in the Western tradition, for example, the restriction most frequently imposed is that of rhythm based on stress or vowel quantity. In other cultures, syntactic and semantic prescriptions can produce the same effect.

For both poetic and prose texts, the discovery and description of the author's style are essential to analysis. In contrast to the methods of traditional literary criticism, linguistics offers the possibility of quantitative stylistic analysis. Computer-aided analysis yields textual statistics based on an examination of various features of phonology and grammar. The results will often place an author within a literary period, confirm his region or dialect, explain the foreign-vocabulary influences, describe syllabication in terms of vowel and consonant count, list euphemisms and metaphors, and delineate sentence structure with regard to subordinating elements, to mention some of the possibilities. All of these applications are based on the taxemes of selection employed by an individual author.

Of all literary endeavors, literary translation seems to stand in the closest possible relationship to linguistics. The translator must perform his task within the framework of an awareness, be it conscious or intuitive, of the phonology, syntax, and morphology of both the source language and the target language. Like the linguist, he should also be acquainted in at least a rudimentary fashion with the society that has produced the text he is attempting to translate. His work involves much more than the mechanical or one-to-one exchange of word for word, phrase for phrase, or even concept for concept. The practice of translation makes possible the scope and breadth of knowledge encompassed in the ideal of liberal arts, and without translation relatively few scholars could claim knowledge and understanding of many of the world's great thinkers and literary artists.

BIBLIOGRAPHY

Akmajian, Adrian, et al. *Linguistics: An Introduction to Language and Communication*. Cambridge, Mass.: MIT Press, 2001. The first part of this work deals with the structural and interpretive parts of language, and the second part is cognitively oriented and includes chapters on pragmatics, psychology of language, language acquisition, and language and the brain.

Beekes, Robert S. P. *Comparative Indo-European Linguistics: An Introduction*. Philadelphia: John Benjamins, 1996. Examines the history of Indo-European languages and explores comparative grammar and linguistics.

Cavalli-Sforza, L. L. *Genes, Peoples, and Languages*. Berkeley: University of California Press, 2001. Cavalli-Sforza was among the first to ask whether the genes of modern populations contain a historical record of the human species. This collection comprises five lectures that serve as a summation of the author's work over several decades, the goal of which has been nothing less than tracking the past hundred thousand years of human evolution.

Chomsky, Noam. *Language and Thought*. Wakefield, R.I.: Moyer Bell, 1998. Presents an analysis of human language and its influence on other disciplines.

Lycan, William G. *Philosophy of Language: A Contemporary Introduction*. 2d ed. New York: Routledge, 2008. Introduces nonspecialists to the main issues and theories in the philosophy of language, focusing specifically on linguistic phenomena.

Pinker, Stephen. *The Language Instinct: How the Mind Creates Language*. New York: HarperPerennial Modern Classics, 2009. Explores how humans learn to talk, how the study of language can provide insight into the way genes interact with experience to create behavior and thought, and how the arbitrary sounds people call language evoke emotion and meaning.

Ruhlen, Merritt. *The Origin of Language: Tracing the Evolution of the Mother Tongue*. New York: John Wiley & Sons, 1996. Provides an accessible examination of nearly 100,000 years of human history and prehistory to uncover the roots of the language from which all modern tongues derive.

Trudgill, Peter. *Sociolinguistics: An Introduction to Language and Society*. 4th ed. New York: Penguin Books, 2007. Examines how speech is deeply influenced by class, gender, and ethnic background and explores the implications of language for social and educational policy.

Vygotsky, Lev S. *Thought and Language*. Edited by Alex Kozulin. Rev. ed. Cambridge, Mass.: MIT Press, 1986. A classic foundational work of cognitive science. Vygotsky analyzes the relationship between words and consciousness, arguing that speech is social in its origins and that only as a child develops does it become internalized verbal thought. Revised edition offers an introductory essay by editor Kozulin that offers new insight into the author's life, intellectual milieu, and research methods.

Yule, George. *The Study of Language*. 4th ed. New York: Cambridge University Press, 2010. Revised edition includes a new chapter on pragmatics and an expanded chapter on semantics; incorporates many changes that reflect developments in language study in the twenty-first century.

Donald D. Hook

GLOSSARY OF POETICAL TERMS

Accentual meter: A base meter in which the occurrence of a syllable marked by a stress determines the basic unit, regardless of the number of unstressed syllables. It is one of four base meters used in English (accentual, accentual-syllabic, syllabic, and quantitative). An example from modern poetry is "Blue Moles" by Sylvia Plath, the first line of which scans: "They're out of the dark's ragbag, these two." Because there are five stressed syllables in this accentually based poem, the reader can expect that many of the other lines will also contain five stresses. See also *Scansion.*

Accentual-syllabic meter: A base meter that measures the pattern of stressed syllables relative to the unstressed ones. It is the most common base meter for English poetry. In the first line of William Shakespeare's sonnet 130, "My mistress' eyes are nothing like the sun," there is a pattern of alternating unstressed with stressed syllables, although there is a substitution of an unstressed syllable for a stressed syllable at the word "like." In the accentual-syllabic system, stressed and unstressed syllables are grouped together into feet.

Allegory: A literary mode in which a second level of meaning—wherein characters, events, and settings represent abstractions—is encoded within the surface narrative. The allegorical mode may dominate the entire work, in which case the encoded message is the work's primary excuse for being, or it may be an element in a work otherwise interesting and meaningful for its surface story alone.

Alliteration: The repetition of consonants at the beginning of syllables; for example, "Large *m*annered *m*otions of his *m*ythy *m*ind." Alliteration is used when the poet wishes to focus on the details of a sequence of words and to show relationships between words within a line. Because a reader cannot easily skim over an alliterative line, it is conspicuous and demands emphasis.

Allusion: A reference to a historical or literary event whose story or outcome adds dimension to the poem. "Fire and Ice" by Robert Frost, for example, alludes to the biblical account of the flood and the prophecy that the next destruction will come by fire, not water. Without recognizing the allusion and understanding the bib-

lical reference to Noah and the surrounding associations of hate and desire, the reader cannot fully appreciate the poem.

Anacrusis: The addition of an extra unstressed syllable to the beginning or end of a line; the opposite of truncation. For example, anacrusis occurs in the line: "their shoul/ders held the sky/suspended." This line is described as iambic tetrameter with terminal anacrusis. Anacrusis is used to change a rising meter to falling and vice versa to alter the reader's emotional response to the subject.

Anapest: A foot in which two unstressed syllables are associated with one stressed syllable, as in the line, "With the sift/ed, harmon/ious pause." The anapestic foot is one of the three most common in English poetry and is used to create a highly rhythmical, usually emotional, line.

Anaphora: The use of the same word or words to begin successive phrases or lines. Timothy Steele's "Sapphics Against Anger" uses anaphora in the repetition of the phrase "May I."

Approximate rhyme: Assonance and half rhyme (or slant rhyme). Assonance occurs when words with identical vowel sounds but different consonants are associated. "Stars," "arms," and "park" all contain identical *a* (and *ar*) sounds, but because the consonants are different the words are not full rhymes. Half rhyme or slant rhymes contain identical consonants but different vowels, as in "fall" and "well." "Table" and "bauble" constitute half rhymes; "law," "cough," and "fawn" assonate.

Archetype: 1) Primordial image from the collective unconscious of humankind, according to psychologist Carl Jung, who believed that works of art, including poetry, derive much of their power from the unconscious appeal of these images to ancestral memories. 2) A symbol, usually an image, that recurs so frequently in literature that it becomes an element of the literary experience, according to Northrop Frye in his extremely influential *Anatomy of Criticism* (1957).

Assonance: See *Approximate rhyme*

Aubade: A type of poem welcoming or decrying the arrival of the dawn. Often the dawn symbolizes the separation of two lovers. An example is William Empson's "Aubade" (1937).

Ballad: A poem composed of four-line stanzas that alternate rhyme schemes of *abab* or *abcb*. If all four lines contain four feet each (tetrameter), the stanza is called a long ballad; if one or more of the lines contain only three feet (trimeter), it is called a short ballad. Ballad stanzas, which are highly mnemonic, originated with verse adapted to singing. For this reason, the poetic ballad is well suited for presenting stories. Popular ballads are songs or verse that tell tales, usually impersonal, and they usually impart folk wisdom. Supernatural events, courage, and love are frequent themes, but any experience that appeals to people is acceptable material. A famous use of the ballad form is *The Rime of the Ancient Mariner* (1798), by Samuel Taylor Coleridge.

Ballade: A popular and sophisticated French form, commonly (but not necessarily) composed of an eight-line stanza rhyming *ababbcbc*. Early ballades usually contained three stanzas and an envoy, commonly addressed to a nobleman, priest, or the poet's patron, but no consistent syllable count. Another common characteristic of the ballade is a refrain that occurs at the end of each stanza.

Base meter: Also called metrical base. The primary meter employed in poems in English and in most European languages that are not free verse. Based on the number, pattern, or duration of the syllables within a line or stanza, base meters fall into four types: accentual, accentual-syllabic, syllabic, or quantitative. Rhythm in verse occurs because of meter, and the use of meter depends on the type of base into which it is placed.

Blank verse: A type of poem having a base meter of iambic pentameter and with unrhymed lines usually arranged in stichic form (that is, not in stanzas). Most of William Shakespeare's plays are written in blank verse; in poetry it is often used for subject matter that requires much narration or reflection. In both poetry and drama, blank verse elevates emotion and gives a dramatic sense of importance. Although the base meter of blank verse is iambic pentameter, the form is very flexible, and substitution, enjambment, feminine rhyme, and extra syllables can relax the rigidity of the base. The flexi-

bility of blank verse gives the poet an opportunity to use a formal structure without seeming unnecessarily decorous. T. S. Eliot's "Burnt Norton," written in the 1930's, is a modern blank-verse poem.

Cadence: The rhythmic speed or tempo with which a line is read. All language has cadence, but when the cadence of words is forced into some pattern, it becomes meter, thus distinguishing poetry from prose. A prose poem may possess strong cadence, combined with poetic uses of imagery, symbolism, and other poetic devices.

Caesura: A pause or break in a poem, created with or without punctuation marks. The comma, question mark, colon, and dash are the most common signals for pausing, and these are properly termed caesuras; pauses may also be achieved through syntax, lines, meter, rhyme, and the sound of words. The type of punctuation determines the length of the pause. Periods and question marks demand full stops, colons take almost a full stop, semicolons take a long pause, and commas take a short pause. The end of a line usually demands some pause even if there is no punctuation.

Cinquain: Any five-line stanza, including the madsong and the limerick. Cinquains are most often composed of a ballad stanza with an extra line added to the middle.

Classicism: A literary stance or value system consciously based on the example of classical Greek and Roman literature. Although the term is applied to an enormous diversity of artists in many different periods and in many different national literatures, classicism generally denotes a cluster of values including formal discipline, restrained expression, reverence for tradition, and an objective rather than a subjective orientation. As a literary tendency, classicism is often opposed to Romanticism, although many writers combine classical and romantic elements.

Conceit: A type of metaphor that uses a highly intellectualized comparison; an extended, elaborate, or complex metaphor. The term is frequently applied to the work of the Metaphysical poets, notably John Donne.

Connotation: An additional meaning for a word other than its denotative, formal definition. The word "mercenary," for example, simply means a soldier who is paid to fight in an army not of his own region, but connotatively a mercenary is an unprincipled scoundrel who kills for money and pleasure, not for honor and patriotism. Connotation is one of the most important devices for achieving irony, and readers may be fooled into believing a poem has one meaning because they have missed connotations that reverse the poem's apparent theme.

Consonance: Repetition or recurrence of the final consonants of stressed syllables without the correspondence of the preceding vowels. "Chair/star" is an example of consonance, since both words end with *r* preceded by different vowels. Terminal consonance creates half or slant rhyme (see *Approximate rhyme*). Consonance differs from alliteration in that the final consonants are repeated rather than the initial consonants. In the twentieth century, consonance became one of the principal rhyming devices, used to achieve formality without seeming stilted or old-fashioned.

Consonants: All letters except the vowels, *a, e, i, o, u,* and sometimes *y;* one of the most important sound-producing devices in poetry. There are five basic effects that certain consonants will produce: resonance, harshness, plosiveness, exhaustiveness, and liquidity. Resonance, exhaustiveness, and liquidity tend to give words—and consequently the whole line if several of these consonants are used—a soft effect. Plosiveness and harshness, on the other hand, tend to create tension. Resonance is the property of long duration produced by nasals, such as *n* and *m,* and by voiced fricating consonants such as *z, v,* and the voiced *th,* as in "them." Exhaustiveness is created by the voiceless fricating consonants and consonant combinations, such as *h, f,* and the voiceless *th* and *s.* Liquidity results from using the liquids and semivowels *l, r, w,* and *y,* as in the word "silken." Plosiveness occurs when certain consonants create a stoppage of breath before releasing it, especially *b, p, t, d, g, k, ch,* and *j.*

Controlling image/controlling metaphor: Just as a poem may include as structural devices form, theme, action, or dramatic situation, it may also use imagery for structure. When an image runs throughout a poem, giving unity to lesser images or ideas, it is called a controlling image. Usually the poet establishes a single idea and then expands and complicates it; in Edward Taylor's "Huswifery," for example, the image of the spinning wheel is expanded into images of weaving until the reader begins to see life as a tapestry. Robert Frost's "The Silken Tent" is a fine example of a controlling image and extended metaphor.

Couplet: Any two succeeding lines that rhyme. Because the couplet has been used in so many different ways and because of its long tradition in English poetry, various names and functions have been given to types of couplets. One of the most common is the decasyllabic (ten-syllable) couplet. When there is an end-stop on the second line of a couplet, it is said to be closed; an enjambed couplet is open. An end-stopped decasyllabic couplet is called a heroic couplet, because the form has often been used to sing the praise of heroes. The heroic couplet was widely used by the neoclassical poets of the eighteenth century. Because it is so stately and sometimes pompous, the heroic couplet invites satire, and many poems have been written in "mock-heroic verse," such as Alexander Pope's *The Rape of the Lock* (1712, 1714). Another commonly used couplet is the octasyllabic (eight-syllable) couplet, formed from two lines of iambic tetrameter, as in "L'Allegro" by John Milton: "Come, and trip as we go/ On the light fantastic toe." The light, singsong tone of the octasyllabic couplet also invited satire, and Samuel Butler wrote one of the most famous of all satires, *Hudibras* (1663, 1664, 1678), in this couplet. When a couplet is used to break another rhyme scheme, it generally produces a summing-up effect and has an air of profundity. William Shakespeare found this characteristic particularly useful when he needed to give his newly invented Shakespearean sonnet a final note of authority and purpose.

Dactyl: A foot formed of a stress followed by two unstressed syllables ($\prime\,\breve{}\,\breve{}$). It is fairly common in isolated words, but when this pattern is included in a line of poetry, it tends to break down and rearrange itself into components of other types of feet. Isolated, the word "meaningless" is a dactyl, but in the line "Polite/ meaning/less words," the last syllable becomes attached to the stressed "words" and creates a split foot, forming a trochee and an iamb. Nevertheless, a few dactylic poems do exist. "After the/pangs of a / desperate/lover" is a dactyllic line.

Deconstruction: An extremely influential contemporary school of criticism based on the works of the French philosopher Jacques Derrida. Deconstruction treats literary works as unconscious reflections of the reigning myths of Western culture. The primary myth is that there is a meaningful world that language signifies or represents. The deconstructionist critic is most often concerned with showing how a literary text tacitly subverts the very assumptions or myths on which it ostensibly rests.

Denotation: The explicit formal definition of a word, exclusive of its implications and emotional associations (see *Connotation*).

Depressed foot: A foot in which two syllables occur in a pattern in such a way as to be taken as one syllable without actually being an elision. In the line: "Tŏ eách/ hĕ boúl/děrs (thăt have)/fállĕn/tŏ eách," the base meter consists of five iambic feet, but in the third foot, there is an extra syllable that disrupts the meter but does not break it, so that "that have" functions as the second half of the iambic foot.

Diction: The poet's "choice of words," according to John Dryden. In Dryden's time, and for most of the history of English verse, the diction of poetry was elevated, sharply distinct from everyday speech. Since the early twentieth century, however, the diction of poetry has ranged from the banal and the conversational to the highly formal, and from obscenity and slang to technical vocabulary, sometimes in the same poem. The diction of a poem often reveals its persona's values and attitudes.

Dieresis: Caesuras that come after the foot (see *Split foot* for a discussion of caesuras that break feet). They can be used to create long pauses in the line and are often used to prepare the line for enjambment.

Dramatic dialogue: An exchange between two or more personas in a poem or a play. Unlike a dramatic monologue, both characters speak, and in the best dramatic dialogues, their conversation leads to a final resolution in which both characters and the reader come to the same realization at the same time.

Dramatic irony: See *Irony*

Dramatic monologue: An address to a silent person by a narrator; the words of the narrator are greatly influenced by the persona's presence. The principal reason for writing in dramatic monologue form is to control the speech of the major persona through the implied reaction of the silent one. The effect is one of continuing change and often surprise. In Robert Browning's "My Last Duchess," for example, the duke believes that he is in control of the situation, when in fact he has provided the emissary with terrible insights about the way he treated his former duchess. The emissary, who is the silent persona, has asked questions that the duke has answered; in doing so he has given away secrets. Dramatic monologue is somewhat like hearing one side of a telephone conversation in which the reader learns much about both participants.

Duration: The length of the syllables, which is the measure of quantitative meter. Duration can alter the tone and the relative stress of a line and influence meaning as much as the foot can.

Elegy: Usually a long, rhymed, strophic poem whose subject is meditation on death or a lamentable theme. The pastoral elegy uses the natural setting of a pastoral scene to sing of death or love. Within the pastoral setting the simplicity of the characters and the scene lends a peaceful air despite the grief the narrator feels.

Elision: The joining of two vowels into a single vowel (synaeresis) or omitting of a vowel altogether (syncope), usually to maintain a regular base meter. Synaeresis can be seen in the line "Of man's first disobedience, and the fruit," in which the "ie" in "disobedience" is pronounced as a "y" ("ye") so that the word reads dis/o/bed/yence, thereby making a five-syllable word into a four-syllable word. An example of syncope is when "natural" becomes "nat'ral" and "hastening" becomes "hast'ning." Less frequent uses of elision are to change the sound of a word, to spell words as they are pronounced, and to indicate dialect.

Emphasis: The highlighting of or calling attention to a phrase or line or a poem by altering its meter. A number of techniques, such as caesura, relative stress, counterpointing, and substitution can be used.

End rhyme: See *Rhyme*

End-stop: A punctuated pause at the end of a line in a poem. The function of end-stops is to show the relationship between lines and to emphasize particular words or lines. End-stopping in rhymed poems creates more emphasis on the rhyme words, which already carry a great deal of emphasis by virtue of their rhymes. Enjambment is the opposite of end-stopping.

Enjambment: When a line is not end-stopped—that is, when it carries over to the following line—the line is said to be "enjambed," as in John Milton's: "Avenge, O Lord, thy slaughtered saints, whose bones/ Lie scattered on the Alpine mountains cold." Enjambment is used to change the natural emphasis of the line, to strengthen or weaken the effect of rhyme, or to alter meter.

Envoy: Any short poem or stanza addressed to the reader as a beginning or end to a longer work. Specifically, the envoy is the final stanza of a sestina or a ballade in which all the rhyme words are repeated or echoed.

Epic: A long narrative poem that presents the exploits of a central figure of high position.

Extended metaphor: Metaphors added to one another so that they run in a series. Robert Frost's poem "The Silken Tent" uses an extended metaphor; it compares the "she" of the poem to the freedom and bondage of a silken tent. See also *Controlling image/controlling metaphor*.

Eye rhyme: Words that appear to be identical because of their spelling but that sound different. "Bough/ enough/cough" and "ballet/pallet" are examples. Because of changes in pronunciation, many older poems appear to use eye rhymes but do not. For example, "wind" (meaning moving air) once rhymed with "find." Eye rhymes that are intentional and do not result from a change in pronunciation may be used to create a disconcerting effect.

Fabliau: A bawdy medieval verse, such as many found in Geoffrey Chaucer's *The Canterbury Tales* (1387-1400).

Falling rhyme: Rhyme in which the correspondence of sound comes only in the final unstressed syllable, which is preceded by another unstressed syllable. T. S. Eliot rhymes "me-tic-u-lous" with "ri-dic-u-lous" and creates a falling rhyme. See also *Feminine rhyme*; *Masculine rhyme*.

Falling rhythm: A line in which feet move from stressed to unstressed syllables (trochaic or dactyllic). An example can be seen in this line from "The Naming

of Parts," by Henry Reed: "Glistens/like cor/al in/all of the/neighboring/gardens." Because English and other Germanic-based languages naturally rise, imposing a falling rhythm on a rising base meter creates counterpointing.

Feminine rhyme: A rhyme pattern in which a line's final accented syllable is followed by a single unaccented syllable and the accented syllables rhyme, while the unaccented syllables are phonetically identical, as with "flick-er/snick-er" and "fin-gers/ma-lin-gers." Feminine rhymes are often used for lightness in tone and delicacy in movement.

Feminist criticism: A criticism advocating equal rights for women in a political, economic, social, psychological, personal, and aesthetic sense. On the thematic level, the feminist reader should identify with female characters and their concerns. The object is to provide a critique of phallocentric assumptions and an analysis of patriarchal ideologies inscribed in male-centered and male-dominated literature. On the ideological level, feminist critics see gender, as well as the stereotypes that go along with it, as a cultural construct. They strive to define a particularly feminine content and to extend the canon so that it might include works by lesbians, feminists, women of color, and women writers in general.

First person: The use of linguistic forms that present a poem from the point of view of the speaker. It is particularly useful in short lyrical poems, which tend to be highly subjective, taking the reader deep into the narrator's thoughts. First-person poems normally, though not necessarily, signal the use of the first person through the pronoun "I," allowing the reader direct access to the narrator's thoughts or providing a character who can convey a personal reaction to an event. See also *Third person*.

Foot/feet: Rhythmic unit in which syllables are grouped together; this is the natural speech pattern in English and other Germanic-based languages. In English, the most common of these rhythmic units is composed of one unstressed syllable attached to one stressed syllable (an iamb). When these family groups are forced into a line of poetry, they are called feet in the accentual-syllabic metrical system. In the line "My mis/tress' eyes/are noth/ing like/the sun" there are four iambic feet ($\smile\prime$) and one pyrrhic foot ($\smile\smile$), but in the line "There where/the vines/cling crim/son on/the wall," there are three substitutions for the iamb—in the first, third, and fourth feet. The six basic feet in English poetry are the iamb ($\smile\prime$), trochee ($\prime\smile$), anapest ($\smile\smile\prime$), dactyl ($\prime\smile\smile$), spondee ($\prime\prime$), and pyrrhus ($\smile\smile$).

Form: The arrangement of the lines of a poem on the page, its base meter, its rhyme scheme, and occasionally its subject matter. Poems that are arranged into stanzas are called strophic, and because the strophic tradition is so old, a large number of commonly used stanzas have evolved particular uses and characteristics. Poems that run from beginning to end without a break are called stichic. The form of pattern poetry is determined by its visual appearance rather than by lines and stanzas, while the definition of free verse is that it has no discernible form. Some poem types, such as the sestina, sonnet, and ode, are written in particular forms and frequently are restricted to particular subject matter.

Formalism, Russian: A twentieth century Russian school of criticism that employed the conventional devices used in literature to defamiliarize that which habit has made familiar. The most extreme formalists treated literary works as artifacts or constructs divorced from their biographical and social contexts.

Found poetry: Poems created from language that is "found" in print in nonliterary settings. They can use any language that is already constructed, but usually use language that appears on cultural artifacts, such as cereal boxes. The rules for writing a found poem vary, but generally the found language is used intact or altered only slightly.

Free verse: A poem that does not conform to any traditional convention, such as meter, rhyme, or form, and that does not establish any pattern within itself. There is, however, great dispute over whether "free" verse actually exists. T. S. Eliot said that by definition poetry must establish some kind of pattern, and Robert Frost said that "writing free verse is like playing tennis with the net down." However, some would agree with Carl Sandburg, who insisted that "you can play a better game with the net down." Free verse depends more on cadence than on meter.

Ghazal: A poetic form based on a type of Persian poetry. It is composed of couplets, often unrhymed,

that function as individual images or observations but that also interrelate in sometimes subtle ways.

Gnomic verse: Poetry that typically includes many proverbs or maxims.

Haiku: A Japanese form that appeared in the sixteenth century and is still practiced in Japan. A haiku consists of three lines of five, seven, and five syllables each; in Japanese there are other conventions regarding content that are not observed in Western haiku. The traditional haiku took virtually all of its images from nature, using the natural world as a metaphor for the spiritual.

Half rhyme: See *Approximate rhyme*

Heroic couplet: See *Couplet*

Historical criticism: A school of criticism that emphasizes the historical context of literature. Ernst Robert Curtius's *European Literature and the Latin Middle Ages* (1940) is a prominent example of historical criticism.

Hymn stanza: See *Ballad*

Hyperbole: A deliberate overstatement made in order to heighten the reader's awareness. As with irony, hyperbole works because the reader can perceive the difference between the importance of the dramatic situation and the manner in which it is described.

Iamb: A foot consisting of one unstressed and one stressed syllable ($\smile\prime$). The line "So long/as men/can breathe/or eyes/can see" is composed of five iambs. In the line "A cold/coming/we had/of it," a trochaic foot (a trochee) has been substituted for the expected iamb in the second foot, thus emphasizing that this is a "coming" rather than a "going," an important distinction in T. S. Eliot's "The Journey of the Magi."

Iambic pentameter: A very common poetic line consisting of five iambic feet. The following two lines by Thomas Wyatt are in iambic pentameter: "I find no peace and all my war is done,/ I fear and hope, I burn and freeze like ice." See also *Foot/feet*; *iamb*.

Identical rhyme: A rhyme in which the entire final stressed syllables contain exactly the same sounds, such as "break/brake," or "bear" (noun), "bear" (verb), "bare" (adjective), "bare" (verb).

Imagery: The verbal simulation of sensory perception. Like so many critical terms, imagery betrays a visual bias: It suggests that a poetic image is necessarily visual, a picture in words. In fact, however, imagery calls on all five senses, although the visual is predominant in many poets. In its simplest form, an image re-creates a physical sensation in a clear, literal manner, as in Robert Lowell's lines, "A sweetish smell of shavings, wax and oil/ blows through the redone bedroom newly aged" ("Marriage"). Imagery becomes more complex when the poet employs metaphor and other figures of speech to re-create experience, as in Seamus Heaney's lines, "Right along the lough shore/ A smoke of flies/ Drifts thick in the sunset" ("At Ardboe Point"), substituting a fresh metaphor ("A smoke of flies") for a trite one (a cloud of flies) to help the reader visualize the scene more clearly.

Interior monologue: A first-person representation of a persona's or character's thoughts or feelings. It differs from a dramatic monologue in that it deals with thoughts rather than spoken words or conversation.

Internal rhyme: See *Rhyme*

Irony: A figure of speech in which the speaker's real meaning is different from (and often exactly opposite to) the apparent meaning. Irony is among the three or four most important concepts in modern literary criticism. Although the term originated in classical Greece and has been in the vocabulary of criticism since that time, only in the nineteenth and twentieth centuries did it assume central importance. In Andrew Marvell's lines, "The Grave's a fine and private place,/ But none I think do there embrace" ("To His Coy Mistress"), the speaker's literal meaning—in praise of the grave—is quite different from his real meaning. This kind of irony is often called verbal irony. Another kind of irony is found in narrative and dramatic poetry. In the *Iliad* (c. 750 B.C.E.; English translation, 1611), for example, the reader is made privy to the counsels of the gods, which greatly affect the course of action in the epic, while the human characters are kept in ignorance. This discrepancy between the knowledge of the reader and that of the character (or characters) is called dramatic irony. Beyond these narrow, well-defined varieties of irony are many wider applications.

Limerick: A comic five-line poem rhyming *aabba* in which the third and fourth lines are shorter (usually five syllables each) than the first, second, and last lines, which are usually eight syllables each. The limerick's anapestic base makes the verse sound silly; modern limericks are almost invariably associated with bizarre indecency or with ethnic or anticlerical jokes.

Line: A poetical unit characterized by the presence of meter; lines are categorized according to the number of feet (see *Foot/feet*) they contain. A pentameter line, for example, contains five feet. This definition does not apply to a great deal of modern poetry, however, which is written in free verse. Ultimately, then, a line must be defined as a typographical unit on the page that performs various functions in different kinds of poetry.

Lyric poetry: Short poems, adaptable to metrical variation, and usually personal rather than having a cultural function. Lyric poetry developed when music was accompanied by words, and although the lyrics were later separated from the music, the characteristics of lyric poetry have been shaped by the constraints of music. Lyric poetry sings of the self, exploring deeply personal feelings about life.

Mad-song: Verse uttered by someone presumed to have a severe mental illness that manifests in a happy, harmless, inventive way. The typical rhyme scheme of the mad-song is *abccb*, and the unrhymed first line helps to set a tone of oddity and unpredictability, since it controverts the expectation that there will be a rhyme for it. The standard mad-song has short lines.

Marxist criticism: A school of criticism based on the nineteenth century writings of Karl Marx and Friedrich Engels that views literature as a product of ideological forces determined by the dominant class However, many Marxists believe that literature operates according to its own autonomous standards of production and reception: It is both a product of ideology and able to determine ideology. As such, literature may overcome the dominant paradigms of its age and play a revolutionary role in society.

Masculine rhyme: A rhyme pattern in which rhyme exists in the stressed syllables. "Men/then" constitute masculine rhyme, but so do "af-tĕr-nóons/spoóns." Masculine rhyme is generally considered more forceful than feminine rhyme, and while it has a variety of uses, it generally gives authority and assurance to the line, especially when the final syllables are of short duration.

Metaphor: A figure of speech in which two strikingly different things are identified with each other, as in "the waves were soldiers moving" (Wallace Stevens). Metaphor is one of a handful of key concepts in modern literary criticism. A metaphor contains a "tenor" and a "vehicle." The tenor is the subject of the metaphor, and the vehicle is the imagery by which the subject is presented. In D. H. Lawrence's lines, "Reach me a gentian, give me a torch/ let me guide myself with the blue, forked torch of this flower" ("Bavarian Gentians"), the tenor is the gentian and the vehicle is the torch. This relatively restricted definition of metaphor by no means covers the usage of the word in modern criticism. Some critics argue that metaphorical perception underlies all figures of speech. Others dispute the distinction between literal and metaphorical description, saying that language is essentially metaphorical. Metaphor has become widely used to identify analogies of all kinds in literature, painting, film, and even music. See also *Simile*.

Meter: The pattern that language takes when it is forced into a line of poetry. All language has rhythm; when that rhythm is organized and regulated in the line so as to affect the meaning and emotional response to the words, then the rhythm has been refined into meter. Because the lines of most poems maintain a similar meter throughout, poems are said to have a base meter. The meter is determined by the number of syllables in a line and by the relationship between them.

Metrical base. See *Base meter*

Metonymy: Using an object that is closely related to an idea stand for the idea itself, such as saying "the crown" to mean the king. Used to emphasize a particular part of the whole or one particular aspect of it. See also *Synecdoche*.

Mnemonic verse: Poetry in which rhythmic patterns aid memorization but are not crucial to meaning. Ancient bards were able to remember long poems partly through the use of stock phrases and other mnemonic devices.

Mock-heroic: See *Couplet*

Modernism: An international movement in the arts that began in the early years of the twentieth century. Although the term is used to describe artists of widely varying persuasions, modernism in general was characterized by its international idiom, by its interest in cultures distant in space or time, by its emphasis on for-

mal experimentation, and by its sense of dislocation and radical change.

Multiculturalism: The tendency to recognize the perspectives of works by authors (particularly women and non-European writers) who, until the latter part of the twentieth century, were excluded from the canon of Western art and literature. To promote multiculturalism, publishers and educators have revised textbooks and school curricula to incorporate material by and about women, ethnic and racial minorities, non-Western cultures, gays, and lesbians.

Myth: Anonymous traditional stories dealing with basic human concepts and antinomies. Claude Lévi-Strauss says that myth is that part of language where the "formula *tradutore, traditore* reaches its lowest truth value. . . . Its substance does not lie in its style, its original music, or its syntax, but in the story which it tells."

Myth criticism: A school of criticism concerned with the basic structural principles of literature. Myth criticism is not to be confused with mythological criticism, which is primarily concerned with finding mythological parallels in the surface action of a narrative.

Narrator: The person who is doing the talking—or observing or thinking—in a poem. Roughly synonymous with persona and speaker. Lyric poetry most often consists of the poet expressing his or her own personal feelings directly. Other poems, however, may involve the poet adopting the point of view of another person entirely. In some poems—notably in a dramatic monologue—it is relatively easy to determine that the narrative is being related by a fictional (or perhaps historical) character, but in others it may be more difficult to identify the "I."

New Criticism: A formalist movement whose members held that literary criticism is a description and evaluation of its object and that the primary concern of the critic is with the work's unity. At their most extreme, these critics treated literary works as artifacts or constructs divorced from their biographical and social contexts.

Occasional verse: Any poem written for a specific occasion, such as a wedding, a birthday, a death, or a public event. Edmund Spenser's *Epithalamion* (1595), which was written for his marriage, and John Milton's "Lycidas," which commemorated the death of his schoolmate Edward King, are examples of occasional verse, as are W. H. Auden's "September 1, 1939" and Frank O'Hara's "The Day Lady Died."

Octave: A poem in eight lines. Octaves may have many different variations of meter, such as ottava rima.

Ode: A lyric poem that treats a unified subject with elevated emotion, usually ending with a satisfactory resolution. There is no set form for the ode, but it must be long enough to build intense emotional response. Often the ode will address itself to some omnipotent source and will take on a spiritual hue. When explicating an ode, readers should look for the relationship between the narrator and some transcendental power to which the narrator must submit to find contentment. Modern poets have used the ode to treat subjects that are not religious in the theological sense but that have become innate beliefs of society.

Ottava rima: An eight-line stanza of iambic pentameter, rhyming *abababcc*. Probably the most famous English poem written in ottava rima is Lord Byron's *Don Juan* (1819-1824), and because the poem was so successful as a spoof, the form has come to be associated with poetic high jinks. However, the stanza has also been used brilliantly for just the opposite effect, to reflect seriousness and meditation.

Oxymoron: The juxtaposition of two paradoxical words, such as "wise fool" or "devilish angel."

Pantoum: A French form of poetry consisting of four quatrains in which entire lines are repeated in a strict pattern of 1234, 2546, 5768, 7183. Peter Meinke's "Atomic Pantoum" is an example.

Paradox: A statement that contains an inherent contradiction. It may be a statement that at first seems true but is in reality contradictory. It may also be a statement that appears contradictory but is actually true or that contains an element of truth that reconciles the contradiction.

Pentameter: A type of rhythmic pattern in which each line consists of five poetic feet. See also *Accentual-syllabic meter*; *Foot/feet*; *Iamb*; *Iambic pentameter*; *Line*.

Periphrasis: The use of a wordy phrase to describe something that could be described simply in one word.

Persona: See *Narrator*

Phenomenological criticism: A school of criticism that examines literature as an act and focuses less on individual works and genres. The work is not seen as an object, but rather as part of a strand of latent impulses in the work of a single author or an epoch. Proponents include Georges Poulet in Europe and J. Hillis Miller in the United States.

Point of view: The mental position through which readers experience the situation of a poem. As with fiction, poems may be related in the first person, second person (unusual), or third person. (The presence of the words "I" or "we" indicates singular or plural first-person narration.) Point of view may be limited or omniscient. A limited point of view means that the narrator can see only what the poet wants him or her to see, while from an omniscient point of view the narrator can know everything, including the thoughts and motives of others.

Postcolonialism: The literature that emerged in the mid-twentieth century when colonies in Asia, Africa, and the Caribbean began gaining their independence from the European nations that had long controlled them. Postcolonial authors, such as Salman Rushdie, V. S. Naipaul, and Derek Walcott, tend to focus on both the freedom and the conflict inherent in living in a postcolonial state.

Postmodernism: A ubiquitous but elusive term in contemporary criticism that is loosely applied to the various artistic movements that followed the era of so-called high modernism, represented by such giants as writer James Joyce and painter and sculptor Pablo Picasso. In critical discussions of contemporary fiction, postmodernism is frequently applied to the works of writers such as Thomas Pynchon, John Barth, and Donald Barthelme, who exhibit a self-conscious awareness of their modernist predecessors as well as a reflexive treatment of fictional form. Such reflexive treatments can extend to poetry as well.

Prose poem: A poem that looks like prose on the page, with no line breaks. There are no formal characteristics by which a prose poem can be distinguished from a piece of prose. Many prose poems employ rhythmic repetition and other poetic devices not normally found in prose, but others use such devices sparingly if at all. Prose poems range in length from a few lines to three or four pages; most prose poems occupy a page or less.

Psychological criticism: A school of criticism that places a strong emphasis on a causal relation between the writer's psychological state, variously interpreted, and his or her works. A notable example of psychological criticism is Norman Fruman's *Coleridge, the Damaged Archangel* (1971).

Pun: The use of words that have similar pronunciations but entirely different meanings to establish a connection between two meanings or contexts that the reader would not ordinarily make. The result may be a surprise recognition of an unusual or striking connection, or, more often, a humorously accidental connection.

Pyrrhus: A poetic foot consisting of two unstressed syllables, as in the line "Appear/and dis/appear/in the/ blue depth/of the sky," in which foot four is a pyrrhus.

Quatrain: Any four-line stanza. Aside from the couplet, it is the most common stanza type. The quatrain's popularity among both sophisticated and unsophisticated readers suggests that there is something inherently pleasing about the form. For many readers, poetry and quatrains are almost synonymous. Balance and antithesis, contrast and comparison not possible in other stanza types are indigenous to the quatrain.

Realism: A literary technique in which the primary convention is to render an illusion of fidelity to external reality. Realism is often identified as the primary method of the novel form: It focuses on surface details, maintains a fidelity to the everyday experiences of middle-class society, and strives for a one-to-one relationship between the fiction and the action imitated. The realist movement in the late nineteenth century coincides with the full development of the novel form.

Regular meter: A line of poetry that contains only one type of foot. Only the dullest of poems maintain a regular meter throughout, however; skillful poets create interest and emphasis through substitution.

Relative stress: The degree to which a syllable in pattern receives more or less emphasis than other syllables in the pattern. Once the dominant stress in the line has been determined, every other syllable can be assigned a stress factor relative to the dominant syllable. The stress factor is created by several aspects of prosody: the position of the syllable in the line, the position of the syllable in its word, the surrounding syllables, the type of vowels and consonants that constitute the syllable, and the syllable's relation to the foot, base meter, and caesura. Because every syllable will have a different stress factor, there could be as many values as there are syllables, although most prosodists scan poems using primary, secondary, and unstressed notations. In the line "I am there like the dead, or the beast," the anapestic base meter will not permit "I" to take a full stress, but it is a more forceful syllable than the unstressed ones, so it is assigned a secondary stress. Relative to "dead" and "beast," it takes less pressure; relative to the articles in the line, it takes much more.

Resolution: Any natural conclusion to a poem, especially to a short lyric poem that establishes some sort of dilemma or conflict that the narrator must solve. Specifically, the resolution is the octave stanza of a Petrarchan sonnet or the couplet of a Shakespearean sonnet in which the first part of the poem prents a situation that must find balance in the resolution.

Rhyme: A correspondence of sound between syllables within a line or between lines whose proximity to each other allows the sounds to be sustained. Rhyme may be classified in a number of ways: according to the sound relationship between rhyming words, the position of the rhyming words in the line, and the number and position of the syllables in the rhyming words. Sound classifications include full rhyme and approximate rhyme. Full rhyme is defined as words that have the same vowel sound, followed by the same consonants in their last stressed syllables, and in which all succeeding syllables are phonetically identical. "Hat/ cat" and "laughter/after" are full rhymes. Categories of approximate rhyme are assonance, slant rhyme, alliteration, eye rhyme, and identical rhyme.

Rhyme classified by its position in the line includes end, internal, and initial rhyme. End rhyme occurs when the last words of lines rhyme. Internal rhyme occurs when two words within the same line or within various lines recall the same sound, as in "Wet, below the snow line, smelling of vegetation" in which "below" and "snow" rhyme. Initial rhyme occurs when the first syllables of two or more lines rhyme. See also *Masculine rhyme*; *Feminine rhyme*.

Rhyme scheme: A pattern of rhyme in a poem, designated by lowercase (and often italicized) letters. The letters stand for the pattern of rhyming sounds of the last word in each line. For example, the following A. E. Housman quatrain has an *abab* rhyme scheme.

> Into my heart an air that kills
> From yon far country blows:
> What are those blue remembered hills,
> What spires, what farms are those?

As another example, the rhyme scheme of the poetic form known as ottava rima is *abababcc*. Traditional stanza forms are categorized by their rhyme scheme and base meter.

Rime royal: A seven-line stanza in English prosody consisting of iambic pentameter lines rhyming *ababbccc*. William Shakespeare's *The Rape of Lucrece* (1594) is written in this form. The only variation permitted is to make the last line hexameter.

Romanticism: A widespread cultural movement in the late eighteenth and early nineteenth centuries, the influence of which is still felt. As a general literary tendency, Romanticism is frequently contrasted with classicism or neoclassicism. Although there were many varieties of Romanticism indigenous to various national literatures, the term generally suggests an assertion of the preeminence of the imagination. Other values associated with various schools of Romanticism include primitivism, an interest in folklore, a reverence for nature, and a fascination with the demoniac and the macabre.

Rondeau: One of three standard French forms assimilated by English prosody; generally contains thirteen lines divided into three groups. A common stanzaic grouping rhymes *aabba, aabR, aabbaR*, where the *a* and *b* lines are tetrameter and the *R* (refrain) lines are dimeter. The rondel, another French form, contains fourteen lines of trimeter with alternating rhyme (*ababab ababab*) and is divided into two stanzas. The rondeau and rondel forms are always light and playful.

Rondel: See *Rondeau*

Rubaiyat stanza: An iambic pentameter quatrain that has a rhyme scheme of *aaba*.

Scansion: The assigning of relative stresses and meter to a line of poetry, usually for the purpose of determining where variations, and thus emphasis, in the base meter occur. Scansion can help explain how a poem

generates tension and offer clues as to the key words. E. E. Cummings's "singing each morning out of each night" could be scanned in two ways: (1) singing/each morn/ing out/of each night or (2) sing/ing each/morning/out of/each night. Scansion will not only affect the way the line is read aloud but also influences the meaning of the line.

Secondary stress: See *Relative stress*

Seguidilla: An imagistic or mood poem in Spanish, which, like a haiku, creates emotional recognition or spiritual insight in the reader. Although there is no agreement as to what form the English seguidilla should take, most of the successful ones are either four or seven lines with an alternating rhyme scheme of *ababcbc*. Lines 1, 3, and 6 are trimeter; lines 2, 4, 5, and 7 dimeter.

Semiotics: The science of signs and sign systems in communication. Literary critic Roman Jakobson says that semiotics deals with the principles that underlie the structure of signs, their use in language of all kinds, and the specific nature of various sign systems.

Sestet: A six-line stanza. A Petrarchan or Italian sonnet is composed of an octave followed by a sestet.

Sestina: Six six-line stanzas followed by a three-line envoy. The words ending the lines in the first stanza are repeated in different order at the ends of lines in the following stanzas as well as in the middle and end of each line of the envoy. Elizabeth Bishop's "Sestina" is a good example.

Shakespearean sonnet: See *Sonnet*

Simile: A type of metaphor that signals a comparison by the use of the words "like" or "as." William Shakespeare's line "My mistress' eyes are nothing like the sun" is a simile that establishes a comparison between the woman's eyes and the sun. See also *Metaphor*.

Slant rhyme: See *Approximate rhyme*

Sonnet: A poem consisting of fourteen lines of iambic pentameter with some form of alternating rhyme and a turning point that divides the poem into two parts. The sonnet is the most important and widely used of traditional poem types. The two major sonnet types are the Petrarchan (or Italian) sonnet and the Shakespearean sonnet. The original sonnet form, the Petrarchan (adopted from the poetry of Petrarch), presents a problem or situation in the first eight lines, the octave, then resolves it in the last six, the sestet. The octave is composed of two quatrains (*abbaabba*), the second of which complicates the first and gradually defines and heightens the problem. The sestet then diminishes the problem slowly until a satisfying resolution is achieved.

During the fifteenth century, the Italian sonnet became an integral part of the courtship ritual, and most sonnets during that time consisted of a young man's description of his perfect lover. Because so many unpoetic young men had generated a nation full of bad sonnets by the end of the century, the form became an object of ridicule, and the English sonnet developed as a reaction against all the bad verse being turned out in the Italian tradition. When Shakespeare wrote "My mistress' eyes are nothing like the sun," he was deliberately negating the Petrarchan conceit, rejoicing in the fact that his loved one was much more interesting and unpredictable than nature. Shakespeare also altered the sonnet's formal balance. Instead of an octave, the Shakespearean sonnet has three quatrains of alternating rhyme and is resolved in a final couplet. During the sixteenth century, long stories were told in sonnet form, one sonnet after the next, to produce sonnet sequences. Although most sonnets contain fourteen lines, some contain as few as ten (the curtal sonnet) or as many as seventeen.

Speaker: See *Narrator*

Split foot: The alteration of the natural division of a word as a result of being forced into a metrical base. For example, the words "point/ed," "lad/der," and "stick/ing" have a natural falling rhythm, but in the line "My long/two-point/ed lad/der's stick/ing through/a tree" the syllables are rearranged so as to turn the falling rhythm into a rising meter. The result of splitting feet is to create an uncertainty and delicate imbalance in the line.

Spondee: When two relatively stressed syllables occur together in a foot, the unit is called a spondee or spondaic foot, as in the line "Appear/and dis/appear/in the/blue depth/of the sky."

Sprung rhythm: An unpredictable pattern of stresses in a line, first described near the end of the nineteenth century by Gerard Manley Hopkins, that results from taking accentual meter is to its extreme. According to Hopkins, in sprung rhythm "any two stresses may either follow one another running, or be divided by one, two, or three slack syllables."

Stanza: A certain number of lines meant to be taken as a unit, or that unit. Although a stanza is traditionally considered a unit that contains rhyme and recurs predictably throughout a poem, the term is also sometimes applied to nonrhyming and even irregular units. Poems that are divided into fairly regular and patterned stanzas are called strophic; poems that appear as a single unit, whether rhymed or unrhymed, or that have no predictable stanzas, are called stichic. Both strophic and stichic units represent logical divisions within the poem, and the difference between them lies in the formality and strength of the interwoven unit. Stanza breaks are commonly indicated by a line of space.

Stichic verse: See *Stanza*

Stress: See *Relative stress*

Strophic verse: See *Stanza*

Structuralism: A movement based on the idea of intrinsic, self-sufficient structures that do not require reference to external elements. A structure is a system of transformations that involves the interplay of laws inherent in the system itself. The study of language is the primary model for contemporary structuralism. The structuralist literary critic attempts to define structural principles that operate intertextually throughout the whole of literature as well as principles that operate in genres and in individual works. The most accessible survey of structuralism and literature is Jonathan Culler's *Structuralist Poetics* (1975).

Substitution: The replacement of one type of foot by another within a base meter. One of the most common and effective methods by which the poet can emphasize a foot. For example, in the line "Thy life/a long/dead calm/of fixed/repose," a spondaic foot (′ ′) has been substituted for an iambic foot (◡ ′). Before substitution is possible, the reader's expectations must have been established by a base meter so that a change in those expectations will have an effect. See also *Foot/feet*; *iamb*; *spondee*.

Syllabic meter: The system of meter that measures only the number of syllables per line, without regard to stressed and unstressed syllables.

Symbol: Any sign that a number of people agree stands for something else. Poetic symbols cannot be rigidly defined; a symbol often evokes a cluster of meanings rather than a single specific meaning. For example, the rose, which suggests fragile beauty, gentleness, softness, and sweet aroma, has come to symbolize love, eternal beauty, or virginity. The tide traditionally symbolizes, among other things, time and eternity. Modern poets may use personal symbols; these take on significance in the context of the poem or of a poet's body of work, particularly if they are reinforced throughout. For example, through constant reinforcement, swans in William Butler Yeats's poetry come to mean as much to the reader as they do to the narrator.

Synaeresis: See *Elision*

Synecdoche: The use of a part of an object to stand for the entire object, such as using "heart" to mean a person. Used to emphasize a particular part of the whole or one particular aspect of it. See also *Metonymy.*

Tenor: See *Metaphor*

Tercet: Any form of a rhyming triplet. Examples are *aaa bbb*, as used in Thomas Hardy's "Convergence of the Twain"; *aba cdc*, in which *b* and *d* do not rhyme; *aba bcb*, also known as terza rima.

Terza rima: A three-line stanzaic form in which the middle line of one stanza rhymes with the first line of the following stanza, and whose rhyme scheme is *aba bcb cdc*, and so on. Since the rhyme scheme of one stanza can be completed only by adding the next stanza, terza rima tends to propel itself forward, and as a result of this strong forward motion it is well suited to long narration.

Theme: Recurring elements in a poem that give it meaning; sometimes used interchangeably with motif. A motif is any recurring pattern of images, symbols, ideas, or language, and is usually restricted to the internal workings of the poem. Thus, one might say that there is an animal motif in William Butler Yeats's poem "Sailing to Byzantium." Theme, however, is usually more general and philosophical, so that the theme of "Sailing to Byzantium" might be interpreted as the failure of human attempts to isolate oneself within the world of art.

Third person: The use of linguistic forms that present a poem from the point of view of a narrator, or speaker, who has not been part of the events described and is not probing his or her own relationship to them; rather, the speaker is describing what happened without the use of the word "I" (which would indicate first-person narration). A poet may use a third-person point of view, either limited or omniscient, to establish a distance between the reader and the subject, to give credi-

bility to a large expanse of narration, or to allow the poem to include a number of characters who can be commented on by the narrator.

Tone: The expression of a poet's attitude toward the subject and persona of the poem as well as about himself or herself, society, and the poem's readers. If the ultimate aim of art is to express and control emotions and attitudes, then tone is one of the most important elements of poetry. Tone is created through the denotative and connotative meanings of words and through the sound of language (principally rhyme, consonants, and diction). Adjectives such as "satirical," "compassionate," "empathetic," "ironic," and "sarcastic" are used to describe tone.

Trochee: A foot with one stressed syllable and one unstressed syllable (ˊ˘), as in the line: "Dóublĕ/dóublĕ toíl ănd/troúblĕ." Trochaic lines are frequently substituted in an iambic base meter in order to create counterpointing. See also *Foot/feet; iamb.*

Truncation: The omission of the last, unstressed syllable of a falling line, as in the line: "Týgĕr,/týgĕr/búrnĭng/bríght," where the "ly" has been dropped from bright.

Vehicle: See *Metaphor*

Verse: A generic term for poetry, as in *The Oxford Book of English Verse* (1939); poetry that is humorous or superficial, as in light verse or greeting-card verse; and a stanza or line.

Verse drama: Drama that is written in poetic rather than ordinary language and characterized and delivered by the line. Verse drama flourished during the eighteenth century, when the couplet became a standard literary form.

Verse paragraph: A division created within a stichic poem (see *Stanza*) by logic or syntax, rather than by form. Such divisions are important for determining the movement of a poem and the logical association between ideas.

Villanelle: A French verse form that has been assimilated by English prosody, usually composed of nineteen lines divided into five tercets and a quatrain, rhyming *aba, bba, aba, aba, abaa*. The third line is repeated in the ninth and fifteenth lines. Dylan Thomas's "Do Not Go Gentle into That Good Night" is a modern English example of a villanelle.

BIBLIOGRAPHY

CONTENTS

ABOUT THIS BIBLIOGRAPHY

This bibliography contains three main sections. The first, "General Reference Sources," lists books that treat poetry of all time periods and countries, including European poets. The section "History of World Poetry" covers sources primarily relevant to poetry from these countries written in three different eras. The final section, "Poets by Country or Region," divides poets and poetry geographically.

GENERAL REFERENCE SOURCES

BIOGRAPHICAL SOURCES

Colby, Vineta, ed. *World Authors, 1975-1980*. Wilson Authors Series. New York: H. W. Wilson, 1985.

_____. *World Authors, 1980-1985*. Wilson Authors Series. New York: H. W. Wilson, 1991.

_____. *World Authors, 1985-1990*. Wilson Authors Series. New York: H. W. Wilson, 1995.

Cyclopedia of World Authors. 4th rev. ed. 5 vols. Pasadena, Calif.: Salem Press, 2003.

Dictionary of Literary Biography. 254 vols. Detroit: Gale Research, 1978-   .

International Who's Who in Poetry and Poets' Encyclopaedia. Cambridge, England: International Biographical Centre, 1993.

Serafin, Steven R. *Encyclopedia of World Literature in the Twentieth Century*. 3d ed. 4 vols. Detroit: St. James Press, 1999.

Seymour-Smith, Martin, and Andrew C. Kimmens, eds. *World Authors, 1900-1950*. Wilson Authors Series. 4 vols. New York: H. W. Wilson, 1996.

Solé, Carlos A., ed. *Latin American Writers*. 3 vols. New York: Scribner, 1989.

Thompson, Clifford, ed. *World Authors, 1990-1995*. Wilson Authors Series. New York: H. W. Wilson, 1999.

Wakeman, John, ed. *World Authors, 1950-1970*. New York: H. W. Wilson, 1975.

_____. *World Authors, 1970-1975*. Wilson Authors Series. New York: H. W. Wilson, 1991.

Willhardt, Mark, and Alan Michael Parker, eds. *Who's Who in Twentieth Century World Poetry*. New York: Routledge, 2000.

CRITICISM

Brooks, Cleanth, and Robert Penn Warren. *Understanding Poetry*. 4th ed. Reprint. Fort Worth, Tex.: Heinle & Heinle, 2003.

Classical and Medieval Literature Criticism. Detroit: Gale Research, 1988-   .

Contemporary Literary Criticism. Detroit: Gale Research, 1973-   .

Day, Gary. *Literary Criticism: A New History*. Edinburgh, Scotland: Edinburgh University Press, 2008.

Draper, James P., ed. *World Literature Criticism 1500 to the Present: A Selection of Major Authors from Gale's Literary Criticism Series*. 6 vols. Detroit: Gale Research, 1992.

Habib, M. A. R. *A History of Literary Criticism: From Plato to the Present*. Malden, Mass.: Wiley-Blackwell, 2005.

Jason, Philip K., ed. *Masterplots II: Poetry Series, Revised Edition*. 8 vols. Pasadena, Calif.: Salem Press, 2002.

Krstovic, Jelena, ed. *Hispanic Literature Criticism*. Detroit: Gale Research, 1994.

Literature Criticism from 1400 to 1800. Detroit: Gale Research, 1984-   .

Lodge, David, and Nigel Wood. *Modern Criticism and Theory*. 3d ed. New York: Longman, 2008.

Magill, Frank N., ed. *Magill's Bibliography of Literary Criticism*. 4 vols. Englewood Cliffs, N.J.: Salem Press, 1979.

MLA International Bibliography. New York: Modern Language Association of America, 1922-   .

Nineteenth-Century Literature Criticism. Detroit: Gale Research, 1981-   .

Twentieth-Century Literary Criticism. Detroit: Gale Research, 1978-   .

Vedder, Polly, ed. *World Literature Criticism Supplement: A Selection of Major Authors from Gale's Literary Criticism Series*. 2 vols. Detroit: Gale Research, 1997.

The Year's Work in Modern Language Studies. London: Oxford University Press, 1931.

Young, Robyn V., ed. *Poetry Criticism: Excerpts from Criticism of the Works of the Most Significant and Widely Studied Poets of World Literature*. 29 vols. Detroit: Gale Research, 1991.

DICTIONARIES, HISTORIES, AND HANDBOOKS

Carey, Gary, and Mary Ellen Snodgrass. *A Multicultural Dictionary of Literary Terms*. Jefferson, N.C.: McFarland, 1999.

Deutsch, Babette. *Poetry Handbook: A Dictionary of Terms*. 4th ed. New York: Funk & Wagnalls, 1974.

Drury, John. *The Poetry Dictionary*. Cincinnati, Ohio: Story Press, 1995.

France, Peter, ed. *The Oxford Guide to Literature in English Translation*. New York: Oxford University Press, 2000.

Henderson, Lesley, ed. *Reference Guide to World Literature*. 2d ed. 2 vols. New York: St. James Press, 1995.

Kinzie, Mary. *A Poet's Guide to Poetry*. Chicago: University of Chicago Press, 1999.

Lennard, John. *The Poetry Handbook: A Guide to Reading Poetry for Pleasure and Practical Criticism*. New York: Oxford University Press, 1996.

Matterson, Stephen, and Darryl Jones. *Studying Poetry*. New York: Oxford University Press, 2000.

Ostle, Robin, ed. *Modern Literature in the Near and Middle East, 1850-1970*. Routledge/SOAS Contemporary Politics and Culture in the Middle East Series. New York: Routledge, 1991.

Packard, William. *The Poet's Dictionary: A Handbook of Prosody and Poetic Devices*. New York: Harper & Row, 1989.

Preminger, Alex, et al., eds. *The New Princeton Encyclopedia of Poetry and Poetics*. 3d rev. ed. Princeton, N.J.: Princeton University Press, 1993.

Prusek, Jaroslav, ed. *Dictionary of Oriental Literatures*. 3 vols. Vol. 1, *East Asia*, edited by Z. Shupski; Vol. 2, *South and South-East Asia*, edited by D. Zbavitel; Vol. 3, *West Asia and North Africa*, edited by J. Becka. New York: Basic Books, 1974.

Shipley, Joseph Twadell, ed. *Dictionary of World Literary Terms, Forms, Technique, Criticism*. Rev. ed. Boston: Writer, 1970.

INDEXES OF PRIMARY WORKS

Frankovich, Nicholas, ed. *The Columbia Granger's Index to Poetry in Anthologies*. 11th ed. New York: Columbia University Press, 1997.

_____. *The Columbia Granger's Index to Poetry in Collected and Selected Works*. New York: Columbia University Press, 1997.

Guy, Patricia. *A Women's Poetry Index*. Phoenix, Ariz.: Oryx Press, 1985.

Hazen, Edith P., ed. *Columbia Granger's Index to Poetry*. 10th ed. New York: Columbia University Press, 1994.

Hoffman, Herbert H. *Hoffman's Index to Poetry: European and Latin American Poetry in Anthologies*. Metuchen, N.J.: Scarecrow Press, 1985.

Hoffman, Herbert H., and Rita Ludwig Hoffman, comps. *International Index to Recorded Poetry*. New York: H. W. Wilson, 1983.

Kline, Victoria. *Last Lines: An Index to the Last Lines of Poetry*. 2 vols. Vol. 1, *Last Line Index, Title Index*; Vol. 2, *Author Index, Keyword Index*. New York: Facts On File, 1991.

Marcan, Peter. *Poetry Themes: A Bibliographical Index to Subject Anthologies and Related Criticisms in the English Language, 1875-1975*. Hamden, Conn.: Linnet Books, 1977.

Poem Finder. Great Neck, N.Y.: Roth, 2000.

POETICS, POETIC FORMS, AND GENRES

Attridge, Derek. *Poetic Rhythm: An Introduction*. New York: Cambridge University Press, 1995.

Brogan, T. V. F. *Verseform: A Comparative Bibliography*. Baltimore: Johns Hopkins University Press, 1989.

Fussell, Paul. *Poetic Meter and Poetic Form*. Rev. ed. New York: McGraw-Hill, 1979.

Hollander, John. *Rhyme's Reason*. 3d ed. New Haven, Conn.: Yale University Press, 2001.

Jackson, Guida M. *Traditional Epics: A Literary Companion*. New York: Oxford University Press, 1995.

Padgett, Ron, ed. *The Teachers and Writers Handbook of Poetic Forms*. 2d ed. New York: Teachers & Writers Collaborative, 2000.

Pinsky, Robert. *The Sounds of Poetry: A Brief Guide*. New York: Farrar, Straus and Giroux, 1998.

Preminger, Alex, and T. V. F. Brogan, ed. *New Princeton Encyclopedia of Poetry and Poetics*. 3d ed. Princeton, N.J.: Princeton University Press, 1993.

Spiller, Michael R. G. *The Sonnet Sequence: A Study of Its Strategies*. Studies in Literary Themes and Genres 13. New York: Twayne, 1997.

Turco, Lewis. *The New Book of Forms: A Handbook of Poetics*. Hanover, N.H.: University Press of New England, 1986.

Williams, Miller. *Patterns of Poetry: An Encyclopedia of Forms*. Baton Rouge: Louisiana State University Press, 1986.

Wimsatt, William K., ed. *Versification: Major Language Types: Sixteen Essays*. New York: Modern Language Association, 1972.

POSTCOLONIAL POETRY

Benson, Eugene, and L. W. Connolly. *Encyclopedia of Post-Colonial Literatures in English*. 2 vols. London: Routledge, 1994.

Bery, Ashok. *Cultural Translation and Postcolonial Poetry*. New York: Palgrave Macmillan, 2007.

Lawson, Alan, et al. *Post-Colonial Literatures in English: General, Theoretical, and Comparative, 1970-1993*. A Reference Publication in Literature. New York: G. K. Hall, 1997.

Mohanram, Radhika, and Gita Rajan, eds. *English Postcoloniality: Literatures from Around the World*. Contributions to the Study of World Literature 66. Westport, Conn.: Greenwood Press, 1996.

Parekh, Pushpa Naidu, and Siga Fatima Jagne. *Postcolonial African Writers: A Bio-Bibliographical Critical Sourcebook*. Westport, Conn.: Greenwood Press, 1998.

Patke, Rajeev S. *Postcolonial Poetry in English*. New York: Oxford University Press, 2006.

Ramazani, Jahan. *The Hybrid Muse: Postcolonial Poetry in English*. Chicago: University of Chicago Press, 2001.

Williams, Mark. *Post-Colonial Literatures in English: Southeast Asia, New Zealand, and the Pacific, 1970-1992*. Reference Publications in Literature. New York: G. K. Hall, 1996.

HISTORY OF WORLD POETRY

ANCIENT TO EIGHTEENTH CENTURY

Carter, Steven D., ed. *Medieval Japanese Writers*. Dictionary of Literary Biography 203. Detroit: Gale Group, 1999.

_____. *Waiting for the Wind: Thirty-six Poets of Japan's Late Medieval Age*. Reprint. New York: Columbia University Press, 1994.

Cyzevkyj, Dmytro. *A History of Ukrainian Literature: From the Eleventh to the End of the Nineteenth Century*. Translated by Dolly Ferguson, Doreen Gorsline, and Ulana Petyk, edited by George S. N. Luckyi. 2d ed. New York: Ukrainian Academic Press, 1997.

Frolov, D. V. *Classical Arabic Verse: History and Theory of 'arud*. Boston: Brill, 2000.

Herdeck, Donald E., ed. *African Authors: A Companion to Black African Writing, 1300-1973*. Dimensions of the Black Intellectual Experience. Washington, D.C.: Black Orpheus Press, 1973.

Husain, Iqbal. *The Early Persian Poets of India (A.H. 421-670)*. Patna, India: Patna University, 1937.

Jackson, A. V. Williams. *Early Persian Poetry, from the Beginnings Down to the Time of Firdausi*. New York: Macmillan, 1920.

Lienhard, Siegfried. *A History of Classical Poetry: Sanskrit, Pali, Prakrit*. Wiesbaden, Germany: Harrassowitz, 1984.

Meisami, Julie Scott. *Medieval Persian Court Poetry*. Princeton, N.J.: Princeton University Press, 1987.

Ooka, Makoto. *The Poetry and Poetics of Ancient Japan*. Translated by Thomas Fitzsimmons. Santa Fe, N.Mex.: Katydid Books, 1997.

Owen, Stephen. *The Making of Early Chinese Classical Poetry*. Cambridge, Mass.: Harvard University Asia Center, 2006.

Shirane, Haruo. *Traditional Japanese Literature: An Anthology, Beginnings to 1600*. Rev. ed. Translated by Sonja Arntzen et al. New York: Columbia University Press, 2007.

_____, ed. *Early Modern Japanese Literature: An Anthology, 1600-1900*. Translated by James Brandon et al. New York: Columbia University Press, 2002.

Thông, Huynh Sanh, ed. and trans. *An Anthology of Vietnamese Poems: From the Eleventh Through the Twentieth Centuries*. New Haven, Conn.: Yale University Press, 1996.

NINETEENTH CENTURY

Berrian, Brenda F., and Aart Broek. *Bibliography of Women Writers from the Caribbean, 1831-1986*. Washington, D.C.: Three Continents Press, 1989.

Cyzevkyj, Dmytro. *A History of Ukrainian Literature: From the Eleventh to the End of the Nineteenth Century*. Translated by Dolly Ferguson, Doreen Gorsline, and Ulana Petyk, edited by George S. N. Luckyi. 2d ed. New York: Ukrainian Academic Press, 1997.

De Souza, Eunice, ed. *Early Indian Poetry in English: An Anthology, 1829-1947*. New Delhi: Oxford University Press, 2005.

Herdeck, Donald E., ed. *African Authors: A Companion to Black African Writing, 1300-1973*. Dimensions of the Black Intellectual Experience. Washington, D.C.: Black Orpheus Press, 1973.

Poggioli, Renato. *The Poets of Russia, 1890-1930*. Cambridge, Mass.: Harvard University Press, 1960.

Shirane, Haruo, ed. *Early Modern Japanese Literature: An Anthology, 1600-1900*. Translated by James Brandon et al. New York: Columbia University Press, 2002.

Singh, Amritjit, Rajiav Verma, and Irene M. Johsi. *Indian Literature in English, 1827-1979: A Guide to Information Sources*. American Literature, English Literature, and World Literatures in English: An Information Guide Series 36. Detroit: Gale Research, 1981.

Thông, Huynh Sanh, ed. and trans. *An Anthology of Vietnamese Poems: From the Eleventh Through the Twentieth Centuries*. New Haven, Conn.: Yale University Press, 1996.

Tschizewskij, Dmitrij. *History of Nineteenth-Century Russian Literature*. Translated by Richard Noel Porter, edited by Serge A. Zenkovsky. Nashville, Tenn.: Greenwood Press, 1974.

TWENTIETH CENTURY AND CONTEMPORARY

Berrian, Brenda F., and Aart Broek. *Bibliography of Women Writers from the Caribbean, 1831-1986*. Washington, D.C.: Three Continents Press, 1989.

De Souza, Eunice, ed. *Early Indian Poetry in English: An Anthology, 1829-1947*. New Delhi: Oxford University Press, 2005.

Haft, Lloyd, ed. *The Poem*. Vol. 3 in *A Selective Guide to Chinese Literature, 1900-1949*. New York: E. J. Brill, 1989.

Herdeck, Donald E., ed. *African Authors: A Companion to Black African Writing, 1300-1973*. Dimensions of the Black Intellectual Experience. Washington, D.C.: Black Orpheus Press, 1973.

Kim, Jaihiun. *Traditional Korean Verse Since the 1900's*. Seoul, South Korea: Hanshin, 1991.

Lin, Julia C., trans. and ed. *Twentieth-Century Chinese Women's Poetry: An Anthology*. Armonk, N.Y.: M. E. Sharpe, 2009.

Morton, Leith. *Modernism in Practice: An Introduction to Postwar Japanese Poetry*. Honolulu: University of Hawaii Press, 2004.

Natarajan, Nalini, ed. *Handbook of Twentieth-Century Literatures of India*. Westport, Conn.: Greenwood Press, 1996.

Poggioli, Renato. *The Poets of Russia, 1890-1930*. Cambridge, Mass.: Harvard University Press, 1960.

Singh, Amritjit, Rajiav Verma, and Irene M. Johsi. *Indian Literature in English, 1827-1979: A Guide to Information Sources*. American Literature, English Literature, and World Literatures in English: An Information Guide Series 36. Detroit: Gale Research, 1981.

Thông, Huynh Sanh, ed. and trans. *An Anthology of Vietnamese Poems: From the Eleventh Through the Twentieth Centuries*. New Haven, Conn.: Yale University Press, 1996.

POETS BY COUNTRY OR REGION

AFRICA

Blair, Dorothy S. *African Literature in French: A History of Creative Writing in French from West and Equatorial Africa*. New York: Cambridge University Press, 1976.

D'Almeida, Irène Assiba, ed. *A Rain of Words: A Bilingual Anthology of Women's Poetry in Francophone Africa*. Translated by Janis A. Mayes. Charlottesville: University of Virginia Press, 2009.

Elimimian, Isaac Irabor. *Theme and Style in African Poetry*. Lewiston, N.Y.: E. Mellen, 1991.

Fraser, Robert. *West African Poetry: A Critical History*. Cambridge, England: Cambridge University Press, 1986.

Herdeck, Donald E., ed. *African Authors: A Companion to Black African Writing, 1300-1973*. Dimensions of the Black Intellectual Experience. Washington, D.C.: Black Orpheus Press, 1973.

Killam, Douglas, and Ruth Rowe, eds. *The Companion to African Literatures*. Bloomington: Indiana University Press, 2000.

Larrier, Renée Brenda. *Francophone Women Writers of Africa and the Caribbean*. Gainesville: University Press of Florida, 2000.

Limb, Peter, and Jean-Marie Volet. *Bibliography of African Literatures*. Lanham, Md.: Scarecrow Press, 1996.

Lindfors, Bernth. *Black African Literature in English: A Guide to Information Sources*. American Literature, English Literature, and World Literatures in English: An Information Guide Series 23. Detroit: Gale Research, 1979.

_____. *Black African Literature in English, 1977-1981 Supplement*. New York: Africana, 1986.

_____. *Black African Literature in English, 1982-1986*. New York: Zell, 1989.

_____. *Black African Literature in English, 1987-1991*. Bibliographical Research in African Literature 3. London: Zell, 1995.

Lindfors, Bernth, and Reinhard Sander, eds. *Twentieth-Century Caribbean and Black African Writers: First Series*. Dictionary of Literary Biography 117. Detroit: Gale Research, 1992.

_____. *Twentieth-Century Caribbean and Black African Writers: Second Series*. Dictionary of Literary Biography 125. Detroit: Gale Research, 1993.

_____. *Twentieth-Century Caribbean and Black African Writers: Third Series*. Dictionary of Literary Biography 157. Detroit: Gale Research, 1996.

Moore, Gerald, and Ulli Beier, eds. *The Penguin Book of Modern African Poetry*. 4th ed. New York: Penguin, 2007.

Ojaide, Tanure. *Poetic Imagination in Black Africa: Essays on African Poetry*. Durham, N.C.: Carolina Academic Press, 1996.

Ojaide, Tanure, and Tijan M. Sallah, eds. *The New African Poetry: An Anthology*. Boulder, Colo.: Lynne Rienner, 1999.

Parekh, Pushpa Naidu, and Siga Fatima Jagne. *Postcolonial African Writers: A Bio-Bibliographical Critical Sourcebook*. Westport, Conn.: Greenwood Press, 1998.

Scanlon, Paul A., ed. *South African Writers*. Dictionary of Literary Biography 225. Detroit: Gale Group, 2000.

ARABIAN PENINSULA

Allen, Roger. *An Introduction to Arabic Literature*. Cambridge, England: Cambridge University Press, 2001.

Badawi, M. M. *A Critical Introduction to Modern Arabic Poetry*. New York: Cambridge University Press, 1975.

_____. *Modern Arabic Literature*. New York: Cambridge University Press, 1992.

Meisami, Julie Scott, and Paul Starkey, eds. *Encyclopedia of Arabic Literature*. New York: Routledge, 1998.

CARIBBEAN AND WEST INDIES

Allis, Jeannette B. *West Indian Literature: An Index to Criticism, 1930-1975*. Reference Publication in Latin American Studies. Boston: Hall, 1981.

Arnold, A. James, ed. *A History of Literature in the Caribbean*. 3 vols. Philadelphia: J. Benjamins, 1994.

Berrian, Brenda F., and Aart Broek. *Bibliography of Women Writers from the Caribbean, 1831-1986*. Washington, D.C.: Three Continents Press, 1989.

Bloom, Harold, ed. *Caribbean Women Writers*. Women Writers of English and Their Work. Philadelphia: Chelsea House, 1997.

Breiner, Laurence A. *An Introduction to West Indian Poetry*. Cambridge, England: Cambridge University Press, 1998.

Brown, Stewart, and Mark McWatt, eds. *The Oxford Book of Caribbean Verse*. New York: Oxford University Press, 2005.

Burnett, Paula, ed. *The Penguin Book of Caribbean Verse in English*. London: Penguin Global, 2006.

Dance, Daryl Cumber, ed. *Fifty Caribbean Writers: A Bio-Bibliographical Critical Sourcebook*. New York: Greenwood Press, 1986.

Dawes, Kwame, ed. *Talk Yuh Talk: Interviews with Anglophone Caribbean Poets*. Charlottesville: University Press of Virginia, 2001.

Fenwick, M. J. *Writers of the Caribbean and Central America: A Bibliography*. Garland Reference Library of the Humanities 1244. New York: Garland, 1992.

Goslinga, Marian. *Caribbean Literature: A Bibliography*. Scarecrow Area Bibliographies 15. Lanham, Md.: Scarecrow Press, 1998.

Haigh, Sam, ed. *An Introduction to Caribbean Francophone Writing: Guadeloupe and Martinique*. New York: Berg, 1999.

Herdeck, Donald E., ed. *Caribbean Writers: A Bio-Bibliographical-Critical Encyclopedia*. Washington, D.C.: Three Continents Press, 1979.

Hughes, Roger, comp. *Caribbean Writing: A Checklist*. London: Commonwealth Institute Library Services, 1986.

Hurley, E. Anthony. *Through a Black Veil: Readings in French Caribbean Poetry*. Trenton, N.J.: Africa World Press, 2000.

James, Conrad, and John Perivolaris, eds. *The Cultures of the Hispanic Caribbean*. Gainesville: University Press of Florida, 2000.

Jenkins, Lee M. *The Language of Caribbean Poetry: Boundaries of Expression*. Gainesville: University Press of Florida, 2004.

Jordan, Alma, and Barbara Comissiong. *The English-Speaking Caribbean: A Bibliography of Bibliographies*. Reference Publication in Latin American Studies. Boston: Hall, 1984.

Larrier, Renée Brenda. *Francophone Women Writers of Africa and the Caribbean*. Gainesville: University Press of Florida, 2000.

Lindfors, Bernth, and Reinhard Sander, eds. *Twentieth-Century Caribbean and Black African Writers: First Series*. Dictionary of Literary Biography 117. Detroit: Gale Research, 1992.

_____. *Twentieth-Century Caribbean and Black African Writers: Second Series*. Dictionary of Literary Biography 125. Detroit: Gale Research, 1993.

_____. *Twentieth-Century Caribbean and Black African Writers: Third Series*. Dictionary of Literary Biography 157. Detroit: Gale Research, 1996.

Martinez, Julia A., ed. *Dictionary of Twentieth-Century Cuban Literature*. Westport, Conn.: Greenwood Press, 1990.

Miller, Kei, ed. *New Caribbean Poetry: An Anthology*. Manchester, England: Carcanet, 2007.

Narain, Denise DeCaires. *Contemporary Caribbean Women's Poetry: Making Style*. New York: Routledge, 2002.

CHINA

Barnstone, Tony, and Chou Ping, eds. *The Anchor Book of Chinese Poetry: From Ancient to Contemporary, the Full 3,000-Year Tradition*. New York: Anchor Books, 2004.

Cai, Zong-qi, ed. *How to Read Chinese Poetry: A Guided Anthology*. Bilingual ed. New York: Columbia University Press, 2007.

Chang, Kang-i Sun, and Haun Saussy, eds. *Women Writers of Traditional China: An Anthology of Poetry and Criticism*. Stanford, Calif.: Stanford University Press, 1999.

Haft, Lloyd, ed. *The Poem*. Vol. 3 in *A Selective Guide to Chinese Literature, 1900-1949*. New York: E. J. Brill, 1989.

Lin, Julia C., trans. and ed. *Twentieth-Century Chinese Women's Poetry: An Anthology*. Armonk, N.Y.: M. E. Sharpe, 2009.

Lynn, Richard John. *Guide to Chinese Poetry and Drama*. 2d ed. Boston, Mass.: G. K. Hall, 1984.

Lupke, Christopher, ed. *New Perspectives on Contemporary Chinese Poetry*. New York: Palgrave Macmillan, 2008.

Nienhauser, William, Jr., ed. *The Indiana Companion to Traditional Chinese Literature*. Bloomington: Indiana University Press, 1986.

Owen, Stephen. *The Making of Early Chinese Classical Poetry*. Cambridge, Mass.: Harvard University Asia Center, 2006.

Wu-chi, Liu. *An Introduction to Chinese Literature*. Bloomington: Indiana University Press, 1966.

Yip, Wai-lim, ed. and trans. *Chinese Poetry: An Anthology of Major Modes and Genres*. 2d ed. Durham, N.C.: Duke University Press, 1997.

INDIA AND SOUTH ASIA

Agrawal, K. A. *Toru Dutt: The Pioneer Spirit of Indian English Poetry—A Critical Study*. New Delhi: Atlantic, 2009.

De Souza, Eunice, ed. *Early Indian Poetry in English: An Anthology, 1829-1947*. New Delhi: Oxford University Press, 2005.

Dimock, Edward C., Jr., et al. *The Literatures of India: An Introduction*. Chicago: University of Chicago Press, 1974.

Gerow, Edwin. *Indian Poetics*. Wiesbaden, Germany: Harrassowitz, 1977.

King, Bruce. *Modern Indian Poetry in English*. Rev. ed. New Delhi: Oxford University Press, 2001.

Lienhard, Siegfried. *A History of Classical Poetry: Sanskrit, Pali, Prakrit*. Wiesbaden, Germany: Harrassowitz, 1984.

Mahmud, Shabana. *Urdu Language and Literature: A Bibliography of Sources in European Languages*. New York: Mansell, 1992.

Naik, M. K. *A History of Indian English Literature*. New Delhi: Sahitya Akademi, 1989.

Natarajan, Nalini, ed. *Handbook of Twentieth-Century Literatures of India*. Westport, Conn.: Greenwood Press, 1996.

Rajan, P. K., and Swapna Daniel, eds. *Indian Poetics*

and Modern Texts: Essays in Criticism. New Delhi: S. Chand, 1998.

Rama, Atma. *Indian Poetry and Fiction in English*. New Delhi: Bahri Publications, 1991.

Sadiq, Mohammed. *A History of Urdu Literature*. Delhi: Oxford, 1984.

Saran, Saraswiti. *The Development of Urdu Poetry*. New Delhi: Discovery Publishing House, 1990.

Singh, Amritjit, Rajiav Verma, and Irene M. Johsi. *Indian Literature in English, 1827-1979: A Guide to Information Sources*. American Literature, English Literature, and World Literatures in English: An Information Guide Series 36. Detroit: Gale Research, 1981.

Singh, Kanwar Dinesh. *Contemporary Indian English Poetry: Comparing Male and Female Voices*. New Delhi: Atlantic, 2008.

Sinha, R. P. N. *Indo-Anglican Poetry: Its Birth and Growth*. New Delhi: Reliance Publishing House, 1987.

Thayil, Jeet, ed. *The Bloodaxe Book of Contemporary Indian Poets*. Cambridge, Mass.: Bloodaxe, 2008.

JAPAN

Bownas, Geoffrey, and Anthony Thwaite, eds. and trans. *The Penguin Book of Japanese Verse*. Rev. ed. London: Penguin Books, 2009.

Brower, Robert, and Earl Miner. *Japanese Court Poetry*. 1961. Reprint. Stanford, Calif.: Stanford University Press, 1988.

Carter, Steven D., comp. and trans. *Traditional Japanese Poetry: An Anthology*. Stanford, Calif.: Stanford University Press, 1991.

_____, ed. *Medieval Japanese Writers*. Dictionary of Literary Biography 203. Detroit: Gale Group, 1999.

_____. *Waiting for the Wind: Thirty-six Poets of Japan's Late Medieval Age*. Reprint. New York: Columbia University Press, 1994.

Hisamatsu, Sen'ichi, ed. *Biographical Dictionary of Japanese Literature*. New York: Harper & Row, 1976.

Miner, Earl Roy, Hiroko Odagiri, and Robert E. Morrell. *The Princeton Companion to Classical Japanese Literature*. Princeton, N.J.: Princeton University Press, 1985.

Morton, Leith. *Modernism in Practice: An Introduction to Postwar Japanese Poetry*. Honolulu: University of Hawaii Press, 2004.

Ooka, Makoto. *The Poetry and Poetics of Ancient Japan*. Translated by Thomas Fitzsimmons. Santa Fe, N.Mex.: Katydid Books, 1997.

Rimer, J. Thomas. *A Reader's Guide to Japanese Literature*. 2d ed. New York: Kodansha International, 1999.

Rimer, J. Thomas, and Van C. Gessel, eds. *The Columbia Anthology of Modern Japanese Literature*. 2 vols. New York: Columbia University Press, 2005-2007.

Rimer, J. Thomas, and Robert E. Morrell. *Guide to Japanese Poetry*. Asian Literature Bibliography Series. 2d ed. Boston, Mass.: G. K. Hall, 1984.

Sato, Hiroaki, ed. and trans. *Japanese Women Poets: An Anthology*. Armonk, N.Y.: M. E. Sharpe, 2007.

Shirane, Haruo. *Traditional Japanese Literature: An Anthology, Beginnings to 1600*. Rev. ed. Translated by Sonja Arntzen et al. New York: Columbia University Press, 2007.

_____, ed. *Early Modern Japanese Literature: An Anthology, 1600-1900*. Translated by James Brandon et al. New York: Columbia University Press, 2002.

KOREA

Kim, Jaihiun. *Modern Korean Poetry*. Fremont, Calif.: Asian Humanities Press, 1994.

_____. *Traditional Korean Verse Since the 1900's*. Seoul, South Korea: Hanshin, 1991.

Korean Poetry: An Anthology with Critical Essays. Seoul, South Korea: Korean Culture and Arts Foundation, 1984.

Lee, Young-gul. *The Classical Poetry of Korea*. Seoul, South Korea: Korean Culture and Arts Foundation, 1981.

McCann, David R. *Form and Freedom in Korean Poetry*. New York: Brill, 1988.

Who's Who in Korean Literature. Korean Culture & Arts Foundation. Elizabeth, N.J.: Hollym, 1996.

MEXICO AND CENTRAL AMERICA

Agosín, Marjorie, and Roberta Gordenstein, eds. *Miriam's Daughters: Jewish Latin American Women*

Poets. Foreword by Agosín. Santa Fe, N.Mex.: Sherman Asher, 2001.

Cortes, Eladio. *Dictionary of Mexican Literature.* Westport, Conn.: Greenwood Press, 1992.

Dauster, Frank N. *The Double Strand: Five Contemporary Mexican Poets.* Louisville: University Press of Kentucky, 1987.

Fenwick, M. J. *Writers of the Caribbean and Central America: A Bibliography.* Garland Reference Library of the Humanities 1244. New York: Garland, 1992.

Foster, David William. *Mexican Literature: A Bibliography of Secondary Sources.* 2d ed. Metuchen, N.J.: Scarecrow Press, 1992.

_____, ed. *Mexican Literature: A History.* Austin: University of Texas Press, 1994.

González Peña, Carlos. *History of Mexican Literature.* Translated by Gusta Barfield Nance and Florence Johnson Dunstan. 3d rev. ed. Dallas: Southern Methodist University Press, 1968.

Nicholson, Irene. *A Guide to Mexican Poetry, Ancient and Modern.* Mexico: Editorial Minutiae Mexicana, 1968.

Vicuña, Cecilia, and Ernesto Livon-Grosman, eds. *The Oxford Book of Latin American Poetry: A Bilingual Anthology.* New York: Oxford University Press, 2009.

Washbourne, Kelly, ed. *An Anthology of Spanish American Modernismo: In English Translation, with Spanish Text.* Translated by Washbourne with Sergio Waisman. New York: Modern Language Association of America, 2007.

PERSIA

Husain, Iqbal. *The Early Persian Poets of India (A.H. 421-670).* Patna, India: Patna University, 1937.

Jackson, A. V. Williams. *Early Persian Poetry, from the Beginnings Down to the Time of Firdausi.* New York: Macmillan, 1920.

Meisami, Julie Scott. *Medieval Persian Court Poetry.* Princeton, N.J.: Princeton University Press, 1987.

Thackston, W. M. *A Millennium of Classical Persian Poetry: A Guide to the Reading and Understanding of Persian Poetry from the Tenth to the Twentieth Century.* Bethesda, Md.: Iranbooks, 1994.

Thiesen, Finn. *A Manual of Classical Persian Prosody: With Chapters on Urdu, Karakhanidic, and Ottoman Prosody.* Wiesbaden, Germany: O. Harrassowitz, 1982.

RUSSIA AND UKRAINE

Blok, Aleksandr. *Us Four Plus Four: Eight Russian Poets Conversing.* New Orleans, La.: UNO Press, 2008.

Bunimovitch, Evgeny, and J. Kates, eds. *Contemporary Russian Poetry: An Anthology.* Translated by Kates. Champaign: Dalkey Archive Press, University of Illinois, 2008.

Cornwell, Neil, ed. *Reference Guide to Russian Literature.* Chicago: Fitzroy Dearborn, 1998.

Cyzevkyj, Dmytro. *A History of Ukrainian Literature: From the Eleventh to the End of the Nineteenth Century.* Translated by Dolly Ferguson, Doreen Gorsline, and Ulana Petyk. Edited by George S. N. Luckyi. 2d ed. New York: Ukrainian Academic Press, 1997.

Kates, J., ed. *In the Grip of Strange Thoughts: Russian Poetry in a New Era.* Brookline, Mass.: Zephyr Press, 2000.

Nabokov, Vladimir Vladimirovich, comp. and trans. *Verses and Versions: Three Centuries of Russian Poetry.* Edited by Brian Boyd and Stanislav Shvabrin. Orlando, Fla.: Harcourt, 2008.

Piaseckyj, Oksana. *Bibliography of Ukrainian Literature in English and French: Translations and Critical Works, 1950-1986.* University of Ottawa Ukrainian Studies 10. Ottawa: University of Ottawa Press, 1989.

Poggioli, Renato. *The Poets of Russia, 1890-1930.* Cambridge, Mass.: Harvard University Press, 1960.

Polukhina, Valentina, and Daniel Weissbort, eds. *An Anthology of Contemporary Russian Women Poets.* Iowa City: University of Iowa Press, 2005.

Rydel, Christine A., ed. *Russian Literature in the Age of Pushkin and Gogol: Poetry and Drama.* Dictionary of Literary Biography 205. Detroit: Gale Group, 1999.

Tschizewskij, Dmitrij. *History of Nineteenth-Century Russian Literature.* Translated by Richard Noel Porter. Edited by Serge A. Zenkovsky. Nashville, Tenn.: Greenwood Press, 1974.

Wachtel, Michael. *The Cambridge Introduction to Russian Poetry*. New York: Cambridge University Press, 2004.

_____. *The Development of Russian Verse: Meter and Its Meanings*. New York: Cambridge University Press, 1998.

SOUTH AMERICA

Agosín, Marjorie, and Roberta Gordenstein, eds. *Miriam's Daughters: Jewish Latin American Women Poets*. Foreword by Agosín. Santa Fe, N.Mex.: Sherman Asher, 2001.

Brotherston, Gordon. *Latin American Poetry: Origins and Presence*. New York: Cambridge University Press, 1975.

Perrone, Charles A. *Seven Faces: Brazilian Poetry Since Modernism*. Durham, N.C.: Duke University Press, 1996.

Rowe, William. *Poets of Contemporary Latin America: History and the Inner Life*. New York: Oxford University Press, 2000.

Smith, Verity, ed. *Encyclopedia of Latin American Literature*. Chicago: Fitzroy Dearborn, 1997.

Stern, Irwin, ed. *Dictionary of Brazilian Literature*. Westport, Conn.: Greenwood Press, 1988.

Vicuña, Cecilia, and Ernesto Livon-Grosman, eds. *The Oxford Book of Latin American Poetry: A Bilingual Anthology*. New York: Oxford University Press, 2009.

Washbourne, Kelly, ed. *An Anthology of Spanish American Modernismo: In English Translation, with Spanish Text*. Translated by Washbourne with Sergio Waisman. New York: Modern Language Association of America, 2007.

TIBET

Cabezon, Jose I., and Roger R. Jackson. *Tibetan Literature: Studies in Genre*. Ithaca, N.Y.: Snow Lion, 1995.

Hartley, Lauran R., and Patricia Schiaffini-Vedani, eds. *Modern Tibetan Literature and Social Change*. Durham, N.C.: Duke University Press, 2008.

Jinpa, Thupten, and Jas Elsner. *Songs of Spiritual Experience: Tibetan Buddhist Poems of Insight and Awakening*. Boston: Shambhala, 2000.

TURKEY

Andrews, Walter G., Jr. *An Introduction to Ottoman Poetry*. Minneapolis: Bibliotheca Islamica, 1976.

Gibb, E. J. W. *A History of Ottoman Poetry*. 6 vols. Cambridge, England: Published and distributed by the Trustees of the "E. J. W. Gibb Memorial," 1963-1984.

VIETNAM

Thông, Huynh Sanh, ed. and trans. *An Anthology of Vietnamese Poems: From the Eleventh Through the Twentieth Centuries*. New Haven, Conn.: Yale University Press, 1996.

"Vietnamese Poetry and History." In *Crossroads: An Interdisciplinary Journal of Southeast Asian Studies* 7, no. 2. De Kalb, Ill.: Center for Southeast Asian Studies, Northern Illinois University, 1992.

Maura Ives; updated by Tracy Irons-Georges

GUIDE TO ONLINE RESOURCES

The following sites were visited by the editors of Salem Press in 2010. Because URLs frequently change, the accuracy of these addresses cannot be guaranteed; however, long-standing sites, such as those of colleges and universities, national organizations, and government agencies, generally maintain links when their sites are moved.

African Literature and Writers on the Internet
http://www-sul.stanford.edu/depts/ssrg/africa

This page is included in the Africa South of the Sahara site created by Karen Fung of Stanford University. It provides an alphabetical list of links to numerous resources about African poets and writers, online journals and essays, association Web sites, and other materials.

A Celebration of Women Writers
http://digital.library.upenn.edu/women

This site is an extensive compendium on the contributions of women writers throughout history. The "Local Editions by Authors" and "Local Editions by Category" pages include access to electronic texts of the works of numerous writers. Users can also access biographical and bibliographical information by browsing lists arranged by writers' names, countries of origin, ethnicities, and the centuries in which they lived.

LitWeb
http://litweb.net

LitWeb provides biographies of hundreds of world authors throughout history that can be accessed through an alphabetical listing. The pages about each writer contain a list of his or her works, suggestions for further reading, and illustrations. The site also offers information about past and present winners of major literary prizes.

The Modern Word: Authors of the Libyrinth
http://www.themodernword.com/authors.html

The Modern Word site, although somewhat haphazard in its organization, provides a great deal of critical information about writers. The "Authors of the Libyrinth" page is very useful, linking author names to essays about them and other resources. The section of the page headed "The Scriptorium" presents "an index of pages featuring writers who have pushed the edges of their medium, combining literary talent with a sense of experimentation to produce some remarkable works of modern literature."

Poetry in Translation
http://poetryintranslation.com

This independent resource provides modern translations of classic texts by famous poets and also provides original poetry and critical works. Visitors can choose from several languages, including English, Spanish, Chinese, Russian, Italian, and Greek. Original text available as well. Also includes links to further literary resources.

Poetry International Web
http://international.poetryinternationalweb.org

Poetry International Web features information on poets from countries such as Indonesia, Zimbabwe, Iceland, India, Slovenia, Morocco, Albania, Afghanistan, Russia, and Brazil. The site offers news, essays, interviews and discussion, and hundreds of poems, both in their original languages and in English translation.

Poet's Corner
http://theotherpages.org/poems

The Poet's Corner, one of the oldest text resources on the Web, provides access to about seven thousand works of poetry by several hundred different poets from around the world. Indexes are arranged and searchable by title, name of poet, or subject. The site also offers its own resources, including Faces of the Poets—a gallery of portraits—and Lives of the Poets—a growing collection of biographies.

Voices from the Gaps

http://voices.cla.umn.edu/

Voices from the Gaps is a site of the English Department at the University of Minnesota, dedicated to providing resources on the study of women artists of color, including writers. The site features a comprehensive index searchable by name, and it provides biographical information on each writer or artist and other resources for further study.

ELECTRONIC DATABASES

Electronic databases usually do not have their own URLs. Instead, public, college, and university libraries subscribe to these databases, provide links to them on their Web sites, and make them available to library card holders or other specified patrons. Readers can visit library Web sites or ask reference librarians to check on availability.

Bloom's Literary Reference Online

Facts On File publishes this database of thousands of articles by renowned scholar Harold Bloom and other literary critics, examining the lives and works of great writers worldwide. The database also includes information on more than forty-two thousand literary characters, literary topics, themes, movements, and genres, plus video segments about literature. Users can retrieve information by browsing writers' names, titles of works, time periods, genres, or writers' nationalities.

Literary Reference Center

EBSCO's Literary Reference Center (LRC) is a comprehensive full-text database designed primarily to help high school and undergraduate students in English and the humanities with homework and research assignments about literature. The database contains massive amounts of information from reference works, books, literary journals, and other materials, including more than 31,000 plot summaries, synopses, and overviews of literary works; almost 100,000 essays and articles of literary criticism; about 140,000 author biographies; more than 605,000 book reviews; and more than 5,200 author interviews. It also contains the entire contents of Salem Press's MagillOnLiterature Plus.

Users can retrieve information by browsing a list of authors' names or titles of literary works; they can also use an advanced search engine to access information by numerous categories, including author name, gender, cultural identity, national identity, and the years in which he or she lived, or by literary title, character, locale, genre, and publication date. The Literary Reference Center also features a literary-historical time line, an encyclopedia of literature, and a glossary of literary terms.

Literary Resource Center

Published by Gale, this comprehensive literary database contains information on the lives and works of more than 130,000 authors in all genres, in all time periods, and throughout the world. In addition, the database offers more than 70,000 full-text critical essays and reviews from some of Gale's reference publications, including *Contemporary Literary Criticism*, *Literature Criticism from 1400-1800*, *Nineteenth-Century Literature Criticism*, and *Twentieth-Century Literary Criticism*; more than 7,000 overviews of frequently studied works; more than 650,000 full-text articles, critical essays, and reviews from about three hundred scholarly journals and literary magazines; more than 4,500 interviews; and about five hundred links to selected Web sites. Users can retrieve information by browsing author name, ethnicity, nationality, or years of birth and death; titles of literary works; genres; selected literary movements or time periods; keywords; and themes of literary works. Literary Resource Center also features a literary-historical time line and an encyclopedia of literature.

MagillOnLiterature Plus

MagillOnLiterature Plus is a comprehensive, integrated literature database produced by Salem Press and available on the EBSCOhost platform. The database contains the full text of essays in Salem's many literature-related reference works, including *Masterplots*, *Cyclopedia of World Authors*, *Cyclopedia of Literary Characters*, *Cyclopedia of Literary Places*, *Critical Survey of Poetry*, *Critical Survey of Long Fiction*, *Critical Survey of Short Fiction*, *World Philosophers and Their Works*, *Magill's Literary Annual*, and

Magill's Book Reviews. Among its contents are articles on more than 35,000 literary works and more than 8,500 poets, writers, dramatists, essayists, and philosophers; more than 1,000 images; and a glossary of more than 1,300 literary terms. The biographical essays include lists of authors' works and secondary bibliographies, and hundreds of overview essays examine and discuss literary genres, time periods, and national literatures.

Rebecca Kuzins; updated by Desiree Dreeuws

Time Line

c. 2000 B.C.E.   The main portion of *Gilgamesh* (*Gilgamesh Epic*, 1917) is written on cuneiform clay tablets. This epic, which is the oldest surviving poem, recounts the exploits of Gilgamesh, the legendary king of Uruk and the first literary hero.

c. 500 B.C.E.   Vālmīki, whom Indian tradition credits with having invented poetry, composes *Rāmāyaṇa* (*The Ramayana*, 1870-1874). Written in Sanskrit, this poem is the national epic of India and will continue to influence poetry, art, drama, and religion in South and Southeast Asia into the twenty-first century.

c. 400 B.C.E.-400 C.E.   The *Mahābhārata* (*The Mahabharata*, 1834), the longest surviving poem in any language, is written in Sanskrit. This epic records political, ethical, mythological, and philosophical thought in ancient India.
The *Bhagavadgītā* (*The Bhagavad Gita,* 1785), a Hindu devotional text composed between c. 200 B.C.E.-200 C.E., is preserved as an interlude in the *Mahābhārata*.

210   Ruan Ji is born in Weishi, China. He will compose eighty-two verses designated as *yonghuai shi* (poems singing of my emotions), which will be studied and imitated by subsequent Chinese poets.

689   Meng Haoran, the first great poet of the Tang Dynasty, is born in Xianyang, China.

701   Li Bo, one of the two greatest poets in Chinese literature, is born in what is now Chinese Turkistan.

712   Du Fu, one of the two greatest poets in Chinese literature, is born in Gongxian, China.

mid-eighth century   *Manyōshū* (*The Collections of Ten Thousand Leaves*; also as *The Ten Thousand Leaves*, pb. 1981, and as *The Manyoshu*, 1940), an anthology of more than 4,500 Japanese poems, is compiled.

c. 1010   The Persian poet Firdusi creates the Iranian national epic, *Shahnamah* (*Sah-name*, 1906), or "the book of kings." Later translations of this epic will influence the work of Western poets.

twelfth century   Omar Khayyám, a Persian poet, composes *Rubā'īyāt* (*True Translation of Hakim Omar Khayyam's "Robaiyat,"* 1994; commonly known as *Rubáiyát of Omar Khayyám*). The work is a series of *ruba'i*, or individual quatrains.

1320   Hafiz, the master of the *ghazal*, or lyric poem, is born in Shīrāz, Persia (now in Iran).

1644   Matsuo Bashō, considered by many to be the greatest of the haiku poets, is born in Ueno, Igo Province, Japan.

November, 1648   Sor Juana Inés de la Cruz, the major writer of colonial Spanish America, is born in New Spain (now Mexico). She will write more than four hundred poems, as well as plays and prose works.

1820   *Ruslan i Lyudmila* (*Ruslan and Liudmila*, 1936), the first long poem by Alexander Pushkin, is published. Pushkin is the first poet to write in a purely Russian style.

1888   *Azul*, a collection of works by Nicaraguan poet Rubén Darío, is published, receiving praise from both South American and European critics. Darío is one of the founders of the *Modernismo* literary movement, and his poetry features innovative themes, language, meters, and rhymes.

1889	Anna Akhmatov is born near Odessa, Ukraine. She will become one of the leading poets of the Russian Acmeist movement.
1913	Indian poet Rabindranath Tagore receives the Nobel Prize in Literature.
1924	*Haru to shura* (*Spring and Asura*, 1973), by Japanese poet Kenji Miyazawa, is released. This collection becomes the only volume of Miyazawa's poetry published during his lifetime.
1945	Gabriela Mistral is the first Latin American writer to receive the Nobel Prize in Literature.
1961	"Babii Yar," Yevgeny Yevtushenko's poem castigating Soviet anti-Semitism, is published.
1964	*Rediscovery, and Other Poems*, the first book by Ghanian writer Kofi Awoonor, is published.
1971	Chilean poet Pablo Neruda receives the Nobel Prize in Literature.
1973	Nigerian writer Chinua Achebe publishes *Christmas in Biafra, and Other Poems*.
1986	Wole Soyinka of Nigeria receives the Nobel Prize in Literature.
1987	Joseph Brodsky, a Soviet writer exiled in the United States, receives the Nobel Prize in Literature. Brodsky wrote his poetry in Russian, and it was translated into many languages, with the English translations earning him high regard in the West.
1990	Mexican writer Octavio Paz is awarded the Nobel Prize in Literature.
1992	West Indian writer Derek Walcott receives the Nobel Prize in Literature.
2006	Nicaraguan writer Claribel Alegría is awarded the Neustadt International prize for her body of work.

Rebecca Kuzins

Major Awards

Adonais Prize for Poetry

The Adonais Prize for Poetry, or Premio Adonáis de Poesía, is awarded annually in Spain to an unpublished Spanish-language poem from any country; winners have come from the Dominican Republic, Honduras, Costa Rica, Venezuela, El Salvador, and Mexico.

1943: José Suárez Carreño (Spain)—"Edad del hombre"; Vicente Gaos (Spain)—"Arcángel de mi noche"; Alfonso Moreno (Spain)—"El vuelo de la carne"

1944: no award

1945: no award

1946: no award

1947: José Hierro (Spain)—"Alegría"

1948: no award

1949: Ricardo Molina (Spain)—"Corimbo"

1950: José García Nieto (Spain)—"Dama de soledad"

1951: Lorenzo Gomis (Spain)—"El caballo"

1952: Antonio Fernández Spencer (Dominican Republic)—"Bajo la luz del día"

1953: Claudio Rodríguez (Spain)—"Don de la ebriedad"

1954: José Angel Valente (Spain)—"A modo de esperanza"

1955: Javier de Bengoechea (Spain)—"Hombre en forma de elegía"

1956: María Elvira Lacaci (Spain)—"Humana voz"

1957: Carlos Sahagún (Spain)—"Profecías del agua"

1958: Rafael Soto Verges (Spain)—"La agorera"

1959: Francisco Brines (Spain)—"Las brasas"

1960: Mariano Roldán (Spain)—"Hombre nuevo"

1961: Luis Feria (Spain)—"Conciencia"

1962: Jesús Hilario Tundidor (Spain)—"Junto a mi silencio"

1963: Félix Grande (Spain)—"Las piedras"

1964: Diego Jesús Jiménez (Spain)—"La ciudad"

1965: Joaquín Caro Romero (Spain)—"El tiempo en el espejo"

1966: Miguel Fernández (Spain)—"Sagrada materia"

1967: Joaquín Benito de Lucas (Spain)—"Materia de olvido"

1968: Roberto Sosa (Honduras)—"Los pobres"

1969: Angel García López (Spain)—"A flor de piel"

1970: Pureza Canelo (Spain)—"Lugar común"

1971: José Infante (Spain)—"Elegía y no"

1972: José Luis Alegre Cudos (Spain)—"Abstracción de Mío Cid con Cid Mío"

1973: José Antonio Moreno Jurado (Spain)—"Ditirambos para mi propia burla"

1974: Julia Castillo (Spain)—"Urgencias de un río interior"

1975: Angel Sánchez Pascual (Spain)—"Ceremonia de la inocencia"

1976: Jorge G. Aranguren (Spain)—"De fuegos, tigres, ríos"

1977: Eloy Sánchez Rosillo (Spain)—"Maneras de estar solo"

1978: Arcadio López-Casanova (Spain)—"La oscura potestad"

1979: Laureano Albán (Costa Rica)—"Herencia del otoño"

1980: Blanca Andreu (Spain)—"De una niña de provincias que vino a vivir en un Chagall"

1981: Miguel Velasco (Spain)—"Las berlinas del sueño"

1982: Luis García Montero (Spain)—"El jardín extranjero"

1983: Javier Peñas Navarro (Spain)—"Adjetivos sin agua, adjetivos con agua"

1984: Amalia Iglesias Serna (Spain)—"Un lugar para el fuego"

1985: Juan Carlos Mestre (Spain)—"Antífona de otoño en el valle del Bierzo"

1986: Juan María Calles (Spain)—"Silencio celeste"

1987: Francisco Serradilla (Spain)—"El bosque insobornable"

1988: Miguel Sánchez Gatell (Spain)—"La soledad absoluta de la tierra"

1989: Juan Carlos Marset (Spain)—"Puer profeta"

1990: Diego Doncel (Spain)—"El único umbral"

1991: Jesús Javier Lázaro Puebla (Spain)—"Canción para una amazona dormida"

1992: Juan Antonio Marín Alba (Spain)—"El horizonte de la noche"

1993: María Luisa Mora Alameda (Spain)—"Busca y captura"

1994: Ana Merino (Spain)—"Preparativos para un viaje"

1995: Eduardo Moga (Spain)—"La luz oída"

1996: Rosario Neira (Spain)—"No somos ángeles"

1997: Luis Martínez-Falero (Spain)—"Plenitud de la materia"

1998: Luis Enrique Belmonte (Venezuela)—"Inútil registro"

1999: Irene Sánchez Carrón (Spain)—"Escenas principales de actor secundario"

2000: Joaquín Pérez Azaústre (Spain)—"Una interpretación"

2001: José Antonio Gómez-Coronado (Spain)—"El triunfo de los días"

2002: Adrián González da Costa (Spain)—"Rua dos douradores"

2003: Javier Vela (Spain)—"La hora del crepúsculo"

2004: José Martínez Ros (Spain)—"La enfermedad"

2005: Carlos Vaquerizo (Spain)—"Fiera venganza del tiempo"

2006: Jorge Galán (pseudonym of George Alexander Portillo; El Salvador)—"Breve historia del Alba"

2007: Teresa Soto González (Spain)—"Un poemario (Imitación de Wislawa)"

2008: Rogelio Guedea (Mexico)—"Kora"

2009: Rubén Martín Díaz (Spain)—"El minuto interior"

ANDREI BELY PRIZE

The Andrei Bely Prize in Russian Literature was founded in 1978 and honors literature in various categories, such as poetry, prose, criticism, and humanitarian investigations. The prize is one ruble, a bottle of vodka, and an apple. The poetry winners are listed below.

1978: Victor Krivulin

1979: Elena Shwartz

1980: Vladimir Aleinikov

1981: Alexander Mironov

1982: no award

1983: Olga Sedakova

1984: no award

1985: Alexei Parschikov

1986: no award

1987: Genady Aigi

1988: Ivan Zhdanov

1989: no award

1990: no award

1991: Alexander Gornon

1992: no award

1993: no award

1994: Shamshad Abdulayev

1995: no award

1996: no award

1997: Victor Letsev

1998: Mikhail Eremin

1999: Elena Fanailova

2000: Yaroslav Mogutin

2001: Vasily Filipov

2002: Mikhail Gronas

2003: Mikhail Eisenberg

2004: Elizabeth Mnatsakonova

2005: Maria Stepanova

2006: Alexander Skidan

2007: Aleksei Tvetkov

2008: Vladimir Aristov and Sergei Kruglov

2009: Nikolai Kononov

MIGUEL DE CERVANTES PRIZE

Spain's ministry of culture awards its prize to honor the lifetime achievement of an outstanding writer in the Spanish language. Recipients, nominated by the language academies of Spanish-speaking countries, can be of any nationality; winners have come from Argentina, Mexico, Cuba, Colombia, and Chile. The list below includes only poets who have received the award.

1976: Jorge Guillén (Spain)
1978: Dámaso Alonso (Spain)
1979: Jorge Luis Borges (Argentina) and Gerardo Diego (Spain)
1981: Octavio Paz (Mexico)
1982: Luis Rosales (Spain)
1983: Rafael Alberti (Spain)
1990: Adolfo Bioy Casares (Argentina)
1992: Dulce María Loynaz (Cuba)

1996: José García Nieto (Spain)
1998: José Hierro (Spain)
2001: Álvaro Mutis (Colombia)
2002: José Jiménez Lozano (Spain)
2003: Gonzalo Rojas (Chile)
2005: Sergio Pitol (Mexico)
2006: Antonio Gamoneda (Spain)
2007: Juan Gelman (Argentina)
2009: José Emilio Pacheco (Mexico)

GOLDEN WREATH AWARD

Struga Poetry Evenings, a major international poetry festival in Macedonia, presents its award to living poets for lifetime achievement.

1966: Robert Rozhdestvensky (Soviet Union)
1967: Bulat Okudzhava (Soviet Union)
1968: László Nagy (Hungary)
1969: Mak Dizdar (Bosnia and Herzegovina)
1970: Miodrag Pavloviá (Serbia)
1971: W. H. Auden (United States)
1972: Pablo Neruda (Chile)
1973: Eugenio Montale (Italy)
1974: Fazıl Hüsnü Dağlarca (Turkey)
1975: Léopold Senghor (Senegal)
1976: Eugène Guillevic (France)
1977: Artur Lundkvist (Sweden)
1978: Rafael Alberti (Spain)
1979: Miroslav Krleža (Croatia)
1980: Hans Magnus Enzensberger (Germany)
1981: Blaže Koneski (Macedonia)
1982: Nichita Stănescu (Romania)
1983: Sachchidananda Hirananda Vatsyayan Agyey (India)
1984: Andrey Voznesensky (Soviet Union)
1985: Yiannis Ritsos (Greece)
1986: Allen Ginsberg (United States)
1987: Tadeusz Rózewicz (Poland)

1988: Desanka Maksimović (Serbia)
1989: Thomas W. Shapcott (Australia)
1990: Justo Jorge Padrón (Spain)
1991: Joseph Brodsky (United States)
1992: Ferenc Juhász (Hungary)
1993: Gennadiy Aygi (Chuvash Republic)
1994: Ted Hughes (England)
1995: Yehuda Amichai (Israel)
1996: Makoto Ooka (Japan)
1997: Adunis (Syria)
1998: Lu Yuan (China)
1999: Yves Bonnefoy (France)
2000: Edoardo Sanguineti (Italy)
2001: Seamus Heaney (Northern Ireland)
2002: Slavko Mihalić (Croatia)
2003: Tomas Tranströmer (Sweden)
2004: Vasco Graça Moura (Portugal)
2005: W. S. Merwin (United States)
2006: Nancy Morejón (Cuba)
2007: Mahmoud Darwish (Palestine)
2008: Fatos Arapi (Albania)
2009: Tomaž Šalamun (Slovenia)
2010: Ljubomir Levčev (Bulgaria)

JNANPITH AWARD

The Indian literary and research organization Bharatiya Jnanpith presents its annual award for lifetime achievement in literature, including poetry, written by an Indian citizen in any of several Indian languages. The list below includes only poets who have received the award.

1965: G. Sankara Kurup
1967: Kuppali V. Puttappa and Umashankar Joshi
1968: Sumitranandan Pant
1969: Firaq Gorakhpuri
1970: Viswanatha Satyanarayana
1971: Bishnu Dey
1972: Ramdhari Singh Dinkar
1973: Dattatreya R. Bendre
1976: Ashapurna Devi
1978: Sachchidananda H. V. Ajneya
1980: S. K. Pottekkatt
1981: Amrita Pritam
1982: Mahadevi Varma
1983: Maasti V. Ayengar
1986: Sachidananda Routroy
1987: V. V. S. Kusumagraj

1988: C. Narayana Reddy
1990: V. K. Gokak
1991: Subhash Mukhopadhyaya
1992: Naresh Mehta
1993: Sitakant Mahapatra
1994: U. R. Anantha Murthy
1997: Ali Sardar Jafri
2000: Indira Goswami
2001: Rajendra Shah
2003: Vinda Karandikar
2004: Rahman Rahi
2005: Kunwar Narain
2006: Satya Vrat Shastri
2007: Akhlaq Mohammed Khan (Shahryar)
2008: O. N. V. Kurup

MASAOKA SHIKI INTERNATIONAL HAIKU PRIZE

Beginning in 2000, the Haiku Grand Prize and several Haiku Prizes have been given every two years at the International Haiku Symposium to raise international awareness of the poet Masaoka Shiki and his chosen form, the haiku. Ehime Prefecture, birthplace of the poet, sponsors the award.

2000: Grand Prize — Yves Bonnefoy (France); Haiku Prize — Li Mang (China), Bart Mesotten (Belgium), Robert Speiss (United States), Kazuo Sato (Japan)
2002: Grand Prize — Cor van den Neuvel (United States); Haiku Prize — Satya Bhushan Verma (India), Shigeki Wada (Japan)
2004: Grand Prize — Gary Snyder (United States);

Haiku Prize — Hidekazu Masuda (Brazil), Ko Reishi (Taiwan), Bansei Tsukushi (Japan)
2006: No awards
2008: Grand Prize — Tota Kaneko (Japan); Haiku Prize — Biwao Kawahara (Japan); Sweden Award: Sonoo Uchida (Japan), O-Young Lee (South Korea)

NEUSTADT INTERNATIONAL PRIZE FOR LITERATURE

Awarded biennially since 1970, this award sponsored by the University of Oklahoma honors writers for a body of work. The list below includes only poets who have received the award.

1970: Giuseppe Ungaretti (Italy)
1974: Francis Ponge (France)

1976: Elizabeth Bishop (United States)
1978: Czesław Miłosz (Poland)

1980: Josef Škvorecky (Czechoslovakia/Canada)
1982: Octavio Paz (Mexico)
1984: Paavo Haavikko (Finland)
1990: Tomas Tranströmer (Sweden)
1992: João Cabral de Melo Neto (Brazil)
1994: Edward Kamau Brathwaite (Barbados)

2000: David Malouf (Australia)
2002: Alvaro Mutis (Colombia)
2004: Adam Zagajewski (Poland)
2006: Claribel Alegría (Nicaragua/El Salvador)
2010: Duo Duo (China)

NOBEL PRIZE IN LITERATURE

Awarded annually since 1901, this prize is given to an author for his or her entire body of literary work. The list below includes only the poets who have been so honored.

1901: Sully Prudhomme
1906: Giosuè Carducci
1907: Rudyard Kipling
1913: Rabindranath Tagore
1923: William Butler Yeats
1945: Gabriela Mistral
1946: Hermann Hesse
1948: T. S. Eliot
1956: Juan Ramón Jiménez
1958: Boris Pasternak
1959: Salvatore Quasimodo
1960: Saint-John Perse
1963: George Seferis
1966: Nelly Sachs
1969: Samuel Beckett

1971: Pablo Neruda
1974: Harry Martinson
1975: Eugenio Montale
1977: Vicente Aleixandre
1979: Odysseus Elytis
1980: Czesław Miłosz
1984: Jaroslav Seifert
1986: Wole Soyinka
1987: Joseph Brodsky
1990: Octavio Paz
1992: Derek Walcott
1995: Seamus Heaney
1996: Wisława Szymborska
2005: Harold Pinter
2009: Herta Müller

JUAN RULFO PRIZE FOR LATIN AMERICAN AND CARIBBEAN LITERATURE

The Guadalajara International Book Fair presents its annual literary award to a writer from the Americas who writes in Spanish, Portuguese, French, or English. Award organizers include Mexico's National Council for Culture and Arts and the University of Guadalajara. The list below includes only poets who have received the award.

1991: Nicanor Parra (Chile)
1993: Eliseo Diego (Cuba)
1998: Olga Orozco (Argentina)
2000: Juan Gelman (Argentina)
2002: Cintio Vitier (Cuba)

2004: Juan Goytisolo (Spain)
2005: Tomás Segovia (Mexico)
2007: Fernando del Paso (Mexico)
2009: Rafael Cadenas (Venezuela)

CHRONOLOGICAL LIST OF POETS

This chronology of the poets covered in this volume serves as a time line for students interested in the development of poetry in Russia, Asia, Latin America, Africa, and the Middle East from the sixth century B.C.E. to modern times. The arrangement is chronological on the basis of birth years, and the proximity of writers provides students with some insights into potential influences and contemporaneous developments.

BORN BEFORE 1000
Vālmīki (fl. c. 500 B.C.E.)
Ruan Ji (210)
Tao Qian (365)
Xie Lingyun (385)
Meng Haoran (689)
Li Bo (701)
Wang Wei (701)
Du Fu (712)
Firdusi (Between 932 and 941)

BORN 1001-1800
Omar Khayyám (May 18, 1048?)
Li Qingzhao (1084)
Saʿdi (c. 1200)
Rūmī, Jalāl al-Dīn (c. September 30, 1207)
Hafiz (c. 1320)
Matsuo Bashō (1644)
Cruz, Sor Juana Inés de la (November, 1648)
Issa (June 15, 1763)
Pushkin, Alexander (June 6, 1799)

BORN 1801-1900
Lermontov, Mikhail (October 15, 1814)
Hernández, José (November 10, 1834)
Annensky, Innokenty (September 1, 1855)
Tagore, Rabindranath (May 7, 1861)
Darío, Rubén (January 18, 1867)
González Martínez, Enrique (April 13, 1871)
Yosano Akiko (December 7, 1878)
Blok, Aleksandr (November 28, 1880)
Khodasevich, Vladislav (May 28, 1886)
Mistral, Gabriela (April 7, 1889)
Reyes, Alfonso (May 17, 1889)
Akhmatova, Anna (June 23, 1889)

Pasternak, Boris (February 10, 1890)
Mandelstam, Osip (January 15, 1891)
Vallejo, César (March 16, 1892)
Tsvetayeva, Marina (October 8, 1892)
Mayakovsky, Vladimir (July 19, 1893)
Esenin, Sergei (October 3, 1895)
Miyazawa, Kenji (August 27, 1896)
Borges, Jorge Luis (August 24, 1899)

BORN 1901-1930
Hikmet, Nazim (January 20, 1902)
Drummond de Andrade, Carlos (October 31, 1902)
Neruda, Pablo (July 12, 1904)
Senghor, Léopold (October 9, 1906)
Césaire, Aimé (June 26, 1913)
Paz, Octavio (March 31, 1914)
Parra, Nicanor (September 5, 1914)
Amichai, Yehuda (May 3, 1924)
Alegría, Claribel (May 12, 1924)
Cardenal, Ernesto (January 20, 1925)
Walcott, Derek (January 23, 1930)
Pagis, Dan (October 16, 1930)
Achebe, Chinua (November 16, 1930)

BORN 1931 AND AFTER
Okigbo, Christopher (August 16, 1932)
Ko Un (January 8, 1933)
Voznesensky, Andrei (May 12, 1933)
Yevtushenko, Yevgeny (July 18, 1933)
Soyinka, Wole (July 13, 1934)
Awoonor, Kofi (March 13, 1935)
Brodsky, Joseph (May 24, 1940)
Cliff, Michelle (November 2, 1946)
Zamora, Daisy (June 20, 1950)
Seth, Vikram (June 20, 1952)

INDEXES

GEOGRAPHICAL INDEX OF POETS

ROMANIA
Pagis, Dan, 213

RUSSIA
Akhmatova, Anna, 3
Annensky, Innokenty, 21
Blok, Aleksandr, 33
Brodsky, Joseph, 44
Esenin, Sergei, 90
Khodasevich, Vladislav, 133
Lermontov, Mikhail, 142
Mandelstam, Osip, 163
Mayakovsky, Vladimir, 176
Pasternak, Boris, 222
Pushkin, Alexander, 236
Tsvetayeva, Marina, 293

Voznesensky, Andrei, 311
Yevtushenko, Yevgeny, 339

ST. LUCIA
Walcott, Derek, 317

SENEGAL
Senghor, Léopold, 264

SOUTH KOREA
Ko Un, 138

SOVIET UNION. *See* **RUSSIA; UKRAINE**

SPAIN
Vallejo, César, 300

TURKEY. *See also* **ASIA MINOR**
Hikmet, Nazim, 117
Rūmī, Jalāl al-Dīn, 255

UKRAINE
Akhmatova, Anna, 3

UNITED STATES
Brodsky, Joseph, 44
Cliff, Michelle, 61

WEST INDIES
Césaire, Aimé, 56
Cliff, Michelle, 61
Walcott, Derek, 317

CATEGORIZED INDEX OF POETS

Categorized Index of Poets covers three primary subject areas: Culture/Group Identities, Historical Periods/ Literary Movements, *and* Poetic Forms and Themes.

Cultural/Group Identities

Historical Periods/Literary Movements

Poetic Forms and Themes

ACMEIST POETS
Akhmatova, Anna, 3
Annensky, Innokenty, 21
Mandelstam, Osip, 163
Pasternak, Boris, 222

AFRICAN AMERICAN CULTURE
Cliff, Michelle, 61

AVANT-GARDE POETS
Esenin, Sergei, 90
Pagis, Dan, 213
Vallejo, César, 300

Critical Survey of Poetry Series: Master List of Contents

The Critical Survey of Poetry, Fourth Edition, *profiles more than eight hundred poets in four subsets:* American Poets; British, Irish, and Commonwealth Poets; European Poets; *and* World Poets. *Although some individuals could have been included in more than one subset, each poet appears in only one subset. A fifth subset,* Topical Essays, *includes more than seventy overviews covering geographical areas, historical periods, movements, and critical approaches.*

AMERICAN POETS

BRITISH, IRISH, AND COMMONWEALTH POETS

EUROPEAN POETS

WORLD POETS

TOPICAL ESSAYS

CUMULATIVE INDEXES

SUBJECT INDEX

All personages whose names appear in **boldface type** in this index are the subject of articles in *Critical Survey of Poetry, Fourth Edition*.

"A Víctor Hugo," 73

About That (Mayakovsky), 179

Accentual meter, defined, 380

Accentual-syllabic meter, defined, 380

Acemeist poets. *See* Categorized Index

Achebe, Chinua, 1-3; *Christmas in Biafra*, 2; *Collected Poems*, 2

Adonais Prize for Poetry, 408

"Aeneas and Dido" (Brodsky), 48

African American culture. *See* Categorized Index

After-Dinner Declarations (Parra), 221

Águila o sol?. See *Eagle or Sun?*

Akhmatova, Anna, 3-9; *Anno Domini MCMXXI*, 6; *Belaya staya*, 6; *Chetki*, 5; *A Poem Without a Hero*, 8; *Requiem*, 7; *Vecher*, 5

Alcayaga, Lucila Godoy. *See* Mistral, Gabriela

Alegría, Claribel, 9-14; *Casting Off*, 13; *Flores del volcán/Flowers from the Volcano*, 11; *Fugues*, 12; *Luisa in Realityland*, 11; *Sorrow*, 12; *Woman of the River*, 12

Alguma poesia (Drummond de Andrade), 80

All Soul's Day (Esenin), 93

All You Who Sleep Tonight (Seth), 275

Allegory, defined, 380

Alliteration, defined, 380

Allusion, defined, 380

Amichai, Yehuda, 14-21; *Open Closed Open*, 19

Anacrusis, defined, 380

Anapest, defined, 380

Anaphora, defined, 380

Andrade, Carlos Drummond de. *See* Drummond de Andrade, Carlos

Andrei Bely Prize, 409

Andreyevna Gorenko, Anna. *See* Akhmatova, Anna

Anna Snegina (Esenin), 95

Annensky, Innokenty, 21-25; "Depression," 22; "The Double," 22; "Poetry," 23; "The Steel Cicada," 24; "To a Poet," 23

Anno Domini MCMXXI (Akhmatova), 6

"Año lírico, El" (Darío), 74

Another Life (Walcott), 320

Approximate rhyme, defined, 380

Archetype, defined, 380

"Arfy i skripki" (Blok), 36

Argentina. *See* Geographical Index

Arkansas Testament, The (Walcott), 322

Artefactos (Parra), 221

Asia Minor. *See* Geographical Index

Aubade, defined, 380

Avant-garde poets. *See* Categorized Index

Awards, 408-412

Awoonor, Kofi, 25-32; *Latin American and Caribbean Notebook*, 31; "The Sea Eats the Land at Home," 29; "Songs of Sorrow," 28; *Until the Morning After*, 31; "We Have Found a New Land," 30; "The Weaver Bird," 29; "The Years Behind," 30

Azul (Darío), 74

Azure (Esenin), 94

"Babii Yar" (Yevtushenko), 344

"Ballad" (Khodasevich), 136

Ballade (poetic form), defined, 381

Ballads. *See* Categorized Index

Ballads, defined, 381

Base meter, defined, 381

Bashō. *See* Matsuo Bashō

Basoalto, Neftalí Ricardo Reyes. *See* Neruda, Pablo

Beastly Tales from Here and There (Seth), 275

Belaya staya (Akhmatova), 6

"Bird, The" (Paz), 232

Black Heralds, The (Vallejo), 303

"Black Woman" (Senghor), 269

Blanco (Paz), 234

Blank verse, defined, 381

"Blazon" (Darío), 75

Blok, Aleksandr, 33-39; "Arfy i skripki," 36; "Gorod," 36; "I Go into Darkened Temples," 37; "I Have a Premonition of You," 37; *Nechayannaya radost*, 37; *The Twelve*, 38

Boitempo (Drummond de Andrade), 82

Borges, Jorge Luis, 39-44; *Dream Tigers*, 42; *Fervor de Buenos Aires*, 42; *The Gold of Tigers*, 42

Bounty, The (Walcott), 324

"Brain" (Pagis), 215

"Bratsk Station" (Yevtushenko), 344

Brazil. *See* Geographical Index

Brodsky, Joseph, 44-51; "Aeneas and Dido," 48; Anna Akhmatova, 8; "A Halt in the Wilderness," 49; *A Part of Speech*, 49; *So Forth*, 50; "Sonnet," 47; *To Urania*, 50

Bronze Horseman, The (Pushkin), 242

Bustos Domecq, H. *See* Borges, Jorge Luis

Bustos, F. *See* Borges, Jorge Luis